KEY

Capital City	■
Other city/town	●
Village	○
Main road	
Other road	
Airport/airfield	✈ ✈ +
International boundary	
State boundary	

Windsurfing in Margarita
page 185

GRENADA

EA

Isla de
Margarita

PORLAMAR
Península de Paria

Güiria

TRINIDAD &
TOBAGO

BARCELONA

CUMANÁ

Sucre

ATLANTIC

Pedernales

MATURÍN

ANZOÁTEGUI

MONAGAS

OCEAN

Tucupita

DELTA
AMACURO

CIUDAD
BOLÍVAR

Orinoco

CIUDAD GUAYANA

Dam

GEORGETOWN

Cerro
Bolívar

Guri Lake

El Dorado

BOLÍVAR

Canaima

Angel Falls
page 268

Caura

Angel Falls
(979m)

GUYANA

Auyantepui
2,510m

Paragua

Juan
Manapiare

Caroní

Roraima
2,810m

*La Gran
Sabana*

Santa Elena
de Uairén

Trekking to Roraima
page 283

La Esmeralda

Orinoco

BOA VISTA

↓ *Manaus*

B R A Z

D0736295

Venezuela
Don't
miss...

Hiking to the *Lost World* summit of Mount Roraima

Join a trek to the top of this mysterious *tepui*, with its unique ecosystem and strange rock formations
(SS) page 283

Robinson Crusoe islands of Los Roques

Relax in the warm waters of this laid-back archipelago that has played host to Hollywood A-listers, top models and singers
(BG/H/A) page 134

Wildlife wonders of Los Llanos
Join hardy cowboys on horseback to explore these seasonally flooded plains, home to more birds than you can count in a day
(GL/FLPA) page 237

White-water rafting in Barinas
Go thrill-seeking at the camps on the Acequias, Siniguis, Santo Domingo and Canagua rivers
(FAB) page 250

Eating *pabellón criollo*
The national dish is just one of many tasty culinary treats on offer in Venezuela
(RM) page 58

left Caracas Cathedral boasts some amazing treasures, including gilded altars and paintings attributed to Rubens and Murillo (SS) page 106

below left The Universidad Central de Venezuela in Caracas is dotted with artwork and murals by artists such as Alexander Calder and Jean Arp and has been declared a UNESCO World Heritage Site (SS) page 108

bottom Caracas nestles at the base of a huge forested mountain, the Ávila, which is the lungs of the city and a lush green contrast to the concrete jungle of the valley below (VVP/A) page 87

top   One of the most popular trails from the city of Mérida is to the picturesque mountain village of Los Nevados at 2,750m, with excellent views over the valleys below (RM) page 373

above   The Iglesia de San Martín de Tours in Colonia Tovar is unique in Venezuela for its black timber architecture, which harks back to the Black Forest and the town's German roots (SS) page 126

below   Ciudad Bolívar has a beautifully restored colonial centre that in centuries past was a port-of-call for Spanish conquistadors, missionaries, and seekers of the golden city of El Dorado (SS) page 255

Los Roques Caribbean

Venezuela

La Cigala,
Specialising in bonefish
fishing and kite surfing
www.lacigala.com

--

Posada La Cigala
Los Roques
+58-414-236.5721
posadalacigala@gmail.com
lacigala@gmail.com
www.lacigala.com

AUTHOR

British journalist **Russell Maddicks** lived and worked
in Venezuela for more than 12 years. Initially drawn to
the country by his interest in anthropology, he was
soon working alongside Pemón Indians as a jungle
guide in Canaima and taking tourists to Angel Falls.
Now covering Latin American politics for a major UK
broadcaster, he maintains his ties with Venezuela
through regular visits.

A keen wildlife watcher with a love of adventure, he
is never happier than when observing the world from
the top of a far-flung *tepui* mountain. During his many
road trips to the interior, he has eaten cow-heel soup,
crunchy termites and even fried piranha in his quest for the tastiest treats in
Venezuela. Very often these delicacies are accompanied by a homemade alcoholic
beverage, such as the deadly *chuchuguasa* (Andean firewater that can only be
tolerated in small sips by the uninitiated). Over the years he has developed a knack
for finding the best food in every region of the country and has mastered the skill
of rustling up a plate of black beans and stewed shredded beef like a native –
something his Venezuelan wife much appreciates.

AUTHOR OF PREVIOUS EDITIONS

This book began in 1989 with the publication of the groundbreaking *No Frills
Guide to Venezuela* by Hilary Dunsterville Branch, the first English-language guide
to Venezuela published outside the country. From its humble beginnings leading
adventurous travellers to the summit of Mount Roraima and by canoe down the
Caura River it grew into the most complete guide to the country and did much to
stimulate the country's fledgling adventure and ecotourism industry.

Hilary was a keen traveller and wrote about her experiences of South America
for *Life en Español* and Venezuela's *The Daily Journal*, where she later worked. For
many years she worked as editor of *Ve Venezuela* tourism magazine, as well as going
orchid hunting with her parents. After years of intrepid exploration around her
adopted country and four editions of the Bradt guide to Venezuela, Hilary sadly
died in 2005. She is sorely missed.

PUBLISHER'S FOREWORD   *Adrian Phillips, Publishing Director*

This book conjures feelings of both sadness and pleasure. The sadness stems from the death five years ago of its original author, Hilary Dunsterville Branch. When first published in 1989 – as the *No Frills Guide to Venezuela* – this was the only guide available in English, and over subsequent editions Hilary ensured that it was a must-have resource for those visiting the country. The pleasure comes from the book's revival, and from seeing the devotion that Russell Maddicks has shown in updating and overhauling its information. His knowledge of the country, his passion for its people and places, and his wish to honour Hilary's memory through his own research, make this a new edition of which she herself would have been deeply proud.

Fifth edition published January 2011
First published 1993

Bradt Travel Guides Ltd, 23 High Street, Chalfont St Peter, Bucks SL9 9QE, England
www.bradtguides.com
Published in the USA by The Globe Pequot Press Inc, PO Box 480, Guilford,
Connecticut 06437-0480

Text copyright © 2011 Bradt Travel Guides Ltd
Maps copyright © 2011 Bradt Travel Guides Ltd
Photographs © 2011 Individual photographers (see below)
Project Manager: Elspeth Beidas

ISBN-13: 978 1 84162 299 6
British Library Cataloguing in Publication Data
A catalogue record for this book is available from the British Library

Photographs Neil Bowman/FLPA (NB/FLPA), Fabiana Arroyo Buzzo (FAB), De Agostini/Photoshot (DA/P), Tui De Roy/Minden Pictures/FLPA (TDR/MP/FLPA), Patrick Escudero/Hemis/Alamy (EP/H/A), FB-Fischer/Alamy (FBF/A), Bertrand Gardel/Hemis/Alamy (BG/H/A), Bob Gaspari/Alamy (BG/A), Imagebroker/Michael Krabs/FLPA (I/MK/FLPA), Gerard Lacz/FLPA (GL/FLPA), Russell Maddicks (RM), Thomas Marent/Minden Pictures/FLPA (TM/MP/FLPA), Loren McIntyre/Alamy (LM/A), Nicholas Pitt/Alamy (NP/A), Juergen Richter/Alamy (JR/A), Kevin Schafer/Minden Pictures/FLPA (KS/MP/FLPA), SuperStock (SS), World Pictures/Alamy (WP/A)
Front cover Angel Falls (DA/P)
Back cover Choroní (EP/H/A), Yanomami Indian (LM/A)
Title page Los Roques (SS), Andean cock of the rock (SS), *Tepui*, Gran Sabana (SS)

Maps David McCutcheon, Dave Priestley (colour map)

Typeset from the author's disc by Wakewing
Production managed by Jellyfish Print Solutions; printed in India

To Hilary Dunsterville Branch,
author of the first four editions of this guide.
Describing herself as British by descent, American by birth
and Venezuelan as a '*re-encauchada*' (literally a 're-tread'),
this sweet, unassuming woman was one of those unique individuals
who seem to pack so much into one life.
She spent more than 40 years travelling around her adopted country,
but to the end she was still planning trips
from her base in the coffee hills south of Caracas
that she shared with her husband Douglas Branch.

My love affair with Venezuela began the moment I first stepped off the plane. It was the blast of hot Caribbean air that enveloped me in its warmth as I walked down the ramp that did it, and the impossibly clear sky above, the loud, happy energy of the people in the airport, and the infectious tropical tunes blasting out on the bus. I'd never felt anything like that before. It was love at first sight. Like arriving in a place and feeling immediately at home. After several years beavering away in London in the bowels of the British Museum as a curator of South American artefacts I was suddenly in South America and the experience was overwhelming. I'd only planned a two week holiday but everything was on a bigger scale than I was used to, and each new place was completely different from the one before. I couldn't get enough of food like *arepas* and impossibly tasty tropical fruit. And the people were so open. Everybody wanted to be my *pana*, my friend, and beautiful women wanted to show me how to dance.

After the beaches and clubs of Margarita I headed for Puerto Ayacucho and the jungle, to visit the Yanomami Indians whose bows and arrows I'd catalogued in London. As I trekked through the rainforest to make contact with the tribe I realised that it would be madness to stay in Venezuela only two weeks. A whole new world was opening up to me and if I left I might never come back. So I chucked in my job in London and stayed. That's my story: I went to Venezuela for two weeks and stayed 11 years. Each weekend I would explore a different beach – Choroní, the islands of the Parque Nacional Morrocoy, Puerto Maya – or a different trail up the Ávila Mountain, where in 15 minutes you can be bathing in a freezing waterfall or watching an electric blue morpho butterfly flutter by.

After a few years the chance came to work as a jungle guide in a Canaima camp and I jumped at the opportunity. It wasn't hard to give up a comfortable bed in Caracas for a magnificent view of Angel Falls from my hammock. Further explorations led to a job at the local English-language newspaper, *The Daily Journal*, where I was able to combine travelling and writing. Along the way I lived through turbulent times, including political unrest and two *coups d'etat*. However, I was lucky to arrive at the same time as the first Bradt guide to Venezuela came out, written by a remarkable woman I was lucky enough to meet in person, Hilary Dunsterville Branch. That first book became my travel bible and I religiously ventured to each and every place she wrote about until I'd seen them all. When Bradt offered me the chance to write this update I felt it would be a fitting tribute to Hilary's memory and a perfect way for me to share my unique and extensive knowledge of a country that is largely undiscovered. I hope, dear reader, that this book equips you to safely explore a country that is full of amazing destinations and life-affirming experiences. Happy travels.

Acknowledgements

I would like to thank my Venezuelan wife Yadira for her support and encouragement for this project over the last two years. Her patience and understanding during my extended trips to the farthest corners of Venezuela and the long days and nights of writing and research on return enabled me to exceed my expectations and produce a comprehensive guide to her native country. I'd also like to extend my gratitude to Señora Maria, my mother-in-law, who was always there to meet me in Caracas with a smile and a cup of coffee to perk up my spirits after marathon bus journeys from ever more remote destinations. My own parents, Derek and Shirley, have also been unwavering in their support for this endeavour. A month-long trip to Caracas, Mérida, Margarita and the Orinoco region with my parents, my sister Sara and my uncle Alfred gave me an invaluable insight into the difficulties of travelling in Venezuela when you don't speak Spanish and helped to fine-tune the tips and advice in the destination chapters and expand the language section. To list all the Venezuelans who have helped me during my years of travelling in their incredible country could fill another book. However, I would like to extend a special thanks to fellow journalist Carlos Camacho in Caracas for being such a good friend over nearly 20 years and for all the nights we have spent dissecting the music, history, sport, politics, economics and quirky traits of Venezuela over beer and pizzas in El Leon. In Choroní, I owe a big hug to my friend 'Palomino', a former lifeguard who now dedicates his time to making *guarapita*, a deceptively sweet and fruity blend of passion fruit juice and fire water that fuels the local *fiestas* and drum dancing. Juan Carlos Ramirez of Akanan Travel & Adventure also deserves a nod for sharing his wealth of knowledge of off-the-beaten-path destinations and where to see wildlife. In Puerto Ayacucho, tour leader and expert on indigenous arts and crafts Vicente Barletta opened his home to me and taught me much about the Piaroa and Yekuana Indians of the Orinoco region on our trip to the Autana tepui. I am also indebted to Jonas Camejo, who taught me how to fish at night on the banks of the Rio Caura with just a flashlight and a machete. Dichenedu Ye'Kwana, also known by his Creole name Miguel Estaba, is another native of the Rio Caura who gave me a deeper understanding of Yekuana culture and introduced me to the residents of El Playón. Back home in England, I must thank Bradt founder Hilary Bradt and Publishing Director Adrian Phillips for believing that we could revive the Bradt Guide to Venezuela after many years without an update. I also owe a great debt of thanks to my ever-patient project editor at Bradt, Elspeth Beidas, for the months she spent nurturing this project and the hours of painstaking copy editing she put in to make this humble guide worthy of the Bradt name.

Contents

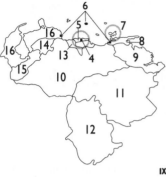

LIST OF MAPS

NOTE ABOUT MAPS

Several maps use grid lines to allow easy location of sites. Map grid references are listed in square brackets after listings in the text, with page number followed by grid number, eg: [156 C3].

Introduction

Venezuela is best known for its outspoken and charismatic president Hugo Chávez, its huge oil resources, and its record-breaking roster of international beauty queens (it boasts more Miss Worlds and Miss Universes than any other country). However, it is Venezuela's natural beauty that has the biggest impact on visitors, most notably through the incredible diversity of its geography and its teeming wildlife. Many people will already have heard of Angel Falls, the highest waterfall in the world, but there is much more to discover in this multi-faceted destination – which is still the best-kept secret in the Caribbean.

At the top of South America, tucked between Colombia and Guyana, and bordered in the south by Brazil and the northern limits of the Amazon Forest, Venezuela is just a few degrees above the Equator and is blessed with the longest coastline in the Caribbean. It is listed as one of 17 'mega-diverse countries' by the UN's World Conservation Monitoring Centre, an initiative designed to highlight the most biologically remarkable nations on the planet, harbouring the most species.

Trekkers looking for a special, once-in-a-lifetime experience should head for Mount Roraima, the most accessible of the mysterious table-top *tepui* mountains of the southern Gran Sabana. It is formed from the oldest rocks on the planet and was once part of the super continent of Gondwana, when present-day Africa, Australia and South America were all joined together. Roraima was also the inspiration for Arthur Conan Doyle's novel *Lost World*, an adventure yarn featuring dinosaurs and derring-do that continues to inspire travellers.

Other natural attractions to explore include the beautiful beaches of the coast and islands, the remote rainforest and indigenous tribes of the Orinoco basin, the arid deserts of the Guajira Peninsula, and the long chain of Andean mountains that stretch from the Colombian border in the far west to the finger of land that points out to Trinidad in the east. Windsurfers will find all they need to plan a trip to Margarita Island's El Yaque beach – now a major centre for the sport – while those seeking the milder pleasures of wildlife watching will find a rundown of the cattle ranches in the Llanos region and jungle camps in Amazonas and the Orinoco Delta.

History buffs will enjoy visiting Macuro, believed to be the only place where Christopher Columbus ever set foot on the South American continent, on his third voyage in 1498. Finding the native inhabitants of the Paria Peninsula 'happy, amiable and hospitable people', Columbus called it Tierra de Gracia, or 'Land of Grace'. Venezuelans continue to be fun-loving party people and the whole place – including the buses – throbs with the bump and grind of tropical salsa and merengue, as well as traditional folk music played on harps or drums. Any beat will do, as long as you can dance to it.

Fans of independence hero Simón Bolívar will find a bust or statue of the great man in every city, town and village. There are countless museums and houses dedicated to his exploits in driving the Spanish Empire out of South America and achieving independence for the modern nations of Venezuela, Colombia, Panama, Peru, Ecuador and Bolivia.

The colourful and controversial Venezuelan president, Hugo Chávez, has revived Bolívar's dreams in recent years, renaming the country the Bolívarian Republic of Venezuela and launching a series of programmes called 'missions'. These are all named after independence heroes and are aimed at using the country's vast oil wealth to provide education, healthcare and job opportunities for the poor majority. A bombastic, larger-than-life character, President Chávez challenges Venezuela's popular soap operas with his own TV show – a mix of serious politics, folksy jokes employing local slang and romantic songs.

This guide is not intended to be a complete rundown of every hotel and restaurant in every city in the country but to provide all the necessary practical advice for travellers to this exciting country, whether you want to locate the steamiest salsa bars in the capital Caracas, paraglide among Andean peaks or fish for piranhas from a dugout canoe in the Orinoco Delta. There is a strong emphasis on ecotourism and responsible travel throughout, with suggestions on how to give something back and travel sensitively to local customs.

Part One

GENERAL INFORMATION

Official name República Bolívariana de Venezuela

Population 28.6 million (2010 est)

Location On the north coast of South America, bordering the Caribbean Sea, between Colombia in the west, Guyana in the east and Brazil in the south

Size 912,050km² (352,144 square miles). Larger than Spain, Portugal, the UK and Ireland together, or the states of California, Oregon and Washington.

Type of government Democratic Federal Republic

Head of state President Hugo Rafael Chávez Frías (since 1999)

Independence 5 July 1811 (from Spain)

Capital Caracas (Pop: 4.2 million)

Climate Average daytime temperature: 25°C. Dry season: December–April, rainy season: May–November. Steamy tropical jungles in the south, hot arid deserts along the coast, cool Andes Mountains in the west.

Topography Flat coastal plains, seasonally flooded lowland plains, high Andes Mountains, mesa mountains of Guiana Shield

Highest point Pico Bolívar (5,007m, 16,427ft)

Coastline 2,800km (1,700 miles)

Major rivers Orinoco, Río Caroní

Currency Bolívar fuerte (BsF)

Rate of exchange US$1=BsF4.43, £1=BsF6.63, €1=BsF5.52 (September 2010)

Economy GDP: US$357.6 billion (2009 est), or US$13,100 per capita. Main exports: oil (75%), bauxite and aluminium, steel, chemicals, cocoa, coffee, rum.

Language Spanish, more than a dozen Indian languages spoken by 34 ethnic groups

Literacy 96%

Religion Catholic (90%), growing Evangelical presence, Jewish, Hindu, indigenous faiths

Time GMT –4.5

International dialling code +58

Electricity 110V, 60Hz (plugs with US-style two flat blades)

Flag Three equal horizontal bands: yellow (top), blue (centre), red (bottom), with a central arc of eight stars in the blue band. Designed by Francisco de Miranda in 1806, the yellow represents the wealth of the country, blue the sea separating it from Spain and red the blood spilled to secure Independence.

National anthem *Gloria al Bravo Pueblo* (Glory to the Brave People)

National bird *Turpial* (troupial)

National flower Orchid

National tree *Araguaney* (yellow paui)

Public holidays 1 January (New Year's Day), 6 January (*Reyes Magos*, Epiphany), 19 March (Saint Joseph's Day), 19 April (Declaration of Independence), 1 May (Labour Day), 24 June (Battle of Carabobo), 29 June (Saint Peter, Saint Paul), 5 July (Independence Day), 24 July (Simón Bolívar's birthday), 12 October (Indigenous Resistance Day), 7 December (Immaculate Conception), 25 December (Christmas Day). Carnival (February/March) and Easter (March/April) are moveable feasts.

Background Information

GEOGRAPHY

The Bolivarian Republic of Venezuela is the sixth largest country in South America, covering an area of 912,050km², making it twice the size of California and nearly five times larger than Great Britain. It is blessed with the longest coastline in the Caribbean (some 2,800km), the world's highest waterfall, and lies in the tropics between latitude 12° and less than 1° north of the Equator. Terrain and climate go from hot and sticky at sea level to icy cold on Andean peaks, although most of the land lies at under 1,000m. The country can be divided into three geographical regions with radically contrasting scenery: the north coast and the Andean mountains; the central plains and Orinoco Delta; and the Guiana Highlands and Amazonian forests south of the Orinoco.

THE NORTH COAST The north coast is bordered for long stretches by semi-arid hills, interrupted by lush coastal valleys such as Caracas, Choroní and Chichiriviche. The densely populated coastal region contains nearly 85% of the population and is bordered by three major mountain ranges, which are spurs of the Andes. Rising in the west to over 5,000m, the Cordillera de Mérida winds its way through Táchira, Mérida and Trujillo states, before ending in Lara. Lush, forested valleys are cultivated with coffee, fruit and vegetables. The Sierra Nevada de Mérida is the section with the highest peaks in Venezuela, including the highest of them all Pico Bolívar (5,007m), reached by a permanent glacier that has retreated significantly in recent years. The Cordillera de Mérida also borders the southern shores of Lake Maracaibo (13,210km²), the largest lake in South America, and one of the oldest in the world according to geologists, who date its formation to 36 million years ago. It is still rich in oil after 80 years' exploitation. The Sierra de Perijá, another spur of the Andes, forms the mountainous border with Colombia in Zulia State and is home to the indigenous Yukpa and Bari. The Cordillera de la Costa extends from Falcón State, where arid coastal conditions have created an extensive system of sand dunes called Los Médanos de Coro, eastwards to Miranda State. The highest point of the mountain range is Pico Naiguatá (2,765m), which rises above Caracas. In the east, the Cordillera Oriental runs through Sucre State to the tip of the Paria Peninsula.

THE CENTRAL PLAINS These are also known as Llanos, and are seasonally flooded plains that slope from the Andes south to the Orinoco River. Including 40,000km² of the Orinoco Delta, this sparsely inhabited region covers nearly a quarter of Venezuela. The mighty Orinoco is the third longest and most voluminous river in South America and travels 2,800km from its source in the Cerro Delgado-Chalbaud in the Sierra de Parima on the border with Brazil to its mouth in the Atlantic Ocean. A major waterway for trade, a dredged channel in the delta makes it navigable by large ore ships as far as the industrial centre of Ciudad Guayana.

The upper Llanos and Andean piedmont in Barinas are extensively cultivated (rice, sorghum, maize, tobacco, oil palm), but the nutrient-poor lower Llanos supports mainly free-range cattle in Apure, Barinas and Guárico states, and pine plantations in eastern Anzoátegui and Monagas states, better known for their extra-heavy oil deposits known as the Orinoco Oil Sands, or Orinoco Tar Sands. Annual rains flood vast stretches of Apure. In the remaining months of drought wildlife concentrates in lagoons, palm stands and marshes.

SOUTH OF THE ORINOCO The Guiana Highlands and the rainforests of Bolívar and Amazonas cover 45% of the country but are home to only 5% of the population. The majestic mesa mountains, or *tepuis*, of the Gran Sabana are remnants of the Guiana Shield, one of the earth's most ancient rock formations. The sandstone formations are sediments eroded from the earth's crust two–three billion years ago. Over 100 *tepuis* rise above the rolling plains. Mount Roraima is the highest of the *tepuis* at 2,810m, while Auyan tepui gives birth to the world's highest waterfall, Angel Falls, at 979m. Although rich in forests, iron, bauxite, gold and diamonds, the region's thin layer of soil is too fragile for sustainable farming. It is an important watershed, however, with the second biggest and longest river, the Río Caroní, feeding into the Central Hidroeléctrica Simón Bolívar, or Guri Dam. This is the third largest hydro-electric dam in the world, and generates more than 70% of Venezuela's electricity. A unique feature of the region is the Casiquiare Canal, which links the Orinoco to the Amazon in Brazil via the Río Negro, making it the only natural waterway to connect two major river systems. Forming the border with Brazil is the Cerro de la Neblina mountain range, with Pico da Neblina in Brazil (2,994m) the highest peak in South America east of the Andes. The Amazonian forests continue into the Orinoco basin in an uninterrupted carpet of green in a huge protected area covered by the Parque Nacional Serranía de la Neblina and the Parque Nacional Parima-Tapirapecó, inhabited by remote tribes of Yanomami Indians.

EARTHQUAKES These are not uncommon in Venezuela. They are related to three main geological faults, all of which have experienced quakes of great magnitude in the last 500 years (albeit rarely). The Boconó system runs through the Andes, the San Sebastian or Caribe system runs through the central coast, and the El Pilar fault is in the east. San Sebastian and El Pilar are both seismically active and run along the boundary of the South American and Caribbean tectonic plates on the coast. The biggest quake in recorded history occurred on 26 March 1812, when a quake measuring 7.5 on the Richter scale shook La Guaira, Caracas, Barquisimeto, Mérida and San Felipe. Some 15,000–20,000 people perished and Simón Bolívar, who was in Caracas and saw the terrible destruction wreaked by the earthquake, said the immortal lines: 'If nature opposes us, we shall fight against it and make it obey.' The last major destructive event to hit Caracas was in July 1967 on the city's 400th anniversary, when a quake measuring 6.5 on the Richter scale killed about 240 people and caused widespread damage in Los Palos Grandes and Altamira. Buildings in Caracas are now required to have earthquake-proof measures built in, and the metro was designed to withstand severe quakes. The last fatal quake occurred in Cariaco, near Cumaná, in July 1997: 73 people died.

CLIMATE

Venezuela's tropical climate is divided into a rainy season called winter (*invierno*), from late May to November, and a dry season called summer (*verano*), from December to April. The hottest months are usually April to August when the sun is directly overhead, and the coolest months are December and January. Torrential rains (over 3,000mm yearly in southern rainforests) peak in June and July, when short heavy downpours can cause flash floods. But it rarely rains all day and the clouds are dramatic and beautiful. Altitude, humidity and winds all contribute to a variety of temperatures across the country with snow sometimes falling in the high Andes from September to November. Annual temperatures in Margarita average 27°C; Caracas at 850m, 24°C; Mérida at 1,645m, 19°C; and the Andean village of Mucuchíes at 2,938m, 11°C. Hikers may experience sharp temperature variations of 10–20°C between noon and night temperatures, so while temperatures at the top of Roraima may exceed 25°C at midday, by night they can fall to a chilly 5°C – add rain and a strong wind and you'll be glad you packed a fleece and waterproof jacket.

NATURAL HISTORY with Mike Unwin

Venezuela offers a feast of wildlife to the visitor. Indeed, the UN body in charge of assessing global biodiversity, the World Conservation Monitoring Centre, includes the country in its list of the 17 most bio-diverse on earth, alongside the likes of Brazil, Australia, India and South Africa. Its prolific variety of both flora and fauna is due to its great variety of habitats combined with its location at the centre of the naturally abundant Neotropic ecozone. Venezuela also ranks among the world's top 20 countries in terms of endemism, with, for example, 38% of its plants and more than half its amphibians found nowhere else.

HABITATS Venezuela comprises a number of different bio-geographical regions. These include the lush Lake Maracaibo basin, enclosed west and south by mountains; the arid Coro system, stretching along the coast from the Guajira Peninsula on the Colombian border to the Paraguaná Peninsula in Falcón State; the Andes, where ecosystems include low-lying deciduous forest, cloudforest at mid-level, the desert-like páramo in the high valleys and glaciers below Pico Bolívar; the Cordillera de la Costa Central to the Paria Peninsula; Margarita, the Los Roques Archipelago and the offshore islands; the Llanos or central plains; the Orinoco Delta system; and the region south of the Orinoco, which is made up of four sub-regions, including the Caura and Caroní basins; the Upper Orinoco; and the Guiana Highlands of the Gran Sabana.

Of particular interest to naturalists are the *tepuis*, or mesa mountains, which harbour unique ecosystems of plants, insects and animals adapted to survive on the ancient rainswept and sun-baked sandstone of their lofty summits. These unique *tepui*-top environments, sometimes referred to as '*pantepui*' environments, have long been isolated from the forest below and support some weird and wonderful wildlife, including carnivorous plants such as sundews and pitcher plants, tiny orchids and primitive hop-less frogs.

The **Llanos**, meanwhile, hosts a spectacular abundance of wildlife, which gathers around the waterholes in great numbers in the dry season. The open terrain makes this an especially rewarding habitat for the visitor, with large numbers of caiman and capybaras guaranteed, along with countless water birds and a chance of sighting such specialities as anaconda and jaguar.

In the Andes, the moor-like *páramos* above 3,000m offer another unique ecosystem, and one that occurs almost exclusively in Colombia, Ecuador and Venezuela. When the wildflowers come into bloom in October, they create a living tapestry of yellow, white, orange and blue in the high valleys. This profusion can be compared to the meadows of northern climates and many *páramo* species are now cultivated in Europe, including the nasturtium, aster, clematis, gentian, befaria and calceolaria. The most memorable plants on the *páramo* are the many species of *frailejón* (*Espeletia*), which grow into tall triffid-like columns, with furry leaves and yellow flowers that emerge on antennae-like stalks. First described by the German scientist and explorer Alexander von Humboldt in 1801, there are some 88 species of *frailejón*. The name means 'big friar', because the tall columns that dot the high *páramo* look brown from a distance, like wandering holy men.

FAUNA

Mammals Venezuela is home to 327 species of mammal, including most of South America's 'must-see' species. Top of many visitors' wish list is the magnificent **jaguar** (*Panthera onca*), the country's most powerful predator and largest big cat of the Americas. This elusive feline is sometimes encountered in the Llanos, as are its smaller cousins the **puma** (*Puma concolor*) and **ocelot** (*Leopardus pardalis*).

Other notable members of the order Carnivora are the raccoon-like **South American coati** (*Nasua nasua*), a sociable creature with a long banded tail; the **giant river otter** (*Pteronura brasiliensis*), which roams lowland rivers in lively fishing parties; and the endangered Andean or **spectacled bear** (*Tremarctos ornatus*), which lives a precarious existence in the forests of the Parque Nacional Sierra Nevada and the Sierra de Perijá,

Easier to see than any predator, however, are monkeys, of which Venezuela is home to a number of species. The roaring dawn chorus of **howler monkeys** (*Alouatta* spp) is one of South America's most distinctive forest sounds. Closely related are **spider monkeys** (*Ateles* spp), which move with great agility through the canopy, often suspended by their tails, while noisy groups of **capuchins** (*Cebus* spp) work their way through the lower levels.

Among hoofed mammals are **brocket deer** (*Mazama* spp) and **white-tailed deer** (*Odocoileus virginianus*), while two species of **peccary** (family Tayassuidae), notoriously aggressive pig-like animals, root through the forest floor in gangs of 50 or more. The lucky visitor may even encounter a **Brazilian tapir**, or *danta* (*Tapirus terrestris*), South America's heaviest land mammal. This long-nosed relative of rhinos is most abundant in the Orinoco rainforest but threatened everywhere by hunting and deforestation.

Venezuela's four species of **sloth** (see box on pages 114–15) are among its more fascinating creatures, leading a low-octane, leaf-eating lifestyle high in the canopy. Belonging to the same order (Pilosa) are the four species of anteater (see box on page 239), of which the 2m **giant anteater** (*Myrmecophaga tridactyla*) is much the largest and cuts a distinctive profile on open grasslands. The endangered **giant armadillo**, or *cuspón* (*Priodontes maximus*), with its armoured plates and long front claws – used for tearing open termite mounds – looks like a living fossil and has a special significance to the natives of the Gran Sabana, in whose myths it is an ancestor. Much more common, however, is the smaller **nine-banded armadillo** (*Dasypus novemcinctus*), which is often seen on roads at night. Like the armadillos, Venezuela's marsupials are among South America's most primitive mammals and comprise more than 20 species of **opossum** (family Didelphidae), all of which carry their young in a pouch.

Rodents are prolific, and vary from mice weighing just 10g to the 45kg **capybara**, or *chigüire* (*Hydrochoerus hydrochaeris*), which is the world's largest. This sheep-sized, semi-aquatic grazer gathers in large number on the wetlands of the Llanos, where it is prey for everything from anacondas to jaguars. Other notable rodents include the rabbit-sized **agouti** (Dasyprocta spp), which play an important role in dispersing rainforest seeds, and **Brazilian porcupine** (*Coendou prehensilis*), which uses its prehensile tail when climbing trees.

Even more prolific than rodents are bats, of which Venezuela has more than 150 species. Most are adapted to a diet of either fruit, nectar or insects, but the common vampire bat (*Desmodus rotundus*) feeds on the blood of cattle. Alexander von Humboldt was keen to experience a vampire bat bite, writing: 'Many a night have I slept with my foot out of the hammock to tempt this winged surgeon, expecting that he would be there; but it was all in vain; the vampire never sucked me, and I could never account for his not doing so.' Other notable species include **bulldog bats** (family Noctilionidae), which snatch fish from the surface of lowland rivers, and the **tent-making bat** (*Uroderma bilobatum*), which nibbles through the ribs of large leaves to collapse them in a tent shape, inside which the colony roosts.

Two aquatic mammals are of particular interest. The **West Indian manatee** (*Trichechus manatus*), weighing up to 500kg, is the largest member of the order Sirenia (sea cows), and grazes on aquatic vegetation in coastal area and river estuaries. The **Amazon river dolphin**, or *boto* (*Inia geoffrensis*), feeds in silty waters in the Amazon and Orinoco river basins, and locates fish using its sonar-like echolocation.

Birds Venezuela's list of 1,392 recorded bird species is the seventh highest of any country on earth and includes 42 found nowhere else. As many as 250 species have been spotted around a single camp in Amazonas, 315 in the Llanos, and a record 578 in Henri Pittier National Park. Even in Caracas there are numerous beautiful birds to be seen at the botanical gardens and on the forested trails of the Ávila Mountain. The first-time visitor cannot fail to be impressed by the sheer colour and variety, while the hardened birder will find a wealth of enticing specialities for their life list. (For practical tips on birding in Venezuela see page 82.)

Wetlands support numerous long-legged waterbirds, such as the enormous **jabiru stork** (*Jabiru mycteria*), the attractive **agami heron** (*Agamia agami*) and the cryptically camouflaged **sunbittern** (*Eurypyga helias*). A colony of flamboyant **scarlet ibis** (*Eudocimus rubber*) has even adopted the artificial lakes of Parque del Este/Francisco de Miranda as a new home. **Black skimmers** (*Rynchops niger*) cruise the waterways, snapping up prey in their outsized bills, while **Anhingas** (*Anhinga anhinga*) use their serpentine necks to capture fish beneath the surface and kingfishers, such as the **Amazon kingfisher** (*Chloroceryle amazona*), plunge down from overhanging perches.

The giant **harpy eagle** (*Harpia harpyja*) holds pride of place among the country's raptors. This endangered species – a major draw for birders worldwide – uses its huge talons to capture sloths and monkeys in the rainforest canopy. Other eagles include the attractive **ornate hawk-eagle** (*Pizaetus ornatus*), while the **northern caracara** (*Caracara cheriway*) is a ubiquitous scavenging relative of the falcons. A visit to the Andes may even afford a glimpse of the enormous and recently reintroduced **Andean condor** (*Vultur gryphus*).

Among Venezuela's more intriguing birds are the primitive-looking **hoatzin** (*Opisthocomus hoazin*) (see page 240), whose chicks are born with claws on their wings, the **yellow-knobbed curassow** (*Crax daubentoni*), which struts around like a long-tailed turkey, and the **greater potoo** (*Nyctibius grandis*), a nocturnal insect-eater that camouflages itself as a dead tree stump by day. Another nocturnal species, the **oilbird** (*Steatornis caripensis*), is one of the very few birds to use echolocation, its stream of continuous high-pitched calls enabling it to navigate around its cave roosts in the pitch blackness, just as bats do.

Most eye-catching are the numerous species of parrot, such as the **scarlet macaw** (*Ara macao*), which draw attention to themselves with dazzling plumage and shrieking calls. Other more subtle beauties, such as the **violaceous trogon** (*Trogon violaceus*) and **paradise jacamar** (*Galbula dea*), bring splashes of colour to the forest canopy, while toucans, such as the **keel-billed toucan** (*Ramphastos sulfuratus*), use their preposterous bills to pluck fruit and raid other birds' nests.

Venezuela is also home to an amazing 97 species of hummingbird (family Trochilidae). These feathered dynamos consume more than their own body weight in nectar each day and include such as gems as the endemic **golden-tailed starfrontlet** (*Coeligena eos*) of montane forest in the Andes.

Among the wealth of songbirds that make up the order Passeriformes is a pageant of colourful cotingas, manakins, cardinals, tanagers, orioles and others. Notable species include **Andean cock-of-the-rock** (*Rupicola peruvianus*), **capuchinbird** (*Perissocephalus tricolor*), **bearded bellbird** (*Procnias averano*), **scarlet-horned manakin** (*Pipra cornuta*) and **spangled cotinga** (*Cotinga cayana*). Of more interest to many serious birders, however, are such 'small brown jobs' as the many elusive ant-birds, spine-tails, pygmy-tyrants and others that lurk deep in the foliage and offer the trickiest challenges to identification.

Reptiles and amphibians The largest reptile in Venezuela is the critically endangered **Orinoco crocodile**, or *caimán del Orinoco* (*Crocodylus intermedius*), which can reach over 6m in length. Today this species is bred in captivity for release into the wild in an attempt to create viable breeding numbers. The related **American crocodile** (*Crocodylus acutus*) survives in brackish coastal lagoons such as the Laguna de Tacarigua. The smaller *baba* or **spectacled caiman** (*Caiman crocodilus*) is much more common, and can be seen in the creeks and ponds of the Llanos, where it breakfasts on waterfowl, fish and turtles.

Lizards range in size from the 6cm-long **dwarf geckos** (*Sphaerodactylus* spp), bold insect-hunters, to the shy vegetarian **common iguana** (*Iguana iguana*), a speedy saurian that may top 1.5m in length and often plunges into the water when fleeing a treetop predator. Other notable species include the **black tegu** (*Tupinambis teguixi*), a heavily built omnivore that resembles the monitor lizards of the Old World, and the **common basilisk** (*Basiliscus basiliscus*), a fleet-footed, semi-aquatic species with an ability to sprint across the water's surface that has earned it the local name *lagarto de Jesus Cristo* ('Jesus lizard'). Lizards, including a friendly black relative of the **jungle racerunner** (*Cnemidophorus lemmiscatus nigricolor*), are the only terrestrial reptiles on the Los Roques Archipelago.

A number of sea turtles, including **green turtle** (*Chelonia mydas*), **loggerhead turtle** (*Caretta caret*) and **hawksbill turtle** (*Eretmochelys imbricata*) come ashore to lay their eggs on sandy beaches. All are now endangered and some are still hunted illegally in places. River turtles, particularly the **large arrau** (*Podocnemis expansa*), used to be so numerous that, according to 19th-century explorers, they blocked river traffic at egg-laying time. These days you can see them sunning themselves on rocks as you come around a river bend on the Río Caura.

Snakes live in most parts of Venezuela, from the apparently lifeless sand dunes of Coro and the cold windswept Andes, to the humid Amazonian jungles and lowland rivers. However, as most are nocturnal they are seldom seen. Those that are active in daylight prefer shady forests that protect them from the sun. Largest by far is the **green anaconda** (*Eunectes murinus*), the heaviest snake in the world, which can grow to 6m long, weigh as much as a grizzly bear and swallow a deer whole. A constrictor that spends most of its time in rivers and lakes – notably in the Llanos and jungle rivers such as the Caura – this monster asphyxiates its prey in its coils before swallowing it headfirst. Smaller constrictors include the beautifully patterned **rainbow boa** (*Epicrates cenchria*) and **red-tailed boa** (*Boa constrictor*).

Of the 182 species of snake recorded in Venezuela, only a dozen or so are poisonous enough to pose a threat to humans. These including five subspecies of the **South American rattlesnake** (*Crotalus durissus*), known as *cascabel*, and the aggressive **lancehead pit viper** (*Bothrops venezuelensis*), known as *mapanare*, *tigra mariposa* or *macagua*. The largest pit viper in South America is the **bushmaster**

(*Lachesis muta*), known locally as a *cuaima* – a name also applied, incidentally, to a nagging wife. Like other pit vipers it has highly sensitive heat sensors located between its eyes and nasal openings, which allow it to find prey. **Coral snakes** (*Micrurus* spp), with their distinctive yellow, red, black and white banding, are also highly venomous, but these relatives of the Old World cobras are no more than 20cm long and their jaws are too small to pose a realistic threat to people unless handled. The similar-looking but relatively harmless **false coral snake** (*Erythrolamprus aesculapii*) is thought to gain some protection from predators by mimicking its more venomous relative. An old rhyme to help distinguish between the two goes: 'Red on yellow kills a fellow, but red on black, venom lack.' This is not reliable, however, and the best advice is to steer clear altogether.

Venezuela is home to more than 280 species of amphibian, with 62 species of frog in the Cordillera de Mérida alone, many of them endemic. Among the more distinctive are the so-called **poison-arrow frogs** (family Dendrobatidae), whose fluorescent colours warn predators of their highly toxic skin. Others include **tree frogs** (family Hylidae), which use sucker pads on their toes to climb foliage, **glass frogs** (family Centrolenidae), whose virtually transparent skin reveals their internal organs and skeleton beneath, and the hefty and voracious **marine toad** (*Bufo marinus*) – also known as *cane toad* – which has become notorious as an invasive species in Australia and the southern US. Few, however, are more bizarre than the diminutive **pebble toad** (*Oreophrynella nigra*), found on isolated *tepuis*, which rolls itself into a rubber ball and bounces down rock faces to escape from predatory tarantulas.

Fish Recent bio-geographical studies give fascinating clues to the astonishing diversity of tropical fish species, which have been inventoried in eastern South America at a rate of 35 new species a year since 1960. This diversity of over 1,000 species in the Orinoco and 2,000 in the Amazon (with a basin five times larger) is rooted in geological time, perhaps 15 million years ago. In that era the Orinoco and western Amazon were one great river bordering the Andes, flowing north to exit in the Caribbean (near present-day Coro). However, when the Venezuelan Andes rose eight to ten million years ago, the river was cut off from its Caribbean delta and the Orinoco became separated from the Amazon. Both rivers then turned eastwards to flow into the Atlantic.

Such continental upheavals and changing environments account for today's thousands of fish species, as very few of the ancient fish types were extinguished. The murky-brown Orinoco River is home to giant catfish, such as the **goliath catfish** (*Brachyplatystoma*), with trailing whiskers; the **arapaima** (*Arapaima gigas*) or *pirarucu* (as it is known in Brazil), the world's largest freshwater fish; the legendary fang-toothed **vampire fish**, or *payara* (*Hydrolycus scomberoides*); and **peacock bass**, or *pavon* (*Cichla* spp). The latter two are popular game fish. The feared piranha is another denizen of Venezuela's rivers, found from the Llanos to the Caura and Orinoco. Only a few species of piranha are carnivorous; the **red-bellied piranha** (*Pygocentrus nattereri*) has the worst reputation. Scientists have recently published studies downplaying the danger and ferocity of piranhas, but in the Llanos they are feared, and anybody who gets a finger too close to their razor-sharp teeth when fishing for them will soon realise why. The **Electric eel** (*Electrophorus electricus*) is not a true eel but belongs to the knifefish group. Either way, this 2m denizen of shallow, lowland rivers can generate an electric current of up to 500 volts – enough to knock a person senseless.

Insects and other invertebrates Venezuela hosts a staggering wealth of creepy crawlies, particularly in the lowland rainforests. Beetles (Celeoptera) are the most abundant order of life on the planet and comprise approximately one-third of the world's 1.75 million animal species described by science. Notable examples include giants such as the 12cm-long **rhinoceros beetles** (subfamily Dynastinae), which sport impressive horns, and **fire-flies** (family Lampyridae) – really beetles – which produce luminous displays along river edges. Other insects that the visitor cannot fail to notice are ants, which comprise up to one tenth of the total rainforest animal biomass. Notable are the **leaf-cutter ants** (*Atta/Acromyrmex* spp.), which harvest foliage in order to cultivate a fungus that feeds their colony, and **army ants** (subfamily *Ecitoninae*), whose long trails across the forest floor generate a flurry of fleeing insects that attracts other insectivorous creatures, such as **antbirds** (family *Thamnophilidae*). **Termites** (order Isoptera) are master builders, like ants, but are more primitive insects that are closely related to cockroaches. Some species build arboreal nests in forests; others raise impressive baked-earth mounds on open grasslands. Among the most spectacular of a dazzling array of butterflies are the **morphos** (*Morpho* spp.), distinguished by their large size and iridescent blue wings.

Spiders (class Arachnida) include the elegant **golden orb-weavers** (*Nephila* spp.), which spin a giant web of strong gold silk across forest gaps and trails. **Tarantulas** (family Theraphosidae), by contrast, do not trap prey in webs but actively hunt it in swamp vegetation or other damp habitats. These large hairy spiders may be the stuff of nightmares for arachnophobes but pose no threat to humans. Many **centipedes** (class Chilopoda), however, have a venomous and extremely painful bite and should be avoided.

CONSERVATION The main dangers to fauna and flora in Venezuela, as elsewhere, are hunting and habitat loss through burning, logging and development. Mining and agriculture also contaminate rivers. Since the creation of its first national park in 1937, Venezuela has brought 141,043km² of wilderness, an area twice the size of the Republic of Ireland, into a system of national parks and natural monuments. These represent over 15% of the country and cover almost all ecosystems. But legal protection is one thing, and effective management another. Few parks actually have guards or rangers, and the national parks institute, Inparques, is small and understaffed. Although trade in wildlife is banned by international pact, an intense illegal traffic in thousands of parrots and songbirds finds an outlet via the Orinoco Delta to dealers in Trinidad and Guyana. The *Red Book of Threatened Fauna in Venezuela* lists 28 mammals (11 endangered), including the giant armadillo, manatee, Margarita deer and monkey, giant otter and spectacled bear. The Orinoco and coastal crocodiles are so rare that they are seldom seen in the wild. The arrau river turtle and five sea turtles are all protected by law but, like crocodiles, their future is uncertain as if they are not killed outright their eggs are taken.

See page 75 for details of environmental NGOs working in Venezuela.

HISTORY

Venezuelan history is dominated by larger-than-life individuals: the liberators, dictators and democrats who have helped shape the country. No-one has had a greater impact on Venezuela than Simón Bolívar, the independence hero whose image and name adorns every square in every town and city in the country. A diminutive visionary who gave up a life of wealthy indulgence and overcame great physical trials to liberate six modern countries from the Spanish yoke, Bolívar's name is sacred across Latin America, where he has inspired both left-wing revolutionaries and right-wing despots. Bolívar lamented that Latin America was being held back by the 'triple yoke of ignorance, tyranny, and vice', and died a disillusioned man aged just 47. Under President Chávez the cult of Bolívar has taken on a new significance and his name is now included in the country's official title and even the president's personal brand of socialist politics, Bolivarianism. A charismatic firebrand, who courts controversy wherever he goes, President Chávez is another unforgettable character. Able to engage emotionally with Venezuela's poor, speaking the language of Che Guevara and Fidel Castro, and unafraid to take on the leader of the US, or anybody else for that matter, President Chávez, with his trademark red beret, has become the darling of left-wingers the world over. Supporters see in his 21st-century socialism an antidote to the greed and destruction of Western capitalism. His opponents, meanwhile, paint him as a reckless authoritarian who allows no dissent and tries to gag the media, using petro-dollars to raise his profile abroad while serious problems of poverty and spiralling crime remain unsolved at home.

EARLY SETTLERS Venezuela has the distinction of being the first place on the American continent where Columbus set foot. Contemporary map-makers labelled it simply *'terra firma'*. Columbus landed on the Paria Peninsula on his third voyage of discovery in 1498. At first he thought that Paria was an island and called it Isla de Gracia, or 'Land of Grace', for its 'happy, amiable and hospitable' people. This easy-going state did not last long as disparate tribes were unable to repel the Spaniards who followed in the early 1500s, enslaving the natives to dive for pearls at the rich pearl beds found around the small island of Cubagua, off the coast of Margarita.

The earliest settlement on the mainland was Cumaná, founded in 1515 by Franciscan missionaries and again in 1521 after fierce resistance by local tribes. Coro, founded in 1527, was the first permanent settlement.

Once the oyster beds of Cubagua were exhausted, the conquistadors sought in vain for El Dorado, subduing the indigenous tribes they met along the way with great brutality, especially under the rule of the German banking family, the Welsers, who were granted permission in 1528 to explore and settle Venezuela by the Holy Roman Emperor Charles V. Gradually, missionaries penetrated the vast hinterland of the country, followed by miners, plantation owners and settlers who built ports and towns along the main rivers. The Welsers organised the first shipments of African slaves and by the late 16th century Dahomey, Congo and Ashanti people from the Gold Coast, Benin and Angola were being brought in by Portuguese, French and English slave ships to work the plantations of cacao, sugarcane and indigo.

TOWARDS INDEPENDENCE The Spanish colony's first stirrings of independence came in 1795 with the slave uprising in Coro of José Leonardo Chirino, who wanted a republic on French lines and was inspired by the Haitian Revolution. Then in 1806 Francisco de Miranda, who had been living in London to drum up support for the independence cause, sailed from New York to Venezuela with a group of 500 American volunteers, on an ill-planned attempt to overthrow the Spanish ruling powers. Miranda managed to escape after two of his three ships were captured, but 63 American volunteers were imprisoned and the officers hanged in Puerto Cabello. Another attempt to take Coro was also unsuccessful. However, after independence was declared in 1810, Miranda was asked to command the First Republic's revolutionary army. After a few successful engagements against the Spaniards, Miranda saw the tide turning and sued for peace with the Spanish, hoping to fight another day. Incensed by this act of seeming betrayal, a young Simón Bolívar seized Miranda and handed him over to the Spanish, who imprisoned him in La Carraca armoury in Cadiz, where he died in 1816 aged 66. Bolívar then took over the leadership of the patriots, as the Venezuelan independence fighters were called, and decreed a 'war to the death'. The turning point in the patriots' long struggle came when they captured Angostura (now Ciudad Bolívar) in 1818. With

16000–14000BC First indigenous hunter-gatherers arrive after crossing Bering Strait from Siberia and making their way through the continent.

1498 Christopher Columbus lands on the Paria Peninsula on his third voyage to the New World, making him the first European to see the South American mainland, but is unaware of what he has found.

1499 Alonso de Ojeda and Amerigo Vespucci sail into Lake Maracaibo and, seeing the indigenous stilt houses called *palafitos*, Vespucci calls the place 'Venezuela' or 'Little Venice'.

1500 Spanish conquistadors found Nueva Cadiz on Cubagua Island to exploit pearl beds.

1500 Juan de la Cosa who sailed with Ojeda includes the name Venezuela on his *Mappa Mundi*.

1521 Cumaná, the first Spanish settlement on the mainland, is founded.

1527 Santa Ana de Coro becomes the first capital; Spaniards stick to the coast.

1528 German banking family the Welsers granted special concession by Charles V to settle and exploit western Venezuela. Ambrosius Ehinger and Nikolaus Federmann begin bloody conquest of indigenous tribes in hunt for gold and riches. Ehinger founds Maracaibo in 1529. Federmann leads expeditions in search of mythical land of El Dorado.

1567 Diego de Losada kills local indigenous chiefs Guaicaipuro, Tamanaco, Paramaconi and Terepaima, and Caracas is founded.

1777 Captaincy General of Venezuela is formed, encompassing most of modern-day Venezuela.

1783 Simón José Antonio de la Santísima Trinidad Bolívar Palacios y Blanco, better known as Simón Bolívar is born on 24 July.

1795 José Leonardo Chirino, inspired by the liberation struggle in Haiti, leads a slave revolt in Coro calling for an end to slavery and a French-style republic. The revolt is violently put down and Chirino beheaded in the central plaza in Caracas. His family is sold into slavery.

1806 Francisco de Miranda, who has fought in the French Revolution and lived in London, launches the first unsuccessful attempt to gain independence.

1810 Venezuela declares independence from Spain on 19 April.

1811 First Republic created on 5 July with signing of Independence Act.

1812 Earthquake reduces Caracas to rubble. Catholic priests say it is divine retribution for independence moves, Bolívar says: 'if nature opposes us we shall fight against it.'

1813 Bolívar declared El Libertador in Mérida after returning from successful campaign in Colombia and significant military victories over Spanish royalist forces.

1819 Bolívar proclaimed President of Gran Colombia (Venezuela, Colombia, Ecuador) by Congress of Angostura, while war of independence continues. The short-lived republic later included present-day Peru and Bolivia.

1821 Decisive victory over Spanish at Battle of Carabobo on 24 June secures Venezuelan independence.

1830 Venezuela breaks with Gran Colombia under José Antonio Páez as president.

1830 Bolívar dies of TB in Santa Marta, Colombia, on 17 December. In one of his last letters he writes: 'He who serves a revolution ploughs the sea.'

1908–35	Dictatorship of Juan Vicente Gómez, the 'Tyrant of the Andes', who runs Venezuela like his private ranch.
1914	Mene Grande oilfield discovered near Maracaibo on 15 April. By 1918 first exports of oil begin.
1947	Novelist Romulo Gallegos becomes president in first democratic elections.
1948	Military junta led by Marcos Pérez Jiménez topples Gallegos government and rules until 1958. Caracas modernised and many large-scale infrastructure projects carried out, including the cable car in Mérida.
1989	Newly re-elected, President Carlos Andrés Pérez announces petrol-price hikes and austerity measures sparking widespread protests, riots and looting on 27 February. The 'Caracazo' as it is known, is swiftly followed by a military crackdown in which an estimated 2,000 die, mainly in shantytowns.
1992	Lt-Colonel Hugo Chávez leads an unsuccessful coup d'etat on 4 February and is caught and imprisoned. Utters immortal words *'por ahora'* ('for now') when asked to tell the nation that the coup attempt is over on national TV. Another coup in November also fails.
1994	Chávez pardoned by President Rafael Caldera.
1998	Chávez wins presidential elections with 56% of the vote and immediately launches referendum on new constitution, which is approved in 1999. Country's name changed to República Bolivariana de Venezuela.
1999	Massive mudslides devastate Vargas State in December, killing tens of thousands and making 75,000 people homeless.
2000	Chávez is re-elected with 59% of the vote for a six-year term.
2002	After a protest march on 11 April ends in deaths of protesters Chávez is removed and provisional government sworn in with Pedro Carmona as leader. Constitution is suspended. Huge popular protests outside presidential palace in favour of Chávez see him returned and re-installed as president after only 47 hours.
2002–03	General strike called by opposition leaders, major companies and state oil firm executives in December–January causes economic chaos but Chávez survives and extends control over oil industry.
2004	Opposition gather 3.4 million signatures to force referendum on removing Chávez from power. President wins referendum.
2006	In a speech at the UN General Assembly in September, Chávez calls US President George W Bush 'the devil', remarking on the 'smell of sulphur' at the podium where Bush had spoken.
2006	In December Chávez wins re-election with 63% of the vote.
2007	Spanish king gets annoyed with Chávez at Ibero-American Summit in November and says 'Why don't you shut up!'.
2007	Referendum to end limits on presidential term narrowly defeated in December by 51% of votes, in Chávez's first loss at the ballot box.
2009	Chávez secures an end to term limits in February referendum, allowing him to stand for re-election in 2012.
2010	Government forced to devalue currency by 17% to tackle black market in dollars and increase revenue.

British and Irish recruits making up the British Legion and the fearless horsemen of the Llanos led by General José Antonio Páez, the ragged army then marched over the Andes to free modern-day Colombia in 1819. This led to the proclamation of the Republic of Gran Colombia, made up of present-day Venezuela, Colombia, Ecuador, Peru and Panama. Venezuela's independence was sealed at the Battle of Carabobo on 24 June 1821, and two years later the last remnants of the Spanish army were finally forced out of Venezuela.

A SOVEREIGN STATE The union of Gran Colombia soon broke down and José Antonio Páez declared Venezuela a sovereign state, becoming president of the new country. Bolívar lived just long enough to see his dream of a unified South America shattered into pieces. He died in 1830, his health laid low by tuberculosis, bitter at how futile his monumental struggle against Spain had been. Venezuela, already devastated by 12 years of wars, was to be battered by continuous civil strife for the rest of the century. After the first president of the new republic came a series of *caudillos*, or 'strongmen', who ruled by force of arms. The most enlightened of these despots was Antonio Guzmán Blanco, a liberal who ruled Venezuela from 1870 to 1877 and again in 1879–84, introducing free compulsory schooling, cracking down on the power of the Catholic Church, constructing the Capitol building, theatres, a railway to La Guaira on the coast and putting up statues to Bolívar and himself. Blanco liked to be addressed as the 'Illustrious American', although he followed the ostentatious fashions of France as did most of Caracas society at the time.

DICTATORS AND DEMOCRACY An illiterate Andean named Juan Vicente Gómez arrived in Caracas in 1899 with the army of another usurper, the *caudillo* Cipriano Castro. In 1908 Gómez took power and held it for 27 years with great cunning and cruelty. He acquired vast properties and ran the country from his house in Maracay as if it was one of his ranches. Those who disagreed with him were clapped in leg irons and thrown in prison, and the student-inspired opposition were forced underground or into exile, rising later to lead the country into democracy. In the meantime, the discovery of oil in Zulia in 1914 was to change the economy permanently, with oil becoming Venezuela's primary export as early as 1926. Gómez died in 1935, but not before using prison labour to build two escape routes over the mountains north of Maracay to Choroní and Ocumare.

Two transitional military presidents followed: Eleázar López Contreras and Isaías Medina Angarita. Medina began a series of civil and political reforms and legalised labour unions and political parties, including the Communist Party, but a military coup led by a young colonel, Marcos Pérez Jiménez, toppled the government in 1945. Rómulo Betancourt, a founder member of Acción Democrática (AD), prepared the first democratic elections in 1947, which was the first time women were allowed to vote. The elections were won by popular novelist Rómulo Gallegos, with an astonishing 74% of the vote. However, this first flowering of true democracy was not to last. Pérez Jiménez led a military junta that brought down Gallegos after just eight months and embarked on a huge programme of splashy public works, investing the country's growing oil wealth in four-lane highways, concrete housing blocks, five-star hotels, a race-track, the cable car systems in Mérida and Caracas and the iconic Hotel Humboldt on top of the Ávila mountain. While Pérez Jiménez's public works were seen as modernising a backward country, his dictatorship was tainted by corruption and an infamous secret police force. On 23 January 1958, the dictator's ten-year run came to an end after growing public protests. He fled the country with his family from La Carlota airport in Caracas and flew to Spain.

In 1959, Rómulo Betancourt, leader of AD, became the first democratically elected president to complete a term, after the two main parties, AD and the Social Christian Party (COPEI), agreed a power-sharing deal known as the Punto Fijo Pact that lasted 40 years. He also oversaw Venezuela's founding role in the Organisation of Petroleum Exporting Countries with Iran, Iraq, Kuwait and Saudi Arabia. In 1963 Betancourt won the extradition of Pérez Jiménez from the USA and brought him to trial for misappropriation of public funds. In 1968, the former dictator was sentenced to four years in prison but, having already spent five years in jail, was released. Betancourt handed power over to Raúl Leoni, also of AD. COPEI then won the elections of 1969 with President Rafael Caldera. Under Carlos Andrés Pérez (1974–79), the price of oil shot to over US$30 a barrel, the oil and steel industries were nationalised and Caracas became one of the world's most expensive cities. This was the start of a period known as 'Venezuela Saudita'; it was a time when Venezuelans were known in the shops and boutiques of Miami as '*da me dos*' ('give me two'), because money was no object. Meanwhile, peasants deserted the countryside and flooded to the shantytowns of the big cities to benefit from the oil bonanza. The economic bubble couldn't last, however, and it burst during the administration of Luís Herrera Campins of COPEI (1979–84) which had to shoulder astronomical foreign debt and was forced into a major devaluation in 1983 known as Black Friday. The bolivar went from four bolivares to the US dollar to 15 bolivares, wiping out savings overnight. By the time Carlos Andrés Pérez was re-elected in 1989 oil prices and income had fallen by half. When the AD president reneged on his election promises of plenty to pursue World Bank and IMF-imposed austerity measures the pressure cooker of growing poverty blew a gasket. On 27 February 1989 a hike in the price of petrol combined with shortages and an end to subsidies, led to a major outbreak of rioting and looting in the capital and other cities that came to be known as El Caracazo. The government's response to the violence was to declare martial law and send in troops to recover stolen goods, resulting in thousands of deaths in the poor neighbourhoods of Caracas.

THE RISE OF CHÁVEZ The 'Caracazo' caused widespread dissatisfaction with the Punto Fijo Pact system, which was seen as perpetuating corrupt parties and governments to the detriment of democracy. In 1992, a group of disaffected military officers led by a charismatic paratrooper, Lieutenant-Colonel Hugo Rafael Chávez Frías, staged a dramatic coup attempt on 4 February to topple President Pérez. The tanks that tried to knock down the doors of Miraflores Presidential Palace narrowly missed a fleeing Perez and the National Guard remained loyal to the president. Chávez, realising he had missed his moment and keen to avert more bloodshed, surrendered and asked if he could broadcast a message to tell his troops in Maracay to lay down their arms. His short, defiant speech acknowledging defeat ended with the words '*por ahora*' ('for now'), which became a rallying cry for the growing opposition to the traditional parties. Although he was immediately imprisoned, the young soldier's serious bearing made him a national hero among the many disaffected Venezuelans who longed for change.

Chávez's coup attempt was given further legitimacy when Congress impeached Pérez in June 1993 on corruption charges, sentencing him to two years' imprisonment under house arrest. In the elections of December 1993, former president Rafael Caldera, 75, was returned to power by a coalition of 16 splinter parties under the banner of Convergence, thus technically breaking the two-party system. One of the most significant acts of his presidency was to pardon Chávez, releasing him from prison and allowing him to stand for election.

Desperate for change from self-enriching political models, the country sought new leadership in the elections of December 1998. Among independent candidates heading their own parties were Hugo Chávez and his Movimiento Quinta República (MVR, Fifth Republic Movement) on an anti-corruption ticket, and Irene Sáez, a blonde former Miss Universe and mayor of the upmarket neighbourhood of Chacao. Except for AD, no traditional party put up a candidate, seeing the anti-party writing clearly on the wall.

The result was a landslide victory for Chávez, 44, with 56% of the vote. Although Chávez's power base was the impoverished majority he also had the support of liberals, intellectuals, artists and environmentalists, who saw him as an idealist able to break the mould of entrenched politics. For a while there was a euphoric feeling that Venezuela would finally shake off the deep-seated corruption holding it back, more people would benefit from the country's rich natural resources and a brighter future beckoned. By exploiting that optimism, Chávez was able to pass a referendum on a new constitution. He changed the country's name to the Bolivarian Republic of Venezuela, in honour of his idol Simón Bolívar, and was re-elected with an even bigger percentage of the vote in 2000.

VENEZUELA UNDER CHÁVEZ The president began his new mandate with an ambitious array of state-sponsored social programmes aimed at alleviating the worst problems of the 80% of Venezuelans living below the poverty line. These *Misiónes* bypassed the crumbling public sector hospital and education systems to take healthcare and literacy projects into the poorest neighbourhoods. Working with his close ally, Cuba's Fidel Castro, Chávez arranged for Cuban doctors to set up free clinics inside shantytowns in return for Venezuelan oil sent to Cuba. Called Misión Barrio Adentro, the project had an immediate impact, although Venezuelan doctors grumbled about the quality of the Cuban medical staff. Misión Robinson saw thousands of teachers sent out to provide basic literacy and numerical skills, raising Venezuela's literacy levels to 93% – among the highest in South America. Misión Ribas went a step further and offered another chance at high school education for those who missed it first time round. Other programmes offer university places and free meals in communal kitchens for those living on the streets. Misión Mercal has grown into a national network of markets and stores selling subsidised basic foodstuffs.

Defining his political position further, the president declared himself a 21st-century socialist, allied himself with Cuba, Iran and China and began to rail at 'the evil empire of the north' and George W Bush, whom he nicknamed 'Mr Danger' for starting wars in Afghanistan and Iraq.

The basic tenets of Bolivarianism, the president's core set of ideals, are taken from Simón Bolívar, other independence heroes and Jesus Christ, whom he calls the first socialist. He also quotes Karl Marx, Fidel Castro and Noam Chomsky, slams 'savage neoliberalism' for creating all of the world's ills, and says 'the people' rule through him.

Increasingly under attack from the private media, whom he accuses of lying about the achievements of his Bolivarian Revolution, Chávez started his own Sunday TV and radio show in 1999 called *Aló, Presidente* (Hello, President). The show can last up to five hours or more, depending on the president's mood, and features chats with his supporters, attacks on his enemies, folk songs, jokes and serious discussions of new policies.

After a brief honeymoon period, the country has settled into a stand-off between *Chávistas*, as the president's supporters are called, and the opposition. The rough dividing line is wealth and class, with the majority of the poor forming the president's strongest supporters, and the middle class and the very rich keen to see him go. However, a new class has emerged known as the *Boliburgesia* (Bolibourgeoise), from those who have made their money by supporting Chávez and the Bolivarian Revolution.

However, it has not been plain sailing for the president. On 11 April 2002 he was briefly toppled by a coup, after an opposition march on the Presidential Palace in Caracas was fired on and 17 people were killed, both supporters and opponents of the president. Many of those killed were shot in the head; two more victims died later. The actual details of the massacre, the president's removal and replacement by an ill-advised interim government led by businessman Pedro Carmona, and Chávez's subsequent rescue by loyal garrisons, is still a mystery that may never be clarified. *The Revolution Will Not Be Televised*, a fascinating documentary by two Irish filmmakers who happened to be in Miraflores as the events unfolded, shows firsthand the huge smiles and backslapping that went on among business leaders, media owners and high Church officials as Carmona cancelled all constitutional guarantees and suspended the supreme court.

Despite the obvious outpouring of affection for the president during the coup, when thousands of his supporters surrounded Miraflores demanding to see him, his problems continued that year. An oil strike was called by managers at the state oil firm Petróleos de Venezuela (PDVSA), which again aimed at bringing down the government. Instead, people grew tired of the conflict and the president had to sack 19,000 workers and take even greater control over PDVSA and its revenues, which represent over 50% of the government's revenue.

Since then, the president has won a recall referendum brought by the opposition to try and unseat him in 2004, and in 2006 he won the presidential election with a convincing 63% of the vote. Bolstered by the victory he has accelerated a programme of land redistribution and the nationalisation of large farms and foreign firms, something that business leaders have said is scaring away investment and causing distortions in the economy. In foreign affairs Chávez has allied Venezuela with the left-wing governments of Cuba, Bolivia, Ecuador and Nicaragua in a regional bloc called Alianza Bolivariana para los Pueblos de Nuestra América (ALBA, The Bolivarian Alliance for the Peoples of Our America). Relations with Colombia have deteriorated to an all-time low over Colombian claims that Venezuela has given safe haven to FARC guerrillas – which Chávez has denied – leading to verbal spats with President Álvaro Uribe.

Stepping up the anti-US rhetoric, the president has also sought closer ties with Iran, China and Russia. China helped to launch a Venezuelan communications satellite and Russia has signed oil, gas and arms deals with Venezuela. In 2008, the USA was not pleased to see its old Cold War rival back in the hemisphere, when the Russian navy visited and Russian war planes flew over the Caribbean.

In 2009, Chávez won a referendum allowing him to stand for election indefinitely, and despite growing dissatisfaction with violent crime and rising inflation eroding earnings, the opposition have still not come up with a candidate that could challenge him in the 2012 elections.

GOVERNMENT AND POLITICS

Under the 1999 constitution, the Venezuelan president is elected by universal suffrage for a six-year term and is both head of state and head of government, appointing the vice-president and cabinet. Anybody over 18 can vote and voting is not compulsory. Since a referendum was held in 2009, there are no longer any limits on how many times a president can stand for re-election. The legislative branch is made up of a unicameral parliament, the Asamblea Nacional (National Assembly), which has 167 deputies who are elected to five-year terms. In 2005, the opposition boycotted the legislative elections giving the pro-government parties complete control. After his re-election in 2006, the president called for all the groups supporting him to join the Partido Socialista Unido de Venezuela (PSUV), although some of his previous allies, such as Patria Para Todos (PPT) and Podemos have refused.

The opposition is made up of parties that existed under the Punto Fijo Pact, such as AD, COPEI and Movimiento al Socialismo (MAS), and the new groups Primero Justicia (PJ) and Un Nuevo Tiempo. Riven with internal divisions, the opposition's main problem has been finding a unity candidate with the charisma and policies needed to unseat the president. They point to intimidation of individuals in the media and opposition by the government as a form of authoritarianism.

ECONOMY

A founder member of OPEC, Venezuela is the world's fourth-biggest oil exporter and continues to be heavily dependent on oil revenues to fund social programmes, despite government efforts to increase tax revenue and stimulate exports in other sectors. The state oil firm Petróleos de Venezuela (PDVSA) is the third largest oil firm in the world; oil still provides 80% of export revenues and a third of the country's estimated US$357.6 billion GDP. Venezuela also has the cheapest petrol prices in the world, with a litre of petrol at the pump costing just US$0.20.

Given the regular attacks President Chávez makes on the US and its 'savage neoliberalism', it is ironic that the US is Venezuela's most important trading partner and oil importer. Venezuela's overseas earnings are also boosted by PDVSA's US subsidiary Citgo, which contributes about a third of PDVSA's income from refining fuels including petrol sold at 14,000 Citgo-branded outlets.

PDVSA is involved in the exploration, production, refining and exporting of oil and, increasingly, natural gas. Venezuela's proven oil reserves total some 99.5 billion barrels, and deposits of extra-heavy crude and bitumen in the Orinoco Heavy Oil Belt are estimated at 513 billion barrels, with an extra 135 trillion cubic feet of natural gas. Venezuela is working closely with China to boost oil exports to the Asian country and create joint ventures for heavy crude extraction in Venezuela. Also, under a programme called Petrocaribe, Venezuela has been expanding exports to its neighbours in the Caribbean and Latin America.

PDVSA is already the largest employer in Venezuela and new jobs are expected to accompany the exploitation of its natural gas reserves. Venezuela has proven gas reserves of 176 trillion cubic feet, the second largest in the Western Hemisphere after the US and eighth largest in the world.

One of the reasons Venezuela is so dependent on power generated by hydro-electric dams is to maximise petroleum exports, but that policy had some costly side effects in early 2010, when a severe drought reduced the rivers and dried up the lake feeding the massive Guri Dam, which along with Macagua I, Macagua II and Caruachi, provides over 70% of the country's electricity. The result was government-controlled energy rationing, late opening and early closing of offices and shopping malls, a ban on air conditioning during the hottest months of the year and rolling blackouts across the country that dented the government's popularity.

Non-oil exports are led by steelmaker Sidor, Venezuela's single biggest exporter after oil, which was re-nationalised by President Hugo Chávez in 2008. Aluminium, petrochemicals and textiles are also high on the export list. Other natural resources are iron, bauxite, coal, nickel, gold, diamonds and timber. Agricultural production includes tobacco, beef, chicken, rice, coffee, cocoa and fresh fruit, but local farmers fail to meet more than a third of the nation's food needs, meaning the rest has to be imported.

A government programme of expropriating land considered 'idle' that is suitable for agricultural use has seen some important cattle ranches being taken over in the Llanos region, which had previously been used for conservation and wildlife-watching tours. So far there has been no resulting boost to local food production, which has instead fallen in recent years, partly due to government attempts at price controls, rampant inflation of 25–30% and a lack of private investment in the food sector.

PEOPLE

Venezuelans are easy-going, open and generous people, who like a laugh and don't stand on ceremony. At the same time they are proud and place great value on respect, something to bear in mind when speaking to authority figures such as the police or National Guard. Social life is very important and the usual greeting for women is a kiss on one cheek, while men shake hands with each other or bear hug and backslap animatedly.

While work and study are considered important, with many Venezuelans doing both to try and get ahead, they also love to kick back and enjoy a cool beer or two with friends. Sometimes referred to as the Irish of Latin America, Venezuelans consume the most beer in the region and are proud of their local lagers, which dominate the market. More upwardly mobile drinkers opt for Scottish whisky and Venezuela is an important export market for all the main whisky producers.

Visitors are sometimes surprised by the lack of service culture in Venezuela, which is partly due to never having had a serious tourism industry and partly to the sense of pride that comes from being a major oil exporter. Shop staff can seem surly or sometimes overfriendly due to the familiarity with which they address strangers. A typical greeting to a thin person might be: *'Epale, flaco, en que te puedo ayudar?'* ('Hey there, slim, what can I do for you?'). Venezuelans are not used to haggling for things, so even market traders will refuse to budge on a given price, regardless of whether it means losing a sale.

Venezuelans are also among the vainest people in the world, according to a global survey carried out in 2000, and this is clear from the prevalence of plastic surgery and the effort people take in their appearance, whatever their socio-economic background. It is not uncommon to see girls proudly walking around with bandages on their nose, to show they've had a nose job, and boob jobs are a common present for girls reaching the magic age of 15.

According to the survey, 65% of Venezuelan women said they thought about their looks all the time, compared with only 27% of US women. This is not surprising in a country obsessed with beauty queens and the Miss Venezuela contestants who go on to win crowns at the top international pageants. Venezuela has won a record-breaking six Miss Universe titles and five Miss World titles. Another record was broken in 2009 when Stefanía Fernández picked up the Miss Universe crown from the previous winner, Venezuela's Dayana Mendoza, giving the country back-to-back victories. So obsessed are people with beauty queens that the country's oil tankers are named after them and a popular *arepa* filling made of shredded chicken, avocado, mayonnaise and peas is called La Reina Pepiada (The Curvy Queen) in honour of Susana Dujim, Miss World 1955.

Macho traits are still prevalent among men, and many women are left to raise the family and run the home on their own. But there is sexual equality in the workplace and women occupy some of the top government and banking jobs and outnumber men as civil servants and teachers.

ETHNIC GROUPS IN VENEZUELA

A beautiful *café con leche* skin tone predominates in Venezuela where 70% of the population are a mix of white, Amerindian and African ancestry. Whites make up 20%, blacks account for a further 8%, and Amerindians about 2%. Post-war immigration from Spain, Hungary, Portugal and Italy was followed in later decades by over a million immigrants from Colombia, Ecuador and Peru, plus refugees from the right-wing dictatorships in Argentina, Uruguay and Chile. In the past, a subtle racism existed that was reflected on TV and in adverts by blonde, blue-eyed models in all the main roles, but this has been replaced in recent years by a stronger sense of national identity in the Chávez era.

Members of Venezuela's 24 indigenous tribes are also becoming more evident in the media and in politics. Most belong to the Carib or Arawak language families. The largest group are the Guajiros or Wayúu (297,400) from Zulia State, who are also the most economically competitive, raising cattle and running businesses in Maracaibo and cross-border trading with Colombia. In the east, the Warao people (36,000) live an almost timeless existence in the Orinoco Delta in their *palafito* stilt houses with very few material goods. In the Guiana Highlands, some Pémon (27,300) now run their own travel firms, taking tourists to the *tepuis* of the Gran Sabana. In Amazonas State, the remote Yanomami and related Sanema (18,000) face invasion of their forest privacy by gold miners. The Yekuana or Makiritare (6,700), meanwhile, are fighting for their land rights in the Río Caura and have already mapped their ancestral territory with the aid of global positioning technology. The Panare (4,300), Piaroa (15,000) and Kariña (16,000) continue to defend their cultural traditions.

The constitution of 1999 marked an important step for Indian rights, guaranteeing indigenous peoples' rights to communally occupied land and to the use of their own language. It also guaranteed Indian participation in the government by reserving three seats, elected by ethnic groups, in the National Assembly. These rights have raised self-confidence and opportunities.

LANGUAGE

Spanish is the official language of Venezuela and is softer than that spoken in Spain, clearer to understand and without the lisp, although people do swallow the last consonant on words and leave out the 's' when speaking fast. The people of the Andes have a reputation for speaking well, the inhabitants of Caracas for speaking fast and the Llaneros for a slightly nasal delivery (for basic vocabulary, see *Appendix 1*, page 423). English is studied as a second language but few people can speak it.

Apart from a bilingual menu in places like Margarita Island, the only English you can expect to hear outside Caracas is Spanglish. This hybrid of Spanish and English is most apparent in sports like *beisbol* and *futbol*, but you'll also hear people say *'estoy full'*, when they can't eat any more and the security guard at your local supermarket may be referred to as *'el guachiman'*.

The only way to communicate with people properly is to learn Spanish, either before you arrive or at one of the local schools. In Caracas, the Centro Venezolano Americano (*www.cva.com.ve*) runs courses in Las Mercedes. In Mérida, there are several schools to choose from, including Venusa (*www.venusacollege.org*), the friendly Iowa Institute (*www.iowainstitute.com*) and Jakera (*www.venezuelaspanishschool.com*) which has classes and homestays and another school on Playa Colorado beach near Puerto la Cruz. In Margarita, CELA (*www.cela-ve.com*) offers Spanish courses with cooking and salsa classes.

RELIGION

Along with Spanish, Columbus brought Catholicism to the New World and Venezuelans are still 95% Catholic. Visits to Venezuela by Pope John Paul II in 1985 and 1996 left no doubt about the country's continuing devotion to the Catholic Church as hundreds of thousands turned out *en masse* in the streets on both occasions to see him. But for many people, religion is something you're born with and they happily live with common-law spouses, practise family planning and eat meat on Friday. Increasingly, Protestant Evangelists are making inroads into the culture, especially Brazilian-based church groups such as No Pare de Sufrir which employ impassioned preachers and TV ads to spread the good word. Indeed, the most vigorous religious groups today are the Baptists, Jehovah's Witnesses and Pentecostal groups who have made thousands of converts in small towns all over the country.

SHAMANISM AND CULTS Indigenous groups have their own religious beliefs, many based on a shamanistic system of learning handed down by elders and explained through ancient myth. While many indigenous groups have been converted to Christianity by missionaries, most conserve parts of their tradition.

Local religious cults also have disciples. The María Lionza cult has a sacred site on the mountain of Sorte near Chivacoa, where followers enter into trances and observe rituals in front of images of religious, mythical and historical figures. The pantheon is led by the Tres Potencias (Three Powers): María Lionza, a forest spirit who rides a tapir, the black patriot Negro Felipe, and the Indian chief Guaicaipuro (see *Yaracuy* on page 343*)*.

EDUCATION

Following a major campaign by the government called Misión Robinson, which saw teachers dispatched all over the country and to remote indigenous communities, basic literacy has risen by 3% to just over 95%. This high figure also reflects a history of free education in state schools and universities. Public education is compulsory up to the ninth grade (*ciclo básico*), but 75% of students leave school by the age of 15 or soon after – although other government programmes are offering free classes to adults who want to finish high school. President Chávez eliminated registration fees in a bid to make free education even more accessible, and thousands more poor children have enrolled. Over the past four decades the number of universities quadrupled from seven to 32 and more than 90 technical and university institutes were established with three-year study courses. The Universidad Central de Venezuela (UCV) is the oldest and largest in the country with some 58,000 students; it was founded as a royal seminary in 1721. Its main campus, the University City of Caracas, on which construction was begun in the 1940s, is dotted with artworks and murals and has been declared a UNESCO World Heritage Site for its synthesis of art and architecture. It is one of the few modern examples of a large compound designed and built by a single architect, Carlos Raúl Villanueva. The next oldest is Mérida's Universidad de los Andes (1810), which has some 40,000 students.

CULTURE

As part of the Bolivarian Revolution, art is trying to shed its elitist image and become more accessible to ordinary people. Government spending on culture has doubled and besides the 36 state-supported cultural institutions, orchestras, theatre groups and excellent museums, there are more provincial cultural centres. Playwrights and novelists continue a long literary tradition and ballet, dance, opera and theatre companies all contribute to the nation's lively cultural scene. Annual and biennial events include international theatre, music and graphic arts festivals, with several book fairs.

Misión Cultura is all about promoting folk arts and removing the divisions between high art and local folk culture. The scheme involves giving free access to classical concerts and ballet performances at the Teresa Carrreño theatre in Caracas, radio legislation that sets quotas for the percentage of local music played, affordable bookshops and funding for folkloric events. This isn't the first time it has been tried: a boom in local music in the 1980s saw the emergence of a group of musicians and singers who benefited from a quota system for radio play.

Venezuela is a nation of music makers. Throughout the plains and mountains, people make and play the local four-stringed guitar or *cuatro*, violin, maracas, harp and drums. Less common are the native pan flute, bone flute and deer horn. Despite pop, salsa and foreign influences, there has been a huge resurgence of folk music. Traditional rhythms such as the *joropo*, *golpe* and *décima* are alive and well. In the Llanos, masters of *contrapunteo* verses, often made up on the spot, sing alternately in a duet. At Christmas no-one can escape the *gaita*, the music of Maracaibo in Zulia State, with its insistent beat and satirical or nostalgic lyrics. It is played on local instruments such as the *charrasca*, a rasp, and the odd-looking *furruco*, a drum with a stick attached to the skin head that is played as if the musician is plunging a blocked sink, creating a noise similar to the instrument's onomatopoeic name.

While detractors believe these schemes are simply pandering to the lowest common denominator, the results are there for all to hear. The Metro system in Caracas was once silent but now moves to the sound of *joropos* from the Llanos, and groups playing Afro-Venezuelan drums, or *tambores*, now play at free events in parks and museum spaces. A boom in community radio stations and courses in learning to play the *cuatro*, and other indigenous instruments is also raising the quality of musicians and giving them more places to perform. Instead of fine arts, crafts are now emphasised and indigenous groups have more outlets to show and sell their wood carvings, ceramics and basket-work.

SPORT Unlike the rest of South America, where football reigns supreme, Venezuelan sport is dominated by *beisbol*, a game brought to the country by the US engineers who came to work in the oil camps. Local contests between the top baseball clubs are electric affairs that can unite the country in its national passion and divide the loyalties of families as fans scream for their teams in the stadium and at home. The biggest rivalry is between Los Leones de Caracas and Los Navegantes del Magallanes, now based in Valencia. Caracas have won more championships but Magallanes have a good record of beating Caracas when they meet. There's a party atmosphere when the two teams play and men and women don their baseball shirts and caps and drink large amounts of beer and whisky while they cheer their team. Everything stops when the game starts and even Chávez would never dare interrupt a baseball game with one of his marathon TV interventions. The electricity problems in February 2010 sparked an unprecedented political protest at the Caracas/Magallanes games with fans holding banners saying '*Un, dos, tres. Luz, agua, inseguridad. Presidente, estas ponchao!*' ('One, two, three. Electricity, water, crime. President, you've struck out!'). The slogan was quickly taken up by the opposition. The president was a promising player in his early years and could have turned pro, something his detractors lament. On one of his trips to Cuba he realised a life-long dream by playing in an all-star team against Fidel Castro. Chávez once joked during a run of poor performances by his team, Los Magallanes, that Magallaneras would make good wives, because they stay faithful despite poor results. Venezuelans have made important contributions to Major League Baseball in the US, with 175 players making the move since 1939, such as Luis Aparicio (who played for the Chicago White Sox and Boston Red Sox), Omar Vizquel, Andrés Galarraga, Dave Concepcion and more recently Omar Visquel, Magglio Ordóñez and Johan Santana. Oscar Guillen, the manager of the White Sox, is another famous role model.

While football barely touches baseball in popularity, the national team La Vinotinto (The Burgundy) were once the laughing stock of South America but have come from nowhere to build a team showing great promise. Of the ten countries in the South American qualifying zone, Venezuela are the only one never to have qualified for a World Cup. But they are getting closer to that dream. Solid performances in World Cup qualifiers in the last few years have seen them beating Ecuador, Colombia and Bolivia. Leading the attack are strikers like Juan Arango, who plays for Borussia Mönchengladbach in Germany's first division. Much of the credit for the transformation of the national side can be laid at the door of coach Richard Paez, and the young players who have stuck with a sport that initially offered none of the financial incentives of baseball.

2

Practical Information

WHEN TO VISIT

Venezuela is in the tropics, just a few degrees north of the Equator. It has a bright, sunny climate with no hot or cold extremes, making it a year-round destination for beach lovers, sightseers, wildlife watchers and hikers. Even in the wet months of the rainy season the sun shines for an average of seven to nine hours a day, with heavy downpours punctuated by sunny spells and only a few days lost completely to bad weather. The hottest months are usually April to August when the sun is directly overhead. Travellers who want to see Llanos wildlife should plan to visit in the dry season, known locally as the *temporada seca* (December to April), while Angel Falls is best visited in the rainy season, *temporada de lluvia* (May to November), when higher river levels allow boats to travel to the base of the falls. There are regional differences, too: rains are generally light in Los Roques and Margarita Island and the coastal areas of Coro and Cumaná. The best all-round months to visit are November to January when sunny skies are glorious and nights are cool.

SPECIALIST-INTEREST GROUPS

Avoiding insect bites People allergic to the bites of midges, mosquitoes and ticks should try and travel in the dry season when insect pests, or *plaga*, are fewer, even in the Orinoco Delta. As a general rule, pests are not present at altitudes over 1,200m and are less of a problem on black-water rivers like the Caura River.

Camping, climbing and hiking These activities are best suited to the dry season. For hiking to Roraima in the Gran Sabana, the weather can be less predictable as the mesa mountains have their own weather machines for churning up storms. The dry season is ideal for hiking in the Andes where mud and fog can be downright dangerous. Do not camp on beaches or islands in October and November when winds can drop and tiny gnats can bite mercilessly all night.

Fishing For those interested in deep-sea fishing, Venezuela is a year-round destination, while December to April is best for river fishing and March to September for trout fishing in the Andes.

Photography Go in the rainy season for lush vegetation, blue skies and impressive waterfalls. During the dry season visibility can be poor for panoramas due to the heat haze and dust and smoke in the air.

River travel The dry season is the best time for river travel, with the notable exception of Angel Falls river trips which are made by operators *only* in the wet season as navigation is faster and easier in high water. In general, during the rains biting insects are torture on slow rivers like the Orinoco, its delta and the Llanos tributaries. Travel on the Caura and other swift black-water rivers is splendid in the dry months when waters sparkle and sandbanks grow into beaches for swimming.

Wildlife Animals are amazingly plentiful on the Llanos, or 'plains', during the dry season when waterholes shrink. The number of wading birds is astounding. Birdwatchers should plan well in advance for the Llanos lodges.

Windsurfing Conditions at El Yaque on Margarita Island and Coche – and emerging kitesurfing and windsurfing spots in the Paraguaná and Araya peninsulas – are ideal year round, although the trade winds slacken a little from September to November.

BUSY PERIODS Unless you really want a wild party or are interested in specific festivals, such as the carnival in El Callao or the Corpus Christi devil dancing in Yare, try and avoid the major holidays. Venezuelans flock to the festivals and the beaches during these times, making it near impossible to book hotel rooms, get seats on planes, buses and ferries, or escape from the riotous sounds of full-volume salsa, merengue and reggaeton.

The peak tourism periods in Venezuela are Christmas, which runs from mid-December to 6 January, the moveable feasts of Carnival and Easter (see list of public holidays on pages 64–5) and, to a lesser extent, the school holidays from late July to September.

Other mini-exoduses to the beaches occur around any national holidays falling near a weekend, when Venezuelans make use of the *puente* (literally, 'bridge') to maximise their vacation time.

Taking an international flight is also unadvisable during peak periods but if you must fly, allow three to four hours before departure as there will be queues for seats.

On the other hand, the big cities are at their best during such holidays and the greater influx of local tourists to the Gran Sabana and Amazonas can make it cheaper to get on a group tour to Roraima, the Caura River or Autana Tepui.

HIGHLIGHTS

Venezuela is blessed with spectacular natural treasures, from picture-postcard Caribbean beaches to tropical rainforests, mist-topped mesa mountains, savannas teeming with birds and wildlife and lofty Andean valleys. The new tourism trends are in adventure sports like white-water rafting, paragliding and kitesurfing. Jungle tours in dugout canoes up the Caura River to visit Yekuana Indians and learn about their culture are also growing in popularity, as are detours to the sacred mountain of Sorte for a spiritual immersion in the bizarre cult of Maria Lionza. Travellers are also linking up trips from different hubs, starting in Mérida before making trips to Catatumbo and Los Llanos, then down to Ciudad Bolívar to see Angel Falls and the Orinoco Delta, finishing off in Santa Elena, on the border with Brazil, to visit Roraima and the waterfalls of the Gran Sabana region. This new approach of locally organised tours is partly to do with security concerns and a desire to pack in more activities, and partly due to travellers trying to avoid staying in Caracas. This is a shame because the capital has plenty to offer in terms of restaurants, culture and nightlife – although it's not easy to find safe, reasonably priced accommodation.

ANGEL FALLS This is the top sight for those travellers who can afford to fly to the jungle camp of Canaima where tours to the falls begin. Known as Salto Angel in

Spanish and Parekupai-Meru in the native Pemon, Angel Falls is the world's highest waterfall, with a staggering drop of 979m. Hidden deep in a canyon in southern Venezuela, it wasn't measured until 1948, and can only be seen by plane (dry season) or by a two-day river trip in dugout canoe (rainy season). The people at Disney-Pixar were so inspired by the falls they featured it in the award-winning animated movie *Up* as Paradise Falls.

MOUNT RORAIMA This is another of the wonders of Venezuela's Guayana Highlands, and is among the oldest mountains on earth, dating 3,000 million years to the ancestral super-continent of Gondwana. A six-day trek from Santa Elena to the *Lost World* summit of Roraima, the tallest of the towering table mountains, makes for an unforgettable adventure.

LOS LLANOS Venezuela's cowboy country of seasonally flooded savannas offers an unmatched opportunity to soak up exotic wildlife, including hundreds of bird species from prehistoric hoatzins to giant storks, herons, macaws, scarlet ibis, hawks and eagles. Stay at a cattle ranch and fish for piranhas in rivers filled with spectacled caimans, or take a safari to spot anacondas, howler monkeys, capybaras and even jaguars, if you're lucky.

THE CAURA RIVER Located in the southern state of Bolívar, this is a truly magnificent black-water river of swirling currents that passes through one of the world's last great untouched areas of pristine rainforest. Dugout canoe trips of five to six days include visits to indigenous communities of Sanema and Yekuana Indians before reaching the idyllic riverside beach of El Playon at the base of the portage route to the thundering Salto Para waterfalls.

MÉRIDA This city in the cooler Andes is a backpackers' delight, offering travellers good value accommodation, great food, lively bars and clubs, as well as mountain walks through picturesque villages reached by 4,000m passes. Overlooking the city are the sometimes snowy peaks of the Sierra Nevada and Venezuela's highest point, Pico Bolívar, which at 5,007m is just 242m above the world's highest cable car system (sadly, undergoing a major refurbishment at the time this guide went to press). Mérida has become a base for exploring the rest of Venezuela with tour companies offering climbing, canyoning, rafting, paragliding, horse- and bike-riding tours locally, affordable nature safaris to small ranches in the Llanos region of Barinas, and longer circuits of the country's top tourism destinations.

MUCUPOSADAS IN MÉRIDA These are small *posadas* set up in the farmhouses of local families living far off the beaten track in the high Andean valleys or *páramos* surrounding Mérida. This highly successful responsible tourism project, supported by an EU grant, aims to allow visitors more time to savour the natural beauty of the remote valleys and learn about the lifestyles of the people who inhabit them, as well as generating income for local people.

MARGARITA ISLAND This sun-kissed island boasts lovely sandy beaches and warm seas next to fine hotels and resorts. It also has arguably the best nightlife in Venezuela. But it is the diving opportunities and the year-round, world-class windsurfing at El Yaque, near the airport, that is increasingly bringing watersports enthusiasts to the island.

CORO A colonial city founded in 1527, Coro has pride of place as the oldest continuously settled town in Venezuela with the most handsome colonial architecture and has been given UNESCO heritage status. The city makes a great springboard for trips to the Lawrence-of-Arabia sand dunes of the Médanos and the desert-dry Paraguaná Peninsula, with its fine old village churches. It is also a good stopping point between the beaches of Choroní, the Parque Nacional Mochima and the mountains of Mérida.

LOS ROQUES ARCHIPELAGO This a Blue Lagoon paradise of white sand islands lapped by warm, transparent waters. A short 40-minute flight from the main international airport takes visitors to the airstrip at Gran Roque. The islands are a magnet for honeymooners, who come here to laze on the beaches, while the more adventurous head further out to snorkel, dive or kitesurf and sport-fishermen amuse themselves with the world-class bonefishing.

THE CULT OF MARÍA LIONZA IN YARACUY STATE This is a mysterious and magical local religion unique to Venezuela. A form of folk Catholicism mixed with African and indigenous ritual and belief, it is practised in the mountains of Sorte at special sites where, to the sounds of Afro-Venezuelan drums, mediums channel the spirits of indigenous figures such as María Lionza, Guaicaipuro and a host of other colourful characters. The María Lionza Cult can be equated with Cuba's santeria or Haiti's voodoo and tourism to Sorte has increased recently, following a spate of magazine and newspaper articles about it.

GUÁCHARO CAVE IN CARIPE There are no words that can accurately describe the experience of entering the dark cavern of the Guácharo Cave in Caripe, Monagas State, and hearing for the first time the riotous noise of the strange oilbirds who live there. Squawking away like a flock of demented Daffy Ducks, these nocturnal creatures live completely in the dark, using echolocation to find their way around, and emerge *en masse* from the cave as the light fades in search of food in a spectacular nightly ritual.

CHORONÍ Reached only by a windy road of hairpin turns from the city of Maracay up and over the lush, cloudforest heights of the Parque Nacional Henri Pittier, the village of Choroní and fishing port of Puerto Colombia make for a truly unforgettable Venezuelan destination. Days are spent under palm trees sipping coconut milk on the crescent beach of Playa Grande, while nights are fuelled by fried snapper and Cuba Libre cocktails while you dance to the sound of Afro-Venezuelan drums. Throw in boat trips along the coast to the historic cocoa plantations of Chuao to find out where chocolate comes from and you have yourself a relaxing way to wind down after all those adventure trips.

SUGGESTED ITINERARIES

Venezuela is a vast country and travelling around can be time consuming and exhausting. Night buses from Caracas to Mérida or Ciudad Bolívar can take up to 12 hours. Santa Elena, the starting point for Roraima treks, is a 23-hour bus ride from Caracas and has no scheduled flights to its tiny airport. Travellers from Caracas or Mérida who want to climb the famous *tepui* have to fly to Puerto Ordaz and make the final 12-hour journey by road. Factor in the six-day trek to the top and you have already filled a week. Angel Falls is easier to organise, as in the rainy season boat trips to the base of the falls can be done in two days and one night, while five-seat Cessnas leave Ciudad Bolívar for Canaima every morning when full. Solo travellers or those travelling in twos and threes will have to factor in delays getting on locally organised trips to Los Llanos, Roraima, Angel Falls, Río

Caura and the Delta Amacuro as most operators will only travel with a minimum of four tourists. The benefit of having everything arranged before you arrive is that you can keep these delays to a minimum and maximise your time in the country. Below are some suggested itineraries to help you plan your trip to Venezuela. They all assume that Caracas is the start and end point of your visit. If you have more specific aims, such as birding particular areas or tracking down wildlife, then you will have to adapt your plans accordingly.

A WEEKEND If you only have a weekend free in Caracas you might want to escape from the concrete jungle and explore the leafy forest paths and cascading waterfalls of the Ávila Mountain, starting in Altamira. If you want to travel further out by car or bus you can head for the picturesque valley of Colonia Tovar to enjoy a blowout on German-style sausages and strawberries and good souvenir shopping. Fresh mountain air and cool nights make a welcome respite from the heat of the city.

Alternatively, sunseekers with cash to spare might want to fly to the Blue Lagoon islands of Los Roques and spend a relaxing weekend swimming in warm, translucent waters and enjoying fabulous fish and seafood at one of the many *posadas* that offer lodging on Gran Roque, the tiny capital.

ONE WEEK A week in Venezuela is enough time to do any of the activities listed above but it also gives you enough time to explore the coast and visit fishing villages, such as Choroní and its fine palm-fringed beach Playa Grande, or the beautiful islands of Parque Nacional Morrocoy. Once tanned, relaxed and in step with the laid back Venezuelan attitude to time you might want to head off to the Andean city of Mérida for a few days of gentle mountain walking, or action-packed adrenaline sports such as paragliding, mountain-biking and white-water rafting. From Mérida, it's possible to take a trip to the wildlife wonderland of Los Llanos for few days of birding, anaconda-spotting or piranha-fishing, before returning once more to Caracas.

The more adventurous might want to head straight down to Ciudad Bolívar, with its well-preserved colonial architecture, and take a flight from there to the jungle camp of Camaima to take in the spectacular sight of Angel Falls, the world's highest waterfall. The return journey could take in the mysterious Cueva de los Guácharos, a large cave inhabited by screeching nocturnal oilbirds.

TWO WEEKS A fortnight allows further exploration around the safe base of Mérida and a trip to the remote southern shores of Lake Maracaibo, the largest lake in South America. There you can experience El Relámpago de Catatumbo, a natural phenomenon of thunder-less lightning that lights up the sky for 140 to160 nights of the year.

Another circuit, using Ciudad Bolívar as a hub, would allow a trip to one of the riverside jungle camps in the Orinoco delta and a few days spent wildlife watching and piranha fishing with the Warao indigenous people, famed for their dugout canoes and knowledge of jungle plants.

Serious hikers coming purely for the challenge of climbing to the summit of Mount Roraima will want to head straight down to Santa Elena, on the border with Brazil, and start their six-day hike. The second week can be spent swimming and snorkelling on the beaches and islands of the Parque Nacional Mochima, reached via Ciudad Bolívar, and possibly also include a visit to the Cueva de los Guácharos or two days in Canaima to see Angel Falls.

THREE WEEKS With three full weeks to play with it's much easier to get the full Venezuelan experience of Caribbean beaches, Andean mountains and tropical jungle. A circuit starting in Mérida could include a hike to one of the isolated Andean guesthouses, known as Mucuposadas, for an overnight stay with a local family in a beautiful valley. The whitewater rafting rivers of Barinas would then take you to Los Llanos and on to Ciudad Bolívar and trips to either Angel Falls or Delta Amacuro, followed by the trek to Roraima, and ending up with a few days chilling at the beach in either Los Roques, Morrocoy, or the lively Caribbean resort island of Margarita.

FOUR WEEKS With a month to spend you might want to canoe up the Río Caura for five days, through one of Venezuela's most pristine forests, to spend time with the Yekuana indigenous group at El Playón, a white beach on the banks of the river below the majestic Salto Para waterfalls. You could also squeeze in a trip to the spectacular but little-visited beaches of the Peninsula Paria, such as Playa Medina, a perfect crescent of palm trees giving on to orange sands and Kodak-moment sunsets. Alternatively, you could break up a trip to Morrocoy or Mérida by fitting in a few days at the Unesco heritage site of Coro, a city of beautifully-preserved historic buildings and close to the rolling sand dunes of the Médanos de Coro that rise out of the surrounding scrubby desert like a Lawrence of Arabia mirage.

TOUR OPERATORS

UK

Audley Travel New Mill Lane, Witney, Oxon OX29 9SX; 01993 838000, 01993 838650; www.audleytravel.com

Dragoman Camp Green, Debenham, Stowmarket, Suffolk IP14 6LA; 01728 861133; e info@ dragoman.co.uk; www.dragoman.com

Explore Nelson Hse, 55 Victoria Rd, Farnborough, Hants GU14 7PA; 0845 0131537; e res@ explore.co.uk; www.explore.co.uk

Geodyssey 116 Tollington Pk, London N16 3RB; 020 7281 7788; e enquiries@geodyssey.com; www.geodyssey.com

Journey Latin America 12–13 Heathfield Terr, London W4 4JE; 020 8747 8315; www.journeylatinamerica.co.uk

Last Frontiers The Mill, Quainton Rd, Waddesdon, Bucks HP18 0LP; 01296 653000; e info@ lastfrontiers.com; www.lastfrontiers.com

Latin American Travel Association 020 8715 2913; e info@lata.org; www.lata.org

Naturetrek Cheriton Mill, Cheriton, Alresford, Hants SO24 0NG; 01962 733051; e info@ naturetrek.co.uk; www.naturetrek.co.uk

Reef & Rainforest Tours Dart Marine Pk, Steamer Quay, Totnes, Devon TQ9 5AL; 01803 866965; e mail@reefandrainforest.co.uk; www.reefandrainforest.co.uk

Sunvil Sunvil Hse, Upper Sq, Old Isleworth, Middx TW7 7BJ; 020 8568 4499; e latinamerica@ sunvil.co.uk; www.sunvil.co.uk

US

Adventure Center 1311 63rd St, Suite 200, Emeryville CA 94608; +1 800 486 9096; e explore@ adventurecenter.com

GAP Adventures 364 Av of the Americas, New York NY 10011-8402; +1 212 228 6655; e greenwichstore@gap.ca; www.gapadventures.com

Iexplore 833 W Jackson, Suite 500, Chicago, IL 60607; +1 800 439 7567; www.iexplore.com

Lost World Adventures 217 East Davis St, Decatur GA

30030; +1 404 373 5820; e info@ lostworld.com; www.lostworld.com

Miller South America 3003 Van Ness St NW Ste S-823, Washington DC 20008; +1 202 250 6004; e info@miller.travel; www.miller.travel

Victor Emanuel Nature Tours 2525 Wallingwood Dr, Suite 1003, Austin TX 78746; +1 512 328 5221; e info@ventbird.com; www.ventbird.com

AUSTRALIA

GAP Adventures Level 1, 172 Bridge Rd, Richmond, VIC 3121, Melbourne; +61 1300 796 618;

e melbourne@gapadventures.com.au; www.gapadventures.com

IN VENEZUELA Travellers on tight schedules who want to pack in as much as possible should consider the many multi-destination options being offered by local Venezuelan operators. Increasingly, agencies and well-established *posadas* in the main independent traveller destinations of Caracas, Mérida, Ciudad Bolívar and Santa Elena are linking up to offer the same deals to tourists as they would get locally. The alternative, if you really want to save money and don't mind waiting a few days to get a group together, is to take a chance and negotiate the best price at the closest jump off point to your desired destination. So Santa Elena or San Francisco de Yuruani would be the cheapest place to pick up a Roraima tour and the airport in Ciudad Bolívar the best place to get a last-minute rainy season bargain to Canaima and Angel Falls (see relevant destination sections as well as below for local operators).

Akanan Travel Edificio Grano de Oro, Planta Baja, Local C, Calle, Bolívar, Chacao, Caracas 1060; ✎ 0212 264 2769, 0212 715 5433, 0212 715 5433, 0212 266 8663; e akanantours@akanan.com, akanantravel@gmail.com; www.akanan.com; Skype: akanantravel. Juan Carlos Ramirez has been organising expeditions & leading film crews into the wilds to make documentaries for years & is a pioneer of eco-friendly tours & many new routes, including mountain biking to Canaima in the Gran Sabana & visits to the less-visited *tepui* mountains. Akanan organise regular trips to Auyan-tepui, Caura River, Paria Peninsula & canyoning, diving & jungle survival courses, with a dedicated team & well-maintained 4x4 vehicles. Clients are also offered a mobile phone to use while on their trip. The friendly English-speaking office close to the main square in Chacao has a wealth of maps & other resources & offers free internet for Bradt readers.

Alpitour Torre Centro-piso 1, Parque Boyacá, Av Sucre, Los Dos Caminos, Caracas; ✎ 0212 283 1433, 0212 283 1033; e linda.sonderman@alpi-group.com; www.alpi-group.com. Alpi is run by an avid fisherwoman, Linda Sonderman, who can arrange bonefishing trips to Los Roques, payara & peacock bass fishing in Amazonas & Bolívar, & tarpon & snook on the coast. She also arranges charters for crewed sailboats, yachts & 4–30-seater planes.

Angel Eco-Tours Shares its office with Osprey at Av Casanova, Sabana Grande, 2da Av de Bello Monte, Edificio La Paz, Piso 5, Oficina 51, Caracas 1050, ✎ 0212 762 5975; e info@angel-ecotours.com; www.angel-ecotours.com. The company offers some more upmarket accommodation options than Osprey on some of its adventure trips.

Montaña Adventure Edf Las Americas, 3 pb, Av Las Americas, Apartado Postal 645, Mérida, Estado Mérida; ✎ 0274 266 1448; e info@venadventure.com; www.venadventure.com. Andean ecotourism firm headed by Jerry Keeton makes treks with porters & pack animals from *pueblo* to *pueblo*; birdwatching from the *páramo* down to the plains & mountain biking. Also Gran Sabana tours, Roraima.

Natoura Travel & Adventure Tours Calle 31 Junín, entre Av Don Tulio y prolongación, Av 6 No 5–27, Mérida, 5101; ✎ 0274 252 4216, 0274 252 4075; e info@natoura.com; www.natoura.com. José Luis Troconis & Renate Reiners run one of the leading travel companies in Mérida, offering local mountain treks & tours, trout fishing, accommodation, transport, bilingual guides, plane tickets & help with reservations as well as tours to Roraima, Angel Falls, Los Llanos, birdwatching trips & mountain biking. Very friendly, helpful, & offer competitive rates.

Orinoco Tours Torre A-piso 7, Galerías Bolívar, Bd de Sabana Grande, Caracas; ✎ 0212 761 8431; e info@orinocotours.com; www.orinocotours.com. A small outfit in Sabana Grande offering Ávila trips on foot or by jeep, Parque Nacional Henri Pittier, wildlife lodges in Los Llanos, by river into the delta, up the Caura, or from Canaima to Angel Falls — at reasonable rates.

Osprey Travel Av Casanova, Sabana Grande, 2da Av de Bello Monte, Edificio La Paz, Piso 5, Oficina 51, Caracas 1050; ✎ 0212 762 5975, 0212 762 9890; e ben@ospreyexpeditions.com, benrodriguez@yahoo.com; www.ospreyexpeditions.com; Skype: ospreyexpeditions. A young, friendly, English-speaking team offer good advice on budget tours around the country, including all the major adventure spots, Los Roques, Mérida, Orinoco Delta & multi-destination packages.

See *Chapter 3* for tour operators who can assist with trips involving special-interest sports.

RED TAPE

All travellers should have a passport valid for at least six months from their date of arrival in Venezuela. Vaccination or health certificates are not required to enter the country but a yellow-fever vaccination certificate will be needed for onward travel to Brazil through a land border.

Nationals of the UK, USA, Ireland, Australia, South Africa, Canada, New Zealand and Japan do not need a visa for short tourist trips of up to 90 days. Airlines and cruiseships are authorised to issue you a 90-day **tourist card** (*tarjeta de ingreso*), at no cost. While in Venezuela always keep your tourist card and passport with you as photocopies are not acceptable as identity documents.

Extensions for periods of up to 60 days can be obtained in Caracas from the Servicio Administrativo de Identificación, Migración y Extranjería (SAIME; Administrative Service for Identification, Migration and Foreigners) at the central SAIME office in the Mil building in Plaza Miranda along Avenida Baralt in the centre of town. Extensions, or *prórrogas*, cost about US$70 and the whole process can be a major headache, including an early start to find the right office and hours waiting in line. You will need two passport photos, a letter in Spanish written on lined legal paper (*papel sellado*) stating the reason for extending your stay and a photocopy of your plane ticket (see SAIME website for latest regulations: *www.saime.gob.ve*). If you have all the right papers it takes two days for the extension to come through. It's actually easier to leave the country and fly back in with a new tourist card!

For entry by land from Colombia or Brazil a tourist visa is no longer strictly needed. Although a multiple-entry one-year tourist visa obtained in your country of residence would avoid all problems, free tourist cards *should* be issued at border crossings to the nationals listed above. As this may depend on the guard officer on duty, who may not know official requirements, go to a Venezuelan consulate early in your travels and early in the day, in the bigger the city the better (ie: Bogotá or Cartagena), before you get to Cúcuta. Even then, the consulate may be out of cards and offer only a tourist visa, which must be paid for (US$40). If consuls in Manaus or Boa Vista in Brazil are away on a trip, you may have to hang around. On the other hand, if you arrive near the end of the week you may be asked to pay for *habilitación*, which is the consul's service when he's off-duty, even if the tourist card is free.

Your passport and tourist card must both be stamped by immigration officials on entering and leaving the country. If the SAIME office is not at the border itself make sure you go to the nearest one during office hours. Make photocopies of the information page of your passport and your ticket in case of loss.

Travellers under the age of 18 unaccompanied by a relative are required to have a letter of authorisation signed by their parents or legal guardian, with a photocopy of their identity document.

Don't accept a **transit visa** (*tránsito*) unless you are headed for the airport. It is only good for emergencies, is valid for 72 hours, and cannot be extended or changed into a tourist visa. Transit visas are intended for passengers, airline staff and sailors who can prove imminent departure.

A **transient visa** (*transeunte*) allows you to work or study, but requires health and 'good conduct' certificates, a sponsor or job, prior SAIME approval, US$50, and a great deal of patience. Legally, transient visas should be applied for outside Venezuela.

Ⓔ EMBASSIES

ABROAD
Australia Culgoa Circuit O'Malley, ACT 2606, Canberra; \ 6290 2967, 6290 2968; e embaustralia@ venezuela-emb.org.au; www.venezuela-emb.org.au;

🕐 10.00–113.00 Mon, Tue & Thu, 10.00–14.00 Wed & Fri

Canada 32 Range Rd ON – KIN 8J4, Ottawa; ☎ 613 235 5151; e info.canada@misionvenezuela.org; www.misionvenezuela.org

France 11, rue Copernic, Paris 75116; ☎ 01 45 53 29 98; e info@amb-venezuela.fr; www.embavenez-paris.fr; ⏰ 09.30–17.30 Mon–Fri

Germany Schillstrasse 9-10, 10785 Berlin; ☎ 030 832 2400; e embavenez.berlin@botschaft-venezuela.de; www.botschaft-venezuela.de; ⏰ 10.30–13.30 Mon–Thu

Spain Calle Capitán Haya 1, planta 13, Edf Eurocentro Madrid, 28020; ☎ 91 598 1200; www.embajadadevenezuela.es; ⏰ 09.30–14.00 & 15.00–16.00 Mon–Fri

UK Cromwell Rd, London SW7 2HW; ☎ 020 7584 4206, 020 7581 2776; e info@venezlon.co.uk; www.embavenez-uk.org; ⏰ 09.00–13.00 & 14.00–17.00 Mon–Fri

US 1099 30th St, NW, Washington, DC 20007; ☎ 202 342 2214; e apaiva@embavenez-us.org; www.embavenez-us.org; ⏰ 09.00–13.00 & 14.00–17.00 Mon–Fri

IN VENEZUELA Consulates in the abbreviated list below are generally open to the public for visas on weekday mornings, 09.00–13.00, except where noted.

Australia Has no embassy in Venezuela. The Canadian embassy handles Australia's consular affairs.

Canada Av Francisco de Miranda con Av Sur, Altamira, Caracas; ☎ 0212 600 3000, 0212 600 3042, 0212 600 3043; e crcas@international.gc.ca; www.canadainternational.gc.ca/venezuela; ⏰ 07.30–16.30 Mon–Thu, 07.30–13.00 Fri

France Calle Madrid at Av Trinidad, Las Mercedes; ☎ 0212 909 6500; e infos@francia.org.ve; www.francia.org.ve

Germany Edif La Castellana-p10, Av José Angel Lamas at Av Principal de La Castellana; ☎ 0212 219 2500; e info@caracas.diplo.de, embajadaalemanacara@cantv.net; www.caracas.diplo.de

Ireland Torre Alfa, PH, Av Principal de Santa Sofia, El Cafetal; ☎ 0212 959 8754, 0212 959 9049; e irlconven@cantv.net

Netherlands Edif San Juan, Piso 9, Av San Juan Bosco at Trans 2, Altamira; ☎ 0212 276 9300; e car@minbuza.nl; www.mfa.nl/car/homepage

Spain Quinta Embajada de Espana Av Mohedano, 1ra y 2da Transversal, La Castellana, PO Box 62297, Chacao; ☎ 0212 263 2855, 0212 263 3876, 0212 263 0932, 0212 263 1956; e emb.caracas@mae.es

UK Torre La Castellana, 11th Flr, Av Principal de La Castellana, La Castellana, Caracas 1061; ☎ 0212 263 8411; www.ukinvenezuela.fco.gov.uk; ⏰ 08.00–12.30 & 13.30–16.30 Mon–Thu, 08.30–13.15 Fri. For out of hours emergency assistance call ☎ 0212 263 8411 & your call will be redirected.

US Calle F at Calle Suapure, Colinas de Valle Arriba; free phone: ☎ 0800 100 5154; ☎ 0212 975 6411; e irccaracas@state.gov, acsvenezuela@state.gov; http//caracas.usembassy.gov; ⏰ 08.00–17.00 Mon–Fri

GETTING THERE AND AWAY

✈ BY AIR

Flying from the UK There are no direct scheduled flights to Venezuela from UK airports. The only option is to fly via a European or US hub. There is little difference in price between the two options (roughly £500–800 depending on time of year) but it is worth bearing in mind that there is more red tape involved now in passing through US airports as a transfer passenger due to increased security measures.

Buy a return ticket as discounted airfares are harder to come by in Venezuela and it will be cheaper to book all your flights from the UK.

Check for deals with several UK travel agents or online before booking as there are significant differences in low- and high-season fares. To find cheap tickets to Venezuela from the UK try Expedia (*www.expedia.co.uk*), Cheap Flights (*www.cheapflights.co.uk*), Skyscanner (*www.skyscanner.net*) or Opodo (*www.opodo.co.uk*). For specialist advice contact Trailfinders (☎ *020 7938 3939; www.trailfinders.com*), which has several offices in the UK offering cheap flights, accommodation, a vaccination centre and insurance scheme, or Travelbag (☎ *020 7810 6645; www.travelbag.co.uk*).

All journeys via Europe require a transfer at a European airport and the main airlines flying to Caracas are Lufthansa (*www.lufthansa.com*) via Frankfurt, Air France (*www.airfrance.com*) via Paris, Iberia (*www.iberia.com*) via Madrid, and Alitalia (*www.alitalia.com*) via Rome.

Flying from the US The airlines travelling to Venezuela via the US are American Airlines (*www.aa.com*) via Dallas, New York, or Miami, Delta (*www.delta.com*) via Atlanta, and Continental (*www.continental.com*) via Houston. Chilean airline LAN (*www.lan.com*) flies from Miami to Caracas on Mondays and Fridays. TACA (*www.taca.com*) flies daily from Los Angeles to Caracas. Avianca (*www.avianca.com*) flies from Miami to Caracas via Bogotá. A return ticket from Miami costs about US$600–800 depending on time of year.

To find cheap tickets to Venezuela from the US check the following companies: Cheap Flights (*www.cheapflights.com*), Orbitz (*www.orbitz.com*) and LowestAirfare (*www.lowestairfare.com*).

Flying from Canada The only direct flight to Caracas is with Air Canada (*www.aircanada.com*) from Toronto (starting at about US$700 return up to about US$1200 depending on time of year). Other alternatives are to fly to US hubs like Miami and transfer to a US or South American carrier.

Flying from elsewhere There are direct flights to and from Venezuela from:

Aruba Aserca (*www.asercaairlines.com*) and Avior (*www.avior.com.ve*) fly to Caracas.

Brazil TAM (*www.tam.com.br*) flies daily from Manaus and Río de Janeiro while TACA (*www.taca.com*) and TAM fly from Sao Paulo to Caracas.

Colombia Avianca (*www.avianca.com*) has four flights daily from Bogotá to Caracas (about US$500 return trip) and Panamanian airline COPA (*www.copaair.com*) flies from Cartagena on Tuesdays, Thursdays and Saturdays. Avianca and COPA also fly from Medellin to Caracas.

Curaçao Avior, Aserca and Dutch Antilles Express (*www.flydae.com*) fly to Caracas.

Ecuador Colombian airline Avianca flies from Guayaquil daily to Caracas.

Panama COPA has a daily flight to Caracas, as does Venezuelan airline Santa Barbara (*www.sbairlines.com*).

On arrival Most visitors fly into Venezuela through the Simón Bolívar International Airport in Maiquetía (*www.aeropuerto-maiquetia.com.ve*), the country's main airport, about an hour's drive away from the capital Caracas. See page 90 for details of getting to/from the airport. Charter flights for package tours from Germany and Canada fly to the Santiago Marino Airport in Margarita. Caracas and Margarita airports have flights to airports in Barcelona, Barquisimeto, La Vigia (for Mérida), Los Roques and Maracaibo.

On departure Check-in times are three hours before international flights and one to two hours before domestic flights, but queues may form even earlier as new anti-drug measures have been implemented by the National Guard, including luggage checks and full body scans of random passengers, which are very time consuming. See page 90 for further information.

Departure tax Many operators in Europe and the USA will advise that all taxes are included in your ticket, but when leaving Venezuela on an international flight all passengers are required to pay a departure tax – BsF165 (about US$40) in late 2010. This must be paid in cash, but if you run out of bolivares you can change US dollars or euros in the airport. Remember: because of exchange controls you will not be able to change any bolivares back into dollars or euros (see *Exchanging money*, page 51).

BY BOAT A service between Trinidad and eastern Venezuela is offered once a week by Acosta Asociados (*for reservations in Trinidad* \ *868 634 4472; in Güira* \ *0294 982 0058;* e *grupoacosta@cantv.net*). The modern, air-conditioned 150-passenger ship sails from Trinidad to Güira in Sucre State on Wednesday morning and returns the same afternoon; the crossing takes four hours and costs around US$100 one way. There are extra sailings during Carnival but call the office in Güira before making any plans as the service is sometimes interrupted and they rarely reply to email. (For details see page 219.)

BY BUS There are no bus companies at the moment offering through journeys from Brazil, Colombia and Ecuador to the main Venezuelan cities. Travellers coming to Venezuela from Colombia must take a bus to Cúcuta to cross the border at San Antonio del Táchira and then continue by bus or plane from San Cristóbal (see page 387). The other crossing point in Colombia is Maico, in the northern Guajira region, where you can catch a bus to Maracaibo (see page 412).

From Brazil, buses from Manaus or Boa Vista reach the border at Santa Elena on the Venezuelan side, where you can catch a bus to Ciudad Bolívar and Caracas (see page 289).

A valid passport and visa are required when crossing borders and a yellow-fever vaccination certificate is compulsory for entry to Brazil.

✚ HEALTH *with Dr Felicity Nicholson*

Venezuela is not a primitive country. Private hospitals and clinics in all the major cities and towns are good and surgeons are excellent, but this is a tropical country and it's important to take into account the special health considerations that apply in some areas. Some parts of Venezuela, including the more remote areas of the Orinoco Delta, Bolívar State and Amazonas, carry a risk of malaria, yellow fever and other insect-borne diseases.

IMMUNISATION Preparations to ensure a healthy trip to Venezuela require checks on your immunisation status: it is wise to be up to date on tetanus, polio and diphtheria (now given as an all-in-one vaccine, Revaxis, that lasts for ten years), and hepatitis A. Immunisations against hepatitis B and rabies may also be recommended. Proof of vaccination against yellow fever is needed for entry into Venezuela if you are coming from another yellow fever endemic area. The World Health Organisation (WHO) recommends that this vaccine should be taken for Venezuela by those over nine months of age, although proof of entry is only officially required for those over one year of age. If the vaccine is not suitable for you then obtain an exemption certificate from your GP or a travel clinic.

Hepatitis A vaccine (Havrix Monodose or Avaxim) comprises two injections given about a year apart. The course costs around £100, but may be available on the NHS; it protects for 25 years and can be administered even close to the time of departure. Hepatitis B vaccination should be considered for longer trips (two months or more) or for those working with children or in situations where contact with blood is likely. Three injections are needed for the best protection and can be given over a three-week period if time is short for those aged 16 or over. Longer schedules give more sustained protection and are therefore preferred if time allows. Hepatitis A vaccine can also be given as a combination with hepatitis B as 'Twinrix', though two doses are needed at least seven days apart to be effective for the hepatitis A component, and three doses are needed for the hepatitis B. Again this schedule is only suitable for those aged 16 or over.

The newer injectable typhoid vaccines (eg: Typhim Vi) last for three years and are about 85% effective. Oral capsules (Vivotif) may also be available for those aged six and over. Three capsules over five days last for approximately three years but may be less effective than the injectable forms They should be encouraged unless the traveller is leaving within a few days for a trip of a week or less, when the vaccine would not be effective in time.

Vaccinations for rabies are ideally advised for everyone, but are especially important for travellers visiting more remote areas, especially if you are more than 24 hours from medical help and definitely if you will be working with animals (see *Rabies*, page 44).

Experts differ over whether a BCG vaccination against tuberculosis (TB) is useful in adults: discuss this with your travel clinic.

In addition to the various vaccinations recommended above, it is important that travellers should be properly protected against malaria. For detailed advice, see below.

Ideally you should visit your own doctor or a specialist travel clinic (see opposite) to discuss your requirements if possible at least eight weeks before you plan to travel.

MALARIA Seek advice from a travel clinic (see opposite) on the best anti-malarial tablets to take. Different parts of Venezuela require different tablets, depending on the resistance patterns of the malaria. Trips to the Angel Falls, Delta Amacuro and parts of Bolívar State all pose malaria risks as do deep jungle trips in Amazonas State, the region in southern Venezuela bordered by Colombia and Brazil. If mefloquine (Lariam) is suggested, start this 2½ weeks before departure to check that it suits you; stop it immediately if it causes depression or anxiety, visual or hearing disturbances, severe headaches, fits or changes in heart rhythm. Side effects such as nightmares or dizziness are not medical reasons for stopping unless they are sufficiently debilitating or annoying. Anyone who has been treated for depression or psychiatric problems, is diabetic on oral therapy or who is epileptic (even if the fits were in the past), or has a close blood relative who is epileptic, should avoid mefloquine.

Malarone (proguanil and atovaquone) is as effective as mefloquine. It has the advantage of having few side effects and need only be continued for one week after returning. However, it is expensive and because of this tends to be reserved for shorter trips. Malarone may not be suitable for everybody, so advice should be taken from a doctor. The licence in the UK has been extended for up to three months' use and a paediatric form of tablet is also available, prescribed on a weight basis.

The antibiotic doxycycline (100mg daily) is a viable alternative when either mefloquine or Malarone are not considered suitable for whatever reason. Like Malarone, it can be started one day before arrival. Unlike mefloquine, however, it may also be used in travellers with epilepsy, although certain anti-epileptic medication may make it less effective. Users should be aware of the possibility of about 1–3% of people developing allergic skin reactions in sunlight. The drug should be stopped if this happens. Women using an oral contraceptive should use an additional method of protection for the first four weeks when using doxycycline. It is unsuitable in pregnancy or for children under 12 years.

All prophylactic agents should be taken with or just after the evening meal and should be washed down with plenty of water. Alcohol is usually compatible with all malaria tablets but should not be used to help swallow the medication! Always complete the course as recommended (one to four weeks after your return, depending on the regime) unless there is a medical reason not to do so.

In Venezuela, anti-malaria pills are dispensed only by agencies of the Health Ministry, Ministerio de Sanidad y Asistencia Social, but it is unlikely you will be near one. You should get your tablets before you leave home from a reliable source.

Travellers to remote parts may wish to consider carrying a course of treatment to cure malaria. At present Malarone or Coarthemeter is the favoured regime, but it would be best to take up-to-date advice on the current recommended treatment. Self-treatment is not without risks and generally people over-treat themselves. If at all possible consult a doctor if you are taken ill since diagnosing malaria is difficult without laboratory facilities.

The symptoms of malaria appear from one week to a year after exposure and may be no worse than a dose of flu initially but more often there is high fever, shivering, chills, profuse sweating, nausea and even diarrhoea and vomiting. In *falciparum* malaria there may be all this plus hallucinations, headache, numbness of the extremities and eventually fits or coma. Given prompt treatment, most people (99%) recover. A number of effective drugs treat malaria. Indeed quinine, derived from the Amazonian cinchona tree, was widely used from 1700, before the disease was understood.

No prophylactic is 100% protective but those on prophylactics who are unlucky enough to catch malaria are less likely to get rapidly into serious trouble. Whether or not you are taking malaria tablets, or carrying a cure, it is important to protect yourself from mosquito bites.

TRAVEL CLINICS It is wise to visit a travel clinic – if you can – a couple of months before departure to arrange your immunisations. As well as providing an immunisation service, travel clinics usually sell a good range of mosquito nets, treatment kits, repellents and malaria medicines.

A full list of current travel clinic websites worldwide is available on www.istm.org/. For other journey preparation information, consult www.nathnac.org/ds/map_world.aspx. Information about various medications may be found on www.netdoctor.co.uk/travel.

UK

Berkeley Travel Clinic 32 Berkeley St, London W1J 8EL (near Green Park tube station); ☏ 020 7629 6233; ⏰ 10.00–18.00 Mon–Fri, 10.00–15.00 Sat
Edinburgh Travel Health Clinic 14 East Preston St, Newington, Edinburgh EH8 9QA; ☏ 0131 667 1030; www.edinburghtravelhealthclinic.co.uk; ⏰ 09.00–19.00 Mon–Wed, 09.00–18.00 Thu & Fri. Travel vaccinations & advice on all aspects of malaria prevention. All current UK prescribed anti-malaria tablets in stock.
Fleet Street Travel Clinic 29 Fleet St, London EC4Y 1AA; ☏ 020 7353 5678; e info@fleetstreetclinic.com; www.fleetstreetclinic.com; ⏰ 08.45–17.30 Mon–Fri. Injections, travel products & latest advice.
Hospital for Tropical Diseases Travel Clinic Mortimer Market Centre, Capper St (off Tottenham Ct Rd), London WC1E 6JB; ☏ 020 7388 9600; www.thehtd.org; ⏰ 09.00–16.30 Mon, Tue & Fri, 10.00–16.30 Wed. Offers consultations & advice, & is able to provide all necessary drugs & vaccines for travellers. Runs a Travellers' Healthline Advisory Service (☏ 020 7950 7799) for country-specific information & health hazards. Also stocks nets, water purification equipment & personal protection measures. Travellers who have returned from the tropics & are unwell, with fever or bloody diarrhoea, can attend the walk-in emergency clinic at the hospital without an appointment.
InterHealth Travel Clinic 111 Westminster Bridge Rd, London SE1 7HR; ☏ 020 7902 9000; e info@interhealth.org.uk; www.interhealth.org.uk; ⏰ 08.30–17.30 Mon–Fri. Competitively priced, one-stop travel health service by appointment only.
MASTA (Medical Advisory Service for Travellers Abroad) At the London School of Hygiene & Tropical Medicine, Keppel St, London WC1E 7HT; ☏ 09068 224100 (this is a premium-line number, charged at 60p per min); e enquiries@masta.org; www.masta-travel-health.com. For a fee, they will provide an individually tailored health brief, with up-to-date information on how to stay healthy, inoculations & what to take.

MASTA pre-travel clinics ☏ 01276 685040; www.masta-travel-health.com/travel-clinic.aspx. Call or check the website for the nearest; there are currently 50 in Britain. They also sell malaria prophylaxis, memory cards, treatment kits, bednets, net treatment kits, etc.
NHS travel websites www.fitfortravel.nhs.uk, www.fitfortravel.scot.nhs.uk. Provide country-by-country advice on immunisation & malaria prevention, plus details of recent developments, & a list of relevant health organisations.
Nomad Travel Clinics Flagship store: 3–4 Wellington Terrace, Turnpike Lane, London N8 0PX; ☏ 020 8889 7014; e turnpike@nomadtravel.co.uk; www.nomadtravel.co.uk; walk in or appointments ⏰ 09.15–17.00 every day with late night Thu. Also has clinics in west & central London, Bristol, Southampton & Manchester — see website for further information. As well as dispensing health advice, Nomad stocks mosquito nets & other anti-bug devices, & an excellent range of adventure travel gear. Runs a Travel Health Advice line on ☏ 0906 863 3414.
The Travel Clinic Ltd, Cambridge 41 Hills Rd, Cambridge CB2 1NT; ☏ 01223 367362; e enquiries@travelclinic.ltd.uk; www.travelcliniccambridge.co.uk; ⏰ 10.00–16.00 Mon, Tue & Sat, 12.00–19.00 Wed & Thu, 11.00–18.00 Fri
The Travel Clinic Ltd, Ipswich Gilmour Piper, 10 Fonnereau Rd, Ipswich IP1 3JP; ☏ 01223 367362; ⏰ 09.00–19.00 Wed, 09.00–13.00 Sat
Trailfinders Immunisation Centre 194 Kensington High St, London W8 7RG; ☏ 020 7938 3999; www.trailfinders.com/travelessentials/travelclinic.htm; ⏰ 09.00–17.00 Mon, Tue, Wed & Fri, 09.00–18.00 Thu, 10.00–17.15 Sat. No appointment necessary.
Travelpharm www.travelpharm.com. The Travelpharm website offers up-to-date guidance on travel-related health & has a range of medications available through their online mini-pharmacy.

Irish Republic
Tropical Medical Bureau 54 Grafton St, Dublin 2; ☏ +353 1 2715200; e graftonstreet@tmb.ie; www.tmb.ie; ⏰ until 20.00 Mon–Fri & Sat

mornings. For other clinic locations, & useful information specific to tropical destinations, check their website.

Any prolonged immobility including travel by land or air can result in deep vein thrombosis (DVT) with the risk of embolus to the lungs. Certain factors can increase the risk and these include:

- Previous clot or close relative with a history
- People over 40 but increased risk in those aged over 80 years
- Recent major operation or varicose veins surgery
- Cancer
- Stroke
- Heart disease
- Obesity
- Pregnancy
- Hormone therapy
- Heavy smokers
- Severe varicose veins
- People who are very tall (over 6ft/1.8m) or short (under 5ft/1.5m)

A deep vein thrombosis (DVT) causes painful swelling and redness of the calf or sometimes the thigh. It is only dangerous if a clot travels to the lungs (pulmonary embolus). Symptoms of a pulmonary embolus (PE) include chest pain, shortness of breath, and sometimes coughing up small amounts of blood and commonly start three to ten days after a long flight. Anyone who thinks that they might have a DVT needs to see a doctor immediately.

PREVENTION OF DVT
- Keep mobile before and during the flight; move around every couple of hours
- Drink plenty of fluids during the flight
- Avoid taking sleeping pills and excessive tea, coffee and alcohol
- Consider wearing flight socks or support stockings (see www.legshealth.com)

If you think you are at increased risk of a clot, ask your doctor if it is safe to travel.

Practical Information HEALTH

2

USA
Centers for Disease Control 1600 Clifton Rd, Atlanta, GA 30333; 800 232 4636 or 800 232 6348; e cdcinfo@cdc.gov; www.cdc.gov/travel. The central source of travel information in the USA. Each summer they publish the invaluable *Health Information for International Travel*.

IAMAT (International Association for Medical Assistance to Travelers) 1623 Military Rd, #279 Niagara Falls, NY 14304-1745; 716 754 4883; e info@iamat.org; www.iamat.org. A non-profit organisation with free membership that provides lists of English-speaking doctors abroad.

Canada
IAMAT (International Association for Medical Assistance to Travellers) Suite 10, 1287 St Clair St West, Toronto, Ontario M6E 1B8; 416 652 0137; www.iamat.org

TMVC Suite 314, 1030 W Georgia St, Vancouver, BC V6E 2Y3; 604 681 5656; e vancouver@tmvc.com; www.tmvc.com. One-stop medical clinic for all your international travel health & vaccination needs.

Australia and New Zealand
IAMAT (International Association for Medical Assistance to Travellers) 206 Papanui Rd, Christchurch 5, New Zealand; www.iamat.org

TMVC (Travel Doctors Group) 1300 65 88 44; www.tmvc.com.au. 30 clinics in Australia & New Zealand, including: *Auckland* Canterbury Arcade, 174

It is dehydration that makes you feel awful during a bout of diarrhoea and the most important part of treatment is drinking lots of clear fluids. Sachets of oral rehydration salts give the perfect biochemical mix you need to replace what your body has lost but they do not taste very nice. Any dilute mixture of sugar and salt in water will do you good, so if you like Coke or orange squash, drink that with a three-finger pinch of salt added to each glass. Otherwise make a solution of a four-finger scoop of sugar with a three-finger pinch of salt in a glass of water. Or add eight level teaspoons of sugar (18g) and one level teaspoon of salt (3g) to one litre (five cups) of safe water. A squeeze of lemon or orange juice improves the taste and adds potassium, which also needs to be replaced. Drink two large glasses after every bowel action, and more if you are thirsty. If you are not eating you need to drink at least three litres a day. If you feel like eating, choose a bland, high-carbohydrate diet; heavy greasy foods will give you cramps.

If the diarrhoea is bad, you are passing blood or have a fever, you will probably need antibiotics in addition to fluid replacement. Ciprofloxacin, norfloxacin are good antibiotics for dysentery or bad diarrhoea and a three-day course is usually sufficient. These are a far better treatment than the 'blockers' like Imodium although there may be situations where you need both. Be careful about what you take from local pharmacies: drugs like chloramphenicol (sold as Chloromycetin, Catilan or Enteromycetin) and the sulpha antibiotics (eg: Streptomagma) have too many serious side effects to be worth the risk in treating simple diarrhoea. Do not take them!

Queen St, Auckland 1010, New Zealand; ✆ 9 373 3531; e auckland@traveldoctor.co.nz; *Brisbane* 75a Astor Terrace, Spring Hill, Brisbane, QLD 4000, Australia; ✆ 3815 6900; e brisbane@traveldoctor.com.au; *Melbourne* 393 Little Bourke St, Melbourne, Vic 3000, Australia; ✆ 9935 8100; e melbourne@traveldoctor.com.au; *Sydney* 428 George St, Sydney, NSW 2000, Australia; ✆ 9221 7133; e sydney@traveldoctor.com.au

South Africa
SAA-Netcare Travel Clinics ✆ 011 802 0059; e travelinfo@netcare.co.za; www.travelclinic.co.za. 11 clinics throughout South Africa.

TMVC NHC Health Centre, Cnr Beyers Naude & Waugh Northcliff; ✆ 0861 300 911; e info@traveldoctor.co.za; www.traveldoctor.co.za. Consult the website for clinic locations.

Venezuela
Vacuven Edificio Centro Uno, Av Mariscal Sucre; ✆ 0212 551 2641/7271; e vacuven@cantv.net; www.vacuven.com.ve. This is a vaccination centre in Caracas located a block north of the Centro Medico hospital in San Bernardino. It provides all the standard immunisation shots such as hepatitis A & B, influenza, tetanus, polio, yellow fever, respiratory infections & anti-venom for snake bites (you can also buy the serum). However, it is always best to obtain vaccinations prior to departure to ensure that they are working before you arrive.

POSSIBLE MEDICAL PROBLEMS
Travellers' diarrhoea Travellers' diarrhoea is common amongst those visiting Venezuela, and the newer you are to exotic travel, the more likely you will be to suffer. Yet simple precautions against diarrhoea will also protect you from typhoid, cholera, hepatitis, dysentery, polio and worms. Travellers' diarrhoea and other faecal-oral diseases most often occur when cooks do not wash their hands after a trip to the toilet; yet if your food has been thoroughly cooked and arrives piping hot, you will be safe despite this. The maxim to remind you what you can safely eat is:

This means that fruit you have washed and peeled yourself or hot foods should be safe but raw foods, cold cooked foods and salads are risky. A local practice is to sprinkle plenty of vinegar on simple salads of tomato, carrot and onion and leave for a few minutes before digging in. Foods kept luke-warm in hotel buffets can also be dodgy.

It is much rarer to get sick from drinking contaminated water but it can happen, so never drink from the tap in Venezuela, although it's OK to clean your teeth with tap water. Water should have been brought to the boil, or passed through a good bacteriological filter or purified with chlorine dioxide. Most restaurants serve filtered water in a jug. Bottled water in Venezuela is generally safe, but insist that bottles are opened at the table.

Insect bites

Avoiding insect bites Pack long, loose, 100%-cotton clothes and use a spray, repellent stick or roll-on containing 50% DEET (N,N-diethyl-meta-toluamide) such as Repel, which offers a good range from 20 to 100% DEET (sadly, vitamin B alone does not work). Keep this to hand at all times and even spray some on your mosquito net or under the hammock to stop insects biting through the net if you roll against it.

Night-biters Mosquitoes and sandflies can transmit malaria and leishmania between dusk and dawn, so at sundown don long clothes and apply repellent on any exposed flesh. Malaria mosquitoes are voracious and hunt at ankle-level so apply repellent under your socks too. Sleep under a bed net or fan, or in an air-conditioned room.

Day-biters During days out in the forest, it is wise to wear long, loose clothes with trousers tucked into socks. This will help to protect you from the day-biting *Aedes* mosquitoes, which can spread dengue and yellow fevers, and also against ticks and chiggers. Minute pestilential blackflies are also active during the day and spread river blindness in some parts of tropical South America, although this is very rare in Venezuela. The disease is caught close to fast-flowing rivers where the flies breed. Eucalyptus-based natural repellents do not work against them but DEET-based repellents will offer some protection.

Sandflies These insects are very small and most active at twilight but bite throughout the night. Some transmit leishmania, a protozoan disease causing painless tropical sores that, in extreme cases, eat away at the flesh leaving leprosy-like lumps or holes in the skin. Sandflies are able to penetrate mosquito netting but treating the net with insecticide keeps them out. Ceiling fans – if available – will help keep them off. Sandflies are the biggest problem in rainforests. Leishmania is relatively common and difficult to treat, so precautions against being bitten must be taken seriously. The severe and untreatable form of the lowland disease is called espundia.

Dengue fever The day-biting *Aedes aegypti* mosquito is responsible for spreading dengue fever, and therefore it is wise to apply repellent if you see any mosquitoes around. This disease may mimic malaria but there is no prophylactic treatment available. Symptoms include strong headaches, rashes, excruciating joint and muscle pains and high fever, hence its other name: breakbone fever. Dengue fever only lasts for a week or so and is not usually fatal. Complete rest, paracetamol and plenty of fluids are often all that is required. It is especially important to protect yourself if you have had dengue fever before: a second infection with a different strain can result in the potentially fatal dengue haemorrhagic fever. However, dengue is not a threat in wilderness areas because it has no animal vectors: the mosquito must breed within 100m of human habitation. There have been epidemics in several cities including Caracas, where a quarter of cases were the serious haemorrhagic sort requiring hospitalisation, but this is a reflection of the previous exposure of the local population and not an immediate cause for panic.

Chagas' disease Chagas' disease or American Trypanosomiasis is a potentially serious disease caused by the protozoan *Trypanosoma cruzi* and is spread by the biting or Reduviid 'kissing' bug (*Panstrongylus megistus*) which is endemic in Central and South America. The disease is most prevalent in rural areas where the bugs live in mud walls and only come out at night. Avoidance is the best method so when travelling through an endemic region try not to sleep in adobe huts where the locals sleep, keep away from walls when sleeping and use mosquito nets. Spraying the insides of rooms with an insecticide spray is also a good idea.

Symptoms include swelling around the site of the bite followed by enlargement of the lymph glands and fever. Long-term symptoms include damage to the heart causing sudden death and paralysis of the gut causing difficulty in swallowing and severe constipation.

There is no preventative vaccine or medication for Chagas' disease and treatment is difficult as agents toxic to the trypansomes are also toxic to humans.

Flesh maggots The macaw or warble-fly lays her eggs on mosquitoes so that when the mosquito feeds, the warble infants can burrow into the victim's skin. Here they mature to cause an inflammation, which will need surgical removal. Now there's another reason to avoid mosquito bites!

Jiggers or sandfleas (niguas) These are minute flesh-feasters, not to be confused with chiggers (see opposite). They are spread by wildlife and dogs and latch on if you walk barefoot in contaminated places (locals will know where). You do not see them or feel them, until about a week after exposure when an irritation becomes noticeable on the soles of your feet or at the side of a toenail: this is not a bite but the egg sac. These need to be picked out by a local expert; if the distended flea bursts during eviction the wound should be dowsed in spirit, alcohol or kerosene to avoid infection.

The best protection is to avoid going barefoot; beach shoes are advisable for river trips.

Ticks Ticks transmit a variety of unpleasant infections in the Americas including Rocky Mountain spotted fever, but there is no Lyme disease in Venezuela. Ticks should ideally be removed as soon as possible as leaving them on the body increases the chance of infection. They should be removed with special tick tweezers that can be bought in good travel shops. Failing that you can use your finger nails: grasp the tick as close to your body as possible and pull steadily and firmly away at right angles to your skin. The tick will then come away complete, as long as you do not jerk or twist. If possible douse the wound with alcohol (any spirit will do) or iodine. Irritants (eg: Olbas oil) or lit cigarettes are to be discouraged since they can cause the ticks to regurgitate and therefore increase the risk of disease. It is best to get a travelling companion to check you for ticks; if you are travelling with small children, remember to check their heads, and particularly behind the ears.

Spreading redness around the bite and/or fever and/or aching joints after a tick bite imply that you have an infection that requires antibiotic treatment, so seek advice. However, it is normal for the welt left by a tick bite to itch for weeks.

The chigger, chivacoa or itch mite Both ticks and these pestilential microscopic mites can be kept off by spraying repellent on your boots and tucking trousers into socks. If you sit down on a trail and break out later (the next day) with red bites, particularly under your belt, waste no time in using an antihistamine cream. To cut down itching, as standard practice on returning from the field, scrub well with antiseptic soap and leave the lather on for three minutes.

Bees Africanised bees are present all over Venezuela, even in cities. Danger comes frighteningly fast when they are disturbed by noise or vibrations, for instance bush-whacking with a machete or using a chainsaw. Unlucky victims can avoid the bees by diving into the nearest pond, where possible, but multiple bee stings can produce a life-threatening crisis. In this event shock can only be met swiftly with anaphylactic injections. People who have experienced any allergic reactions to food or insect stings should carry an emergency anaphylaxis kit (epinephrine). There is a ready-to-use one available in the US and UK called an EpiPen. You can only get an EpiPen on prescription from a GP or other doctor in the UK.

Bilharzia Bilharzia or schistosomiasis (*Schistosoma mansoni*) occurs only in Lake Valencia, Camatagua Reservoir and some coastal rivers of the Litoral and Barlovento. It can be avoided by knowing a little about the parasite, which is acquired by bathing, swimming, paddling or wading in fresh water in which people with bilharzia have excreted. Getting out of the water within ten minutes and vigorously towelling yourself dry should reduce the risk to a minimum. Avoid bathing or paddling on shores within 200m of villages or places where people use the water a great deal, especially shores where there is lots of waterweed. Covering yourself with DEET insect repellent before swimming is also protective, but this may detract from the joy of bathing.

If your bath water comes from a risky source try to ensure that the water is taken from the lake or river in the early morning and stored snail-free, otherwise it should be filtered or have Dettol or Cresol added. Well water should be safe. Bathing early in the morning is safer than bathing in the afternoon or evening. If you think you have exposed yourself to bilharzia parasites, arrange a screening blood test (your GP can do this) more than six weeks after your last possible contact with suspect water.

Skin infections Skin infections set in remarkably easily in warm climates and any mosquito bite or tiny cut is a potential entry point for bacteria. It is essential, therefore, to clean and cover even the slightest wound. Creams are not as effective as a good drying antiseptic such as dilute iodine, potassium permanganate (a few crystals in half a cup of water) or crystal (or gentian) violet. One of these should be available in most towns. If the wound starts to throb or becomes red and the redness spreads or the wound oozes, and especially if you develop a fever, antibiotics will probably be needed; flucloxacillin (250mg capsules four times a day) or cloxacillin (500mg four times a day). For those allergic to penicillin, erythromycin (500mg twice a day) for five days should help. See a doctor if the infection does not improve in 36–48 hours.

Fungal infections also get a hold easily in hot moist climates so wear 100%-cotton socks and underwear and shower frequently. An itchy rash in the groin or flaking between the toes is likely to be a fungal infection. This needs treatment with an antifungal cream such as Canesten (clotrimazole). If this is not available try Whitfield's ointment (compound benzoic acid ointment) or crystal violet (although this will turn you purple!).

Sun protection
Prickly heat A fine pimply rash on the torso is likely to be heat rash; cool showers, dabbing dry (not rubbing) and talc will help. If it's bad you may need to check into an air-conditioned hotel room for a while. Slowing down to a more relaxed schedule, wearing only loose, baggy, 100%-cotton clothes and sleeping naked under a fan can help to reduce the problem.

Sunburn The incidence of skin cancer is rocketing as Caucasians are travelling more and spending more time exposing themselves to the sun. Sun exposure also ages the skin, making people prematurely wrinkly; cover up with long, loose clothes, put on plenty of suncream and wear a hat when you can. Remember that the sun's rays are very direct (even when skies are overcast), and get stronger as altitude rises. Keep out of the sun in the middle of the day and if you must expose yourself, build up gradually from 20 minutes per day. Be especially careful of sun reflected off water and wear a T-shirt and lots of waterproof SPF15 suncream when swimming; also Bermuda shorts when snorkelling or you may get scorched thighs.

Heatstroke You are most likely to suffer from heatstroke within the first week or ten days of arriving in a hotter, more humid climate. It is important to slow down, drink plenty of fluids and avoid hard physical exercise in the middle of the day, particularly at first. Treatment for heat exhaustion is rest in the shade and sponging with cool water, plus lots to drink.

Dehydration The key when in the tropics is to drink more than normal and before you get thirsty, especially at first. The telltale sign is not always thirst, but dark urine, irritability and fatigue (leading to mental confusion). Catch it early as, if undiagnosed, the syndrome can develop serious, long-lasting consequences, especially in older travellers. Beer is no substitute for water!

Foot injuries If you wear light canvas shoes on sea or river trips where you need to get in and out of the water, you are more likely to avoid injury and less likely to get venomous fish spines in your feet. If you do tread on a venomous fish or a stingray strikes you, soak the foot in hot (but not scalding) water until well after the pain subsides: this may take 20–30 minutes. Remember to take your foot out of the water when adding more hot to avoid scalding yourself. If the pain returns, re-immerse the foot. Once the venom has been heat-inactivated, get a doctor to check the wound and remove any bits of fish spines.

Rabies If you are venturing into the rainforest ask around about dangerous wildlife. When sleeping outside, a net will keep off vampires as well as smaller biters. Any mammal can carry rabies and the disease is common in bats (especially vampires); village dogs that attack and draw blood must also be assumed to be rabid. Following suspected exposure (bites, scratches, licks to open wounds) scrub the wound with soap and running water for ten minutes and then flood with local spirit or dilute iodine. Also be aware that rabies can be contracted from inhalation of bat droppings!

At least two post-exposure rabies injections are needed for those who have been immunised; the un-immunised need even more injections, together with rabies immunoglobulin (RIG). RIG is expensive (around US$900 a dose) and is also in very short supply, which is a good reason for taking the pre-exposure vaccine.

You should always seek help immediately, ideally within 24 hours, but since the incubation period for rabies can be very long it is never too late to bother. Death from rabies is probably one of the worst ways to go.

DANGEROUS ANIMALS

Snakes Despite their reputation, snakes rarely attack unless provoked and travellers are most unlikely to get bitten. All the same, wearing stout shoes and long trousers when in the forest is a sensible precaution. Most snakes are harmless and many of the highly venomous and brightly coloured coral snakes have such small mouths they are unlikely to be able to bite you unless you offer them an ear lobe to nibble. Even those larger venomous species capable of harm will dispense venom in only about half of their bites; bearing this in mind may help you to stay calm in the unlikely event of being bitten. Most first-aid techniques do more harm than good: cutting into the wound is harmful and tourniquets are dangerous; suction and electrical inactivation devices do not work; the only treatment is antivenom. In case of a bite that you fear may have been from a venomous snake:

- Try to keep calm – venom may not have been dispensed
- Stop movement of the bitten limb by applying a splint
- Keep the bitten limb below heart height to slow the spread of any venom
- If you have a crepe bandage, bind up as much of the bitten limb as you can, but release the bandage every half hour
- Get to a hospital that has antivenom as soon as possible
- Never give aspirin; you may offer paracetamol, which is safe
- Never cut or suck the wound
- Do not apply ice packs
- Do not apply potassium permanganate

If the offending snake can be captured without the risk of someone else being bitten, take this to show the doctor, but beware since even a decapitated head is able to dispense venom in a reflex bite.

Local snake antivenom (*suero antiofídico*) is effective against both the rattlesnake (*cascabel*) and fer-de-lance (*mapanare*); it should be administered by medical experts. In Caracas you will find such doctors at the Periférico de Coche Emergency Hospital, Clínica El Ávila and Hospital Urológico (see *Travel clinics* on page 37). Antivenom is also sold and administered by the Vacuven vaccination centre (*Av Mariscal Sucre, Edif Medicentro, San Bernardino;* \ *0212 551 2641; www.vacuven.com.ve*).

Self-prescribing has its hazards so if you are going anywhere very remote consider taking a health book (see *Appendix 2, Further information* on page 432).

Stingrays and piranhas There are plenty of venomous creatures in the sea but be aware that South America also boasts freshwater stingrays whose barbed tails inflict damage as well as dispensing venom. Candirú fish make fine travellers' tales for scaring the uninitiated; stories are exaggerated to the level of fiction. Don't worry about piranhas, or caibes as they are known locally, in black-water rivers where there are few. However, they are altogether a different kettle of fish in the muddy white-water rivers of the Llanos where it's difficult to tell their true numbers, especially in the dry season when watercourses shrink. In these slower rivers, ask the locals for advice and swim only where they swim. For what to do about stingray spines, see *Foot injuries* opposite.

SEX Travel in a beautiful tropical paradise can sometimes lead to sexual adventures, especially when alcohol reduces inhibitions. Remember the risks of sexually transmitted infection are high, whether you sleep with fellow travellers or with locals. About half of HIV infections in British heterosexuals are acquired abroad. Make sure you pack plenty of condoms or femidoms, as they are hard to find in some parts of Venezuela. If you notice any genital ulcers or discharge get treatment promptly; sexually transmitted infections increase the risk of acquiring HIV. AIDS is known as SIDA in Spanish. The Fundacion Daniela Chappard (*www.salvasida.org*) is a private Caracas-based organisation working to raise awareness about the disease and has useful information on specialised clinics around Venezuela. There are more than 110,000 people with HIV in Venezuela (2003 figures) and the stigma that still surrounds the disease means that many more prefer not to come forward. HIV/AIDS is prevalent in areas visited by tourists and precautions should be taken.

FIRST-AID KIT No visitor to Venezuela planning to spend time on jungle journeys or visiting remote areas should travel without a decent first-aid kit. If you plan to trek in heat take plasters and rehydration sachets. Repellent is a must in most areas outside the main towns and cities. Here is a checklist of useful items you might want to pack:

- Anti-diarrhoea tablets – loperamide or diphenoxylate
- Antifungal cream
- Anti-inflammatory tablets – ibuprofen
- Antiseptic cream or wipes
- Bandages and plasters
- Blister patches
- Glucose energy tablets
- Iodine tincture or tablets for water purification
- Painkillers – paracetamol or aspirin
- Mosquito repellent containing DEET in cream and spray
- Rehydration sachets
- Scissors, tweezers

SAFETY

Venezuela has high levels of violent crime in some of its major cities, such as the capital Caracas, Valencia and Maracaibo, and in the border regions with Colombia. All visitors must exercise caution during their time in the country, especially when arriving at Maiquetía Airport. Frightening news reports of murders, muggings, kidnappings and so-called express kidnappings (*secuestro express*) – where victims are held for short periods, or taken to an ATM and made to empty their accounts – can make some people give up on the idea of visiting Venezuela completely. The country's reputation wasn't helped by a 2008 article in *Foreign Policy* magazine that dubbed Caracas the murder capital of the world, easily beating Cape Town, New Orleans and Moscow. A 2009 study saw the Caracas murder rate surpassed by Ciudad Juarez in Mexico, which was at the centre of a war between drug cartels and the government at the time. Newspapers in Caracas report a regular tally of 50 murders every weekend in the capital alone. However, it should be noted that the crime figures reflect the grim reality of life in Venezuela's poorest neighbourhoods, where most murders occur, and the majority of visitors will travel without incident.

The UK Foreign Office advises that visitors exercise caution in the capital Caracas to avoid pickpockets and to avoid all shantytown areas. It also advises against visiting areas of Táchira, Zulia and Apure states bordering Colombia as guerrillas, paramilitaries and organised crime gangs have carried out kidnappings in those regions.

Exchange controls and a lucrative black market for local currency also present security problems for visitors, who should be wary of changing money on the streets or in the main airport of Maiquetía near Caracas.

One of the reasons why Mérida has boomed as a travel destination is because it is seen as a safer alternative to Caracas. The rise in multi-destination packages being sold by Venezuelan tour operators is also an attempt to offer visitors a safer experience, because they have something organised for every stage of the trip, reducing the amount of time spent hanging around bus stations or looking for places to stay in unknown destinations.

To reduce the risk of crime:

- Always follow advice about places to avoid. Don't wander into shantytown areas, *barrios*, or walk around alone at night in unfamiliar neighbourhoods.
- Avoid travel on public transport during peak hours when buses and subway carriages are packed and pickpockets, especially kids, are harder to avoid.
- When travelling or sightseeing don't wear expensive chains, rings or watches (don't take them to Venezuela at all) and keep valuables such as iPods, digital cameras or mobile phones out of sight as much as possible.
- Keep money in a money belt or locked in a hotel safe. If you are mugged, do not put up resistance. It is always good to have some spare money to hand over, kept separately from your money belt, and a separate stash in a sock or shoe to get you back to your hotel.
- Be cautious of accepting food and drinks from strangers and try to travel in a group.
- When travelling by car, leave valuables out of sight or locked in the boot.
- Carry your passport and tourist card with you at all times. People found by the police or National Guard to be *indocumentado*, without valid ID, are liable to be fined, imprisoned or at the very least harassed. Carry your passport well hidden in an inside pocket or money belt, separate from your money. As a precaution against loss, scan the main pages of your passport and email yourself a copy; keep a photocopy of your airline ticket and all other documents as well, and leave copies at home with family or friends.

See also *Exchanging money* on page 51.

SOLO TRAVELLERS Venezuela is no harder or easier than other places in South America for lone travellers. You have to pay more for a room, it can be harder to organise tours, you have to ask strangers to look after your stuff when you go for a swim at the beach and it can get lonely, especially if you can't speak the language. There are very few English-speakers outside the main cities in Venezuela so every word and expression you learn before you go will help to make travelling easier and increase the chance of striking up friendships along the way. It will also make your travels safer as you can get advice from the locals on where to go and where to avoid. Most solo travellers head for the places where they know they will meet other travellers, such as Mérida – a good place to organise tours to other parts of the country as you can easily find others to hook up with and bigger groups get better deals on price. Bigger groups also offer more safety – you can take it in turns to look after bags at bus stations and you present less of a target to muggers and opportunists. For women travelling solo, this is an even greater reason to seek out travel buddies; see overleaf for more information.

WOMEN TRAVELLERS Like most of Latin America, Venezuela is a macho country where men feel the need to demonstrate their masculinity by showing their appreciation of women, in some cases every woman they come across. This includes whistling through their teeth to get attention or blowing a few kisses and following up with lame chat-up lines, or *piropos*, that are so old they probably came over with Columbus. These *piropos* generally include references to angels falling from heaven and the word '*mamacita*', meaning 'little mummy'. Venezuelan women are used to this and generally ignore all unwanted comments, good and bad, by putting on an indifferent expression and staring straight ahead as if they heard nothing. As a rule it's best to follow that procedure and ignore any comments rather than taking the bait and saying something as this will only encourage further banter. Blonde-haired, blue-eyed lady travellers will get more attention because they stand out more and single females will get a lot more attention than those travelling in a group with men.

However, it is also worth stating that Venezuelan men are also very friendly and charming and will make flattering remarks to women friends, colleagues and acquaintances as a matter of course, without meaning any disrespect.

For safety, females travelling solo should be cautious when first arriving in the country until they settle in, should not take taxis at night unless from a taxi rank and should avoid arriving in bus stations either very early in the morning or at night. If possible, it is best to take tours with other travellers and stick to places where other travellers congregate, such as Choroní, Mérida, Santa Elena and El Yaque in Margarita, which are more laid back, self-contained and easier to navigate. Women travellers should always be cautious about accepting drinks from strangers due to the availability of date rape drugs.

Venezuelan women may appear in the tiniest of *tangas* (g-strings) on the beach but Venezuela is still a conservative country and it is better to err on the side of caution when choosing an outfit until you feel comfortable in your surroundings. While it may be acceptable in other countries, topless bathing is illegal in Venezuela and generally frowned upon. Foreign women who sunbathe topless in Margarita or mainland beach resorts will only attract the wrong kinds of attention.

GAY/LESBIAN TRAVELLERS Gay men may find themselves stared at if they hold hands or kiss in public and '*marico*', meaning 'gay', is still used as an insult among macho men. Venezuela has not yet passed a law allowing same-sex marriages but the government has agreed in principle to extending gay rights to civil marriages and attitudes towards homosexuality and homosexuals are definitely moving towards greater acceptance. The annual Gay Pride march held every 4 July in Caracas has grown from 100 or so marchers in 2000 to several thousand and has spread to other cities. Gay activists are also getting more involved in politics and protests. In 2010 a 'Miss Fat Gay Venezuela' beauty pageant was held in Caracas aimed at breaking down stereotypes with humour. A Venezuelan Gay, Lesbian, Bisexual and Transgender (GLBT) group on Facebook has over 500 members and is used to promote awareness as well as being a place to make friends and discuss issues.

Gay and lesbian travellers will find a very inviting and vibrant local gay and lesbian scene, especially in the main cities and resorts. There are a host of gay nightclubs in Margarita and Caracas (see *Gay Caracas*, page 99). A Turkish baths scene in the main cities and beaches such as Playa El Agua in Margarita and Playa Grande in Choroní are well-known gay holiday spots.

An online magazine and chat group at www.orbitagay.com also has up-to-date information on events and parties in the main Venezuelan cities.

WHAT TO TAKE

Common sense will tell you what to pack: if it's a beach holiday with swimming and snorkelling, bring lots of suncream (SPF15 and above), sunblock for your face, and a mask and snorkel. If you plan only to visit coastal areas such as Margarita or Los Roques and you have room in your luggage bring your own flippers too, as hire costs add up. Bring a floppy hat to protect shoulders and the base of your neck from sunburn, as well as a baggy long-sleeved T-shirt and long surfing shorts or a sarong for when the sun gets too much. Canvas shoes are a cheap way to protect feet from sharp coral or sea urchins when snorkelling and flip-flops with straps are a great investment. (See *Chapter 6*, page 133, for further advice on what to take when visiting the marine national parks.)

If you are backpacking in the Andes, or climbing Roraima, remember it may be alternately hot during the day and cold at night. You will need light rainwear and layers of clothes – two thin wool sweaters, or a zip-up hoody and a sweatshirt will be more practical than a thick jumper, which is bulky and impractical for the rest of your trip. If you are camping on your own rather than with an organised tour, you'll need all the usual gear: light tent, stove (Bluet Gaz canisters are available in cities), three-season sleeping bag and thermal sleeping mat. Decent mountain gear, although expensive, can be found in sports shops in Caracas and Mérida.

Those travelling on their own to remote regions should take or buy a fine mesh mosquito net (the self-standing sort is unavailable in Venezuela), malaria pills, light cotton clothes, a light blanket for chilly tropical nights, and plastic bags to keep clothes and cameras dry. Insect repellent is essential, both spray and cream, and the best protection is to wear a long-sleeved shirt, long trousers and long socks (spray socks and cuffs). A hat is essential for river travel and savanna walking and so is a water bottle.

Everyone should have a rain poncho (cheap, plastic) or light cagoule, a torch and a small head torch (essential for a night-time trip to the loo in the jungle), a couple of toilet rolls in a waterproof bag and a basic first-aid kit (see *Health* on page 46). Also handy are earplugs (for noisy hotels or buses), strong needles and thread or dental floss for repairs, and a disposable lighter.

A good Spanish phrasebook and pocket dictionary will also come in handy for getting around and as a conversation starter. Any attempt to speak the lingo, however badly, will be most appreciated.

Coffee is excellent in Venezuela but tea drinkers should bring their own supply, as tea is regarded as a drink for sick people (and sometimes, shudder, a teabag is dangled in a cup of hot milk).

$ MONEY

On 1 January 2008 Venezuela changed its currency from the bolívar (Bs) to the bolívar fuerte (BsF), effectively knocking three noughts off the old currency so that Bs1,000 became BsF1. New notes are in circulation of BsF2, 5, 10, 20, 50 and 100 and coins of BsF1 and small denomination coins of 1, 5, 10, 12.5, 25 and 50 centavos (cents). Given the confusion created by having old and new currency, travellers should check notes carefully before accepting them. The BsF100 has a picture of Simón Bolívar, BsF50 shows Simón Rodriguez, Bolívar's teacher, BsF20 shows Independence heroine Luisa Caceres de Arismendi, BsF10 shows Indian chief Guaicaipuro, BsF5 shows Independence hero Pedro Camejo, or *Negro Primero* and BsF2 shows Francisco de Miranda.

CREDIT CARDS In cities credit cards are useful in the larger hotels, shops and supermarkets. They are required for car hire and, more importantly, for medical care as private hospitals require deposits before accepting patients. Many small-town hotels and businesses are not affiliated to credit card companies because they are charged a 7–10% commission. Visa and MasterCard are the most widely used (issued by a dozen different banks), then American Express. Diners is the least accepted. Cash advances from abroad by credit card are fast and easy; however, this service may be unavailable outside major cities. Let your bank or credit card company know that you will using your card abroad to avoid a stop being put on transactions.

☞ **WARNING:** Credit cards are vulnerable to a practice known as skimming, by which an impression is taken of your card, enabling it to be reproduced. Never let the card out of your sight at a hotel or restaurant.

EXCHANGING MONEY The exchange rate is fixed by the government, and buying and selling bolivares outside Venezuela is almost impossible, except perhaps on eBay. The exchange rate at the time of publication is BsF4.43 to US$1, after being increased from BsF2.60 to US$1 in July 2009.

ATM withdrawals with Visa or MasterCard are calculated at the official exchange rate of BsF4.30.

Italcambio (**e** *info@italcambio.com*) has exchange booths at the main airports and in Caracas. Before changing money, count your notes in full view of the teller to avoid a bill getting 'lost' afterwards. Always change money before leaving major cities. It is useful to carry some small denomination dollar bills for emergencies.

NB: the fixed-rate exchange system, and controls on how many dollars Venezuelans can exchange for business trips or holiday travel, has given rise to a so-called 'parallel market' for dollars and euros that offers higher rates. Some hotels and tour companies will offer these parallel rates when discussing prices. It must be kept in mind that exchanging money unofficially is illegal and great caution should be exercised when approached at the airport or in the street by people wanting to change money. Criminals are aware that tourists are coming into the country with large quantities of dollars in cash to take advantage of the higher parallel rates, which raises the risk of muggings. There have been cases of fake notes being exchanged, sleight of hand tricks or simply enticing tourists to 'a quiet place' to undertake a transaction and then robbing them.

A further complication of the currency controls is that you cannot change back any bolivares at the end of your trip. So only change as much as you will need, taking into account the departure tax you must pay to leave the country.

Cash Although there is a market for euros and they can be exchanged in most major cities in Venezuela, it is much easier to exchange dollars, even in some small towns. There is no point trying to exchange UK pounds except perhaps in Caracas.

Travellers' cheques American Express travellers' cheques can be exchanged in *casas de cambio* and most five-star hotels but other travellers' cheques are more difficult. Given the parallel market encouraging visitors to bring cash in dollars, and the ease of withdrawing money from ATMs with Visa and MasterCard, travellers' cheques are being used less often.

BANKS Banking hours are 08.30–15.30 Monday–Friday. In December banks work later hours and Saturday mornings. To make up for such overtime, bank holidays are observed on the Monday following: 6 January – Three Kings, 19 March – St Joseph, June (40th day after Easter) – Ascension Day, 29 June – St Peter, 15 August – Assumption, 1 November – All Souls' Day, and 8 December – Immaculate Conception. Late banking hours are the rule in various new shopping malls such as El Recreo and the Sambil in Caracas, and Sambil in Valencia and Porlamar which are open ⏱ 10.00–21.00 every day, 365 days a year.

Most banks will not change dollars except for account holders but the majority have ATMs that will accept MasterCard and Visa cards.

Some card holders find they are asked for six digits at ATMs in Venezuela, when their PIN has only four digits. Try adding two zeros at the end as this sometimes does the trick.

☞ **WARNING:** To reduce the risk of robbery, look for a bank with an inside ATM. Use your ATM card during banking hours, if possible, to enable you to get help if a card sticks or if the machine gives no money. Foreign card holders will only get the withdrawal statement from their home bank, and this may take months.

ELECTRONIC TRANSFER If you're stuck and need money, a Moneygram from home could be the answer. Italcambio (*www.italcambio.com*) provides electronic transfer of funds to an authorised bank or agency for pick-up. Italcambio has two dozen branches in airports and towns around Venezuela, plus four in Caracas. Alternatively, Grupo Zoom (\ *0212 204 6700; www.grupozoom.com*) represents Western Union in Venezuela and has branches in all major cities. Electronic transfer of funds to Venezuela is quick and efficient but the name on the money transfer must be exactly the same as on the recipient's passport, and the recipient should know in advance how much is being transferred and to where.

TIPPING Service in restaurants and bars in Venezuela is generally very good and waiters are usually friendly and attentive. However, in some places service can vary from obsequious, with a waiter at your elbow all through the meal, to curt and indifferent. Any tip you might leave depends entirely on how well you feel you've been treated. Tipping is not compulsory in Venezuela and there are no hard and fast rules on how much to tip. Some Venezuelans are happy to leave some small change behind, while others will happily walk away without leaving anything. Remember that most restaurants will already have added a 10% service charge on top of the printed menu prices.

With taxis, there are no meters so all fares must be agreed beforehand or you could get seriously ripped off. Venezuelans rarely if ever tip taxi drivers, but if you meet an especially friendly and useful taxi driver who goes out of their way to show you around feel free to offer them BsF10 or BsF20 as a thank you.

In most hotels it is acceptable to give a few coins to the porter who carries up your bags, but in high-class establishments you should reach for BsF10 as a start.

There is no need to tip hairdressers or barbers unless you feel they have made a special effort for you.

On tours, especially jungle tours in the Delta Amacuro or on a trek in the Gran Sabana, keep in mind that your tour guides and porters, many of whom come from local indigenous tribes, are paid very low wages and often support large families. Rather than hand over money to the head guide to distribute, it is always better to hand out tips individually. If you travel in a large group to the top of Roraima, for example, you can all put some money into a central pot and share it out amongst the porters on the last night. Alternatively, you can wait until you get to the nearest bar or restaurant and buy them all a beer.

BUDGETING Prices in Venezuela go from ridiculously cheap to ridiculously expensive. A coffee in a chic café in Caracas can cost the same as in Berlin, Paris or London, while a beer at the beach can be a third of the price paid in Europe. Very often it is what you get for your money – or not – that makes the biggest impression. Travellers to the island paradise of Los Roques will find themselves paying four- or five-star prices for one-star accommodation, albeit with lots of trimmings. This is because everything has to be flown in and there are strict

SOME AVERAGE PRICES

Beer in a bar	US$2.00
Can of beer in a supermarket	US$0.30
Single trip on Caracas metro	US$0.20
A litre of petrol	US$0.20
A litre of bottled water	US$0.80
Coffee in a bakery	US$1.20
A French stick from a bakery	US$0.50
An *empanada* in the street	US$1.00
An *arepa*	US$6.00
A litre bottle of Cacique rum	US$15.00
Dinner for two in a medium restaurant	US$30.00
Fixed menu lunch for one	US$10.00
Bus trip from Caracas to Ciudad Bolívar (10 hours)	US$15.00

restrictions on air conditioning and building regulations aimed at keeping the *posada*-style hotels small.

High inflation, topping 30% in 2010, has seen prices rise rapidly in recent years and the emergence of a 'parallel' exchange rate, following the government's decision to fix exchange rates, has also affected the affordability of travelling in Venezuela. Prices tend to follow the parallel rate closely and those who change money on the black market essentially pay much less for hotels and excursions.

The most noticeable price difference is between water and petrol. A litre of mineral water costs around BsF3–4 (just under US$1), while a litre of petrol is four times cheaper at 90 centavos (about 20 US cents).

GETTING AROUND

✈ BY AIR Air travel is not as cheap as it was a few years ago, given poorer exchange rates and high inflation, but it is still the best way to cross the vast distances between Caracas and the adventure-travel hotspots in Mérida and the Gran Sabana. It's worth asking about discounts. If you're travelling with kids, for example, you can get discounts of up to 50% for children aged between two and 11 years old and up to 50% for senior citizens (*tercera edad*) of 60 or 65 years of age and over, depending on the airline. Ask also about any discounts for students, groups or early purchase (30 days in advance). To purchase air tickets you need a photocopy of your passport. Take student ID if asking for a special student rate, although few companies accept ISIC.

Domestic airlines New, competitive airlines have at last opened routes linking small provincial towns. More ambitious still, they are making alliances and flying international routes. Avior serves 16 towns with over 260 flights a day. Aserca makes 300 flights a week nationally and others to Aruba. Santa Bárbara flies to Miami and Madrid in Spain. All lines serve Caracas (Maiquetía Airport).

Aereotuy (TUY) ☎ 0212 212 3110–14, 0212 212 3106; e sramirez@tuy.com; www.tuy.com. Daily flights to Los Roques from Maiquetía & Porlamar in Margarita. Flights & tours to Canaima & Kavak in the Gran Sabana.

Aeropostal (VH) ☎ 0800 284 6637, 0212 708 6220, 0212 708 6226; e reservaciones@aeropostal.com, tarifas@aeropostal.com; www.aeropostal.com. Daily flights between Caracas & Barquisimeto, Maracaibo, Maturín, Puerto Ordaz & Porlamar in Margarita. International flights to Trinidad (Mon, Wed, Fri & Sat).

Aserca (R7) ✆ 0800 648 8356, 0212 953 3004; www.asercaairlines.com. From Caracas to 8 major cities in Venezuela. International flights to Aruba & Curacao.

Avior (9V) ✆ 0501 284 67737, 0501 237 28467, 0212 213 0611; e reservaciones@avior.com.ve; www.aviorairlines.com. Daily flights from Caracas to over 14 destinations including Canaima, Carúpano, Puerto Ayacucho; from Porlamar to 7 cities including Güiria, Tucupita, Valencia & Los Roques. International flights to Miami, Aruba & Curacao.

Conviasa (VO) ✆ 0500 266 84272, 0212 303 7337, 0212 716 5770; e ventas@conviasa.aero, reservas.caracas@conviasa.aero; www.conviasa.aero. State-owned airline flies to Margarita, Puerto Ayacucho, Maracaibo & other national destinations, as well as Trinidad, Grenada, Dominica, Iran & Syria.

Laser (QL) ✆ 0212 202 0100, 0212 355 3100, 0295 263 9195; www.laser.com.ve. Weekday flights Caracas–Porlamar–Valencia; good prices.

Rutaca (RUT) ✆ 0212 355 1838, 0285 600 5300–15, 0501 788 2221, 0800 788 2221, 0285 632 0304; www.rutaca.com.ve. Flights to Ciudad Bolívar, Barinas, Barcelona, Caracas, Maturín, Porlamar, Puerto Ordaz & Santo Domingo.

SBA (S3) ✆ 0212 204 4000; www.sbairlines.com. Flights from Caracas to Valencia, Maracaibo, El Vigia & Las Piedras. International flights to Madrid & Tenerife in Spain, Quito & Guayaquil in Ecuador, Panama City & Miami with alliance partners Air Europa, Spanair.

BY BUS Buses are a cheap and easy way to get to all over the country. Each town has its connecting lines and central bus station, called the *terminal de pasajeros*. Caracas has two terminals: La Bandera, supposedly for south and west travel, and the Terminal de Oriente for eastern destinations, although La Bandera now has buses going to all destinations.

Fares are not expensive, ranging from US$10 to US$12 to San Fernando de Apure (8 hours), US$20–25 to Maracaibo (11–12 hours), US$20–25 to San Cristóbal (13 hours) and US$30–40 to travel as far as Santa Elena de Uairén (23 hours).

It is always best to travel midweek or buy your bus ticket (*boleto*) a few days in advance of travelling, especially on long weekends when all the buses to the beaches are crammed. The best advice for travelling during the major holidays is to leave very early or wait until the mid-point lull.

Ordinary buses are cheaper than more luxurious options, travel by day, stop frequently and have windows you can (sometimes) open. The downside is that they have no air conditioning.

Expresos usually travel by night, and are fast and comfortable but have the air conditioning set to Arctic. They are so cold that Venezuelans take blankets, duvets and woolly hats on board with them to keep warm. *Expresos* leave at set hours and have fixed rest stops. The coaches have tinted windows, making it difficult to see out.

Ejecutivo buses are fancier and the most luxurious ones, called *buscamas* (bed buses), have reclining seats and a toilet. The downsides of these are that you cannot open the windows and you must not touch the curtains, because it allegedly interferes with the freezing air conditioning. This can be frustrating when you want to see the countryside outside as you arrive early in the morning in an exciting new place.

A few bus companies such as Aeroexpresos Ejecutivos (*www.aeroexpresos.com.ve*) and Rodovías (*www.rodovías.com*) have modern offices and websites showing routes and fares, but the majority of Venezuela's bus lines operate solely from the main terminals and generally sell tickets only from their bus terminal kiosks on the day of departure or 24 hours ahead.

WARNING: Never travel without passport or ID papers. Bus passengers are open to hassle from police or National Guards searching for drugs and illegal immigrants. Mask your anger if shaken awake in the early hours by a couple of teenagers in uniform with scary-looking guns – they are just doing their job. Always be polite when speaking to security officials.

🚕 BY TAXI

Por puesto Long-distance taxis called *carritos*, or *carritos por puestos* (literally 'by the seat cars') are usually found outside bus terminals. As the name indicates, they charge by the seat and will only leave when they are full. Routes have set fares but you can hire all the seats of a *por puesto* for a *viaje expreso*, which saves time and may be more comfortable but could work out at double the bus fare. One good thing about *por puestos* is that they will stop to let you buy some street food or go to the toilet in times of need.

In cities, owner-operated *por puestos* have grown into small buses providing most of the urban transportation. The tropical tunes being played on these city buses is almost always set to extra loud but it's amazing to look back at the passengers and see almost everybody mouthing nearly every word of every salsa or merengue track played. There are no set bus stops on these routes. To indicate your stop you can clap your hands or shout '*la parada, por favor*'.

Standard taxis The other word for a taxi in Venezuela is 'a *libre*', meaning 'available'. Every district has its *línea de taxi*, operating during the day. There are no meters so *always* negotiate a price before you get in. Rates have risen with inflation but are not exorbitant: a short ride in Caracas can cost US$5–6; a long one US$10; Caracas to the airport is about US$30–35. Venezuelans do not tip taxi drivers. Radio-taxis provide reliable service day and night; phone ahead to request wake-up and a car for the airport.

Apart from the airport, where the official taxis are black, most legal taxis in Caracas are a uniform white with a checkered yellow-and-black band and have telephone numbers painted on the body.

Unlicensed taxis, known as *piratas*, do not have the required yellow number plates and for safety reasons should be avoided. Always try and use a taxi from a taxi rank – outside a hotel or shopping mall – or ask locals at your hotel or *posada* for the numbers of taxi companies you can call to pick you up. Taxis should be used where possible if going out in the major cities at night, when buses should be avoided and walking is not recommended.

In view of high car-rental rates, travellers report that combining taxis and bus services is more flexible and economical for a morning's tour. This also has the added advantage of no parking and no car theft. Always negotiate the cost before setting out, on the basis of the car, not per passenger.

🚗 BY CAR

Car hire Driving in Venezuela can be an adventure in itself. In theory there are speed limits of 40km/h in cities and 80km/h on main roads, and drivers must wear seat belts and always carry a reflector triangle in the boot to place behind the car in the event of breakdown or accident. In reality, the rules are rarely respected. Drivers jump red lights at night, especially in cities, right of way goes to the largest, most aggressively driven vehicle and drink-driving is endemic. If you fancy having a go, half-a-dozen international car-rental firms, including Hertz (*www.hertz.com*), Avis (*www.avis.com*) and Budget (*www.budget.com.ve*), compete with local rental companies at every airport. All require credit cards and stipulate that drivers must be over 21, or 25 for any 4x4 (known as a *vehículo rustico*). A 4x4 works out at nearly double the cost of a small car, already a stiff US$40–60 per day/US$240 a week without the 12% value-added tax.

It's probably more convenient to book from home with one of the international car-rental firms, although some small firms in Margarita or Ciudad Bolívar may offer better rates than the big companies. Ask about charges for additional drivers and returning the car to a different city and make sure to clarify all insurance included.

The advantage of working with a large franchise is a greater supply of cars, not better service. You must still check basic points such as tyres, brakes, belts – as well as any dents and all extra equipment (tools, security devices) as you will be liable for damages and loss. When you reserve a car from abroad and the chosen model proves unavailable, the company must assign you a better model at no extra cost.

Automobile club If you need advice on driving conditions, insurance, rules or vehicle documentation, the automobile association can help. The Touring & Automóvil Club de Venezuela (TACV) (*piso 15, Torre Phelps, Plaza Venezuela;* \ *0212 781 9743, 0212 794 1278;* e *desiree@automovilclubvenezuela.com; www.automovilclubvenezuela.com*) is affiliated with international groups such as the AAA and RAC and extends its services to their members. Among services on offer are 24-hour towing, coverage of hotel bills and transfers resulting from car accident or theft, assistance with documents, legal matters and licence renewals. TACV provides international licences for Venezuelan drivers, and the triptych for border crossings for cars with Venezuelan plates. It has offices in Maracaibo and San Cristóbal.

Ⓜ BY METRO In a hectic city, the Caracas metro is an oasis of relative calm (outside the peak hours of 06.00–10.00 and 16.00–18.00) and a great way to get round the city quickly. The first line opened in 1983 and now there are four lines, with more offshoots planned. A 9.5km extension to the Caracas suburb of Los Teques will bring the total length east to west to 50km and make commuting much easier for thousands of Tequeños. Maracaibo is now engaged in building a metro system and another is underway in Valencia.

🚂 BY TRAIN Unlike other countries in South America, Venezuela has never had an extensive railway system. Only a few vestiges remain of the trains that did operate on limited commercial lines, such as the Puerto Cabello to Barquisimeto train, which no longer takes passengers. It was built in the 1950s when there were still trains running between Caracas and Valencia, and Caracas and La Guaira. Now, an ambitious new national railway project is taking shape with the 2006 opening of an electric railway line from the metro stop at La Rinconada in Caracas to Charallave and Cúa in the Tuy Valley. This is the only train line currently operating for passengers in Venezuela, and the train operates like an overground extension of the Metro; there is no advance booking, you just buy your ticket when you want to travel. Over 40km the line rises 625m in altitude and the longest of the line's 23 tunnels is 6.8km. The US$1,900 million system, built by an Italian, French and Venezuelan consortium, operates with 13 Japanese-made trains, each with four cars, travelling at 120km/h. Studies are already complete for a second stage, from Puerto Cabello to Cagua.

🚢 BY FERRY Ferries to Margarita Island leave from Puerto La Cruz, Cumaná and Chacopata on Araya. The larger of the two lines is Conferry (\ *0212 709 0000; www.conferry.com*), and the other is Naviarca-Gran Cacique (\ *0281 263 0935; www.grancacique.com.ve*). See page 163 for prices.

🏠 ACCOMMODATION

Venezuela has a wide range of accommodation options from five-star luxury hotels in all major cities to rainforest camps offering hammocks strung up under straw roofs in indigenous-style huts.

Hotels distinguish between two kinds of double room: *habitación doble* meaning twin beds, and *matrimonial* with a double bed. Single rooms differ little from the *matrimonial* and cost about the same. Many economy hotels offer only double beds, but you can ask for an extra single bed or cot at low cost. Cheap hotels and *pensiones* provide dim lighting, indifferent mattresses and bathrooms with a cold shower. However, they can also be clean, humble and owner-maintained. Other places may turn out to be Love Hotels, known as *hoteles de cita*, or, more crudely, as

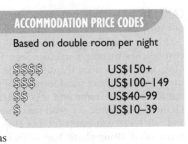

ACCOMMODATION PRICE CODES

Based on double room per night

$$$$	US$150+
$$$	US$100–149
$$	US$40–99
$	US$10–39

mataderos (slaughterhouses), where guests by the hour are preferred and the sheets are still warm. Extras at Love Hotels may include a jacuzzi, special programmes on the TV and mirrored ceilings. Given the fact that so many Venezuelans live with their parents until they are married, it's not surprising there are so many Love Hotels in most cities and towns.

IN TOWNS AND CITIES All cities and most towns have a range of hotels from first class to the anonymous hostel. Caracas has the highest rates and the price categories below make allowances for this, as well as for low-/high-season changes. A reasonable hotel in Caracas may cost US$50 for a double, whereas in Mérida you would expect to pay US$35. This does not reflect the quality, which may actually be better in a smaller hotel. During high season city hotels, if anything, are likely to lower their rates to attract cash-strapped Venezuelans (such bargains are not always offered to foreigners). High season (*temporada alta*) covers Christmas, New Year, Carnival, Easter and the school holidays in July–August. To secure a reservation in peak periods, you may be asked make a deposit to the hotel's bank account and fax them the bank slip. It is a good idea to reconfirm reservations before arrival.

International chain hotels such as the Hesperia, Inter-Continental or Melia catering to businessmen charge US$150–200 for a double. All have swimming pools, nightclubs, shops and five-star facilities. Dropping steeply in price but still expensive in local terms are the better hotels with rates of US$100–149 for a double. Mid-range hotels provide the best combination of quality, price and location for around US$40–99. Economy hotels are those charging US$10–39. There is a 12% value-added tax (IVA) and a 1% tax which supports tourism promotion and training; hotel rates usually include taxes in the room price. Always ask if the tax is included in the quoted price, so as not to get stung later.

IN THE COUNTRYSIDE Country lodgings may be a beautifully kept ranch, a converted home, an old colonial house given new life, or just 'rustic' village rooms, meaning one step away from primitive. *Posadas* are family-run guesthouses or inns (some do not provide meals), which can be small and economical, or quite exclusive and upmarket with full meals. They are multiplying in the Andes where tourism is expanding fast. A *pensión* or *residencia* is a low-cost boarding house popular with workers, where little space is left for travellers.

In wilderness areas safari camps, rainforest lodges and *hatos* (ranches) often provide first-class lodging, all meals and excursions.

RESORT HOTELS Margarita Island, specifically Playa El Agua, comes closest to being a holiday resort where new hotels and holiday homes are springing up in growing numbers. Mérida State, now with over 140 hotels and 170 guesthouses (16,000 beds) is *the* mountain resort area. It attracts not only Venezuelan families but also many outdoor enthusiasts, adrenaline junkies and language learners from abroad.

2

▲ CAMPING

A tent site is called *sitio para campar* (whereas a *campamento* may be a lodge) but such facilities are almost unknown outside a few national parks. Venezuelans do love to camp, but generally only during the main holidays when the country's best beaches become tent cities for a few days or weeks. Foreigners who want to camp in Venezuela are reasonably safe away from main roads in the Gran Sabana, the Llanos, the Andes and in national parks, but you must ask first locally to find out if it is safe to camp and if permission is needed. Some beaches, such as Playa Grande in Choroní, are good for camping, but beaches near towns attract robbers and wherever you camp (except atop Roraima) you cannot not leave your tent unattended. Bring plastic bags to pick up rubbish.

Short tropical days mean that camp must be made early; the sun sets by 18.30 (an hour later in July). And if you don't string up a roof or tarpaulin, it will surely rain.

COMPLAINTS ABOUT ACCOMMODATION The government's consumer protection institute, Indecu, obliges all hotels, camps and *posadas* to display a complaints' book in reception. These books are audited by Indecu. If you have a complaint make sure you give vent to your frustrations in the book.

✕ EATING AND DRINKING

FOOD Venezuelans love their food, which is hearty and filling, relying on seasonings such as cumin, fresh coriander and garlic rather than on spicy peppers. Traditional dishes still make up the bulk of the diet, with meat or fish accompanied by rice and *caraotas negras* – the black beans that set Venezuelans apart from their Latin American neighbours. A simple tomato, grated carrot, onion and lettuce salad is sometimes served on the side. This kind of salad is usually safe, but to be sure sprinkle some vinegar on it, give it a stir and leave for a few minutes before eating.

Breakfast traditionally consists of *arepas*, baked or fried cornmeal buns that are opened like a pocket and buttered or stuffed with cheese, ham and other fillings. *Arepas*, and a mini version called *arepitas*, are also served with lunch and dinner in place of bread. Fast-food outlets called *areperas* sell *arepas* all day long, with a variety of odd fillings that include *morcilla* (black pudding), *huevos de codorniz* (quail eggs) and the queen of *arepas* the *reina pepiada*, a gooey mixture of shredded chicken, peas, mayonnaise and avocado. Rather than stumbling off to the kebab shop after a night on the lash, Venezuelans head for a late-night *arepera* to soak up the booze.

Pasta is also a very important staple, although few Italians would understand the Venezuelan love of eating plain boiled pasta with mayonnaise or ketchup.

Variety is provided by the many reliable Italian, Spanish and Chinese restaurants. McDonald's and other US fast-food places can be found in all the major shopping malls for those hankering after a taste of home.

Local dishes The national dish is called *pabellón criollo*, literally 'Creole flag', a tasty and filling combo platter of *carne mechada* (shredded beef), *arroz* (white rice), *tajadas* (fried plantains) and black beans. In Margarita and other beach resorts the beef is replaced with *cazón*, or baby shark.

On the coast, try the excellent fish such as *pargo* (red snapper), *mero* (grouper) or *carite* (kingfish). In the Andes, the best fish dish is the *trucha* (trout).

Barbecued steaks, chicken and sausages are served at *parilla* restaurants, normally accompanied by fried yuca (known as *manioc* or *cassava*) and *guasacaca*, an exquisite drizzling sauce made from avocados, fresh parsley, coriander leaves, green bell pepper, garlic, oil and vinegar. *Guasacaca* and *picante* (hot sauce) are always available at street stands selling *empanadas* (fried maize-dough turnovers stuffed with beef,

Some local dishes, drinks, and better-known tropical fruits and vegetables:

ají	Peppers, either hot *ají picante*, or sweet *ají dulce*.
apio	Yellow root (*arracacha*) like turnip or swede, good in soup.
arepa	Cornmeal griddle bun, staple in place of bread, filled with cheese, chicken, black beans, shredded beef.
asado	Pot roast, usually *muchacho asado*, rump.
batido	Juice of freshly blended fruit such as mango, *lechosa* (papaya); sugar or water may be added.
cachapa	Pancake of freshly grated young maize, typically served with margarine, white cheese.
cambur	Banana. In slang, *cambur* is used figuratively to mean a soft job, often bureaucratic; *policamburista* is a person holding several such jobs.
caña	Alcoholic drink distilled from sugarcane, especially *aguardiente* (firewater).
carne en vara	Side of beef roasted on a spit.
casab cassava	Flat dry 'bread' of grated yuca (*manioc*) root. Staple diet of Indian groups.
empanada	Fried cornmeal turnover filled with cheese, chicken, mincemeat or baby shark.
guarapo	Pressed sugarcane juice, also called *jugo de caña*.
hallaca	Christmas special: a tamale envelope of cornmeal with filling of chicken, pork and olives wrapped in banana leaves and boiled.
hervido	Soup made with a base of beef (*res*) or chicken (*gallina*), onions, pumpkin and roots such as yuca and yam. When made with both beef and chicken it is *cruzado*; when made with fish, it is usually called *sancocho*.
jojoto	An ear of fresh maize.
lagarto	Pot roast of shank (not lizard).
mondongo	Hearty soup of vegetables, tripe and hoof, a guaranteed hangover cure.
nata	Thick salty cream used in place of butter.
queso de mano	Fresh white cheese, also called *queso guayanés*.
pastelito	Wheat flour version of the *empanda*, a quick snack half the price of an *arepa*.
tajadas	Fried slices of ripe plantain (cooking banana, *plátano*).
tequeño	Fried cheese-stick in pastry; must be eaten hot.
teta	Homemade ice lolly frozen in small plastic bag, (literally, tit).
tortilla	Omelette (unless in a Mexican restaurant).
tostones	Thin rounds of green plantain, fried like potato crisps.
tuna	Fruit of cactus; tuna fish is *atún*.
yuca	*Manioc*. Varieties of this root, whether the sweet or bitter kind, have poisonous properties when raw. *Yuca* must be well boiled, or the juice expressed as when making *cassava*.

chicken or cheese). Avoid *bistek*, which is tough fried meat, not to be compared with *lomito*, a sirloin steak.

Most towns have chicken rotisseries preparing inexpensive and delicious *pollo a la brasa*.

Christmas for Venezuelans is all about eating, and the big family meal is a real blowout, eaten late and including the unmissable *hallaca*, a sort of maize tamale filled with a stew of chicken, pork, olives and capers, wrapped in a banana leaf, tied up like a parcel and boiled. Tradition has it that the *hallaca* harks back to slave days when the scraps from the master's table would be combined with the plain boiled

maize dough that the slaves subsisted on. Other Christmas dishes include chicken and potato salad, pork shoulder and *pan de jamón*, a soft rolled bread stuffed with ham and raisins.

The universal hangover cure is a bowl of *hervido*, a stew of hen, beef or fish with chunks of onions, maize and roots such as *manioc* (yuca), *ñame* (yam) and *ocumo* (dasheen). Although these roots are called *verduras*, there is little green in the national diet. Vegetarian travellers will soon become eager to eat anything rather than roots.

Most city dwellers rely on beans, rice, spaghetti and tuna, and that is the basic diet on treks and excursions to Roraima and Angel Falls. Other staples vary regionally, with maize in central areas, potatoes in the Andes, and potatoes and yuca in the south and east. *Casabe* is made of bitter yuca, grated, pressed and dried into flat cakes that are dipped in sauce or water to soften them before eating. *Casabe* is the perfect preserved food and lasts forever, and no Indian will travel without a supply. Too bad it has little taste, although it is a great source of fibre. Try it with *catara*, or *katara*, a spicy sauce made by indigenous groups in Amazonas from the *bachaco culon* (literally, 'big-arse ant'). The sauce is made by boiling down the water pressed out of yuca in the process of making *casabe* and adding chilli and herbs. It is so popular nowadays that you find it on sale all over the Amazonas capital Puerto Ayacucho. A variation on the sauce made by the Pemon Indians of the Gran Sabana includes termites as well. Make sure you get some from the roadside stalls at San Francisco de Yuruani, the starting point for Roraima treks.

Snacks Venezuelans love tasty street food and snacks and fresh fruit such as bananas and mangoes are easily available, which is a good thing for travellers on a budget.

Empanadas (fried turnovers) are the cheapest popular snacks and are a great way to fill up for lunch. They are stuffed with cheese, shredded chicken, minced beef, black beans and even baby shark at the beach. When they're made with wheat flour instead of maize, they are called *pastelitos*.

Cachapas are thick pancakes made from roughly grated sweetcorn, usually served with margarine and soft white cheese called *queso de mano* (hand cheese) in the Guayana region and *queso guayanés* in Caracas. When fresh, the slightly sweet mozzarella-like cheese is delicious on the salty *cachapa*. For a full meal, go for the *cachapa con cochino*, with cheese and a pork chop.

Another delicious creation, invented in Los Teques, is the *tequeño*, a cheese finger encased in twisted dough and deep fried.

A nutritious pack snack is the guava bar, sold in supermarkets as *bocadillos de guayaba* – pure fruit plus sugar. You'll probably discover Venezuelan chocolate for yourself. *Chuao* cocoa beans are highly prized by chocolatiers in Europe and the USA for their fine quality and rich taste. If you visit the village of Chuao, near Choroní, you can pick up a ball of the homemade local chocolate, which is melted in milk to make a delicious hot chocolate.

Eating etiquette 'Buen provecho' means 'enjoy your meal' and is a typical way to address fellow diners before tucking in. After a meal, show your appreciation to the cook with a smile and the phrase: 'muy sabroso, gracias!' ('very tasty, thanks!'). When drinking, it is usual to say 'salud' (health) when raising or clinking glasses, but you do sometimes hear the quaint-sounding 'chin-chin'.

If you are invited to dine out your host will generally pick up the tab, and will be offended if you insist too doggedly on paying your share. Equally, if you ask people to eat out with you they will assume you will pay. Venezuelan women are not accustomed to paying for anything when out on a date and will be horrified at any suggestion they go Dutch.

DRINK One of the best things about the tropics is the abundance of fresh fruit and Venezuela is no exception in this respect. Dozens of fresh fruit juices called batidos (made with water) are available in most places, including lechosa (papaya), melon (melon), watermelon (patilla), mango (mango), guava (guayaba), soursop (guanábana), and the super-healthy tres-en-uno (three-in-one), made of carrot, orange juice and beetroot. Venezuelans have a sweet tooth and batidos of pineapple (piña), passionfruit (parchita) and strawberry are made with sugar and ice. If you find the juices too sweet ask for a batido sin azucar. Great milkshakes made with fresh fruit are called merengadas.

Bakeries sell processed juices but they tend to be high in sugar. Other drinks sold in cartons are chocolate milk and chicha, a mix of milk and rice that is sweet and custardy. Bottled water is sold either plain or carbonated (sin gas/con gas) in restaurants, cafés and bars.

Water It is not safe to drink tap water in Venezuela, although you can clean your teeth with it. Ice is generally safe in restaurants as it is made with filtered water (agua filtrado), which is also served in jugs in many restaurants. Bottled water is sold either plain or carbonated (sin gas/con gas) and is available in most places around the country. Insist that bottles of water are opened at the table in restaurants.

Alcoholic drinks Wherever you go in Venezuela, you're never far from an ice-cold cerveza, sold anywhere you see the polar-bear brand mark of the biggest

COFFEE FOR ALL TASTES

Coffee drinking is an art cultivated by Venezuelans and Venezuelan Arabica coffee compares well with the best in the world. In the shops a pound of coffee costs the equivalent of US$1.50. In the countryside the owner of even the remotest farm or mining camp will proudly share their hospitality, often with a tiny cup of sweet black coffee – over a wood fire the cook makes café de olla (pot coffee), bringing the coffee, sugar and water to a boil and letting the grounds settle to make a basic, rewarding brew. In towns or pueblos, drip coffee or café colado is traditional for its smoothness. Strong Italian-style coffee is called café de máquina and is popular in cities where espresso machines are installed in every coffee bar and bakery.

When ordering coffee Venezuelans do not just ask for un café but specify a certain kind or colour: black (negro, negrito); long or short (largo or corto); strong (fuerte, cargado); bitter (amargo, cerrero); weak (suave, claro); thin (guayoyo); or weak and sweet (guarapo). Plain coffee with milk is café con leche; when it is more milk than coffee it is sometimes called a tetero (baby's bottle). Coffee can also be served darker or lighter brown (marrón or marrón claro), or topped with whipped cream in a rich capuchino. If you like coffee laced with rum, ask for a café bautizado.

brewer and posters of the latest batch of bikini-clad beer models. Venezuelans are the biggest beer consumers in Latin America, quaffing 87 litres of the amber nectar per person in 2008, and drinking the USA and Spain under the table. Local brewer Polar had a virtual monopoly of beer sales until the 1990s and still controls nearly 75% of the market. Regional has about 18% and Brahma, a Brazilian brand now owned by a Belgian group, has about 8%. The lager-style beer is drunk in small bottles and cans so it doesn't get warm and the new trend is towards 'Ice' (4%) and 'Light' (4.5%) beers, which are lower in alcohol content. Traditional Polar, which hasn't changed much since the brand was launched in 1941, is now known as Polar Pilsen (5%) and is sold in small bottles called *polarcitas* and a larger *tercio* (a third of a litre). President Chávez has cracked down on TV advertising in an attempt to cut down on drinking but giant billboards featuring scantily clad models sipping icy brews still sit provocatively alongside posters of the president calling for 'Fatherland, Socialism, or Death'.

Despite producing superb-quality rums (see page 66), Venezuelans are also the biggest whisky drinkers in Latin America, favouring Johnnie Walker Black Label and Chivas Regal over cheaper brands. One of the strange sights you come across on the beach in Venezuela is people pulling ice out of the cool-box to serve whisky with coconut milk mid-morning.

For a true flavour of life on the central coast seek out a bottle of the local homemade hooch, *guarapita*, a super-sweet cocktail of passion-fruit juice, sugar,

CORPUS CHRISTI: WHEN DANCING RED DEVILS RULE FOR A DAY

Every year on the moveable feast of Corpus Christi, sacred brotherhoods in 14 Venezuelan towns and villages act out a centuries-old tradition of devil dancing that was brought to these shores from Spain but which grew to incorporate the slaves' defiance and rejection of being left outside the church during the Catholic mass. This ancient tradition, a fusion of Spanish and African elements, goes back to the earliest days of the colony and is one of the most interesting spectacles in Venezuela's rich cultural calendar.

The most famous example of these Diablos Danzantes, or 'Devil Dancers', is in the sleepy town of San Francisco de Yare, about two-hours' drive from Caracas in the Tuy valley, which fills with thousands of tourists on the Thursday of Corpus Christi for the morning rituals. The central focus is the parade of red-dressed devils with their horned papier-mâché masks and maracas. Yare has the distinction of being the sole place where Diablos Danzantes wear only red; elsewhere, such as the cocoa plantation of Chuao, the devils wear costumes made from colourful rags. The day starts at the ceremony where the devils pay their respects to those who dance only in spirit. After visiting a few altars in private houses the devils then march around town to the beat of maracas and drums before dancing in the square outside the whitewashed 18th-century church of San Francisco de Paula. The priest then makes the call to mass and the devils try to storm the church. Three times they surge forward and each time they are beaten back by the force of good in the shape of the Holy Eucharist held aloft by the priest. Finally, their efforts exhausted, the devils take off their masks, prostrate themselves before the priest and receive a blessing. At this point, masks are removed and the festival takes on more of a party atmosphere with music and dancing.

While the festival of the Diablos Danzantes is promoted as a tourist attraction – and the influx of outsiders drinking and merry-making gives the event a carnival atmosphere – there is nothing fake about this profound demonstration of religious devotion, which is a fragmented remnant of an ancient Passion play pitting the forces of good against the forces of evil.

and raw cane alcohol. Sold in recycled *aguardiente* bottles in Choroní and Chuao, *guarapita* is a great way to loosen your hips for the *tambores* dancing. Just go easy – *guarapita* might taste like fruit juice but it has a kick like a mule and the beach is no place for a bad head the morning after.

PUBLIC HOLIDAYS

Venezuelans take holidays seriously. Families migrate to the coast in peak beach weather (January–April). Traffic is frantic, roads are clogged and bus and plane terminals mobbed. If you are travelling during these periods, wait for people to leave the city and then you may find transportation. On New Year's Day everything closes; even if you are lucky enough to find a taxi you won't find anywhere open to get something to eat. Even petrol stations are closed.

If a public holiday falls on a Thursday or Tuesday, many people make a *puente* (bridge) to take a four-day weekend. This often makes appointments difficult to keep. In December, government offices close early, working roughly 07.30–15.30. From 15 to 18 December onwards, rule out any idea of business until schools open again after 6 January, Los Reyes Magos, the day when the Three Kings bring children presents. Work does not begin again in earnest until 15 January. The same applies to the days before Carnival weekend and the pre-Easter week when many businesses are shut. Banks are the major exception, working full hours except on the legal holidays.

The dancers are all local men who belong to a *cofradía* or 'religious brotherhood', which has organised the event for centuries. There is a strict hierarchy, with the chief devil or 'Capataz' ('Overseer') the only one allowed three horns on his mask. Each dancer makes a solemn vow to dance for a number of years, some for life, to give thanks for favours granted by God and prayers answered, usually connected to an illness in the family. The dancers put on their costumes and masks to represent Lucifer and his fallen angels, but not before first protecting themselves against evil spirits by taking ritual baths, being blessed with holy water and wearing protective amulets and palm-leaf crosses.

The eve of Corpus Christi is a good time to see the preparations the devil dancers go through and to visit the **Casa de Los Diablos Danzantes** on Calle Rivas, which has old photographs of the devil dancing, altars and masks, and is where the devils congregate for ceremonies. On other days the house is open from 09.00 to 17.00 but if it's closed just ask somebody at the house next door to go and get the key – everybody knows everybody in Yare. The other two places worth visiting are the workshops on Calle Ribas of the master mask makers Juan Morgado, and Manuel Sanoja, known as 'El Mocho', who sadly died in March 2010 aged 73, and whose sons carry on the tradition.

PRACTICALITIES Sadly there are no decent places to stay in San Francisco de Yare. The sleazy Love Hotels that do exist all get booked up well in advance of Corpus Christi. The best option for attending the festival is to set out very early from Caracas, take the 20-minute train from La Rinconada to Charallave (operating 06.00–22.00) and then one of the frequent *por puestos* that travel via Ocumare del Tuy to Yare.

UPCOMING DATES Corpus Christi is due to fall on the following days: 23 June 2011, 7 June 2012, 30 May 2013, 19 June 2014, and 4 June 2015.

1 January	New Year's Day
Carnival	Monday–Tuesday before Lent
Easter	Holy Thursday, Good Friday
19 April	Proclamation of Independence
1 May	Labour Day
24 June	Battle of Carabobo (the decisive battle in Venezuela's war of independence against Spanish control is celebrated with military parades)
5 July	Independence Day
24 July	Bolívar's Birth
12 October	Indigenous Resistance Day – (a public holiday formerly known as Columbus Day)
25 December	Christmas Day

FESTIVALS Cities and towns honour their patron saints with processions, masses and street dances deeply engrained in folklore. In many cases these fiestas are three-day affairs fuelled by rum. Citywide *ferias*, lasting one to two weeks, celebrate a saint's day with agricultural fairs, religious, cultural and sports events. Below is a partial list.

2 January	Virgen de Coromoto, patroness of Venezuela; masses at the National Sanctuary south of Guanare.
6 January	Los Reyes Magos, 'Three Kings' Day'; San Miguel de Boconó turns out for a *Romería* and bottle dance.
14 January	Feria de la Divina Pastora; Barquisimeto's week-long festival for the Divine Shepherdess.
20 January	Feria de San Sebastian; San Cristóbal opens a two-week fair of music, sports and bullfights.
2 February	Los Vasallos de La Candelaria, 'the Vassals of Our Lady of Candelaria'; Mérida State.
February/March	**Carnival** Street parties and parades in many towns. The best carnival celebrations are held in Carúpano and El Callao. Mérida City celebrates Carnival with the ten-day Feria del Sol. On Ash Wednesday El Entierro de la Sardina, 'The Sardine's Funeral', is enacted in Naiguatá and Macuto.
19 March	San José, 'St Joseph's Day'; fiestas and bullfights in Maracay.
March/April	**Easter** Semana Santa, 'Holy Week'; in Caracas starts on Palm Sunday with blessing of palm leaves in Chacao and open-air mass in Plaza Caracas, 11.00. On Wednesday evening, Nazarene procession from the Basílica de Santa Teresa to Plaza Caracas. The Passion of Christ is acted out on Good Friday at Plaza Caracas, at El Hatillo's church, and in many, many *pueblos*, especially La Parroquia in Mérida and Ureña, Táchira. In Puerto Cabello the Blessing of the Sea takes place on Easter Sunday at a huge sunrise mass by the marina. Easter ends on Sunday afternoon with the Quema de Judas, burning Judas's effigy.
3 May	Velorio de la Cruz de Mayo; altars to the May Cross coincide with planting and the Southern Cross in the sky; widespread, especially in Puerto La Cruz and the east.
15 May	San Isidro Labrador; in Mérida State – Apartaderos, Jají, Lagunillas, Tovar.
June	Corpus Cristi; celebrated on the 9th Thursday after Holy Thursday. Venezuela's famous Diablos Danzantes, or 'Devil

	Dancers', perform traditional dances and rituals in horned papier-mâché masks outside churches in San Francisco de Yare, Chuao and 12 other villages.
13 June	San Antonio; people of El Tocuyo, Quíbor and Sanare stage the Tamunangue's complex dances and mock battles.
23–24 June	Fiesta de San Juan; three days and nights of African drums celebrate St John the Baptist in Curiepe and Birongo in Miranda State, and coastal towns: Cuyagua, Choroní, Puerto Maya, Chichiriviche, Chuspa.
29 June	San Pedro y San Pablo; a costumed folklore street play in Guatire.
25 July	Santiago Apóstol, 'St James the Apostle'; Caracas honours its patron with a cultural festival. Religious processions in Mérida: Ejido, Jají, Lagunillas.
8 August	Nuestra Señora de las Nieves, Our Lady of the Snows, leads Ciudad Bolívar's Feria del Orinoco.
8 September	La Virgen del Valle; the patroness of Margarita and all seafarers inspires masses, processions in El Valle, Margarita, and the blessing of fishing craft also in Puerto La Cruz and eastern Venezuela.
8 September	La Virgen de Coromoto, Guanare. Pilgrimage honours the Patroness of Venezuela on the anniversary of Chief Coromoto's conversion in 1651.
24 September	San Miguel Arcángel, Archangel Michael; drums and dances in Puerto Maya, Jají, Mérida City.
12 October	Dia de la Raza is the biggest festival in the year for the Cult of Maria Lionza, with thousands of her devotees travelling to the Mountain of Sorte in Yaracuy State to bathe in the river, take part in cleansing rituals with candles and watch the mass fire walking ceremony that closes the day.
18 November	Feria de la Chinita; Maracaibo goes all out for the Virgin of Chiquinquirá, known to devotees as La Chinita, in ten-day festivities led by a queen: parades, races, music, folklore.
25 December	*Navidad*; Christmas masses on the eve, at the midnight Misa de Gallo, the 'Cock's Mass'.
27–29 December	San Benito; costumed dancers fete Venezuela's black saint in Zulia and Mérida states: 27 December Sinamaica, El Moján; 28 December Gibraltar, Bobures, Palmarito; 29 December Mucuchíes, Timotes.
28 December	Día de Los Inocentes, 'Innocents' Day'; this recalls the slaughter of infants by Herod. It is a day for practical jokes, in the same vein as April Fool's Day (not observed in Venezuela).

🛒 SHOPPING

From colourful street markets selling spicy sauces made from termites and ants to sophisticated shopping malls called *centros comerciales* (CC), Venezuela caters for most shopping needs. Caracas, Barquisimeto, Mérida, Puerto La Cruz, Puerto Ordaz, Maracay, Maracaibo and Porlamar in Margarita all have shiny, new malls. Bright and modern, they are well stocked with everything from designer brands and beachwear, to music shops and pharmacies. In Caracas there are several swanky shopping centres, including the Sambil, near the Chacao metro station, said to be the largest in South America, with over 500 shops, banks, fast-food outlets, cinemas, a giant aquarium and a rooftop fun park for kids. Venezuelans go to shopping malls for day-long entertainment as they are open ☉ 10.00–21.00 every day, 365 days a year – revolutionary in a country where commerce has always shut down for a long siesta lunch.

The good news for visitors is that virtually everything you might need is available in these mega malls, including banks, but the bad news is that prices are invariably higher than at home, because everything is imported. The best bargains are the country's excellent coffee beans, connoisseur's sipping rums and indigenous crafts. The quirkiest and most rewarding finds are to be had in the countryside, or in indigenous villages, where you can buy your beads and blowpipes direct from the people who make them.

PRESENTS AND SOUVENIRS

Indigenous crafts Crafts are on sale at the airport and in specialist shops near Caracas, such as Hannsi (see *El Hatillo*, page 117), but the best place to pick up handmade Indian baskets, wood carvings and necklaces is by visiting the indigenous communities on organised trips. If you travel to the Orinoco Delta to see the Warao look out for the beautiful hammocks they make from Moriche palm called *chinchorros*.

If you travel to the Caura River try and pick up one of the wooden shaman's benches carved by the Yekuana in the form of a jaguar, armadillo, tapir or monkey.

Puerto Ayacucho in Amazonas State has an Indian market with a host of treasures on offer from a number of surrounding tribes, including a spicy sauce made from ants called *catara*.

In Zulia, the local Wayuu Indians make woven string bags of exuberant colours that have a mythical significance. Wayuu women wear long flowery robes called *mantas*, which are also sold in Zulia and make unusual gifts.

In Lara State, weavers make blankets and rugs, woodworkers turn fine bowls in semi-precious woods, and potters make pre-Columbian reproductions.

Rum Venezuelan rums are among the best sipping rums in the world and are coveted for their smooth taste and complex flavours. Look for top brands such as Pampero Aniversario, which comes in a leather pouch, Cacique 500, Diplomatico Reserva Exclusiva, Santa Teresa 1796 or the special edition Cacique Antiguo. All rums in Venezuela have to be aged for four years before they can be sold, so even cheaper brands will taste good and be great for making Cuba Libre cocktails back home.

Coffee beans Venezuela exports little of its coffee, unlike Colombia, so the local market is well served with high-quality local produce. Venezuelans like their coffee roasted dark, Italian style, which makes for a strong cup of java. If you're out in the countryside in Cumana, Caripe or Mérida look out for coffee from small local *haciendas*, although supermarkets also stock good quality beans.

☻ ARTS AND ENTERTAINMENT

ART Caracas is the arts centre of Venezuela with many private galleries and museums such as the Museo de Bellas Artes, Galeria de Arte Nacional and the Contemporary Arts Museum, which put on shows of international quality. Artists of note include the 19th-century master Arturo Michelena (1863–98), an accomplished oil painter who won the highest honour for a foreign artist at the Paris Salon in 1887. His greatest masterpiece, on show at the national art gallery, is a painting of independence hero Francisco de Miranda languishing in a Spanish jail called *Miranda en la Carraca*. Armando Reveron (1889–1954) was a groundbreaking painter who explored elements of both Impressionism and Expressionism. He gradually stripped his palette to shades of white to recreate the blinding light of the central coast, where he lived a Robinson Crusoe existence with his maid Juanita. Contemporary painters, sculptors and graphic designers of international repute are the pop artist Marisol Escobar, who now lives in New York's trendy Tribeca, José Hernández-Diez, Alirio Palacios, Jacobo Borges and Alejandro Otero. Venezuela's most famous artist is Jesús Rafael Soto (1923–2005), part of the Kinetic art movement who won France's *Grand Prix de l' Esculture* in 1995. His shimmering sculptures of brightly coloured tubes adorn public spaces in France and the United States and are prominent landmarks in Venezuela. A museum dedicated to his life and work in his hometown of Ciudad Bolívar has a couple of his 'penetrables', large cubes made of coloured plastic tubes that gallery-goers can walk through. Designs by Carlos Cruz-Diez, another Kinetic artist, appear prominently at Maiquetía Airport, on the metro system and in the Guri Dam.

CINEMA Venezuelans are keen cinema-goers and most large shopping malls have multiplex cinemas showing all the big Hollywood releases in English with Spanish subtitles. Indie and foreign film seasons are shown at arthouse venues, such as the Cinemateca and Transnocho cinemas in Caracas. Tickets are half price on Monday nights and there are discounts for over 65s.

The local film scene has been boosted by the creation of the Villa de Cine, a government initiative that President Chávez has said will break 'the dictatorship of Hollywood'. Movies sponsored so far include historic dramas about independence heroes Francisco de Miranda, and a later revolutionary called Ezequiel Zamora. *Lethal Weapon* actor Danny Glover has also been in talks with the president to produce a movie about Haitian independence leader Toussaint L'Ouverture. One of the best recent films to come out of the initiative is *Postales de Leningrado*, a whimsical and touching depiction of a group of guerrillas in the 1960s from director Mariana Rondon that owes much to Gabriel Garcia Marquez's brand of magical realism. The movie has picked up a handful of international awards. Another recent success was Alberto Arvelo's 2007 movie *Cyrano Fernandez*, a complicated love story set against the violence of shantytown life, which brings the Cyrano de Bergerac story of a big-nosed poet with a heart bang up to date. The movie stars Edgar Ramirez, a Venezuelan actor who has had international success in *The Bourne Ultimatum* alongside Matt Damon and in *Domino* alongside English actress Keira Knightley.

Venezuelan actresses working in Hollywood include Maria Conchita Alonso (*Running Man, Desperate Housewives*) and the former supermodel Patricia Velasquez (*The Mummy, The Mummy Returns, Ugly Betty*).

The biggest international success for a Venezuelan movie in recent years is *Secuestro Express*, a Tarantino-style black comedy by debut director Jonathan Jakubowicz. The film follows a middle-class couple, kidnapped after a night on the town and taken on a terrifying rollercoaster ride with their captors to the seediest corners of the capital's most violent *barrios*. The film was condemned by some ministers as an attempt to discredit the government but it went on to become Venezuela's highest grossing movie at the local box office.

Venezuela has also been the backdrop for international movies, including the 1990 horror comedy *Arachnophobia* and the 1997 Tim Allen comedy *Jungle 2 Jungle*, both shot in Canaima. The most recent film to feature Venezuela is the cartoon *Up*, about a grumpy old man who hitches his house to thousands of balloons and flies off to Roraima and Angel Falls.

THEATRE Theatre, ballet, and opera companies are an essential part of cultural life and the main companies share the installations of the Complejo Cultural Teresa

Carreño in Caracas (see page 98). An International Theatre Festival brings first-rate groups from many countries to Caracas in April–May with many street performances by Australian, Chinese, Czech or Danish groups.

MUSIC Everywhere you go Venezuela is alive with the sound of music, from the salsa and merengue blasting from bus stereos to the folk music played in the metro. At the beach, music is a constant companion and during the peak holidays you can find yourself wedged between competing sound systems, one playing reggaeton and the other soppy love ballads.

Venezuelans are great dancers too and no party is complete without couples dancing to tropical salsa, merengue, Colombian vallenato or local folk music. The idea is for everybody to get a turn on the dance floor, so don't be surprised if you're asked to join in.

Music shops in all the big cities are well stocked and sell tropical, pop, and classical CDs for around US$10–15 but many Venezuelans buy pirate CDs and DVDs from street stalls or vendors in bus stations where they retail for about US$1.

Tropical, pop and rock The most famous homegrown music star is Oscar D'Leon, the Lion King of salsa, a truly international star who is as big in Venezuela, Cuba and Miami as he is in Japan. Another major export is the group Los Amigos Invisibles, whose infectious blend of tropical boogaloo, acid jazz and electronica is a guaranteed party starter. Signed to David Byrne's Luaka Bop label in 1998, the Amigos have since brought their unique blend of Latin grooves to New York. In 2009 they were rewarded with a Latin Grammy for their sixth album *Comercial*.

Ska is very popular in Venezuela and veteran group Desorden Publico continue to release hits after 25 years at the top. Younger rock acts making a splash are Mermelada Bunch, La Vida Boheme, Nana Cadavieco and hip-hop trio Tres Dueños.

Folk music Head into the countryside and you're in for an immersion course in Venezuela's *joropo* folk music, which is virtually unknown outside the country. The jaunty music of Los Llanos, *joropo*, mimics the galloping steps of a young colt and is danced in couples, like a waltz with some fast cockroach-crushing steps thrown in towards the end. Played on harp, maracas and small four-stringed guitar called a *cuatro*, the *joropo* has lent itself to classical arrangements by instrumental artists such as Juan Vicente Torrealba, and nostalgic ballads that hark back to the working songs of the ranch by Simon Diaz, a national treasure. In village festivals, the raw-throated contests between competing singers are called *contrapunteo*, and test the wit and lyrical skills of the contestants as they strive to outdo each other.

Nothing beats the raw power of Afro-Venezuelan *tambores*, a lively folk tradition that harks backs to slave days and is popular in the old plantation towns along the central coast, such as Choroní, Chuao, Puerto Maya and the beach towns of Barlovento. The infectious music is played on long *cumaco* drums made from hollowed-out avocado tree trunks with deer or cowhide skins. One drummer sits astride the drum and plays the skin, while two others play on the trunk with hard sticks called *palillos* or *laures* that give the distinctive taca-ta-taca-ta sound that drives the dancing. The singer or *cantor* is accompanied by a chorus, in a typical Afro-Caribbean call-and-response style. The hip-swivelling dancing takes place in a circle, with the boys trying to get as close as they can to the *muchachitas*, who spin around to avoid them. Anybody, male or female, can cut in at any time and take over and the dancing goes on until the last sweaty dancer gives up or the rum runs out. In May, during the Cruz de Mayo celebrations the drumming and singing is accompanied by *cuatro* and there is no dancing.

Classical Classical music is another highlight of any visit to Venezuela. There are 30 symphony orchestras in the country and 125 youth orchestras, including five full orchestras in Caracas, plus three youth orchestras and many chamber groups. The reason for this incredible flowering of classical music is El Sistema (The System), a foundation started in 1975 by economist José Antonio Abreu that currently teaches music to 250,000 children, the vast majority of whom are from the poorest neighbourhoods of Venezuela. *Gramophone* magazine called El Sistema 'probably the most ambitious programme of music education and orchestra training in the world' and fans include the guitarist John Williams and the conductor Simon Rattle. Julian Lloyd Webber said the Simon Bolívar Youth Orchestra's electrifying performance at the Proms in London was 'quite simply miraculous'. One of the big stars to emerge from El Sistema, and one of the hottest properties in classical music at the moment, is the mop-haired conductor Gustavo Dudamel. After leading the Simon Bolívar Youth Orchestra on critically acclaimed tours of Europe that saw standing ovations for nearly every number, he now shuttles between Sweden, where he is the principal conductor of the Gothenburg Symphony Orchestra, and the United States, where he's the musical director of the Los Angeles Philharmonic. Not bad for a poor boy from Barquisimeto who turned 29 in 2010.

PHOTOGRAPHY

Although batteries and memory cards are available for all major digital cameras in all major cities, make sure you bring everything you need as prices for imported electrical goods are generally high. If travelling on excursions into jungle areas, doing the Roraima trek or spending time in Los Llanos on a wildlife safari, you should bring an extra battery for your camera and extra memory cards. There is nothing more frustrating than a dead battery when every minute could bring a once-in-a-lifetime photo opportunity. Typically, Llanos tours last for a few hours at a time, six hours maximum, but a river boat trip to Angel Falls lasts three days, with two nights in jungle camp, and hiking to the top of Roraima takes six days.

When taking photos remember that light conditions vary greatly during the day, with softer light and more colours in the early morning and late in the afternoon and harsh light at midday.

Always carry a couple of waterproof plastic bags when visiting waterfalls and on jungle river trips and boat excursions to keep cameras dry. To protect against loss or damage of expensive camera equipment insurance is strongly recommended.

When photographing people, especially indigenous groups, always ask first before taking photographs. The beauty of digital cameras is that an initial refusal can sometimes be gently overcome by taking a few photos of your surroundings or fellow travellers and showing them around to break the ice. Avoid the temptation to take photographs surreptitiously when you've been told not to.

⟩ MEDIA AND COMMUNICATIONS

TELEVISION Venezuela's polarised political situation has turned the country's sophisticated media environment into a battleground, with President Chávez accusing private media outlets of working with the oligarchy and foreign interests to try and undermine the government. The private media, in turn, have accused the president of being a dictator and attacking freedom of expression. The conflict came to a head in 2007 when the government refused to renew the operating licence of the TV channel Radio Caracas TV (RCTV; *www.rctv.net*), the oldest TV station in Venezuela, saying that it had backed the April 2002 coup when the president was briefly removed. The channel has continued to broadcast on satellite and its signal has been taken over by the state-owned channel TVES, which has a minimal audience. The other main opposition TV station is the 24-hour news channel Globovision (*www.globovision.com*). The other two privately owned TV channels have toned down their opposition to the government in recent years. Venevision (*www.venevision.net*) now has the biggest audience since RCTV moved to satellite, and Televen (*www.venevision.net*) shows mainly Brazilian soap operas and US series. Government-run channel Venezolana de Televisión (VTV; *www.vtv.gob.ve*) relies heavily on news shows and documentaries and broadcasts President Chávez's weekly Sunday show *Aló, Presidente*, a folksy, informal chat show in which the president discusses the issues of the day, rails against capitalism, the USA and the private media, sings the odd song and tells a few jokes. There is no set time for the show, which can run for up to five hours. The president can also force all TV channels to carry his broadcasts any time he wants to speak to the nation, in what are called *cadenas nacionales*.

NEWSPAPERS Venezuela has a strong independent press, which is also divided into papers that oppose the president and others which have tried to remain neutral. The main opposition newspapers are *El Nacional* (*www.el-nacional.com*), *Tal Cual* (*www.talcualdigital.com*) and *El Universal* (*www.eluniversal.com*), which has a daily news section in English. The best-selling national daily is *Ultimas Noticias* (*www.ultimasnoticias.com.ve*), a tabloid. Government-run dailies include *Diario Vea* (*www.diariovea.com.ve*) and *Correo del Orinoco* (*www.correodelorinoco.gob.ve*), which

---

PHOTOGRAPHIC TIPS
Ariadne Van Zandbergen

EQUIPMENT An SLR camera with one or more lenses is recommended for serious photography. The most important component in a digital SLR is the sensor, either DX or FX. The FX is a full size sensor identical to the old film size (36mm); the DX sensor is half size and produces less quality. The type of sensor will determine your choice of lenses as the DX sensor introduces a 0.5x multiplication to the focal length. FX ('full frame') sensors are the future, so I will further refer to focal lengths appropriate to the FX sensor.

Always buy the best lens you can afford. Fixed fast lenses are ideal, but very costly. Zoom lenses offer good flexibility with composition. If you carry only one lens a 24–70mm or similar zoom should be ideal. For a second lens, a lightweight 80–200mm or 70–300mm or similar will be excellent for candid shots and varying your composition. Wildlife photography requires at least a 300mm lens. For a small loss of quality, teleconverters are a cheap and compact way to increase magnification: a 300 lens with a 1.4x converter becomes 420mm, and with a 2x it becomes 600mm. NB: 1.4x and 2x teleconverters reduce the speed of your lens by 1.4 and 2 stops respectively.

For ordinary prints a 6-megapixel camera is fine. For better results, the possibility to enlarge images and for professional reproduction, higher resolution is available up to 21 megapixels.

It is important to have enough memory space. You should calculate how many pictures you can fit on a card and either take enough cards or take a storage drive onto which you can download the cards' content.

Remember that digital camera batteries, computers and other storage devices need charging so make sure you have all the chargers, cables and converters with you.

DUST AND HEAT Keep your equipment in a sealed bag, and avoid exposing equipment to the sun when possible. Digital cameras are prone to collecting dust particles on the

also has an English edition on Fridays. Newsstands carry foreign papers and sell a range of international magazines. Hundreds of radio stations carry music and news programmes.

✉ **POST** The postal system is run by Ipostel (Instituto Postal Telegráfico; *www.ipostel.gov.ve*) and is slow and unreliable. Letters take a fortnight or longer for delivery (and some never get there). Allow a month for a postcard to arrive and be pleased if it takes less. There is no point mailing packages to Venezuela. The stamps cost as much as the contents and, if the parcel arrives, the receiver must not only make one or more trips to Customs, but also pay duty on the contents and then travel to the central post office to collect it. If you want to send a postcard, get stamps from a large hotel and post it there or at the airport. A short airmail letter costs US$0.80 in stamps.

✆ **TELEPHONE** The country code for Venezuela is 0058; area codes are given under each destination in the relevant chapters.

The state-controlled telephone company CANTV (*www.cantv.com.ve*) was re-nationalised in 2007 and is the sole landline provider. It also operates call centres known as *Centros de Comunicacion*, located in shopping malls, airports, bus stations and on the main streets of all cities and most towns, where you can make national and international calls and access the internet. Mobile phone provider Movistar also runs its own *Centro de Comunicaciones* in most places and there is little difference in rates. Expect to pay just under BsF0.70 for each minute for local calls and about BsF2 (US$0.50) a minute for international calls.

sensor which results in spots on the image. The dirt mostly enters the camera when changing lenses, so be careful when doing this. You can have your camera sensor professionally cleaned, or you can do this yourself with special brushes and swabs, but note that touching the sensor might cause damage and should only be done with the greatest care.

LIGHT The most striking outdoor photographs are often taken during the hour or two of 'golden light' after dawn and before sunset. Shooting in low light may enforce the use of very low shutter speeds, in which case a tripod/beanbag will be required to avoid camera shake. The most advanced digital SLRs have very little loss of quality on higher ISO settings, which allows you to shoot at lower light conditions. It is still recommended not to increase the ISO unless necessary.

Generally, it is best to shoot with the sun behind you. When photographing animals or people in the harsh midday sun, images taken in light but even shade are likely to look nicer than those taken in direct sunlight or patchy shade.

PROTOCOL In some countries it is unacceptable to photograph local people without permission, and many will refuse to pose or will ask for a donation. Don't try to sneak photographs. Even the most willing subject will often pose stiffly when a camera is pointed at them; relax them by making a joke, and take a few shots in quick succession to improve the odds of capturing a natural pose.

Ariadne Van Zandbergen is a professional travel and wildlife photographer specialised in Africa. She runs 'The Africa Image Library'. For photo requests, visit the website www.africaimagelibrary.co.za or contact her direct at e ariadne@hixnet.co.za.

Public phone boxes are now virtually redundant (as very few actually work) although you can still buy phone cards for public phones from newspaper kiosks. It's easier to head for the nearest call centre or one of the tables set up on the street by vendors hiring out mobile phones (see below).

MOBILE PHONES Mobile phones are big business in Venezuela, which has the highest mobile-phone per-capita rate in Latin America at close to 99.2%, with 28.9 million mobile phones in use in 2009. This is partly due to the red tape and endless waiting time involved in getting a landline installed in your home or office by CANTV and partly due to heavy marketing by the mobile-phone firms.

Service is provided by three main rivals: Movistar, owned by Spanish firm Telefonica, uses 0414 and 0424 numbers; Movilnet is owned by CANTV and uses 0416 and 0426; Digitel is owned by the Cisneros group and uses 0412. Calls between Movistar, Movilnet and Digitel accounts can be expensive and many Venezuelans carry two or three mobile phones to minimise costs. In most towns and cities and at bus stations, street vendors rent out mobile phones to make short calls. Show them the number you want to call and they will select the phone for you to use. Short local calls cost around US$0.15 a minute; texts are much cheaper. One way of using your existing phone while in Venezuela is to buy a local SIM card (US$10) and a top-up scratch card (US$5–20). Be aware that not all SIMs will work in all phones, so check with your mobile-phone company before travelling to see if your phone is compatible. Digitel has the worst coverage outside big cities and Movistar has the best.

Venezuelans are keen users of BlackBerrys, with over a million users (2½ times the Latin American average) but bear in mind that they are highly sought after by thieves. The cheapest phone on the market is manufactured by the government in co-operation with China and is called El Vergatario. The rather vulgar name, pronounced with relish by President Chávez at the launch in May 2009, is a slang term for penis used in Maracaibo. The term is used to say something is 'the best', just as Londoners might use 'the dogs' bollocks'. Retailing at about US$15, El Vergatario is one of the cheapest mobile phones in the world and stocks sold out in hours when it was first introduced.

INTERNET Venezuela has some nine million internet users and cyber cafés are found virtually everywhere, offering broadband connection for millions of people who have no computer or fixed phone line to access the net. More than half the population are expected to have internet access by 2012. In the city of Mérida internet access is so widespread that it is said there are more computer users per capita than in Tokyo. Every city also has a state-equipped **Infocentro** in libraries and cultural centres such as museums, equipped with ten to 15 computers with high-speed internet access, colour printers and scanners. A national telecommunications plan backs not only the Infocentros but is also trying to expand internet access to schools, colleges and remote indigenous communities, such as the Pemon village in Canaima. The cost per hour at cyber cafés varies from a low of US$0.50 in Mérida to US$1.50 an hour in Caracas; expect to pay more in hotels and at the airport. Most hotels and many *posadas* geared for foreign tourists offer free Wi-Fi.

There has been an explosion in the use of social networking sites in the last two years, with 86% of Venezuelan internet users having a Facebook account in 2009. Twitter use has also boomed, with much of the polarised political debate taking place in cyberspace. The Twitter account of opposition news channel Globovision led the field with 260,000 followers before President Chávez decided to join the fray in April 2010 and take on his critics head on. After signing up 95,000 followers in the first 36 hours of opening his account @chávezcandanga, the president has since had to take on 200 assistants to cope with the messages he receives from critics, supporters and Venezuelans petitioning for jobs. In late May 2010 the president had more than 420,000 followers.

BUSINESS

Venezuelans are early risers and by 07.00 the day's first rush hour builds into a jam of people going to work. Business hours vary, with most companies starting at 08.00; almost all close at lunch for one to two hours. The five-day week is standard. (Half-day work on Saturdays was called *sábado inglés*.) For what goes on behind the scenes in business, consult people in the know. The Venezuelan American Chamber of Commerce (*www.venamcham.org*), is a highly organised group of more than 4,500 US and Venezuelan businessmen. VenAmCham publishes a monthly magazine called *Business Venezuela*.

CULTURAL ETIQUETTE

Venezuelans are laid back and friendly and will usually greet new acquaintances and friends in the same informal way. Women and men greet each other with a single kiss to the right cheek and men will shake hands with each other or even move into a bear hug, sometimes with back slapping. They will also slip immediately into the informal '*tu*' form when speaking, which at least makes it easier for novices in Spanish.

Social graces are important. When people meet, the custom is to enquire about the welfare of the entire family before getting down to business. Be complimentary first, make your complaints later, and try to find the other person a way out of the difficulty he has caused you without losing face.

If invited to a barbecue or party it is best to take a bottle of wine or whisky but never take a cheap bottle of whisky as Venezuelans are picky and will see anything less than Chivas Regal or Johnnie Walker Black Label as a snub.

Venezuelans are also a proud people who react quickly to a slur on their cultural identity. Simón Bolívar, as their highest role model and liberator of five South American countries (six, if you include Panama) is honoured with a statue in virtually every town and village and if you find yourself in Plaza Bolívar you should never show disrespect for Bolívar's statue by loitering about in beach clothes. Respect for Bolívar also extends to his printed likeness. The editors of one newspaper were made to recall all copies because a currency devaluation report was illustrated with a banknote torn in half through Bolívar's face.

Equally, avoid talking about politics unless you are sure of your audience. Venezuela is a highly polarised society and strong opinions on President Chávez and his Bolivarian revolution from a foreigner may not be well-received. It might be better to ask questions about the situation in the country than give opinions. Never assume that just because a Venezuelan is unhappy about aspects of their country they will be happy to hear criticism of Venezuela from you. It is far more productive to focus on the positive aspects of the country when trying to start conversations, such as the natural beauty of the beaches and *tepuis*, than tackling a potential hot potato like politics.

To disrespect someone is to *faltarle el respeto*, a grave wrong. Although a uniformed official may be overstepping his authority, be careful in word (and looks) when addressing representatives of the law: never demean their position or dignity. (They are always in the right.) You could begin: '*Con todo respeto, oficial...*' ('With all due respect, officer…') Explain that whatever you might have done was unintentional: '*Perdón, fue sin intención*'.

Flattery may not get you everywhere, but it will go a long way. Try not to be *antipático*, disagreeable or negative. If there is nothing good to say about a roadblock, a missed plane, or an outboard engine that fails, try to be *simpático* to the traffic policeman, the overworked employee or the sweating mechanic. They all have families and problems.

TOILET TIPS Venezuelan loos are very particular. You mustn't flush toilet paper down the loo as it blocks up the narrow pipes. A small basket is always provided in the toilet in which to place paper. Usually there's a sign saying *'No botar papel en la poseta'* ('Don't flush paper down the toilet') to remind you. There are few public toilets so take advantage of fast-food outlets in cities. Buses on cross-country journeys tend to stop at grotty service stations where the public toilets have an attendant who will try and charge you BsF1 for two squares of flimsy toilet paper as you go in. Always be prepared with a few rolls of your own toilet paper when travelling and keep them safe in a waterproof bag.

TRAVELLING POSITIVELY

Venezuela not only offers travellers the opportunity to enjoy great beaches, fantastic scenery and exhilarating adventures, it also provides plenty of practical ways to show your appreciation for the hospitality you receive in the places you visit. Giving something back doesn't have to be a grand gesture; small contributions can be just as important. One traveller, for example, donated inflatable map globes to remote schools, another took Frisbees to hand out on a Gran Sabana trek. If carrying gifts is not always possible, paper and pencils can easily be bought at a bookshop (*librería*) on the way. **Terekay Adventures** (*www.terekay.com.ve*) in Puerto Ayacucho encourages visitors to take school supplies on its boat trips to the small Piaroa community of Raudal de Ceguera, opposite Autana Tepui. **Akanan Adventures** (*www.akanan.com*) can also help with suggestions on useful donations to the local communities visited on its trips.

Andes Tropicales www.andestropicales.org. This organisation helps local communities with its Mucuposada programme, fitting out farmhouses to receive guests in the high Andean *páramos*, thereby allowing tourist dollars to benefit the people directly. The hikes between Mucuposadas are not physically demanding & offer an incredible way to see firsthand how Andean traditions survive in these remote locations.

Cocolight www.cocolight.com. A tour company run by Alan Highton in Mérida that takes visitors to see the Catatumbo Lightning, Cocolight is working with the people of the Sur del Lago stilt villages of Congo & Ologa to find solutions to the lack of safe drinking water.

Peace Village Foundation Lomas de Piedra, Santa Elena de Uairén; ╲ +58 289 416 0718; e mail@ peacevillages.org; www.peacevillages.org. A volunteer programme in the Gran Sabana run by an experienced German charity worker, Manfred Mönnighoff, who previously worked in Mérida & the *barrio* of Petare in Caracas before setting up

Fundacion Aldea de Paz in Santa Elena in 2003. The charity aims to give educational support to local indigenous Pemon & works with disabled children. Volunteers pay a weekly financial contribution that goes towards the educational & therapy programmes & covers bed & board in dorm-style accommodation. There are also homestays with local families as part of a language-learning programme. Popular with gap-year students, there are no restrictions on age, experience or background. Volunteers get to decide how much of their time they divide between teaching, or construction projects & equine therapies, or exploring the *tepuis* & waterfalls of the Gran Sabana.

SOS Children's Villages www.soschildrensvillages.org.uk. A UK-based charity that runs orphanages in El Topita & Ciudad Ojeda, near Maracaibo, & another in Maracay. Called 'Children's Villages', they combine living quarters, cooking, play & teaching facilities for hundreds of abandoned & orphaned children, as well as hundreds more from low resource families who need day care. The first Venezuelan Children's Village was opened in 1976. The group relies on financial support from donors who can sponsor a child in Venezuela (or another of the hundred countries they work in), or you can make a donation to a particular project. **Veniños – Venezuelan Children In Need** UK: London St, Reading, RG1 4QD; ☏ +44 07906 901796; ✉ info@veninos.org; USA: Suite 2633, 14781 Memorial Av, Houston, Texas, TX 77079; ☏ +1 888 5 836 4667; ✉ usa@veninos.org; www.veninos.org. A registered charity supporting groups working with street & shantytown children in a number of places in Venezuela (see box below). Regular fundraising events in the UK & USA include concerts of Venezuelan music, gastronomic events & sponsored walks & marathon runs. In 2008, co-founder Lisa Tylee cycled 9,000 miles around the USA to raise funds for the organisation, despite being born with

Practical Information **TRAVELLING POSITIVELY**

2

UK CHARITY LENDS SUPPORT TO SHANTYTOWN KIDS

Venezuelan Children in Need, or Veniños for short (*www.veninos.org*), is a UK- and US-registered charity dedicated to improving the lives of street and shantytown children. It is an example of how committed individuals can make positive contributions in the countries that they visit. It was founded by two British women who met in Venezuela and decided to act on their shared desire to make a difference, however small, by supporting local groups working with orphans and underprivileged kids in the *barrios* of Venezuela's big cities. Co-founder Lisa Tylee first travelled to Venezuela in 1986 as an exchange student and spent a year living with the Angulo family near Valencia, where she was impressed by the warmth of the people and the diverse geography of the country. Born without a knee in her left leg and adopted at birth, she became conscious in Venezuela that in comparison to many, she had been lucky to have a very fortunate upbringing in England.

Lisa later returned to Venezuela to work as a volunteer with children's groups and met Jane Blake, another British expatriate whose husband worked in the oil industry. Jane had never worked with street children previously but, seeing the obvious needs of the large numbers of children living rough and wanting to give something back, she decided to get involved. Guided by Lisa initially, Jane did some voluntary work with local orphanages and NGOs in Caracas, something that changed her life:

> As I got to know some of the street and shantytown kids it became apparent that they had exactly the same aspirations as any other children, to be sports stars, astronauts, much like my own children, yet the contrast in their lives and therefore opportunities in life, were stark.

Back in the UK, the two friends decided to continue with their fundraising work and on 18 September 2003 launched Veniños, quickly building a strong support base and sponsorship from the Dorset chocolate makers Chococo (*www.chococo.co.uk*), who use Venezuelan cocoa in their creations.

Among the projects they support is a day care centre for the children of sex workers run by a group called Ambar, and a programme promoting sports as an alternative to gang mebership in the Caracas *barrio* of El Saman. One of their most affecting projects is an orphanage run by nuns in Caracas for abandoned babies and young children, many of whom have suffered abuse and neglect. Despite very limited resources the orphanage does everything in its power to provide a family atmosphere and keep siblings together for as long as possible.

Following interest from US groups – both Americans who had lived in Venezuela and Venezuelan expatriates – Veniños was registered as a US charity in 2006.

Since then, Lisa, who was awarded an MBE from the Queen in 2000 for her charity work in Venezuela, has raised funds for the group by walking the entire length of Great Britain from Land's End to John O'Groats and cycling 9,000 miles around the USA, pedalling all the way with her right leg on a specially adapted bike.

only one knee & having to pedal the whole way with just one working leg. Other supporters have taken part in the London Latin American Dance Marathon & the Adidas 5km Women's Challenge.

ENVIROMENTAL NGOS

Environmental groups vary from small associations to NGOs of over 1,000 members. What they have in common is the goal of guaranteeing a better quality of life for future generations through study and protection of Venezuela's biodiversity.

Econatura Apartado 63109, Caracas 1067A; ✆ 0212 238 1039, 0212 975 0911; e econatul@ telcel.net.ve. Priorities: research grants for undergraduate & postgraduate students, training for park guards, resource management, & conflict solving in national parks.

Fudena Oficina 611-A, Centro Empresarial Senderos, Trans 2 at Av Principal, Los Cortijos de Lourdes, Caracas 1071; ✆ 0212 238 2930; e fudena@ fudena.org.ve, dbigio@fudena.org.ve, snarciso@fudena.org.ve; www.fudena.org.ve. Projects support sustainable use of natural resources, beach cleaning, protection of sea turtles & Orinoco crocodile. Fudena also manages protected areas such as the Cuare Wildlife Refuge in Morrocoy.

Fundación Proyecto Paria Calle Rivero, Casa 50, Río Caribe, Estado Sucre; ✆ 0294 646 1223; e fppcarlos@cantv.net; www.fproyectoparia.com. Focus on conservation & social programmes on the Paria Peninsula.

Fundacion Tierra Viva Edif Imperial, Piso 7, Ofic 7-B, La Candelaria, Caracas 1011; ✆ 0212 576 6242, 0212 576 1927; e info@tierraviva.org, ftv.tierraviva@gmail.com; www.tierraviva.org. Priorities: environmental education projects involving schools, communities & companies in self-help action; responsible tourism & agro-tourism initiatives, such as their Organic Cocoa Trail Project, taking groups to visit small cacao producers in Birongo, Cata & Cumboto.

Provita Piso 15, Ofic-15 Norte, Edif La Previsora, Av Las Acacias, Los Caobos, Caracas; ✆ 0212 794 2234, 0212 794 1291; e provita@provitaonline.org; www.provita.org.ve. Provita uses community-based education programmes to highlight the endangered status of 20 threatened species including the spectacled bear, the manatee, Margarita parrots & Andean frogs. Provita also publishes the *Libro Rojo de la Fauna Venezolana (Red Book of Venezuelan Fauna)*, a guide to Venezuela's most endangered species, available to download as a PDF from the website.

Sociedad Científica Amigos del PN Henri Pittier Apartado Correos 4626, Maracay, Estado Aragua; ✆ 0243 245 3470; e ernestofernandez@ hotmail.com. Local group from Maracay that studies the cloudforest & birdlife of the Parque Nacional Henri Pittier. Can advise on staying at Rancho Grande.

Sociedad Conservacionista Audubon de Venezuela Apartado Postal 80450, Caracas 1080A; ✆ 0212 272 8728; e audubon@cantv.net; www.audubonvenezuela.org. Venezuela's leading bird conservation group & a magnet for all serious birdwatchers in the country, it is also involved in a range of other environmental projects & organises hiking & birdwatching trips to mountains, plains & parks; non-members welcome but members come first in reservations.

Sociedad Conservacionista de Mérida SOCOME Apartado 241, Mérida; ✆ 0274 244 6409; e psalinas@ula.ve. Priorities: cloudforest conservation, training for environmental teachers.

3

Activities

VISITS TO NATIONAL PARKS

Venezuela has an impressive 43 national parks and 20 natural monuments covering all the country's major wildlife areas: the Andean valleys, the mysterious and unique table mountains, or *tepuis*, of Bolívar and Amazonas states and the major water basins. An incredible 141,000km² or over 15% of the country falls under some sort of protection, although managing such a vast network of parks and monuments is no easy task for the Instituto Nacional de Parques (Inparques), the National Parks Institute.

The headquarters of Inparques is located in Caracas a short walk east of Parque del Este/Francisco de Miranda metro station on Avenida Rómulo Gallegos (\ *0212 273 2860, 0212 273 5056; www.inparques.gob.ve;* ⊕ *08.30–12.30 & 13.30–17.00 Mon–Fri, except in Dec, when the hours are 07.30–15.30*).

PERMITS People planning a scientific, filming, caving or diving expedition in a national park should request special permission in writing 60 days in advance. Write to the Director, Parques Nacionales, stating your objectives and listing group members with their passport numbers, and Venezuelan affiliations. Other enquiries may be directed to the Inparques regional offices, listed on page 79.

In most national parks there is a nominal fee or no charge for users, but hikers should sign in at the local ranger post, or *Puesto de Guardaparque* (PGP).

If you plan to stay in a national park overnight, request a *permiso de pernocta*. This permit costs very little and applies to parks with shelters called *kioscos* and areas designated for tents, such as Guaramacal, Guatopo, Laguna de Tacarigua, Sierra Nevada, and Yacambú.

Two parks have very cheap dormitories: Guatopo and Los Venados on the Ávila in Caracas, which sleep some 30 people; as they are booked months ahead, written requests for reservations must be directed to Parques Nacionales in Caracas.

Park entrance fees are charged on arrival at **Los Roques** (about US$19 for non-residents) and **Canaima** (US$9).

No permits are being issued for *tepui* expeditions, except to licensed tour operators, although treks to Roraima are allowed.

The marine and coastal park of **Morrocoy** restricts overnight stays to the islands of Cayo Sal, Paiclá, Sombrero and Cayo Muerto; the permit costs the equivalent of about US$1 per person per day and is available from the Inparques office in Tucacas (see *Chapter 6, Other practicalities*, page 149).

Campers bound for island beaches in **Mochima** pay a nominal fee of US$0.30 a night per tent, deposited beforehand in a bank; people staying in the village of Mochima or Santa Fe who visit the park by boat do not pay any park fee.

Travel on the Orinoco River in Amazonas State is restricted beyond the mission of La Esmeralda as this is the entry to the **Alto Orinoco Biosphere Reserve**.

NATIONAL PARKS AND NATURAL MONUMENTS

Venezuela's national parks cover a total area of 129,805km²

NATIONAL PARK	AREA (KM²)	NATIONAL PARK	AREA (KM²)
Aguaro-Guariquito	5,857	Mariusa	3,310
Archipélago Los Roques	2,211	Médanos de Coro	913
Canaima	30,000	Mochima	949
Cerro El Copey	71	Morrocoy	321
Cerro Saroche	323	Páramos Batallón La Negra	952
Chorro El Indio	170	Parima-Tapirapeco	34,200
Ciénaga del Catatumbo	2,500	Península de Paria	375
Cinaruco-Capanaparo	5,844	Río Viejo	682
Cueva de la Quebrada del Toro	49	San Esteban	435
Dinira	420	Serranía de La Neblina	13,600
Duida-Marahuaca	2,100	Sierra de Perijá	2,952
El Ávila	818	Sierra de San Luis	200
El Guácharo	627	Sierra La Culata	2,004
El Guache	167	Sierra Nevada	2,764
El Tamá	1,090	Tapo-Caparo	2,050
Guaramacal	210	Terepaima	186
Guatopo	1,225	Tirgua	910
Henri Pittier	1,078	Turuépano	700
Jaua-Sarisariñama	3,300	Yacambú	146
Laguna de la Restinga	189	Yapacana	3,200
Laguna de Tacarigua	391	Yurubí	237
Macarao	150		

NATURAL MONUMENTS

Abra Río Frio	
Cerro Autana	Las Tetas de María Guevara
Cerro Platillón	Loma de León
Cerro Santa Ana	María Lionza
Cerros Matasiete-Guayamurí	Meseta de la Galera
Chorrera de las González	Morros de Macaira
Cueva Alfredo Jahn	Morros de San Juan
Cueva del Guácharo	Pico Codazzi
Laguna de las Marites	Piedra del Cocuy
Laguna de Urao	Piedra La Tortuga, La Pintada
	Tepuis (25 in all, 10,698km²)

Fishing permits Seasonal permits for sport fishing (*pesca deportiva*) are issued by local Inparques offices in Laguna de Tacarigua and Los Roques. The permit specifies a catch limit and minimum size for each species on the basis of catch-and-release. For information about fees, which vary by boat type and by park, enquire at the regional Inparques offices listed opposite.

For rivers and lakes outside national parks, tour operators will be able to provide permits or you can get your own (US$25) at the Instituto Socialista de la Pesca y Acuicultura (*Socialist Institute of Fishing and Aquaculture; www.insopesca.gob.ve*), which has offices all around the country, including Delta Amacuro (*Paseo Manamo, Sede del MPPAT, al lado de la Guardia Nacional Tucupita;* \ *0287 721 1132*), Margarita (*Calle Cazorla, Granja Salamanca, Municipio Arismendi, La Asunción;* \ *0295 242 4255*), and Mérida (*Edificio UEMPPAT, Av Urdaneta, Piso 2, Municipio Libertador;* \ *0274 262 3842*).

INPARQUES REGIONAL OFFICES

Amazonas Edif Funeraria Amazonas, end of Calle La Guardia, Barrio Unión, Puerto Ayacucho; ☏ 0248 521 4771

Anzoátegui Parque Andrés Blanco, Paseo Colón, Puerto La Cruz; ☏ 0281 267 8973

Apure Edif Pasquali, Calle Bolívar opposite Palacio Los Barbaritos, San Fernando de Apure; ☏ 0247 341 3794

Aragua Zoológico Las Delicias, Maracay; ☏ 0243 241 3933

Bolívar Edif Centro Empresarial Alta Vista, Piso 8, Puerto Ordaz; ☏ 0286 966 2033

Carabobo Parque Metropolitano, Sector Rosarito, Av Paseo Cabriales, Valencia; ☏ 0241 859 2459, 0241 859 0530

El Ávila Los Venados; ☏ 0212 860 0690

Falcón Jardín Xerófito de Coro León Croizat, Intercomunal Coro-La Vela; ☏ 0268 277 8582

Guárico La Represa, Calabozo; ☏ 0246 871 3523

Laguna de Tacarigua ☏ 0234 871 1143

Lara Av Los Leones facing CC Las Trinitarias, Barquisimeto; ☏ 0254 254 3577

Los Roques ☏ 0237 221 1332; m 0414 907 3220

Mérida Headquarters in Sector Fondur, opp McDonald's, Av Las Américas; ☏ 0274 262 1529

Miranda Parques Nacionales HQ, Av Rómulo Gallegos, Santa Eduvigis, Caracas; ☏ 0212 285 4859

Monagas & Delta Amacuro Parque Andrés Eloy Blanco, Carretera Vía Sur, Maturín; ☏ 0291 641 7543

Nueva Esparta Margarita Calle Sta Lucía, La Asunción; ☏ 0295 242 0306

Paria Inparques, Av Principal Campo Claro, Irapa

Portuguesa Av Eduardo Chulet at Av Páez by bus terminal, Acarigua; ☏ 0255 623 4611

San Esteban Inparques, opp Puerto Cabello Airport, no phone

Sucre Parque Guaiquerí, Av Arismendi, Cumaná; ☏ 0293 431 4873

Táchira Parque Metropolitano, Av 19 de Abril, San Cristóbal; ☏ 0276 346 6544

Trujillo Oficentro Pavón, Piso 1, No 4, Av 11 at Calle 12, Valera; ☏ 0271 221 2458

Yaracuy Parque Leonor Bernabó, Av Los Baños, San Felipe; ☏ 0254 234 4553

Zulia MARNR bldg, Cabecera Puente sobre el Lago, Sector Punta de Piedra, Maracaibo; ☏ 0261 761 9298

SPECIAL-INTEREST ACTIVITIES

The list of adventure sports being practised in Venezuela grows by the year, as does the number of specialist operators and instructors who offer excursions and courses. Mountain biking, scuba diving, paragliding, windsurfing, kitesurfing, canyoning and white-water rafting are not only being offered in Mérida, Los Roques and Margarita but all over the country. Here's a list of a few top operators and instructors.

CAVING Venezuela has more than 1,500 caves, including the spectacular **Cueva del Guácharo** in Monagas State, and the **Cueva Alfredo Jahn** in Birongo. For information on speleology and spelunking contact Akanan Travel and Adventure or the **Sociedad Venezolana de Espeleología** (*Apartado 47334, Caracas 1041A;* ☏*0212 242 9001;* m *0414 246 5712; www.sve-espeleologia.org.ve, www.sve-espeleologia.org.ve*), who do field work and publish an annual scientific bulletin.

CLIMBING The Andean peaks of Mérida offer mountaineers several options and mountain climber and paragliding champion Jose Albarran of **Fanny Tours** (*www.fanny-tours.com*) organises trips to Pico Humboldt and Pico Bolívar, the highest peaks in Mérida. **Federación Venezolana de Montañismo & Escalada** (*www.fevme.com.ve*) has a calendar of courses and competitions. Affiliated groups meet in Barquisimeto, Caracas, San Cristóbal, Trujillo and Valencia. Mountaineering groups in Mérida include: **Grupo Andino de Rescate** (☏ *0274 244 4666*) and the **Asociación Merideña de Andinismo** (☏ *0274 252 6806*).

CYCLING A number of mountain-bike treks are organised around the country by **Akanan Travel and Adventure** (www.*akanan.com*), including a trip through the *Lost World* of the Gran Sabana from La Paragua to Canaima camp and a trip

3

from the mountain valleys of Colonia Tovar down to Puerto Maya or Chichiriviche de la Costa.

In Mérida, **Montaña Adventure** (*www.venadventure.com*) use a support vehicle to carry cyclists' camping gear up the high Andean *páramos* to reach the picturesque mountain village of Los Nevados, for an exhilarating trip back over mountain trails.

Fanny Tours, also in Mérida (*www.fanny-tours.com*), are specialists in mountain-biking trips and organise a three- to four-day cycling tour of mountain villages around La Azulita, site of an annual international mountain-biking competition.

DIVING With such a long Caribbean coastline and outlying islands, Venezuela has a host of excellent dive sites and good quality instructors. All the major certification courses are on offer, including PADI, NAUI and SSI, as well as everything from one-day taster immersions to Open Water Diver/Instructor, cave diving, night diving and wreck diving.

In Caracas, **Aquasub** (*www.aquasub.com.ve*), based in Parque Cristal, offers PADI courses and can arrange diving trips all over Venezuela.

Los Roques is a diving hot spot with four centres on the main Island Gran Roque, including **Ecobuzos** (*www.ecobuzos.com*), **Aquatics Dive Center** (*www.scubavenezuela.com*) and **Eco Challenge** (*www.ecochallenge.ws/roques_venezuela.html*).

Chichiriviche Divers (*www.chidivers.com.ve*) provide a centre for courses, tank fills, equipment rental and boat trips in Chichiriviche de la Costa, just west of Maiquetía Airport.

In Mochima, Rodolfo Plaza runs the **Mochima Dive Center** (*www.laposadadelosbuzos.com*), offering dive packages, an intensive course for CMAS certification, plus lodging at the **Posada de Buceo**.

In Puerto La Cruz, **Aquatic Adventures** (*www.aquaticadventures-mochima.net.tc*) also take divers out to reefs in the Parque Nacional Mochima and run certification courses.

The **Tienda de Buceo** (*www.venezueladiving.com*) offers diving off the coast of Puerto Cabello and San Esteban and has three dive boats to explore sunken ships around Isla Larga and Alcatraz, and the reefs of Morro de Turiamo.

In Morrocoy, divers have a choice of the excellent **Frogman Dive Center** (*www.frogmandive.com*) run by Manuel Collazo, who also organises diving trips to Bonaire, and scuba pioneer Mile Osborne at **Submatur** in Tucacas.

In Margarita there are several outfits operating from Playa El Agua, including **Enomis** (*www.scubadivemargarita.com*) and **Margarita Divers** (*www.scubadiving-margarita.com*) who offer the chance to dive off the islands of Los Frailes, Coche and Cubagua.

HIKING AND TREKKING Venezuela offers world-class trekking, from the glaciers of Pico Humboldt and Pico Bolívar, to six-day treks to the top of Mount Roraima in the *Lost World* region of the Gran Sabana. New trails being offered in Mérida include trips between remote mountain-valley farmhouses known as Mucuposadas. This innovative community tourism initiative is designed and run by **Andes Tropicales** (*www.andestropicales.org*).

In Amazonas State, **Terekay Adventures** (*www.terekay.com.ve*) run a five-day trip to the mysterious Lago Leopoldo – an isolated lake in the middle of a low-lying *tepui* named after Belgian King Leopold. The trip includes navigating a small tributary of the Orinoco, sleeping in hammocks and tents and trekking in rainforest.

In Caracas, there are many trails up the Ávila Mountain offering different levels of difficulty from a 25-minute hike up to Sabas Nieves to an all-day trek to Pico Naiguata, the highest peak, for great views of the city on one side and the

Caribbean Sea on the other. The **Centro Excursionista Caracas** (*www.centroexcursionistacaracas.org.ve*) organise Ávila trips for those who'd like company and post a schedule of upcoming hikes on their website.

The Caracas Runners (*www.caracasrunners.org*) meet regularly to run at Parque del Este/Francisco de Miranda and on the Ávila. The **Caracas Hash House Harriers** (*www.jaychristopherson.com/CHHH/*) are a group of expatriates who describe themselves as a 'drinking club with a running problem' and meet alternate Sunday afternoons for events.

KAYAKING Venezuela has excellent kayaking opportunities both in sea and river settings, from the Caribbean keys and islands of Los Roques, Mochima and Morrocoy to the rivers of the Gran Sabana and the Delta Amacuro. **Jakera** (*www.jakera.com*), a tour agency run by a Scot, Chris Patterson, organises kayaking trips to the Laguna de Tacarigua and longer trips to the Orinoco Delta, where kayakers get the chance to visit isolated river communities and meet the indigenous Warao, known as 'the boat people'.

In Amazonas, **Aguas Bravas** (*www.raftingorinoco.com*) offer kayak courses and trips on the Orinoco run by Venezuelan champions in the sport.

PARAGLIDING Paragliding, known as *parapente*, is hugely popular in Venezuela and there are many sites to fly from, including La Victoria near Colonia Tovar and Las Gonzales in Mérida.

One of the best outfits offering paragliding tours, tandem flights and base jumping experiences, for the more extreme thrill seekers, is the Caracas-based tour company **Autana** (*autana.org*). One of the most spectacular trips they offer is paragliding from Kuravaina Tepui, with an overflight of Canaima Lagoon, the base for trips to Angel Falls.

Close to Colonia Tovar and an easy morning's trip from Caracas is a paragliding centre called **Soaring** (*www.volarparapente.com.ve*). It is run by Orlando Leyton and Mari Nouel at Placivel, on the Colonia Tovar–La Victoria road. They offer tandem flights, courses and rooms for guests.

WINDSURFING, KITESURFING AND SAILING With its year-round winds and tropical sunshine the beach resort of El Yaque, on Margarita Island's south coast, has become a firm fixture on the international windsurfing and kitesurfing circuit. International competitions are held here each year and an international kitesurfing competition is now held at the nearby island of Coche.

In Los Roques, **Vela Windsurf** (*www.velawindsurf.com*) offer courses and equipment hire in the paradise isles, while Adícora, on the Paraguaná Peninsula, and the barren Araya Peninsula have good wind, but less infrastructure.

WHITE-WATER RAFTING Rafting was launched by Jorge Buzzo in a big way in the Orinoco's fearsome Atures rapids, using a specially built, powered raft; levels 3 and 4. Now, rafting on the fast Acequias River (levels 3 and 4) in the Andean state of Barinas has become popular, led by his son Alejandro Buzzo.

Other Mérida tour operators who offer rafting on the Acequias are **Guamanchi Expeditions** (*www.guamanchi.com*), **Arrasari Trek** (*www.arassari.com*) and **Fanny Tours** (*www.fanny-tours.com*). Most tour operators in Mérida also offer **canyoning**.

BIRDWATCHING With its distinctive geographic areas encompassing Caribbean beaches and Andean mountains, and its location on a major migration route, Venezuela has a growing reputation as one of the most spectacular countries in the world for birdwatching, or 'birding' as it is known to practitioners.

Chris Sharpe

Venezuela is one of the so-called 'mega-diversity countries' – a handful of nations that contain the lion's share of the world's biodiversity – so it is no surprise to find that it is the world's sixth-most bird-species-rich nation, with over 1,380 species recorded. Of these, 45 are found only in Venezuela (ie: they are political endemics) and a further 120 or so have most of their distribution within Venezuela. Examples of avian endemics include the tepui tinamou, Táchira antpitta, Caracas tapaculo, Mérida flowerpiercer and Guaiquinima whitestart.

In addition, Venezuela harbours a number of well-known, charismatic species that are highly prized by birders. These include birds like torrent duck, agami heron, scarlet ibis, harpy eagle, sunbittern, four species of large macaws, hoatzin, 100 hummingbirds, four quetzals, 16 toucans, over 90 antbirds, over 160 flycatchers, two species of cock-of-the-rock, white and bearded bellbirds, black-capped donacobius, musician wren, over 100 tanagers and the red siskin.

Venezuela's geographical location also makes it important for migrant birds from both the northern and southern hemispheres. About 100 species are regular migrants and a further 50 or so are vagrants. During the northern winter, the Venezuelan Andes are home to a variety of boreal breeders, including a colourful selection of warblers.

Given its position in the global tables of bird diversity, Venezuela is a world-renowned birding destination and there is a long and distinguished ornithological tradition with a wealth of published information. The twin testaments are Mary Lou Goodwin's *Birding in Venezuela* which advises on where to go, and Steve Hilty's *Birds of Venezuela* which helps you to identify what you see. The existence of a reliable transport infrastructure and specialised bird tour agencies has helped make birding in Venezuela an experience that is hard to beat.

A birding trip to Venezuela will typically aim to see as many endemic species as possible and accrue a large total number of species, usually by combining time in several eco-regions. A good two-week introductory trip might comprise visits to the Coastal Cordillera, the Andes and the Llanos and would typically produce about 500 species – not far off the total number ever recorded in the UK. With a further two weeks, the Guiana Highlands can be added, together with other titbits that would make up a satisfying eastern Venezuela tour. Variations might include the arid northwest or the Maracaibo basin. On the other hand, there is nothing as relaxing as a week spent leisurely birding in the Llanos at one of the famous wildlife ranches or *hatos*. For those who like to be challenged, that week might better be spent chasing specialities at an Amazonian lodge, hiking in the *tepuis* or seeking out those enigmatic birds that have not been seen in recent decades. In short, the birding possibilities in Venezuela are endless.

Chris Sharpe is a Yorkshire-born birder and author of several books on birds and conservation who has been leading birding tours around Venezuela since 1988. His website www.birdvenezuela.com is full of information and tips for twitchers wanting to get the most out of a visit.

International twitchers flock to the Llanos to see elegant white egrets, prehistoric hoatzins and giant jabirus. Others visit the cloudforests of the Parque Nacional Henri Pittier, on the roads to Cuyagua or Choroní, to see rufous-cheeked tanagers and white-tipped quetzals, or trek through the jungles of Amazonas State to try and catch a rare glimpse of the large and powerful harpy eagle, a magnificent predator that can snatch a monkey or a sloth from the high canopy without missing a wing beat.

Few visitors can fail to be impressed by the Guacharo Cave in Caripe and the nocturnal oilbirds that fly out *en masse* to feed as the sun sets.

Specialist birding lodges include the working cattle ranch **Hato El Cedral** (*www.elcedral.com*) in Los Llanos, **Posada Casa Vieja** (*www.casa-vieja-merida.com*) near the Andean town of Tabay in Mérida, and the **Barquilla de Fresa** (*www.strawberrybirds.com*) in La Escalera, a forested region at the start of the Gran Sabana.

Part Two

THE GUIDE

4

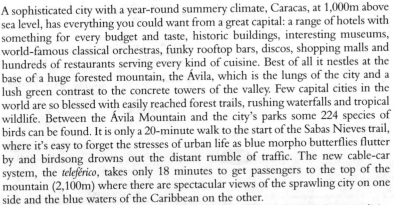

Caracas

Telephone code: 0212

A sophisticated city with a year-round summery climate, Caracas, at 1,000m above sea level, has everything you could want from a great capital: a range of hotels with something for every budget and taste, historic buildings, interesting museums, world-famous classical orchestras, funky rooftop bars, discos, shopping malls and hundreds of restaurants serving every kind of cuisine. Best of all it nestles at the base of a huge forested mountain, the Ávila, which is the lungs of the city and a lush green contrast to the concrete towers of the valley. Few capital cities in the world are so blessed with easily reached forest trails, rushing waterfalls and tropical wildlife. Between the Ávila Mountain and the city's parks some 224 species of birds can be found. It is only a 20-minute walk to the start of the Sabas Nieves trail, where it's easy to forget the stresses of urban life as blue morpho butterflies flutter by and birdsong drowns out the distant rumble of traffic. The new cable-car system, the *teleférico*, takes only 18 minutes to get passengers to the top of the mountain (2,100m) where there are spectacular views of the sprawling city on one side and the blue waters of the Caribbean on the other.

With a population edging towards seven million and social inequalities continuing to divide rich and poor (despite concerted government action to improve conditions), Caracas can feel hectic, crowded and overwhelming to first-time visitors. This is not helped by the very real dangers that may be encountered in some areas, especially in the off-limits *barrios*, the shantytowns clinging precariously to the hills ringing the valley. For that reason, some people try to avoid Caracas completely, travelling to the Andean city of Mérida, which is a tourist hub, or flying directly to the Los Roques Archipelago, with its three sandy streets and laid-back vibe.

But it would be hard to understand Venezuela without visiting Caracas, a vibrant city that begs to be explored. Caracas is the birthplace of Simón Bolívar, the most famous independence hero in South America who liberated five countries from Spanish rule. It is also the political, cultural and business capital of the country, and its shiny glass skyscrapers and traffic jams of brand-new 4x4 cars reflect the country's immense oil wealth and create a dramatic contrast with the shantytowns. All that is required of visitors is a little patience, a cultural readjustment to the more elastic Venezuelan concept of time and the sometimes frustrating bureaucracy involved in the simplest of tasks. Caracas is relatively easy to explore. Traffic may grind to a standstill at peak hours and walking any distance may be foolhardy given the fact that the city is carved up by four-lane highways, but most of the main museums, shopping malls and hotels are close to stations on the modern and very efficient metro system. When it comes to lodging, the safest – and priciest – area to stay is in the east of the city around Altamira in the affluent municipality of Chacao, where there are plenty of restaurants, bars and clubs and it's possible to walk around in the evenings. The Altamira metro stop is also the starting point for hikes to the Ávila Mountain, and the trail up to the ranger post at Sabas Nieves.

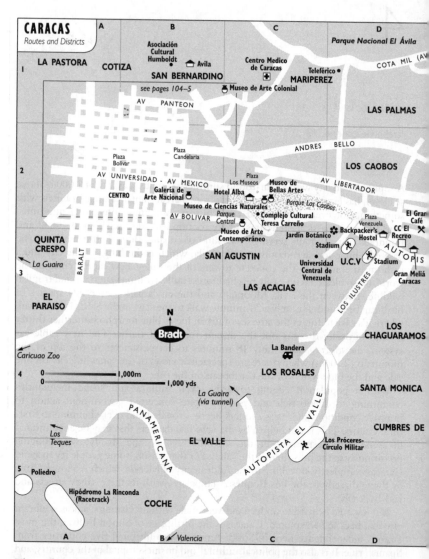

CARACAS
Routes and Districts

A   **B**   **C**   **D**

Parque Nacional El Ávila

LA PASTORA   COTIZA

Asociación Cultural Humboldt ●
▲ Ávila

Centro Medico de Caracas ✚

Teleférico ●

COTA MIL (AV

SAN BERNARDINO

MARIPEREZ

see pages 104–5

🏛 Museo de Arte Colonial

LAS PALMAS

AV PANTEON

ANDRES BELLO

LOS CAOBOS

Plaza Candelaria

Plaza Bolívar

Plaza Los Museos

Museo de Bellas Artes

AV LIBERTADOR

2

AV UNIVERSIDAD - AV MEXICO

Galería de Arte Nacional 🏛

CENTRO

Hotel Alba 🏛

Museo de Ciencias Naturales

Parque Los Caobos

El Gran Café ✕

AV BOLIVAR

Parque Central 🏛

● Complejo Cultural Teresa Carreño

Plaza Venezuela

CC El Recreo

QUINTA CRESPO

Museo de Arte Contemporáneo

Jardín Botánico

Backpacker's Hostel 🏠

BARALT

← La Guaira

SAN AGUSTIN

Stadium 🚹

AUTOPIS

Universidad Central de Venezuela

U.C.V 🚹 Stadium

EL PARAISO

LAS ACACIAS

Gran Meliá Caracas

LOS ILUSTRES

3

LOS CHAGUARAMOS

La Bandera 🚌

Caricuao Zoo

4

0   1,000m
0   1,000 yds

LOS ROSALES

SANTA MONICA

La Guaira (via tunnel) ↗

Los Teques ←

PANAMERICANA

EL VALLE

AUTOPISTA EL VALLE

CUMBRES DE

Los Próceres-Círculo Militar 🚹

Poliedro

5

Hipódromo La Rinconda (Racetrack)

COCHE

A   **B** ↙ Valencia   **C**   **D**

The west of the city is the historic centre focused around the Capitolio and
Silencio metro stops, where you find Plaza Bolívar, the National Congress and
Simón Bolívar's birthplace. This area is best visited during the day and avoided at
night. Wherever you end up in the city, remember that if you can see the Ávila
Mountain, which is in the north, you can get a rough idea of where you are.

GETTING THERE, AWAY AND AROUND

BY AIR The Aeropuerto Internacional Simón Bolívar (*www.aeropuerto-
maiquetia.com.ve*), also known as Maiquetía Airport (MIQ), is on the coast, about
30km from midtown Caracas. The international terminal is modern, clean and well
organised, with good shops and services, fast-food restaurants and coffee shops, and
a range of nearby hotels for overnight stays (see *Chapter 5, Maiquetía Airport hotels,*

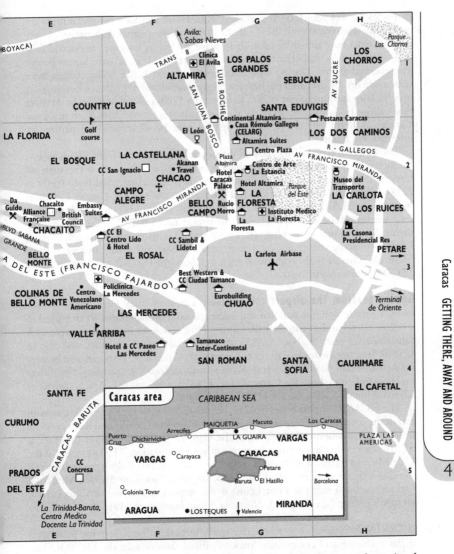

page 119). A free shuttle service carries passengers the 300m between the national and international terminals, but it takes only five to ten minutes to walk.

For help, there is a passenger advice counter (⊕ *08.00–20.00 daily*) on Level 2, near the arrivals section, and there is a tourist office with maps on the lower floor, where the check-in desks are located.

Airline counters are open at flight times only. There is a CANTV Communications Centre on the upper floor by arrivals, which is open ⊕ 08.00–20.00 daily for international or local calls, and manned phone booths offering the same service are located in departures. Money exchange is available at Italcambio branches located on the lower floor next to departures and the upper floor near arrivals and there are branches of Banco de Venezuela, Banesco and Banco Industrial de Venezuela with ATMs that accept Visa and MasterCard. Car-hire agencies require credit card, foreign or international licence, and a minimum age of

21 (or 25 for 4x4 vehicles). Avis, Budget, Aco, Hertz and local car-rental firms are open daily from 06.00 until the last flight arrives, closing earlier on Sundays.

With strict new anti-drug controls in place, including baggage checks and full-body scans, it is important to be at the airport at least two hours before international flights. During local holidays the airport is like a department store with a sale on. Be prepared for heavy weekend traffic when queues of beach-goers may back up at tunnels (one is 2km long) on the 17km tollway or *autopista*. At these times allow 1½ hours instead of the usual 45 minutes for the drive from midtown Caracas. A hefty exit tax (US$38) must be paid by all travellers departing on international flights.

The national terminal handles all **domestic flights**, apart from flights to Los Roques which leave from the auxiliary terminal (after check-in at the national terminal). Passenger assistance is available at the national terminal from 05.00 to 22.00 daily. For domestic carriers and telephone numbers see *Chapter 2, Getting around*, page 53. You should aim to be at the airport two hours before flights during long weekends and holidays. There is an airport tax of BsF32.50 for all domestic flights. Services include left luggage, a government tourism booth (usually with an English-speaking attendant), car rental, bank, ATMs, coffee bars that open from 04.30, and charter flight companies such as Chapi Air (\ *0212 355 1965;* m *0414 323 2457; www.chapiair.com*).

Getting to/from the airport Official taxis, a fleet of black Ford Explorers, are located outside both the national and international terminals; fares are displayed in a yellow booth in the customs hall. Journeys to Caracas for up to four people with four suitcases start at about US$33 at the official rate of exchange and rise to US$40. It is not customary to tip taxi drivers in Venezuela. Taxis can also be pre-booked through Taxi To Caracas (*www.taxitocaracas.com*), a company that offers pickup and transfers to Caracas for US$55 and to the beach town of Choroní/Puerto Colombia for US$150 (*4–5 hours*).

The UCAMC airport buses (\ *0212 352 4818;* ⊕ *04.00–19.00*) outside the main exit of the international airport charge US$5 for fares to Caracas and leave every 30 minutes or so when full, stopping at the Gato Negro metro station (not safe at night), where you can continue by metro to your destination. The last stop is at the UCAMC bus terminal in Parque Central, beneath Avenida Bolívar; from here you can take a taxi or walk two blocks to the Bellas Artes station on Avenida México. If you are staying a night at a hotel close to the airport, in Macuto or Catia la Mar, arrange a pickup (see *Chapter 5, Maiquetía Airport hotels*, page 119).

☞ *WARNING:* Swarms of touts operate in the airport, offering arriving passengers dollar exchange and cheap taxis. Stick to official taxis or take the UCAMC bus. Some unwary passengers have been held up at gunpoint after getting into a pirate cab and been stripped of all their belongings before being dumped on the highway in their underwear.

BY BUS There are two different bus terminals for catching **long-distance buses** to all other parts of the country, located at separate ends of the city. The **Terminal de Oriente** [89 H3] serves destinations in eastern Venezuela. This well-organised bus station is located on the Guarenas highway, 3km beyond the metro stop of Petare and is open 24 hours a day. There are shops selling drinks, water, basic snacks such as *empanadas*, and toilet facilities. **Local buses** take passengers from outside the Petare metro stop to the terminal. **La Bandera** [88 C4] is a short walk from the metro station of the same name on Line 2 from Plaza Venezuela. It is supposedly designed to serve destinations in central and western

Venezuela, but you can get buses to most places in the country from here and it is also open 24 hours a day. Apart from scheduled departures on express buses, it also has fast *por puesto* services to Maracay, Valencia and San Felipe that leave when they're full. La Bandera handles more than 25,000 passengers a day and can be a hectic experience, from the ten-minute walk from the metro past gas stations and street vendors that crowd the pavement, to the chaos as you climb three stories up a ramp to the main entrance. You buy tickets direct from the bus company booths on the left as you enter and there are shops selling drinks, water, basic snacks such as *empanadas*, and toilet facilities. To find a bus company going to the destination you want visit the information desk in front. Never buy a ticket from anybody loitering in front of the offices no matter how much they insist they work for the bus company as there plenty of scam artists about. There is no booking beforehand and in most cases tickets can only be bought on the day of departure or 24 hours before.

Bus fares change but on going to press the following fares were available at La Bandera to Barinas (9 hours, US$14), Barquisimeto (5 hours, US$12), Ciudad Bolívar (11 hours, US$15), Coro (7 hours, US$15), Maracaibo (11 hours, US$20), Maracay (1½ hours, US$4), Mérida (12 hours, US$15–19), San Cristóbal (13 hours, US$20), Valencia (2½ hours, US$5).

During holidays ticket costs can soar by 20% and advance purchase is recommended, although some companies insist on selling same day tickets. Arrive at least two hours before departure to ensure you get a ticket and load luggage. It's safer to take a taxi from inside the terminal at night. They leave from the same place as intercity *por puestos* to Valencia and Maracay.

Private bus lines with their own terminals offer more comfortable buses with air conditioning, video, reclining seats and for a bit extra you can travel on a *bus-cama* (bus-bed).

🚌 **Aeroexpresos Ejecutivos** Av Principal de Bello Campo, Chacao; ☏ 0212 266 2321; e info@ aeroexpresos.com.ve; www.aeroexpresos.com.ve. There are 27 departures daily to Barquisimeto, Maracaibo, Maracay, Maturín, Puerto La Cruz, San Felix & Valencia.

🚌 **Expresos Camargüi** Calle Sucre at Calle Nueva, behind Bloque de Armas, San Martín; ☏ 0212 471 7437, 0212 471 4614. Executive & ordinary buses cover 22 towns in eastern Venezuela: Cumaná, Carúpano, Maturín, El Tigre, Puerto Ordaz.

🚌 **Expresos Flamingo** Av Francisco Miranda, Santa Cecilia; ☏ 0212 239 4910. Close to the Parque del Este/Miranda metro stop & Museo de Transporte, it runs buses to San Cristóbal, Mérida, Maracaibo & Barinas.

🚌 **Rodovias** 100m west of Colegio de Ingenieros metro station, Av Amador Bendayán, Quebrada Honda; ☏ 0212 577 6622; e info@rodovias.com.ve; www.rodovias.com. There are daily departures for Barquisimeto, Carúpano, Ciudad Bolívar, Maturín, San Felix, Upata & Valencia.

Other buses leave from the chaotic Nuevo Circo terminal by **La Hoyada metro station** [105 E5] to Miranda towns such as Los Teques, Santa Teresa and Ocumare, but the train from La Rinconada metro station is a better option. Buses currently park in the empty lot on Avenida Lecuna opposite the former Nuevo Circo.

Inner-city buses are dominated by owner-operated *por puestos*, small buses that work fixed routes that are identified in the front window of the bus. A list of fares is posted near the driver, who may collect either as the passenger gets on or off. The crowded buses, with loud salsa or merengue music blasting away inside, stop and start as passengers clap their hands to get off or call out to be dropped at the next stop '*la parada por favor*'.

The only other buses operating in Caracas are the efficient Metrobuses that link stations. Tickets, called '*boleto integrado*', are sold in Metro stations and combine a return journey on the subway with a Metrobus journey. You can also buy a ten-journey Metro and Metrobus ticket known as a 'Multiviaje Intregrado' that costs about US$2 (see *By metro*, below).

BY TAXI Officially licensed taxis are white and have yellow number plates, although taxi ranks at major hotels may have their own colours. Taxis do not have meters so always negotiate a price before getting in. For trips around the city, expect to pay about US$4–9 according to distance. Unfortunately, anybody can stick a plastic taxi sign on the top of their car and cruise the streets for business but visitors should always avoid pirate taxis for safety reasons. Late at night when leaving clubs and bars seek advice from door staff or call one of the 24-hour taxi companies, such as Teletaxi (✆ *0212 751 2379*), Taxi Movil (✆ *0212 577 0922*) or Taxitour (✆ *0212 794 1264, 0212 793 9744*) who also provide airport transfers.

Mototaxis are scooters or motorbikes that aim to beat the gridlock in Caracas, often by mounting the pavement and squeezing between cars and trucks on the highway. Some 30,000 of these unregulated mototaxis ply their trade in the city, offering cheap fares and a helmet to those brave enough to take a chance in the traffic. Not recommended.

BY METRO The longest underground system in South America, the Caracas metro (*www.metrodecaracas.com.ve*) operates daily from 05.30 to 23.00 and has four lines. Clean, fast and efficient, it is the saviour of the city, making up for the chaos above ground. Avoid peak times in the early morning and evening as main-line stations are becoming increasingly congested now that free travel is given to over-65s and metro fares are lower than *por puesto* buses. There is still no easier way to cross the city. Line 1, which opened in 1983, covers the 40km from Propatria in the west to Palo Verde in the east and is the busiest section. Line 2 travels from Caricuao to El Silencio, where it joins Line 1. Line 3 links Plaza Venezuela on Line 1 to La Rinconada and the railway connection to Charallave, Cua and the Tuy Valley. Line 4 runs between Capuchinos on Line 2 and Zona Rental, which links to Line 1 at Plaza Venezuela. Line 5 is currently under construction and will extend Line 4 to Bello Monte, Las Mercedes, the cable-car station at Mariperez and Petare.

There are shops and occasional art shows in the metro stations – but no public toilets. Tickets for one stop are 500 centavos (US$0.10), round-trip tickets (*ida y vuelta*) 900 centavos and a *multiabono* ticket, for ten rides costs BsF4.50. An *integrado* ticket includes a journey on the metro and the metrobus, modern buses linking subway stations with outlying districts such as San Bernardino, El Cafetal, Baruta and El Hatillo. A *multiabono integrado* costing BsF6 covers ten journeys by metro and metrobus.

☞ **WARNING:** People riding the metro escalators have had necklaces and wallets taken by pickpockets, sometimes children, who take advantage of the crush at peak times. Be careful with your belongings when entering and leaving the trains and on escalators. Carry daypacks in front, wear no jewellery or watch and keep your wallet in a safe pocket. One scam involves two men, one who rides in front of you on the escalator and trips or bends down just as you get to the top, and another stands behind you and goes through your pockets, snatching your valuables as you bump into the man in front. See also *Security*, page 101.

TOURIST INFORMATION

The National Tourism Institute, **Inatur** (*www.inatur.gob.ve*), is the entity in charge of promotion and comes under the Tourism Ministry, **Mintur** (*www.mintur.gob.ve*). It has booths at the international and national terminals at Maiquetía Airport,

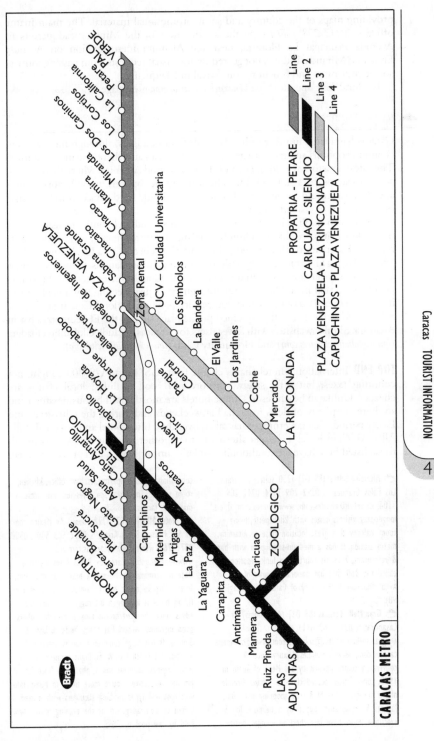

CARACAS METRO

Bradt

Line 1 PROPATRIA - PETARE
Line 2 CARICUAO - SILENCIO
Line 3 PLAZA VENEZUELA - LA RINCONADA
Line 4 CAPUCHINOS - PLAZA VENEZUELA

PALO VERDE
Petare
La California
Los Cortijos
Los Dos Caminos
Miranda
Altamira
Chacao
Chacaíto
Sabana Grande
PLAZA VENEZUELA
Colegio de Ingenieros
Bellas Artes
Parque Carabobo
La Hoyada
Capitolio
EL SILENCIO
Caño Amarillo
Agua Salud
Gato Negro
Plaza Sucre
Pérez Bonalde
PROPATRIA

Zona Rental
UCV – Ciudad Universitaria
Los Símbolos
La Bandera
El Valle
Los Jardines
Coche
Mercado
LA RINCONADA

Parque Central
Nuevo Circo
Teatros
Capuchinos

Maternidad
Artigas
La Paz
La Yaguara
Carapita
Antímano
Mamera
Ruiz Pineda
LAS ADJUNTAS

ZOOLOGICO
Caricuao

93

providing maps of the country and some promotional material. The main Inatur office (\ *0212 208 4886*) is in the south tower of the Mintur headquarters in Avenida Principal La Floresta, near the Altamira metro station on Avenida Francisco Miranda, but it is not geared up for casual requests from passing tourists so get your maps and brochures on arrival in Maiquetía.

For local tour operators see *Venezuelan tour operators* on page 31.

WHERE TO STAY

Caracas has a large number of hotels for different budgets, although there are few economic options and rates are generally higher than anywhere else in the country. The safest area to stay is in the east of the city around Altamira, where there is easy access to shops, bars and nightlife. There are budget options in the historic centre and the area around Sabana Grande but visitors should heed advice from hotel staff on safe places to visit after dark.

Those who don't mind sharing with a stranger and feel confident using social networking sites, could try **Couch Surfing** (*www.couchsurfing.org*), which puts registered users in touch with individuals offering a bed or sofa for the night. With over 100 users in Caracas, many with multiple recommendations, Couch Surfing is a way to discover the city with a friendly local. Couch Surfers tend to be young people interested in speaking a foreign language or just meeting new people. Even if you don't need accommodation you can arrange to meet local Couch Surfers for a drink and a chat at a well-frequented public place such as the El Leon pizza bar in Altamira. Similar websites, with fewer users for Caracas, include Global Freeloaders (*www.globalfreeloaders.com*) and Hospitality Club (*www.hospitalityclub.org*).

TOP END International hotel chains charge from US$150 to US$300 a night, not counting taxes, but offer safety, comfort and good facilities; local chains are cheaper. Unlike in beach resorts, these hotels are mostly used by businessmen and so there are plenty of deals to be had at weekends and during the Christmas and Easter period. The government has taken over the Hilton hotel and renamed it the Alba, which provides a cheaper alternative to the other five-star hotels in town. All those listed here have air conditioning and a swimming pool, except where noted.

Altamira Suites [89 G2] (250 suites) 1st Trans, Los Palos Grandes; \ 0212 209 3474, 0212 209 3104; e info@alsuites.com; www.alsuites.com. Offers longer-stay visitors suites with kitchenette, living room, balcony & a great location close to Altamira metro station. It has a medium-sized pool with bar & restaurant, 2 tennis courts & a funky rooftop bar called the 360 that has panoramic views of the Ávila Mountain & the valley of Caracas (see page 98). $$$$

Gran Meliá Caracas [88 D3] (430 rooms) Av Casanova; \ 0212 762 8111; e gran.melia.caracas@solmelia.com; www.gran-melia-caracas.com, www.solmelia.es. Luxury hotel & convention centre opened by Sol Meliá of Spain in 1998. Conveniently located close to Sabana Grande metro station & the El Recreo shopping mall. Bar, Jacuzzi, 5 restaurants, topped by a heliport. Top 5 executive floors have fast check-in lounges, business,

computing support. Apartments have office, kitchen, room service. The Royal Spa gives full anti-stress massages, facials. $$$$

Hotel Alba [88 C2] (728 rooms) Av México con Av Sur Mexico, Bellas Artes; \ 0212 503 5000, 0500 887 4766; www.hotelalbacaracas.com.ve, www.venetur.gob. Located by Bellas Artes metro & close to terminal for Maiquetía buses, art museums, Teresa Carreño music & arts complex. This former Hilton hotel is looking a bit raggedy around the edges since the government took it over but offers good discounts & still has filling buffet b/fasts & dinners. It has large conference rooms, internet available at snack bar, Wi-Fi, flight confirmation at travel agency, souvenir shops, pharmacy. Once full of Japanese executives, you're more likely to bump into local political types rubbing shoulders with invited Cuban or Bolivian guests at the evening music shows held by the pool. $$$$

Hotel Caracas Palace [89 G2] (212 rooms) Av Miranda at Plaza Altamira; \ 0212 771 1000, 0212 771 2000; e information@caracaspalace.com; www.caracaspalace.com. Formerly the Four Seasons, this upmarket option on the corner of Plaza Altamira is well situated in a safe area. Business centre, athletics club, outdoor & covered pools with Jacuzzi, pretty view over La Estancia/Parque del Este. $$$$

Lidotel [89 F3] (92 rooms) Av Tamanaco, El Rosal; \ 0212 957 7777; e reservas@ hotelcentrolido.com; www.lidotel.com.ve. Calling itself a boutique hotel, this very smart option in the CC Sambil shopping mall is between Chacaito & Chacao metro stations. Business centre, Wi-Fi & 15th-floor restaurant. No pool. Ask for w/end discounts. $$$$

Paseo Las Mercedes [89 F4] (194 rooms) Paseo Las Mercedes shopping mall; \ 0212 991 0033, 0212 991 0077; e reservas@hotelpaseolasmercedes.com; www.hotelpaseolasmercedes.com. Located in shopping mall close to nightlife, dining areas & cinema. Swimming pool, sunbathing terrace, small business

centre with internet. Reasonable rates, good value. $$$$

Pestana Caracas Hotel & Suites [89 H2] (195 rooms) Ira Av, Santa Eduvigis; \ 0212 208 1900, 0212 208 1916; e reservas@pestanacaracas.com; www.pestana.com. Close to Parque Cristal shopping mall, this ultra-swanky new hotel is part of the Lisbon-based Pestana group & comes with all mod cons, including colourful retro furniture, conference centre & 18th-floor pool & jacuzzi area boasting a popular bar with wood-decking & comfy sofas offering panoramic views of the city. $$$$

Tamanaco Inter-Continental [89 F4] (600 rooms) Las Mercedes, opp Paseo Las Mercedes mall; \ 0212 909 7111; e caracas@interconti.com; www.ichotelsgroup.com. A hotel in the Las Mercedes area highly rated for its setting, with huge pool offering great views of the Ávila, tennis courts, gym, Wi-Fi, shops, travel agency, good restaurants & nightclub. Popular with business travellers it has convention facilities for 2,000. $$$$

MID RANGE AND BUDGET

Ávila [88 B1] (113 rooms) Av Washington, San Bernardino; \ 0212 555 3000; e reservaciones@ hotelávila.com.ve; www.hotelávila.com.ve. Set among tropical gardens, this gracious 4-storey hotel with 5 conference rooms was built by Nelson Rockefeller in the 1930s & designed by Wallace Harrison, architect of the UN building in New York City. The faded glory is clear in the furnishings, but good bar, restaurant & pool make it a safe oasis of calm, although a little isolated. No AC but cool due to proximity to mountain. Jeeps for Galipan on the Ávila depart from outside gate. $$$

Hotel Altamira [89 G2] (80 rooms) Av Jose Felix Sosa at Av Sur Altamira; \ 0212 267 4255, 0212 267 4284; e hotelaltamira@telcel.net.ve. A large hotel a block south of Plaza Altamira, well placed for access to Sambil shopping centre, Altamira metro station, restaurants & bars. Basic rooms with AC, TV, some with balcony. Indifferent staff, you pay for the location. $$

La Floresta [89 G2] (82 rooms) Av Ávila Sur, Plaza Altamira; \ 0212 263 1955;

e hotellaflorest@cantv.net; www.hotellafloresta.com. Basic & tired rooms, functional restaurant, but great location near Plaza Altamira. Ask to see the rooms first & try to get one with a view. $$

Backpacker's Hostel [88 D3] Av Casanova con Calle El Colegio, next to El Arabito restaurant; \ 0212 761 5432, 0212 762 1788. Also known as Nuestro Hotel, this serves as a 'Love Hotel' when it's not hosting backpackers & the area is not safe at night. Portuguese lady Rosita makes foreigners feel at home & some info on things to do in town is available. Budget option only. $

Plaza Catedral [104 D3] Plaza Bolívar in Capitolio; \ 0212 564 2111; e plazacatedral@ cantv.net. Bang in the heart of the historic centre of town you can hear the cathedral's bells chiming from your room. The rooftop restaurant, El Grisol, offers a view over the plaza with b/fast, which is included in the price. A budget option for those desperate to stay in the centre as it's too quiet to be safe on the streets after dark. $

✖ WHERE TO EAT

Free-spending Caraqueños eat out a lot and the capital is known for its many good restaurants. The range is good too, from fast-food outlets to world-class gourmet dining, sushi and modern fusion food that blends local Creole dishes with pan-Asian flourishes. Places are constantly opening, changing owners, remodelling. Executives and politicians like to talk business over quality whiskies like Chivas

Regal and Johnnie Walker Black Label, favouring classy restaurants in eastern Caracas and in the San Ignacio shopping mall – easy to spot by the fancy cars parked three deep. Students normally head to cheap and cheerful pizza places, like El Leon in Altamira, where Polar beer is the tipple of choice. For visitors, however, Caracas is no longer the cheap eating option it once was as inflation and fixed exchange rates have forced prices up. If you're on a budget buy fruit from supermarkets and stick to snacks such as *empanadas* and toasted sandwiches from *panaderias* (bakeries). Hearty traditional Venezuelan soups and staples such as *pabellón criollo* will also fill you up cheaply. Lunch menus are more reasonable than dinner and a fixed-price *menú ejecutivo*, *menú del día*, or *sopa y seco*, will generally include soup, main course and dessert or coffee. Note that servings of steaks and mixed grills may be larger than one person can manage, so try sharing. After tax, most restaurants add a 10% service charge, whether the service was good or not, so tipping is entirely optional. There are too many restaurants and snack bars to list them all but here are a selection of some of the recommended options to suit a range of tastes. (See inside front cover for price bands.)

PLAZA BOLÍVAR AND EL CENTRO

✗ **La Tertulia** [105 G4] Alcabala a Urapal, La Candelaria; ☎ 0212 574 1476. This authentic *tasca* is one of a number in a little enclave of Basque & Spanish restaurants in La Candelaria, near Parque Carabobo metro & a block from the church. Very popular at midday, you can nibble on tapas at the bar while waiting for a table. *Fabada Asturiana*, squid in its own ink, stuffed peppers, rabbit are all on the menu. Other *tascas* nearby are la Cita, Bar Basque & Guernica. **$$**

✗ **Les Grisons** [103 D3] Hotel Plaza Catedral, Esq La Torre, Plaza Bolívar; ☎ 0212 564 2111; ⊕ all day. The rooftop restaurant of the Hotel Plaza Catedral has a nice view over Plaza Bolívar & serves economic local dishes & some unexpected Swiss options. Not what it was, but an escape from the bustle below. **$$**

✗ **Café del Sacro** [104 D4] Museo Sacro, Plaza Bolívar; ⊕ Tue–Sat. Excellent light lunches served in the pretty colonial courtyard with its ancient statues. **$**

✗ **La Ataraya** [104 D4] Plaza El Venezolano, Esq San Jacinto; ☎ 0212 545 8235; ⊕ 08.00–20.00. Budget Venezuelan cooking prevails at this busy lunchtime option in a 19th-century house on Plaza El Venezolano by Bolívar's birthplace. Serves *arepas*, *cachapas* & juice at the bar, full dinners, including roast chicken, inside. **$**

SABANA GRANDE AND CHACAITO

✗ **Dena Ona** 52 Av Tamanaco, El Rosal, behind Centro Lido shopping mall; ☎ 0212 953 2060; ⊕ 11.00–23.00. A good lunch option for a seafood splurge. Some Spanish dishes but the specialities are the soups, squid, grouper & lobster, when it's in season – Nov–Apr. **$$$$**

✗ **Da Guido** [89 E2] Av Francisco Solano, Sabana Grande; ☎ 0212 763 0937. An Italian restaurant that has had a devoted following since the 1960s. Pastas, chicken, good soups & good service. **$$$**

✗ **El Rugantino** Av Francisco Solano, Sabana Grande; ☎ 0212 762 0562; ⊕ 10.00–23.00. This Italian restaurant at Hotel Tampa has a reliable kitchen serving pastas & risottos, with live music at night. **$$$**

✗ **Urrutia** Av Solano López, on the corner of Calle Los Manguitos, Sabana Grande; ☎ 0212 763 0448; ⊕ 12.00–23.00. Known as the best Basque restaurant in Caracas, it's worth trying to get a seat to sample the seafood paella, stuffed peppers, squid & fish dishes in *salsa verde*. A minor splurge if you fancy something more formal. **$$$**

✗ **El Arabito** Av Casanova con Calle Villaflor, Sabana Grande; ☎ 0212 761 7989; ⊕ 10.00–22.00. A popular restaurant which, despite awful décor, not only serves *kibbe*, *labne*, *hummus* (chickpea) & *babaganush* (eggplant) dips, but also oriental delicacies, sweets & nuts. **$$**

✗ **Misia Jacinta** Av Tamanaco con Av Principal de Las Mercedes, El Rosal; ☎ 0212 951 6550; ⊕ 24hrs. Opposite McDonald's on the road from Chacaito to Las Mercedes this is a Venezuelan fast-food joint serving soups, *arepas* in all varieties & healthy juices. Remember to specify 'sin azucar' if you want your juice unsweetened. **$$**

✗ **Mi Tasca** Av Francisco Solano, Esq Los Apamates, Sabana Grande; ☎ 0212 763 2478; ⊕ 12.00–24.00. A basic Spanish place with a

convivial atmosphere where people crowd in for beer, wine, shrimp & squid appetisers at lunchtime & after work. Good portions of Spanish omelette. Across the road from the salsa joint El Mani Es Asi. $$
✗ **El Gran Café** [88 D2] Sabana Grande Bd, Calle Pascual Navarro, Sabana Grande; ☎ 0212 763 1493; ◷ 08.00–24.00. At the western end of the pedestrian boulevard this historic café is only a shadow of the place run by the French convict Papillon in the 1960s. It's still a good place to take a break, have a coffee & a snack & watch Caracas go by – the shoppers, salesmen, peddlers, office

LAS MERCEDES
✗ **Astrid y Gastón** Calle Londres entre Av Caroní y Nueva York, Las Mercedes; ☎ 0212 993 1119; www.astridygaston.com. Award-winning Peruvian chef Gaston Acurio is a global phenomenon, with restaurants in Peru, Chile, Colombia, Ecuador, Mexico, Spain & Argentina. Here, he adds Venezuelan Creole flavours to his trademark Peruvian fusion dishes such as ceviche & chupe in one of the most talked-about restaurants in town. $$$$

ALTAMIRA AND LA CASTELLANA
✗ **Samui** Av Andrés Bello con 1ra Transversal, Los Palos Grandes; ☎ 0212 285 4603; ◷ 12.00–24.00. One of the few Thai options in town & the first, this expensive restaurant owned by a French restaurateur is decorated with all the Asian trimmings but has lost some of its edge. $$$$
✗ **Mamma Nostra** Av San Juan Bosco, between 2nd/3rd Transversal, Altamira; ☎ 0212 263 5554; ◷ 12.00–24.00. Just 2 blocks north of Plaza Altamira, this large, mid-range Italian restaurant has 32 variations on the cheese pizza to choose from, pastas, cakes & desserts. $$$
✗ **Rucio Moro** [89 G2] Av Principal, Bello Campo; ☎ 0212 263 6596; www.ruciomoro.net; ◷ 12.00–24.00. Only a Llanero would name a restaurant after his horse, but that's what Llanero singer Reynaldo Armas has done at this huge barn of a place that serves up big steaks & the harp music of the Llanos. The whisky menu is as long as the dinner menu, which features carne en vara, fried yuca, goat & rabbit, & many of the diners come in cowboy hats & boots. Reynaldo often shows up in person to sing with his mates, the top joropo artists of the day. If you like the music ask to be seated nearer the stage. $$$
✗ **Tarzilandia** Av San Juan Bosco, 10ma Transversal; ☎ 0212 261 8419; www.tarzilandia.com; ◷ 12.00–24.00. At the foot of the Ávila by the

girls, street kids & motorcycle cops. From lunchtime to late they serve soups, Caesar salad & a decent mixed grill. $
✗ **Jugos Chacaito** Plaza Brion, in front of Chacaito metro entrance; ◷ 07.30–20.00. This hole in the wall juice & empanada place has some of the best deals in town. Chicken, beef & cheese empanadas fresh from the frier, tasty salsa picante & guasacaca sauces to drizzle over them, & the best tres en uno (beet, orange & carrot juice) in town. A great way to start the day. $

✗ **La Casa del Llano** Av Río de Janeiro, Las Mercedes; ☎ 0212 991 7342; ◷ 24hrs. Traditional Venezuelan arepas, hearty soups & big plates of pabellón criollo, with black beans, rice & fried plantains to fill you up. Polar beer served cold at any time of the day or night. Popular with party people when the bars shut. $$

entrance to Sabas Nieves, this old-school restaurant serves good soups, steaks & international dishes in a cool, quiet space surrounded by jungle vegetation & caged parrots. A popular Sun lunch option since it opened in the 1950s it now has Wi-Fi for businessmen on the go. $$$
✗ **Arabica Cafe** Av Andrés Bello con 1ra Transversal, Los Palos Grandes; ☎ 0212 286 3636; ◷ 07.00–23.00 Mon–Wed, 07.00–24.00 Thu–Sun. Next to Thai restaurant Samui, this upmarket coffee place serves good quality java for discerning palates & cakes & snacks on a pleasant terrace with views of the street. A small shop sells the best coffee beans from all over Venezuela. $$
✗ **Saint Honore** Av Andres Bello con 1ra Transversal, los Palos Grandes; ☎ 0212 286 7982; www.sthonore.com.ve; ◷ 07.00–12.00. The best cakes & pastries in Caracas are sold at this chic café, which also serves up soups, gourmet sandwiches, ham & eggs & pizzas. Expect to wait for a table at midday. A good place to check out the beautiful people of the area over a cappuccino. $$
✗ **El Budare** Av Principal de La Castellana; ☎ 0212 263 2696; ◷ 24hrs. An arepa place near Altamira with all the traditional options, including the queen of arepas, La Reina Pepiada, a mix of chicken, mayo & avocado that is said to be a good hangover cure after a night on the town. $

Caracas has a lively music and theatre scene with free weekend concerts in parks, banks, museums and galleries. Classical concerts by Venezuela's internationally acclaimed Simón Bolívar Youth Orchestra are regular features on the bill at the **Complejo Cultural Teresa Carreño** [89 C2] (*www.teatroteresacarreno.gob.ve*), home to the Ballet Nacional de Caracas and the national opera. Weekend editions of *El Nacional* and *El Universal* list concerts, art exhibitions, festivals and gastronomic events. The main party areas in Caracas are in Altamira, the Centro San Ignacio shopping mall, and Las Mercedes, where you can easily walk around exploring the bars and restaurants. For up to the minute information on clubs, bars and live music check the website of **Rumba Caracas** (*www.rumbacaracas.com*).

BARS

♀ **Lounge Bar Ávila** [89 H2] 18th Flr, Pestana Caracas Hotel & Suites, Ira Av, Santa Eduvigis; ☎ 0212 208 1900; www.pestana.com; ⏰ 12.00–02.00. The new place to be seen is a poolside bar on the roof of the city's newest 5-star hotel, with low lighting, cocktails, comfy sofas & panoramic views of the city, popular midday & after work. **$$$**

♀ **Suka Bar** Centro Comercial San Ignacio, La Castellana; ☎ 0212 263 5249; ⏰ 19.00–02.00. An ultra-hip lounge bar with a Moroccan theme, cool cocktails & Venezuela's top alternative DJs playing jazz, funk, electronic & hip hop & the occasional live act. Very popular with the young, trendy & well heeled, it has a terrace for when things get too hot inside. **$$$**

♀ **Bar 360** [89 G2] 19th flr, Hotel Altamira Suites; ☎ 0212 209 3474; www.alsuites.com; ⏰ 17.00–24.00. The first rooftop bar in the Altamira area & still popular, the cocktails & classy lounge music make it a hip venue for young professionals hoping to hook up. The bar is named for the fantastic views of the city from here, especially at sunset, so don't forget your camera. **$$**

♀ **Birras Pub & Café** Av Principal de Las Mercedes, edif ITACA; ☎ 0212 992 4813; ⏰ 18.00–03.00.

A cheap & cheerful place to start a night out in Las Mercedes. The owners just pull a few tables out onto the street, set up a terrace bar & start serving ice-cold beer to thirsty punters. Attracts a young crowd. **$**

♀ **El Leon** [89 F2] Plaza la Castellana; ☎ 0212 263 6014; ⏰ 12.00–03.00. The easiest place to meet for an informal drink & a pizza, this very popular outdoor venue overlooks Plaza La Castellana & is a short walk from Altamira metro station. Young & old flock here at night & tables overflow with bottles as everybody tries to keep count of the tab to avoid arguments with the waiter when the bill arrives. Try the fried cheese & pastry twists called *tequeños* & get here early at w/ends as tables fill up fast. Highly recommended. **$$**

♀ **El Naturista** 2da Transversal, next to McDonald's, La Castellana; ☎ 0212 263 5350; ⏰ 12.00–03.00. Across the street from El Leon, this unremarkable *tasca* serves cheap beers & attracts a student crowd. Menu specials include the *parilla mixta*, a mixed grill of chicken & beef served on a bed of French fries that the whole table can pick at to soak up the beer. A counter at the far end serves *arepas* & juices to passers-by. **$**

LIVE MUSIC

El Mani Es Asi Calle el Cristo, Av Francisco Solano, Sabana Grande; ☎ 0212 763 6671; www.elmaniesasi.com; ⏰ 10.00–late. This converted house on a side street is known as the Temple of Salsa & every Venezuelan salsa musician worthy of a pair of maracas has played here. Faded black-&-white photos of Fidel Castro, Muhammad Ali & salsa stars cover the walls & the bar runs out of beer when they want you to switch to Cuba Libre cocktails or buy a bottle of rum or whisky. But the real action takes place on the postage-stamp-sized dance floor directly in front of the tiny

stage. Salsa doesn't get more intimate than this. A cover charge, which includes a house cocktail, is sometimes made.

El Puto Bar Av Libertador, edificio Planinco, behind McDonald's de Chacao; ⏰ 09.00–late. The sound of the metro can be heard at this intimate & iconic venue, formerly La Mosca, & sometimes referred to as BarNuvo. The place is so small it's like watching the band play in your living room. Cheap beers & a chance to see the best new bands & DJs in town, with guest appearances by famous faces. Nominal cover charge includes a cocktail.

GAY CARACAS

There are dozens of gay venues in the city, where they are known as bars *de ambiente*, literally 'with atmosphere'. The thriving GLBT scene is most visible during the annual Gay Pride march through the streets of Caracas, held on 4 July. The march only began in 2000 when a few hundred people turned out, but the tenth anniversary march in 2010 brought thousands of supporters onto the streets in a colourful parade starting at Parque del Este/Francisco de Miranda. Popular gay meeting places include Plaza Francia by Altamira metro station and nightspots such as the boisterous **La Fragata** (*Calle Villaflor, Sabana Grande;* \ *0212 762 6857;* ⊕ *18.00–late*). In Paseo Las Mercedes there is the old-school vibe of **La Cotorra**, discreet and sober from the outside, and the chic bar of the **Transnocho Cultural** (*www.trasnochocultural.com*). **Copas Dancing Bar** (*Torre Taeca, Calle Guaicaipuro, El Rosal;* ⊕ *19.00–late Wed–Thu, 21.00–late Fri–Sat*) is a mixed venue for guys and gals with weekend shows. The big night out is at the disco **Triskel** (*CC Placette, Piso 2, Av San Juan Bosco, 3ra Transversal, Altamira;* \ *0212 265 9036; www.triskelclub.com;* ⊕ *23.00–04.00 Thu–Sat*), which plays banging electronica in three rooms called Hell, Paradise and Purgatory.

El Teatro Torre DyD, Av Orinoco, Las Mercedes; www.elteatro.com.ve; ⊕ 17.00–04.00. Large, busy venue with events all week, from stand-up comedy on Mon to live bands & DJ sets throughout the week. This is the place to hear Venezuela's talented rock bands do their thing one night & rave to house the next.

Latinos All Stars Centro Comercial Los Chaguaramos, Los Chaguaramos; \ 0212 693 6695; m 0412 378 1520; ⊕ 20.00–late Wed–Sat. A relatively small venue for salsa dancers, Latinos has live bands playing classic salsa dura, merengue & other tropical rhythms. Semi-formal dress code, no sneakers.

CINEMAS Shopping malls, like the Sambil and Centro Plaza have multiplex cinemas showing the latest Hollywood movies in English with Spanish subtitles. For art-house movies and Latin American cinema try the **CELARG** [89 G2] (*Casa de Romulo Gallegos, Av Luis Roche, Altamira; www.celarg.org.ve*), a cultural centre that has regular art exhibitions and film festivals. The **Cinemateca Nacional** is at the **Museo de Bellas Artes** [88 C3], near the Bellas Artes metro station, and can be combined with a visit to the museum as films are shown at 16.15. The details of what's showing are pinned up on a board at the museum entrance by the shop. The **Cine Trasnocho** (*www.trasnochocultural.com*) in Paseo las Mercedes [89 F4] also has film seasons of international movies.

CULTURAL ASSOCIATIONS There are a number of organisations where English, French or German is the first language and all have libraries. Cultural activities of general interest to travellers include lectures, films, recitals, music, jazz and dance events, often free.

Alliance Française [89 E2] Edif Centro Solano, Av Solano López at Av 3 de Las Delicias, Chacaito; www.afvenezuela.org. There are branches in La Castellana, La Tahona & Las Mercedes in Caracas & Valencia, Barquisimeto, Mérida & Maracaibo. French courses & workshops in theatre, music, cinema & cooking are available.
Asociación Cultural Humboldt [88 B1] Av Jorge Washington at Juan Germán Roscío, San Bernardino;

www.asociacionculturalhumboldt.com. ACH has a theatre, multimedia library & a replica of Alexander von Humboldt's 19th-century study. German studies & scholarships are sponsored by the Goethe Institute. There is a quarterly magazine, *Encuentros*.
British Council [89 E2] 3rd Flr, Torre Credicard, Av Principal del Bosque, north of Chacaito; www.britishcouncil.org/es/venezuela.htm. The main offices provide English teaching, preparation for TEFL

qualifications & sponsor cultural events. There is a branch in Maracaibo. **Centro Venezolano Americano** [89 E3] Northwest end of Av Principal, Las Mercedes; www.cva.org.ve. The CVA offers English teaching & Spanish classes for English-speakers. The well-stocked library has magazines & books in English. Branches at Esquina Mijares downtown, & in La Trinidad.

SHOPPING

Window shopping is a popular Caracas pastime and shopping malls provide safe places to visit banks, restaurants, supermarkets and cinemas, make phone calls and surf the internet. The biggest mall of all is the shiny **Sambil** shopping mall [89 F3] on Avenida Libertador, south of the Chacao metro station. Hailed as the largest shopping and recreation centre in South America, it has 540 shops, businesses and banks, ten cinemas, a food fair with 20 fast-food options, an aquarium and a rooftop amphitheatre for open-air concerts. There is a branch of the Jacobo Borges Art Museum, a 24-lane bowling alley that converts into a disco at weekends and for the kids a space travel simulator, robotland and fun-fair. All businesses in the mall stay open until 21.00, 365 days a year.

Other shopping centres offering a full range of services are **Centro Plaza** [89 G2], two blocks east of the Altamira metro station, **CC El Recreo** [88 D3] on Avenida Casanova in Sabana Grande; the **Centro Lido** [89 E3] on Avenida Francisco Miranda, between Chacaito and Chacao metro stations; and the **CC San Ignacio** [89 F2] on Avenida Blandín in La Castellana, with a lively bar scene at night, five long blocks up from the Chacao metro station.

HANDICRAFTS Artisans from the Guajira, the Delta Amacuro, the Andes, Ecuador and Colombia have a permanent craft market, the **Mercado Guajiro**, in Paseo Las Flores off Plaza Chacaito. Look for the steps down to the left by the Kuai Mare bookshop. Besides a great number of souvenirs, there's a variety of hammocks for one person (*individual*) or a couple (*matrimonial*). Compare the cotton hammocks with the more expensive *chinchorros* made of *moriche* palm fibre by the Warao Indians – beautiful and smooth but heavy. Hand-knotted hammocks in nylon thread are light and last forever. **Casa Curuba** (*Calle Andrés Bello, between Trans 1–2, Los Palos Grandes;* \ *0212 283 1857*) displays fine local treasures chosen by artists and designers. This is the best place in Caracas to buy exquisite wooden furniture, boxes, bowls, spoons, fruit and figures carved from tropical hardwoods by Venezuelan master craftsmen, particularly those in Quíbor, Lara State. Prices reflect the quality of the carving. The gift shops at the **Museo de Arte Contemporáneo** [88 C2] and the **Museo de Bellas Artes** [88 C2] also have some good Venezuelan handicrafts, although not the cheapest. Look out for the tall, spindly carvings of Simón Bolívar and other historical Venezuelan figures. By far the biggest collection of shops selling handicrafts from all over the country is in El Hatillo, just south of Caracas, especially **Hannsi**, a warehouse-sized store near Plaza Bolívar (see page 117).

BOOKS Lavishly illustrated coffee-table books about Venezuela's *Lost World tepui* mountains, the Andes, colonial architecture, flora and fauna make good souvenirs and can be found at book stores in hotels and shopping centres. **Tecni-Ciencia Libros** (*www.techniciencia.com*) is a chain of bookshops handling a very large and varied stock from cookbooks to guides and maps and has branches in the Sambil, CC El Recreo, CC San Ignacio, Ciudad Tamanaco and Centro Lido. They sell a good range of English-language books and guides. **Librería La France**, in CC Chacaito, specialises in French books. For books in German visit the **Librería Alemana** in CC El Bosque. The **American Book Shop** is the only dedicated

English-language bookshop in Caracas and can be found in the basement of the Centro Plaza shopping mall in Altamira.

MUSIC There are plenty of street vendors selling pirate copies of the latest CDs and DVDs near the Chacaito metro, including compilations of local artists that you will find nowhere else. For the genuine article, head to **Esperanto**, which has stores in the Centro San Ignacio [89 F2] and CC Paseo Las Mercedes [89 F4]. They have the best selection of modern Venezuelan rock, pop, salsa, jazz, classical and indie bands. **Don Disco** in front of CC Chacaito [89 E2] has a good selection of hard to get Venezuelan artists, classical, jazz and folk music.

FESTIVALS

The major religious festival of Semana Santa (Easter) is celebrated in Caracas with a number of parades. The biggest visual spectacle for tourists is the annual Palm Sunday celebrations in Chacao, when a group of local men known as 'Los Palmeros' descend from the Ávila at about 10.00 with bunches of palms that they have cut from a place high on the mountain. They then walk down to the church in Chacao where the local priest gives a blessing to the men and the palms before they are handed out to the faithful.

On the Wednesday after Palm Sunday there are colourful night time processions at a number of churches in the capital where the faithful, dressed in purple robes, parade a statue of Jesus slowly around the parish.

Although there is no longer a wild Carnival in Caracas these days, children do dress up in costumes and parade up and down Sabana Grande on the main days of the February holiday and bands play free concerts at several points in the city.

OTHER PRACTICALITIES

SECURITY Caracas is a big city and the best way to avoid crime is to stick to safer areas, be cautious at night, take taxis to nightclubs in areas you don't know, hide your valuables and never wear gold or silver jewellery or a watch. Avoid carrying large amounts of cash but keep some handy in case you are mugged and always have some emergency money tucked away somewhere. Take precautions in crowded places such as metro station entrances and when getting on and off the trains. Never resist an armed robbery, stay calm and do as you are told – it is better to lose your money and valuables than your life. Dial ⏧ **171** nationwide for the police. Altamira, with its own Chacao police force, is the safest district for moving around at night. See also page 92 for security advice for when travelling on the metro.

MEDICAL SERVICES Pharmacies such as **Farmatodo** and **Farmahorro** are found all over the city and in major shopping malls and are well stocked for minor emergencies. At night, pharmacies that are open for business display a neon sign saying '*Turno*'; just ring or knock to be served. All public hospitals will treat patients free of charge but if you have medical insurance, and you have a health emergency, or need a quick test for parasites, it is better to visit one of the main private clinics, some of which are listed below.

✚ **Centro Medico de Caracas** [88 C1] Plaza El Estanque, San Bernardino; ⏧ 0212 555 9111, 0212 552 9418; www.centromedicodecaracas.com.ve

✚ **Centro Medico Docente La Trinidad** [89 E5] Carretera towards El Hatillo in La Trinidad; ⏧ 0212 949 6411; www.cmdlt.edu.ve/index.html

✚ Clínica El Ávila [89 F1] 6th transversal with Av San Juan Bosco, Altamira; ✆ 0212 276 1111; www.clinicaelavila.com
✚ Hospital de Clínicas Caracas Av Panteon, Centro; ✆ 0212 508 6111; www.clinicaracas.com
✚ Instituto Medico La Floresta [89 G2] Av Principal de la Floresta & Av Fco Miranda, La Floresta; ✆ 0212 209 6222; www.clinicalafloresta.com
✚ Policlínica Las Mercedes [89 E3] Av Principal Las Mercedes, Calle Monterrey; ✆ 0212 993 2059; www.clinicalasmercedes.com

MONEY The best place for changing dollars and euros at the official exchange rate is at a *casa de cambio*. All the top hotels will be able to do this for you or you can visit a branch of **Italcambio** (*www.italcambio.com;* ⊕ *08.30–17.00 Mon–Fri, 08.30–12.30 Sat*), with branches at the Simón Bolívar Airport in Maiquetía, Sabana Grande (*Edif Adriático, Av Casanova*) and in Altamira (*Edif Belmont, Av Roche, Plaza Altamira Sur*), beside the Flor de Castilla café. If you need to withdraw cash from an ATM, most banks accept Visa or MasterCard and the branches in the Sambil shopping centre stay open until late. Some ATMs ask for six digits when most foreign cards have four-digit PINs. Inputting two zeros at the end sometimes does the trick.

Bank transfers to Venezuela from abroad can be complicated and involve plenty of red tape. If you run out of money, you could have funds transferred to your UK or US account and then withdraw the cash from an ATM. To have money wired to you, Italcambio offers a MoneyGram service and **Zoom** (*www.grupozoom.com*) is Western Union's representative in Venezuela.

PHONE, INTERNET AND POST The majority of the big hotels and many smaller ones now have free **internet** or a cyber café on site, or offer Wi-Fi free or for a daily tariff. If you can't make a **local or international phone call** or surf the web from your hotel, or you just want a cheaper option, look out for a Centro de Comunicaciones run by the state phone company CANTV or one of its mobile phone competitors Movistar or Digitel. All the big shopping malls will have one of these centres offering both phone and internet communication for a reasonable price. Also, as phonecards and phone boxes have gone out of use, enterprising Venezuelans now offer mobile phone calls on the street, setting up a table with an umbrella and an assortment of different phones. If you want to call a Movistar number they give you a phone with a Movistar account so the call is cheaper. These little tables come in very handy for keeping in touch in town.

If you just want internet, **private cyber cafés** are to be found all over the city and most stay open until late; just ask a local. If you're strapped for cash, government-sponsored **Infocentros** (*www.infocentro.net.ve*) offer free internet access at most public libraries and some museums such as the **Galería de Arte Nacional** [105 H5]. Local tour operator **Akanan Travel and Adventure** [89 F2] (*Edificio Grano de Oro, Calle Bolívar; www.akanan.com*) also offers free web browsing and a free coffee for Bradt-guide readers at their office near the main plaza in Chacao.

The **post** has never been efficient in Venezuela and with the coming of the internet it is used even less. Trying to get a stamp (*timbre*) to send a postcard can be a trial except at major hotels. The state-run postal service is called **Ipostel** [104 C3] (*Esquina Carmelitas, Av Urdaneta; www.ipostel.gov.ve;* ⊕ *08.00–18.00 Mon–Fri, 08.00–17.00 Sat–Sun*) and has a philately department at its office in Carmelitas selling first issues (⊕ *09.00–16.00*). The poste restante address is: Lista de Correos, Ipostel, Carmelitas, Avenida Urdaneta, Caracas 1010. Other Ipostel branches are closed on weekends; the smaller post offices may also close at midday.

Caracas is not a pedestrian-friendly city, carved up as it is by highways and overpasses, but if you explore it in sections there are many areas to discover on foot and the most important historic sites, museums, theatres, cafés, shops and parks can all be reached using Line 1 of the metro. Bear in mind that museums and parks are closed for maintenance on Mondays.

HISTORIC CENTRE To explore the old colonial part of the city start at the Capitolio metro station in the heart of downtown Caracas, close to places linked to the birth, boyhood and burial of Independence hero Simón Bolívar. This intense, passionate and idealistic young man gave his strength, fortune and ultimately his health to his country, a sacrifice that means a great deal to Venezuelans. A town is not a town, they say, until it has a Plaza Bolívar. The houses where Bolívar lived hark back to an era that has left only faint traces after the brutal modernisation of the city by the dictator Marcos Pérez Jiménez.

El Capitolio [104 C4] (*Plaza Bolívar;* ◷ *09.00–11.00 & 14.00–16.00 Tue–Sun; admission free*) This is the centre of government, the Capitol, built by the Paris-inspired president Antonio Guzmán Blanco in the 1870s in a bid to transform the Spanish colonial character of Caracas. To do so he razed a convent, another indication of his republican sentiments. The building's distinctive dome was brought from Belgium in 1891 and replaced in the 1960s with aluminium. Show your passport to guards at the west gate to enter. Visitors are shown the ceremonial Salón Elíptico. This oval hall, where the Venezuelan Declaration of Independence is kept in a locked casket, is noted for canvases of the battles of Carabobo, Junín and Boyacá, painted in Paris by Venezuelan artist Martin Tovar y Tovar and later

Caracas WHAT TO SEE AND DO

4

WILD AND ESCAPED PARROTS ADOPT CARACAS

If parrots like Caracas, all is not lost. Every time a band of large, loud yellow-headed parrots crosses the eastern sky early in the morning, their squawks and trills recall the rivers and forests of Amazonas. That's where this Amazona genus belongs, not in the capital where space is haggled over by some four million people.

Yet many parrots, including foreign species and other escapees from houses, have found their niche in Caracas. Watch for the Amazon parrots at dusk when, two-by-two, flocks of 30 or more settle for the night in Las Mercedes in trees lining the Guaire River, little more than a sewer. Even the trees are not natives either; many are African tulip trees.

A small, brilliant green cloud settles in a *mamón* tree at a busy corner in Las Mercedes – it is a flock of tiny parrotlets (*Forpus passerinus*), the kind people used to sell in the market (this is now outlawed). A macaw screeches above a construction site – the big red bird is perched on a crane, calling for its mate. In San Bernardino, late every afternoon a pair of green macaws descends by an apartment block to roost in royal palms.

During the day these parrots fly off to feed on the Ávila range or in Parque del Este where more parrots live. In season, mango trees and palms provide them with food in Caracas. Not all the parrots are naturalised. Some are migratory, like the maroon-faced parakeets (*Pyrrhura emma*) that visit when palm nuts are ripe, and the brown-throated parakeets (*Aratinga pertinax*) that may fly by on their way to a greener part of the range. These parakeets hollow out nests in large termite mounds on trees, cohabiting peacefully with the insects.

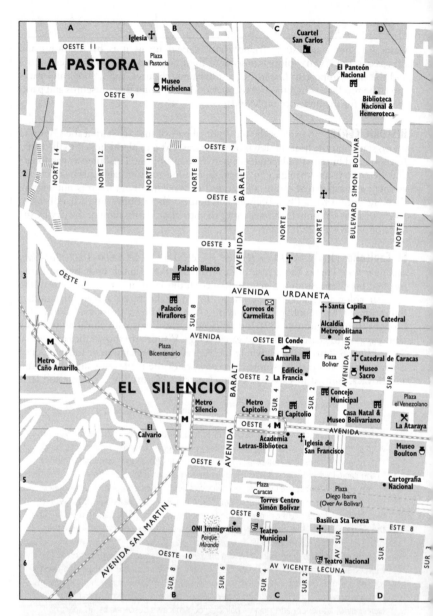

glued in place. The next hall has a huge triptych by Tito Salas showing Simón Bolívar on Monte Sacro, crossing the Andes and on his deathbed. When Congress is in session you can request permission to visit the galleries above the National Assembly facing Avenida Universidad. The ironwork in the Capitol was brought over from England.

Plaza Bolívar [104 C4–D4] Called the Plaza Mayor in colonial days, it was laid out by the Spanish conquistador Diego de Losada, who founded Santiago de León de Caracas on 27 July 1567. Losada arrived in the Caracas Valley from El Tocuyo at

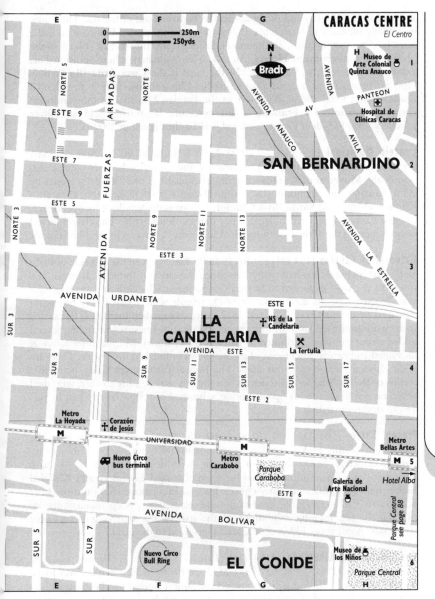

the head of a group of 950 followers and soldiers including 20 cavalrymen and an assortment of mules, pigs and sheep. Every year the city's anniversary is celebrated on the day of St James (Santiago), patron saint of Spain, 27 July, with theatre and music festivals. The shady square is home to pigeons, black squirrels and a couple of sloths, who sometimes come down from their trees. It had many guises before it became Plaza Bolívar in 1883. It was the Plaza de Armas where rebels were hanged, later a marketplace, a bullfight plaza and in republican times the Plaza La Constitución. The famous equestrian statue of Bolívar by Adam Tadolini is a copy of one in Lima. It was cast in Munich and shipped in pieces, but the ship ran aground in Los Roques and the boxes had to be fished out of the sea. The statue was finally unveiled in November 1874 by President Guzmán Blanco who had a 'time box' containing coins, documents and a map sealed into its base. North of the plaza is the **Government House** (Alcaldía Metropolitana), where occasional art exhibitions are open to the public. In the west is the **Casa Amarilla** (Yellow House), infamous as a royal prison in the 17th century, later a presidential residence and today the headquarters of the Foreign Ministry. In the southwest corner is **Edificio La Francia**, a famous centre for buying gold and silver jewellery until President Chávez ordered it to be shut down in 2009.

Concejo Municipal [104 C4] (⊕ 09.00–12.00 & 14.00–18.00 Tue–Sun; admission free) A large colonial building with an attractive interior patio, the town council also houses the **Museum of Caracas**, a series of miniatures of 1930s daily scenes by Raul Santana and paintings by Emilio Boggio. Ask to see the Concejo's handsomely restored **Santa Rosa Chapel**, famous as the 'cradle of Independence' because Congress declared Independence here on 5 July 1811. The chapel served as a seminary in the 17th century and the University of Caracas in the 18th century.

Catedral de Caracas [104 D4] (⊕ 10.00–16.00 Tue–Sun) On the east side of Plaza Bolívar, this church has had many lives since the city was founded. It began as a mudwalled chapel dedicated to St James or Santiago. The church that replaced it was destroyed by an earthquake in 1641, rebuilt with a bell tower but again damaged by the quakes of 1766 and 1812. After this the bell tower was left as it is today without the top level. Inside you can see amazing treasures, including several gilded altars, paintings attributed to Rubens (*Resurrection*), Murillo (*Presentation of the Virgin*) and Arturo Michelena's *Last Supper*, an unfinished final work. There are eight elaborate side crypts with altars. The Bolívar family crypt holds the marble tombs of Bolívar's father, who died when the boy was 2½, his mother, who died when he was nine, and his Spanish bride, who died of yellow fever when he was 18 (he never remarried).

Museo Sacro [104 D4] (⊕ 10.00–16.00 Tue–Sun; small admission fee) The restoration of this ex-Episcopal college built in 1884, revealed a 17th-century church cemetery. Stoop through a massive stone doorway to get to the dark ecclesiastic jail. The osarium behind has been excavated 2.5m deep and 12 sealed niches hold the remains of early church leaders. In a colonnaded patio the little Café Sacro (⊕ Tue–Fri) serves sandwiches and salads. There is a permanent display of religious art, rotating exhibitions in the gallery and free recitals on some weekends. A gift shop, El Vitral de Caracas, gives on to the plaza.

Casa Natal del Libertador [104 D4] (*Esquina San Jacinto a Traposos, Plaza El Venezolano;* \ 0212 545 7693, 0212 541 2563; ⊕ 10.00–16.30; admission free) Just a block east of Plaza Bolívar is the house where Simón Bolívar was born on 24 July 1783, the fourth child of a wealthy aristocratic couple. Reconstructed after neglect by later owners, the Casa Natal is a tourist 'must'. The **Museo Bolivariano** next door has Bolívar's uniform and documents, Independence memorabilia, period weapons and furniture.

Iglesia de San Francisco [104 C5] (*Av Universidad;* ⊕ 06.00–12.00 & 15.00–18.00) South of Congress, this historic church also figures in Bolívar's career. Founded as a monastery in 1575 and rebuilt after the 1641 earthquake, the church was the setting for the proclamation of Bolívar as Liberator, when he was 30 years old. Today it seems miraculous that so young and slight a man should have been instrumental in freeing from Spanish control the area which is now Venezuela, Colombia, Panama, Ecuador, Peru, and Bolivia – named in his honour. In the process he sacrificed his health and succumbed to tuberculosis. Bolívar died penniless and despondent in Santa Marta, Colombia, in 1830. His remains were finally repatriated in 1842, when the streets, houses and churches of Caracas were draped in black for the biggest ceremony ever held: the Liberator's funeral at San Francisco Church. He was buried in the family crypt in the cathedral. The church has a statue to San Onofre, believed to bring help in finding employment and all around it are plaques and offerings of thanks from successful jobseekers. Next to the church are the neo-Gothic spires of the **Palacio de las Academias**, once the San Francisco convent and then home of the Central University, and the **Biblioteca** or central library.

El Panteón Nacional [104 D1] (*Av Panteon con Av Norte, 5 blocks directly north of Plaza Bolívar;* ⊕ *09.00–12.00 & 14.00–16.30; admission free*) Rebuilt by President Guzmán Blanco in 1876 to hold the remains of Simón Bolívar, this former church has become a shrine to the Liberator and other independence heroes. Outside, soldiers stand guard in full ceremonial dress. Every 25 years the president opens the bronze casket to verify that the remains are undisturbed. One of the five people buried alongside Bolívar in the central nave is his Irish aide-de-camp, Daniel O'Leary. Ceiling paintings are by Tito Salas. In all, 138 founding fathers and national figures are interred in the Panteón, including two women: independence heroine Luisa de Cáceres and pianist Teresa Carreño. Two empty tombs await the remains of Francisco de Miranda, who died in a Spanish prison and was buried in a mass grave, and Antonio José de Sucre, assassinated in Colombia. Tradition has it that when the original church (completed the year of Bolívar's birth) was destroyed in the 1812 earthquake, part of a pillar rolled downhill to the Plaza and smashed the gallows, giving the revolutionaries a moral boost.

Next to the Panteón is the concrete building of the **Hemeroteca** (✆ *0212 564 1215;* ⊕ *09.00–16.45 Mon–Sat*), which holds an archive of newspapers and magazines, and a well-used reading room, where you can consult magazines from around the world, including the first newspaper printed in Venezuela (1808) and the world's smallest newspaper, the thumbnail *Colosso* published in Altagracia de Orituco.

Museo de Arte Colonial Quinta Anauco [105 H1] (*Av Panteón, San Bernardino;* ✆ *0212 551 8190; www.quintadeanauco.org.ve;* ⊕ *09.00–11.30 & 14.00–16.30 Tue–Fri, 10.00–16.00 Sat–Sun; admission US$2.50 adults, US$1.25 children/students*) This lovingly restored colonial house with its period furnishings and artworks is a window into the past and an oasis of calm in this hectic city, screened as it is by high walls and trees. Admission includes a guided tour of the gracious residence dating from 1797, including its kitchens, stables and even a bath fed by a stream. The Marquis of Toro gave a ball here on 15 July 1827 for his friend Simón Bolívar, who was to spend his last night in Caracas in Quinta Anauco, never to return. Chamber music concerts are sometimes held here; check the website for upcoming events. To get here take metrobus route 421 from the Belles Artes metro station.

BELLAS ARTES AND ALTAMIRA The main art museums are located close to the **Bellas Artes** metro station and the **Plaza Los Museos**.

Museo de Arte Contemporáneo [88 C2] (*Parque Central, near Alba Hotel;* ✆ *0212 573 7289;* ⊕ *10.00–18.00 Tue–Sun; admission free*) Recognised as one of the finest modern art museums in South America, it has a collection of engravings by Picasso on permanent display, paintings by Francis Bacon, Fernand Léger, Georges Braque, Marc Chagall, Miró, a sculpture by Henry Moore and a big bronze cat by the Colombian artist Botero. Venezuelan artists include Jesus Soto, Carlos Cruz-Diez and Armando Reverón. There is a 175-seat theatre, an excellent reference library of art books and audiovisuals, a gift shop in Sótano 1 and a small restaurant in the entrance garden.

Museo de los Niños [105 H6] (*Parque Central;* ✆ *0212 576 4249, 0212 575 0695; www.maravillosarealidad.com;* ⊕ *09.00–17.00 Mon–Fri, 10.00–17.00 Sat–Sun; admission BsF23 adults, BsF20 children*) You can't miss the bright Lego colours on the outside of this building, close to the Contemporary Art Museum. The concept continues inside with hands-on activities for fun and learning. Aimed at younger kids, there's plenty to do and a separate charge gains you admission to the small planetarium for a 20-minute look at the stars and the origin of the universe. Best avoided during school holidays.

Galeria de Arte Nacional [105 H5] (*Av Mexico, between Bellas Artes & Parque Carabobo metro stations;* ✆ *0212 576 8707; www.fmn.gob.ve/fmn_gan.htm;* ⊕ *09.00–17.00 Mon–Fri, 10.00–17.00 Sat–Sun; admission free*) Transferred from its former neo-Classical home in Plaza de Museos to this huge, concrete building on the main avenue so that more of its 6,000 pieces could be displayed, this impressive collection of Venezuelan art extends from pre-Colombian figurines to ultra-contemporary conceptual pieces. The best of the collection is still the 19th- and 20th-century masters, especially Arturo Michelena's portrait of the Independence hero Francisco de Miranda languishing in a Spanish jail, Armando Reverón's Expressionistic paintings of the coast and shimmering Kinetic sculptures by Jesus Soto.

Museo de Bellas Artes [88 C2] (*Plaza de los Museos, near Bellas Artes metro;* ✆ *0212 578 0275; www.fmn.gob.ve/fmn_mba.htm;* ⊕ *09.00–16.00 Mon–Fri, 10.00–17.00 Sat–Sun; admission free*) Covering contemporary art from around the Americas and a permanent display tracing the evolution of Cubism, the museum has expanded into the Galeria de Arte Nacional's former home in the exquisite 1938 building designed by Carlos Raúl Villanueva. A good place to escape the city, it has well-lit rooms around a green patio, weeping willow and pool, and there are sometimes free concerts on Sunday afternoons. The **Cinemateca Nacional** shows art-house movies from around the world. In 1976, Villanueva also designed the museum's four-storey concrete and glass installation next door. Don't miss the outdoor sculpture garden with a wind-driven Kinetic piece by Alejandro Otero and the rooftop sculpture garden with views of Parque Los Caobos, which is better viewed from above than visited on foot for safety reasons.

Museo de Ciencias Naturales [88 C2] (*Natural History Museum, Plaza Los Museos;* ✆ *0212 577 5103, 0212 577 5094; www.fmn.gob.ve/fmn_mc.htm;* ⊕ *09.00–17.00 Mon–Fri, 10.30–18.00 Sat–Sun; admission free*) Pre-Columbian ceramics, a sabre-toothed tiger and a collection of stuffed animals from around the world make up the eclectic collection of this interesting museum, with informative exhibitions on natural history, ecology and science.

Universidad Central de Venezuela [88 C3] (*Ciudad Universitaria; www.ucv.ve*) This sprawling campus of 26 Modernist buildings was declared a World Heritage Site by UNESCO in 2000 as a masterwork in city planning by Carlos Raúl Villanueva. The campus is dotted with some 80 frescoes, murals, stained-glass windows and sculptures, including works by Léger, Arp, Laurens, Kandinsky and

Pevsner as well as Venezuelan artists Francisco Narváez, Jesus Soto, Alejandro Otero, and Hector Poléo. Saunter around the grounds with some of the 62,000 students, or go to a concert at the 3,000-seat **Aula Magna**, where the ceiling has acoustic clouds by Alexander Calder, a great friend of Villanueva. From the Plaza Venezuela metro station you can walk across the *autopista* bridge, but it's safer to take a taxi to the main entrance. Pedro León Zapata's spectacular 150m mural greets visitors. The cartoonist said he wanted to entertain drivers stuck in traffic with his depiction of Venezuela's leaders, past and present as *Conductores de Venezuela* (drivers/leaders).

Casa de Rómulo Gallegos – CELARG [89 G2] (*Av Luis Roche, Altamira;* \0212 285 2644, 0212 285 2721; *www.celarg.gob.ve;* ⊕ 10.00–21.00; admission free) Modern space with regular art exhibitions, a bookstore and a café as well as a fine restaurant, Vizio's. Worth a look after a walk up the Ávila. The cinema shows art-house movies in the evening and there are regular concerts.

Centro de Arte La Estancia [89 G2] (*Av Francisco de Miranda, Altamira;* \0212 208 0413, 0212 208 0427; e *laestancia@pdvsa.com; http://laestancia.pdvsa.com;* ⊕ 09.00–17.00 Mon–Thu, 09.00–19.00 Sat–Sun; admission free) A hidden gem in Altamira, tucked behind high walls, is an old colonial coffee plantation, the Hacienda La Floresta, which gave its name to this area of town. Bought by the state oil firm PDVSA and completely restored, the house and luxuriant grounds were opened in 1995 as an exhibition and concert space. Free concerts are held most Saturday and Sunday afternoons, featuring folk groups or one of the country's excellent youth orchestras. A small restaurant under the trees serves elegant brunches and lunch.

PARKS AND ZOOS
Jardín Botánico [88 D2] (*Av Salvador Allende, Universidad Central de Venezuela;* \ 0212 605 3989, 0212 605 3994; *www.fibv.org.ve;* ⊕ 08.30–16.30 Mon–Sun; admission: BsF1 adults, 50 centavos children) Occupying an old family farm, the Hacienda Ibarra, the 150-acre botanical gardens are planted with lilies, cacti, orchids and dozens of palm species, plus plenty of lawn space for a picnic (toilets, too). The entrance is just before the university gates. Guided visits in English can be arranged for large groups if you call ahead. There is a library and Botanical Institute housing the national herbarium.

Parque Generalísimo Francisco de Miranda, Parque del Este [89 G3] (*Av Francisco de Miranda, Parque del Este metro station;* ⊕ 08.00–17.00 Tue–Sun; admission free) Probably the only place that most people will see a jaguar in Venezuela is at this popular park with its 200 acres of lawns, a boating lake, zoo, aviary, planetarium and terrarium filled with snakes and creepy-crawlies. It was originally called Parque del Este Rómulo Betancourt after the president who, in 1961, asked Brazilian landscape architect Roberto Burle Marx to transform this old coffee hacienda into a park worthy of the city. Home to storks, egrets, parrots and sloths, who freely take advantage of the trees and ponds, it also has an aviary with colourful Venezuelan birds, including a fearsome-looking harpy eagle. The open zoo area has an otter pool, an anaconda moat, a monkey island, a jaguar pit, crocodiles and caimans and a lagoon with scarlet ibis. There is also a replica of Francisco de Miranda's ship *Leander*. The **Planetario Humboldt** (\ 0212 234 9188; *www.planetariohumboldt.com;* ⊕ 12.00–16.00 Sat–Sun; admission US$1) has a fabulous three-ton mechanical Zeiss machine with 200 separate projectors, a 1952 classic brought to Venezuela by the dictator Marcos Pérez Jiménez and the last working model of its kind. The hourly shows at the weekend are well worth

4

seeing. The **Terrarium** (✆ *0212 976 9582;* m *0414 662 3566, 0424 122 1052;* *www.terrario.org.ve;* ⊕ *09.00–17.00 Tue–Sat; admission BsF5 adults, BsF3.5 concessions Tue–Fri; BsF6.5 adults, BsF4.5 Sat–Sun*) has more than 50 species on show, including Venezuela's largest and most venomous snakes, scorpions and spiders, a good introduction for those heading out to the jungle.

Caricuao Zoo

[88 A4] (*Av Ppal La Hacienda, Caricuao;* ⊕ *09.00–16.30 Tue–Sun; admission free*) Take Line 2 to Zoologico metro station to see spider and howler monkeys playing freely in the trees of this 1,200-acre park. Many native animals are on display here, including armadillos, opposums, anteaters and wading birds like flamingos and ibis that roam free. An African section has giraffes, elephants and rhinos.

THE ÁVILA MOUNTAIN

The coastal range that includes the Parque Nacional El Ávila separates Caracas from the Caribbean Sea, reaching a lofty 2,765m (9,071ft) at Pico Naiguatá, the highest peak. The park stretches 86km from east to west and covers an area of 850km², much of which is wild. The changes in climate, fauna and flora as you go up are fascinating. Some 200 kinds of bird and 130 mammal and reptile species live here. Although most walkers will spot electric blue hummingbirds, yellow and blue jays and small lizards, few see the howler monkeys that prefer the mountain's wilder Caribbean slopes. This is also true of capuchin monkeys and many other species. Only the very lucky will ever see the ocelots, margays, racoons, armadillos, agoutis, porcupines, foxes, rabbits, deer, and skunks that live in the forests of El Ávila or the honey-bears, sloths and squirrels that hide in the treetops. With its well-marked trails, shelters and ranger stations, the high mountain offers plenty of walks at different grades. The Ávila is an oxygen-maker, and Caraqueños walk up the mountain for the exhilarating air as well as magnificent views.

Geologically speaking, the Cordillera de la Costa is fairly young, uplifted by the collision of the South American and Caribbean tectonic plates only some 40 million years ago.

The first ascent of the **Pico Oriental** (2,640m) was made in 1800 by Alexander von Humboldt and Aime Bonpland, aided by 80 porters and peons cutting a trail up the Sabas Nieves route. **Naiguatá** was first climbed in 1872 by a group including German painter Anton Goering and British traveller James Mudie Spence. In his book, *The Land of Bolívar*, Spence related that from the peak he could see as far as Los Roques Archipelago and the plains of Guárico.

Today, there are three ways to reach the lofty ridge of the mountain: on foot, by cable car or by jeep, using the 4x4s that operate from outside Hotel Ávila.

Walking the Ávila

Trail to Sabas Nieves Experienced Venezuelan hikers can walk to the highest peak, Pico Naiguatá, and return the same day but anybody new to the mountain should start with the main trail from Altamira, which begins at the park entrance near Tarzilandia restaurant. From here, there is a 25-minute walk up a steep, windy path to the Sabas Nieves ranger post, which has taps with fresh water from the mountain and homemade iced lollies. This is a safe route and the one preferred by the beautiful people of Caracas who climb up here most mornings and evenings to keep in shape (there are even bars for doing dips and sit-ups). The pleasant trail passes through forest and gives good views of the city as you get towards the ranger station. Expect to see birds and butterflies and lots of people in Lycra. For those who start very early and want to go further than Sabas Nieves, there is a trail above the ranger station that forks left and down to the waterfalls at Quebrada Chacaito, about 20 minutes away. If you want to reach Pico Oriental – and have come prepared with water, food, a flashlight and something warm in case you get caught in cloud – turn right and walk up a steep trail to a shelter at *No Te Apures* (Don't Hurry), reached in about 1½ hours. From here it is up all the way to the ridge at *La Silla* (The Saddle), which is the dip between Pico Occidental (2,478m) and Pico Oriental (2,640m). The climb from La Silla to Pico Oriental is about 45 minutes, with spectacular views over the Caribbean and the coast. Total journey time from the park entrance to the peak is just over four hours. The descent is quicker but can be hard on the knees. The Ávila's paths are steep enough to set your heart pounding and are good training for expeditions to Roraima or the Andes, but take plenty of rest stops if you're feeling the heat and drink lots of water. When you get to the bottom you can pick up a fresh juice from the stall by the National Guard post and there are other stalls selling coconut milk, natural yoghurt, health foods and energy drinks.

An alternative route from the park entrance goes to the waterfall at Quebrada Quintero, following a thickly forested trail that is not as steep as the Sabas Nieves route. The waterfall cascades down a huge rock wall and the pool below is deep enough to submerge yourself if you can brave the freezing water.

Permits and emergencies Park rangers at guard posts, *puestos de guardaparques* (PGP), monitor the activities of hikers, who must sign in if they plan to walk to the peaks. No permits are required to walk the main trails. Remember to bring your passport as the National Guard at the start of the trail to Sabas Nieves may ask you for identification. Always bring water, some snacks and a small flashlight or head torch in case it gets dark.

Bear in mind that the Ávila is a big, bold mountain and careless walkers can come to grief when straying from paths, walking at dusk or in mist. The park guards' job is to bring you safely down in the case of accident, but they cannot do this speedily if you are not on a trail. Do not attempt shortcuts; do not run downhill. Smoking and camp fires are forbidden due to the risk of fire, a constant hazard in the dry season.

Organised walks A good way to explore the park safely and enjoyably is to join a walking party. The most established group is the **Centro Excursionista Caracas** (*www.centroexcursionistacaracas.org.ve*) who organise regular hikes to the Ávila and other national parks.

Camping on the Ávila The campsites mentioned below are those with toilet facilities. There are many other places in the park flat and clear enough to serve as a campsite. All human waste should be properly buried and garbage carried out. The park is generally clean considering the number of visitors. **Los Venados** is a large recreation area that was part of a former coffee plantation. Its centre is the handsome old great house embracing an enormous coffee-drying patio. There is an Inparques office here, a cafeteria, museum and library. Campsites are available and also kiosks, which are handy in case of rain. This area is very popular at weekends and on school holidays. **Sabas Nieves** is popular with trekkers overnighting in Caracas. There is a camping area on flat ground above the park ranger's house.

Visting the mountain by cable car The **Waraira Repano** cable car, or *teleférico* (*www.warairarepano.gob.ve*; ⊕ *13.00–18.00 Tue, 10.00–21.00 Wed–Sat, 10.00–18.00 Sun; admission BsF35 adults, BsF15 children*) has some 70 cars that take 18 minutes to travel the 3.5km from Mariperez station to the cable-car installations on the Ávila Mountain at 2,105m above sea level. Very popular at weekends and on holidays, visitors are greeted by a fresh breeze and fantastic views of the city of

4

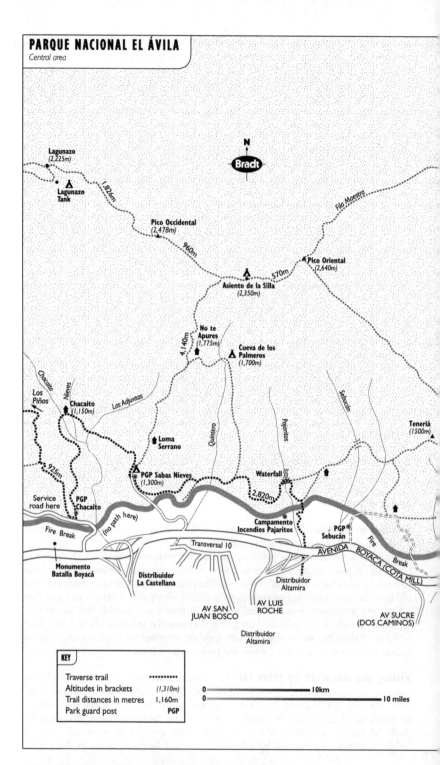

PARQUE NACIONAL EL ÁVILA
Central area

Lagunazo (2,225m)

Lagunazo Tank

Pico Occidental (2,478m)

Pico Oriental (2,640m)

Filo Maestra

1,826m

960m

570m

Asiento de la Silla (2,350m)

No te Apures (1,775m)

Cueva de los Palmeros (1,700m)

4,140m

Chacaito

Nieves

Los Piños

Chacaíto (1,150m)

Las Adjuntas

Quintero

Sebucán

Pajaritos

Tenería (1500m)

Loma Serrano

925m

PGP Sabas Nieves (1,300m)

Waterfall

2,820m

Service road here

PGP Chacaíto

(no path here)

Campamento Incendios Pajaritos

PGP Sebucán

Fire Break

Fire Break

Monumento Batalla Boyacá

Transversal 10

Distribuidor La Castellana

AVENIDA BOYACA (COTA MILL)

Distribuidor Altamira

AV SAN JUAN BOSCO

AV LUIS ROCHE

AV SUCRE (DOS CAMINOS)

Distribuidor Altamira

KEY

Traverse trail	••••••••
Altitudes in brackets	(1,310m)
Trail distances in metres	1,160m
Park guard post	PGP

0 ———— 10km
0 ———— 10 miles

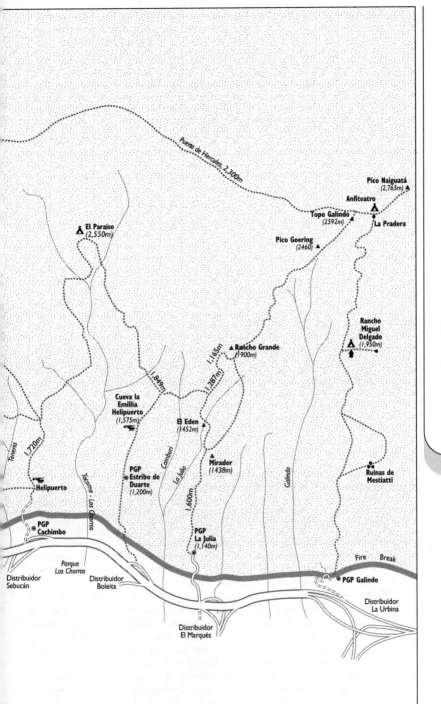

Pico Naiguatá
(2,765m) ▲

Anfiteatro

Topo Galindo
(2592m) ▲

La Pradera

Pico Goering
(2460) ▲

Puerto de Hercules, 2,300m

El Paraíso
(2,550m)

Rancho
Miguel
Delgado
(1,950m)

▲ Rancho Grande
(1900m)

1,165m

1,287m

849m

Cueva la
Emillia
Helipuerto
(1,575m)

El Eden
(1452m) ▲

Ruinas de
Mestiatti

Mirador
(1438m) ▲

1,720m

Teneria

Tocome - Los Chorros

Cambiri

La Julia

Galindo

PGP
Estribo de
Duarte
(1,200m)

1,600m

Helipuerto

PGP
Cachimbo

PGP
La Julia
(1,140m)

Fire   Break

Distribuidor
Sebucán

Parque
Los Chorros

Distribuidor
Boleita

PGP Galindo

Distribuidor
La Urbina

Distribuidor
El Marqués

Caracas to the south and the Caribbean coast to the north. Kiosks sell homemade cakes and fruit juices, as well as raspberries, peaches and jams from the mountain community of Galipán. There are short walks up to the **Hotel Humboldt**, which looks like something out of an old James Bond movie with its iconic circular tower and 1960s furnishings. The luxury 14-floor hotel designed by architect Tomás Sanabria boasted a ballroom with heated marble floors, a heated indoor pool and a revolving discotheque where guest stars included salsa legends Celia Cruz and Tito Puentes. It has not been in use as a hotel for more than 40 years. The cable-car system and hotel were opened in December 1956 by the dictator Marcos Pérez Jiménez. A year later his mistress jumped from the seventh floor after being caught having an affair with one of the workers; her ghost is said to roam the corridors. Pérez Jiménez never had time to enjoy his creation and was overthrown and forced to flee the country on 23 January 1958. Another cable-car route travelling the 7.6km down to Macuto on the Caribbean coast is sadly out of action but the state-run cable-car company has plans to reopen it. When it does, visitors will be able to avoid the weekend traffic and enjoy a day at the beach with a stop on the mountain. To get to Mariperez take a taxi, as there is no direct bus service.

Galipán When the national park was established in 1958, 100 families in Galipán were left in legal limbo on their farms high on the Ávila's north side. The Galipaneros, among them descendants of the original Canary Islanders who arrived two centuries ago, fought for their homes and in 1982 finally won the right to stay.

SLOTHS, THE CHAMPION SURVIVORS

One slow but magical creature you may encounter while walking the trails of the Ávila is a sloth (*pereza* in Venezuela), although you have to be lucky as they stick to the canopy during the day, move very little, and are hard to spot among the leaves. Both two-toed and three-toed sloths are found in Venezuela but it is the brown-throated three-toed sloth (*Bradypus variegata*) that you find in the mountains of the Ávila and the Parque Nacional Henri Pittier as their main geographic distribution is along the central coast. The pale-throated three-toed sloth (*Bradypus tridactylus*) is found in the Orinoco Delta and south of the Orinoco in Bolívar State. Occupying the same area is the southern two-toed sloth (*Choloepus didactylus*), which also extends to the forests in the far south of Amazonas State. Hoffman's two-toed sloth (*Choloepus hoffmani*) is limited to the forested mountains west of Lake Maracaibo and north of the Andes. Two-toed sloths have only two long curved claws on their front feet that they use to hook onto the trunks and branches of trees, while three-toed sloths have three. All the sloth species have three claws on their back limbs. Their grip is like iron and the males use their claws as a terrible weapon in territorial fights, which can end in the death of a rival. They spend most of their lives upside down, a position they can sleep in. To make life a little easier from this back to front position their round heads can rotate through more than 90°. Of all the mammals, *Bradypus tridactylus* has the most neck vertebrae (nine) and can turn its head nearly 180°.

Sloths wear a bemused half-smile at all times, whether upset or frightened. How do they survive? Very well, thank you. The leaves of various trees give them both water and food which they digest in a many-chambered stomach. Called *perezas* in Spanish, they belong to the primitive order of Edentata – meaning 'toothless', although they do have teeth which grow as they are worn down. Sloths have little need to come to ground as they live in forests where branches touch and will move through the canopy from tree to tree, although they will descend once a week to defecate, clinging to the trunk and making a neat hole with their stumpy tail. If they need to cross a river during wet season floods it's no problem as they can float and swim well. Like some moth-eaten mat trying

In 1995 the first paved road arrived, bringing a stream of weekend visitors and giving farmers better access to Caracas for selling flowers and vegetables, their traditional livelihood, and high school and job opportunities for their children. There are three Galipán communities: San Isidro at 1,800m altitude, the highest and closest to the Ávila cable-car terminal; San Antonio at 1,500m, 3.5km farther; and San José at 800m, some 4km downhill. Now the cable car service is in good order and working regularly, it is easier than ever to visit some of the high-quality gourmet restaurants in Galipán that offer good food and great views of the coast from your table. You can either take a Jeep from the cable car installations at the top of the mountain, or drive up from Hotel El Ávila in one of the 4x4s that operate from there.

✖ Where to eat

✖ **Casa Pakea** Sector Manzanare de Galipan; ☎ 0212 415 5353; m 0414 195 7800; ⊕ 12.00–17.00 Wed–Sun. A transplanted Basque Juan Manuel Bereciartu, better known as Señor Pakea prepares a changing feast of baked red snapper, roast lamb, grouper pie & Basque specialities at this mountain retreat. Seating for 55 & very popular despite pricey menu, so reserve well in advance. Transport organised from Hotel El Ávila or cable car station. **$$$**

✖ **Granja Natalia** Sector Manzanare de Galipan; m 0416 621 6687, 0414 126 7166; ⊕ 12.00–20.00 Wed–Sun. A granja is a farm, & this one is surrounded by organically grown leeks, lettuce, parsley, chives, oregano & mint – a cook's delight. Two-thirds of the ingredients that Angel Sánchez & his wife Alejandra use are locally grown. When you ring for reservations, they will suggest a main course, perhaps roast duck or rabbit; when you arrive there are also terrine or mousse entrées,

to swim, a sloth on the ground is virtually helpless as its legs cannot hold up its belly. In fact a certain moth actually lives on the algae which grows in patches on the sloths' fur, giving it a greenish hue. These moths are thought to be beneficial, causing the sloth to scratch and increase circulation to its skin.

When motorists see a sloth painfully crossing the road, the driver will often stop to lend a hand. This is done safely by holding the sloth firmly under the armpits from behind, so that its long claws with their terrible grip cannot hook on to the rescuer.

Rescued *perezas* are often put in town squares and if you look high in the treetops in Plaza Bolívar in Caracas you may see a sloth scratching, or sleeping curled in a ball. They are not early risers and doze until the sun warms them, having a variable blood temperature (24–33°C).

They are not as slow as believed and given a few moments will disappear into the canopy, camouflaged by the algae that grows on their fur. The coarse fur, growing from the belly to the back, sheds rainwater while the sloth eats upside down. Sloths make almost no alarm cry, grunting softly or hissing. They appear to see poorly, and locate each other with a high thin whistle. If a baby is separated from its mother, or falls out of the tree, it stands a poor chance of finding her again. Mothers bear a single young which rides clasped to her chest for six to nine months. As William Beebe observed, the babies are able to walk upright on branches before learning to hang upside down. Hunters in Venezuela shun sloths as having more mat than meat, and even boys think it unsporting to kill so sluggish an animal. Their main predator is the powerful harpy eagle (*Harpia harpyja*), which can take an adult sloth from the canopy without slowing down, spearing the cranium with its five-inch killing claw. Zoos don't want sloths because they do not adapt well to captivity. A clue to the reason for this lies in the umbrella-leaved cecropia or *yagrumo*, a tree often preferred by sloths. These trees have hollow stems colonised by ants. Apparently it's not freedom that sloths pine for in zoos, but something lacking in their diet akin to formic acid (a fatty acid found in ants).

cream soups of garden vegetables, homemade pastas served with dried tomatoes & chopped cashews, fruit crêpes with real cream, cakes, coffee & liqueur. Angel has another restaurant close by called **Le Galipanier** (*www.legalipanier.com*) that specialises in Swiss dishes & fondues, just right when the clouds descend & the evening turns cool. **$$$**

AROUND CARACAS

EL HATILLO Only around 20km outside Caracas, El Hatillo (altitude 1,150m) is a pretty village that has managed to conserve its charm in the face of massive development around it. Houses are painted every colour of the rainbow, with few over two storeys high. The whitewashed church is simple but quaint and the Plaza Bolívar is decorated with dovecotes, a perfect setting for shops selling knick-knacks, handicrafts and funky furniture items. This is where Caraqueños come on Sundays to browse the boutiques and lunch alfresco. It is a great stop for tourists looking for last-minute gifts at **Hannsi**, a huge barn of a place packed to the rafters with Venezuelan handicrafts from all over the country; see *What to do* opposite for more detail.

History At the foot of a mountain range reaching 1,490m in Alto Hatillo, the village nestles in a valley where cattle once grazed, known as a *hatillo* or 'little ranch'. In 1784 a local resident, Don Balthasar de León, together with 180 families from the area, won permission to officially found a town. They began by making a plaza and building the church of Santa Rosalía de Palermo. Closely linked with El Hatillo's church, Balthasar de León was imprisoned in Spain in 1751 with his Canary Islander father, Juan Francisco de León, and his brothers for rising up against the Spanish trading monopoly in Venezuela, the Compañía Guipuzcoana. When smallpox struck the prison, taking Juan Francisco as its first victim, the prison chaplain called on Santa Rosalía for help and the epidemic receded. (Saint Rosalía, who lived in Sicily in the 12th century, was venerated for her miraculous cures; she had renounced a privileged life as the daughter of a counsellor to King Roger II of Sicily to become a hermit.) When Balthasar finished his prison term and returned to Venezuela, he resolved to build a church for the saint.

The village grew very slowly and even after electricity was installed in 1935 it remained such a quiet spot that distance and bad roads kept away most visitors except for those on horseback. All that changed when city workers came to live in new land developments in the 1950–60s such as Las Marías, Loma Larga and Oripoto. The opening of the exclusive Lagunita Country and Golf Club transformed El Hatillo into an upper-class enclave and precipitated the boom of patio restaurants and boutique stores.

Getting there Metrobus route 212 leaves from Avenida Principal del Bosque, up from Plaza Chacaito, stopping at La Trinidad and El Hatillo. Alternatively, *por puesto* buses to El Hatillo leave as soon as they are full from Avenida Humboldt near the Chacaito metro station.

If driving, take the road from Las Mercedes to the Baruta Autopista and follow the signs to El Hatillo.

✖ **Where to eat** The village is bursting with inviting little restaurants, cafés and pizzerias – over 40 at the last count – and competition has kept prices fairly reasonable. Below are a few suggestions to get you started.

✖ **Das Pastelhaus** Lower west side of Plaza Bolívar; ☏ 0212 963 5486, 0212 963 7655; ⏰ 07.00–23.00. With an attractive terrace facing onto the plaza & a menu of pastries, cakes & simple but freshly made margherita, diavola & calzone pizzas, this is one of the most popular places in town. Try the zingy passion-fruit mousse. $$$

✗ **Las Tapas del Hatillo** Calle Bolívar 15; \ 0212 961 3721; ⊕ 12.00–23.00. Opposite Hannsi, this intimate Spanish-style restaurant is popular for its small bar & seafood tapas options. $$$

✗ **El Fogón del Hatillo** 10 Calle La Paz; \ 0212 963 1068; ⊕ 12.00–22.30. Longstanding El Hatillo eatery with no frills but tasty Venezuelan staples such as arepas Andinas, maize cachapas with cheese. $$

✗ **Padrísimo Taqueria** Calle Miranda con calle Escalona; \ 0212 961 5801; ⊕ 12.00–22.00. At the top of the plaza, this is another fast-food Mexican place with just 6 tables & a tasty list of tacos, tortillas & spicy soup. $$

✗ **Pizza La Grotta** Calle Comercio facing Plaza Sucre; \ 0212 961 3266; ⊕ 12.00–23.00 Tue–Sun.

A good place for simple but honest wood-oven pizzas, lasagne & beer; music at w/ends. $$

✗ **Capri** Calle 2 de Mayo, 2nd flr; \ 0212 963 4653, 0212 961 2655; e bettinvzla@cantv.net; ⊕ 12.00–23.00. Good Italian home cooking with hearty portions served up by Señora Ita Bettin; w/end diners should reserve ahead. $

✗ **La Gorda** Calle Santa Rosalía; \ 0212 963 7476; ⊕ 12.00–15.00 Tue–Fri, 08.30–17.00 Sat–Sun. Traditional soups & hearty Venezuelan classics at this small place with its home-style criollo lunches. $

✗ **Los Compadres** Calle La Paz; \ 0212 961 4664; ⊕ 17.00–22.30 Wed–Fri, 13.00–22.30 Sat–Sun. Tacos & tostadas filled with chicken, pork, beef & a vegetarian version make this cheap & cheerful Mexican place worth visiting. They also have tamales & salads. $

Festivals Founder's Day is celebrated on 12 June, and Santa Rosalía's Day, 4 September, is marked with a three-day celebration. Among Easter observations, the people of El Hatillo hold processions from Wednesday to Good Friday's Passion Play, when the tiny **Capilla de El Calvario** (across the high street north of Calle Bolívar) opens for the faithful. There is a jazz festival in early October and a busy calendar of music, dance and crafts events during the year.

What to do Stroll around the pleasant **Plaza Bolívar** and treat yourself to a frozen yoghurt or *churros* (hot, crinkly doughnut sticks) and hot chocolate at one of the cafés to give you the energy to browse in the boutique, curio and craft shops that fill the small side streets.

Hannsi (*12 Calle Bolívar, up from the church;* \ *0212 963 5577, 0212 963 6513;* e *info@hannsi.com.ve; www.hannsi.com.ve;* ⊕ *09.00–19.00 Mon–Sat, 10.30–19.30 Sun*) is the one store you mustn't miss, even if you just want to compare prices with cheaper places around town. Nowhere has as much stuff as Hannsi. It will take you a good two hours to browse through the hand-woven hammocks, Indian baskets, Andean wood carvings, pottery, weaving, masks, candles – you name it. You'll pay five times more here for that bead necklace you could have picked up for peanuts at the Indian market in Puerto Ayacucho, but the advantage is having everything under one roof.

5

Central Coast and Colonia Tovar

The towns and beaches of the central coast in Vargas State, known here as the Litoral Central, hold few attractions for visitors due to security concerns following the devastating flooding and landslides of 1999, which washed whole resorts and beaches away and knocked out most of the tourist infrastructure. While the beaches of this long strip of coast are still popular with the crowds from Caracas, especially during the busy holiday seasons, foreigners would do better to head for safer destinations in Choroní–Puerto Colombia, Mochima and Santa Fé, or Tucacas and Chichiriviche in the Parque Nacional Morrocoy.

Until the situation improves, the main reason for coming to La Guaira Catia la Mar and Macuto is their proximity to the Simón Bolívar International Airport at Maiquetía, offering overnight accommodation for those who don't want to spend a night in Caracas before catching a flight to Los Roques, Ciudad Bolívar, Mérida, or back home.

West of La Guaira Catia la Mar, on a stretch of coast also reached from the high valleys of Colonia Tovar, are Chichiriviche de la Costa, good for diving, and the more isolated Puerto Maya, which is culturally closer to the cacao plantation villages of Aragua State, and from where boats can take you along the coast to Cepe and Chuao.

Colonia Tovar, a pretty town with historic links to Germany's Black Forest (Shwarzwald) region, is set in a beautiful mountain valley. It continues to be a popular weekend escape for Caraqueños seeking cool breezes and good food, with sausages and strawberries high on the list of local specialities. For foreign visitors, Colonia Tovar makes a nice break from the usually hectic pace in Venezuela, offering good hiking possibilities, ancient petroglyphs and jeep tours to sights of interest.

MAIQUETÍA AIRPORT HOTELS Telephone code: 0212

Anybody arriving at the main international airport in Maiquetía after 16.00, who wants to fly on to Los Roques, or other destinations with no late flights, will have to either spend the night in Caracas (about 1–1½ hours away, depending on traffic) or overnight close to the airport in Catia La Mar or Macuto (10–15 minutes by car or taxi). Most hotels will arrange pickup from the airport and early transfer the next day, which is good as Catia la Mar and Macuto are not safe for evening strolls around the streets away from the main areas. While the more expensive options offer swimming pool, sea views, bars and restaurants, cheaper options are just a place to spend the night, have breakfast and make that early connection.

GETTING THERE

By bus The distance from midtown Caracas to La Guaira is some 36km (about a 50-minute trip). Take almost any *litoral* bus from Caracas to the coast, except those for Maiquetía and Catia La Mar (west). City buses pick up passengers on Avenida Universidad between Avenida Baralt and Norte 8 by El Silencio metro station. Big buses of the Excarguaica line and *por puestos* leave for La Guaira and Maiquetía from Avenida Sucre at the Gato Negro metro station.

By car Take the Caracas–La Guaira highway from the Francisco Fajardo.

☞ *WARNING*: If you arrange pickup at Maiquetía Airport ask for a description and the name of the person picking you up. Many touts operate in the airport, trying to change money or get you into a taxi. If you are approached by someone, make sure you ask them for the name of the person they are waiting for and the name of the hotel. Don't offer the information first, because touts will just nod, smile, say everything is fine and take you to a taxi, for which you will then be charged an exorbitant amount on arrival at the hotel. If you do take a taxi from the airport, only take official taxis with yellow number plates and agree the fare with the driver before getting in or placing your luggage in the boot.

WHERE TO STAY
Catia La Mar

⌂ **Marriott Hotel Playa Grande** (194 rooms) Av El Hotel, Playa Grande; ☎ 0212 535 2222, 0212 535 6350; www.marriott.com. This newish, 5-star hotel is just 5mins' drive from the airport. Built on 12 floors with sea views, swimming pool, restaurant with buffet, internet & Wi-Fi. $$$$

⌂ **Hotel Catimar** (75 rooms) Av Ppal de Puerto Viejo; ☎ 0212 351 9097, 0212 351 7906; m 0416 611 0938; e contacto@hotelcatimar.com; www.hotelcatimar.com. Reasonable option offering clean rooms with AC, *tasca* bar, restaurant, free transfers to/from airport if arranged in advance. $$

⌂ **Hotel La Parada** (10 rooms) Av Atlántida con Calle 10; ☎ 0212 351 2148, 0212 351 2626; e hotel_la_parada@hotmail.com. One of the best basic options close to the airport with *tasca*-style restaurant, rooms with AC, TV, & internet available in reception to check emails. Most Venezuelan tour operators send people here. $$

⌂ **Parador Turistico y Posada Il Prezzano** (63 rooms) Av Principal de Playa Grande; ☎ 0212 351 2626; e reserva@ilprezzano.com.ve; www.ilprezzano.com.ve. Another clean, budget option with AC, hot water, TV, restaurant serving Italian food. They now operate 2 hotels jointly. $$

Macuto

⌂ **Hotel Olé Caribe** (126 rooms) Av Intercomunal, El Playon; ☎ 0212 620 2000; e info@ hotelolecaribe.com; www.hotelolecaribe.com. A 5-star hotel set above Macuto with fine sea views, impressive swimming pool, sauna, gym, tennis courts. Rooms & suites with AC, fridge & bar. Ask about off-season rates with b/fast. The hotel's **Cascada Restaurant & Tasca Los Molinos** are good dining choices on the Litoral Central. $$$$

⌂ **Hotel Santiago** (84 rooms) Av La Playa at Calle 2; ☎ 0212 334 1837; m 0414 922 3168. Known for its busy waterfront seafood restaurant, pool with Ávila view, rooms & suites with AC. $$

⌂ **Posada de Hidalgo** (34 rooms) Av La Playa at Calle 3; ☎ 0212 414 8460, 0212 414 7991. Rooms with AC. Spanish *tasca*-style restaurant has good seafood, waiters have to cross the road to serve the seaside tables. $$

⌂ **Hotel Plazamar** (22 rooms) In central Macuto on the plaza at Calle del Medio; ☎ 0212 344 1271. A quiet, family-run budget option on 2 floors, rooms with fan & TV but no hot water. $

COLONIA TOVAR TO WESTERN COVES

The mountain retreat of Colonia Tovar, with its picturesque black-and-white houses, hotels and restaurants, sauerkraut, homemade jams and hiking trails in the cloudforests around Codazzi Peak (2,425m), is second only to the beaches of the Litoral Central as a weekend destination for Caracas residents. The main route to Colonia Tovar from Caracas runs from La Yaguara in Caracas via El Junquito (63km), but there are also three lesser-travelled winding roads that descend to the coast: one to the isolated beaches and fishing villages of Puerto Cruz and Puerto

Maya; one to the diving centre of Chichiriviche de la Costa; and another to Carayaca, which continues to Catia La Mar and the airport at Maiquetía.

At 2,000m above sea level, Colonia Tovar has a cool climate, great food and gives Venezuelan tourists the chance to visit an 'authentic' German village. It was founded in 1843 by peasants from the villages of Wyhl, Edingen and Oberbergen in the Black Forest, who were brought here to work the land. Virtually abandoned and almost totally isolated for the next hundred years these hardy German settlers farmed, planted coffee and clung to their Black-Forest customs and language (see box, *A hard life for pioneers*, page 125). They lived on the food they grew and by taking a mule trail down to La Victoria to trade coffee for clothes and tools. Finally, a road to Caracas was built in the 1950s. When it was paved in 1963 the area opened up to tourism, from which it has thrived ever since, and the population of the valley grew from 1,500 to over 14,000 today.

COLONIA TOVAR (*Telephone code: 0244*) It's clean, green and a refreshing relief from the sweltering heat of the coast, but Colonia Tovar is also different from everywhere else in Venezuela. There's a slightly cheesy, theme park quality to the kitsch souvenirs, the waitresses done up in pigtails and traditional dress, and the Teutonic Olde Worlde signs on restaurants and hotels. Speak German to most people in town and you'll get a bemused look and a shake of the head. Scratch a bit deeper, however, and the fascinating history of this Shwarzwald Shangri-La is all around: from surnames like Breidenbach, Muttach, Pfaff, Schmuck and Strubinger to the blond-haired, blue-eyed farm girls with ruddy cheeks tending their strawberries. A popular destination for day-trippers, prices are slightly higher than average, but it's a very safe, well-organised place to spend a few days, offering excellent food and accommodation options and an ideal base for walkers and campers. Except for Mérida and the Parque Nacional Ávila no area has as many wooded paths. The average temperature is 16°C, dropping at night to a chilly 8°C, so warm clothing such as a jacket or fleece is a must.

Getting there The popularity of Colonia Tovar with weekenders can make traffic a nightmare on Saturdays and Sundays, so try and arrive and leave during the week. Although the distance from western Caracas to Colonia Tovar is only about 60km, the road winds up from industrial Antímano through crowded *barrios* and it can take 1½ hours. When you add fog or rain to the traffic, the queues of cars can slow to a tortuous crawl. Day-trippers in search of rural delights such as strawberries and sausages (*chorizos*) also throng to El Junquito (27km), a less-than-attractive market town and the halfway point in the journey from Caracas to Colonia Tovar.

Small buses leave Caracas to El Junquito from outside La Yaguara metro station on weekdays from 05.00 until mid-morning. Change buses in El Junquito for the final stretch to Colonia Tovar. Once past El Junquito, traffic thins and the road winds around a ridge with good views. Colonia Tovar is 8km past the archway marking the Aragua State border. An alternative route back to Caracas is to take a *por puesto* jeep to La Victoria on a mountain road that descends 1,250m in 30km down a wide valley. From La Victoria, buses travel frequently to Caracas (1½ hours). The route passes a popular paragliding spot close to Colonia Tovar at Loma de Brisas. On weekends you can watch experienced pilots soar high above the valley or experience the adrenaline rush yourself on a short tandem flight.

Tourist information This is available from the **Instituto Autonomo de Turismo** (\ *0244 611 5123*), which has a kiosk by Plaza Bolívar, next to the church. This is the place to get maps and ask about scheduled events, parks, petroglyphs and a list of guesthouses and restaurants.

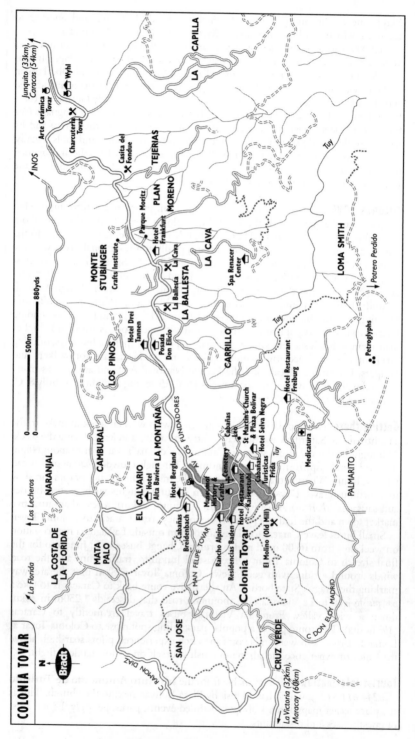

COLONIA TOVAR

N

Bradt

0   500m
0   880yds

Junquito (33km),
Caracas (54km)

INOS

LA CAPILLA

Wyhl

Arte Cerámica Tovar

Charcutería Tovar

Casita del Fondue

TEJERÍAS

PLAN MORENO

Parque Moritz

Hotel Frankfurt

MONTE STUBINGER

Crafts Institute

LA CAVA

La Cava

Spa Renacer Center

La Ballesta

LA BALLESTA

LOMA SMITH

Tuy

Potrero Perdido

Hotel Drei Tannen

Posada Don Elicio

LOS PINOS

CARRILLO

Tuy

Petroglyphs

Hotel Restaurant Freiburg

LOS FUNDADORES

Cabañas Leo

Cabañas
St Martin's Church & Plaza Bolívar
Hotel Selva Negra

LA MONTAÑA

Hotel Alta Baviera

Hotel Bergland

EL CALVARIO

CAMBURAL

NARANJAL

Los Lecheros

Museum of History & Crafts

Cemetery

Cabañas Turísticas Frida

Hotel Restaurant Kaierstuhl

Medicatura

PALMARITO

Cabañas Breidenbach

Rancho Alpino

Residencias Baden

Colonia Tovar

El Molino (Old Mill)

C MAN FELIPE TOVAR

MATA PALO

LA COSTA DE LA FLORIDA

La Florida

SAN JOSE

C RAMON DIAZ

CRUZ VERDE

C DON ELOY MADRID

La Victoria (32km),
Maracay (60km)

Tuy

122

The website www.coloniatovar.net also has information in Spanish on local sites, accommodation and restaurants.

🏠 **Where to stay** Set among hilly flower gardens, new hotels and cottages are expanding Colonia Tovar's roster of traditional lodgings. All have private bath and hot water and some offer bed and breakfast. Reservations with bank deposits are required for weekends and high season, especially the December–January holidays, when most places stipulate a two-day minimum stay and reservations up to two weeks in advance. Ask for discounts during the week. The larger guesthouses usually accept credit cards.

On the entrance road

🏠 **Posada Don Elicio** (11 rooms) Carretera Principal, entering village; ☎ 0244 355 1254; m 0414 308 9666, 0416 242 4248; e posadadonelicio@hotmail.com; www.posadadonelicio.com. A kind of Black-Forest boutique hotel, the dining area is tastefully decorated with antiques & dark wood furniture, the dining room has a fireplace for the cool nights & landscaped gardens have great views over the valley. Rooms are cosy, service is excellent; hot water, Wi-Fi, classical music. Reservation essential. $$$

🏠 **Hotel Drei Tannen** (9 rooms) On the right above the road; ☎ 0244 355 1264. This B&B option offers simple but cosy rooms & suites for 2–5 guests, attended by owner Rudolf Klampferer; hearty b/fasts home-cooked by Frau Klampferer. $

In the village

🏠 **Hotel Restaurant Freiburg** (9 rooms, 6 cabins) Calle E. Fon Keller; ☎ 0244 355 1313, 0244 417 5990; m 0414 333 5007; e freiburg@cantv.net. Located 700m beyond El Molino restaurant & the Tuy River bridge. Neat lawns & flowering shrubs, good views, rooms with hot water, heating, TV. There's a large, reasonable restaurant with nice German touches, open ⊕ midday–21.00. $$

🏠 **Rancho Alpino** (16 rooms) On the right as you turn down Calle Museo from the high street; ☎ 0244 355 1470; www.hotelranchoalpino.com. Large, clean rooms with hot water, TV, in B&B option with little local character. Traditional restaurant, with sausage, egg & cheese for b/fast. $$

🏠 **Cabañas Tuiristicas Frida** (6 rooms & cottages) Opposite El Molino restaurant; ☎ 0244 355 1033; m 0414 492 8725; e folc@cantv.net. Attractive option that only operates on w/ends & holidays. Rooms with TV, hot water, some with refrigerator & kitchen. $

By the church

🏠 **Hotel Restaurant Kaiserstuhl** (21 rooms) Calle Bolívar; ☎ 0244 355 1859. A block above the church, the Kaiserstuhl is a handsome structure with Germanic touches, Gothic letters & waitresses in Black-Forest fancy dress. 2 restaurants, terrace dining. Rooms rented with B&B, some gloomy, ask to see a couple before deciding. $$

🏠 **Hotel Selva Negra** (46 rooms) Located below the church down a short, steep driveway; ☎ 0244 355 1415, 0244 355 1715; e selvanegra@cantv.net; www.hotelselvanegra.com. Colonia Tovar's first (1938) & leading hotel has spacious grounds, beautiful views across the valley, a medium-sized swimming pool, sauna, heated carpeted bungalows, & a couple of very good restaurants with dark wood furniture & Germanic touches. It is now run by Ronald Gutmann, an enthusiastic chef & hotel manager who trained in Europe & has reinvigorated the menu with traditional recipes from the Black Forest region. A historic hotel that is worth a visit, even if you don't stay here. $$

🏠 **Cabañas Leo** (2 rooms, 3 cabins) Down from the plaza; ☎ 0244 355 1623; m 0414 110 1308. Well-kept rooms with TV, hot water & cabins for 5–6 people with kitchen. Owned by Leonidas de Rudman. $/$$

Upper sector

🏠 **Cabañas Breidenbach** (18 rooms) El Calvario; ☎ 0244 355 1211. In front of the Bergland & with fantastic views of Colonia Tovar. Rooms with hot water, TV, some cabins with kitchens. Wi-Fi, café, terrace. $$

Hotel Bergland (15 rooms) El Calvario; ☎ 0244 355 1229; e bergland@cantv.net. Located on the road out of Colonia Tovar to La Victoria, it has 7 heated cabins/houses in the pretty garden with panoramic views over the valley. B&B offered Mon–Thu only. Reservation essential. $$

Health spa
Spa Renacer Center, Quinta Mi Refugio Left from the main road down to La Cava sector; ☎ 0244 355 1504; m 0412 218 2811, 0414 331 0939; e renacerspacenter@cantv.net; www.renacerspa.com. This upmarket spa is the place for pricey pampering, aimed at mending spirit as well as body. Chocolate, honey & yoghurt treatments; massages to treat pain from migraines, muscle strain, cancer; therapies from aroma to laser & ultrasound are available. Pleasant gardens, fountains, music, outdoor jacuzzi, dining in a thatch-roofed *caney* – vegetarian & non-vegetarian options. Lodging in 8 bungalows, each with 3 sgl beds. Day plan without lodging (includes use of installations, some massages, treatments & lunch) is about US$100. Packages available. $$$$

Shopping On the way into Colonia Tovar, the **Charcutería Tovar** makes pickles, *knockwurst* (German seasoned sausage), smoked sausages and all kinds of picnic goodies. In the upper part of town you can buy Cerveza Tovar, which is no longer brewed here since the company expanded and moved to La Victoria. Liqueurs and wines made from strawberries and blackberries (*mora*) make good presents. All over Colonia Tovar there are shops and stalls selling mustards, sauces, sauerkraut, jam and biscuits. The market down by the church specialises in fresh local farm produce, such as garlic and apricots.

Festivals The **International Chamber Music Festival** held in March draws musicians and singers from Germany, Italy, the United States and even China to join Venezuelan chamber groups. The Selva Negra, Freiburg and other local hotels offer settings for this festival.

Carnival is high season when the Tovarenses take to the streets in costumes led by traditional *jokili*, or 'jesters', dressed in Mr Punch masks, belled caps and stripey outfits. The *jokili* have their own society and meeting place, the Jokili Heim, not far above the Edelweiss Hotel. **Founder's Day** is 8 April when the anniversary of the 1843 founding of Colonia Tovar is marked by cultural events. **Easter** and **Corpus Christi** are observed with processions and mass in many outlying *pueblos*.

No German village worth its sauerkraut would be without its beer-swilling **Oktoberfest** and Colonia Tovar does not disappoint. To keep things lively and inject extra authenticity, the German embassy brings over oompah groups for thigh-slapping good times. On 11 November, the day of Martín de Tours, the patron saint of Colonia Tovar, there is a craft, fruit and flower fair.

Other practicalities Access to the **internet** is available from Ciber Welt in the Mini Centro Gotingen at the top of town and Inversiones Das Glück, which is above the **Banco de Venezuela**, which has an ATM. Down by the church there is a communications centre with internet and phone booths for national and international calls.

In addition to Banco de Venezuela, the jeep tour firms and hotels can help with changing money if you get short.

There are a couple of pharmacies in town but any medical emergency would mean transfer back to a hospital or private clinic in Caracas.

What to see and do
Colonia Tovar on foot Walk along the high street, **Calle Codazzi**, from the arch. Besides souvenir and crafts shops you will find banks, a bakery and a supermarket. Among the small shops, don't miss the little *bodega* or general store called **La**

Siempre Viva near the far end. It's one of the few surviving structures from the horse-and-cart days and was built by Jacob Ruh in 1897. It is run by his granddaughter's family, the Breidenbachs. Relics of the past can be seen on weekends in Nestor Rojas's private **Museum of History and Crafts**, Calle Museo (🕐 *10.00–16.00*). The display includes photos of the early colonists, farm

A HARD LIFE FOR PIONEERS

Venezuela needed farmers to work the land after the devastating Independence wars. Don Martín Tovar, a congressman and supporter of immigration, put up a 60,000-peso loan to back a colony of Germans. His nephew, Manuel Felipe Tovar (later president of the country) set aside a mountain tract west of Caracas. Two foreigners were key to the settlement's success: Agustín Codazzi, an Italian geographer, and a young engraver from the Kaiserstuhl, mapmaker Alexander Benitz whom Codazzi had met in a Paris print shop. Together they visited sites in Venezuela at the government's request. Codazzi returned to France to hire the emigrants' ship and buy food and equipment such as a printing press and sawmill. Benitz signed up land-hungry peasants and craftsmen; he also signed on as an immigrant himself. On 11 January 1843, both Benitz and Codazzi sailed aboard the *Clemence* from Le Havre with the emigrants, in all 392.

Things did not go well. On the 52nd day of the voyage to La Guaira several lives were lost to smallpox, giving rise to a three-week quarantine on board. Luckily, Codazzi had the quarantine switched to a landing near Choroní. Next, the settlers shouldered their gear up the cordillera and over to Maracay. There they were welcomed with a big barbecue by the President of Venezuela, General José Antonio Páez. Páez offered some wagons to take women and children to La Victoria, the starting point for the trek up to Tovar. Skirting chasms and tripping over roots, the colonists, who now numbered 374, finally arrived on 8 April at a clearing where a few dismal huts stood among burnt stumps. Each settler was indebted for 2ha of this wilderness (children under one received 1ha), as well as for the voyage, food and gear.

The debt was interest-free and could be paid off in work. There were typesetters, carpenters, a blacksmith, shoemaker, tailor, baker, brewer (who made the first beer in Venezuela), barrel-maker and teacher. Classes began on the fourth day for some 80 children under the age of 14. As their leader and later mayor, Benitz helped the colonists tackle hardship, disease and isolation. He was named chief justice, replacing Codazzi – an army colonel who brought in soldiers to enforce the colonists' labours.

Desertions soon depleted the colony and among the first to go were the teacher, doctor and typesetter. The *Colonia Tovar Bulletin*, in German and Spanish, ceased publication. The priest from La Victoria came only once a year. Remote and unprotected, the colony was sacked during civil wars. A project to open a road to Caracas failed. The colonists worsened their isolation by banishing members who married outside and confiscating their lands. This led to inbreeding and cultural poverty. Illiteracy, once only 5%, grew to 40%.

However, new immigrants arrived and there were still leaders. One mother gave classes in reading and writing; her daughter helped a Swiss physician for two years, then treated the sick herself; botanist Karl Moritz led Bible studies and gave horticulture lessons. Coffee growing brought some degree of prosperity. But, even in the 20th century, teachers and priests sent from the outside world could not stick Tovar's rigidity. It was not until 1942, when Colonia Tovar became a township and Spanish became the official language, that land could be bought by anyone and colonists could marry freely. Finally, with the opening of an earth road to Caracas in 1950, Tovar's mulish isolation ended and Caraqueños 'discovered' Tovar.

tools, the original printing press that produced Venezuela's first newspaper, and even a petroglyph.

The **cemetery**, close to the museum, traces the colony's growth, with wooden crosses for early leaders such as mayor Alexander Benitz (d.1865) and botanist Karl Moritz (d.1866), who planted the cypress still growing here; and marble mausoleums for later prosperous residents. The earliest gravestone is that of Joseph Müssle who died in May 1843.

Iglesia de San Martín de Tours, an attractive black-and-white building with a tower built in 1862, is named after the colony's patron saint. During the *fiestas patronales* on 11 November and the closest weekend, the statue of St Martin, which was brought from Germany by the colonists, is taken out in procession. The church's black timbers make it unique in Venezuela. Although the rebuilt tower has some painted 'beams', the wall and windows next to the bell tower are original. Inside, you will see the twin naves that once separated men from women.

Among Tovar's oldest wooden houses are the **Villa Jahn** where mapmaker Agustín Codazzi lived and the 1846 **Benitz House**, now the Muuhstall Café. Alexander Benitz, guiding spirit of the colony, had a brewery (the first in Venezuela), print shop and store in his house, today Colonia Tovar's oldest structure.

Jeep tours Two tour companies offer similar excursions in 4x4 vehicles to the Parque Nacional Codazzi, nearby petroglyph sites. In low season they can arrange visits to the village of El Jarillo (a smaller, less touristy version of Colonia Tovar founded 100 years ago by German settlers), and the beaches of Puerto Maya, Puerto Cruz and Chichiriviche, for a minimum of four people. The cost per person varies with group size and time, from about US$10–40.

Regenwald Tours 2nd flr at Novedades Burkheim shop, Calle Bolívar; \ 0244 355 1662; m 0416 646 8497, 0416 234 7857; e regenwald@ cantv.net. Tours to local sites in distinctive red-&-black vehicles. Can help with renting apartments, cabins, camping, paragliding, mountain biking or estimates for transfers anywhere by car.

Rustic Tours At the entrance to town by the arch; \ 0244 355 1908; m 0416 740 0255; e rustictours@cantv.net. Tours to the cloudforest of the Pico Codazzi Natural Monument (2hrs), giant cedar, visits to strawberry & apricot farms, pottery factory or petroglyphs in jeeps.

Hike to the petroglyphs During his field trips in 1844, naturalist Hermann Karsten found the way to a set of carved boulders known as the **Piedras de Los Indios** in a place called **Potrero Perdido**. Nobody has been able to date or decipher the meaning of these petroglyphs of anthropomorphic and zoomorphic figures, but they were made by local Indians long before the arrival of Europeans. It's a good walk of some 14km round trip to Potrero Perdido, starting downhill from the church, following the signs to the Medicatura. At the first fork turn right and follow a steep concrete road passing the Evangelist chapel. Cross the bridge over the upper Tuy and continue, keeping left on the road and asking everybody you meet along the way for directions. The views back over the valley and Colonia Tovar are worth the walk. After climbing through coffee farms and gardens, the road comes to a building with a bridge; turn right up to Potrero Perdido (5km from Tovar) and the petroglyphs are close to some abandoned buildings. Unfortunately, someone has painted the petroglyphs a gaudy blue, probably to photograph the incised designs. If you don't want to walk, Rustic Tours and Regenwald Tours drive up here (see above).

Codazzi Natural Monument Feeding the watersheds of rivers in Vargas, Aragua and Miranda states, Codazzi Peak at 2,429m is one of the highest in the Cordillera de la Costa. This natural monument is particularly important because its 11,850ha provide an ecological corridor linking Parque Nacional Macarao in Miranda State with the Parque Nacional Henri Pittier in Aragua State. Its upper cloudforests are largely undisturbed, sheltering in their cathedral gloom elegant tree ferns, philodendrons and orchids. Rainfall is plentiful, some 2,000–4,000mm a year. One giant Spanish cedar is so imposing that it draws admirers from many lands: clouds veil the canopy 60m up, the trunk has a circumference of 8m, and, on the ground, the giant's base measures 35m around.

You have only to ask at the Alta Baviera or Edelweiss hotels for paths uphill to strawberry fields near the INOS watertanks, to the chapel of the Virgen de los Dolores, named after an image the settlers brought from the Black Forest, or to the woods by an area called Los Lecheros.

For **Codazzi Peak** take the road out of town towards La Victoria. After about 3.5km, where a cross stands by the road, go right (left for Capachal). Less than ten minutes uphill where the road goes over a brook, look on the left for a path leading through bamboos. The walk through woods and shrubs to the top takes half an hour. The view is breathtaking when clear: east to Naiguatá Peak above Caracas, north to the sea, west as far as Lake Valencia.

Paragliding Halfway down the hill from Colonia Tovar to La Victoria, paragliders gather on Fridays, Saturdays and Sundays at Loma Brisa (Windy Hill), also known as Placivel. You can watch the pilots gently swoop and pirouette in the sky overhead or join the group in the Casa de Los Parapentes, where there is a sandwich and juice bar. Orlando Leyton and Marisabel Nouel who run this two-storey centre have a paragliding school called **Soaring** (\ *0212 985 0418;* e *soaring@cantv.net; www.volarparapente.com.ve*). No experience is needed to take an adrenaline-boosting tandem flight with an instructor. Anybody wanting to fly should weigh no more than 100kg and wear training shoes and a sweater or warm top. Flights last about 15 minutes, depending on the wind and thermals. Soaring also run five-hour courses over four weekends, offering enough theory and practice for solo flying, accompanied by an instructor on a radio.

Colonia Tovar to the sea on foot There are long walks from Colonia Tovar down to the Costa Maya coast, mostly along jeep tracks, but unless you can hitch a ride, transport back is a problem. British tour guide and paraglider **Douglas Pridham** (m *0416 743 8939;* e *trekadventure@gmail.com*) – who is based in Colonia when he's not hiking up Roraima or leading jungle expeditions to meet the isolated Shirian tribe – organises hikes down to Tuja and Cepe, in Aragua State. The three-day excursion, sleeping in the forest in tents, is mostly downhill. Doug drives the first 50km in a jeep to a cloudforest camp at the trailhead called Las Caras (The Faces), named for dozens of boulders covered in petroglyphs. The next day, walking for seven hours, hikers reach the cacao groves and old plantation house of Cepe about 5km from the sea. At the beach, trekkers stay at the *posada* of a marine biologist, before travelling by fishing boat to Choroní where a car awaits for the return drive.

BY ROAD TO PUERTO CRUZ DEL LIMÓN, PUERTO MAYA AND CHICHIRIVICHE DE LA COSTA
If exploring by car, remember to fill up first because there are no services at all on the paved roads down to the sea. From the petrol station at the Aragua State arch, the road descends through cool forests down to coffee groves shaded by tall *bucares*, the immortelle trees whose blooms are a vivid coral colour in February and March. On the coast are the villages of Puerto Cruz, Puerto Maya and Chichiriviche de la Costa.

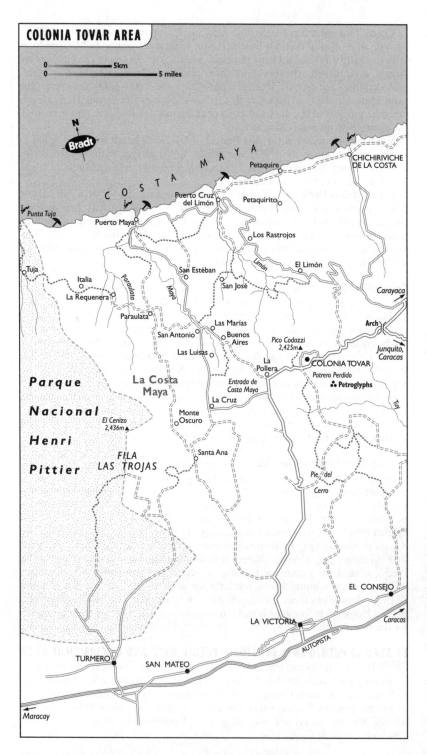

COLONIA TOVAR AREA

0 ————— 5km
0 ————————— 5 miles

N
Bradt

C O S T A   M A Y A

Petaquire

CHICHIRIVICHE
DE LA COSTA

Punta Tuja

Puerto Cruz
del Limón

Petaquirito

Puerto Maya

Los Rastrojos

Limón

El Limón

Carayaca

Tuja

Italia

La Requenera

San Estéban

San José

Arch

Paraulata

Paraulata

Maya

Junquito,
Caracas

San Antonio

Las Marías

Buenos
Aires

Pico Codazzi
2,425m ▲

COLONIA TOVAR

Las Luisas

La
Pollera

Potrero Perdido

Petroglyphs

Tuy

Parque

Nacional

Henri

Pittier

La Costa
Maya

El Cenizo
2,436m ▲

Entrada de
Costa Maya

Monte
Oscuro

La Cruz

*FILA
LAS TROJAS*

Santa Ana

Pie del
Cerro

EL CONSEJO

LA VICTORIA

Caracas

TURMERO

SAN MATEO

AUTOPISTA

Maracay

El Limón to Puerto Cruz This road has more twists than a snake so allow four hours or more for the round trip if you plan on returning to Colonia Tovar. The distance is 43km to the tranquil little bay of Puerto Cruz. This is one of the most beautiful drives on the coast as clouds roll down dramatically from the heights to forested flanks above steep valleys, and mist outlines vines, orchids and bromeliads on huge trees. Halfway down is the coffee hacienda of El Limón; there are few other communities and no restaurants, although people in Puerto Cruz prepare fried fish for weekend visitors.

As you drive down to the beach look for a sign on the right-hand side that says 'Museo de Petroglifos' or 'Panarigua', about 20km down from the arch at Aragua State. The small house shaded by huge trees and surrounded by flowers and birds was the home of retired archaeologist Luis Laffer who died in 2000. Margarita, his gracious widow, will show you around his small but interesting collection of prehistoric pots, shards and stone axes. The house has a wealth of books and sound recordings. Luis Laffer, a Hungarian, spent much of his life recording and cataloguing the native music of Venezuela, from Barlovento to Sinamaica. In El Limón he catalogued the area's many petroglyphs. If you have time, ask Margarita how to get to local sites, especially the spectacular ridge on the other side of the valley, crossing the river, where there is a cluster of large stones engraved with jaguars and faces.

Puerto Cruz del Limón This remote fishing village offers a near crescent beach of fine sand, with a few trees that are good for hanging hammocks. Some houses in the village rent rooms so if you want to stay, ask around. The bay and beach are largely deserted from Monday to Friday except for fishermen. Local ladies make *empanadas* and serve fried fish and *tostones* (fried bananas) on weekends to the regular beach-goers.

A stony, tortuous jeep track crosses the sun-baked promontory eastward to Chichiriviche de la Costa (25km) but it is not recommended as there is no help if you get into difficulties. Another track leads west to Puerto Maya; it's 16km and a lot better. You can also hire a fishing boat to take you the 25 minutes to Puerto Maya. Ask for Chencho, who guards cars for guests at Posada Punta Maya. A return boat trip to Puerto Maya costs about US$25 round trip, shared by up to six passengers. Pay half on arrival and the other half on the way back.

Puerto Maya This picturesque fishing village in a narrow, crescent bay, with high bluffs falling into the sea on either side, is on the edge of the Parque Nacional Henri Pittier in Aragua State. The road from Puerto Cruz del Limón is steep in parts, but quite good. However, it's more fun and faster to get a fishing boat to take you from there. As you skirt the coast in a small boat under cliffs sculpted by the surf, you slip into another time: one framed by the sea, steep headlands and the rising cordillera walls. As you arrive in Puerto Maya you see a dozen colourful fishing boats moored in the bay; on the sand fishermen mend nets. Under coconut palms a street doubles as a basketball court; school is out and children are everywhere. During the holidays, the villagers set up shacks selling fish, beer and *empanadas* and the beach fills with hammocks and tents. At night the locals sing call-and-response songs inspired by African rhythms played on the *cumaco* drums – made from hollow avocado trunks – in the same style as Chuao and Choroní. In Puerto Maya everyone seems to be related, like one big family, and houses are placed wherever their owners decide. There is no Plaza Bolívar and no founding date; just two small *abastos* (groceries), one policeman and one chapel, which is always open.

As a fishing community, Puerto Maya until recently had few land visitors; there is still no link with mountain cultures such as Colonia Tovar. These are black people and they live well off the sea. The price of fish is high in La Guaira, less than

5

two hours away, and that is where the fishermen go to sell their catch, refill, buy clothes and supplies, or seek hospital care. New fibreglass *lanchas* are bought in Tacarigua de la Laguna where they are made.

The women meanwhile tend maize, yuca, pigs and chickens. Descendants of African slaves, the people of Maya laugh, dance, play the big drums and drink quarts of alcohol at Carnival and traditional *fiestas* such as San Juan, a three-day party in honour of Saint John the Baptist around 24 June, and the *fiesta* for Archangel Michael, the patron saint, on 24 September.

Behind the village, the Río Maya rushes between boulders on its way to the sea. Walk up beside the river to fine pools for bathing and the Pozo de los Perros, a rock-slide into a deep pool. When the water level is too high it's best avoided, but in the dry season this natural feature set in the tropical forest is more magical than any theme park could dream up. The pure mountain water in Puerto Maya is so sought after it is pumped through a pipeline to supply Catia and La Guaira. The villagers see this as fair because in return they get their electricity.

Where to stay and eat You can pitch a tent on the beach, hang a hammock or ask around the village for a house to rent. On the seafront, some villagers rent out simple rooms with fan.

Posada Punta Maya (8 rooms) m 0414 114 4216, 0414 922 7799, 0412 639 3607; e puntamaya@hotmail.com; www.puntamaya.blogspot.com. The only proper lodging option in town, this comfortable guesthouse with restaurant at the beach's western edge is run by the Lemoine family. Rooms have fan, private bath with hot water & packages (US$35pp, low season) include hearty b/fasts & dinner. Special dishes such as lobster are extra. The Lemoines can arrange for car transfer from Caracas or a boat from Puerto Cruz, scuba diving & local excursions. There is a little restaurant, La Negra, serving *pargo* (red snapper), *mero* (grouper), paella & shellfish. Alternatively, buy your fish from the fishermen. $-$$

Chichiriviche de la Costa
The road from the Colonia Tovar arch follows the Puerto Cruz road, taking a turn-off at the second right after 10km (the first fork goes to Carayaca). The next 25km offers fine views of farms, mountains and sea. On the last stage, which is a protected watershed, ferns and heliconias proliferate by the road; there are fewer dwellings. Because this part is not paved and crosses the tumbling Chichiriviche River many times (some concrete aprons but no access ramps), a car with ample clearance is needed. The road and river, which even has hot springs, come out at a growing beach community on a clean crescent bay enclosed by promontories. The village, church and coffee-drying patio of Chichiriviche proper are set back 1km from the sea. There is good fried fish to be had.

Stands of immense mahoganies shade houses behind the beach. At the east entrance there is a well-stocked food and liquor shop called La Parada. But no public transportation stops here, or anywhere. In order to continue to Catia or Maiquetía, you must have a car.

Whales have been sighted off this coast. The sperm whale is more or less resident, while the humpback comes from the north in winter and as many as 20 have been seen only 200m offshore. When this happens, you can approach in a fishing boat for a closer look. Ask **ChiDivers** (see opposite) for the best time to see whales.

Where to stay and eat

Hotel & Restaurant El Montero (14 rooms) 3 blocks from the beach at the east entrance; \ 0212 311 1751; m 0412 964 1200; e info@ elmontero.com; www.elmontero.com. The first lodging option in the village & still the best is this German-run *posada* with dbl & trpl rooms, private baths (mostly with cold water); also a cabin for 6 with equipped kitchen, dining area, swimming pool. The cost of rooms includes b/fast & dinner, lobster from the fish tank is extra. Specialise in scuba-diving courses, submersions. Owner Bruno Sponsel will arrange excursions with fishermen. $$

🏠 **Posada La Quilla** (9 rooms) ✆ 0212 345 1153; e lrojasmac@cantv.net. Better known locally as La

Posada de Loli. The 2-floor house with garden & parking in the rear is located a block from the sea. Loli & her husband offer rooms for 2–8 guests, some with AC, private bath, aimed at divers. There's also a restaurant where Loli cooks up a storm. The room price includes 2 meals; w/end rates cover 1 night & 4 meals. Call for information about transfer service from Caracas. $$

What to do

Scuba diving Excellent underwater banks account for Chichiriviche's growing fame as the best diving area on the Vargas coast. Fishermen will take you out to Banco Los Arenales, Los Barriles or Noche y Día.

↙**ChiDivers** ✆ 0212 731 1556, 0212 731 1410; m 0416 623 9551; e info@chidivers.com.ve; www.chidivers.com.ve. Run by José Antonio Rodriguez, a very experienced dive instructor who also has an office in Caracas, this dive centre offers SSI courses

from Try Scuba to Open Water & advanced. The 2-storey dive centre is in the middle of the village & has 8 rooms offering beds for 30, with hot showers, fan & AC. Just an hour from Maiquetía, transfers from Caracas arranged.

6

Los Roques, Morrocoy and Mochima

THE ROBINSON CRUSOE EXPERIENCE

With the longest coastline in the Caribbean, Venezuela is blessed with more than its fair share of beautiful beaches and warm seas. But to live out a *Blue Lagoon* castaway fantasy of having an island all to yourself, with nothing on the horizon but a green fringe of mangroves and calm, crystalline waters protected by coral reefs, then you need to head for Los Roques, Morrocoy and Mochima. Safely tucked away to the south of the Caribbean's hurricane belt, enjoying year-round sun and a stable climate, these three island chains have been declared national parks to protect their fragile ecosystems of coral reefs, mangroves, turtles and teeming undersea life.

The Los Roques Archipelago lies about 150km off the coast of La Guaira and can only be reached by air or sea, making it the most expensive option, albeit the most breathtaking. Much more affordable trips can be made to the islands of Morrocoy in Falcón State, which are reached by fast launches from the mainland towns of Tucacas or Chichiriviche, and to Mochima, in Anzoátegui State, which is accessible from a number of points on the mainland, including Puerto La Cruz, Santa Fé and the fishing village of Mochima.

PLANNING A VISIT

All three island groups have established tourism infrastructures in place and offer a range of services to travellers depending on which islands are visited. If you intend to camp, make sure to pack emergency food and water as the itinerant vendors who operate on some of the islands may fail to show up when expected. For Los Roques, the 10kg luggage restrictions on all flights can make it difficult to bring sufficient supplies for camping, and visitors should take this into account when planning their trip.

After water, which is essential, the most important consideration is the **sun**. White coral beaches and silvery seas reflect the sun's rays, increasing the risk of sunburn, while cool breezes can mask the danger signs. Be warned: more than one sun-seeker has overdone it on the first day and been laid up with painful burns in a darkened room for days afterwards because they didn't take adequate precautions. On the islands the sun can be fierce and unrelenting, and if you're dependent on a fisherman to pick you up then be aware that they are notorious for turning up late, leaving you to fry. A floppy hat is an essential requirement and sunglasses will help to ease the midday glare. It's important to put on sunblock before you set out on any boat trips and make sure to slather cream onto tender spots, such as the backs of knees and the tops of feet, which rarely get this kind of exposure. Take plenty of suncream (minimum SPF15) and reapply after each immersion in the sea, and use a total sunblock or zinc cream for nose, lips and ears. After 10.00 newcomers and young children should wear an old T-shirt, especially when snorkelling, and bring loose, light clothes to cover up with when the sun gets too much. Make sure you have some kind of sunshade with you, even if it's just a sarong or large towel you can tie to a couple of sticks. If you can afford a beach umbrella, rent one before you get on the boat to your island. Take hammocks if there are trees big enough on your island destination as this will also give you a break from the sun.

Take plenty of repellent for the sandflies and mosquitoes that come out around 17.00 as the sun starts to go down and avoid the windless months of October to mid-January, when tiny biting midges can make camping miserable, or even intolerable, after sundown as they pass through the finest netting. There are many cases of fishermen having to rescue campers who have spent the night in the sea to escape these *puri-puri* or 'no-see-'ems'.

Finally, try to plan your stay to avoid long weekends and school holidays when even remote beaches get invaded by Venezuelan sun-seekers and your peaceful, paradise island can turn into a noisy, all-day drinking party.

PARQUE NACIONAL ARCHIPELAGO LOS ROQUES

There are travellers who have been known to fly into Venezuela at Maiquetía and immediately board a waiting plane for Los Roques. Ten days later, having explored the keys by fishing boat and spent their days swimming, snorkelling, diving, kitesurfing, bonefishing, or just idly sailing around the archipelago, they go home to Europe, Canada or the USA without so much as a glance at Caracas. Antonio Banderas, Naomi Campbell, Leonardo DiCaprio and Colombian hip-shaker Shakira are just some of the A-list celebrities who have fallen for the charms of Los Roques and it's easy to see why. Virtually uninhabited except for the main island and entry point of Gran Roque, the marine park shares many similarities with the coral atolls of the Pacific, comprising about 50 named islands and keys and a further 200 or so sandbanks, rocky bumps and coral reefs set in shallow translucent seas. The archipelago curves 46km east to west, and 26.6km north to south, an extension of 2,250km² of islands and sea. It was declared a national park in 1972.

Gran Roque is the main entry point, the only island of any size and the only place offering accommodation in *posadas*. It lies some 156km north of La Guaira, the closest port to Caracas, and is reached by small charter planes and regular services from Maiquetía and Porlamar in Margarita.

All the islands except Gran Roque, which rises to a hill of 130m, are low lying with fine coral sands, scrubby vegetation offering little shade and with water temperatures in the shallows reaching a bath-like 30°C. Barrier reefs in the east and south drop off into ocean water 500–1,000m deep, offering exceptional coral walls for divers to explore. The birdlife is also impressive with frigate birds wheeling overhead and pelicans plummeting into the sea to dive for fish, while brown boobies like nothing more than to bob in rows on the sand.

Well appointed, with pretty-but-pricey *posadas* and a few budget options on the main island of Gran Roque, Los Roques is so breathtaking that after a week surrounded by turquoise water, reefs and birds you may not want to leave.

WILDLIFE The archipelago is home to 42 species of birds from petrels, pelicans, frigate birds and flamingos to canaries. A further 50 migratory visitors come to spend the winter, or touch down on their way south. Selesquí, Bequevé, Canquises and Cayo Bobo Negro are noted for birdlife.

There are funny little black lizards (*Cnemidophorus lemmiscatus nigricolor*) who will nibble your toes if you fall asleep on the beach, but no snakes and no native land mammals except for a fishing bat. Four native turtle species are all on the endangered list, the most persecuted being the green turtle (*Chelonia mydas*).

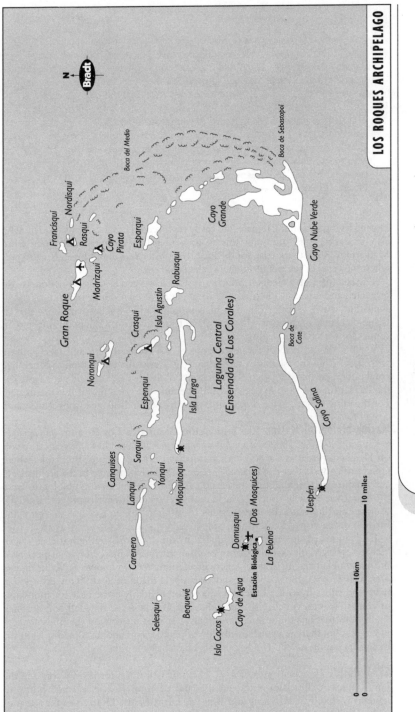

LOS ROQUES ARCHIPELAGO

The islands' odd names come largely from old English map makers who turned the Indian *cayo* into 'key'; these names were then borrowed back into Spanish. *Espenquí* evolved from Spanish Key, *Lanquí* Long Key, *Sarquí* Salt Key, *Nordisquí* Northeast Key, *Selesquí* Sails Key, *Esparquí* Spar Key, *Rabusquí* Robert's Key and *Domusquí* from Domain Key. *Uespén* was once West Point and *Cayo Mosquito* was Musket Key. *Madrizquí* is different; it was called Namusquí or Rataquí until the 1960s when a man named Juancho Madriz got a 100-year concession to develop the island for tourism. He died in 1972 but his heirs sold these rights to some powerful Caracas families who built weekend houses there. Besides this key, the only permanently inhabited islands are Gran Roque, Francisquí with its tourist camp, fishing settlements on Isla Fernando and Pirata, and the biological station on Dos Mosquises (Domusquí).

During laying season the females are easily captured on beaches by fishermen, who also steal the eggs, although this is now illegal. Fishermen still come from Margarita, 300km to the east, for the lucrative lobster season in November to April, when they stay in temporary shelters called *rancherías*.

The beautiful queen conch, which was once harvested to near extinction, is also protected and it is now illegal to sell or eat conch (*botuto*). Huge mounds of conch shells line many islands. Valued as high-protein food, conches have been part of island diet since prehistory, when mainland tribes from near Valencia came here in canoes for seasonal harvesting.

Visitors should respect the regulations of the national park and take nothing with them from the islands or reefs they visit. Resist the temptation to touch live coral underwater or drag your feet across it. Firstly because you will get a nasty cut that is painful and slow to heal, secondly because the coral dies if it is mistreated. For the same reason, make sure your boatman doesn't drop anchor over the coral.

Marine biological station The **Fundación Científica Los Roques** (*headquarters in Caracas;* \ *0212 892 8868; www.fundacionlosroques.org*) operates a biological station on Dos Mosquises in the southern archipelago. There are breeding tanks where green turtles and other endangered species are raised for release in the archipelago, and a nature trail highlighting the island's ecosystems. The station's biologists were the first to raise queen conch larvae in captivity. Visitors are welcome on Saturdays, Sundays and holidays. Boat excursions from Gran Roque to Cayo de Agua, the furthest of the visited keys, usually stop here.

Excavations made on Dos Mosquises in the 1980–90s by Venezuelan–Polish archaeologists Marlena and Andrzej Antczak uncovered incredibly well-preserved pre-Colombian clay figurines – many in a feminine form known as Venus figures – as well as pots, tools, spoons and ornaments made of shell. This proves that mainland tribes from the Lake Valencia region regularly came here for thousands of years to harvest conch, fish and gather salt. It is believed they left empty conch shells in formations to capture scarce rainwater. The majority of the finds are kept in Caracas but there is a small exhibition of photographs and texts on display at the biological station called 'The Sacred Isle of Prehistoric Venezuela'.

GRAN ROQUE (*Telephone code: 0237*) The only island not formed by corals in the Los Roques Archipelago is the main island of Gran Roque, a small hump of igneous rock only 3.5km long and 1km wide. It rises just 130m from the sea at its highest point and is topped with an old lighthouse, like a wonky birthday cake.

About half of the native Roqueños make a living from fishing, the rest from tourism, and there are an incredible number of Italians, who run the majority of the town's upmarket *posadas*.

Gran Roque is expensive; some would say unjustifiably so. Everything has to come from the mainland – the food mostly by air, as the supply boat comes only twice weekly. Commercial fishing is prohibited in the park, so sometimes your fish dinner may come from La Guaira.

Everything is packed into Gran Roque's six little sandy streets, where you find a Guardia Nacional post, a Plaza Bolívar, a primary school, a medical dispensary, a bar, a couple of restaurants, a food shop, a pizza parlour, a kiosk selling *arepas*, a small disco and a bank. Best of all, the island is traffic-free – the only vehicles being a water truck, a rubbish truck and a few golf carts used by the *posadas*. Telephone service is provided by cellular companies with fixed terminals and there are a couple of shops offering internet services, although the connection is erratic. Given the growing demands of tourism, a new desalination plant and generator have been brought in to provide more water and electricity, allowing the use of air conditioners at last. Other improvements are also underway. With the aid of a Spanish co-operation agency, Gran Roque has become the first Venezuelan town to classify its solid waste for recycling and there is an ecological furnace for other waste.

The governing body in the islands is the **Autoridad Unica Los Roques** (\ *0212 408 2050;* e *secretaria@losroques.gov.ve*).

History Occupied seasonally for centuries by native tribes from the mainland who came here to fish and gather salt, Los Roques was used as a bolt hole by Caribbean pirates in the 17th and 18th centuries. The Dutch then moved in from the neighbouring Netherlands Antilles and exploited salt, guano and a dye taken from the red mangroves, until the beginning of the 20th century, when Venezuela began to exercise its sovereignty over the island and the Dutch were eased out. For Venezuelans, the modern history of Los Roques begins in 1906 when a woman named Gabriela Estrada first settled in Gran Roque. She was followed by fishermen from Margarita, drawn by the abundant lobster and fish. In those days, all fresh water had to be brought in on navy ships and life was hard.

As recently as 1987 there were only 807 people in the archipelago, a quarter of them temporary fishermen. However, in the 1990s the number of permanent residents doubled as Los Roques entered the tourism market in a big way, especially following the arrival of the Italians who began to improve the accommodation on offer. All materials, even construction sand and water, had to be imported from the mainland as the village grew from a dozen humble, tin-roofed fishermen's houses to nearly 60 *posadas* and guesthouses. The current population is about 1,800.

Getting there and away Although it is possible to find a small fishing boat to Los Roques from La Guaira, it is not recommended. The crossing against sea currents takes some 12 hours, the diesel engines stink and roar without relief and seas can be rough. Air travel is the way to go. Reservations can be made through any travel agency for daily flights from the national terminal in Maiquetía, although agencies will try to sell you a tour. The only two airlines with regular scheduled flights are Aereotuy (\ *0212 212 3110; www.tuy.com*) and Chapi Air (\ *0212 355 1349; www.chapiair.com*). Aereotuy's turboprops leave from the national terminal at Maiquetía Airport at 06.00 and 08.30 and take about 30 minutes; smaller planes flown by Chapi Air leave at 08.30 and take up to 45 minutes. Both airlines have an afternoon flight at 16.00, giving passengers arriving on international flights the chance to get a same-day transfer to the islands. The alternative is a night in a hotel

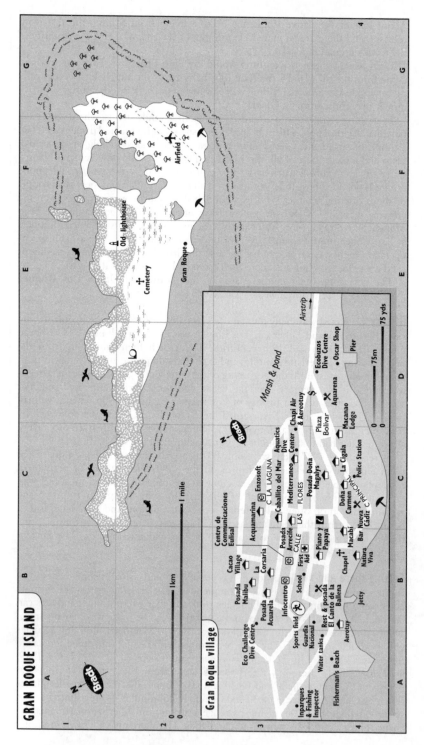

GRAN ROQUE ISLAND

0 1 km
0 1 mile

Gran Roque village

Cemetery

Old lighthouse

Airfield

Gran Roque

75m
75 yds

Eco Challenge Dive Centre

Posada Malibu

Posada Acuarela

Cacao Village

Infocentro

La Corsaria

Centro de Communicaciones Eulisal

Acquamarina

Enzosoft

C LA LAGUNA

Caballito del Mar

Aquatics Dive Center

Chapi Air & Aereotuy

Ecobuzos Dive Centre

School

First Aid

Posada Arrecife

CALLE LAS

Mediterraneo

FLORES

Posada Doña Magalys

Oscar Shop

Sports field

Guardia Nacional

Rest & posada El Canto de la Ballena

Piano y Papaya

Plaza Bolivar

Macanao Lodge

Aquarena

Pier

Water tanks

Chapel

Macabi

Natura Viva

Doña Carmen

La Cigala

Police Station

Aerotuy

Bar Nueva Cadiz

PRINCIPAL

Airstrip

Fisherman's Beach

Jetty

Inparques & Fishing Inspector

Marsh & pond

Bradt

138

close to the airport (see *Chapter 5, Maiquetía Airport hotels*, page 119). Return flights from Los Roques leave for Maiquetía at 17.00 with an extra flight at 16.00 on weekends. One-way fares from Maiquetía are about US$100–130 on weekdays and US$130–150 at weekends, depending on season. From Porlamar in Margarita, Aereotuy charges about US$165. Children aged two to 12 years get 30–50% off. Ask about discounts. All passengers must carry an identity card, or passport and tourist card.

On arrival in Gran Roque all visitors must pay a parks fee of US$5 for residents and US$20 for non-residents at the Inparques kiosk by the landing strip, which covers the duration of their stay. (Also see *Taking a tour*, below.)

☞ **WARNING:** It is not uncommon for passengers leaving Los Roques to be kept waiting on the airstrip. As Gran Roque has no landing lights, and therefore no night flights, you may find yourself leaving the next morning. Do not plan an escapade to Los Roques just before your international flight.

Getting around Once on Gran Roque you can negotiate with local fishermen at the little dock or *muelle* for a *peñero* ride to the islands. The further away you go from Gran Roque, the more isolated the keys and the more expensive the trip. A large group of six or more is needed to visit the more remote islands. All the prices for return trips are written on a board so if you want to haggle, walk up the beach and speak to the fishermen. Larger groups have more chance of getting a bargain so search around for other tourists to make up numbers. Always check whether the price includes beach chairs and parasols, and specify the time you want to be picked up.

The most popular and closest islands are the cheapest to visit with Madrizquí, Francisquí and Rasquí at US$5–6 for a round trip (7–10 minutes), Crasquí, Noronquíses and Rabusquí, US$13 (25 minutes), Sarquí and Espenquí US$16 (35 minutes), Carrenero, US$18 (45 minutes) and Cayo de Agua US$27 (1½ hours). Ask the boatman to point out the best snorkelling spots on each island as you arrive.

Taking a tour One way to visit is on a full-day or two-day/one-night tour, organised by the airline or by individual *posadas*. All-inclusive tours include flight, lodging, meals, soft drinks and beach excursions to Francisquí or Madrizquí with a picnic lunch, beach umbrellas and chairs; masks and flippers are available at extra cost. Aereotuy is the pioneer of these kinds of packages and has its own catamaran to ferry passengers to the islands, which has the added bonus of being a shady place to escape to if the sun gets too hot. Once paid for, day tours cannot be changed and are not refundable in case of cancellation. The cost of a two-day package is US$300–360 depending on choice of lodgings: standard or superior. This means that if you arrive on the morning flight you get dinner, one night's lodging and leave the next day after lunch (two meals). In other words you are paying over US$100 more than for the day tour but can spend only half a day more exploring beaches. While lower-priced packages may seem attractive, they usually only involve tourists being ferried to the closest possible beach on Francisquí to follow a line of fellow bathers snorkelling around an overworked reef and seeing little of paradise. Meals at standard guesthouses may also be disappointing in view of the high prices and tours are even more expensive at weekends and in the high season during Christmas, Easter and Carnival. However, if you have only a day to experience Los Roques a tour is the best option.

If you have more than two days to play with and someone who will share expenses, make your own tour: buy a flight-only ticket, stay in a cheap *posada* (see page 141) and rent a boat to explore different islands each day such as

Crasquí or Carenero, where you will be able to buy fried fish. Fishing boats leave from the jetty by Oscar Shop [138 D4] and prices for all the islands are clearly displayed.

Where to stay Italians have a love affair with Los Roques. You hear Italian everywhere you go: by the dock and in the dive centres, restaurants and guesthouses. Many Italians have opened small *posadas*, bought launches and now show tourists the sights of Los Roques. There are now over 50 *posadas* with two to 15 rooms, jostling elbow-to-elbow in eye-catching Mediterranean colours on Gran Roque's six streets. Facilities vary greatly in quality, particularly the meals, with memorable cuisine offered by some deluxe guesthouses and fried fish and rice the norm in others. Air conditioning and hot water are still rare, but the sea breeze is constant and the water is never too cold for a shower. Reservations are advised for all small guesthouses, even during the low season (as owners may otherwise attend to business on the mainland). Some guesthouses will quote an all-inclusive price covering a range of options, from breakfast only or breakfast and dinner, to all meals and a picnic lunch for the beach, plus a launch service to the closest beach (usually Francisquí). If you want to be free to arrange your own beach transportation, specify room rates *sin lancha a las playas*. Many *posadas* on the abbreviated list below have weekday discounts. Always check if taxes are included in quoted prices.

Upper range

Aereotuy [138 B4] (65 rooms) \ 0212 212 3110; e sramirez@tuy.com; www.tuy.com. The main airline bringing in tourists is also the biggest accommodation provider with rooms ranging from standard to superior, offered as part of inclusive tours. Packages for 2 days/1 night cost around US$150–200 (in addition to air ticket), depending on high/mid/low seasons; this price covers insurance, bilingual guide & outings in Aereotuy's catamarans. Children aged 2–12 pay half price. Ask about low-season offers & remember that it is possible to pay for just B&B. Aereotuy's *posadas* are: **Las Palmeras,** the **Macabí** near the church, the costlier **Posada La Plaza,** & **Vistalmar,** on the beach. $$$

Macanao Lodge [138 C4] (8 rooms) \ 0237 221 1301; m 0414 906 1612; e lodge@ macanaolodge.com; www.macanaolodge.com. Facing the beach near the airstrip, this deluxe guesthouse features lovely Caribbean-style woodwork & tiles, a patio garden & roof terrace with sea views. $$$

Mediterraneo [138 C3] (6 rooms) m 0414 215 2292, 0424 829 4509; e info@ posadamediterraneo.com, infoposadamediterraneo@gmail.com; www.posadamediterraneo.com. A former Italian lawyer, Elena Battani, runs this immaculate *posada* with white Mediterranean interiors & dark wood furniture as if it were a boutique hotel, taking the upmarket Los Roques *posada* experience to its upper limit. À la carte meals served on white

tablecloths by candlelight on romantic roof terrace. Rooms have AC, TV & en suite, & there is a large water tank & generator. Prices good for level of comfort. $$$

Natura Viva [138 B4] (14 rooms) \ 0237 221 1035; m 0414 274 1231, 0414 236 8082; e info@naturavivalosroques.com, posadanaturaviva@hotmail.com; www.naturavivalosroques.com. The ochre & terracotta tones here complement the larger space at this very swanky *posada*, which is more like a hotel, with its central dining area & rooftop bar in the shape of a boat with sea views. Pricey but comfortable, it has its own boat & passengers can leave for trips from the beach behind. $$$

Posada & Restaurant Acuarela [138 B3] (11 rooms) \ 0237 221 1436, 0237 221 1456; m 0414 932 3501; e airmundo@cantv.net. Angelo Belvedere runs this *posada* with an interior garden, beautiful rooms & suites on 2 levels. It also has a restaurant. $$$

Posada Malibu [138 B3] (14 rooms) \ 0237 221 1274; m 0424 222 1322, 0412 388 4237; e info@posadamalibu.com, posadamalibu@cantv.net; www.posadamalibu.com. A spectacular house of wood beams, whitewashed walls & marine themes, this upmarket *posada* has a roof terrace & its own boat for trips to the islands. AC & en-suite bathrooms. $$$

Mid range

⌂ **Acquamarina** [138 C3] (5 rooms) ✆ 0237 221 1161; m 0414 200 4882; e losroques@mail.com, rigovivas@cantv.net. A pretty inn with roof terrace, 5 rooms for 2–3 guests, fridge, satellite TV; own launch; good package offered with airfare included; Italian spoken. $$

⌂ **Caballito del Mar** [138 C3] (5 rooms) m 0414 291 9479, 0414 337 8856;
e posadacaballitodemar@hotmail.com, info@posadacaballitodemar.com. Margarita & Stefano Palmerine have made this most attractive guesthouse one of the homeliest on the island, with an airy open kitchen dominating the living area & good food; ask about their economical packages. Some English spoken. $$

⌂ **La Cigala** [138 C4] (8 rooms) m 0414 236 5721; e posadalacigala@gmail.com; www.lacigala.com. This immaculate, whitewashed *posada* with dark wood furniture & tastefully placed vases looks like something from a *Vogue* fashion shoot & serves incredible food but doesn't cost the earth. The owner, Liana Trevisi Docournau, used to work with yachts & can arrange boat trips & fly-fishing for bonefish. No plasma screen, just relax. Located by the airstrip & Aquarena bar, this is great value for a superior experience. English, French & Italian spoken. $$

⌂ **La Corsaria** [138 B3] (9 rooms) ✆ 0212 951 6994, 0212 952 5981; m 0414 119 9475, 0426 908 9975; e mary@posadalacorsaria.com.ve. A good restaurant plus guesthouse done up in rich colours; large living area, attractive rooms with skylights, safe, fridge; own desalination plant. $$

⌂ **Posada Arrecife** [138 C3] (6 rooms) ✆ 0237 221 1024, 0237 221 1066; m 0414 234 9641, 0414 328 5471; e arrecife@cantv.net. Offers 6 lovely rooms with satellite TV, telephone, optional AC. Italian-speaking staff will arrange fishing & diving; the Arrecife has its own launch. $$

Budget

⌂ **Doña Carmen** [138 C4] (9 rooms) m 0414 318 426, 0414 291 9225, 0414 262 7837;
e richardlosroques@turismodonacarmen.com, reservaciones@turismodonacarmen.com; www.turismodonacarmen.com. The original Doña Carmen was the woman who opened the first guesthouse in Los Roques in 1967, & her son carries on the tradition. Located on Plaza Bolívar next to the fishermen's favourite bar. Most rooms have AC, except the 2 by the beach which catch the breeze. New terrace with sea views & back door that opens onto beach. *Criollo*-style meals are filling & adequate. Good value at low end of the spectrum. $$

⌂ **Piano y Papaya** [138 B4] (5 rooms) m 0414 911 6467, 0414 914 4423; e posada@pianoypapaya.com. An Italian couple run this attractive *posada* behind the church, with living room, garden, roof terrace & b/fast included in the price. The Piacenzas can give you a shiatzu massage or arrange watersports & excursions. $$

⌂ **Posada Doña Magalys** [138 C4] (6 rooms) ✆ 0212 227 8215; m 0414 120 4096. Opposite Doña Carmen, this basic place is good value, considering what others charge for very similar sized rooms. B/fast & dinner included in price. $

Camping The cheapest option for visiting Los Roques is to camp, which is free, but there are serious obstacles to overcome as you can only bring 10kg of luggage per person on the plane. Water and other supplies are exorbitant on Gran Roque so it is advisable to bring them with you, and there are no public toilets or shower facilities for campers, either on Gran Roque or any of the authorised camping beaches. No fires are permitted anywhere.

Free camping permits are issued at the Inparques office at the west end of the shore road at the opposite end of town from the landing strip.

Camping is allowed on Gran Roque near the beach behind the Inparques office [138 A3] and the islands within the so-called 'recreational zone', which are: the nearby Madrizquí and Cayo Pirata, joined by a coral sand bar, where lobster fishermen corral their catch; Francisquí, two small islands joined by a sand bar, with an ocean beach on the north and a lagoon for swimming; and Noronquises and Crasquí, which are 30–40 minutes away by boat.

The best plan is to pitch your tent on Los Roques, which has small shops, a bar and restaurants, and take a boat out to the keys each day, or camp on Crasquí, where there are two fried-fish restaurants with bathrooms, where you can grab a bite and escape the sun. If you have a camping stove, ask the boatmen to bring you a fresh fish or pick one up in the morning before heading out to the keys. A small cool box is a great way to keep water cold (ice is available at a cost in Gran Roque) and pack some limes for drinks and to squeeze over fish.

Island camps

Å Campamento Francisquí m 0414 337 3148. On 1 of a circle of 4 isles, just 5mins northeast of Gran Roque, is a house owned by Marcos Jurado who has a restaurant & 2 rooms for rent with private bath, as well as facilities for campers. Can organise package including flight from Maiquetía, boat transfer, meals, excursions. $$

Å Campamento Rancho Agua Clara on Crasquí \ 0212 243 1843; m 0414 247 3498; e cumaco@ yahoo.com; www.ranchoaguaclara.blogspot.com. For a view of the sea from your bed you could try this converted fisherman's shack run by Roqueño Guayo & his German wife Anya. The house has 2 beds, bathrooms, fresh water is available & there are covered areas to escape the sun. They also rent out tents, provide meals & pick up guests from Gran Roque in their own boat. The camp is midway between Juanita's restaurant & La Punta, the best snorkelling spot on Crasquí. A good way to get the desert-island experience with a few home comforts. $$

On the windward side of Francisquí de Abajo, there's a camp consisting of two old A-frame houses on the tiny **Rasquí** (\ *0212 263 8991;* m *0414 249 3683, 0414 373 1111;* e *miguel@roques.net*) that offers diving, bonefishing tours and windsurfing.

✘ **Where to eat** There are few options for eating out in Gran Roque, as most people are on tours or in *posadas* with meals included in the accommodation price. In the morning you can get filling *arepas* at the kiosk by the bridge leading to the airstrip, including the exquisite decadence of lobster-filled *arepas* during the lobster season (15 November–30 April). A few cheap places in Plaza Bolívar offer pizzas and snacks. The best place to eat in Crasquí is Doña Juanita's fish restaurant on the beach, with the open dining area giving shade from the midday sun and hammocks to laze about in and read a book.

✘ **Aquarena** [138 D4] m 0414 131 1282; e losroques@aquarena.com.ve; www.aquarena.com.ve; ⊕ all day until late. Immaculate beach bar, coffee shop & restaurant in a nice spot near landing strip & boat jetty. Tables under palms, bean bags, funky, laid-back tunes, perfect for sitting under the stars sipping Polar beers or mojito cocktails, depending on your budget. The best place to chill out in the evenings. They also do sushi snacks & can arrange weddings! $$

✘ **El Canto de la Ballena** [138 B4] \ 0237 221 1160; m 0414 333 4092, 0414 291 9021; e ballena@hotmail.com; www.cantodelaballena.com; ⊕ 08.00–late. Nelly Camargo, a likeable Andean lady who makes gourmet meals, runs this restaurant-bar with the strange name of 'The Whale Song' & a Tibetan touch to the funky décor. Wooden tables with candles & cool tunes make this a good place to hang out in the evening but the real draw is the excellent cooking, especially fish & seafood dishes, which include carpaccio & curry. Nelly rents 2 rooms with king-size beds above the restaurant, & is the owner of the 6-room budget *posada* **Ranchito Power**. $$

✘ **Bar Nueva Cadiz** [138 C4] Plaza Bolívar; ⊕ noon–late. This noisy bar loved by local fishermen is a good place to get a flavour of what life was like in Los Roques before the *posadas* came. A massive plasma screen takes over when important baseball games are being played. Beers are cheaper here than in some of the cocktail joints in town. $

Other practicalities Situated at the entrance to town next to the pier, **Oscar Shop** [138 D4] can arrange almost any service available in the archipelago, from beach chairs, parasols, snorkels and flippers, to boat charters, money exchange and finding fishing guides.

Money There is a Banesco branch (✆ *0237 221 1265;* ⏰ *08.00–12.00 & 14.00–17.00 Mon–Fri, 08.00–14.00 Sat*) in Plaza Bolívar, which has an ATM that takes Visa, MasterCard, Cirrus and Maestro cards but is sometimes inoperative. There is a limit of US$90 on ATM withdrawals and about US$350 over the counter, but they can run out. Always bring enough cash with you to cover your stay. Most *posadas* will be able to change dollars.

Communications Internet service to Los Roques can be slow and goes down from time to time. Some *posadas* offer Wi-Fi internet connections, as does the Aquarena restaurant [138 D4] (see opposite). The state-run Infocentro [138 B3] by the school is free but places are seldom available. Centro de Comunicaciones Eulisal [138 B3] (⏰ *08.00–15.00 & 16.30–21.00 Mon–Sun*) just off Plaza Bolívar has both internet, at US$5 an hour, and phone booths for national and international calls. Enzosoft [138 C3] (⏰ *12.00–21.30 Mon–Sun*) also has internet service for the same price but you can haggle if you plan a long session.

Medical services There is a very basic clinic and a pharmacy but any serious medical emergency would mean transfer back to a hospital or private clinic in Caracas.

What to see and do The stunning coral islands of the archipelago are clearly the main attraction but it's worth taking time out to explore Gran Roque as well. Early morning or just before sunset are the perfect times to join the local joggers on a trip up to the lighthouse, or *faro* [138 E2], which is so emblematic of the island. A 30-minute walk on a rough, grassy trail takes you 100m up to the crumbling stone tower on the island's highest point, giving views across Gran Roque and the neighbouring atolls, and great sunset shots if you're here by 17.30. The lighthouse, which operated until the 1950s, dates from the 1870s when the Dutch occupied Gran Roque. Don't forget to take repellent, because as soon as the sun starts to set the midges come out to play.

Yachts and sailboats Crewed yachts and sailboats offer a great way to explore the less-visited islands of Los Roques. If you have a group of four, or even two, sailboats are better value than *posadas*. The food really is superior, the beaches are solitary and the crystalline water has no equal. In Los Roques ask Oscar at Oscar Shop (see *Other practicalities*, opposite) or enquire at La Cigala (see page 141) to find out which yachts are available for hire, or try the Venezuelan charter firm Explore Yachts (*www.explore-yachts.com*). Most boats will require a few days' or a week's notice if they are to be on hand to meet you on arrival in Los Roques.

△ **Alpiturismo** ✆ 0212 283 1433; e alpi@alpi-group.com; www.alpi-group.com. Arranges fishing/diving cruises in 35–52ft craft, luxury 76ft sailboat with 4 cabins, or an AC 54ft yacht. Alpi can arrange snorkelling, surfing & waterskiing, all meals & national drinks, from around US$160 a day pp (4–6 people). Cruises start from Gran Roque.

△ **Auropoltours** ✆ 0212 312 7053; m 0414 324 9210; e auropoltours@yahoo.com; www.auropoltours.com. Run by Jochen Pollosch & his wife Aurora, offering tours of the islands in a 47ft catamaran, one of the biggest, most comfortable boats in Los Roques. You can hire the whole catamaran at a price of US$1,000 a day, or enjoy it for US$150 pp, all-inclusive. Bonefishing packages start at US$300 a day.

△ **Bicho** ✆ 0212 283 4750; m 0414 263 56645; e ttmjpca@cantv.net; www.infolosroques.com/pages/bicho.html, www.roques.org. A 51ft sailing craft captained by Arnaud Dely of Transporte Turístico Marítimo. It has an 85HP engine, phone, GPS & 3 cabins with dbl beds & hot water. Packages include round-trip airfare, all meals & national drinks (locally made rum, beer, whisky, vodka). TTM also sails the

Levante, a catamaran sleeping 10 passengers, with a w/day plan for 2 days & 1 night.
⚠ **Dali, Frida & Picasso** m 0414 315 9001, 0414 321 6614; e santiagomayo@hotmail.com; www.losroquesavela.com. 3 sailboats with 2–4 dbl rooms on board run by Santiago Mayo, ideal for cruising the islands & fishing; US$120–140 daily pp.
⚠ **Pitigüey** 0237 414 5818; m 0414 239 0744, 0414 205 5224; e massimonavarro@hotmail.com, info@losroques.dk;

www.losroquesonline.net. A catamaran run by Massimo Navarro who offers day tours & can also arrange fishing, windsurfing & kitesurfing.
⚠ **Sula Sula** 0212 751 1712; m 0414 237 0863; e sutzimar@telcel.net, info@sula-sula.com; www.sula-sula.com. A 42ft GibSea craft run by Captain Fernando Martínez that carries up to 6 passengers in 4 cabins. Rates include all meals, national drinks & Chilean wine.

Scuba diving The diving is spectacular at Cayo Sal where caves in vertical walls sprout multi-coloured sponges, and in the clear waters of Boca del Medio which teem with corals and fishes. At Boca de Sebastopol, you can see manta rays and sharks. Boca de Cote has a 12–15m wall with abundant sea life and you pass through the central lagoon to get there, which is off-limits for yachts and fishermen. Sleeping sharks are seen in the caves off Rabusquí; lobsters and shipwrecks off Nordisquí. There are dive sites for all levels in Los Roques and four dive centres competing for clients, which keeps prices down.

Park rules limit dive groups to ten, accompanied by a divemaster; divers may not touch or stand on corals and, for health reasons, divers should not take plane flights until 12 hours after their last dive. A dive permit costs US$12.

If you have accreditation from PADI, NAUI or SSI, you can hire equipment and dive. If not you can take a beginner's course for US$80 or an Open Water Diver certificate for US$350 (price includes equipment and boats). Rental equipment such as regulator, wetsuit, fins, tanks and weights are included in the price of packages for full-day trips or courses. The companies offering diving and certified courses in Gran Roque include:

✔**Aquatics Dive Center** [138 C3]
www.scubavenezuela.com
✔**Arrecife** [138 C3] www.divevenezuela.com, www.posadaarrecifelosroques.com
✔**Ecobuzos** [138 D4] m 0414 791 9380, 0414 395 4208; e info@ecobuzos.com; www.ecobuzos.com. A well-organised diving school that operates from a base next to the airstrip. 1-

day tasters with instruction & submersion are about US$80. Certification courses run from basic to professional rescue courses; rates from US$65 a day for 3 dives (maximum) to US$280 for 5 days. Recommended.
✔**Eco Challenge** [138 B3]
www.ecochallenge.ws/roques_venezuela.html. Has its own small *posada*.

Fishing Marlin, sailfish, tarpon, wahoo, barracuda and grouper are a few of the prized catches around Los Roques but the big draw is the world-famous bonefishing. Shallows between the archipelago's islands called 'pancake flats', coral banks and mangroves are perfect for wading out and fly-fishing for bonefish. Serious anglers pay US$200–300 a day and come thousands of miles to catch (and release) these lightning-fast fish, called *pez ratón* or *macabí* in Spanish.

Fishing is good all year, particularly so from June through to December. The sport fishing licence from Inparques costs about US$15 a day.

🎣 **Chapi Sport Fishing** 0212 985 4384, 0212 987 0032; e chapi@net-uno.net; www.chapisportfishing.com. Offers complete service for fishermen from airport reception in Maiquetía & private plane to Los Roques to bilingual guides, at

competitive prices. Chapi works with the Posada Arrecife.
🎣 **Fly Fishing Los Roques** m 0414 121 0157; www.flyfishinglosroques.com. Felipe Reyes is a sports fisherman with over 20 years' experience arranging

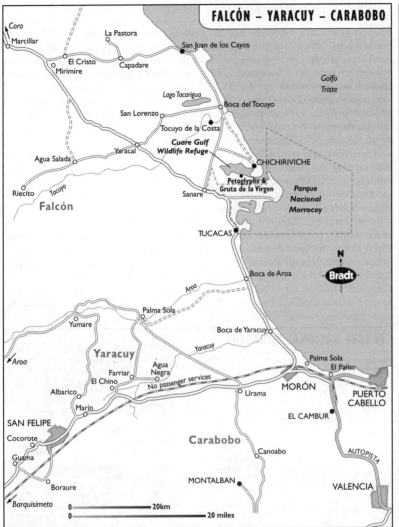

Golfo
Triste

Coro
Marcillar
La Pastora
San Juan de los Cayos
El Cristo
Mirimire
Capadare
Lago Tacarigua
Boca del Tocuyo
San Lorenzo
Tocuyo de la Costa
Cuare Gulf
Wildlife Refuge
Agua Salada
Yaracal
CHICHIRIVICHE
Riecito
Tocuyo
Falcón
Sanare
Petoglyphs &
Gruta de la Virgen
Parque
Nacional
Morrocoy
TUCACAS

N
Bradt

Boca de Aroa
Palma Sola
Aroa
Boca de Yaracuy
Yumare
Yaracuy
Yaracuy
Palma Sola
El Palito
Aroa
Farriar
Agua
Negra
El Chino
No passenger services
Albarico
Urama
MORÓN
PUERTO
CABELLO
Marín
SAN FELIPE
EL CAMBUR
Cocorote
Carabobo
Guama
Canoabo
AUTOPISTA
Boraure
MONTALBAN
VALENCIA
Barquisimeto
0   20km
0   20 miles

fishing trips in Los Roques & can organise full packages & accommodation at Posada Malibu.
⚓ **Pez Ratón Fishing Lodge** \ 0212 975 0906; m 0414 265 3744, 0414 257 0167; e info@pezraton.com; www.pezraton.com. Alejandro Gonzalez has been arranging fishing tours in Los Roques for more than 20 years & provides everything needed for some of the best fly-fishing

in the world; US$350 daily with bilingual guide, lodging based on dbl occupancy at Posada Mediterraneo (see *Where to stay*, page 140), meals & shared boat (if you don't bring rod & reel, it's an extra charge). Their fleet includes skiffs, fibreglass *peñeros* or open fishing boats with outboard, & deep-sea craft.

Windsurfing and kitesurfing
Vela Windsurf m 0414 012 6751; e epernales@hotmail.com; www.velawindsurf.com. Elias Pernales & Liselote run this kitesurfing camp

on Francisquí Abajo & represent Vela Windsurf in the area.

PARQUE NACIONAL MORROCOY

Easy to reach and relatively easy to explore, the Parque Nacional Morrocoy encompasses 320km² of glorious Caribbean exuberance, home to hundreds of coral reefs offering great diving for all levels, a smattering of paradise islands big enough to hang up a hammock and spend hours exploring, turquoise waters, tangled mangroves, ancient Indian rock carvings and one of Venezuela's most important nature reserves, the Cuare Wildlife Reserve. The area was declared a national park in 1974 to protect the fragile coral reefs and halt the runaway development of holiday homes along the coast but sadly the disorganised overdevelopment of apartments and hotels has continued.

The islands and coastal beaches are reached by well-organised and economical boat services from the two gateway points to the park: Tucacas, which has diving schools, and Chichiriviche. The main problem for visitors is finding decent accommodation in these scruffy waterfront towns, which would be better avoided if they didn't offer access to the islands in the park.

So which one to choose? It depends on which islands you intend to visit. Tucacas in the south is good for waterskiing and snorkelling, and has a popular island called Punta Brava with good beaches that you can walk to. Island beaches reached by boat include Playuela and Paiclas, both of which have palm trees and amenities. Chichiriviche, which is less developed and more laid back, is close to Cayo Sal, Cayo Los Muertos, Cayo Pelón and Cayo Peraza, and boat tours can include visits to the Cueva del Indio, a large rock on the coast covered in petroglyphs. One of the

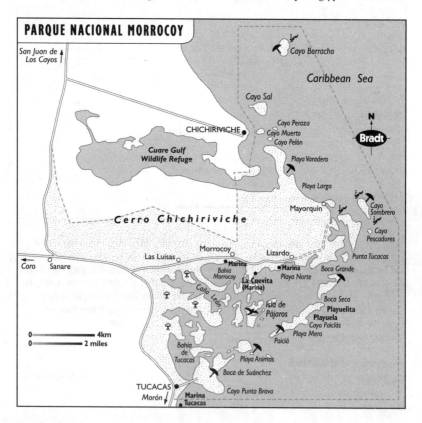

largest and most popular islands is Cayo Sombrero, which has food stalls and palm trees and can be reached from both Tucacas and Chichiriviche.

Although the palm trees, white beaches and translucent waters paint a picture of tropical paradise, the corals in the park are only now recovering from widespread whitening in late 1995, believed to have been caused by a chemical spill. Nothing was ever proved and the reefs have since made a strong recovery, with plenty of undersea life to delight snorkellers and divers, including parrot fish, turtles and conger eels.

☞ **WARNING:** Only three hours' drive from Caracas and close to Valencia, which has direct buses, Morrocoy is overrun by Venezuelan sun-seekers during the Christmas, Easter and Carnival holidays who like nothing better than to set up hammocks, crank up the salsa and consume alcoholic beverages. Accommodation is almost impossible to find during these periods so book well in advance if you want to join the party. From November to February another annoyance is the tiny biting gnats, called *puri puri*, that come out in the early morning and just before sunset, making camping torture if you don't have repellent or a mosquito net for hammocks.

TUCACAS (*Telephone code: 0259*) Tucacas is a hot, pricey town dotted with holiday apartments, private resorts, luxury yacht marinas and a couple of diving centres. It has a bank, food stores, a liquor store on nearly every corner selling ice by the bag, and a massive casino. Small hotels, bakeries and *areperas* are found along the main street, Avenida Libertador, which runs from the Valencia–Coro highway at the top of town to the boat jetty by the sea. Tucacas lives from tourism these days but ships still sail from here to supply fruit and vegetables to the Netherlands Antilles of Aruba, Bonaire and Curaçao.

The main attraction is the access to the spectacular keys and beaches of the national park.

Getting there Tucacas can be reached by car or bus off the main highway between Morón and the city of Coro. Buses from Caracas take 4½ hours via Valencia. Buses from Coro take four hours. Direct buses from Valencia on the Morón–Coro route take 2½ hours. *Por puestos* to Chichiriviche take 25 minutes.

🏠 **Where to stay**
Hotels
🏠 **Sun Way Morrocoy** (201 rooms) Falcón highway at Km 58; ☏ 0259 812 4611, 0259 812 1002, 0212 952 7316. 5-star resort on the main road outside town. Rooms with AC, TV, 3 swimming pools, gym, restaurants, nightclub & top of the line casino. Ask for low-season rates. $$$

🏠 **Hotel Manaure** (45 rooms) Av Silva; ☏ 0259 812 1011, 0259 821 2086; e otumacal@cantv.net. A dignified older hotel with pleasant pool, restaurant & rooms with hot water & AC. $$

Posadas
🏠 **Aparto Posada del Mar** (15 rooms, 5 apts) Calle Páez con Av Silva; ☏ 0259 812 0524, 0259 812 3587; e info@apartoposadadelmar.com; www.apartoposadadelmar.com. Restaurant, swimming pool, garden, sauna & bbq area. 5 nice apts with kitchen, rooms with fridge, AC, satellite TV & hot water. With its own jetty at the back with chairs & mooring for launches & a trimaran, this is

recommended. Good value, especially when beach day-tours are included. $$
🏠 **Posada Balijú** (14 rooms) Calle Libertad; ☏ 0259 812 1580; m 0412 262 3596; e info@posadabaliju.com.ve; www.posadabaliju.com.ve. Very attractive *posada* run by José Jelambi, known as 'Pepe'. Great base for exploring the marine park. Rooms with AC & hot water included in package

along with meals & boat trips to islands from jetty behind. Can also organise horseriding & birdwatching trips. $$

⌂ **Posada Nautica** (8 rooms) ✆ 0259 244 4814, 0259 812 2559; m 0414 430 8660; e posadanautica@hotmail.com; www.posadanautica.com.ve. Rooms with AC, bathrooms, satellite TV, small swimming pool, restaurant, bar, boat for excursions leaves from jetty behind. Good self-contained option, call to reserve. $$

⌂ **Posada Venemar** (8 apts) Av Libertador, Calle La Iglesia; ✆ 0259 812 0515; m 0414 343 1313; e hospedaje@venemar.com.ve. Suite-style rooms with AC, TV, hot water in brick hotel close to bridge & Playa Blanca beach. Ask for room with sea view. Seafood restaurant one of the best in town. $$

⌂ **Posada Amigos del Mar** (9 rooms) Calle Nueva, Barrio Libertador, south of highway; ✆ 0259 812 3962, 0259 812 1754; e amigos-del-mar@cantv.net. Run by Andres Najon of Amigos del Mar dive shop, this gated house with large garden is a basic backpacker option & is used for divers doing courses with Andres. Rooms with bathroom, cold water, use of kitchen. Contact Andres in town so as not to get lost (see *Diving*, page 150). $

⌂ **Posada Carlos, or Hotel Las Palmas** (12 rooms) Av Libertador; ✆ 0259 812 1493. Basic place on main street with no name outside just a sign saying 'rooms'. Popular with backpackers. Most rooms with bathroom, cold water, use of kitchen. Carlos can arrange boat tours. $

Posadas **west of Tucacas** With close proximity to the beaches and keys as their main attraction there are excellent guesthouses out of town. These *posadas* on the bay of Morrocoy's western shore must be reserved in advance and are recommended as upmarket getaways, offering all-inclusive packages and personalised attention. They are reached by an access road that joins the national highway about 8km west of Tucacas.

⌂ **Posada Ardileña** (7 rooms) ✆ 0261 766 5295, 0259 808 8779; m 0414 610 0113; e reservaciones@ardilena.com, info@ardilena.com; www.ardilena.com. This attractive *posada*, with its own jetty & packages including boat trips to the islands, is located out of Tucacas in Agua Salobre & offers a more peaceful way to enjoy the park for those looking for a more pampered experience. TV lounge & dining area. Rooms with AC, fridge, bathroom. $$$

⌂ **El Paraiso Azul** (15 rooms) Cerro El Silencio, sector Lizardo, past the Guardia Nacional post; ✆ 0259 812 0929, 0212 953 2670; m 0414 484 5053; www.paraisoazul.com.ve. Excellent views over islands & canals, English spoken. $$–$$$

⌂ **La Acacia** (6 cabins) ✆ 0259 881 5536; m 0414 481 5536; e julietamed@gmail.com, info@posadalaacacia.com. Another upmarket *posada* in Lizardo offering lodging & excursions to the keys, attended by the owners Julieta & Carlos de Valdés who are excellent cooks. $$

⌂ **Villa Mangrovia** (4 rooms, cabin) ✆ 0259 881 1299; m 0414 941 5176; e posadamangrovia@yahoo.es. Birdwatchers can observe hundreds of birds just sitting on the terrace here. Swimming pool, own jetty & boat for excursions to keys included in lodging packages. Good meals. Long known for gracious hospitality of Irina Jackson, who speaks 5 languages. $$

Posadas **near Sanare**

⌂ **El Solar de La Luna Posada Turistica** (7 rooms) ✆ 0259 881 1010, 0259 881 8800; m 0416 644 0915, 0414 484 5054; e elsolardelaluna@cantv.net; www.circuitodelaexcelencia.com. If you fancy cooling off with a panoramic view of the beaches & islands of the Parque Nacional Morrocoy & an absolutely first-rate dinner, this award-winning *posada* is the place. The area, called Buena Vista, is south of the national highway about 11km west of Tucacas, via a rough, & at times steep, road. With flair & inspired touches, owner Bertapaula has crafted a rambling house with great terrace & 7 guest rooms with hot water, AC & good beds, each room different.

Bertapaula's passion is cooking & besides her own creations she has a sheaf of recipes for Venezuelan specialities from centuries past. Wine served with dinner. Can arrange boat trips. $$

⌂ **La Pradera** (11 rooms) ✆ 0259 881 1222; m 0416 642 2014, 0412 702 0891. Originally a restaurant, it now offers rooms. On the national highway in Sanare at the turning for Chichiriviche, this is a nice place to stop. Swimming pool, terrace with good views up the hill. Chef & hostess Carmen Domínguez has gradually added more rooms with AC, hot water. $$

Camping To limit numbers and support conservation efforts on the islands, camping is restricted to Punta Brava (5,084 tents allowed), Paiclá (276), Cayo Sal (424), Cayo Muerto (364) and Cayo Sombrero (688). Advance reservations have to be made through Inparques and the process is not simple. First, you phone \ 0212 285 3111 to request a reservation. Then you deposit US$2.50 per night (for each camper aged 12+) into a Banesco bank account. When you have the deposit slip, you must ring back with the deposit slip number (don't lose it). Then within 48 hours of your allotted time, you must call to reconfirm or your space will be cancelled. If you are already in Tucacas, check with Inparques to see if there has been any change to this system before making a deposit at Banesco. Campers may not light fires anywhere in the park or consume alcohol.

By far the best place for camping is Cayo Sombrero, which has many palms to sling hammocks from and excellent beaches with the sea breeze helping to keep the midges at bay. The sea inside the reef, named La Piscina or 'pool', is ideal for swimming and snorkelling. The beach is cleaned every day and has many toilets. Bring large containers of water and a load of food, although on weekends the shacks open to sell fried fish and vendors circulate with soft drinks and coconut ice cream. If you plan to stay for a couple of days you can ask the boatmen to bring you more food or water.

✖ Where to eat

✖ **Resturant Venemar** Av Libertador; ⊕ lunch, dinner. Swordfish, red snapper & fresh tuna join shrimp, squid & shellfish on the menu of this good, reasonable option, next to the *posada* of the same name (see *Where to stay*, opposite). Standard chicken & beef main courses if you want a break from seafood. $$

✖ **Panaderia Reina del Mar** Edif Gaeta, Av Libertador; ⊕ 08.00–20.00. They have the best sandwiches in town at this bakery, including large slabs of baguette stuffed with cheese, salami & tomatoes. $

Other practicalities The **Inparques office** (*Av Libertador;* \ *0259 812 2176, 0259 812 0053;* e *pnmorrocoy@inparques.gov.ve;* ⊕ *08.00–12.00 & 14.00–17.00*) is located at the end of Avenida Libertador where the bridge continues on to Punta Brava, and is the place to enquire about camping on the islands. In February 2010 camping was re-allowed after a brief suspension in 2009 to clear up the beaches.

Tucacas is no place to pick up souvenirs, apart from gaudy beach towels, and it's best bring suncreams and repellent with you as choice is limited in the few small supermarkets and pharmacies.

Money There is a **Banesco** bank (*Av Libertador*) on the main street which has an ATM. **Banco Provincial** (*Morón–Coro highway*) also has an ATM but is out of town.

Medical services There are a couple of pharmacies in town, but serious medical emergencies would mean transfer to Valencia.

What to do

Boat trips to the beaches and islands The pier where the boats leave for the *cayos* is called the *embarcadero* and is run by a boatmen's co-operative. Walk down Avenida Libertador and turn left on Avenida Marino to the pier, where someone has painted a map of the islands on the wall, and the prices are displayed next to the kiosk on the jetty. Try and gather a group or join others as the round-trip fare is for the whole boat – up to eight people depending on gear. Prices range from US$20 for a boat to the closest beaches like Paiclá to US$45 for Cayo Sombrero, the farthest. Tell the boatman what time to pick you up for the return trip and remember the name of the boat.

Buy a hammock Local craftsmen make hammocks of hand-knotted coloured nylon strings that are ideal for the beach as they are light, strong and unaffected by water. They cost about US$10–15, depending on size and adornment. Rows of these hammocks are displayed along the Falcón highway, some 10km west of Tucacas near the Cerro de Chichiriviche.

Yaracuy River trip Boats head up the Río Yaracuy among forests of buttressed dragon's blood trees and pink poui, past banks of reeds and bird-of-paradise into a wilderness inhabited by crocodiles, capybaras, and capuchin and howler monkeys. Enquire about tours at Submatur (see *Diving*, below).

Punta Brava You don't need to take a boat to visit the national park. The closest beaches are just a 15-minute walk away from town across the bridge at the bottom of Avenida Libertador, past the Inparques office. Cars pay a small fee to enter but there is no charge for people. Cross the bridge, continue for a kilometre and you are on Punta Brava, the largest of Morrocoy's islands. The sun is *bravo* (fierce) so those on foot should go early. The beach and huge parking lot draw crowds on weekends. However, it is pleasantly empty from Monday to Thursday. Hammocks can be slung from palm trees and camping is permitted.

Diving

✒**Amigos del Mar** 1 Calle Democracia near the Embarcadero; ✆ 0259 812 1754. André Nahon, who worked for many years with Mike at Submatur (see below), offers basically the same services at his own dive school & centre. André has 10 rooms that he rents to divers at low rates.

✒**Frogman Dive Center** CC Bolívar, Local 3, Plaza Bolívar, Tucacas; ✆ 0241 824 3879; m 0414 3401824; e frogmanmorrocoy@cantv.net, collazo60@gmail.com, frogmandive@hotmail.com; www.frogmandive.com. Expert diver Manuel Collazo runs this relatively new operation offering everything from equipment hire to taster dives for beginners (2 immersions US$120) to advanced courses such as Advanced Open Water Diver (US$450). He can also arrange boat trips to beaches & islands off the usual routes run by the boatmen's co-operative & can arrange accommodation.

✒**Submatur** No 6, Calle Ayacucho; ✆ 0259 812 0082; e morrocoysubmatur@cantv.net. Mike Osborn, a pioneer of diving in Morrocoy, has been renting equipment & running courses at this place at the bottom end of Av Libertador for years. Mike is a licensed NAUI instructor & underwater photographer. A 4-day Open Water diving course covers theory, 8 dives, boat & equipment for US$330, & entitles you to a PADI certificate. A day's diving with all equipment runs for US$70 pp, & a 2-day/1-night diving package with food & lodging costs around US$144. Mike is working with the captain of the *Kulkuri*, an 80ft sailboat, taking divers (& companions) on cruises to the uninhabited Archipiélago de Las Aves, 160km north.

CHICHIRIVICHE (*Telephone code: 0259*) An unplanned village that grew into an unplanned town with pot-holed muddy streets: there is little picturesque about Chichiriviche except its name and its access to the stunning keys of Cayo Pelón, Cayo Peraza, Cayo Sal, Cayo Muerto and the distant Cayo Sombrero. However, Chichiriviche's advantages over Tucacas as a jumping-off point for the islands are a sandy shore at the edge of town and a more laid-back atmosphere. The Malecón, or sea wall, with its bars and cheap eating places also makes for a good place to hang out and meet people in the evenings.

Another difference with Tucacas is that boat trips to the keys include an option to visit the ancient petroglyphs of the Cueva del Indio and the nearby Grotto of the Virgin in the Golfete de Cuare. Ask for a *viaje corto* and your boatman will take you on a tour of the gulf before heading to the beach at Varadero or Cayo Muerto.

There are three main roads in Chichiriviche: Avenida Zamora, the road entering the town, with a supermarket, bank, travel agency and bus terminus, ends at the shore; Avenida Playa Norte follows the north shore; and Vía Fabrica de Cemento leaves Avenida Zamora at the Garza Hotel and goes to the bay and cement works.

Getting there Chichiriviche is harder to reach than Tucacas because the only direct bus is from Valencia. These buses run regularly and take 2½ hours (about US$5). From Barquisimeto get a bus to the terminal in San Felipe, catch a bus for Morón and from Morón take a bus to Tucacas/Chichiriviche. If you are coming from Coro, alight at the Sanare fork and wait for a Valencia–Chichiriviche bus to take you the last 22km. Local *por puestos* between Tucacas and Chichiriviche take 20–25 minutes to cover the 35km trip (about US$1) depending on what CDs are playing. The bus stop in Chichiriviche is on Avenida Zamora. Some hotels will arrange transfers from Caracas.

Keep your eyes peeled when travelling along the 12km causeway that links Chichiriviche to the outside world as it crosses the lagoon and marshes of the Cuare Wildlife Refuge; it is not unusual to see spectacular flocks of pink flamingos in the rainy season.

Where to stay Hotels and *posadas* are much pricier at Christmas, Easter and Carnival, when everything is full and the place is filled to bursting with holidaymakers. Always check for midweek discounts in low season. Reasonable boat trips to the *cayos* from hotels can also work out cheaper than taking a boat from the *embarcaderos* if you are in a small group.

Hotels

⌂ **Mario** (114 rooms) Av Zamora; ☎ 0259 818 6811. Big white, 4-star hotel with large swimming pool, restaurant, rooms with AC. Some rooms have seen better days but good value out of season rates. Boat trips to beaches organised as part of w/end packages including meals. $$$$

⌂ **Coral Suites Hotel & Spa** (230 rooms) ☎ 0259 815 1033, 0259 818 6103; e reservaciones@ hotelcoralsuites.com; www.hotelcoralsuites.com. This massive complex on the Via Fabrica de Cemento has 2 restaurants, 2 tennis courts & a huge S-shaped pool. All rooms have AC, en-suite bathrooms, fridge & satellite TV. $$$

⌂ **Capri** (19 rooms) ☎ 0259 818 6026. A small Italian-run hotel on Av Zamora. Rooms with AC & good restaurant make it an economical meeting place for travellers. $$

⌂ **Caribana** (34 rooms) ☎ 0259 818 6837. Rooms with AC, private bath, TV make this a good option. $$

⌂ **Hotel La Garza** (75 rooms) Av Zamora; ☎ 0259 818 6048, 0259 818 6711; e hotellagarza@ hotmail.com. Another old-style 70s' hotel at the top of town, swimming pool with slide, rooms with AC. $$

Guesthouses

Unless noted, the guesthouses on this list have internal bathroom, cold water and fan. Most do not accept credit cards.

⌂ **Casa Manantial** (12 rooms) ☎ 0259 818 6248; e info@posadacasamanantial.com.ve, casamanantial@posadasdemorrocoy.com; www.posadacasamanantial.com. On Av Cuare, right near the beach, on a street leading left from Vía Fábrica de Cemento & opposite Coral Suites, this is a modern *posada* with small but attractive pool, restaurant; rooms with AC, TV, for 2–5 people. $$

⌂ **Morena's Place** (5 rooms) ☎ 0259 815 0936. By the waterfront, 2 blocks north of Av Zamora, this is one of the cheapest dorm-style options in town. 1 room has interior bath, 4 with shared bath. Owners

Editna & Carlos van Marcke offer laundry service, a boat for trips to the keys & kayaks for rent; English & French spoken. $

⌂ **Posada El Profe** (7 rooms) ☎ 0259 416 1166, 0212 235 1116; m 0414 336 3808; e posadaelprofe@ hotmail.com; www.posadaelprofe.com. This friendly, laid-back B&B on 2da Calle la Playa is run by the amiable Aminta & has a terrace & a weights room open to guests. Aminta can arrange birdwatching trips & boat rides to the islands. $

⌂ **Villa Gregoria** (18 rooms) ☎ 0259 818 6359; m 0416 608 6913. On Calle Mariño, a block north of Av Zamora, this is a 2-floor house with porch & hammocks. Run by friendly Spanish owner Aurelio Augustín (speaks English) who offers boat tours & transport round town in his van. Rooms with fan & bathroom. Good prices. $

✕ Where to eat

✕ **Brisas del Mar** Av La Marina, on the Malecón; ⊕ 12.00–23.00. Nelida, the cook, serves up tasty seafood at this local landmark, famous for its squid rings, fried fish & paella. $$

✕ **Restaurant El Txalupa** Calle Marina, on the Malecón; ⊕ 12.00–22.00. A Basque-run seafood restaurant with views of Playa Grande, the islands & the boats at the jetty. $$

✕ **Da Paolo** On the Malecón; ⊕ 12.00–23.00. Pizzas cooked over wood by an Italian chef don't get much better, also offer seafood. $

Other practicalities The **Banco Industrial** (\ *0259 815 0445, 0259 815 0442*; ⊕ *09.30–15.30*) on Avenida Zamora does not cash travellers' cheques but will give money on Visa cards over the counter. It is harder to change dollars in Tucacas and Chichiriviche and rates are lower than in more touristy spots like Margarita, Mérida or Santa Elena. Make sure you bring enough cash with you.

The tourism development corporation (\ *0259 818 6156, 0259 818 6656*) is on Avenida Zamora and has tourist maps and hotel suggestions.

There are several informal internet places in town, including two on Avenida Zamora and another on Paseo Bolívar.

Apart from a couple of pharmacies, there is little in the way of medical facilities. The nearest large private clinics or hospitals are in Valencia.

Shopping is limited to a small supermarket and a liquor store on every corner.

What to do

Boats to the islands It's all about the islands here and there are two points in Chichiriviche to catch boats: Embarcadero Sur, on the beach about 700m south of Avenida Zamora, and Embarcadero Norte, by the Malecón or concrete sea wall. Both co-operatives post a list of islands and prices, and the boatmen can tell you which islands have food stands. As in Tucacas they charge by the boat, with an eight-passenger limit, so it pays to get a group together. A round trip costs about US$20 to the closest keys, Cayo Sal and Isla de los Muertos (large beach, good snorkelling at the south end). Cayo Sombrero and Cayo Pescadores are ten times further away and therefore more expensive. Cayo Borracho is the only island said to have no *plaga* (biting midges), but is currently off-limits to protect regenerating corals.

Petroglyphs and virgins Boats to the closest beaches of Varadero include mini-tours through the Golfete de Cuare to the impressive petroglyphs etched into the walls of the Cueva del Indio, where you can get off the boat and walk on raised platforms to see the pre-Colombian glyphs of anthropomorphic and zoomorphic figures. The next stop is at another cave-like sea wall where images of the Virgin of the Valley, from Margarita, and the Virgin of Carmen are venerated by local fishermen. This grotto takes on a special significance on 8 September when a festival is held in honour of the Virgin of the Valley, with processions, dancing and music.

Cuare Wildlife Refuge The Golfete de Cuare, its wetlands and salt flats, together with the limestone bluffs and forests of Cerro de Chichiriviche and five offshore keys, make up this wildlife refuge, Venezuela's first. The area of 113km² is home to some 315 kinds of bird, including 70% of the aquatic birds found in Venezuela, such as scarlet ibis, roseate spoonbills and egrets. Its wetlands also provide feeding grounds for as many as 20,000 flamingos during the peak birding season from

September to January. They are also one of the last holdouts of the coastal crocodile. There are no organised trips into the wildlife reserve at the moment but you can see flocks of flamingos as you drive in to Chichiriviche along the causeway and boat trips to the Cueva del Indio take you into the Golfete de Cuare, where you can observe the mangroves and roosting birds.

PARQUE NACIONAL MOCHIMA

Stretching across the territory of two states, from Puerto La Cruz in Anzoátegui State east to El Peñon near Cumaná in Sucre State, the Parque Nacional Mochima is Venezuela's second national park, created in 1973 to protect the natural beauty of the islands and halt the haphazard and unregulated building of holiday homes along the coast. Three-fifths of the park's 950km² cover the 30 or so islands and surrounding reefs, while the rest protects the many beaches, mangroves and forests along the coast. Over 200 species of fish have been recorded in its waters. The park takes its name from the Bahía de Mochima, a small fishing village that has adapted, but not much, to cope with the influx of visitors during the high-season holidays. The coastal drive from Puerto La Cruz to Cumaná offers stunning views of tiny sandy coves, long bays and large rocky islands in the blue Caribbean. Some of the larger islands such as Picuda Grande, Los Caracas islands and Isla Venados, are extensions of a sunken mountain range whose valleys now form the gulf in front of the fishing village of Santa Fé, and the dramatic fjord-like bay in front of Mochima. The sea is very calm in these protected bays, home to pods of dolphins that often come close to shore. The main attractions for visitors are snorkelling, deep-water diving and enjoying the numerous sandy beaches on the coast and the islands.

PRACTICALITIES Backed by rocky cliffs and home to iguanas and spiky, cactus-like vegetation, the island beaches are generally small with little natural shade, although some offer refreshments and shacks selling food. When visiting the islands always take sun protection, a hat, a sarong or long-sleeved cover-up, a T-shirt for snorkelling, food and plenty of water. Remember that boat trips feel fresh because of the breeze but you will still be burning, so apply suncream before setting out. Boat trips to the islands normally take you out in the morning and pick you up in the afternoon, so plan for a day of total sun exposure and try to cover up or head for shade before you get too burnt.

Money Changing dollars with *posada* owners is easier in Santa Fé than in the village of Mochima, but there are no banks so bring all the money you need with you.

SANTA FÉ (*Telephone code: 0293*) One of the beaches most prized by travellers is that of Santa Fé, also known as **Playa Cochaima**, a little fishing port east of Punta Colorada, between Puerto La Cruz and Cumaná. Get off the bus at the petrol station on the highway and walk through the rather uninteresting town to the beach, where all the accommodation options are located. The local *posada* owners have long championed the cause of conservation and the beach and nearby streets are cleaned daily. As a result, this long strip of golden sand with its warm, shallow waters and beautiful views across the gulf of Santa Fé has become a magnet for backpackers looking for a change of pace after climbing Roraima in the Gran Sabana or visiting the Delta Amacuro. Once on the beach in Playa Cochaima the vibe is warm, Caribbean and relaxed, a perfect place to hang out and swap stories with other travellers. Everything you need is close at hand with a small market

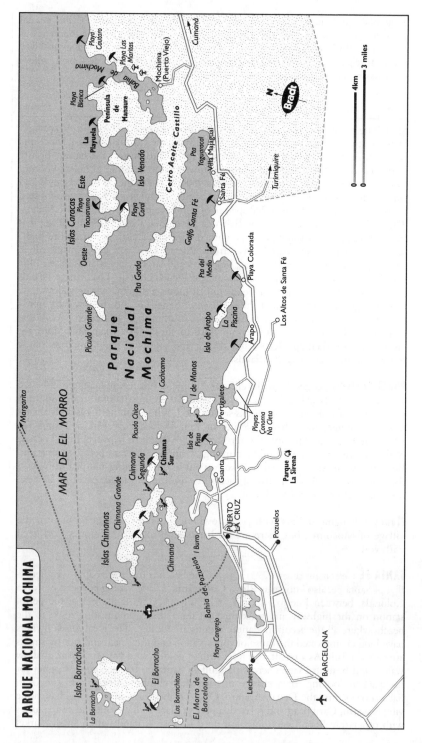

PARQUE NACIONAL MOCHIMA

Islas Borrachas

La Borracha

MAR DE EL MORRO

Margarita

Islas Chimanas

Chimana Grande

Chimana Segunda

Chimana Sur

Chimana

Picuda Chica

Picuda Grande

Isla de Plata

Bahía de Pozuelos

Burro

Los Borrachitos

El Borracho

El Morro de Barcelona

Playa Congrejo

Lecherías

BARCELONA

Pozuelos

PUERTO LA CRUZ

Guanta

Parque La Sirena

Playas Conoma Na Cleta

Pertigalete

Parque Nacional Mochima

I de Monos

I Cachicamo

Isla de Arapo

La Piscina

Arapo

Los Altos de Santa Fé

Pta del Medio

Playa Colorada

Golfo Santa Fé

Santa Fé

Villa Majagual

Pta Yaguaracal

Cerro Aceite Castillo

Pta Gorda

Islas Caracas

Oeste

Este

Playa Tacuarumo

Playa Coral

Isla Venado

La Playuela

Península de Manaure

Playa Blanca

Mochima (Puerto Viejo)

Playa Las Maritas

Bahía de Mochima

Playa Cautaro

Cumaná

Turimiquire

N
Bradt

0   4km
0   3 miles

selling fish and fruit in town next to the beach, and small restaurants and bars in the *posadas* offering snacks and drinks throughout the day.

☞ **WARNING:** The town has had a bad reputation in the past for muggings, and visitors are warned to arrive and leave Santa Fé in the daytime and stick to the beach. Increased police activity in the area has reportedly helped to improve this situation, but it always pays to be alert.

🏠 Where to stay

🏠 **Playa Santa Fé Resort & Dive Centre** (see *Diving*, page 156). $$–$$$
🏠 **Bahia del Mar** (6 rooms) `\` 0293 231 0073; m 0416 386 7930. Another economic *posada* on the beach, run by a French man & a Canadian woman. Rooms with bath, AC & use of kitchen. Palm-thatched caney, cable TV, meals available. Boat trips by arrangement. English & French spoken. $$
🏠 **Café Posada del Mar** (14 rooms) `\` 0293 231 0029. An informal beachside restaurant (low-priced daily menu; ⊕ 07.00–21.00. *Posada* on 2 levels with a roof terrace, especially pleasant upstairs rooms with view, all hand-built by a young German, Matthías Sauter. Dbls with bath, fan & sea view. $
🏠 **La Sierra Inn** (11 rooms) `\` 0293 231 0042; m 0416 681 4678, 0414 993 3116; e cooperativasantafedemisamores@hotmail.com. Owner José Vivas is a journalist, eco-activist & actor who built the Posada Siete Delfines many years ago, starting the beach clean-ups & putting Santa Fé on the international backpacker route. There is a palm-roof caney & barbecue for outdoor eating & a

separate little house on stilts, with kitchen at the back. In the big house there are pleasant dbls with bath & AC, 4 with TV. A fenced rear parking area entered by way of the street behind. José arranges boat tours & is a great source of information on Santa Fé. $
🏠 **Las Palmeras** (10 rooms) `\` 0293 231 0008; m 0414 773 6152. The 2-storey house has a roof terrace with hammocks & tables & a garden. Only ground-floor rooms have hot water. Low-season discounts. French, English & Italian spoken. $
🏠 **Quinta La Jaiba** (4 rooms) `\` 0293 231 0027, 0293 808 8350. Rooms with bath, fridge for guests. Yugoslav owner Miguel Milosevich speaks Dutch, English, German & Italian. $
🏠 **Residencia Los Siete Delfines** (13 rooms) `\` 0293 231 0084; m 0414 815 0228, 0416 317 9290; e oasiskaffe@hotmail.com. Now run by the owners of Oasis Kaffe, this landmark *posada* in the centre of the beach has small rooms but a large, shaded terrace with hammocks overlooking the beach & sea. Rooms with private shower, fan. $

✖ Where to eat

✖ **Bar Restaurant Club Nautico** `\` 0293 231 0026; ⊕ 11.00–21.00, closed Tue. Right at the entrance to Playa Cochaima, this large restaurant has a beachside terrace offering hearty seafood soups, fish dishes, grilled chicken & a very reasonable spaghetti bolognese. $$

✖ **Cafe Posada del Mar** ⊕ 07.00–21.00. You can sit at the wooden tables with your feet in the sand eating b/fast, lunch or dinner, or sip a cocktail watching the sunset. Popular with the backpacker crowd. $
✖ **Snack Carmen** ⊕ 08.00–21.00. A cyber café offering international calls & hamburgers. $

Nightlife Nights in Santa Fé are spent at the beach bars or in *posadas* as the town is not worth a visit and can be unsafe after dark. At weekends night owls can try dancing to tropical tunes at the **Oceanic Café** or **La Tasca** in town, two basic places serving drinks at reasonable prices.

Other practicalities There are no banks in Santa Fe so it's best to bring all the money you need with you. Posada owners can help change money (at low rates) but you can also take a por puesto to Puerto La Cruz if you run short.

There are a couple of pharmacies in town and the closest clinics and hospitals are in Puerto la Cruz.

Internet and international phone calls are available at Snack Carmen and the Sierra Inn also has internet access.

Fresh fruit and fish are available in the market near the start of the beach.

What to do

Boat trips Fishing boats offering trips to the Parque Nacional Mochima leave from the beach just in front of the Posada Los Siete Delfines for the nearby islands and snorkelling spots of La Piscina (30 minutes, beach shacks selling food), Arapo and Arapito (both 35 minutes, food available), Isla Los Venados and Isla Los Caracas (both 45 minutes). Return trips are charged per person not per boat; always specify a pickup time. Some of the *posadas* organise tours taking in a few islands, with a stop at La Piscina to snorkel and then on to Isla Caracas (US$8–15 per person). Snorkels, masks and flippers are sometimes thrown in so shop around. A good thing about visiting the national park on a boat trip from Santa Fé is the high possibility of seeing groups of dolphins when leaving or returning.

Diving

Playa Santa Fé Resort & Dive Centre \ 0293 231 0051, 0293 808 8249; m 0414 773 3777; e santafedive@cantv.net, cpclean@sierra.net; www.santaferesort.com. Run by an American, this *posada*-cum-dive centre has the best & most complete diving services in Santa Fé. Boat trips, hiking, rafting & adventure touring can also be arranged. The *posada* has 10 suites & rooms for 2–4 guests; some rooms have a beach view, some have independent entrance, others a porch. All have private bath with hot water, except the 2 that share a bathroom, plus a kitchen.

AROUND SANTA FÉ

Los Altos de Santa Fé Overlooking the coast at 900m above sea level, Los Altos is a great place to take panoramic photographs of the islands and enjoy cool mountain breezes. The area is famous for its small coffee and cacao plantations, many of which offer accommodation and horseriding, and several artisans and ceramicists have shop studios to sell their handicrafts.

Getting there The turning for Los Altos is about 20km east of Puerto la Cruz on the Santa Fé–Cumaná road. Jeeps from Puerto La Cruz take 40 minutes, taxis from Cumaná an hour.

Where to stay and eat

Neblina Posada & Restaurant (7 rooms) \ 0293 433 1057, 0293 416 9767; e posadaneblina@losaltosdesucre.com. Tucked away in the forest, 500m from the main track through Los Altos, is this charming *posada* with a swimming pool offering B&B. Rooms with bathroom, hot water. Suite with jacuzzi. Birdwatchers itching to set eyes on the majestic harpy eagle use the *posada* as a base to explore. $$

Posada Vista Montaña (10 rooms) \ 0293 431 2541, 0293 432 3542; m 0414 808 6430; e vistamontana@gmail.com; www.posadavistamontana.com. This large, well-appointed *posada* in rustic terracotta tones offers B&B packages in a mountain setting just 20mins' drive from the beach. It has a spa, small zoo, rooftop terrace with hammocks & views over the cloudforest. Rooms have bathroom, hot water, fan. A good restaurant serves fish & barbecued meats. Hiking tours available to local beauty spots. $$

Between Santa Fé and Mochima On the highway, about 6.5km between Santa Fé and Mochima is the entrance to a private road leading to **Villa Majagual** (*12 rooms in 6 cabins;* \ *0212 976 2117;* m *0414 733 0023;* e *majagualv@aol.com;* $$$). This upmarket *posada* on Majagual Point has its own access to a small beach, swimming pool, and tables, where a chef turns Mochima's fresh fish into gourmet dishes followed by local fruit ices. Screened by plants, six lovely cottages have connecting double rooms, all with spring water. Guests may use kayaks and snorkelling masks, or arrange trips to go fishing or exploring beaches. Reservations are required for a two-day minimum stay; enquire about package prices. Transfers arranged from Barcelona or Cumaná airports.

MOCHIMA BAY (*Telephone code: 0293*) Just before Cumaná, on the road from Santa Fé, a fork on the left winds 5km down to the tiny fishing village of **Puerto Viejo de Mochima**, set in a narrow bay penned in by steep-sided cliffs. Mochima has made few concessions to tourism. Constrained by space, it has two main streets, a couple of restaurants, a school, a medical dispensary, a marine biological station, a cock-fighting ring, a little church, two dive centres and a dock from where boat trips begin. In the peak seasons of Christmas, Easter and Carnival it is swamped with sun-seekers and every bed and hammock space is occupied. For the rest of the year, especially midweek, it reverts to a more relaxed rhythm of life, where time slips by slowly, accompanied by the occasional cold beer.

Getting there and around Jeeps leave La Redoma in Cumaná every half hour for the 40-minute journey to Mochima (⊕ *06.30–18.00 Mon–Sat, 06.30–16.00 Sun*). An alternative is to ask on your bus from Cumaná, Puerto La Cruz or Santa Fé to be dropped at the turning on the main highway and either walk the 5km down to the village or wait for a bus to pass.

An Inparques office by the boat jetty has maps showing all the main bays and beaches.

Where to stay Despite its importance as an entry-point to the national park, Mochima has remained a fishing village at heart and the villagers continue to rent out rooms in their houses, or their whole house during peak season. This made for very cheap accommodation options a few years ago but prices have been going up recently. Look for signs saying '*habitación*', which means rooms are available. Bring a hammock at peak time, if you have one, as a hammock space could be all that's available.

Casa de Los Rojas (2 apts) m 0414 773 4839. A 2-storey house near the car park & *abasto* (general store), with 2 good apts each for 2–4 guests, kitchen & bathroom. $$

Posada Gaby (17 rooms) ⏴ 0293 417 2558; m 0414 773 1104. A lilac house at the end of the main street, this is a popular option. Simple rooms have good beds, private bath, TV, AC; lodging includes transfer to beaches. $$

Posada de los Buzos (see *Diving*, page 158). $

Posada El Mochimero (16 rooms) ⏴ 0293 416 3349; m 0414 773 8782, 0414 777 3463. Facing the Mochimero restaurant on the waterfront, it has a great roof terrace for b/fast & dbl or trpl rooms with showers, some with AC. Ask for sea view. $

Posada Girasol (6 rooms) ⏴ 0293 416 0535; m 0414 840 1099. Pleasant rooms with AC, TV, shower & small fridge. Owners can arrange boat tours, snorkelling equipment for hire. $

Where to eat

El Mochimero ⊕ 11.00–21.00. This Spanish-style restaurant run by a Catalan has a nice terrace over the sea & serves good seafood dishes, such as paella & squid rings, as well as chicken & steak. $$

El Rancho de Compa ⊕ 07.00–13.00. Catch a b/fast snack before heading out to the islands at this *arepa* & *empanada* place down by the dock. $

Puerto Viejo ⊕ 11.00–21.00 w/ends & high season, 17.00–21.00 midweek. Down by the dock, this colourful restaurant aims to catch sun-seekers returning from the beach. Good seafood, meat dishes, nice atmosphere. $

Other practicalities There is an Inparques office (no phone) by the jetty, where you pay US$0.50 a night per person for a permit to camp on one of the islands in the park.

There is no bank, so bring all the cash you'll need.

Internet is available from a couple of informal cyber places in town.

Apart from a dispensary and a pharmacy in the village the closest medical services are 40 minutes away in Cumaná.

What to do

Boat trips The fishermen's co-operative offering boat trips to the national park is called Asotumo. Shuttle service to the beaches runs 07.00–18.00 on weekends, later during the week. A price list is posted at the dock. You pay by the boat according to distance (US$12–35) and agree an hour for pickup. The first proper beach is Las Maritas, which is small and overcrowded at weekends. It has food and beer stalls, and palm-roof shelters which fill up quickly. The next beach, Playa Blanca de Guagua, is bigger and better, with food and drinks available but no umbrellas or jetty. Once out of Mochima Bay there are good beaches around the headland west to Playa Manaure and Islas Caracas, and east to Playa Cautaro, Cautarito, Puerto Escondido and Playa Cachimena. These and others further east can also be visited from Cumaná, taking 30–40 minutes by speedboat.

Diving

Aquatics Diving Center Av La Marina, down by the jetty; 0414 777 4894; e info@ scubavenezuela.com; www.scubavenezuela.com. A well-established dive shop with over 17 years experience offering courses & taking divers out to the best spots. Prices similar to Mochima Dive Center.

Mochima Dive Center 0293 416 0856; m 0414 180 6244, 0424 807 7647, 0414 999 8422; e mochimadivecenter@hotmail.com, mochimarafting@hotmail.com; www.laposadadelosbuzos.com. Rodolfo Plaza has been here for years offering diving packages, taster courses & an intensive course for CMAS certification. He also runs the **Posada de Los Buzos** with 4 rooms with sgl & bunk beds. Rodolfo provides instruction, insurance, scuba gear, lodging & boats to the best diving places all year; US$70 a day for diving, US$20 snorkelling. The 5-day Open Water Diver course costs about US$550 & includes instruction, manual, snorkelling practice, all diving equipment & 5 immersions.

7

Margarita

Telephone code: 0295

PEARL OF THE CARIBBEAN

Margarita is now so identified as a holiday island that some Europeans are not even aware that it's part of Venezuela. All round the island you find English, French, Canadians, Germans, Spaniards and even Brazilians: people who came on packages to soak up the sun and then returned to live by the sea and set up guesthouses, windsurfing schools or horseriding stables. It's that kind of place.

Visitors relish the variety of great beaches, tasty fish cooked straight from the sea and varied nightlife. They also have a choice between the laid-back vibe that reigns during most of the year or the mad partying at Christmas, Easter and Carnival, when hordes of young people descend on the island from the mainland and the 4km of golden sand at Playa El Agua becomes a huge open-air concert.

Called the 'Pearl of the Caribbean' for the abundance of pearls found off the nearby island of Cubagua, Margarita today lives on tourism. What fascinates foreigners is swimming with dolphins at Waterland, surfing the waves at Parguito beach, taking a boat through the mangroves of La Restinga, horseriding along the shore of the desert-like Macanao Peninsula, diving off Los Frailes and exploring a new beach every day. The latest wave of tourism to hit the island is the massive boom in windsurfing and kitesurfing in El Yaque and the island of Coche, as the year-round winds and perfect seas attract foreigners intent on improving their surfing by day and bar-hopping at night in the self-contained resorts that have sprung up there.

Then there are the beaches – over 30 strips of sand gracing the island's 170km of shoreline, some of them so deserted that clothes are optional. And those who can tear themselves away from the coast to explore the interior find historic forts built to protect the island from marauding pirates, the oldest church in Venezuela and the basilica of La Virgen del Valle, Margarita's patron saint.

Margariteños are good-humoured and patient with outsiders, and the only ties you see are worn by bankers. Transport from the main cities is plentiful and cheap and little buses can take you nearly everywhere. Public as well as private health services are good. People look satisfied and work hard; street kids are a rare sight. The little fishing villages on the coast are clean and well cared for, plazas are filled with trees and houses overflow with plants. Fresh water is no longer a problem as an undersea pipeline brings mountain water from Turimiquire Dam in Sucre State. Life goes on with little reference to mainland Venezuela and politics takes a back seat to the price of fish.

GEOGRAPHY AND CLIMATE

Part of the Lesser Antilles chain, Margarita is just 25km off the coast of South America. It is the largest of Venezuela's 72 islands, measuring 67km from east to west and 33km north to south, covering 934km². At 11° north of the Equator the island lies south of the hurricane belt. Moderate rains fall mostly in November–January, but it is only below El Copey Mountain that there is enough

Margarita GEOGRAPHY AND CLIMATE 7

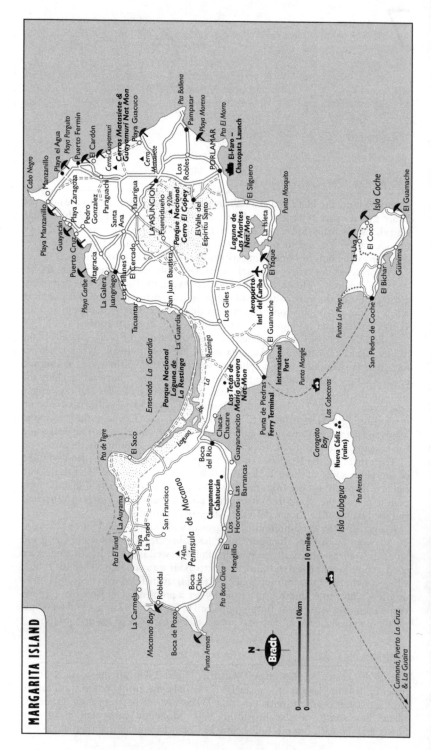

MARGARITA ISLAND

Playa Manzanillo
Cabo Negro
Manzanillo
Playa el Agua
Playa Parguito
Puerto Fermín
El Cardón
Guayacán
Playa Zaragoza
Puerto Cruz
Pedro Gonzalez
Altagracia
Playa Caribe
La Galera
Juangriego
Los Millanes
Santa Ana
El Cercado
Tacuantar
Paraguachí
Cerro Guayamurí
Cerros Matasiete & Guayamurí Nat'Mon
Cerro Matasiete
Pta Ballena
Pta Guacuco
Pampatar
Playa Moreno
Pta El Morro
Los Robles
PORLAMAR
El Faro – Chacopata Launch
El Silguero
Punta Mosquito
LA ASUNCIÓN
Fuentidueño
Parque Nacional – Cerro El Copey 920m
El Valle del Espíritu Santo
Tacarigua
San Juan Bautista
Laguna de Los Marites Nat'Mon
La Isleta
El Yaque
Aeropuerto Intl del Caribe
Los Giles
Los Giles
El Guamache
Isla Coche
El Guamache
El Coco
La Uva
Guinima
El Bichar
San Pedro de Coche
Punta La Playa
El Coco

Ensenada La Guardia
Parque Nacional Laguna de La Restinga
La Guardia
La Restinga
La Restinga
Restingo
El Guamache
El Guamache
Pta de Tigre
El Saco
Laguna
Boca del Río
Guayancancito
Las Tetas de María Guevara Nat'Mon
Chaca-Chacare
Punta de Piedras
Ferry Terminal
International Port
Punta Mangle
Las Cabeceras
Caragato Bay
Nueva Cádiz (ruins)
Pta Arenas

La Auyama
Pta El Tunal
Playa La Pared
San Francisco
Campamento Cabatucán
Las Barrancas
Los Horcones
Península de Macanao
740m
La Carmela
Robledal
Boca Chica
Pta Boca Chica
El Mangillo
Boca de Pozo
Macanao Bay
Punta Arenas

Isla Cubagua

Isla Coche

N
Bradt

10km
0
10 miles
0

Cumaná, Puerto La Cruz & La Guaira

rain to sustain limited agriculture. The sun shines an average of nine hours a day almost all year. There is a constant breeze and even the hottest days begin to cool off by mid afternoon. Day temperatures hover at a 27°C average, while the cooler months of December–March drop to 20–21°C at night. And, most appealing to sea lovers, water temperatures average 26°C.

The eastern and western halves of Margarita, once separate islands, are joined by a narrow isthmus called La Restinga. In the east the highest mountain reaches 920m; in the west, Macanao Peninsula, the high point is 740m. Macanao is beautiful but arid and sparsely populated; a vehicle is a must for exploring.

Margarita makes up Nueva Esparta State, together with the smaller islands of Coche and Cubagua, and the little Los Frailes Archipelago. The capital is La Asunción, a quiet town. Porlamar, the main city, is on the island's southeast coast. Two-thirds of Margarita's population of 430,000 is concentrated between Porlamar and Pampatar. The island also has a floating population of some 100,000 workers and tourists.

HISTORY

THE COLONIAL ERA Called the 'Pearl of the Caribbean', Margarita was first famous for its oyster beds. It was sighted by Columbus in 1498 on his third voyage to the Americas. Contrary to popular belief Columbus did not name the island Margarita after the Greek word for pearl, because he did not land and knew nothing of the fabulous undersea riches to be found here. Instead, he christened the island in honour of Margaret, Princess of Castile, daughter of Maximilian of Austria the Holy Roman Emperor. It was only in 1499 that Spanish conquistadors located the source of pearls worn by local Indians to oyster beds off the tiny island of Cubagua. The first shipment of 80lb of pearls to the Spanish court created an instant frenzy and the rush was on. Pearls from these small islands represented 40% of all the New-World riches transported to Spain between 1500 and 1530 and led to the settlement of Cubagua and Cumaná, which served as the supply centre for fresh water and Indian slaves. On Cubagua, Nueva Cádiz, after a decade of settlement as the first town in Venezuela, received a royal patent as a city in 1528 but it was short-lived. Ruthless exploitation not only exhausted Cubagua's pearl beds but also the supply of Indian divers. The enslaved natives were fed on oysters and forced to work until they died from exhaustion, blood gushing from mouth and nose. The alternative to this ugly death was being eaten by sharks, who were attracted in great numbers and took a heavy toll on the Indian divers. By 1541 when an earthquake and tidal wave devastated Nueva Cádiz it was already abandoned, the pearl beds having been picked clean as bones. Pearl fishing moved on to Coche Island and Margarita, where El Valle and La Asunción were settled as early as 1529 and 1536. (The pearl beds were again ravaged in 1823 when a concession was given to an English company using dredges. In the early 20th century Puerto Fermín saw some pearling activity and in 1943 divers with helmets were successful in gathering almost 1,500kg. Banned in 1962, pearling today is only allowed in season (January–April) every other year.)

During the colonial era a string of seven forts was built to protect Spanish interests from the British and French pirates of the Caribbean. Two have been restored: San Carlos Borromeo in Pampatar and Santa Rosa in La Asunción, both of which withstood pirate attacks and later assaults by royalists and patriots in the Independence wars.

INDEPENDENCE Margarita, and Cumaná on the mainland, were strong supporters of separation from Spain during the Independence wars and two special holidays are celebrated on the island: 4 May, which commemorates Margarita's Declaration of Independence in 1810; and 31 July, the day in 1817 when the patriots vanquished Spanish forces at the Battle of Matasiete by rolling huge boulders down the mountain of the same name.

In 1817, following the victory at Matasiete, La Asunción served as provisional capital of the republic, while an executive triumvirate operated from the Casa Amarilla in Pampatar. Margariteños still speak with pride of their part in the patriot victory and the role of the heroine Luisa Cáceres de Arismendi, wife of Juan Bautista Arismendi who was commander of Margarita's defence forces. While imprisoned in Santa Rosa fortress, this 17-year-old gave birth to a baby girl (who died) and was later sent to Spain where she escaped from captivity, returning to her homeland and husband in 1818. The bravery of such freedom fighters earned the new state the name of Nueva Esparta after the Spartan warriors of ancient Greece. Both Luisa and her husband are buried in the Panteón Nacional in Caracas and Luisa's image appears on the new 20 bolívar fuerte note.

FREE PORT For the next 150 years, life in Margarita centred on the peaceful activities of fishing, some farming and making pots and hammocks. The island was so tranquil, in fact, that it was famous for having no jail. In 1959 a ferry began a regular service to Cumaná. Curiously, when the bridge over Maracaibo Lake was built in 1963, it gave the island a big boost as the four lake ferries were acquired for Margarita duty.

In the 1970s Margarita was declared a free port and exchanged peace and isolation for tourism and shoppers, prompting the construction of a modern airport, highways and frenetic urban development. Currency devaluation attracted foreign investors as Margarita became the country's leading centre of tourism, both national and international. The 1990s were a decade of phenomenal hotel construction on some of the best beaches, starting with the Hilton on Playa Moreno (now operated by the government), Flamingo Beach in Pampatar, the Lagunamar on Gasparico beach, and around the island to the Dunes Hotel, Hesperia and Playa El Agua hotels. Margarita now has a golf course, casinos and the huge Sambil shopping mall. The challenge now is to fill the hotels and shopping malls in the face of economic recession in Venezuela and abroad.

☞ *WARNING:* Another challenge is the increasing security issues on the island, a reflection of the crime increase across Venezuela as a whole. Drugs are also a problem that has touched Margarita and foreign tourists are warned to steer clear of taking or transporting drugs in any form, given the harsh sentences of eight to ten years for possession and trafficking. While once the doors of the island's jail stood open for lack of prisoners, today San Antonio prison near Porlamar is home to several Europeans who made the stupid mistake of getting involved with drugs and are now paying the price.

GETTING THERE AND AWAY

BY AIR Santiago Mariño Airport is situated 20km southwest of Porlamar and has two terminals, national and international, although there are currently no direct international flights except on charter planes transporting European and Canadian package tourists. Travellers will find money exchange desks, duty-free shops, car-rental agencies and a tourism information booth.

For flights to Caracas arrive at least two hours before departure at peak times. Margarita is a popular holiday destination in Venezuela and Aeropostal, Aserca, Avensa, Avior, Conviasa, Laser, Rutaca and Santa Bárbara run more than 20 flights a day to/from Caracas (Maiquetía), a dozen to Barcelona and others to Barquisimeto, Carúpano, Maracaibo, Maturín, Mérida, Ciudad Guayana (Puerto Ordaz) and Valencia. (See *Chapter 2*, pages 53–4 for the airlines' contact details.)

Fares vary according to season and airline. Caracas–Porlamar flights range from about US$80 in low season to over US$120 in high season.

From Margarita it is easy to visit some of Venezuela's most scenic spots, including wilderness camps. Aereotuy (\ *0295 415 5778, 0295 415 5784; www.tuy.com*) flies direct to Canaima (Angel Falls), Arekuna, La Blanquilla Island, Los Roques and Delta Amacuro.

There are no public buses at the airport so take a taxi to get to your destination: Porlamar (20km, 30 minutes, US$10) or La Asunción (24km, 35 minutes, US$14). From downtown Porlamar, there is a bus to the airport from Avenida Miranda on the northwest corner of Plaza Bolívar; check it is still operating.

BY FERRY The ferry terminal is at Punta de Piedras, 29km west of Porlamar. Buses go regularly to Porlamar (35 minutes, BsF5), where they stop on Calle Mariño (the building of a main bus terminal may change this). Taxis to Porlamar charge anything from US$15 to US$25 depending on season and time of day. Punta de Piedras is a small fishing town and many *peñeros* tie up at the dock. At the end of the seaside at Paseo María Guevara are the marine research station, fishing school and oceanological museum of the Fundación La Salle.

From Punta de Piedras there are ferries to Puerto La Cruz and Cumaná. Cumaná offers cheaper routes but passengers can't go on deck. Conventional ferries allow First Class passengers on the upper deck, but not Tourist passengers who are cooped up in the stern over noisy engines.

Avoid taking a ferry on any big holiday or long weekend. Every Easter week Conferry transports some 35,000 people and 7,800 vehicles to Margarita. When it is time for them to return the queues are horrendous.

Conferry In Porlamar: Calle Marcano near Av Santiago Mariño; \ 0295 261 9235, 0295 261 6780; ⊕ 08.00–12.00 & 14.00–17.00 Mon–Fri; www.conferry.com. Over a million people go to & from the island yearly on Conferry's vessels linking Margarita with Puerto La Cruz. Ferries carry passengers & cars. **Regular ferries** leave Puerto La Cruz at 01.00, 08.00, 13.00 & 20.00 every day & take 4½ hrs to make the crossing. There are 2 classes: First Class (US$14 I way), with access to the decks, & Turista (US$10). Vehicle charges vary from US$22 to US$27. All Conferry fares have 50% discounts for children aged 2–7 & adults over 65 (you need a photocopy of passport or ID card). Even with prepaid car reservations drivers should be at the terminal 2hrs before sailing time. **Express ferries** leave Puerto La Cruz at 07.00, 12.00, 15.00, 16.00, 19.30 & 21.00 every day except Wed, when they leave at 12.00 & 19.30. The crossing takes 2hrs & there are 2 classes: VIP (US$40) & First Class (US$22). **Coche Island** ferry *Maria Libre*, run by Conferry, leaves Punta de Piedras at 18.00 Mon–Fri, 08.00 & 18.00 Sat–Sun; & from Coche to Margarita at 06.30 on w/days, 06.30 & 18.00 on w/ends. Fare is a bargain at US$4 & it takes 1hr. Buy tickets at the ferry terminal in Punta de Piedras.

Gran Cacique Express \ 0295 264 2945; www.grancacique.com.ve. Run by Naviarca, this is a Singapore-built hydrofoil that makes the crossing from Puerto La Cruz to Punta de Piedras in 2hrs carrying passengers only: VIP (US$27), Turista (US$18). The AC is cold! From Cumaná, the *Gran Cacique II* hydrofoil makes the 2-hr crossing from Cumaná to Porlamar at 07.00 & 14.00 with VIP (US$23) & Tourist Class (US$18) tickets.

Chacopata launches In Porlamar, look for the ticket kiosk by El Faro (lighthouse) at the end of Paseo Rómulo Gallegos; ⊕ 07.00–16.00. The Empresa Naviera Turismo Chacopata runs a cheap (US$5) passenger service bringing workers from Chacopata, a fishing village at the east end of Araya Peninsula, in *'tapaitos'*, launches with roof & canvas sides to keep out spray; it's an uncomfortable ride on benches with no view & not for those who get seasick. The *tapaitos* leave Chacopata 05.00–13.00, & Porlamar 08.00–16.00.

GETTING AROUND

BY BUS For many staying in resorts along the northern coast transport can be problematic, but those near Porlamar, Pampatar, Juangriego or Playa El Agua will find it easy and cheap to do short day trips to places of interest on the many small buses that travel around the island. Porlamar buses go to Pampatar (8km), La Asunción (10km), Playa El Agua (21km), Juangriego (25km), Boca del Río on Macanao Peninsula (26km), and Punta de Piedras (30km).

Many buses do not run after 21.00 and there is a small additional charge for night hours, holidays and Sundays. The majority of routes originate in Porlamar and fan out across the island. At present, downtown Porlamar is practically one large terminal where the little buses each use a certain street as the starting point of their route. This tradition plays havoc with traffic but is conveniently central. However, plans are underway for a bus terminal. Starting points of some lines are given below but can change at any time, so ask at your hotel:

🚌 **Aeropuerto** Plaza Bolívar, corner of Calle Mariño & Av Miranda.

🚌 **El Valle** Calle Marcano at Av Miranda.

🚌 **Juangriego** (via Santa Ana) Av Miranda between Marcano/Igualdad.

🚌 **La Asunción** Calle Fajardo at Marcano.

🚌 **La Restinga-Macanao** Calle Mariño at Calle Maneiro, until 18.30.

🚌 **Pampatar** Calle Fajardo at Maneiro; number 4 or 5 buses go via Av 4 de Mayo, Diverland & the Sambil shopping mall.

🚌 **Playa El Agua** Calle Guevara at Marcano.

🚌 **Playa El Angel** Buses circulate on Av 4 de Mayo.

🚌 **Playa Guacuco** Calle Fajardo between Igualdad/Velásquez.

🚌 **Punta de Piedras** Calle Mariño between Zamora/Maneiro.

🚌 **San Juan & Fuentidueño** Plaza Bolívar: Calle Velásquez at Mariño.

BY HIRE CAR Renting a car is a good way to see Margarita. At the airport, a dozen agencies, including Avis (\ *0295 269 1230; www.avis.com*), Budget (\ *0295 269 1490; www.budget.com.ve*), Hertz (\ *0295 269 1237; www.hertz.com*) and Margarita Rentals (\ *0295 269 1285*) all have booths and many are open until the last flight arrives. You will find rates are less expensive than the mainland, about US$50 a day for a small car; petrol is cheap so try the plan without *kilometraje* or mileage. Car-hire agencies work with your open credit-card voucher, so make a thorough check of the car before signing to protect against charges for dents and missing accessories that show up on statements once you are at home.

BY TAXI A good alternative, despite rising fares, are the island taxis that can be hired by the trip or by the day. A full-day excursion by taxi will cost around US$85–95, enough time to do a circuit of Pampatar, La Asunción, Playa El Agua, Juangriego and La Restinga. Air-conditioned taxis may charge extra. Always pay the driver at the end of your journey if you plan to make stops along the way. At night it is hard to find taxis to take you to out-of-the-way places, one of the reasons why most tourists stick to places like Porlamar, Juangriego, Playa El Agua and El Yaque where there are restaurants, bars, shops and nightlife. Taxis put prices up by 10% after 21.00 and apply the higher rate on Sundays and holidays. Tipping is not customary. Always agree the price before getting in. Taxi lines operating from the Sambil shopping mall are Luxor (\ *0295 263 7979*), Costa Azul (m *0416 401 1498*), Cexpre (\ *0295 262 4545*) and Union Latina (\ *0295 263 7113*).

TOURIST INFORMATION

The Nueva Esparta State Corporación de Turismo, **Corpotur** (*Centro Artesanal Gilberto Menchini, Los Robles*; \ *0295 262 2322, 0295 262 4511; www.corpoturmargarita.gov.ve*), compiles complete lists of hotels, guesthouses, tourism agencies and money exchange bureaux and has maps and brochures showing main attractions. Their headquarters are 3km northeast of central Porlamar. A booth in the airport has basic information and maps and a government-run website (*www.islamargarita.gob.ve*) has maps and pictures of the island and a list of attractions.

FESTIVALS AND HOLIDAYS

Shops and banks traditionally close on four local holidays as well as national ones: 4 May, Margarita's Independence declaration; 31 May, Free Port Labour Day; 31 July, Battle of Matasiete; 8 September, Virgen del Valle.

OTHER PRACTICALITIES

SECURITY Not everything is idyllic in Margarita and non-Spanish speakers should observe standard precautions, especially in the old town of Porlamar. Don't wear expensive jewellery or watches or count money in the street. Use ATMs inside shopping malls or banks. Be cautious of accepting drinks from strangers. Drug taking and drug smuggling are a problem on the island and specially trained National Guard units operate at the airport, aided by foreign police agencies. Judges tend to be severe on tourists smuggling drugs and an eight- to ten-year sentence is mandatory. Of the 300 or so prisoners in Margarita's state penitentiary in 2010, there were nearly 30 foreigners, mostly tourists. Given the tough conditions in these prisons, never buy or attempt to smuggle drugs and beware of accepting packages from strangers or even friends.

INTERNET Internet service is provided mainly by cyber cafés in Porlamar, Juangriego, Playa El Angel and other tourist centres for about US$1 an hour.

MONEY Credit cards are widely accepted in the main shopping malls and in some restaurants in the main towns but you will need cash for buses, taxis, beach bars, small stores, markets and the hire of jet skis. Remember that money withdrawn from an ATM will be paid out in BsF at the official exchange rate, with a small transaction charge. The parallel rate of exchange offered by some tour companies and small hotels only applies to US dollars and, to a lesser extent, the euro. Some stores in Porlamar on Avenida 4 de Mayo will give discounts of 10% or more for cash. Italcambio (*www.italcambio.com*) has a booth at the international terminal and offers money exchange and Moneygram services at Jumbo mall on Avenida 4 de Mayo and Galerias Fente on the same street. Cambios Cussco, on Calle Velásquez at Santiago Mariño, has branches at the international terminal, opposite Hotel Macanao in Costa Azul, in Playa El Agua, and at Hotel California in El Yaque.

MEDICAL EMERGENCIES The **Hospital Luis Ortega** (\ *0295 261 1101, 0295 262 0366*) is the main hospital in Porlamar and is centrally located on the busy Avenida 4 de Mayo.

PORLAMAR

Porlamar is the only big city in Margarita, home to five-star hotels, casinos, bingo halls, shopping malls, bars and restaurants. Moving away from the Plaza Bolívar and the old centre of town, new developments have changed the focus of the city east towards the outskirts of Pampatar. Together they have some 230,000 inhabitants, whose prosperity is staked on attracting shoppers and tourists.

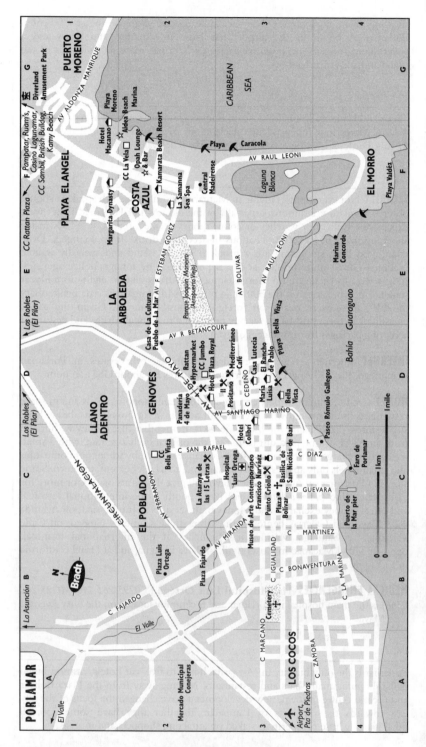

PORLAMAR

PUERTO MORENO

Diverland Amusement Park

Pampatar, Ruam's, Casino Lagunamar, CC Sambil, British Bulldog, Komy Beach

CC Rattan Plaza

Los Robles (El Pilar)

Los Robles (El Pilar)

La Asunción

El Valle

PLAYA EL ANGEL

COSTA AZUL

Hotel Macanao
Playa Moreno
Aldea Beach
Marina

Opah Lounge & Bar
CC La Vela
Kamarata Beach Resort

Margarita Dynasty

La Samanna Sea Spa

Central Madeirense

Playa Caracola

AV ALDONZA MANRIQUE

AV RAUL LEONI

CARIBBEAN SEA

EL MORRO

Playa Valdéz

Laguna Blanca

Marina Concorde

LA ARBOLEDA

Casa de la Cultura
Pueblo de La Mar

Parque Joaquín Maneiro (Aeropuerto Viejo)

AV F ESTEBAN GOMEZ

AV R BETANCOURT

AV BOLIVAR

AV RAUL LEONI

playa Bella Vista

Bahia Guaraguao

GENOVES

Rattan Hypermarket
CC Jumbo
Hotel Plaza Royal
Mediterráneo Café
Panadería 4 de Mayo
Positano
Casa Lutecia
El Rancho de Pablo
María Luisa
Bella Vista

AV DE MAYO
C CEDEÑO
AV SANTIAGO MARIÑO

LLANO ADENTRO

CIRCUNVALACIÓN

EL POBLADO

AV TERRANOVA

CC Bella Vista
La Ataraya de las 15 Letras
Hospital Luis Ortega

Hotel Colibrí

C SAN RAFAEL

Museo de Arte Contemporáneo Francisco Narváez
Punto Criollo
Plaza Bolívar
Basílica de San Nicolás de Barí

BVD GUEVARA

C DIAZ

Paseo Rómulo Gallegos

Faro de Porlamar

C MARTINEZ

Plaza Luis Ortega

Plaza Fajardo

AV MIRANDA

C IGUALIDAD

C BONAVENTURA

Puerto de la Mar pier

LOS COCOS

Mercado Municipal Conejeras

C FAJARDO

El Valle

Cemetery

C MARCANO

C ZAMORA

C LA MARINA

Airport, Pta de Piedras

N

Bradt

0   1km
0   1mile

Before the 1970s Porlamar was still a provincial town of 31,000 people, ending at a small airport east of the present Jumbo mall on Avenida Aeropuerto Viejo. In those days, the elegant Bella Vista was the only luxury hotel. After Margarita was declared a free port in 1970, however, Porlamar began to grow along Avenida 4 de Mayo, sprouting hotels and shopping centres such as the landmark Rattan hypermarket. By 1981 there were 73,700 inhabitants. Despite currency devaluation and hard times, a wave of luxury hotels went up in the 1990s starting with the Margarita Hilton (taken over by the government in 2009 and renamed Hotel Macanao), the Dynasty, Marina Bay, Margarita International Village, Margarita Plaza, and the Flamingo Beach in Pampatar. The trend has continued with new shopping malls, such as the huge Sambil and the latest addition, Centro Comercial La Vela, which opened in 2010.

HISTORY Founded in 1536 as Pueblo (or Puerto) de la Mar at the mouth of El Valle River, Porlamar struggled for survival for three centuries. Destroyed by pirates in 1555 and by Aguirre the Tyrant in 1556, the first settlement with its church was moved in 1567 to the more protected site of La Asunción, leaving the little port inhabited by Indian fisherfolk. Pirate attacks continued, first by the British privateer John Hawkins and then by John Burg in 1593 who, with four ships and 400 men, launched an attack in which Governor Juan Sarmiento de Villandrando was killed defending the town. Then in the 1600s more English, French and Dutch privateers came marauding. Still the settlement hung on. It had grown to some 600 inhabitants by the mid 1700s, only to be razed to the ground in the War for Independence by royalists who even destroyed the church of San Nicolás de Bari. Finally at peace, Porlamar was able at length to rebuild its church in 1853–64. Trade began to flourish and the population rose to 2,655 in 1873. In 1895 the lighthouse was built, followed by a dock and in 1900 the first telephone service.

WHERE TO STAY Every kind of accommodation, from luxury resorts down, is found here. In central Porlamar, except for the Bella Vista, there are no hotels on the beach. However, in the **Costa Azul–Playa Moreno** resort area east of town, the Macanao Hotel (formerly the Hilton) sits on a good stretch of sand and there are many large, posh hotels within a short walk of the long Playa Moreno–La Caracola coastline. All have air conditioning, hot water, restaurants, swimming pool and many offer transportation to beaches and shopping malls.

Hotel Macanao [166 F1] (280 rooms) 0295 262 4111. This deluxe, 10-storey hotel on Playa Moreno was the Margarita Hilton, one of the best hotels on the island, until it was taken over by the government in 2009. It continues to operate with most of the same staff but there have been complaints that standards are slipping. The beach has lifeguards, shelters, jet skis & parasailing. Low-season bargains available. $$$$

La Samanna Sea Spa [166 F2] (64 rooms) Av Esteban Gómez at Bolívar, Costa Azul; 0295 262 2662; www.lasamannademargarita.com. A top-notch health centre & hotel with 64 rooms & suites, balconies with sea view, pool, shops, pharmacy, plus a fine Japanese–Peruvian restaurant. This spa, renowned for thalassotherapy using sea water, gives full health & beauty treatments, massages for sports injuries, gym & t'ai chi classes. It's a shame it doesn't have better access to the beach. $$$$

Bella Vista [162 D3] (305 rooms) Av Santiago Mariño; 0295 261 7222; e ventas@ hbellavista.com; www.hbellavista.com. Porlamar's original (1955) 5-star hotel on Guaraguao Bay, has 2 pools, a bar/nightclub & an old-school Spanish resort vibe. A bit faded around the edges, the service is still passable, the views out to sea over the tall palms still spectacular, although the beach could do with a clean. Try it if you can get a low-season discount. $$$–$$$$

Best Western Margarita Dynasty (150 suites) Costa Azul; 0295 262 1622, 0295 400 8000; e reservaciones@margaritadynasty.com; www.margaritadynasty.com. 4-star hotel located, as it says in the brochure 'close to everything', including the

Sambil shopping mall, bars & restaurants. Some of the rooms, studio apartments & suites with kitchenette for 2–4 people, have seen better days. $$$

🏠 **Casa Lutecia** [166 D3] (10 rooms) Calle Campos between Cedeño/Marcano; ☎ 0295 263 8526; 📱 0414 789 7769. Not a hotel, this is a guesthouse owned & run by a French woman, Colette Pompili. Nicely decorated rooms with bath & AC are complemented by an inviting terrace, bar, swimming pool & French restaurant. $$

🏠 **Hotel Colibri** [166 D3] (70 rooms) Av Santiago Mariño; ☎ 0295 251 5645. A comfortable hotel with a shiny lobby close to Av 4 de Mayo. Japanese–Peruvian restaurant, rooftop pool, B&B rooms with TV, AC, hot water. $$

🏠 **Hotel Plaza Royal** [166 D2] (100 rooms) Calle Fermin con Av 4 de Mayo; ☎ 0295 261 6666; www.hotelplazaroyal.com.ve. A clean, well-run option at the start of the main street on Av 4 de Mayo, close to shops & casinos. Rooms with AC, hot water, TV, internet. Higher floors have better views of the sea, some 5 blocks away. $$

🏠 **Kamarata Beach Resort** [166 F2] (40 suites) Av Bolívar, Costa Azul; ☎ 0295 262 4311; e hotelkamarata@telcel.net.ve. An attractive, small apart-hotel; 40 suites with kitchen for 4–7 people, poolside bar, *tasca* restaurant. $$

🏠 **María Luisa** [166 D3] (98 rooms) Av Raúl Leoni, across the street from the bay; ☎ 0295 263 6737; www.hotelmarialuisa.com.ve. A clean hotel with pool near the Bella Vista Hotel & a few blocks from Av Santiago Mariño. Free Wi-Fi. Ask for room with sea views. Not the best area at night. $$

✗ WHERE TO EAT

Porlamar is a tourist mecca and has plenty of places to eat in the old town, the streets around Avenida 4 de Mayo and the Costa Azul area near Hotel Macanao, where many of the bars and clubs are located. Food ranges from the humble *empanada*, stuffed with cheese, meat or baby shark, to lobster thermidor. For an affordable lunch, go *criollo*, eat local dishes or cheap and cheerful spit-roast chicken, pasta and pizza.

The rise of swanky shopping malls, offering cool interiors for window-shopping and secure environments for partying, has brought a slight decline to the traditional tourist centre of Porlamar. The massive Sambil mall, between Porlamar and Pampatar, has a large food fair area with fast-food options and good restaurants including A Granel, which has live jazz. Reservations are not customary even in expensive restaurants. A service charge is included in the bill, so only tip if you're happy with the service.

✗ **El Rancho de Pablo** [166 D3] Av Raúl Leoni, near Bella Vista Hotel; ☎ 0295 263 1121; ⏰ 08.00–23.00. Open-air terrace with view of beach. Main meals include soups, seafood, grilled fish & lobster. $$

✗ **Il Positano** [166 D3] Calle Fermín at Tubores; ⏰ 17.00–23.00 Tue–Sun. Well-prepared pastas, wood-oven pizza & reasonable prices. $$

✗ **La Atarraya de las 15 Letras** [166 C2] Calle San Rafael at Charaima, north of Av 4 de Mayo; ☎ 0295 261 5124; ⏰ 12.00–23.00. An unpretentious spot recommended for the best Margaritan cooking, including fresh local fish cooked *al ajillo* (with garlic) & a filling *sancocho* soup with seafood, yuca & vegetables. $$

✗ **Mediterráneo Café** [166 D3] Calle Campos at Patiño; ⏰ 11.00–23.00, closed Mon. An Italian restaurant with a romantic patio setting for great ravioli & creative salads. $$

✗ **Panaderia 4 de Mayo** [166 D2] Av 4 de Mayo; ⏰ 07.00–23.00. A busy café on the main street with good coffee & economic sandwiches, snacks, pastries & tables outside to watch the world go by. $

✗ **Punto Criollo** [166 C3] Calle Igualdad at Fraternidad; ⏰ 11.00–24.00. A busy, economical choice downtown below the Porlamar Hotel. The full menu covers pastas, pizza, steaks, chicken, shrimps & *hervido* (stew), *asado* (pot roast), side orders of *tajadas* (fried plantain bananas), fresh milky-white cheese, & *nata* (a tangy sour cream). $

NIGHTLIFE Porlamar hums at night, especially around the main party area of Costa Azul, and some clubs and bars will stay open until the last party-goer stumbles out the door. It is a dynamic, changing scene with new spots opening frequently. Outside high season most places are only open Thursday–Sunday, while at Easter the party never seems to stop as thousands of Venezuelans descend on the island looking for good times. Since Señor Frog's closed down, the *rumba* (party) has moved to places like Stigma in Pampatar and La Aldea. For gay clubs head for Tiffany Beach (*www.tiffanybeach.com*) at Playa El Angel, behind Farmatodo.

☆ **Aldea Beach** [166 F2] Margarita Village, behind Centro Comercial Bayside mall, Costa Azul; ⊕ 09.00–03.00 Thu–Sat. A new beachside disco place similar in concept to Kamy (see below).

☆ **British Bulldog** [166 F1] Av Bolívar, 2nd flr CC Costa Azul; ⊕ 09.00–03.00. This rock bar in Margarita serves up a regular menu of live bands, many playing covers of reggae & classic rock tunes. Beer & snacks available at the bar. No cover charge.

☆ **Kamy Beach** [166 F1] Av Aldonza Manrique, Playa Varadero, Pampatar; ⊕ 09.00–03.00 Thu–Sat. The best & most popular disco on the island, Kamy Beach is right on the beach with a bar & sofas on the sand & a large palm-thatched dance floor where all the action takes place. Young crowd, a mix of funky electronica, chart hits & tropical tunes. US$10 cover includes drinks.

☆ **Opah Lounge & Bar** [166 F2] Av Bolívar, Centro Comercial, Costa Azul; ⊕ 09.00–03.00 Thu–Sat. A disco-lounge for the over 30s, this place has been here for years, with a varied mix of old favourites, current pop hits & tropical rhythms.

☆ **Ruam's** [166 F1] Calle el Cristo, La Caranta, at Hotel Flamingo Beach, Pampatar; ⊕ 08.00–03.00 Thu–Sat. Vast hall that fills up at w/ends with a young crowd, with live music & salsa shows some nights.

Casinos are the hot spots in Porlamar for Venezuelan holidaymakers, they are swanky spaces where drinks are brought to your table and there are big payouts for the lucky winners. Pace yourself. **Casino del Sol** is at the elegant Marina Bay Hotel, Costa Azul. Another option is the **Casino Lagunamar** [166 F1] in Apostadero, a short drive from Pampatar, part of the huge Lagunamar resort complex.

If bingo is your thing head for **Bingo Charaima** (*Av 4 de Mayo, some 4 blocks west of Rattan Hypermarket*), **Reina Margarita** (*Centro Comercial La Redoma, Av Jóvito Villalba*) or the **Caribe Plaza** (*Calle Patiño between Santiago Mariño & Malavé*). These places are nothing like the British seaside-style bingo halls with old ladies in rollers.

SHOPPING Most tourists tend to stick to the beach or the markets, but for an insight into the Venezuelan love of shopping malls there are four large temples to consumerism in and around Porlamar. Open every day until about 21.00 (including the banks), they lure in shoppers with big-name stores selling clothes and the Venezuelan favourites: whisky, wine and cheese. **Centro Comercial Jumbo** [166 D2], on Avenida 4 de Mayo, has four cinemas. **Rattan Plaza** [166 F1] is some 3km further out, where Avenida Jóvito Villalba meets Aldonza Manrique. The largest of them all is **Sambil Margarita** [166 F1], only a kilometre or so before Pampatar, which has seven cinemas, hundreds of shops, bars, restaurants, fast-food outlets and banks. The newest and shiniest is **Centro Comercial La Vela** [166 F2] (*www.cclavela.com.ve*). As there is no value-added tax, prices are attractive. Low-season sales (*ofertas*) are worthwhile, especially in boutiques on Avenida Santiago Mariño and shops along Avenida 4 de Mayo.

The **Rattan Hypermarket** [166 D2] on Avenida 4 de Mayo and Calle Fermín is famous as the first of Margarita's fixed-price giant shops combining supermarket and department store. Years ago when Porlamar first became a free port Rattan started life as a small shop. It grew as its American owner brought supplies from abroad, visiting the US and each year canvassing more and more countries, until today Rattan stores have at least 80,000 different items from around the world.

In the crowded heart of downtown, around Plaza Bolívar, shops line the streets on **Boulevard Guevara** and **Boulevard Gómez** selling cheap clothes and shoes from China, India, the US, Italy, Mexico and Brazil. They seem to have permanent sales (*rebajas*), and shoppers prepared to haggle can often get a further 10–30% off the price. Try shaking your head and saying, '*Es muy caro para mi. Cuál es su mejor precio?*' ('It's very expensive for me. What's your best price?').

WHAT TO SEE AND DO

Basílica de San Nicolás de Bari [166 C3] The basilica, in the shape of a cross, is on the east side of Plaza Bolívar. Religious images include a replica of the black Virgin of Montserrat, the patron saint of Cataluña, Spain. A marble plaque bears the text of Porlamar's founding. Processions on 5 December mark the feast day of San Nicolás.

Museo de Arte Contemporáneo Francisco Narváez [166 C3] (*Calle Igualdad con Díaz;* ℡ *0295 261 8668;* ✆ *08.30–17.00 Tue–Fri, 10.30–15.30 Sat–Sun; admission free*)
An art gallery and a cool retreat from the midday sun, it displays a collection of paintings and sculptures by local artist Francisco Narváez. The artist was born in Porlamar in 1905, worked in Paris as a young man and died in Porlamar in 1982. His delightful sculpture *La Ronda*, showing four children dancing, pigtails flying in the air, is in front of the basilica on Plaza Bolívar.

Paseo Guaraguao [166 C4] A bayside promenade, also known as **Paseo Rómulo Gallegos**, goes from the bottom of Avenida Santiago Mariño to a small lighthouse built in 1895, the **Faro de Porlamar**. Steps form an amphitheatre here for folk spectacles. From the pier daily launches leave for Chacopata. At the foot of Boulevard Gómez stands a single-storey building, the old Aduana or customs house. Walking around here after dark is not recommended.

Mercado Municipal Conejeros [166 A2] The busy public market is on Porlamar's northwest outskirts by the Circunvalación highway. Under one roof you find fresh fruit, vegetable and fish stands, and stalls heaped with inexpensive perfumes, sandals, souvenirs and cotton imports. There are no handicrafts in the concrete market but you can eat cheaply at stands where women serve chicken salad, maize *cachapas* and *arepas* for BsF25, and *empanadas* (turnovers) of white cheese, shredded meat or *cazón* (shark) for about US$1.50. Or try the budget eateries inside the market, where the food is hearty and the boss is the lady cooking the *rueda de carite al ajillo*, fried kingfish with garlic, or the *pabellón Margariteño*, a rice, bean and plantain dish with shredded fish cooked in a sauce. Regular buses come here from Plaza Bolívar.

Casa de La Cultura Pueblo de La Mar [166 D2] (*Av Rómulo Betancourt at Av Aeropuerto Viejo;* ℡ *0295 264 5969;* e *fccpm@hotmail.com*) This handsome cultural centre was inaugurated in 2000. A concert hall, lecture rooms and art gallery are complemented by community workshops in music, ballet and theatre. Also, there's an Infocentro with 11 terminals for computer students and internet surfers (✆ *09.00–17.00 Mon–Fri*). Except for evening cultural events, the centre is open ✆ 08.00–21.00 Monday–Saturday.

Margaritaville–Las Churuatas (*On the Costa Azul beach by Centro Comercial Bayside;* ℡ *0295 267 00503;* e *margaritaville@telcel.net.ve*) This cultural centre includes an art gallery, craft shop and museum housed in striking *churuatas*, the Indian-built structures roofed with intricately woven palm leaves. Another *churuata* is devoted to a large restaurant and piano bar. The nicely maintained beach here is open to all and is used by guests from local hotels.

Diverland [166 G1] (*Av Jóvito Villalba at Av Bolívar near Pampatar;* ℡ *0295 267 0571, 0295 262 0813;* ✆ *18.00–midnight every day in high season, Fri–Sun in low season;*

admission US$5 adult, US$3 child) A large amusement park that's showing its age, Diverland offers visitors a giant Ferris wheel, roller-coaster, haunted house, karting, mini-golf, inflated playgrounds, carousels, swimming pools, water slide and bump'em boats on the lagoon. Bring your swimsuit and a towel. The admission ticket covers unlimited use of all attractions.

Within the Diverland complex, **Waterland** (\ *0295 262 2182;* e *info@ dolphinswin4u.com; www.waterlandmundomarino.com;* ⊕ *10.00, 11.30, 14.30, 16.00*) is an aquarium with performing dolphins and seals, and a specially operated pool where tourists pay about US$50 to swim and play with dolphins for 30 minutes, by prior reservation.

Beaches Porlamar's beaches are not of the white, idyllic variety that make Margarita famous. The Bella Vista beach has palm trees and is convenient, being right at the bottom of Avenida Santiago Mariño, but it can be grubby after major holidays. La Caracola, the 2km-long strand south of Costa Azul, is the favourite beach of joggers, walkers, cyclists and sunbathers; it has food and drink stalls as well as sun shades and chairs for rent. The road between La Caracola beach and Laguna Blanca goes south all the way around Punta El Morro to Playa Valdéz, then west to the Concorde Marina on Avenida Raúl Leoni. North of La Caracola the beach is called Playa Moreno. In a short walk you reach the well-kept sands and palm trees of Margaritaville's restaurant and the marina. Beyond, the beach in front of the Hotel Macanao has stalls hiring jet skis and offering parasailing.

PAMPATAR

Pampatar is 8km east of Porlamar and the land between the towns is filling up with suburbs, shops and hotels. Pampatar, however, retains its charm as a historic port. In Los Robles, on the way to Pampatar, the beautiful white colonial church of El Pilar stands on Plaza Bolívar. On 12 October, the feast day of Nuestra Señora del Pilar (also a national holiday, Día de la Resistencia Indigena), the little statue of 'La Pilarica' heads a procession around the village. A replica of one in Zaragoza, Spain, 'La Pilarica' is said to be of solid gold (she is kept in a bank) and was the gift in 1504 of Queen Juana La Loca, daughter of Fernando and Isabel of Spain. In pedestrian streets around the church cars are replaced with plants and benches; children swarm through the Plaza de La Concha with its small Venus in a shell.

Old houses with tall doors and window grilles, decorative friezes and wrought-iron locks line the entrance to Pampatar. The ruins of La Caranta fort on the eastern bluff afford a magnificent view of Pampatar's San Carlos de Borromeo fortress and the long palm-shaded bay in front with colourful fishing boats and yachts from around the world. One of the oldest towns on Margarita, Pampatar was founded in 1580 as Mampatare, or Pampatar, after an Indian word meaning 'house of salt' (salt pans can still be seen on the east coast of Punta Ballena). The Royal Port of Mampatare on the island's deepest harbour was often attacked by pirate marauders seeking pearls. Tourism is its main livelihood today and there is a choice of hotels.

WHERE TO STAY

🏠 **Flamingo Beach** (159 rooms) Calle El Cristo, Caranta; \ 0295 262 4750; www.hotelflamingobeachmargarita.com. The Flamingo's 5-star facilities include pool, tennis courts, gym & sauna, boutiques, disco, seafood grill, a tiny beach in front of the resort, & free transfers

to Porlamar. Popular with Venezuelan families, it is close to the Sambil shopping mall & main discos in Pampatar. $$$
🏠 **Lagunamar Resort** (400 rooms) Apostadero; \ 0295 400 4035; www.lagunamar.com.ven. This massive hotel & casino complex 15mins from

Porlamar is touted as the island's largest resort. Aimed at families & package tour groups its 300 acres include 9 pools (olympic, cloverleaf, kids & pools with waves, slides, jacuzzi), bowling lanes, 9 tennis courts, theatre, 5 restaurants, bars & disco. Packages available with low-season discounts. $$$

✗ **WHERE TO EAT** Every morning on Pampatar beach kiosks serve up the morning's catch, fresh *pargo* (red snapper) or *carite* (kingfish), with rice and *tajadas* (plantains) on the side, all for about BsF15. Get your order in before the crowd appears at noon. *Empanadas de cazón* (shark turnovers) are the speciality at the stalls.

✗ **Las Algas** By Flamingo beach. A popular shrimp- &-fish place with live music on w/ends. $

✗ **Mora Luna** Calle Nueva Cádiz. A good seafood restaurant. $

✗ **Trismar Restaurant** Pampatar Bay. Makes good, economical Margarita dishes. $

OTHER PRACTICALITIES The main place for shopping in Pampatar is in the enormous Sambil shopping mall, which has banks, supermarkets, clothing stores, pharmacies, restaurants, fast food outlets and cinemas.

Spanish language courses The **Centro de Lingüística Aplicada**, or **CELA** (*Quinta Cela, Calle Corocoro, Urb Playa el Angel;* ✆ *0295 262 8198, 0295 808 8411;* e *info@cela-ve.com; www.cela-ve.com*), is a well-established school run by Sabine Loffler, which offers Spanish language courses from beginners to proficiency level, excursions around the island and homestays with Venezuelan families, as well as cooking and salsa classes. Spanish courses of 25 lessons a week cost US$250. Sabine's website offers lots of practical tips and background on places to visit in Margarita.

WHAT TO SEE AND DO

Castillo de San Carlos Borromeo (⏲ *09.00–17.00 Tue–Sun*) Pampatar's most prized landmark, this attractive fortress was burnt in a Dutch attack and rebuilt over 1664–84 complete with a moat, now dry. The fort's star shape, like the one in Cumaná, is a fine example of Spanish military architecture. Among historical events portrayed in the paintings inside is the imprisonment of Margarita's Independence heroine Luisa Cáceres de Arismendi in 1816. Besides art exhibitions, cultural events are staged in an amphitheatre.

Iglesia de Santísimo Cristo del Buen Viaje The 18th-century church across the plaza from the fort is a place of pilgrimage for Margarita's fishermen, who attribute great powers to the image of Christ over the altar. Legend has it that when the ship transporting the crucifix to Santo Domingo stopped at Pampatar it was unable to continue its voyage until the statue was unloaded, which was interpreted as a sign from above.

Playa Varadero and the western beaches of Pampatar These can be reached by any buses travelling to Playa El Angel from Porlamar, and have good basic restaurants serving fish for lunch or dinner. In front of Pampatar, the beach is lined with palms. Swimmers are recommended to use the clear waters east of Pampatar. Buses will take you as far as La Caranta, by the small hilltop fort, a short walk from two small beaches by the Flamingo Hotel.

EL VALLE DEL ESPÍRITU SANTO

An interesting destination to visit close to Porlamar (3km), you can easily see the sights related to the patron saint of Margarita, La Virgen del Valle (Virgin of the

Valley) in a few hours, or incorporate a trip here with a visit to La Asunción and the Santa Rosa Fort. The little town's lofty name, meaning The Valley of the Holy Spirit, dates to 1528 when the first settlers arrived – three years after the Province of Margarita (Venezuela's first) was created by Spain. When the Spanish governor died in 1526, his daughter and heir, Aldonza Villalobos Manrique, became governor and it was Aldonza's mother, Isabel, who founded El Valle. This was Margarita's capital until Aldonza's grandson, the last Villalobos governor, died in 1593.

WHAT TO SEE AND DO

La Virgen del Valle People come year round to the main square to see the tiny statue of the Virgin displayed behind glass in her cream-and-white neo-Gothic shrine, the twin-spired Santuario de la Virgen. The main pilgrimage is on the Virgin's feast day of 8 September, a state-wide holiday. To Margariteños, the week-long celebrations over 7–15 September are the most important event of the year. The Virgin del Valle is the patron saint of Margarita, Los Roques, Chichiriviche and many other coastal towns. Venezuelan fishermen and sailors traditionally ask for her blessing before going to sea and even the Venezuelan navy pays homage to her on its vessels.

According to local lore, the people of Cubagua had ordered an image of the Virgin Mary from Spain which they received in 1530. A hurricane hit the small island destroying almost everything, but the image was miraculously unscathed. It was decided to bring it to safety and it was brought to El Valle, where a number of shrines were built and the statue gained a reputation for saving sailors at sea, curing illness and working miracles.

During the celebrations on 8 September do not even think of taking a car into the centre; go on foot. People crowd around the basilica, built in 1909 on the site of earlier churches. The entire surroundings and Plaza Mariño are thronged by pilgrims, vendors of religious artefacts, souvenirs and refreshments. Busy shops and stalls selling religious images, handicrafts and homemade honey line the plaza.

Museo Diocesano de la Virgen del Valle (⊕ *09.00–12.00 & 14.00–17.00 Mon–Sat, 09.00–13.00 Sun; admission US$1*) A small museum with images of the Virgin and offerings from pilgrims, including heaps of coins, graduation rings, baseball bats and sports trophies. Faith can move mountains they say, and the odd assortment of silver and gold miniatures of houses, farm animals, hands, cars and eyes, pays tribute to that sentiment. All have been donated as thanks for favours received, wounds healed, diseases cured, exams passed or jobs secured. The navy has also donated insignia and model ships.

Plaza Mariño The town square is named after the Independence hero General Santiago Mariño, who was born in a house a block away, son of an army captain and a Trinidadian mother with Irish roots. He studied in Trinidad and as soon as the Independence struggles broke out was sent as an envoy to ask the British governor of Trinidad for assistance. A great military leader, at the age of only 25 he gathered and trained a military force with Manuel Piar and José Bermúdez and in six months had liberated eastern Venezuela from Spanish control. After reverses in central Venezuela, Mariño sailed with Simón Bolívar to Jamaica and Haiti seeking international support, returning by way of Juangriego in 1816. In the church of Santa Ana, Bolívar was proclaimed supreme head of the republic and Mariño his second in command.

Museo Casa Natal Santiago Mariño (⊕ *09.00–17.00 Mon–Fri, 09.00–14.00 Sat–Sun; admission US$0.25*) The birthplace of Mariño in 1788 is a well-restored house by the river. As you walk up the shady entrance directly west of the church, birdsong replaces traffic noise and centuries fall away. Some 250 years old, the cool Spanish house is today one of the best museums in Margarita. Antique tables, beds and chests fill front rooms, paintings by local artists line the corridors, and in the back a library conserves rare books and Independence documents.

LA ASUNCIÓN

La Asunción (population 22,000) is a sleepy old town of small houses and shady trees that merits a short visit. Although outshone by the modern city of Porlamar (9.5km, 25 minutes by bus), La Asunción is the official capital of Nueva Esparta State and has some well-preserved colonial buildings. It was first settled by the Spanish in 1562, when villagers from Espíritu Santo, fleeing from pirates, took refuge in this fertile valley, which is fed by a mountain stream from Cerro El Copey. The relocation did little to deter the pirates and in 1566 it was completely sacked by the French pirate Jean Bontemps, who was followed by the English privateer John Hawkins. In 1600 it received a coat of arms and became a city and in 1677–83 the splendid Santa Rosa fortress was built.

✗ WHERE TO EAT
Restaurant La Plaza ⏰ 07.00–20.00 Mon–Sat. A café-style restaurant with tables outside serving coffee & snacks on Plaza Bolívar, & tables inside in a pleasant central courtyard of the old house. $$

OTHER PRACTICALITIES In La Asunción there are two banks, a post office, public library, a cultural centre, two museums and a private hospital, the Centro Médico Nueva Esparta (*Sector El Dique;* ✆ *0295 242 0011*), which has a good reputation for modern facilities and emergency attention.

WHAT TO SEE The shady plaza of La Asunción is really two: the south half is **Plaza Bolívar**, the north half is the **Plaza Luisa Cáceres**, identified by a white marble statue of Margarita's Independence heroine. On its east side stands a restored two-storey house where you can buy souvenirs, surf the internet or have a coffee and juice at tables on the street, which is closed to traffic. This is Calle Bolívar which leads to the hills and up to Santa Rosa fortress where Luisa Cáceres was imprisoned.

Castillo de Santa Rosa (⏰ *09.00–16.00 Tue–Sun; admission free*) Less than a kilometre uphill from La Asunción, this historic fort has panoramic views over the valley to the hills of Cerro Matasiete and the distant sea. It is said that during its construction during 1677–83, the fortress was linked to the church, monastery and governor's house below by a kilometre-long tunnel. The moat and drawbridge no longer exist. Period weapons are on display, as well as heavy iron balls once attached to leg irons. Behind the kitchen is a 'bottle' dungeon whose only entrance is a hole in the ceiling. As a pregnant teenage bride in 1815, Independence heroine Luisa Cáceres de Arismendi was imprisoned in a cell here after being captured by the Spanish on 24 September, the day before her 17th birthday. Her husband, Juan Bautista Arismendi, had escaped into the forests of the Cerro Copey and the Spanish hoped her capture would force him to surrender. It didn't work. Four months later she gave birth to a daughter in her cell. The baby died and Luisa was taken to Spain, from where she escaped. Eventually after many trials she was reunited with her husband and had 11 children with him, living to the age of 65. She is one of only two women buried in El Panteón Nacional in Caracas. You can visit the cell she was kept in.

Catedral de Nuestra Señora de La Asunción On the east side, this large, impressive building was begun in 1570, making it Venezuela's oldest church – predating the cathedral of Coro (1583) – and among the first in the Americas. However, as the church remained unfinished, a new structure was begun in 1609 and completed ten years later. Its classic rectangular design and strong, stark lines were a mark of the early years of the Spanish colony, when thick walls were the best protection against pirates and marauders. Inside, two rows of massive columns rise solemnly to the rafters. Outside, the bell tower is unique, the last surviving example of its time; the old bells are now in the plaza. In mid-August the feast day of Our Lady of the Assumption is celebrated with processions and a special mass.

Casa de La Cultura (⊕ *08.00–18.00 Tue–Fri, 08.00–14.00 Sat, 08.00–12.00 Sun*) On the plaza opposite the cathedral, this building has a small theatre and gallery displaying replicas of pre-Columbian pottery made by local artisans. Such replicas can be bought at Cerámica El Cercado near Santa Ana.

Museo Nueva Cádiz (*Calle Independencia on the plaza's northwest corner;* ⊕ *09.00–17.00 Tue–Sun; admission free*) Dating from 1612, this building once housed the Casa Capitular, or 'government seat', with offices upstairs and a jail downstairs. It is famous as the place Margarita declared Independence on 4 May 1810, just weeks after the proclamation in Caracas. In the early 1950s the jail was closed for lack of prisoners and the building was turned into a museum, gallery and library. There is a statue of the tyrant Lope de Aguirre (featured in the movie *Aguirre–Wrath of God* by Werner Herzog, starring Klaus Kinski) who terrorised the island for a brief period in 1561. The colonial bridge over the Río Asunción, two blocks north of the museum, was built in 1609 and was in use until the 1970s, forming the north entrance to La Asunción for more than 350 years.

Casa Natal Juan Bautista Arismendi (*Calle Independencia;* ⊕ *10.00–17.00 Sat–Sun*) The reconstructed birthplace of the Independence hero (1770–1841) and husband of Luisa Cáceres.

Palacio Municipal (*Bd 5 de Julio*) Behind the cathedral are the state government buildings. The **Asamblea Legislativa** is housed in a former Franciscan monastery and later served as a prison and a hospital. On one corner stands a famous sundial, 'Relox Equinoca Inferior', in use ever since it was set up in 1612 by a far-sighted governor.

PARQUE NACIONAL CERRO EL COPEY

Between La Asunción and El Valle del Espíritu Santo is the highest point on the island at Parque Nacional El Copey (⊕ *08.00–16.00 Tue–Sun; information from Inparques office in La Asunción, Calle Unión;* \0295 242 0306). The park is a cool and moist retreat of 7,000ha. At the Guardia Nacional post there is a parking lot and *mirador*, or 'viewpoint', complete with picnic grills, shelters and restroom. Just to the left of the picnic area there is an amazing specimen of the tough-leafed copey tree with waxy white flowers (Clusia family) after which the park is named. It is perhaps 20m in circumference with a girth enclosing a dozen supplementary trunks. The paved path from the entrance takes you on a 5km walk to the peak, known as Las Antenas for its communication towers. At 920m elevation, you are on the highest spot in Margarita and the view to Juangriego is impressive. This is a good place to see cloudforest with its tree ferns, air plants, orchids, mosses, vines and elegant mountain palms. The park is home to the *mono mandarín* (capuchin monkeys) whose mysterious presence on the island has never been explained. Camping is not permitted.

EAST COAST BEACHES

A web of roads links La Asunción with beaches: Juangriego 14km to the west, Playa El Agua 12km north, and Playa Guacuco 6km to the east.

PLAYA GUACUCO This is a fine 2km-long beach, popular as one of the few with changing rooms and showers. Guacuco has chairs and parasols for hire. Palm trees provide shade and the sea is fairly shallow, not too rough. At beachside restaurants the thing to do is eat *guacuco* soup made from the little clams that people dig up right on the beach. From Guacuco a narrow white strand stretches north 3km; here, the road runs between steep hills and the sea. At the bluffs of Arena Cernida or Ranchos de Chana, the road turns inland between Cerro Matasiete (680m) on the south and Guayamurí (480m) on the north – which together form a Natural Monument.

PARAGUACHÍ (LA PLAZA) Paraguachí is an old village with big trees. People come to see the restored 1599 remnants of Iglesia de San José, namely the sacristy and dome to which three naves were added in the 19th century. The French privateer Marquis de Maintenon, who encrusted in the church tower two faience plates (long gone), spared Paraguachí in 1677 when he burned and plundered many settlements.

PARQUE EL AGUA (\ *0295 263 0710; www.parqueelagua.com;* ⊕ *10.00–17.00 Wed–Sun; admission US$20 adults, US$13 children*) One for the kids. This massive amusement park occupies a strip 80m wide stretching from Avenida 31 de Julio down to Cardón beach, entirely landscaped with islands, pools and a river just over 1m deep fed by well water. Water chutes are gentle for the toddlers, as high as three storeys for the daring, and as broad as a bus for rubber rafts. In the centre there's a jacuzzi for 25 people. Lifeguards are everywhere. The park has changing rooms, showers, lockers, and several snack bars and restaurants.

PUERTO FERMÍN This fishing village projects on a little point into El Tirano Bay. To this day, the town is also called El Tirano after the Spanish conquistador Lope de Aguirre, a widely feared tyrant who seized the island briefly in 1561. Descending the Amazon from Peru, the infamous Aguirre terrorised Margarita, murdered the governor and went on to more killings, including his own daughter, before he himself was beheaded and quartered in Barquisimeto. On the point a jetty has been built for fishing boats, which come in with their catch early in the morning. This is the *muelle pescador* and you may ask fishermen here about a boat to **Los Frailes Archipelago** some 15km away; they charge about US$30 per person, round trip, including light lunch and snorkelling; scuba diving costs double.

The village has character, a spacious plaza, and a European-looking church. The crescent of sea north of Puerto Fermín is '*bravo*' – rough and unsuitable for swimming, and the shore road is unpaved.

PLAYA PARGUITO The main entrance to this popular surfers' beach, just before Playa El Agua, is via Avenida 31 de Julio. Parguito's high, rolling breakers are famous among surfers, who study internet satellite images of ocean currents and reports on Atlantic storms so they can anticipate the big waves. International competitions are held here. Coconut palms and sea-grape trees give spectators shade and you can rent chairs and umbrellas. Food stands serve inexpensive fish. Byblos restaurant on the beach is a popular, shady meeting spot with good food.

PLAYA EL AGUA

The most famous beach in Margarita, for Venezuelan tourists Playa El Agua is the place to see and be seen. Tiny *tangas* and Miss Venezuela strutting are the order of the day, as the beautiful people, sometimes with a whisky in hand, promenade back and forth along the beach. During Christmas, Easter and Carnival the crowds from Caracas descend *en masse* and the palm-shaded beachside restaurants at the back are full to bursting as music booms out from stages set up on the sand by the big beer companies. Many people drive their 4x4s onto the north end of the 4km beach during these peak times and bikini-clad beach babes and big-biceped boys in shades and surf shorts form groups around the loud sound systems in their cars. Out of season there are days when you have most of the beach to yourself, with just a smattering of Canadian, German or Italian tourists sticking to their allocated beach chairs at intervals along the sand. Most people find a spot on the beach in front of the restaurant with the best tunes, hire a chair and sunshade and settle in for the day. But you can equally just plop down your towel anywhere you please and soak up the sun. Waiters from the beach bars and itinerant vendors selling cold beers from cool boxes are happy to bring drinks direct to you. You'll also find young guys with buckets selling oysters by the dozen, eaten raw with a squeeze of lime or a splash of Tabasco. For the very brave, there are seafood concoctions of shrimp, oyster, octopus and squid marinated in lemon, tomato and Worcestershire sauce, with strange names such as *Volver a la Vida* (Back to Life) or *Rompe Colchon* (Mattress Breaker). The vendors insist, with a nod and wink, that their wares have proven aphrodisiac qualities. For the not so brave, there are kids selling freshly made cheese and baby shark *empanadas*, which are cheap snacks to keep you going through the day.

If you like beach walking, there's a long stretch of sand to the south that will take you all the way to Playa Parguito (25 minutes), but take a hat and slap on some cream before you set out as the sun is fierce at midday and its burning effects are intensified by the reflection from the white sand and shallow water.

Playa del Humo, another kilometre of beach being developed, lies just north of Playa El Agua, following Avenida 31 de Julio. Here are large hotels such as the 300-room Portofino Mare. Jet-ski facilities are available on the beach.

☞ *WARNING:* The sea is very shallow close to shore on Playa El Agua but there is a dangerous rip tide and bathers should not venture too far out. In January 2009, Scottish cruise-ship passenger Colin Love, 23, was drowned here after just a short time in the water. His mother Julie Love has been campaigning for more warnings to be placed on the beach and for more lifeguards. The waves are calmer during May–October and rougher later in the year.

GETTING THERE Only 30 minutes by taxi from Porlamar (23km), or slightly longer in a bus from Plaza Bolívar (BsF5), it's easy to organise a day trip to Playa El Agua, combining it with a visit to La Asunción or the nearby surfers' beach of Playa Parguito.

WHERE TO STAY Choices are varied, from big five-star resorts to more intimate lodgings on the streets behind the beach. Always enquire about off-season discounts.

🏠 Hesperia Playa El Agua (410 rooms) Av 31 de Julio; www.hesperia.com. This is one of the top hotels here although not by the sea. Rooms & suites in 3 buildings with all-inclusive services, tennis & watersports included. $$$

🏠 Costa Linda Beach (38 rooms) Calle Miragua; ☎ 0295 415 9961, 0295 249 1303; e hotelcostalinda@cantv.net; www.hotelcostalinda.com. Cosy B&B *posada* on the main street, a few mins' walk from beach. Rooms

with AC, hot water, in a charming *criollo*-style layout with verandas, pool, palm trees & potted plants. Beach chairs, parasols included. $$
⌂ **Margarita Tropical Villa** (10 rooms) Av 31 de Julio; ✆ 0295 249 0558; m 0416 695 3704; e margarita.island@gmail.com. Canadian Dan O'Brien & his Dutch wife Trudy run this B&B, formerly Casa Trudel, in their home a short walk from the beach. You'll find terrace & hammocks, plenty of Dutch, English & German books, rooms with king-sized beds, shower, hot water, AC, TV, Wi-Fi, internet, small pool. $$

⌂ **Cocoparaiso** (26 rooms) North part of Bd El Agua; ✆ 0295 249 0117, 0295 249 0274. A pretty B&B hotel with a gym, swimming pool & gardens, a block from the beach. Rooms have terrace with hammocks, built-in safe, phone, fridge. Prices include beach chairs & sun shade. $
⌂ **Posada Nathalie** (12 rooms) ✆ 0295 249 1973; e info@posadanathalie.com; www.posadanathalie.com.ve. Good value smaller hotel set in gardens near beach run by Dutch couple. Simple but clean, rooms with bath, hot water, AC, use of kitchen, on small road behind beach reached from car park. Low-season discounts for longer stays. $

OTHER PRACTICALITIES There are supermarkets, car rentals, money change and tour agencies on Calle Miragua and the boulevard behind the beach.

SANTA ANA AND CRAFT VILLAGES

The road from Porlamar to Juangriego passes through the town of Santa Ana and a number of smaller villages that all specialise in different handicrafts, which are displayed from roadside shops and stalls.

SANTA ANA This attractive little town, founded in 1530 as La Villa del Norte, has beautiful trees, plazas and colonial houses. It is famous for its *chinchorros*, the open-weave hammocks made using fishing-net techniques (see box below).

HAMMOCKS: TRAVELLERS' AND SAILORS' BOON

The first navigators to the New World brought back a great native invention used all over the tropics: the hammock. English ships soon saw the advantage of hammocks below decks and sailors have been swinging ever since. Hammocks are the only traditional furnishings of Warao houses (see *Chapter 9, Monagas and the Orinoco Delta*, page 232). In their language *hanoko* means 'the hammock's place' or 'house' and would seem to be the origin of our word.

In Venezuela two basic kinds are distinguished: the *hamaca* made of woven cloth and the *chinchorro*, which is usually knotted like the fishing net it is named for. Most hardware stores sell pre-cut lengths of *mecate* (rope) for slinging hammocks.

The open weave of the *chinchorro* gives a very cool, comfortable rest, but if you are looking for a hammock to take travelling, remember that bugs and cold air pass easily through the holes. What is a delight in the daytime on the beach may be a misery at night. The ordinary hammock of solid cloth may be less elegant, but it gives more protection and is cheaper (most *chinchorros* are hand-knotted). Remember to get one wide enough to allow you to sleep on the diagonal with a relatively straight back; double-width size is called *matrimonial*. A warmer hammock that you can partially wrap around you will allow you to carry a lighter bedroll and is most appreciated in the predawn chill of tropical nights.

A hammock is a must for the back-country traveller in lowland Latin America. It is used throughout the hot country and allows you to sling your bed up off the (wet, buggy, crawly) ground, and sleep anywhere there are two points to hang it from. You will see truckers in Venezuela snoozing in their slings under the chassis while waiting at a garage, a ferry crossing or road block.

The handsome church, built in 1748–69, has a magnificent bell tower, unusual because it has outside stairs. Now a national monument, the church secured its place in history on 6 May 1816, when Simón Bolívar declared the Third Republic here, and the national assembly proclaimed him supreme chief, with Santiago Mariño as second in command. The chair Bolívar used stands by the baptistry. Parish records list the marriage of the Independence heroes Luisa Cáceres and Juan Bautista Arismendi on 4 December 1814: she was 15, he was 39. Centuries-old houses remain around the church. The former Arismendi residence stands at Number 3 on the south side; Bolívar and Mariño both stayed there. The Casa de Cultura and a restaurant, Casa Antañona, occupy other colonial homes. In front of the church, Plaza Francisco Esteban Gómez honours Santa Ana's hero of the Battle of Matasiete in 1817. His home, a few steps west, is conserved as a museum. On the northern outskirts (via Pedro González) you can find the remains of Fortín España. Look for its obelisk; from here you can see as far as the Macanao Peninsula on the other half of Margarita Island.

OTHER CRAFT VILLAGES In Pedro González the locals make and sell fibre bags called *mapires*. Altagracia, on a northwest road, is known for leather-soled sandals, or *alpargatas*. La Vecindad is another hammock centre. Cotton hammocks made here are sold all along the road to Juangriego. In Los Millanes practised hands roll cigars – the *tabacos* preferred by Margarita's smokers, including many women of the older generation. The tobacco comes from Sucre State and the cigars are said to compare well to Havanas, at a much lower cost.

JUANGRIEGO

Legend says that this charming town takes its name from a Greek sailor called Juan who was wounded and left here by fellow pirates. Local fisherfolk took him in and cured him. As early as 1545, one Juan el Griego is recorded among island residents and in 1661 the name appears on a Spanish map. Juangriego, with a population of around 28,000, is famous for its magnificent sunsets, seen from the terraces of beachside restaurants or the historic hilltop fortress above the town, La Galera. The broad bay is filled with yachts at anchor and colourful fishing boats with eyes painted on the prow to help the fishermen get home – an odd and colourful sight. The day's catch is sorted onshore: some fish go to distant markets, some are set to dry on poles in the sun, others are sold on the spot. Less built up than Porlamar and Pampatar with their posh concrete resorts, the town is small and relaxed, with parades of shops run by Lebanese traders selling cheap clothes and duty-free cheeses. Budget travellers appreciate the smaller scale of things here at Juangriego, with access to economic lodgings and the nearby northern beaches of Playa Caribe and Playa Puerto Cruz.

GETTING THERE Buses to Porlamar (30 minutes) stop near Plaza Bolívar on Avenida Miranda. Other buses leave (every 20 minuntes) for Playa Caribe, Pedro González and Playa Zaragoza.

WHERE TO STAY Prices are generally somewhat lower in Juangriego than on the east coast. Lodgings are divided between large apartment hotels with swimming pools on the outskirts of town and plain hotels with basic amenities downtown. Budget and solo travellers will want to head for the economic options near the beachfront.

▲ **Villa El Griego Resort** [180 D6] (168 apts) Calle Picaquinta, south of the Santa Ana–Juangriego road; ☎ 0295 253 1507; e villaelgriego@cantv.net; www.villaelgriego.com.ve. Many Dutch & Danish

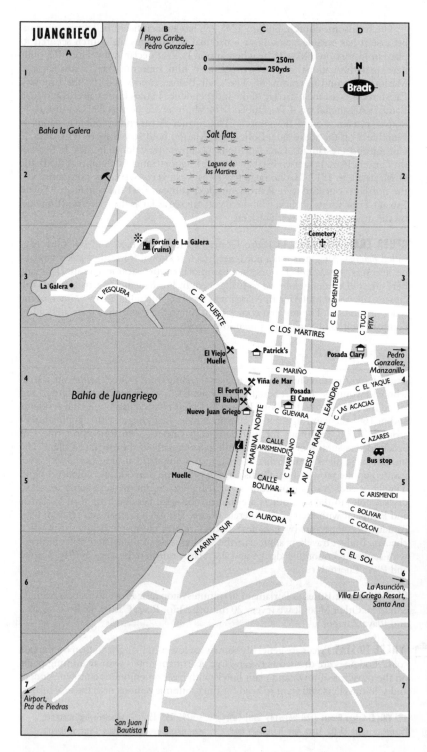

JUANGRIEGO

A

↑ Playa Caribe,
Pedro Gonzalez

Bahía la Galera

0 ————— 250m
0 ————— 250yds

Bradt

N

Salt flats

Laguna de
los Martires

Cemetery ✝

Fortín de La Galera
(ruins)

La Galera ●

L. PESQUERA

C EL FUERTE

C EL CEMENTERIO

C TUCU PITA

Bahía de Juangriego

C LOS MARTIRES

El Viejo
Muelle ✗

Patrick's 🏠

Posada Clary 🏠

Pedro Gonzalez, Manzanillo →

C MARIÑO

Viña de Mar ✗

C EL YAQUE

El Fortín ✗
El Buho 🏠
Nuevo Juan Griego 🏠

Posada
El Caney

C LAS ACACIAS

C GUEVARA

C AZARES

Bus stop 🚐

C MARINA NORTE

CALLE
ARISMENDI

C MARCANO

AV JESUS RAFAEL LEANDRO

Muelle

CALLE
BOLIVAR

✝

C ARISMENDI

C BOLIVAR

C COLON

C AURORA

C MARINA SUR

C EL SOL

La Asunción,
Villa El Griego Resort,
Santa Ana →

↙ Airport,
Pta de Piedras

San Juan
Bautista ↓

180

package tourists favour these pleasant studio apts with balcony, AC, TV, kitchen, just on the way into town. Swimming pools for adults, kids, poolside bar, disco, pizza restaurant. $$

🏠 **Patrick's** [180 C4] (9 rooms) Calle El Fuerte, towards Fortín La Galera; ✆ 0295 253 6218; e info@hotelpatrick.com; www.hotelpatrick.com. A very pleasant *posada* & bar run by Irishman Michael & his wide Odalis, which is easily the best option for budget travellers. Rooms with AC, hot

water, downstairs bar & dining area in pleasant walled garden. Close to beach, transport to Playa El Caribe. $

🏠 **Posada El Caney** [180 C4] (11 rooms) 17 Calle Guevara at La Marina; ✆ 0295 253 5059; m 0416 795 6379; e giulliana@hotmail.com. Alain from Canada & Giulliana from Peru run this place with 1–3 beds in simple rooms with AC, TV, cold water & a guest kitchen with coffee maker. Can organise transport to/from airport or beaches. $

✗ **WHERE TO EAT** The best place to view the spectacular sunset is at one of the rustic restaurants on the bay serving cold beers and seafood dinners along Calle Marina. Recommended are **El Buho** [180 C4], **El Fortín** [180 C4], and **Viña del Mar** [180 C4] with air conditioning inside. Try the tables on the beach at the pricier **El Viejo Muelle** [180 C4], if only to have a beer and listen to the music. Fried fish, chicken and pizza are served at popular pavement tables by the sea at the end of Calle Guevara.

FESTIVALS The year's biggest bash is **Carnival**, when Juangriego takes to the streets with parties, parades, costumes and floats. There are also religious street processions on the feast days of Santa Eduvigis 20 October, and San Juan Evangelista 27 December–3 January.

OTHER PRACTICALITIES There are several banks with ATMs along Calle La Marina, which faces out towards the bay.

Internet and international calls are available from the CANTV call centre on the corner of Calle Bolívar and Calle La Marina.

There are several pharmacies but the nearest private hospitals and clinics are in Porlamar.

WHAT TO SEE AND DO

Fortín de la Galera [180 B3] On the bay's north headland, Fortín de la Galera commands a panorama of neighbouring bays. The fort was taken by Spanish royalists in the Independence wars and burnt down in 1817 but the main structure remains, with a few cannons to help you visualise the fierce battles that took place here. The lake below the fort is called Laguna de los Mártires (Lagoon of the Martyrs), in honour of the Independence troops who tried to draw fire from the Spanish besieging the castle so their comrades could escape. So many died in the gunfight that their blood made the water run red. Ceremonies to mark the event are held on 8 August. Make sure you hear the dramatic story from one of the local children, who for a tip will recite the history of the fort in staccato Spanish as they breathlessly race to the end. Don't interrupt because they have to start from the beginning again!

Playa Caribe A five-minute drive from the foot of the fortress takes you to this beautiful palm-fringed beach with two horseshoe bays and golden-brown sands. The turquoise sea is more tranquil here than at Playa El Agua and the water colder. The most famous restaurant is **La Playya**, run by an Argentine, who serves up chilled-out tunes and fresh seafood on the beach even after the sun sets.

🏠 **Where to stay**

🏠 **Casa Caracol** (10 cabin rooms) Playa Caribe; ✆ 0295 416 8439, 0212 284 2628;

www.caracolgroup.com. Redefining the *posada* experience in Venezuela are this Italian group who have brought the concept of designer décor, fine dining & immaculate attention to detail from their guesthouse in Los Roques to Playa Caribe. With a high wall & no sign outside, you would never know of the luxuries hidden within, including a large freshwater pool, bar, restaurant & cottage-style cabins done out in a Mediterranean-style of whitewashed walls & chic wooden furnishings. They even give you a mountain bike to cycle down to the beach where they have loungers & parasols. By reservation only. $$$

NORTHWEST COAST

The coast road leads to beautiful crescent beaches, some of them over a kilometre long, that are better than Playa El Agua and without the crowds. Playa Zaragoza is also known as Playa Pedro González. It boasts a picturesque row of painted houses on a seaside boulevard. The bay is protected by Zaragoza Point with its lighthouse. The sea is transparent: deep and cold on the beach's left side, shallow and calm on the right. Restaurants offer beach chairs and sun shades; there's water skiing and jet skiing, too.

Just north of Punta Zaragoza is Playa Puerto Cruz. This broad, spectacular crescent of white sand is rated by many as Margarita's finest beach, fanned by a breeze and shaded by palms. At the far west of the beach is a huge sand dune that takes you up to a ridge by the lighthouse, with fantastic views over the sea and coast. However, the surf can be very rough and swimmers are warned of a dangerous undertow. Two major resorts back onto separate ends of the beach. The five-star, Spanish-owned Hesperia Isla Margarita (*www.hesperia.com*) has 312 rooms and an 18-hole golf course, the only one on the island. The hotel, formerly called Isla Bonita, has five desalination plants to water its large swimming pools, a deluxe spa with therapeutic pool and a full range of health and beauty treatments. Dunes Hotel and Beach Resort (*www.dunesmargarita.com*) is mainly dedicated to package tour customers.

Guayacán and Playa Manzanillo are the last northern bays on the ring road before it turns east to Playa El Agua. Hidden by hills, Guayacán is a lively fishing village where almost all the inhabitants are related. It is at the bottom of a steep road; the sea is usually calm and there are trees, and kiosks selling beer and soft drinks. In the same area is Playa Escondida, a hidden beach. Bring food, drink and a hammock, as again there are trees. Playa Manzanillo is getting more popular as Playa El Agua fills up. It has good swimming, beach chairs and umbrellas for rent and you can explore beaches around Cabo Negro (Black Cape) or the island of Los Frailes by hiring a *peñero* (fishing boat). Speak to the fishermen. The fish caught here are sold on the spot as the boats are unloaded, some to Porlamar and some to the restaurants and beach shacks here – it doesn't get much fresher.

LA RESTINGA LAGOON AND NATIONAL PARK

To get closer to nature, learn a bit more about the island and enjoy an adventure, the best place to head is the mangroves and beaches of La Restinga, the largest national park on the island, and the most accessible.

Located in the narrow isthmus (a *restinga* is a sandbar) between the halves of Margarita, which were once separate islands, **Parque Nacional Laguna de la Restinga** (⊕ *07.00–17.00; admission BsF15*) occupies 10,700ha of sea, shore, lagoons, channels and tangled mangroves. A boat trip through the labyrinth of channels to the beach is well worth while. Boats leave from the *embarcadero*, or 'pier', by the park entrance, which is 350m from the main road and 36.5km (40 minutes) from downtown Porlamar. After paying a small park fee you hop aboard one of the scores of *lanchas* waiting by the jetty. A 30-minute trip through the mangroves to La Guardia beach is BsF15; an hour costs BsF20 and you pay on return. Note the name and number of your boat so there's no confusion on the way back. Each boat takes five or six passengers to the beach through fascinating mangrove channels with cheesy names like the Love Tunnel; some are so narrow you can touch the leaves on either side and see oysters clinging to tangled roots. At the far dock by the *balneario* you set a time for the same boat to pick you up, or have the boatman wait an hour. There are clean restrooms; ask a waiter for the key. Open-sided restaurants offer food and shade, so that's where most people go. Check prices, as the closest restaurants are reported to charge more. Sweeping in a long crescent to either side of La Guardia Bay, the bar enclosing the lagoon forms an oceanic beach 10km long; the swimming is good but there is no natural shade and the beach is covered in shells, so bring flip flops, a hat and plenty of sunscreen. In the right season people scoop up bucketfuls of the little clams called *guacucos* at the water's edge, which are good for seafood broth, as well as eating fresh like oysters. The return trip is a fast race back to the *embarcadero* but if you want more mangroves you can tip the boatman to take you through more of the channels or out to sea via Boca del Río, where most of the *lancheros* live.

From La Restinga you can clearly see the two mountains known as **Las Tetas de María Guevara** (Maria Guevara's Breasts) which rise to 130m near the south coast. It's an odd name for a topographical feature but María Guevara did exist. She was born in Cumaná in 1801 and in her twenties married a Margariteño. Having some property, she invested in his fishing fleet in Punta de Piedras. Under her management a well was dug, houses were built for fishermen from Juangriego and the little port grew to be an important fishing centre. The fame of this enterprising lady who lived to be 85 outlived her and sailors gave her name to the hills they used as landmarks to guide them home. Ironically, María Guevara's real lady bumps were said to be small. In 1974 the lopsided hills were declared a natural monument, along with Laguna Las Marites, Cerro Matasiete and Cerro Guayamurí.

GETTING THERE Take a taxi or bus from Porlamar leaving from Calle Mariño between La Marina and Maneiro, about four blocks from Plaza Bolívar (ask first). Go early on Sundays as return buses are scarce in the afternoon.

OTHER PRACTICALITIES There are no shops or banking services on the beach at La Restinga, just a couple of shacks with tables selling cold beer and fried fish with rice, salad and plantains (about US$15) and *empanadas*, so bring everything you need with you. If you leave the beach and walk into the small village of La Restinga the snacks on offer are less expensive.

MACANAO PENINSULA

Across the bridge from La Restinga Lagoon is the 'other side' of Margarita, a rugged, semi-desert, sparsely inhabited land. Macanao's central mountain rises to 760m. Surprisingly, what appears to be wasteland supports varied wildlife: snakes, lizards, foxes, rabbits, the occasional deer and feral goats. Look carefully at the tops of cacti and you will spot songbirds and finches. You may even see flocks of rare Margarita parrots, a species that mates for life and nests in the same hollow tree year after year (see *Margarita Parrot Festival*, overleaf).

Macanao is surrounded by beaches but they have little natural shade and the midday heat is intense in these desert-like conditions, so bring plenty of water, suncream, a hat, and long sleeves or sarong to avoid burning.

GETTING THERE A good road of 68km circles the peninsula. Macanao is served by the Línea La Restinga buses which go to scattered fishing villages as far as Robledal and San Francisco.

WHERE TO STAY

Posada Río Grande (5 rooms) Cabatucán; \ 0295 416 8111; e info@posadariogrande.com. On the same property as the Cabatucán horseriding ranch, this B&B run by Señora Valeria has a swimming pool & dbl rooms with AC, private bath. $$

FESTIVALS

Margarita Parrot Festival On the first Saturday in June, the people of Macanao make merry. This is the day honouring the yellow-shouldered Margarita parrot, or *cotorra Margariteño*, with music and dance in Boca del Río. The little parrots are not there, however; they live on the mountainsides. A few years ago their fate was in doubt as numbers of the *Amazona barbadensis* dwindled to 700. Worried conservation groups began a study and found that the birds' isolated habitat was raided by locals in search of chicks for the pet trade. To reverse this, biologists from the environmental NGO Provita (*www.provita.org.ve*) devised a programme to raise fledglings for return to the wild and raise public awareness of the parrot's plight. Margariteños love parrots and they made the *cotorra* Nueva Esparta's state bird. They are also working with a second endangered parrot, known locally as the *ñángaro* (*Aratinga acuticaudata*), which is down to fewer than 200 birds and lives only in Parque Nacional La Restinga.

WHAT TO SEE AND DO

Boca del Río Macanao's biggest town, Boca del Río is the home port of a large deep-sea fishing fleet. Its name really should be Boca de La Restinga as it is at the lagoon's mouth. The fleet, which also anchors in Chacachacare, is known throughout the Caribbean and northern Atlantic, pursuing grouper and red snapper as far as Suriname and even Brazil. Margarita is an important centre of wooden boat building and Boca del Río is a good place to see ship carpenters at work. The trawler-sized boats called *tres puños* are handmade to a design which has varied little in centuries. Steps lead from the port's boulevard down to the water. Smaller wooden boats, *peñeros*, dock here. As you might expect in a town that makes its living from fish, this is what is served in restaurants. Chucho is the cook at **El Pescador**, and his wife runs **Fríomar**, on Calle La Puntilla as you drive through town; specialities include omelettes of *erizo* (sea urchin), fish sun-dried and then grilled, *arepas* and *empanadas* filled with *chucho* (ray).

Museo del Mar (*Boca del Río;* \ *0295 291 3231;* ⊕ *09.00–16.00; admission US$2 adults, US$1 children*) This two-floor museum of marine life is the pride of Margarita. Live exhibits in 11 salt-water aquariums and a turtle aquarium allow visitors to handle some of the extraordinary creatures that live in the sea including starfish, crabs, lobsters and sea cucumbers. There are plans to build a 35,000-litre shark pool. Models made by local carpenters of Margarita's fishing vessels are on view, plus nets, traps and knots. The 14m skeleton of a whale was rescued and cleaned by students of UDO's school of Applied Marine Science after it died and was washed up on Cubagua.

Horseriding at Campamento Cabatucán (*2km from Guayacancito, Macanao;* \ *0295 416 3584;* m *0416 681 9348;* e *cabatucan@gmail.com; www.cabatucan.com*) A well-established ranch offering two-hour outings, one in the morning and another in the evening, that take riders up into the dry, dusty hills of Macanao and then down for a canter along the beach and in the surf.

Exploring deserted beaches During the week you'll have the beaches of Macanao to yourself, so rent a car and do a circuit of the peninsula or sign for a jeep tour in

Porlamar. Punta Arenas is Margarita's westernmost point, 27km from Boca del Río. Bordered with dunes and seashells, the blazing white beach is hot. There are some palms, a few houses and restaurants selling grilled fish and lobster in season (November–April). Windsurfers are starting to discover this beach. Beyond the salt flats another beach offers chairs, sunshades and enough isolation for a nudist or two. The wild coast northeast of Robledal has isolated beaches used by campers with cars who bring their own food, water and shade. You see jeep tracks cutting off the road through scrub to Playa Carmela or La Mula. La Pared ('the wall') beach and fishing village are at the foot of a bluff 8km from Robledal. There are few services, but above the beach there is a restaurant where the owners prepare fried fish, squid, and maybe a lobster. And you can walk for miles or watch a fantastic sunset over the sea. There is a fishing community at the next northern beach: follow a track of about 1km to the small point of El Tunal sheltering a long curved beach. There is a restaurant renting sunshades. Eastward of Punta El Tunal there is another, longer beach, La Auyama (the pumpkin), but the breakers can be very rough on this bit of unprotected coast.

EL YAQUE

El Yaque, a 2km beach on Margarita's south coast near the airport, is now recognised as a world-class **windsurfing** destination. Enthusiasts come from all over the world to spend some six hours a day on the warm, shallow water and their nights on the beach, roaming the funky bars and restaurants that cater to the scene. It's a tight, friendly community and everybody seems to know everybody, making El Yaque a safe place to spend a week or so. Wherever you go, you find English-, German-, Italian- or French-speakers. But it wasn't always like this. There was nothing here 15 years ago – not even electricity or fresh water. Now there are more than 15 hotels and guesthouses, windsurfing and kitesurfing schools and hire firms, restaurants, bars, tour operators, money changers and a travel agency. The excellent facilities make El Yaque reportedly the best windsurfing spot, with infrastructure, for 80% of windsurfers. The influx of rich foreigners wanting to practice an expensive sport is reflected in the prices at hotels and restaurants, which those on a budget will find slightly high.

The key to its success is the 13km strait between El Yaque and the island of Coche (which some windsurfers have crossed), the shallow waters that are waist deep for more than 300 yards, and steady trade winds, which blow at 25–35km/h nearly all year round (just slacking a little September–November). As a local instructor explained: 'It's like the god of windsurfing sat down to create the perfect spot and came up with El Yaque.' It now hosts international competitions, such as the Margarita Wild Winds, which takes place May/June, drawing some 80 foreign competitors and more and more locals, who are beginning to pick up top trophies.

GETTING THERE El Yaque is 5km south of the airport by way of a fork as you approach the terminal. It is the only village on the road, which ends at Laguna Las Marites. Airport taxis charge about US$10. The lack of regular buses to and from Porlamar (30 minutes) has been resolved by the hotels themselves providing a daily service in a 28-seat bus (late return on Saturday night). Direct buses of the Línea Negro Primero leave twice a day from Calle Arismendi at San Nicolás in Porlamar.

If you are driving you can get straight to the beach by following the road past the entrance to the national park, turning off the main road at the bridge over the lagoon and then turning right on the road to the village of La Restinga.

🏠 **WHERE TO STAY** Lodgings are mainly small-to-medium hotels, that are bright, breezy and relaxed. Most were built in the past ten years on the main street parallel to the beach, opening directly onto sand. The lodging options below all have air conditioning and private bath, unless noted, and hotel rates all include breakfast. El Yaque's high season is from November/December to April.

🏠 **Hotel California** (46 rooms) Opposite El Yaque Paradise; ✆ 0295 263 9494; e calfort@gmail.com; www.elyaque.com. Surrounding a central pool & jacuzzi, the hotel is set back 50m from the beach with leafy gardens & a depository for kitesurf equipment. B&B options for 2, 3 or 4 sharing, some rooms with balconies, sea view. Da Rocco restaurant serves pizza, pasta & grilled fish. Discounts on windsurf classes & equipment rental at the California Beach Club. $$$

🏠 **El Yaque Beach** (12 rooms) Midway on Calle Principal; ✆ 0295 263 8441; e eybeach@cantv.net; www.yaque-beach.com. Rooms & apts with solar-heated water, TV, fridge, B&B, low-season rates. $$

🏠 **El Yaque Motion** (9 rooms) A walled property on the right of Calle Principal; ✆ 0295 263 9742; e info@elyaquemotion.com; www.elyaquemotion.com. Also called the Windsurfer's Guest House. Popular with budget travellers looking for B&B & is a good value option run by Mike Schultze. All rooms have AC, Wi-Fi, use of kitchen. $$

🏠 **Hotel Windsurf Paradise** (62 rooms) ✆ 0295 263 8890, 0295 263 9387; e reservas@hotelsurfparadise.com; www.hotelsurfparadise.com. A large complex with a terrace & swimming pool area overlooking the beach & offering windsurf & kitesurf lessons & equipment hire. Also have kayaks for hire. Standard rooms have AC, cable TV & Wi-Fi, while high-end suites are kitted out with kitchen, fridge & jacuzzi. Best rooms overlook the pool & beach. $$

🏠 **Hotel Yaque Paradise** (26 rooms, 2 suites, 2 penthouse suites) ✆ 0295 263 9810, 0295 263 9418; e ventas@hotelyaqueparadise.com; www.hotelyaqueparadise.com. The first hotel in El Yaque, this is a 3-storey resort-style complex with associated restaurant, beach bar & store for windsurfing & kitesurfing equipment. Half the rooms have a sea view, half face onto the street. Penthouse suites have kitchen & terrace overlooking beach. No swimming pool. Boat transfers to the island of Coche included. $$

🏠 **Jump n' Jibe** (14 rooms) Calle Principal; ✆ 0295 263 8396; e dario@jumpnjibe.com; www.jumpnjibe.com. Small surf hotel on the beach offering B&B rooms with sea view, AC. Works with Mistral. The beachside snack bar serves sandwiches, salads, spaghetti, coffee, beer, inexpensive juice. $$

🏠 **Winds of Margarita** (24 rooms) ✆ 0295 263 9455; e hotelthewinds@cantv.net. One of the first hotels you see on entering El Yaque's hotel row. It's a pretty, single-storey place with beach, garden, popular restaurant, low-season discounts. $$

🏠 **Windsurfer's Oasis** (22 rooms) Calle Principal; ✆ 0295 263 9375; e info@windsurfersoasis.com; www.windsurfersoasis.com. With its fountain, small blue pool & border gardens, the German-owned B&B hotel is true to its name. Spacious rooms with AC, small pool, jacuzzi, snack bar. $$

🏠 **Casa Rita** (20 rooms) Calle Principal, Colinas del Yaque; ✆ 0295 263 1667; e casarita@cantv.net; www.casarita.com. A good, inexpensive B&B, 400m from the beach: rooms with fan, fridge, balcony. Garden & b/fast terrace. $

🏠 **Sail Fast Shop** (4 rooms) Calle Principal; ✆ 0295 263 7486; e sailfastshop@hotmail.com; www.sail-fast.com. Simple, inexpensive rooms in the rear of the shop. Closes 12.00–17.00 to allow owner Herbert Novak to go windsurfing, then reopens until 20.00. Popular with Germans, French & Italians. $

NIGHTLIFE You can't expect to bring windsurfers from around the world without offering something for them to do in the evenings, and El Yaque doesn't disappoint, with beach bars, restaurants and discos to sweat out some of that sea salt. Recommended places are **Shampam Solarium Desk** (⊕*12.00–24.00*), which provides an Ibiza vibe under the palms on the beach in front of Hotel Yaque Paradise. DJ Irak offers champagne and Red Bull cocktails, gourmet snacks, massages, and lounge tunes from the mixing desk. This is the place for beach parties at Easter and Carnival. Other popular places are the **Fuerza 6** bar, run by a Chilean woman called Gaby, which is covered in magazine articles about windsurfing and serves up cheap chicken, pricier seafood and beers. The **Ipanema Beach Bar** (⊕ *12.00–24.00*) in front of Hotel Windsurf Paradise is another cool place to chill after a day on the waves, with sushi and a disco afterwards. The party continues at **Gabi's Grill and Voodoo Lounge** (⊕ *12.00–24.00*) with a barbecue serving fish, Tex Mex and burgers, and a bar with pool tables, live music and tropical sounds for dancing.

OTHER PRACTICALITIES There is no bank in El Yaque but almost all the hotels and *posadas* can change US dollars and the larger hotels will accept payment by Visa or Mastercard.

There are several mini-marts selling fresh fruit, cheese, ham and bread in the street behind the beach and surf shops selling everything from sex wax to T-shirts.

A cyber-café can be found in the Sail Fast shop behind the beach and there is another in Hotel California.

There is a small clinic in town on the main road next to the elementary school that can deal with light emergencies but the nearest hospital is in Porlamar.

WHAT TO DO

Windsurfing International experts based in clubs on the beach can provide windsurf gear and instruction. Ten hours of beginners' classes cost US$200 from Germany's Club Mistral (*www.clubmistral.com*), Planet Windsurf of the USA (*www.planetwindsurfing.de*), or Club Margarita (*www.clubmargarita.com*), a British group whose windsurfers divide the year between El Yaque in winter and Greece in summer. El Yaque is great for learning how to waterstart and jibe because of its safe, shallow water and sandy bottom. Many of the local boys who work in El Yaque get free training and equipment from the windsurf clubs and are now doing very well in international competitions. Boards and sails can be rented at surf hotels and schools, or bought at surf shops.

Kitesurfing Kitesurfing is rapidly gaining adepts and the PKRA (Professional Kiteboard Riders Association) now has competitions every year in April/May. Planet Windsurf gives classes at the Kite beach at Boca del Yaque. Equipment rental costs US$23 per hour and classes cost US$150 for six hours including equipment. Murray Sampson, a pioneer of kitesurfing in El Yaque, runs Margarita Xtreme (*www.margaritaxtreme.com*), giving classes from Hotel Windsurf Paradise. Three times world freestyle windsurfing champion Ricardo Campello sometimes gives clinics on technique at Campello Windcenter (*www.campello.com.ve*) at Hotel Yaque Paradise.

COCHE

Lying between Margarita and the Araya Peninsula on the mainland, the tiny island of Coche (population 8,800) is one of three islands forming Nueva Esparta State. About 13km long by 6km wide, the highest point is a mere 60m above sea level. Famed for its hot sun, dazzling beaches and perfect windsurfing conditions, life moves at the pace of a sleepy fishing village. The lack of shopping malls, fast food joints and noisy nightlife evokes Margarita 50 years ago. Catamarans and pleasure craft from the mainland bring tourists over at weekends to revel in the warm tropical waters that rarely fall below 27°C. The locals make a living from the sea and process their own salt to cure fish. Important pearl beds were exploited in the 1500s and today there is still a small production from eastern banks. All fresh water has to be piped from the mainland and there are weekly beer deliveries by a Polar boat. There is an asthma research clinic, an airfield and virtually no traffic on the surprisingly good roads which link the capital of San Pedro to the fishing communities of El Bichar and Güinima on the west coast, El Amparo and

Guamache in the south, and the wild eastern beaches of La Uva, and El Coco at the foot of astonishing ochre-red cliffs.

Although arid, Coche must once have had trees as its name means 'deer' in Indian tongue. That changed with the Spanish conquest and nowadays all you see is the odd goat. The only trees are the palm trees planted and nurtured by hand. San Pedro de Coche, on the west coast, is a town where lampposts are taller than the houses and the town generator runs day and night. The streets are wide and empty and there are only a handful of shops, a Chinese 'supermarket', beer halls with pool tables and the island's only petrol station. The biggest public building is the school. The former Isla de Coche Hotel now serves as a medical centre. The church, built a bit like a warehouse, is the Iglesia de San Pedro Apostol, scene of island festivities during the main fiesta in honour of San Pedro held 28–29 June.

GETTING THERE AND AWAY From Margarita's airport it is a hop by airtaxi to Coche, although there have been no regular flights for some years. Conferry's vessel crosses from San Pedro de Coche to Punta de Piedras every morning on weekdays at 06.00 to take workers and shoppers, and twice on Saturday and Sunday, at 06.00 and 18.00. The return to Margarita is at 17.00 during the week, and at 08.00 and 15.30 on weekends. The *María Libre* carries passengers (see page 163).

Fishing boats make the crossing from La Isleta (20 minutes, BsF15) on the east side of Laguna Las Marites near El Yaque and the airport. The boats leave for San Pedro through the day taking locals and all their purchases.

From El Yaque, the Paradise hotels run a half-hour launch service twice daily for guests of the Hotel Coche Paradise and Hotel Punta Blanca in Playa La Punta. Non-guests pay BsF50 round trip. There are also day-tour packages and El Yaque fishermen can arrange passage if you can get a group together.

WHERE TO STAY AND EAT Most boats land on the fine white beach of Playa La Punta, in the lee of the island's northern point, where most of the accommodation options are located.

Hotel Coche Paradise (114 cottage-style rooms) \ 0295 265 4444; e reservaciones@ hotelcocheparadise.com; www.hotelcocheparadise.com. The hotel offers all-inclusive packages in cabins with king-size beds, AC, TV. Nothing luxury, food options basic, but the location on the beach is unbeatable for the price, which includes transfer from El Yaque, swimming pool, pitch-&-putt golf course, large open-sided restaurant, windsurf school, kayaks, snorkelling, children's park. Tame macaws & parrots perch by the pool, iguanas run under the sun loungers & donkeys parade on the beach. Low-season discounts. $$

Posada El Oasis & Restaurant (29 rooms) \ 0295 416 9756; e isladecoche@hotmail.com; www.isladecoche.com. Located 3km east of Playa La Punta beyond the pink salt flats, is this simple *posada* built by Elías Pérez & his wife. Elías, an escapee from Margarita, began 10 years ago by planting palms & building a small pool & a house with hammocks, just 80m from the beach & a good snorkelling spot. His green oasis is the setting for one of the few good restaurants on Coche, serving cream of lobster soup, clams in garlic, shrimp pie. The cool bedrooms with TV, AC are of simple design with built-in tables & concrete bed bases. Price includes meals, transfers to beach with chairs & towels, boat from Margarita. $$

OTHER PRACTICALITIES There was no bank or *casa de cambio* operating in Coche at the time of publication so take all the money you will need with you. Hotel Coche Paradise can change dollars and accepts payment by Visa and mastercard.

The resort hotels charge non-guests for internet access.

There is a medical centre in the old Coche Hotel that can treat emergencies but the closest hospital is in Porlamar on Isla Margarita.

CUBAGUA

The small, barren island of Cubagua offers visitors the chance to explore the foundations of historic Nueva Cádiz, the first Spanish city in South America – although little but rubble remains. It's also a great place to go scuba diving. The Spanish established the first settlement here after discovering Cubagua's rich pearl banks in 1499. In the next three decades pearl harvests exceeded 11 tons, a fifth of which went to the Spanish crown. The small town of enslaved native pearl divers and their Spanish overseers quickly grew to 1,000 inhabitants in 1519 when a freshwater supply was organised from Cumaná on the mainland. However, by the time Nueva Cádiz became a city in 1528, the pearl beds were almost exhausted and the settlers started to leave. Finally, on Christmas Day 1541, a tidal wave swept the 'Island of Satan' clean and Nueva Cádiz was abandoned.

Pearling sounds romantic but it was brutal, with countless native pearl divers losing their lives and the oyster beds ravaged. It also destroyed the environment. Archaeological excavations have shown Cubagua was not always barren. Remains of native potsherds and conch tools found at Punta Gorda date to 4,000 years ago and suggest the island had extensive tree cover. It is believed the last few trees were cut down by camps of pearl divers.

Today, Cubagua is uninhabited except for visiting fishermen who have erected shelters on the northern bay of Charagato, and daytrippers on boat tours from Margarita. Scuba divers also come to dive two wrecks, one a barge, the other a ferry grounded when it caught fire, its watery hull still full of cars.

DAY TRIPS Tour agencies offer sailing and diving trips but do not always go to the ruins. The comfortable pleasure boats provide food, drinks and music, perhaps some fishing along the way, lunch on board and beach games. Most boats leave from the Concorde marina, Porlamar, and the crossing takes two hours.

8

The Oriente Coast

The coastal states of Anzoátegui and Sucre, known as El Oriente (The East), stretch from the historic city of Barcelona in the west to the remote cloudforests and secluded coves of the sparsely populated Paria Peninsula, the long finger of land that points to the island of Trinidad. It's an area steeped in the history of the Spanish conquest, blessed with breathtaking beaches and criss-crossed by oil pipelines, the pumping lifeblood of Venezuela's modern economy. Tourists come here to dive in the warm, clear waters of the Caribbean, explore ancient fortresses and shake their stuff at wild carnivals.

ANZOÁTEGUI STATE *Telephone code: 0281*

For Venezuelans Anzoátegui State means beaches – urban in Puerto La Cruz, uninhabited in Mochima – and oil. As you pass through the state you are never far from a pipeline or massive refineries, lit up at night like Christmas trees twinkling with fairy lights. The massive presence of petrochemical plants has altered the coast permanently in Jose, 15km east of Píritu. Pipelines link the refineries at Jose with eastern and southern fields, including the Orinoco heavy oil belt, and have fed the oil and gas bonanza. The once separate cities of Barcelona and Puerto La Cruz have merged into a sprawling conglomeration that is home to over two thirds of the state's 1.5 million inhabitants. Barcelona, with its well-preserved historic centre, still holds on to the past, while Puerto La Cruz is a thoroughly modern resort city, gateway to Margarita Island and the islands of the Parque Nacional Mochima.

BARCELONA The quiet old state capital (population 320,000) has gradually merged with the newer Puerto La Cruz, which is brasher, more competitive and more expensive in every way. Founded on the banks of the Neverí River by the Spanish in 1671, Barcelona became the administrative, religious and economic seat of the region, exporting cacao, cotton, and salted beef from the plains. The two-storey Aduana El Rincón, once a colonial customs house, can still be visited north of the city although mangroves now swallow its former sea access. Barcelona's many green plazas and proudly restored colonial buildings make it a pleasant, old-fashioned city. Nearby is the mega-tourism and housing project El Morro.

Getting there
By air Aeropuerto José Antonio Anzoátegui (*www.sageaca.com*), which also serves Puerto La Cruz, is about 2km south of the town centre. There is a fairly new international terminal but domestic passengers will arrive in the national terminal, which has shops and restaurants, money exchange, banks and car-rental agencies. There are over a dozen flights daily from Caracas by Conviasa (*www.conviasa.aero*), Aserca (*www.asercaairlines.com*) and Avior (*www.avior.com.ve*), costing US$60.

Barcelona–Porlamar is flown mostly by Avior and Rutaca (*www.rutaca.com.ve*), which also serve Ciudad Guayana. Aserca flies to Valencia, San Antonio del Táchira and Maracaibo. Buses to the airport leave from Avenida 5 de Julio.

By bus The main Terminal de Pasajeros is on Calle 4 (San Carlos), two blocks after it intersects with Avenida Fuerzas Armadas. There is a frequent service to Caracas (310km, 4½ hours, US$10); east to Cumaná, (92km, 2 hours), and on to Carúpano; south to Ciudad Bolívar, (295km, 4 hours), and on to Puerto Ordaz. Some lines are: Aerobuses de Venezuela (\ *0281 266 6257*); Tierra Firme (\ *0281 266 7534*); Expresos La Guayanesa (\ *0282 266 6612*). Local buses to downtown Puerto La Cruz go east on the Intercomunal or Vía Alterna (30 minutes). *Por puestos* leave for Santa Fé just outside the station. For the fishing village of Mochima take the *por puesto* to Cumaná but remember to tell the driver to drop you off at Mochima.

By car Barcelona is reached on the main highway from Caracas to Puerto La Cruz.

Tourist information The **Corporacion de Turismo, Coranztur** (*Av 5 de Julio;* \ *0281 275 1469; www.coranztur.com.ve;* ⊕ *08.00–12.00 & 14.00–16.00 Mon–Fri*) office, located in the Palacio del Gobierno, has maps and information in Spanish on tourist attractions in the state.

Where to stay Barcelona's hotels are older, more basic and cheaper than those of Puerto La Cruz.

🏠 **Hotel Barcelona** (70 rooms) Av 5 de Julio & Calle Bolívar; \ 0281 277 1065. Rooms with AC, TV, close to Plaza Boyaca. $

🏠 **Hotel Canarias** Carrera 13 (Bolívar) & Av 5 de Julio; \ 0281 277 1034. A colonial-style house with rooms off a central patio, bath, AC. $

🏠 **Posada Copacabana** (16 rooms) Calle Juncal; \ 0281 277 3473; m 0414 807 1199. Basic option in the historic centre opposite the cathedral. Rooms with bath, TV, AC. $

Where to eat Around Parque El Indio are Lebanese stalls selling falafels and *shawarmas* and there are *panaderias* on Plaza Boyaca selling sandwiches and pastries.

✗ **Gran Palacio Gastronomico** Av 5 de Julio; ⊕ 07.00–22.00. This place is not quite as fancy as the name suggests but serves up cheap & cheerful chicken & burgers. $

✗ **La Villa De Pan** Av 5 de Julio; ⊕ 07.00–22.00. Has a terrace serving coffee & snacks. $

Other practicalities There is a CANTV call centre on Avenida 5 Julio and Calle La Llovizna and another on Avenida 5 de Julio and Calle Maturín on Plaza Miranda.

What to see The city of Barcelona was founded in 1671 and most of the historical sights are found around Plaza Boyaca. The city's founding square honours an Independence battle in Colombia and its local hero, José Antonio Anzoátegui. Avenida 5 de Julio runs south–north through town and is the main business street.

Catedral San Cristóbal Erected on the plaza in 1748–73, the cathedral has a glowing gilded altar screen. The church is famous for the embalmed and robed remains of Italian crusader San Celestino, venerated as having miraculous powers. Celestino is Barcelona's third patron saint; his feast days and procession are on 3–4 May.

Across from the cathedral is the **Palacio Municipal** or Alcaldía, a handsome town hall erected in 1858.

Museo de la Tradición (*Plaza Boyacá;* ⊕ *08.00–12.00 & 14.00–17.00 Tue–Sun; admission free*) The oldest house in the city (1671) has been lovingly restored and opened as a museum, complete with religious objects from the period, furniture, weapons, and the old colonial kitchens. It was once a private residence with a back door leading to the river and later became a maternity hospital. Its historical collection barely fits and the overflow is on view at the nearby Ateneo.

Casa Fuerte (*Av 5 de Julio, Plaza Bolívar*) The story behind the stark ruin of the former Franciscan monastery is one of heroism, defeat and death. When a royalist force of 4,300 occupied the city in 1817 many families took refuge in the Casa Fuerte, defended by 1,400 men under General Pedro María Freites (age 27) and William Chamberlain, Bolívar's young British aide-de-camp. Despite spirited resistance, the Spanish forces prevailed over the defenders and the Casa Fuerte fell on 7 April 1817. Few escaped the massacre that followed and some 1,600 people were killed. The tragic fate of Chamberlain and his beloved companion Eulalia was told and retold in poems and even a play in Europe. One version says that Chamberlain called for a priest, married Eulalia, put a bullet through her brain and then went to give his life on the ramparts.

Gobernación del Estado Opposite Plaza Miranda, the Gobernación del Estado is a pyramidal structure layered with greenery. Gardens extend south to the spacious Plaza de la Raza, while on the east side of Avenida 5 de Julio magnificent royal palms and pink poui trees (*apamate*) announce a trio of plazas: Plaza Miranda, Plaza Tricentenaria and Plaza Bolívar.

Mercado Municipal This market, where you can find stalls of clothing and many typical restaurants, as well as fresh fish and vegetables, is about a kilometre south of Plaza Boyacá, next to the bus terminal.

EL MORRO The showcase El Morro Tourist Complex is a stunning project said to have inspired the creators of Cancún. Thirty-three years ago sailing enthusiast Daniel Camejo envisioned a holiday city on some neglected salt flats. Today canalside homes, hotels, shops, marinas and golf courses have brought Camejo's dream to life. Playa Cocales and Los Canales are the best beaches in Puerto La Cruz, with palm trees and soft sands. Along Avenida Costanera, a broad pedestrian boulevard, showers have been installed for bathers and joggers. Southwest on Paseo Colón Sur is the entrance to a large shopping centre with cinemas, CC Plaza Mayor.

El Morro lies between the two cities that provided the land, and lives independently of both; it is not detailed on maps of Puerto La Cruz or Barcelona. The massive development encloses 20km of navigable canals dredged to give access to the bay and depends on 20 pumps and a sewage treatment system (not always adequate). On the main channel the Américo Vespucio Marina has berths for 80 yachts. There is a shipyard for complete yacht overhaul, the Centro Marino de Oriente (CMO), the country's most modern boatyard with a 70-ton travel lift, shops and a restaurant. The CMO and the new Bahía Redonda Marina with 150 berths and condominiums are reached by road via Puerto La Cruz. For most tourists, El Morro is something to wonder at in the distance as you pass by on a bus or on a boat out to the Parque Nacional Mochima from Puerto La Cruz. While there are large resort-style hotels in El Morro with good nightlife nearby, it is easier to find accommodation in Puerto La Cruz.

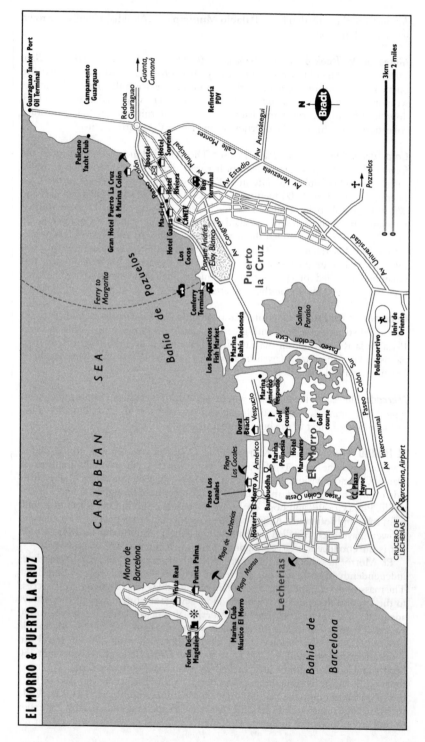

EL MORRO & PUERTO LA CRUZ

Guaraguao Tanker Port Oil Terminal

Campamento Guaraguao

Pelicano Yacht Club

Redoma Guaraguao

Guanta, Cumaná

Refinería PDV

Hotel Sorrento

hostal

Paseo Colón

Gran Hotel Puerto La Cruz & Marina Colón

Hotel Riviera

Macuto

Bus Terminal

Hotel Gaeta

CANTV

Los Cocos

Parque Andrés Eloy Blanco

Ferry to Margarita

Bahía de Pozuelos

Conferry Terminal

Av Congreso

Av Municipal

Av Estadio

Calle Montes

Av Anzoátegui

Av Venezuela

Puerto la Cruz

CARIBBEAN SEA

Los Boqueticos Fish Market

Marina Bahía Redonda

Salina Paraíso

Paseo Colón Este

Av Universidad

Pozuelos

Polideportivo

Univ de Oriente

Marina Américo Vespucio

Doral Beach

Golf course

Playa Los Cocales

Av Américo Vespucio

Marina Polinesia

Hotel Maremares

El Morro

Golf course

Paseo Colón Oeste

Paseo Colón Sur

CC Plaza Mayor

Av Intercomunal

Barcelona, Airport

Paseo Los Canales

Hostería El Morro

Bambuddha

Playa de Lecherías

CRUCERO DE LECHERIAS

N

Bradt

0   3km
0   2 miles

Morro de Barcelona

Vista Real

Punta Palma

Fortín Doña Magdalena

Marina Club Náutico El Morro

Playa Manso

Lecherías

Bahía de Barcelona

Getting there El Morro is wedged midway between Barcelona and Puerto La Cruz and is served by *por puestos* from both cities. The Aeropuerto José Antonio Anzoátegui is 20 minutes away by taxi (US$10).

Where to stay Facilities in the tourist complex are mostly resort hotels vying for dollars, sometimes with good low-season prices.

⌂ **Hotel Maremares** (493 rooms) Av Americo Vespucio; ☎ 0281 281 3022, 0281 281 1011, 0500 887 4766; www.venetur.gob.ve. A 5-star resort now run by the government's tourism agency Venetur. The canal-side complex of pink stucco villas in gardens has an attractive series of swimming pools, 2 tennis courts, convention rooms, 3 restaurants & a daycare centre. Guests ride in electric carts to the 3,000m² lagoonpool. Marina for 50 vessels, boats to island beaches & Parque Nacional Mochima. $$$$

⌂ **Punta Palma** (180 rooms) At the foot of El Morro isthmus; ☎ 0281 500 2200, 0281 500 2389; www.puntapalma.com. Good holiday offers at this hotel with its own marina, pool, tennis & good beach. Seafood specialities at Alcatraz Snack & Grill. Business centre with internet. $$$

⌂ **Hostería El Morro** (140 rooms) West on Av Américo Vespucio; ☎ 0281 281 1312, 0281 281 4335. Good value option with access to Playa Cocales & Los Canales. Rooms with AC. Pool & restaurant. $$

PUERTO LA CRUZ A major tourism centre with its bustling Paseo Colón seafront, filled with restaurants and bars, Puerto La Cruz is the main departure point for ferries to Margarita Island. Although the city beaches are not good for swimming, the western islands of the Parque Nacional Mochima are within easy reach and further east are the beaches of Santa Fé and Cumaná.

History The city gets its name from a cross that stood by an alkaline spring, the Pozo de la Santísima Cruz, which once flowed near Plaza Bolívar. The cross is now kept in the Iglesia de la Santa Cruz, two blocks west of Plaza Bolívar. A few huts housing Margarita fishing families were pretty much all that was here until the country's oil boom and the building of the oil terminal in 1939. Now Guaraguao, near Pozuelos Bay, is one of the world's largest oil ports and pipelines feed heavy, medium and light crude in a totally automated system, loading several ships at a time with as much as 70,000 barrels of oil an hour.

But the economic potential of the large bay of Puerto La Cruz was noted much earlier. In 1878, English traveller James Mudie Spence wrote in his travelogue *In the Land of Bolívar* of his search for a coaling station, because Barcelona's port was inadequate. He began sounding the coast and hit upon a place with sufficient depth: 'It had good anchorage for a thousand vessels and was situated within 4½ miles of the capital. This was on the eastern side of a small peninsula named the Morro de Barcelona.' Spence gave his report, along with a painting by Ramón Bolet of the future port with railways and telegraphs, to President Guzmán Blanco who said: 'In time it will no doubt become the centre of commerce for the eastern section of the republic.' And it did. At the turn of the century coal from the mines of Naricual was brought by train and shipped from Guanta, today the region's busy commercial port.

The area's third impetus came through tourism. Puerto La Cruz has funnelled most of Margarita's visitors on its ferries since they started operating in 1959. The big boost to local tourism came with the opening of the five-star Meliá Hotel (today the Hesperia) in 1974, which launched the town as an international destination.

Getting there
By air Puerto La Cruz is served by Barcelona's Aeropuerto José Antonio Anzoátegui (see page 191).

By bus The large Terminal de Pasajeros is located three blocks south of Plaza Bolívar on Calle Juncal. Coaches and express lines serve the same destinations as from the Barcelona terminal. Caracas is five hours by bus, four by *por puesto*; Ciudad Bolívar (5 hours); Maturín (3 hours); Cumaná (1½ hours). Frequent buses and *por puestos* to Barcelona run from Avenida 5 de Julio near Buenos Aires. Minibuses to Caripe leave from Calle Democracia west of the terminal.

Aeroexpresos Ejecutivos (*www.aeroexpresos.com.ve*) have a bus terminal in the same complex as the Conferry Terminal for ferries to Margarita. They run direct coaches between Puerto La Cruz and Caracas (US$14; at 07.00, 11.30, 15.30, 15.45, 00.30). They also run direct buses to Maracay, Valencia and Barquisimeto. Arrive at the terminal 30 minutes before departure as luggage is put through a security procedure. Well-maintained buses have numbered seats, air conditioning, toilets, video; fine at night, but windows are closed and curtained during the day.

By car Puerto La Cruz is on the main highway from Caracas after passing Barcelona.

By ferry The busiest sea link to Margarita for both passengers and cars is provided by **Conferry** (*www.conferry.com*). The terminal is off Paseo Colón, opposite Parque Andrés Eloy Blanco. Ferry schedules vary according to high or low season; check the website for the latest departure times. The big conventional ferries cross in 4½ hours with four to six sailings daily; the First Class fare for adults is about US$12, Second Class US$8; half price for children and senior citizens. Conferry also runs the modern **Margarita Express** boats that take two hours, with two departures daily on two to four days a week depending on the season; First Class US$30, VIP US$35.

The **Gran Cacique Express** (*www.grancacique.com.ve*) has its offices beside Conferry. There are three sailings a day, at 09.30, 15.30 and 21.00 in high season, and two sailings in low season (US$37 return). This is a fast, modern, passengers-only ferry that makes the crossing to Margarita in two hours.

Tourist information Some information on local sights can be obtained from **Fondoturismo Anzoátegui** (*Calle Bolívar, Edif Araya, local 3;* \ *0281 267 1632;* ⊕ *08.00–12.00 & 14.00–17.00*). Coranztur has a module on the Paseo Colón that is open daily.

Tour operators Local tours can be arranged by **Ma-ci-te** (*CC Paseo Mar, Calle Sucre, Paseo Colón;* \ *0281 265 5703; www.maciteturismo.com*) an Italian-owned agency that can organise paragliding, scuba diving, rafting, trekking, sailing and deep-sea fishing services, as well as air, bus and ferry reservations, guides and interpreters in many languages. They also arrange tours to Isla Tortuga, 30 minutes by private plane from Barcelona Airport, some 90km northwest.

Where to stay Many hotels are on or near the Paseo Colón. For a decent double room you will have to look hard for one at US$25; the better hotels are over US$50 a night (more on holidays). A single costs almost as much as a double. The partial list below does not include apartment hotels, which may require a week's stay at holiday times or two to three nights in low season. All have private bathroom and air conditioning except where noted.

⌂ **Gran Hotel Puerto La Cruz** (217 rooms) \ 0281 500 3611; www.venetur.gob.ve. Now run by the Venezuelan government's Venetur tourism agency, this landmark hotel at the end of Paseo Colón has seen better days & has a retro 1970s' feel. The large central pool & location make it a good option;

tennis courts, car rental & travel agencies, dive shop & adjacent marina. $$$

⌂ **Hotel Riviera** (74 rooms) 33 Paseo Colón; ℡ 0281 267 2111; e hotel-riviera@cantv.com. Located on the seafront, sizeable rooms have AC, TV, B&B, hot water, some with balconies & sea views. $$

⌂ **Hotel Gaeta** (50 rooms) Paseo Colón; ℡ 0281 265 0411. Rooms with TV, AC, hot water, some with sea views, b/fast served on 5th floor. Good location. $

⌂ **Hotel Sorrento** (82 rooms) Av 5 de Julio between Maneiro & Freites; ℡ 0281 268 6745. An economic option with small rooms. $

✖ **Where to eat** Around Paseo Colón are some of the city's best and busiest restaurants – at least 20 of them. They cover a wide price range from grilled chicken at US$4 upwards; seafood is a good choice here although not cheap.

For a reasonable *criollo* brunch, try **Perriven**, on Avenida Bolívar at Arismendi. The **Casa Pueblo**, Calle Carabobo a block from the Paseo, also serves reliable Venezuelan food. **Pastelería Fornos** on the Paseo opposite the Coranztur module bakes excellent pastries, as does **L'Incontro Café** at Plaza Colón. Next to the old standby Parador del Puerto, the **Dulcería Arabe** on the Paseo at Calle Buenos Aires has the reputation for the tastiest coffee in town and amazing Arab sweets. Also on the Paseo is the **Restaurant Arabe**.

Two blocks further west on the Paseo, a pair of hotel restaurants are recommended as reliable and moderate: the **Neptune's** rooftop restaurant, and the **Margelina's** Italian dining room. Pizza and pasta houses on the Paseo include **O Sole Mio** and **Porto Vecchio**. For French food, wine and music, go to the **Chic e Choc** by the Montecarlo.

If your budget is pinched, sample the tacos or burritos sold by Taco To Go carts. Or have an *empanada* (turnover) filled with *cazón* (shark), or *pabellón* (black beans, beef, plantain); these are served day and night at several kiosks in the Conferry Terminal. At lunch ask for fried fish or a *sancocho de pescado*, a soup said to raise the dead.

Nightlife Paseo Colón has lost some of its lustre as the nightlife centre of town, although there are plenty of bars for an evening drink. The new hotspots are in El Morro, especially the uber-funky **Bambuddha Bar** (*Av Americo Vespuccio, between CC Caribbean Mall & Hotel Maremare;* ⊕ *19.00–04.00*), a chic restaurant serving sushi and Thai food with oriental décor that transforms into the hottest place in town after 23.00.

Festivals The four- to five-day **Carnival** is celebrated with dances in clubs, street parades on the Intercomunal, steel bands, and plenty of vigour and liquor. This 'superbonche' ends with Carnival Tuesday. Hotels are fully booked, restaurants crowded and pickpockets overactive during this time.

The **Cruz de Mayo** is a spring festivity heralding the appearance of the Southern Cross constellation at planting time. Altars are decorated in many homes on the eve of 3 May, and the observation begins with a *velorio* or 'vigil', and songs. Puerto La Cruz celebrates with a festival around the cross on Paseo Colón, drawing processions with altars from various parishes. Singers begin the give and take of *contrapunteo* couplets sung to traditional music called the *galerón*.

The **Virgen del Valle**, patroness not only of Margarita but also of all eastern Venezuela, is honoured on 8 September. As many local families come from Margarita, they celebrate in a big way. Fishermen adorn boats with flowers, figurines and banners hailing the Virgin. After the priest says mass, scores of boats sail along the coast towards Puerto La Cruz. The flowerdecked leading *peñero* bears the Virgen del Valle, and fishermen chant prayers and hymns. On shore a procession lets off fireworks.

Other practicalities Booths for international phone calls and internet can be found at **CANTV Centro de Comunicaciones** (*Paseo Colón;* ⊕ *08.00–22.00*).

Another CANTV office at Calle Libertad and Freites shares the building with **Ipostel**, the state postal service.

Cyber cafés are all over town, with several on Paseo Colón (US$1 an hour). Try the Cristóforo Colombo shopping mall.

Inparques has offices in the Parque Andrés Eloy Blanco (↘ *0281 267 8973*). If you need a camping permit, request it in writing, make photocopies of your passport, and be patient.

There is a Banco de Venezuela with an ATM a block south of Plaza Colón on Calle Arismendi.

The usual collection of touristy T-shirt and souvenir stalls can be found along the beachfront Paseo Colón.

There is a 24-hour pharmacy on Plaza Colón.

What to see and do A city with a short past, Puerto La Cruz has no historic monuments and few tourist attractions. Tourists use it as a base to explore the Parque Nacional Mochima (done more cheaply from Santa Fé and Mochima) or as a stop between long journeys.

Paseo Colón, in front of the bay of Pozuelos, is the centre of town life. At its east end is the Gran Hotel. From the bronze statue of Christopher Columbus and the Cross in an oval plaza, the seafront boulevard runs a dozen blocks to the Conferry Terminal and Parque Andrés Eloy Blanco, where it leaves the shore to go southwest around El Morro. By day visitors and locals congregate around the benches, pastry shops and open-air restaurants, soak up the sun on the beach in front (the sea is not clean enough for swimming), and set out in boats for island beaches. In the evenings street vendors sell crafts, souvenirs, toys, CDs and DVDs, paintings and leather sandals, while locals take a promenade along the front. Bars and restaurants open until late.

Fishermen bring their catch early in the morning to the waterfront fish market of Los Cocos just west of the Rasil.

Pozuelos Once a separate village, Pozuelos is now a quiet suburb about 1km south of the Intercomunal and Vía Alterna highways. Named for its springs, whose luxuriant greenery announced water to passing sailors and explorers, Pozuelos is on a steep hill with a wonderful view of the bay. A mission was founded in 1681 to resettle Indians and a little church was built, dedicated to Nuestra Señora del Amparo. A colonial painting of the Virgin stands over the altar.

Diving

✒**Aquatic Adventures** Marina de Puerto Cruz; m 0414 806 3744, 0414 820 8758, www.aquaticadventures-mochima.net.tc. On Paseo Colón in the marina by the Gran Hotel, full dive services are provided, SSI courses & certification, & diving excursions arranged to island reefs. The shop stocks Dacor, Genesis & Sport Divers equipment. ✒**Explosub** Hotel Mare Mare, Paseo Colón; ↘ 0281 282 2818, 0281 281 3022; ⊕ 08.00–17.00 daily. Has a dive shop at the Mare Mare in El Morro, the

Gran Hotel on Paseo Colón & on the beach; they fill tanks & rent masks, scuba equipment, boats, windsails. ✒**Horisub** Marina Americo Vespuccio; ↘ 0281 281 4878; m 0416 680 3800; e horisub@telcel.net.ve; www.horisub.com. A PADI dive resort that offers courses, equipment hire, night dives, & excursions to the Parque Nacional Mochima, La Tortuga, La Blanquilla.

Yachting Puerto La Cruz is the country's biggest watersports centre with over seven marinas and yacht clubs. Right on Pozuelos Bay by the Gran Hotel is the **Marina Gente de Mar** or **Marina Colón** (↘ *0281 269 1517*), which offers visiting yachtsmen a launching service; closed Wednesdays for maintenance. The newest marina, **Bahía Redonda**, is a world-class facility with not only 150 full service berths, but also a swimming pool, hot showers and a communications centre. To reach the marina, follow Paseo Colón past the ferry terminal and at Redoma Los Cerezos go west to Los Boqueticos and the Centro Marino de Oriente shipyard. Enquire about charters, both sail and motor. Other marinas include: the Pelican Yacht Club, and Club Náutico El Chaure in the oil terminal, the Guanta Marina, Hotel Punta Palma's marina, and the pioneer **Marina Club Náutico El Morro** at the isthmus of El Morro Peninsula. It has a restaurant, marine shop, fork-lift service and some space for visiting yachts.

Parque Nacional Mochima (See map on page 154.) Although urban beaches may be clean, the sea currents carry pollutants from the ports and cities. The truly beautiful beaches are on the islands and coasts of Parque Nacional Mochima. A dozen islands lie within easy reach of Puerto La Cruz. Although arid and hilly they are surrounded by clear waters where groups of dolphins play and the coral reefs attract snorkellers and divers. The **Borracha** and **Chimana** island groups lie some 11km and 6km north of Puerto La Cruz. La Borracha has good reefs; **Playa de Guaro** is on the west side. Chimana Grande has protected beaches called **Playa Puinare** and **El Saco** (most popular), sunshades and a well-run restaurant. Chimana Segunda has **El Faro**, a quiet beach with restaurant.

At the east end of Paseo Colón the boatmen's co-operative called **Transtupaco** (\ *0281 267 4263*) has a stand on the jetty by the Gran Hotel. Their 16 *peñeros* equipped with roof, life-jackets and radio are on call every day from 08.30; weekends are crowded. You buy a numbered return ticket for about US$7–10 to visit Playa El Saco, Puinare and El Faro on the Chimanas. **Transtupuerto**, at the other end of Paseo Colón, offer similar tours. Enquire about tours to **Arapo**, an island off the coast east of Puerto La Cruz. If you wish to explore various islands with snorkelling and diving see *Diving* opposite.

Isla de Plata, named for its silverwhite sand, nestles between the headlands of Guanta and Pertigalete. Crystal waters, reefs, umbrellas and food stalls attract plenty of bathers on weekends when the ten-minute shuttle boat from **Pamatacualito** runs from 07.30 until 16.30. Service is less frequent during the week. *Por puestos* to Pamatacualito, about 10km away, leave from Plaza Bolívar in Puerto La Cruz. If you wish to camp overnight, consult the Isla de Plata ferry co-operative first; they will need to know your transportation and food requirements. The boatmen here can also arrange trips to other islands and beaches: Isla de Monos, Ña Cleta, Conomita, Arapo and La Piscina.

Further east along the coast is **Playa Santa Cruz** (30 minutes from Puerto La Cruz), which has a comfortable guesthouse, **Villa La Encantada** (*12 rooms;* m *0414 980 3751, 0416 781 0430*), above the small beach with fine sea views. They have a pool and restaurant (good food) surrounded by flowers, 12 rooms with fans for two to four people at US$40 a double. Ask owner Diane Wilson about scuba diving or boat rides to islands and good beaches around the steep headland.

Fishermen in Valle Seco just beyond Pertigalete will take you to **Conoma**, **Conomita** (10 minutes), **Ña Cleta** (5 minutes) and **Isla de Monos** (18 minutes) which has a small beach and beautiful corals. A narrow road descends from the highway to the community of Valle Seco. Agree on a price per boat round trip, *ida y vuelta*.

Arapo and **Arapito islands** where vendors ply *empanadas*, beer and cold *kolas* or soft drinks, lie opposite the very popular mainland beaches of **Playa Arapito**, **Vallecito** and **Colorada**, 23–26km from Puerto La Cruz. Between the islands is La Piscina, the 'swimming pool', famous for its mirrorlike translucent water. Off Arapo, northwest, is a rocky pelican perch, Isla de Pájaros. Boatmen in Playa

8

Colorada or Arapito charge about US$20 per boat (five passengers) to these islands, returning at an agreed hour.

Playa Colorada is a long crescent beach off the main coastal highway known for its reddish sand and fringe of tall coconut palms, great for slinging hammocks. Shacks of informal restaurants serve fish, snacks and cold beer to the large weekend crowds. You can overnight in your tent or hammock for a fee but security is questionable. Better to cross the road and walk uphill to one of the half dozen good, inexpensive guesthouses. **Jakera Lodge** (\ *0293 808 7057;* e *info@ jakera.com; www.jakera.com*) is a large guesthouse with dorm room accommodation for young foreign travellers who want to learn Spanish, volunteer, dance salsa, and make new friends. Hammocks also available. Run by a Mérida-based group, Jakera can also arrange all transport to the lodge and trips and tours around Venezuela. A French-Canadian couple Jacques and Sonya run **Quinta Jaly** (m *0416 681 8113*), with use of a kitchen, six rooms for one to four guests, fan or air conditioning, hot water, some private baths; about US$18 for two.

El Tucusito or Villas Turísticas (\ *0212 952 1393;* m *0416 482 1749*) has a restaurant, small pool, and six caravans with two bedrooms, kitchen, air conditioning, bath; also 12 smaller suites for two to three persons; US$40 per unit. (See *Chapter 6, Los Roques, Morrocoy and Mochima*, for a map of this coast, the route to Santa Fé and the village of Mochima.)

SUCRE STATE

To most Venezuelans El Oriente stands for Sucre's long Caribbean shore stretching from Parque Nacional Mochima east to Paria Peninsula. The main town is Cumaná, an excellent hub for travel to the beaches of the Paria Peninsula, Margarita, Monagas State and the Orinoco Delta. The area has much to offer: the famous Guácharo Cave is nearby, and the region boasts forests, mountains and laidback rural towns where people still take life slowly. Dialects vary from the rapid accents of Cumaná's fishermen to the English and French influence of patois in the small port of Güiria. Daily life here revolves around fishing and farming. Coconut plantations fringe the bays of Paria, water buffalo are at home in the wetlands, huge trees shade lush cacao groves beyond Carúpano, and sugarcane blooms in the Cariaco and Cumanacoa valleys. Mangoes are so abundant that in season they cover the ground.

CUMANÁ (*Telephone code: 0293*) A historic city that claims to be the oldest on the South American continent (1521), Cumaná looks out towards the Caribbean Sea from its perch at the mouth of the Manzanares River.

A walk through Cumaná's small centre gives little indication of its importance as a state capital and a major seaport with a population of 370,000 (half under the age of 20), although the imposing stone fortress that watches over the city is a reminder of pirate attacks in the colonial past. Most inhabitants live in outlying *barrios* and their daily comings and goings produce a serious gridlock at peak hours. For the traveller, however, the concentration of activity downtown offers unlimited opportunities for peoplewatching. Music is everywhere, from the solitary wanderer singing to the accompaniment of his *cuatro* (a four-stringed guitar), to groups of children drumming on discarded tins, or blaring *minitecas* wheeled around town by sellers of bootleg CDs. It is perfectly acceptable to dance as the mood strikes, whenever and wherever.

History Cumaná was home to the Cumanagoto Indians long before the arrival of Spanish conquistadors. Its claims of being the oldest Spanish town on the

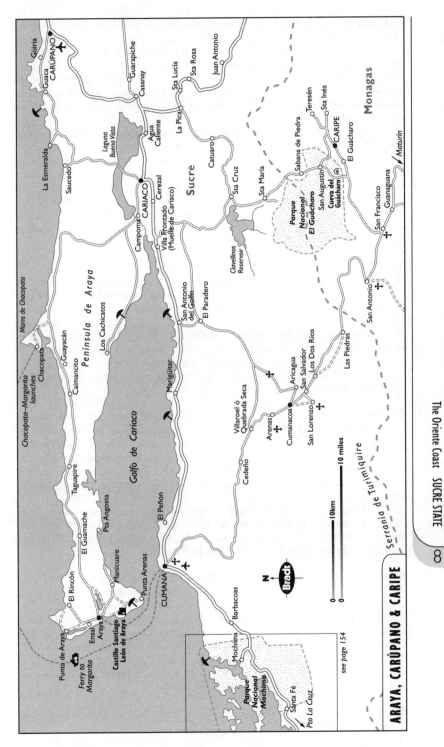

ARAYA, CARÚPANO & CARIPE

see page 154

201

mainland are disputed, but it was certainly the most important native community on the coast. The discovery of pearl beds off Margarita in 1499 made Cumaná an indispensable supply base for fresh water and Indian slaves, who were forced to dive for pearls. The Franciscan missionaries, who arrived in 1515, came to try and protect the Indians from exploitation. What followed were 54 years of massacres as Cubagua's slavers raided the coast again and again, the Indians rebelled against the intrusion by monks, and Spaniards sent punitive expeditions in retaliation.

In 1569 Cumaná received its first permanent settlers and in the 1660s two forts, San Antonio de la Eminencia and Santa María de la Cabeza, were constructed. These forts and the whole city were destroyed several times by earthquakes in 1684, 1797, 1853 and 1929. San Antonio has been partially restored, but of Santa María there remains little. Cumaná joined the Captaincy General of Venezuela in 1777, and during the war for Independence from Spain in the early 1800s played an important part, being taken and retaken a number of times. Sucre State is named after native son Grand Marshal Antonio José de Sucre who fought with Bolívar and liberated Ecuador, Peru and Bolivia. He was Bolivia's first president.

Getting there

By air Aeropuerto Internacional Antonio José de Sucre (10km from downtown Cumaná) doesn't have any international flights at the moment but you can fly to Margarita in 12 minutes with Rutaca (*www.rutaca.com.ve*) – much less time than it takes to board. Flights to Caracas (US$45, 1 hour) on Venezolana (*www.ravsa.com.ve*) and Avior (*www.avioairlines.com*) leave several times a day from 06.00 to 17.30. State airline Conviasa (*www.conviasa.aero*) has also stated its intention to start flights between Cumaná and Caracas. There are no buses from the airport to Cumaná, get a taxi. From town to the airport *por puestos* leave from the river east of the plaza.

By ferry Ferry and launch services go separately to Margarita and to Araya (for details see *Araya*, page 208). Remember that ferry schedules are not written in stone, so be flexible. The ferry terminal is at the foot of Avenida El Islote, several blocks down from the Mercado Municipal. A *por puesto* leaves from Plaza Miranda between the two bridges. It is better not to walk if you are alone or carrying anything, as the waterfront can be a dangerous place for anyone with anything to lose.

For Margarita, the **Gran Cacique** (*www.grancacique.com.ve*) hydrofoil takes two hours to Punta de Piedras, Margarita. Prices for a single fare are: First Class BsF101; Tourist BsF81; children pay half. Sailings from Cumaná are at 07.00 and 14.00, from Punta de Piedras at 11.00 and 18.00.

By bus The Terminal de Pasajeros is on Avenida Las Palomas [203 B3], 3km from the centre of town, and is open all night, when many long-distance coaches arrive and depart. Exercise caution here. Buses leave for Caracas (7 hours) every 30 minutes and through the day to Ciudad Bolívar (7 hours), via Puerto La Cruz (2 hours). For the Guácharo Cave, take the Caripe bus at 07.30 or 12.00. The Caripe service can vary depending on road conditions. Buses go throughout the day to Carúpano (2½ hours) and Güiria (4½ hours). For the Orinoco Delta, head for Maturín where you can get transport to the Delta. *Por puestos* to Mochima and to Santa Fé park a block north of Redoma El Indio.

By car Cumaná is on the main highway Route 9 running from Caracas all the way along the coast to Carúpano.

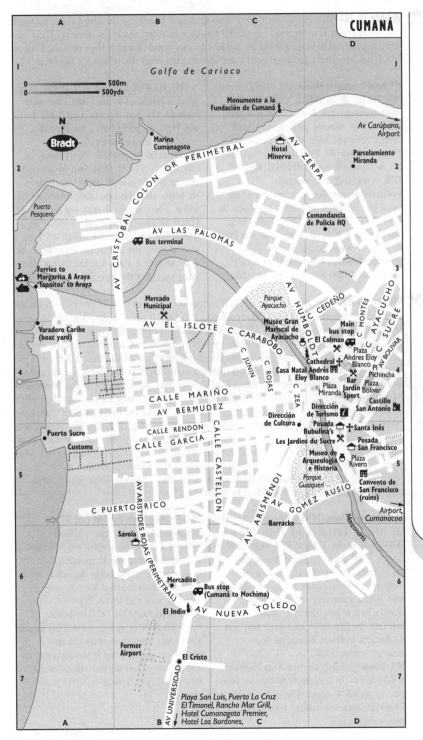

CUMANÁ

Golfo de Cariaco

Monumento a la
Fundación de Cumaná

Av Carúpano,
Airport

Marina
Cumanagoto

Hotel
Minerva

Parcelamiento
Miranda

Puerto
Pesquero

AV CRISTOBAL COLON OR PERIMETRAL

AV LAS PALOMAS
Bus terminal

AV ZERPA

Comandancia
de Policia HQ

Ferries to
Margarita & Araya
'Tapaitos' to Araya

Mercado
Municipal

AV EL ISLOTE

C CARABOBO

AV HUMBOLDT

C CEDEÑO

Parque
Ayacucho

Museo Gran
Mariscal de
Ayacucho

El Colmao

Main
bus stop

C MONTES

C AYACUCHO

C SUCRE

Plaza
Andres Eloy
Blanco

Varadero Caribe
(boat yard)

C JUNIN

C ROJAS

Cathedral

AV BOLIVAR

Casa Natal Andrés
Eloy Blanco

C ZEA

Bar
Jardín
Sport

Pichincha

Plaza
Bolivar

CALLE MARIÑO

AV BERMUDEZ

CALLE RENDON

CALLE GARCIA

CALLE CASTELLON

Plaza
Miranda

Dirección
de Turismo

Castillo
San Antonio

Puerto Sucre

Customs

Dirección
de Cultura

Posada
Bubulina's

Santa Inés

Les Jardins du Sucre

Posada
San Francisco

Museo de
Arqueología
e Historia

Plaza
Rivero

AV ARISTIDES ROJAS (PERIMETRAL)

C PUERTO RICO

AV ARISMENDI

AV GOMEZ RUSIO

Parque
Guaiquerí

Convento de
San Francisco
(ruins)

Airport,
Cumanacoa

Manzanares

Barracks

Savoia

Mercadito

Bus stop
(Cumaná to Mochima)

El Indio

AV NUEVA TOLEDO

Former
Airport

El Cristo

AV UNIVERSIDAD

Playa San Luis, Puerto La Cruz
El Timonel, Rancho Mar Grill,
Hotel Cumanagoto Premier,
Hotel Los Bordones,

0   500m
0   500yds

N

Bradt

The Oriente Coast SUCRE STATE

8

203

Where to stay

Cumaná's four- and five-star beach hotels are clustered at the far west end of Avenida Universidad, about 20 minutes in a taxi from the airport. They can seem empty out of season and a bit isolated but are good bases for trips into the Parque Nacional Mochima (arrange your own with boatmen on the beach for big savings).

Hotel Cumanagoto Premier [203 B7] (163 rooms) Playa San Luis, Av Universidad; \ 0293 430 1400; www.hotelespremier.com. A 5-star hotel on 4 floors, with gym, large swimming pools, access to beach, loungers, restaurants, buffet b/fast & tours. $$$$

Los Bordones [203 B7] (115 rooms) Playa San Luis, Av Universidad; \ 0293 400 0350, 0293 400 0358; e reservas@losbordones.com; www.losbordones.com. This 4-star hotel has a large central pool in front of the beach & buzzes with the sound of slot machines at the bingo centre. Tennis, restaurant, bar & Wi-Fi. Can arrange boat trips from the beach to Parque Nacional Mochima. $$$

Posada Bubulina's & Restaurant [203 D5] (12 rooms) Callejón Santa Inés, near Santa Ines church;

\ 0293 431 4025, 0293 433 4137. Another central option. 2 redecorated houses, 1 with a Venezuelan restaurant, have been joined to create a B&B. Rooms with TV, AC, fan, private bath & hot water off a central patio corridor. Homely. $

Posada San Francisco [203 D5] (10 rooms) 16 Calle Sucre; \ 0293 431 3926. From its tall, narrow entrance, this 300-year-old colonial town house in the historic centre has been totally restored by Rolf Scherer, a Swiss engineer & sailor who has made Cumaná his preferred port-of-call. He rescued the original floor tiles, put in cane ceilings, fans & hot-water plumbing, plus a restaurant serving Venezuelan dishes for lunch & a nice little bar. Ask him about sailing tours along the coast. $

Where to eat

Cumaná is a street food mecca if you want to take the risk and head out to the nationally famous **Mercadito** [203 B6], a noisy collection of 20 or so seafood restaurants north of Redoma del Indio (a cement statue of an Indian holding a fish, said to be the only fish not consumed in Cumaná). Try the *hervido* or *sopa de pescado*, an inexpensive chunky fish soup with all the bones left in. This is a meal in itself and a daily mainstay of coastal diet. It is excellent for an uneasy stomach and when recovering from illness. You may prefer to eat at the **Mercado Municipal** [203 B3] (⏰ 07.00–14.00), which offers the same fare as the Mercadito but in a more secure environment. In the streets and on the beach of San Luis small stalls offer a typical street *parrilla* menu: on a base of *bollitos* (boiled maize meal) is *manioc* (yuca) or *ocumo chino* (taro), grilled beef or pork steak, two kinds of sausage, and *chinchurria* (intestines, in case you want to give it a miss), served with *guasacaca*, a non-*picante* sauce of chopped coriander, parsley, onions, garlic, green pepper and avocado. Top it off with a *jugo de parchita* (passion-fruit juice), and the bill will be about US$4. Best deal in town.

Les Jardins du Sucre [203 D5] Calle Sucre; \ 0293 431 3689; ⏰ 18.00–20.00 Mon, 12.00–15.00 & 18.00–20.00 Tue–Fri, 12.00–15.00 & 18.00–23.00 Sat–Sun. French pastry chef Benoit Bourille gives classics dishes from France a local twist at this remodelled old house opposite Posada San Francisco, where tropical plants bring the jungle indoors, tastefully. Duck in port, lamb in 4 peppers, red wine from Chile, chocolate soufflé, it's a world away from the Mercadito in flavours & price. The best restaurant in town. $$$

El Colmao [203 D4] Calle Sucre, Plaza Pichincha; \ 0293 451 6477; ⏰ 12.00–02.00 Mon–Sat. Locals swear by the fish & seafood dishes at this popular Spanish-style restaurant, including a good paella. Live music sometimes. $$

El Timonel y Ranch Mar Grill [203 B7] Av Universidad, Playa San Luis; \ 0293 451 6477; ⏰ lunch & dinner. Two places in one. El Timonel is a Spanish-style *tasca* with AC, specialising in seafood & decorated like a ship. Rancho Mar Grill is outside & serves up barbecued meat & chicken, when it's open. Live music most w/ends. $$

Bar Jardin Sport [203 D4] Plaza Bolívar; ⏰ 09.00–24.00. An open-air bar that has become a well-known reference point for international travellers, it now has a big TV showing sports. Still a good place to beat the heat with an icecold Polar or fruit juice & watch the action in the plaza. $

Festivals The **Noches de Antaño Festival** held on the last weekend of November is Cumaná's yearly parade and family party. Inspired by yesteryear, this is an evening affair in the historic centre. The note is one of nostalgia and good humour with art and historical exhibitions, antique cars, old-style songs, music and dances by many local groups performing in Plaza Bolívar and the Alcaldía, capped off with a costume parade and prizes.

Other practicalities There are branches of Banco de Venezuela and Banesco on Calle Mariño between Calle Carabobo and Calle Rojas, and a CANTV call centre on Avenida Humboldt in the Centro Comercial San Onofre.

The **Dirección de Turismo** [203 D4] has an office in Calle Sucre next to the Hotel Astoria. Helpful staff have a few pamphlets and can offer advice on visiting local sites and further afield in Sucre State.

What to see and do Cumaná's historic heart is conveniently arranged around Plaza Bolívar and the government buildings. Explore the plaza and the fortress but resist the temptation to wander up into the unsafe old section of town on the hills behind Plaza Rivero and the partly restored ruin of the **Convento de San Francisco** [203 D5] (Cumaná's first university which ended as a soap factory). Also, Cumaná is built on filled swamp. If you visit in the wet season you will note that some parts of the city simply have no drainage.

Castillo San Antonio de la Eminencia [203 D4] (⊕ *10.00–19.00; admission free*) Built out of coral in the shape of a four-pointed star to defend the city against French pirates who attacked in 1654, the castle was completed in 1686 and withstood many attacks and earthquakes. Reached from Plaza Bolívar (follow the signs) or by steps from Calle La Luneta behind the Iglesia Santa Inés, it gives spectacular views over the city and Gulf of Cariaco and Araya. In 1965 it was declared a national monument and archaeologists continue to find secret tunnels under the 2m-thick walls.

Iglesia Santa Inés [203 D5] This church is dedicated to Cumaná's first patron saint, named in 1572 when settlers beat off a dawn attack by Indians. The second patron, St John the Baptist, earned the honour when Walter Raleigh, fresh from an expedition up the Orinoco, failed to take Cumaná and was forced to exchange his prisoner, Trinidad governor Antonio de Berrío, for English casualties. That was on St John's Day, 24 June 1595. The church that you see, raised after the disastrous earthquake of 1929, is the last in a long succession begun in 1637. Up the hill from the church are the inconspicuous ruins of **Santa María de la Cabeza** fort (1673).

Museo Gran Mariscal de Ayacucho [203 C4] (*Parque Ayacucho;* ⊕ *09.00–12.00 & 14.00–18.00; admission free*) Two blocks from the cathedral is this museum to the Independence hero Antonio José de Sucre, Cumaná's most famous son. The ground floor displays portraits, weapons and relics once owned by Sucre, who was born in 1796, the son of the Spanish governor of the Province of Nueva Andalucía and Guayana. He began military training at age ten in the fortress of San Antonio de la Eminencia and before he was 16 he had joined the 'patriot' Independence army of Francisco de Miranda. A brilliant general and strategist, his victory at Pichincha in 1822 liberated Ecuador. Then in 1824 he won the Battle of Ayacucho, which brought independence to Peru, earning him the title of Grand Marshal. The following year he thrashed royalists in Alto Peru and on the creation of Bolivia was elected president, proving to be an able administrator. Perhaps he was too able. Opponents of Simón Bolívar's plan to unify all the countries liberated from Spain into Gran Colombia saw Sucre as his successor. In 1828 an unsuccessful attempt was made on Bolívar's life and on 4 June 1830 Sucre was ambushed and killed near Pasto in southern Colombia, while riding home to his wife. He was 35 years old.

Casa Natal Andrés Eloy Blanco [203 D4] (*Plaza Bolívar; ⊕ 09.00–12.00 & 15.00–18.00 Mon–Fri; admission free*) The birthplace of Venezuela's best-loved poet (1896–1955). The restored 1840s' house where his grandparents and parents lived conserves the period furniture, kitchen, and 200-year-old piano which is still used for recitals. Memorabilia include a desk made by Blanco, a political activist, during the dictatorship of Juan Vicente Gómez, when he couldn't publish. He died in exile in Mexico during the dictatorship of Marcos Pérez Jiménez.

Museo de Arqueología e Historia [203 D5] (*25 Calle Sucre; ⊕ 08.30–12.00 & 14.30–17.30; admission free*) Displays archaeological finds in what was the home of Daniel Beauperthuy, a doctor who discovered the yellow-fever mosquito. It is followed by a cultural centre, housed in the birthplace of poet José Antonio Ramos Sucre.

Mercado Municipal [203 B3] The big market on Avenida El Islote is a must – by far the best public market in all the Oriente; large, open and well organised. Wander through the airy main building where fruit, vegetables and meat are sold, and around the back to the *playa*, the part where the trucks unload and sell directly to the public. In this section you will find the freshest produce and best prices. You will have the opportunity to choose a live chicken and deliver it to be killed and plucked, get your hair cut, select some handmade cigars (a local speciality), buy shoes and clothing at the lowest prices around, eat and drink all manner of interesting things, and generally be dazzled. By the main parking entrance there is an *artesanía* (craft) section that sells pots, hats, birds, herbs, handmade furniture, a good variety of hammocks and souvenirs in general. Open every day till midday, but best and busiest on weekends. During market hours almost all minibuses stop here. Look for the *Mercado* card on the windscreen. All the local colour you can handle and then some.

Beaches Cumaná is known for its long beach and tranquil sea but unfortunately they are polluted by sewage and agricultural chemicals from the Manzanares River.

This does not stop the Cumaneses, however, and on weekends and holidays they flock to the seaside. The main beach is Playa San Luis on Avenida Universidad, reached by minibus. If you must bathe on the Playa San Luis, go to the Hotel Los Bordones or the Cumanagoto and use the patrolled beaches in front. They close the gates at dusk. Do not wander in lesser-used areas of the beach; these are haunts for muggers that even the locals avoid.

ARAYA PENINSULA (*Telephone code: 0293*) Araya is a long desert peninsula. Only a few kilometres across the Gulf of Cariaco from Cumaná, it affords a true escape for seekers of sun, wind and solitude. Beaches on the Caribbean side are of broken shells with generally rough water, but the western shores are wide and tranquil. The gulf is very deep and the water is cooler than one would expect, a welcome contrast to blazing sun. These depths are an important breeding ground for fish, and Araya's inhabitants are by and large fishermen.

Araya's industry is salt; mainstay of the town of Araya. People come daily from Cumaná to work in the salt works. The *salinas* have been worked since 1499 when they were known as the world's richest and they still produce 500,000 tons a year. Seawater is evaporated from the salt, and the evaporation lagoon is an otherworldly pinkish mauve which must be seen to be believed. When you cross from Cumaná to Araya by ferry or launch you will see a mountain of salt off to the north. On working days, 06.00–14.00, you can ask at the Salaraya offices about seeing the salt works. In one of the old salt pans a shrimp farmer is doing quite well breeding sea shrimp for export. The pink colour of the evaporation pools comes, in fact, from microscopic shrimp. If you take the road north of the town to Punta Araya, you get a good view of the rectangular salt pools.

The same winds that dry the salt now make Araya an off-the-beaten-track destination for **windsurfing**. Winds are strong but, with onshore/sideshore direction, not easy for beginners. Adepts use the beach near the fort.

The imposing fortress of **Santiago León de Araya** was built to stop the smuggling of salt – then almost as valuable as gold – by the Dutch and English. Begun in 1622, construction of this massive fortification, known locally as El Castillo, whose partly restored ruins may be visited just south of the town, took 47 years. The workers toiled away at night to avoid the blistering heat of the day. It proved to be Spain's costliest construction and consumed fortunes in maintenance. In 1770 its demolition was ordered, although large parts survived the dynamite intact. You will see the fort as you approach Araya by sea. It is an easy 20-minute walk from the village and has a good beach with a few small *cabana*-type shelters. The fortress has no gate, just wander around and imagine pirates of the Caribbean fighting to the death over gold, booty and... salt.

If you plan to explore Araya's wilder beaches take good shoes for the rugged terrain and ubiquitous cactus. There's no shade here and full desert sun protection is a must. Take a hat, long trousers and long-sleeved shirt, more sunscreen than you plan to use and more water than you plan to drink. Araya's main road is good, with regular traffic, but side roads are generally rough and unmarked, with very little traffic. Wildlife away from the road is surprising: lizards and snakes, birds perched on cactus tops and feral goats everywhere. There are foxes and rabbits as well but these are more difficult to see. The lagoon near Chacopata is known for its birdlife, especially flamingos.

Getting there

By road The circuitous route from Cumaná to Araya is some 150km via Cariaco and Punta Arenas. The scenic, often solitary, peninsular route follows a dramatic coastline of beaches, rocks and cliffs. The only fork is the 3km road to Chacopata, an unkempt village on the northern point. The distance from this fork to the *pueblo* of Araya is 50km, passing communities of subsistence fishermen: Caimancito, Taguapire, El Guamache. Take the ferry.

By bus Don't bother – take the ferry. To get to Araya by bus would mean taking a local *por puesto* from to Cumaná to Cariaco and then another *por puesto* to Chacopata and then another to Guayacán, and service is neither frequent nor reliable on the Araya Peninsula.

By boat Araya is accessible from Cumaná (10km, 1 hour, BsF6) by Naviarca's inexpensive open car ferry (*chalana*) from the main dock at the foot of Avenida El Islote that serves the Margarita ferry and launch. Sailings are *highly* variable: morning (earliest at 06.00, often with a queue), noon and afternoon on weekdays, and once a day at weekends at around 09.00, returning at 15.30. The ferry goes when it fills up, so on arrival check demand for the return so as not to get left high and dry.

A much faster boat service is available in passenger launches called *tapaitos*, which refers to their roofs or *tapas*. The boats leave throughout the day from the ferry terminal in Cumaná to Manicuare (20 minutes, US$1.50), a small village known for its rustic pottery.

Chacopata–Margarita launches A passenger service crossing from Chacopata on the Araya Peninsula to Margarita takes just 1½ hours and is gaining popularity. *Tapaitos* and fishing boats leave when they are full, from about 07.00 to 15.30. The *tapaitos* have canvas sides keeping out spray (and any view) and the ride on hard benches can be cramped, but it is fast. This service is used mainly by residents and workers from eastern Sucre, who reach Chacopata by *por puesto* from Carúpano or Cumaná (1½ hours). Drivers may leave their cars by the National Guard post. Boats can also be contracted to go to Coche Island, 40 minutes away.

Where to stay Inns and hostels on the peninsula are basic, with fans and cold water, operating on a cash-only basis. To find lodgings in Araya village, near the ruins of the fort, ask around Plaza Bolívar.

⌂ **Alojamiento Helen** (23 rooms) Calle Castillo, Araya; ✆ 0293 437 1101; m 0414 392 5422. Near the fort with plain, clean rooms with private bath, TV, some with AC. $

⌂ **Posada Araya Wind** (15 rooms) Calle Castillo, Araya; ✆ 0293 437 1132; m 0414 189 0717. An attractive beachfront *posada* & a magnet for windsurfers who gather at its bar & restaurant, & park their sails at the inn's shelter. Some of the rustic rooms have private bath, AC, TV. $

⌂ **Posada de Arquímedes** (6 rooms) Punta Arenas; ✆ 0293 416 9809; m 0414 993 2683, 0414 393 0622. Also called **Shailili-Ko**, this small *posada* 100m from the beach was the first inn built here by Arquímedes Vargas. It has great views of the sea & 2 rooms have sliding panels so you can sleep

under the stars, no problem in this arid climate. Hammocks, terrace, small pool & garden shelter where Arquímedes serves b/fast & dinner in peak season. Can arrange Cumaná transfers, trips to Parque Nacional Mochima, tours. $

⌂ **Posada Restaurant Araya Mar** (9 rooms) Calle Castillo, Araya; ✆ 0293 437 1132, 0293 437 1382. Good beach, sea views at this small *posada* by the fort. Rooms with AC, TV, cold water. $

⌂ **Vista al Mar** (6 rooms) ✆ 0293 467 2468; m 0416 806 7223. Owner Asdrúbal Cabrera & his wife run this small *posada* near Arquímedes with simple, attractive rooms with dbl & sgl beds, hammocks, all meals included. The *posada* has a small pool. Can arrange boat service to & from Cumaná. $

Other practicalities Bring everything you need with you as apart from a few *posadas* and very basic stores there is nothing on the Araya Peninsula.

EAST SUCRE STATE

The route to Paria Peninsula The road leaving Cumaná follows the lovely, sheltered Gulf of Cariaco eastward to Cariaco, an agricultural town of 15,000 people at the end of the gulf, which bore the brunt of Venezuela's worst earthquake in 30 years on 8 July 1997. The quake of 6.9 on the Richter scale split streets, flattened most homes and buildings, and left over 70 dead, many of them schoolchildren. Cumaná and Cariaco are on not one, but two active geological faults. Hot springs throughout the area are evidence of these faults and several *posadas* and restaurants have set up shop along the road allowing visits to the natural sulphur springs. There are popular thermal pools beyond Cariaco on the road to Casanay.

Where to stay On these tranquil shores there are a few places worth checking for a day's rest.

Balneario Los Cocoteros (30 rooms) \ 0294 331 9240, 0294 414 5749. Take a dip (there's a small fee of about BsF20) in one of various palm-shaded pools at this large complex on the road to Casanay. The hot springs are actually only lukewarm, but are rich in minerals judging from the smell. You can eat at the inexpensive restaurant, or stay over at the hotel. Rooms with bath, AC, TV. $$

Club Maigualida Hotel (8 apts & 16 rooms & suites) \ 0293 839 1070; e info@ maigualida.com; www.maigualida.com. Just before Marigüitar are the jetty, beach, pool & tennis court of this handsome beachfront hotel, a good centre for watersports such as sailing, surfing & fishing (they rent pedal, motor & sailboats). 2 modern buildings have rooms, all with AC, private bath, hot water. The big open-sided restaurant is open to the public & serves good, inexpensive food. $$

Balneario Cachamaure (12 cabins) \ 0293 839 3045, 0293 433 0556. 2km west of San Antonio is this old standby, also economical, in a fenced grassy plot with coconut palms where the attraction is not the beach (rocky) but a pool fed by hot springs, open to non-guests for a small fee. There are showers, shelters & cabins (kitchen but no pots) for 2–6 guests. $

CARÚPANO (*Telephone code: 0294*) Famous throughout Venezuela for its crazy annual carnival, Carúpano is a good base for exploring local beaches, the Gulf of Cariaco and Araya Peninsula and further afield to the famous Guácharo Caves (see *Chapter 9, Monagas and the Orinoco Delta*, page 225) and the Paria Peninsula. With a population of some 150,000, the town has pleasant streets with well-kept old houses around Plaza Santa Rosa de Lima, two blocks from the bay. Plaza Bolívar is 14 blocks north of the coast road. In between, the main shops and office buildings are centred around Plaza Colón.

History Carúpano has a history as a trading and shipping centre for the Paria region. Founded in 1647, the agricultural settlement grew very slowly. Foreign trade was opened in the 1820s, followed by immigration, especially from Corsica. But it wasn't until the 1860s that Carúpano took on importance with direct exports to Europe. From the port it sends over two-thirds of Venezuela's cacao crop to Europe and Japan, and tons of salted fish and shark. Carúpano also enjoys a certain fame for its rum distilleries: Real Carúpano made on Hacienda Altamira, Macarapana, and El Muco made in town; you can visit El Muco's installations.

Getting there

By air Aeropuerto General José Francisco Bermúdez is 5km west of town. Rutaca (*www.rutaca.com.ve*) flies to Porlamar four times a day from 08.30 to 16.00 with four return flights from Porlamar. Avior (*www.avior.com.ve*) had suspended flights to Caracas at the time of publication but they could resume. The state-owned airline Conviasa (*www.conviasa.aero*) has plans to fly from Carúpano.

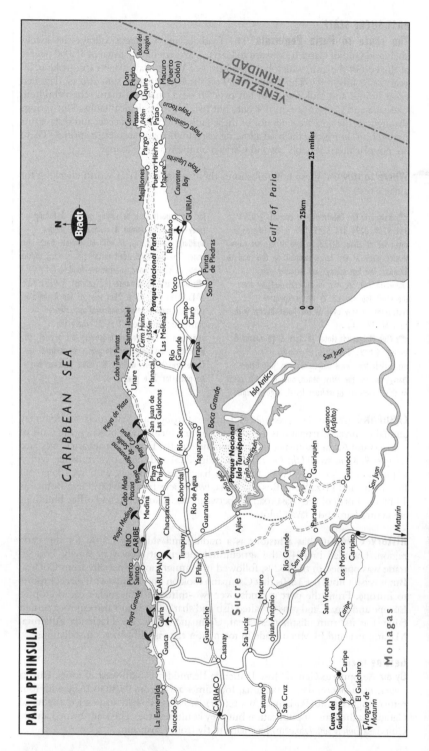

PARIA PENINSULA

CARIBBEAN SEA

Boca del Dragón
Don Pedro
Uquire
Macuro (Puerto Colón)
Cerro Patao
1,048m
Patao
Playa Yacua
Guiriíntita
Playa Uquirito
Puerto Hierro
Mapire
Mejillones
Pargo
Cauranta Bay
GÜIRIA
Río Salado
Parque Nacional Paria
Yoco
Punta de Piedras
Soro
Campo Claro
Cerro Humo
1,356m
Las Melenas
Manacal
Río Grande
Irapa
Santa Isabel
Cabo Tres Puntas
Unare
San Juan de Las Galdonas
Playa de Plata
Río Seco
Yaguaraparo
Playa de Oro
Playa de Cangua
Chaguaramas
Cabo Mala Pascua
Medina
Playa Pui-Puy
Playa Medina
Bohordal
Río de Agua
Guaráunos
RÍO CARIBE
Chacaracual
Tunapuy
Ajíes
Caño Ajíes
Caño Guariquén
Parque Nacional Isla Turuépano
Boca Grande
Puerto Santo
CARÚPANO
El Pilar
Playa Grande
Guiria
Guaca
Guarapiche
Casanay
La Esmeralda
Saucedo
CARIACO
Catuaro
Sta Cruz
Guariquén
Guanoco (Asfalto)
Guanoco
Paradero
Río Grande
San Juan
San Vicente
Los Morros
Caripito
Maturín
Sta Lucía
OJuan Antonio
Macuro
Caripe
San Juan
Isla Antica
Isla Antica
San Juan
Gulf of Paria
VENEZUELA
TRINIDAD

Sucre
Monagas

Cueva del Guácharo
Caripe
El Guácharo
Aragua de Maturín

N
Bradt

25km
25 miles
0
0

210

By bus The Terminal de Pasajeros is midway on Avenida Perimetral. Frequent departures for Caracas (8–9 hours), Cumaná (2 hours), Puerto La Cruz (4 hours), east to Güiria (2½ hours); and south to Ciudad Bolívar (6 hours). Buses to Río Caribe start from Avenida 4-Juncal at Calle 5 and go down to the coast road, stopping at El Kiosko restaurant, eastern Avenida Perimetral. *Por puestos* follow this route, starting from Calle 7. Buses to Chacopata leave from Avenida Perimetral, west, opposite the Mercado Municipal.

By road Carúpano is reached on the Route 9 highway that runs from Caracas to Cumaná.

Tourist information The **Dirección de Turismo** (*1st flr, Edificio Fundabermúdez, Av Carabobo between Calles 6–7;* ✆ *0294 332 0868;* ⊕ *08.00–12.00 & 14.00–17.00 Mon–Fri*) office offers information about sights in Sucre State.

A tourism booth at the airport has maps of local attractions. **Corpomedina** (✆ *0294 331 3021;* e *playamedina@cantv.com*) also has an office there where you can make reservations for Playa Medina and Playa Pui-puy.

Where to stay This is a popular tourist town and prices go up by at least 50% during Carnival and Easter.

⌂ Hotel Euro Caribe (90 rooms) Av Perimetral Rómulo Gallegos; ✆ 0249 331 3911; e hoteleurocaribe@cantv.net. The most expensive & luxurious hotel in town has a bar, restaurant, disco, swimming pool & comfortable rooms with AC, minibar, cable TV, some with sea views. Wi-Fi available in lobby & bingo for those who like a flutter. Pricey for what you get but well-located on the main street down by the seafront. $$$$

⌂ Posada La Colina (17 rooms) Calle Boyacá above the Victoria Hotel; ✆ 0294 332 0527, 0294 332 2915; e ventas@littlesecrets.com.ve; www.littlesecrets.com.ve. Now run by Frenchman Michel Texier, this well-appointed B&B guesthouse in a restored old house has a refreshing sea view, good restaurant. Rooms with AC, TV, hot water, Wi-Fi in lobby. Low-season discounts. $$$

On Playa Copey, a broad beach with good surfing 2km west of Carúpano, there are various guesthouses.

⌂ Posada Nena (7 rooms) On the beach road; ✆ 0294 331 7624; m 0414 807 2304; e info@ posadanena.com; www.posadanena.com. B&B by the beach, recommended for its generous rooms with hot showers, AC, thatch-roofed garden restaurant, & many services including bike rental, internet & tours to Guácharo & Paria arranged by owners Volker & Minerva. $$

⌂ Hotel Bologna (19 rooms) 47 Av Independencia at Calle 4; ✆ 0294 331 1241. Budget option centrally located on Plaza Santa Rosa. Rooms with fan or AC & TV. $

⌂ Hotel Lilma (45 rooms) Av 3 Independencia near Calle 12; ✆ 0294 331 1341, 0294 331 1361; e hotlilma@telcel.net.ve. Basic hotel in a centre with shops, cinema & restaurant. Rooms with AC, hot water, low-season discounts. $

Where to eat Before you leave Carúpano, try the local cured sausages, *chorizos carupaneros*, which are sent all over Venezuela. **La Colina** has a restaurant by the pool, and an air-conditioned *tasca* indoors, both recommended. You can eat inexpensively on the beach at the **Café Boulevard** and the restaurant opposite, **Frente al Mar**, by the port. There is no lack of places in the centre serving pizza, chicken and *arepas* – and the cheaper *empanadas*. Among inexpensive *luncherías*, three on Avenida Juncal towards Plaza Bolívar serve Arab fare, including **Lunchería El Oasis**. One of the specialities of Carúpano are the little handcarts with umbrellas selling cups of shaved ice mixed with coconut

Sucre (which does not mean sugar) has two large sugar-producing areas, the wide valleys around Cumanacoa and Cariaco. In these towns are located big sugar refineries or *centrales azucareros*. Sugarcane has been planted on a large scale here for several hundred years, and the remains of old water-operated mills with their adjacent rum distilleries can still be seen. Sugar production is a difficult business as the world price is low and competition is stiff. Cariaco's *central* is privately owned and its owners have not found it profitable to buy all the local cane, a situation that has caused much distress and many confrontations.

Sugar production is an environmental disaster in all its aspects. A monoculture, cane is chemically fertilised and pesticided: a soil destroyer. Land retired from cane production is so exhausted as to be good for little else. Fertiliser and pesticide residues are washed into local water systems. The Manzanares River passing through Cumanacoa is heavily polluted and all ground water is affected as well. Prior to harvest the fields are burned to clear off the sharp-edged leaves and drive away snakes and insects. In the refineries, bagasse is burned to provide heat for reduction of the juice. Smoke and ash from these processes produce an intense respiratory irritation known locally as *Cumanacoaitis*. It is a vicious cycle, difficult to break because of massive dependence on this one crop.

MAKING SUGAR LOAVES Raw sugar loaves called *papelón* (conical) or *panela* (brick) are made on a small scale at numerous operations dotted around the countryside. The cane is pressed in a *trapiche* or heavy mill powered by a 'one lunger' diesel engine. The cane residue or *bagazo* provides fuel for the reducing process. This is generally a series of three deep iron basins set atop a stone base, mouth at one end to receive dry bagasse, chimney at the other. The raw juice called *guarapo* is poured into the first kettle. When the master stirrer and mixer decides it has reached the proper consistency, he dips it into the next kettle, often with an aluminium hard-hat attached to a long pole. Once concentrated, the syrup goes into a cooling trough hollowed out of a solid log. It is then ladled into fired-clay moulds to cool and harden. The entire operation resembles scurrying slaves attending a dragon breathing fire at one end, expelling smoke at the other, steam rolling off its back, all accompanied by the roar of the mill and motor. The final product has a rich brown colour and, freshly made, the better quality *papelón* will have a flavour not unlike maple sugar.

and fruit flavours, called *raspados* all over Venezuela except here, where they call them *esnobores*.

✕ **El Fogon de la Petaca** Av Perimetral, Bd Bermudez; ☎ 0294 331 2555; ⊕ 12.00–22.00. One of the best restaurants in town, it's in an old house with antique photos of old Carúpano & views of the plaza. Not just great grilled beef & seafood but rarities like shrimp *tequeños*. $$

✕ **Trattoría La Madriguera** Av 3 Independencia; in Hotel Euro Caribe; ☎ 0294 331 9018; ⊕ 12.00–22.00. By Plaza Santa Rosa this place serves the best Italian food in town & some local seafood dishes. $$

✕ **Lilma Restaurant** Av 3 Independencia; ☎ 0294 331 9473; ⊕ 11.30–22.00. Good fish & seafood dishes at this Spanish-style *tasca* in the Hotel Lilma. $

Festivals Carúpano is famous for its **Carnival** celebrations, a week-long *bonche* with street dances day and night, a Carnival queen, parades with floats and costumed figures from folklore such as the donkey-and-rider (the papier mâché donkey is part of the rider's costume), followed on the next weekend by a last gasp called the Octavita. The town fills to bursting during Carnival, with some 400,000 revellers descending on the town in 2010, and anybody without a paid-up hotel reservation months in advance will be lucky to find a mattress on the floor of a hotel lobby or a hammock. Other popular festivals celebrate the feast of **Santa Inés** on 21 January, the **Cruz de Mayo** on 3 May, and the **Día del Carmen**, on 16 July, when the Virgin's statue is brought by sea from Guaca, escorted by fishing boats.

Other practicalities Downtown, you can easily find **Ipostel** (*Av 2-Carabobo at Calle 5;* ⊕ *08.00–12.00 & 14.00–17.00 Mon–Fri*) and **internet** and email services. In the Centro Comercial Rex opposite the Lilma Hotel, formerly a cinema, there is now an internet office in what used to be the balcony, open six days a week. The **internetc@fé** (⊕ *09.30–19.30 Mon–Sat*) is in the Centro Comercial Olas del Caribe, 136 Avenida Independencia.

There's a Banco Caribe (⊕ *08.30–15.30 Mon–Fri*) on Avenida Independencia, and a Banco de Venezuela, also on Avenida Independencia, on the corner with Calle Las Margaritas, but to change dollars ask at the hotels for a better rate.

What to see and do A block from the shore, several historic houses have been renovated around the charming Santa Rosa de Lima plaza.

La Casa del Cable This is a 19th-century building that was the head office of the first telegraph cable linking Europe and South America, laid in 1895 between Marseilles and Carúpano. A century later, the first computer with internet access in the Paria region was donated by a German firm to Corpomedina, the company that acquired and restored the house. It is today a cultural centre and seat of Fundación Thomas Merle (*www.fundacionthomasmerle.org.ve*), which supports environmental education and self-help programmes among five rural communities in the Paria region.

Museo de Historia de Carúpano (⊕ *09.00–12.00 & 14.30–17.30 Mon–Fri; admission free*) This museum houses a sparse collection of historic photographs and early coins of the Republic of Venezuela. Originally the 1880s' home of an English merchant, J M Imery, it passed to a Corsican, Tomás Massiani, and later was occupied variously by consulates, a clinic and a teaching institute.

Iglesia de Santa Rosa Carúpano's cathedral since 2000, it was rebuilt in 1969 after an earthquake damaged the earlier structure raised in 1829.

Ateneo de Carúpano (*Av 2 Carabobo at Calle 7;* \ *0294 332 1124;* ⊕ *08.30–18.30 Mon–Sun*) A cultural centre with gallery, theatre and music school. Dance, ballet, choral and theatre groups for adults and children rehearse here, and there is a full programme of workshops, recitals and meetings. The Ateneo sponsors the penitentiary theatre festival, the Cruz de Mayo festivities, as well as the fiestas honouring Carúpano's patron saint, Santa Rosa de Lima.

RÍO CARIBE The old seaside fishing port of Río Caribe has gained new life from an influx of travellers beguiled by its unhurried ways, chilled-out inhabitants and welcoming *posadas*. It has some restored colonial houses, three very large plazas, two banks, a hospital and the Church of San Miguel, built soon after the settlement's founding in 1713 and rebuilt in 1919. At one time a rich centre of cacao exports from local *haciendas* and the rainy, southern slopes of the Paria Peninsula. In the mid 1800s many immigrants from Corsica settled in the area and began growing coffee and cacao, acquiring large properties. That tradition continues at small plantations that can be visited to see how cocoa is grown, harvested, dried and processed. The harbour shelters a colourful fishing fleet. The fishermen who unload their catch by the Hotel Mar Caribe are able, and usually willing, to take you to beaches along the coast. Local *posadas* can also organise trips to nearby beaches, hot springs and the Museo del Cacao in Chacaracual (see page 216).

Getting there There is no bus terminal; buses to the Terminal de Oriente in Caracas and Cumaná leave from the northeast side of Plaza Bolívar at 19.00 or 20.00 (10 hours, US$23).

The Unión San Miguel, on the north side of Plaza Bolívar, runs taxi *por puestos* to Carúpano (five passengers) all day; you can also contract a *viaje expreso* for yourself alone. Another car line to Carúpano runs from the south side of Plaza Bolívar from 05.00.

There's a daily bus at 07.00 to San Juan de Las Galdonas, leaving from the upper end of town past the petrol station; you wait by the kiosk selling newspapers.

If driving, you can reach Río Caribe via the main coast road from Carúpano.

Tour operators Run by Zoleida and Rufino Gamboa, **Mareaje Tours** (72 *Av Bermúdez;* \ *0294 646 1543;* e *mareajetours@cantv.net*) can provide a car and driver for tours to Playa Medina, San Juan de Las Galdonas in the Paria Peninsula, or the buffalo farm and Aguasal hot springs on the south coast. They can also organise transfers to and from Río Caribe, and make flight and guesthouse reservations.

Where to stay Río Caribe has a good variety of *posadas*. Unless noted otherwise, guesthouses come with fan, cold water and private bath. As a rule they accept only cash.

Posada Caribana (11 rooms) 25 Av Bermúdez; \ 0294 646 1162, 0212 263 3649; e parquenivaldito@gmail.com; www.parquenivaldito.com. Gonzalo Boulton has impeccably restored an 1878 house & converted it into an upmarket *posada* around a traditional patio. B&B rooms with fan or AC, hot water. Offer 3-day/2-night packages including meals, wine with dinner & beach excursions. Ask for low-season discounts. They also offer day tours around Paria by fishing boat to Playa Medina or by car as far away as San Juan de Las Galdonas & Playa Uva, a small, wild beach with a charming *posada* & restaurant, run by the same group. $$

La Posada de Arlet (8 rooms) 22 Calle 24 de Julio; \ 0294 646 1290; m 0416 494 0630. A modern 2-storey house where Arlet Scossa (a Swiss woman who speaks 5 languages) offers tours, mountain bikes, & 8 rooms with private bath, hot water, b/fast optional. $

Posada Shalimar (15 rooms) 54 Av Bermúdez; \ 0294 646 1135; m 0414 898 4797; e info@posada-shalimar.com; www.posada-shalimar.com. Very cosy 2-storey *posada* in colonial house with tropical & oriental touches, funky central swimming pool, bar, restaurant, internet, bikes. Rooms in pastel shades with AC, hot water, Wi-Fi. Boat tours organised to Playa Medina, San Juan de Las Galdonas, cacao museum in Chacaracual. Recommended. $

Villa Antillana (6 rooms) 32 Calle Rivero opposite the police station; \ 0294 646 1413; e villantillana@cantv.net. A charming 1850s' house beautifully restored by architect Rigoberto Aponte & decorated by his wife Hortensia Carrer (she speaks English). B&B rooms with hot water & ceiling fan. Hortensia can arrange excursions to hot springs, Paria beaches & *haciendas*, & also offers yoga, t'ai chi & therapeutic massages. $

Where to eat Ask the *posada* restaurants in advance if you want to eat so they can make arrangements. The Caribana's restaurant is excellent, if pricey. Shalimar is good.

above Parque Nacional Canaima, home to Angel Falls, stretches over 30,000km² and has been declared a World Heritage Site by UNESCO for its beauty and biodiversity (SS) page 279

below For a Lawrence of Arabia experience head for Los Médanos de Coro, an extensive area of shifting sands and 35m dunes whipped by constant trade winds (JR/A) page 397

above Hardy Llanero cowboys — Los Llanos is cattle-raising country, and more cows than people live on these vast open plains. After a day in the saddle they dust off the harp for a jaunty evening of *joropo* music and song (BG/A) page 244

left Corpus Christi Devil Dancing, San Francisco de Yare — held every year, the local men don devilish masks and blood-red costumes to act out a centuries-old Passion play of good against evil (SS) page 62

below Venezuela's Warao Indians, famous for their well-made canoes, still live along the banks of the Orinoco Delta river in traditional stilt houses known as *palafitos* (GL/FLPA) page 231

<table>
<tr><td>above left</td><td>Drying cocoa beans, Chuao — cocoa beans from the isolated coastal plantation of Chuao are highly prized by the top chocolatiers of Europe and the USA for their fine quality and rich taste (SS) page 319</td></tr>
<tr><td>above right</td><td>The Yanomami Indians are one of Venezuela's 24 indigenous tribes and live in remote parts of Amazonas, where they fiercely defend their language, culture and customs (LM/A) page 20</td></tr>
<tr><td>right</td><td>Bottles of catara (or katara), a spicy indian sauce made from leafcutter ants and chilli that is reputed to have strong aphrodisiac qualities (RM) page 60</td></tr>
<tr><td>below</td><td>Believers in the Cult of María Lionza go to the Cerro de María Lionza, also known as Cerro de Sorte, to take part in rituals for healing or for help with practical problems and personal and work relationships (RM) page 345</td></tr>
</table>

above   Fishermen in Puerto la Cruz still use traditional *peñeros* (fishing boats) to bring in the catch and they can be seen at work all along the coast (SS) page 195

below   The Castillo de San Carlos Borromeo is Pampatar's most prized landmark; the attractive fortress had to be rebuilt after a Dutch pirate attack and is now a cool backdrop to Margarita's most happening nightspots (SS) page 172

above left El Yaque is recognised as one of the best windsurfing and kitesurfing spots on the planet and enthusiasts come from all over the world to enjoy its warm waters and constant winds (NP/A) page 185

above right The stunning palm-fringed beach at Choroní is reached via a winding road that snakes up and over the cloud-forested hills of the Parque Nacional Henri Pittier, where an astonishing 550 bird species have been recorded (PE/H/A) page 315

below The only island not formed by corals in the Los Roques Archipelago is the main island of Gran Roque, which makes a great base for exploring this tropical paradise (SS) page 136

above The giant anteater (*Myrmecophaga tridactyla*) is one of the largest and most impressive mammals in the rainforest, growing up to 2.8m long and weighing up to 40kg, surviving on a diet of tiny ants and termites which it hoovers up with its long sticky tongue (TDR/MP/FLPA) page 239

below left The magnificent jaguar (*Panthera onca*), king of the rainforest, is seldom seen in the wild except by very lucky and very patient visitors (KS/MP/FLPA) page 6

below right Several species of turtle, including the hawksbill turtle (*Eretmochelys imbricata*), are found in Venezuela, almost all of them endangered by egg collectors (TM/MP/FLPA) page 8

bottom right Yellow-banded poison arrow frogs (*Dendrobates leucomelas*) can be found in abundance around Salto El Sapo in Canaima and in jungle camps on the Río Caura (TM/MP/FLPA) page 9

above left   Venezuela is home to an incredible 97 hummingbird species, among them the orange-throated sunangel (*Heliangelus mavors*) (NB/FLPA) page 8

above right   The punky-fringed hoatzin, or *chenchena* (*Opisthocomus hoazin*), is an odd bird. It can fly only short distances as its pectoral muscles are too small for sustained flight and the young have claws to help them climb back to the nest if they fall into water (I/MK/FLPA) page 240

right   The spectacled caiman (*Caiman crocodilus*) can be found in the creeks and ponds of the Llanos, where it snaps up unlucky wading birds, fish and turtles (GL/FLPA) page 8

below   Capybaras (*Hydrochoerus hydrochaeris*), known locally as *chigüires*, are the largest rodents in the world and congregate in herds close to the lakes and rivers of Los Llanos (SS) page 6

Watched over by a statue of the Virgin Mary, with its jagged peak jutting above a shrinking white glacier, Pico Bolívar (5,007m) is Venezuela's highest mountain
(FBF/A) page 370

You dream up the trip,
we make it happen!

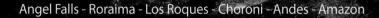

✗ **Doña Eva** Calle Girardot, Plaza Miranda; ⊕ 11.00–23.00. Beer & chicken place serving good *pasticho* (lasagne), fried fish & burgers on a terrace where you can meet the locals over an ice-cold Polar. $
✗ **Manos Benditas** Av Romulo Gallegos, seafront; ⊕ 08.00–21.00. Cosmelina from the defunct

Pariana Café now runs this small place with a West Indian flavour: chicken in curry & ginger, ocra. A nice change from traditional Venezuelan fare. $
✗ **Pizzeria Da More** Av Romulo Gallegos; ⊕ 18.00–23.00. Pizzas, pastas & burgers cooked by an Argentine called Roberto – a change from seafood. $

Festivals Ríocaribeños turn out in full for festivities, and those with jobs in El Tigre and Maturín return home by bus for **Carnival**, quite a sophisticated affair with floats and steel bands. **Easter** processions start from La Ermita above town, a blue-and-white colonial chapel facing the sea; a pilgrimage is made to the Cristo Rey, a large crucifix on a hill. Particularly colourful are traditions linked with the **Virgen del Carmen** whose image is guarded year-round in La Ermita. On 16 July, the Virgin is carried out to sea heading a procession of gaily bedecked fishing boats, for a meeting with San Ramón, patron saint of El Morro de Puerto Santo. Fireworks and rockets sound as the saints greet and separate. The Virgen del Carmen is patron saint of the army, police and forces of law and order in general. Río Caribe's own patron saint is **San Miguel Arcangel**, celebrated by a week-long cultural festival at the end of September with local artists and musicians taking part, including the Río Caribe Children's Symphony Orchestra.

Other practicalities There are a couple of banks on Calle Rivero and there is a Cantv call centre on Calle Rivero for internet and international calls
The **Fundación Proyecto Paria** (*50 Calle River;* ✎ *0294 646 1883; www.fproyectoparia.com*) has good information about local sustainable development projects to stimulate interest in cocoa farms and environmental projects.
There is a pharmacy on the main street and there are some small *abastos* selling bottled water, fruit, crackers and sweets to stock up for excursions.

AROUND RÍO CARIBE
Nearby beaches There are many small, isolated but beautiful beaches close to Río Caribe that are popular with locals at weekends. Most are difficult to reach without a car or boat but transport can be arranged by the *posadas* in Río Chico. **Playa Los Cocos** is a long beach with palms, before Río Caribe. **Playa Caracolito** can be reached on foot or bicycle by taking the road to the Cabañas Costa Caribe where there is a trail; ask in town. Further away is the splendid beach of **Chaguarama de Loero**. If you want to stay at a remote beach, head for the golden sands of **Playa de Uva**, where the owners of Posada Caribana (*www.parquenivaldito.com*) run a rustic camp with a dozen rooms set among citrus groves.

The cocoa trail The green hills around Río Chico are covered in lush shade forests protecting cacao and coffee plants from the blazing sun. Along these roads you get a taste of rural Paria, with huge trees draped in Spanish moss (here called 'English beard' or *barba inglés*) and donkeys carrying large sacks upon their backs.

Hacienda Paria Shakti (✎ *0246 819 6035;* m *0426 906 2401; www.pariashakti.com*) Known for years as Hacienda Bukare, this working cocoa plantation about 14km from Río Caribe, near the village of Chacaracual, has been taken over by Greta Sanchez. The new owner lived for years in California and now offers yoga, chocolate massage and other spa treatments, alongside the traditional guided tours of the cocoa *hacienda* to see how chocolate is made. It's worth making a stop even if you are staying elsewhere as the *hacienda* has been producing some of the world's best cacao beans since 1908. The original name of Bukare came from the trees planted for coffee and cacao shade, whose flame-orange blossoms attract flocks of parakeets. The birds attract twitchers from Europe, who also flock to this *hacienda* ($$). The four simple but ample rooms have private baths, there's a swimming pool and babbling brook and the handsome, reconstructed *hacienda* house has a restaurant where they combine native fruits in delicious sauces and conserves. Airport transfers and tours arranged to beaches and sights around Paria and Río Chico.

Museo de Cacao Pariano (m *0416 680 5214, 0414 780 3560; www.chocolatesparia.com; admission free*) In the village of Chacaracual, 14km from Río Caribe, Chocolates Paria have opened this tasty showcase museum, explaining the steps involved in harvesting, fermenting and drying cocoa beans and the production of chocolate from the resulting cocoa solids and cocoa butter. Best of all, there's a tasting session involved and a chance to try homemade bon bons, hot chocolate and even liquid chocolate.

Posada La Ruta del Cacao (*10 rooms;* m *0414 994 0115, 0416 894 3171,* e *oticampos@yahoo.com;* $$) This guesthouse with stables run by Maria Otilia Campos offers homestays and horseriding through Paria's forested cocoa country, to *haciendas* and beaches.

Playa Medina Described as Venezuela's most perfect beach, Playa Medina is a near perfect crescent, with a lovely palm-lined bay of golden sand framed by two promontories. It's a picture postcard image that has graced almost every tourism campaign in the country and yet very few Venezuelans ever make it here. Part of the reason is its isolation: 3km from the village of Medina and 23km from Río Chico, with the last part of the journey down a dirt track. Come here during the week and most of the time it's all yours to string up a hammock and laze away the day like Robinson Crusoe, although bring some supplies as the ladies who sell fish and *empanadas* at the weekends don't bother if nobody's about. The swimming is good but surprisingly, the sea here is freezing. As dusk falls, stick around for superb shots of a magnificent sunset. The cape on the right was named Cabo de Mala Pascua by Columbus when a storm drove him into the bay in 1498. Camping is not allowed, nor can you stay in hammocks, but under the palms Corpomedina have built eight cabins and a restaurant, which are pricey considering it's dead here after the beach closes. If you don't mind walking it's 2km back into town, or hitch a lift with a local, where cheap rooms are available in the village of Medina.

Where to stay

⌂ **Corpomedina Cabins** (8 cabins) \ 0294 331 5241; e playamedina@cantv.net. They couldn't make it harder to stay at these attractive 2-storey beachside cabins made of rammed-earth walls & red-tiled roofs if they tried. You have to reserve & pay the full amount 14 days before you come if you want to enjoy the privilege of watching the sunset from the restaurant or one of the hammocks swinging from the balconies of the cabins. The price goes up at w/ends & in holiday seasons. They have an office in Carúpano Airport. $$

⌂ **Posada de Angel** (19 rooms) \ 0294 417 8179: m 0416 794 7477. Rooms with hot shower, some with fans, AC, swimming pool, big restaurant serving hearty *criollo* food. $

⌂ **Posada El Milagro** (12 rooms) \ 0294 416 1045, 0294 416 1056. Basic option on the crossroads to Playa Medina, Playa Pui-Puy. Small rooms, some with bunks, cold water, country-style restaurant. $

Playa Pui-Puy About 11km east of the Medina fork the rough road ends at the large, but seldom visited, beach of Pui-Puy, which is an incredible kilometre of soft golden sand where you can camp under palm trees. At the far end there are a couple of general stores used by the local fishermen. The sea is a little rough and the waves can get big enough for bodysurfing and surfing. Come here between February and July and you could wake to the sound of a turtle heaving herself up the beach to lay her eggs in the sand, as the beach is a protected area for marine turtles. There is an economical restaurant open daily, plus 18 reservation-only cabins for two to four, rented for BsF42,000 per person with all meals included. This is another development by Corpomedina (see *Playa Medina* above for contact details). A guard will ask for a small contribution to use a camp bathroom. Otherwise you can stay in the *pueblo* of Pui-Puy where Doña Paula has four rooms at US$10, but it's 4km from the sea. Small local buses make regular journeys from Medina to Pui-Puy.

San Juan de Las Galdonas San Juan, on a promontory above the sea, has not one but four beaches west and east of the village, three *posadas* and an unlikely four-storey hotel. Tradition says that in 1620 Admiral Domingo Galdona sailed from Spain with three ships and a group of would-be settlers. Struck by storms, the little fleet never reached Florida but foundered on the coast of Paria and the settlers arrived in the New World, reported by Columbus in his letters home as a 'Tierra de Gracia' or 'Land of Grace', so rich were the forests and so gentle their inhabitants. Make the journey over the steep sandy hills that wind their way for 22km to get here and San Juan (population 1,500) seems a very special place; somewhere Gabriel Garcia Márquez might set a novel, the end of the road but the start of an adventure as you wind down and explore the beaches of Tucuchire, Sotavento and Barlovento.

Where to stay

🏠 **Hotel Playa Galdonas** (29 rooms) ✆ 0294 332 2915, 0294 331 9494; www.littlesecrets.com.ve. Rising 5 storeys from the beach, this incongruous hotel is the first sight that greets you in San Juan. The rooms filled up quickly when Jean Paul Belmondo's film crew passed through in 2001, but most of the year its jacuzzi & fresh water pool are empty. Built by Egyptian Richard Hassid (who speaks 4 or 5 languages) & opened in 1998, the hotel has 2 restaurants, rooftop bar & fabulous view of sea & coast. It is now being run by Michel Texier & has been spruced up. $$

🏠 **Posada Las Tres Carabelas** (13 rooms) Calle Comercio; ✆ 0294 511 2729; m 0416 894 0914. Opened in 1992, it is the true pioneer of San Juan, with a restaurant terrace that has a 180° view over beaches, sea & the lighthouse of El Morro. The rooms are pleasant, if plain, with bath, AC, cold water, some with sea view. Ask for Lalo, a wiry Spaniard, who leads hikes to Cerro del Humo in the national park, & to the delta wetlands of southern Paria for birdwatching, as well as boat excursions to distant beaches. $

What to see and do

Guided tours of the Paria Peninsula 'Botuto' (✆ 0294 511 1680; m 0416 597 7273), also called Clemente, is a recommended guide who can organise boat tours to the many beaches along the coast as far as Uquire at the tip of the finger pointing to Trinidad. He can also arrange snorkelling, scuba diving and hiking. If you ask in the village everybody knows him.

CARÚPANO TO GÚIRIA
The southern peninsular road rises to verdant hills where cacao trees thrive in deep shade. You can see the beans drying in the sun around El Rincón and El Pilar. On the stretch from El Pilar east to Tunapuy, get off the bus in Guaraúnos (2.5km west of Tunapuy), and go south on the paved road.

Finca Vuelta Larga (✆ 0294 666 9052, 0294 646 7292; e vueltalarga@cantv.net) The home of Klaus Müller and his family is Campamento Vuelta Larga, 800m from the highway. The camp's tall palm-thatched buildings, designed by Klaus with bioclimatic vents in the roof taking the place of fans and large windows of fine netting, are cool and mosquito-free. Most of the handsome furniture was handmade by Klaus and his sons who have a complete carpentry shop. Lodging includes eight rooms, some with private bath. Surrounded by fragrant herb gardens, there are also two attractive cabins with tall ceilings, twin beds, bath and roofed terrace. Credit cards accepted, but if you pay in cash or confirmable cheque there's a 10% discount.

A dormitory and a big open-sided dining room accommodate groups of students and visiting biologists. Together with the International Council for Bird Preservation and Pro Vita, the Vuelta Larga Foundation carries out environmental education work in local schools and communities, encouraging sustainable agriculture outside Paria Park (climate deterioration is evident in Paria, now hotter and drier with less cloud cover). Klaus supports conservation programmes through ecotourism. He and his son Daniel, who both speak German and English, lead hikes in Paria Park and over **Cerro Humo** to Santa Isabel where there is a beach shelter: walking time about six hours. From Santa Isabel hikers can return by sea to Carúpano.

The large *finca* (farm) and nature reserve lie 12km beyond, stocked with water buffalo from Australia. Here in an open meadow three thatched buildings are the centre of another camp with plenty of space for tents. The wetlands are wonderful in late afternoon when parrots return to roost. From an observation hut on stilts in a large lagoon you can see caiman, turtles, capybara, herons, scarlet ibis and many other of the 230 listed bird species.

Klaus runs river trips from one to three days' long on Caño Ajíes, which forms the boundary of **Parque Nacional Turuépano**. These marshes and *caños* or creeks are the habitat of 160 bird species, including 14 kinds of hawk, kite and falcon, eight kinds of woodpecker, the great potoo, little tinamou, toucan and hoatzin. You are sure to see capuchin or howler monkeys, but only if you're very sharp-eyed will you spot the endangered manatee. Other trips visit **Guariquén** where there is a community of Warao Indians. Klaus goes there to trade for the fibre called *tirita*, which he uses to make screens and chair backs. This area has large flocks of scarlet ibis. There are cacao plantations south of Guaraúnos, and then the horizon opens to marshes. The road continues to Ajíes, on Caño Ajíes.

Hacienda Aguasana (\ *0294 417 2944;* m *0414 260 7068; www.ecoparia.com*) On the highway 5km east of Tunapuy, royal palms mark the entrance to a very special set of savanna hot springs. They are neither very hot nor large, and have not been channelled into a swimming pool: quite the reverse. They are of many sizes from baby-bath to small jacuzzi to big fish pond, all in their natural grassy setting. Of the 50 or so individual springs, 17 have been cleared of reeds; one or two are roofed to provide shade for users. And they come in different temperatures and colours: crystalline, blue, green and red tints. Their varying chemical analyses are on record in the office by the guesthouse and small swimming pool. In a sunny yellow-and-green building with screens and porch, the pleasant *posada* has six cool, double-height rooms, half with twin beds and bath, half with four beds, some with hot water. Lodging, two meals and use of thermal pools is about US$50. Or you can use the hot springs and mud for US$10 including fruit juice; lunch to order. The masseuse comes on certain days; call in advance if you have special needs. The friendly manager, Elisa Arraiz, arranges for transfers from Carúpano and day tours to Irapa beaches and Playa Medina.

GÜIRIA (*Telephone code: 0294*) Güiria is at the end of the road, looking out across the Gulf of Paria to Trinidad and Tobago. You immediately get a sense of the links with Trinidad from the town's traditional wooden houses, the odd English words that

Parque Nacional Paria covers 375km² of the northern slopes and crest forming the backbone of Paria Peninsula. A few fishing hamlets dot bays at the foot of the coastal range which rises almost straight from the sea. The highest peak is **Cerro Humo**, at 1,356m. This is an area of superb cloudforest, remarkable because it grows as low as at 800m. Many palms, tree ferns, lianas, epiphytes and huge buttressed trees thrive in the drenching conditions created partly by condensation recycled by the forest itself. These mountains are described as once forming part of a 'forest island' that included Trinidad and as such are the refuge of endemic species. It's a birdwatcher's paradise with rare endemics such as the scissortailed hummingbird, Venezuelan flowerpiercer and whitethroated barbtail. The spiny rat and black nutria are also only found here. However, only half of Cerro Humo is legally protected, and there are only half a dozen *guardaparques* or rangers to patrol the entire park. The forest is affected by farm clearing, especially in the south where villages are expanding.

residents inject into the conversation, the *bati bol* that the kids play (a kind of cricket), and the steel bands that liven up the annual carnival. The peninsula's only large town (population 40,000), Güiria still makes a living from its sizeable fishing port. A huge 5,000-ton freezing plant handles the catch of modern trawlers fishing the gulf. However, the port facilities have been privatised and the future appears to be in gas, with the advent of the huge gas projects in the Gulf of Paria. To have a look at the bay, walk down from the church on Plaza Bolívar; past the international port with its docks and customs hall on the right. On the left (north) of the docks are yards where wooden boats are built and drawn up on the beach for repair. Stalls with a few tables serve inexpensive fried fish and *hervido* (stew). Although the town looks out to sea it lacks any beaches that would attract sunseekers and its main attraction is as a jumping off point for trips to the small village of Macuro at the end of the Paria Peninsula. A road has been bulldozed through to Macuro, but it has stability problems and is impassable after rains so the only way to get there is by sea (see below).

Getting there

By bus From Caracas's Terminal de Oriente, Expresos Güiria, Los Llanos and other lines run through Puerto La Cruz and Cumaná *en route* to Güiria (700km, 12 hours or more). Many buses travel at night, arriving early the next day, and at 07.30 return to Caracas. Buses wait on the streets around the triangular Plaza Sucre at the west edge of town, six blocks from the bay; there is no bus terminal.

Buses from Güiria to Carúpano take 2½ hours and are inexpensive; *por puestos* take two hours but cost 50% more.

By car Güiria is at the end of the Route 9 highway and has a petrol station for refuelling.

By boat A ferry sails every Wednesday at 16.00 for Trinidad, arriving in Chaguaramas near Port of Spain at 19.30. The *Sea Prowler*, a modern 105ft pleasure boat, has a promenade upper deck and a lower deck with lounge. The boat carries 150 passengers; round-trip fare about US$100. There is a port tax and an exit tax. You should be at the dock an hour in advance and have a passport and return ticket or ongoing ticket for the islands. Pier 1 (e *pier1@rave.tt.net*) have a schedule of three-hour pleasure cruises the rest of the week in Trinidad. The Venezuelan agents are **Acosta Asociados** (*Calle Bolívar 31, opposite Unibanca;* \0294 982 1556; e *grupoacosta@cantv.net*).

Boats to Macuro are open fishing *peñeros* which moor near a kiosk called Los Cinco Rumbos at the left end of the bay, bringing shoppers and workers in at 07.00–08.00, and departing when full up, from 10.00 till about 13.00. People start to queue before 08.00. You may find there are few or no boats on Sundays. The 30km trip takes almost two hours and costs BsF25.

🏠 Where to stay

🏠 **El Orly** (12 rooms) Av Paria, on the bay opposite the port administration; ☎ 0294 982 1830. The best hotel in town, which isn't saying much. Rooms on 2 floors with AC, TV, hot water. Ask for a sea view. $

🏠 **Hotel La Posada de Chuchú** (14 rooms) Calle Bideau; ☎ 0294 511 2234. A 2-floor modern building a block from the bus lines, rooms upstairs with AC, TV. $

🏠 **Hotel Plaza** (20 rooms) Calle Vigirima at Bolívar; ☎ 0294 982 0022. Well located on Plaza Bolívar. The modest, Portuguese-run hotel offers good value, starting with the espresso & juice bar on the corner. Inside there's a popular restaurant on the patio. Ask for new rooms. $

Other practicalities There's a Banco República and a Banco Unión on Calle Bolívar. There are a few internet places in town on Calle Bolívar but they aren't very reliable.

MACURO Clinging to the tip of the peninsula, closer to Trinidad than to Güiria, is the rather ramshackle town of Macuro, or Puerto Colón. It is credited with being the only place that Christopher Columbus set foot on the American continent, on his third voyage in August 1498. On the 500th anniversary of this historic event, on 5 August 1998, Macuro was declared the capital of Venezuela for a day and President Caldera led the speeches, promising the town a boat yard, and a 48-passenger launch – sorely needed in a place accessible only by sea. President Hugo Chávez came a year later, bringing a 450kW power plant, a sewage treatment plant and an ambulance boat. Chávez broadcast his Sunday TV show from Macuro by satellite, a novelty for Macureños, who receive most of their TV and radio broadcasts from Trinidad. A new 35km road from Güiria across the peninsula is now surfaced with concrete in places but is still unpassable for most of the year. Once completed it promises to bring an end to Macuro's 500-year isolation and breathe new life into this drowsy tropical outpost. Most of Macuro's 3,000 inhabitants survive from fishing and work at a nearby gypsum mine. There is said to be illegal trading with Trinidad, and the area is a natural sea route for cocaine smuggling from the Gulf of Paria out to the Caribbean Sea through the Bocas del Dragón (Dragon's Mouths). A bronze statue of Columbus is almost the tallest structure in Macuro. It once stood on the steps of El Calvario in Caracas and was brought to Macuro in 1968.

History The names in Columbus's log are still in use: the Indians called the land Paria and their village Amacuro, now shortened to Macuro. Columbus's ships passed from Trinidad, which he named for its triple peaks, through straits roaring with tides of sweet water; he called the straits Serpent's Mouth and Dragon's Mouth. Columbus at first thought Paria was another island and called it 'Isla de Gracia', 'Island of Grace', because he was so impressed by its amiable natives, their farms, houses and pearl necklaces. But after he had sailed for two days into the Gulf of Paria, he wrote that he had either found paradise on earth, or a continent big enough to contain a huge river the likes of which he had never seen. Pressed for time, however, he and his men never entered the Orinoco Delta.

Records give 1783 as the year of Macuro's founding as a Capuchin mission settlement gathering Paria, Warao and Chaima Indians. The mission *pueblo* was called San Carlos Borromeo de Amacuro. It grew to over 200 families in a year, but when smallpox struck the *pueblo* was devastated and only recovered its impetus a century later. Coffee, cacao and indigo exports from Paria led the government to build the port of Cristóbal Colón in 1903. Few structures remain from the port's heyday in the 1920s–30s. There was a governor in residence then and the town was the country's head customs office (dictator Gómez wished to sidestep a debt agreement giving the British in La Guaira rights to collect customs' fees).

The **Museo Macuro** occupies an old house dating from the Gómez era when an escapee from Devil's Island painted a mural showing the harbour full of ships. The museum, created by Eduardo Rothe, houses fossils, pre-Columbian pottery, even a handmade aeroplane. Rothe calls Macuro 'the first and last town in Venezuela'.

Where to stay Lodging options are limited to a few houses that take in guests such as **Posada Beatriz** and **Posada Marlon**; look for a place where you can use the kitchen. A simple room with bath and ceiling fan is about US$10 per person; meals are provided for US$5. Or you can camp with a tent or hammock. There's plenty of firewood on the little beach and you can buy fresh fish from fishermen. Don't buy the meat or eggs of turtles – *tortugas* – as they are all endangered species. Other food supplies should be brought with you since they are very expensive in Macuro.

Other practicalities Macuro consists of no more than a dozen streets, with a pre-school, medical aid post, library and museum, but no telephones. The beach is not idyllic because the water is brown from the Orinoco Delta. Macureños go up to a little rocky river for swimming.

What to see and do Two trails lead from Macuro, involving about six hours' hard walking to the north coast where there are crystal clear waters, rocky shores and two villages: Uquire, and Don Pedro. **Uquire** is a large village with a fantastic beach, good snorkelling and palm trees. **Don Pedro**, two hours by trail from Uquire, is smaller, like a village abandoned by time. You should be able to return to Macuro by boat.

From Macuro, you walk up through shady coffee and cacao plantations to enter the wilder national park. You will probably hear, if not see, the red howler monkeys, among the few noisy wild animals. The tail end of the Serranía de Paria is here, not much over 1,000m altitude. On the way down you see signs of the woods having been disturbed by hunters. The trail divides, east for Don Pedro and west for Uquire. You thread through plantations of cacao, mango, avocado and banana as the path, and a little river, come down to the sea. The park guard lives in a house under palm trees, one of about two dozen dwellings. Prepare yourself for an idyllic half-moon bay, backed by forest, edged by beach. At either end there are cliffs and in the cliffs there are sea caves, home to *guácharos* (the oilbirds that also live in the Guácharo Cave). Uquire has little in the way of supplies, except for a well-patronised bar. The boat ride back to Macuro takes two hours in an open *peñero* or fishing boat.

Guides and tours As there are no marked trails and the paths constantly change course to new plots or *conucos*, you will need a guide. The park guard can locate guides – there is none better than a local farmer (*conuquero*) who is expert with a machete and knows how to deal with snakes. Paria is known for its bushmasters or *cuaimapiñas*, and fer-de-lances (a type of snake) or *mapanares*. Give your guide US$10 for a day on the trails. Water is available in mountain streams. Take plenty of insect repellent.

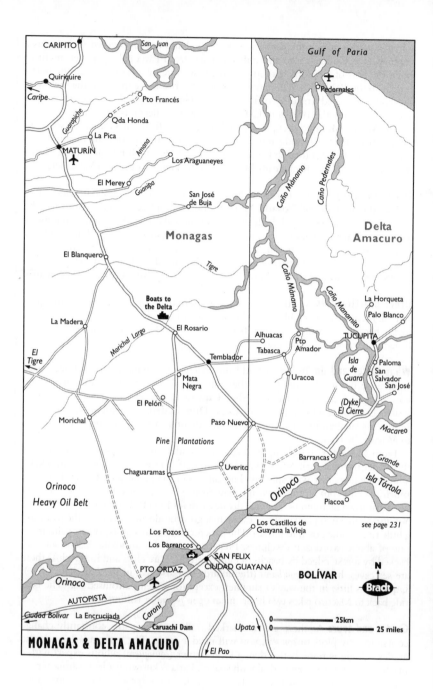

CARIPITO

San Juan

Gulf of Paria

Quiriquire

Pedernales

Caripe

Pto Francés

Qda Honda

Guarapiche

La Pica

Amana

MATURÍN

Los Araguaneyes

El Merey

Guanipa

San José
de Buja

Caño Mánamo

Caño Pedernales

Delta
Amacuro

Monagas

El Blanquero

Tigre

Caño Mánamo

La Horqueta

Boats to
the Delta

Palo Blanco

La Madera

El Rosario

Morichal Largo

Alhuacas

Pto
Amador

TUCUPITA

Caño Manamito

*El
Tigre*

Tabasca

Temblador

Isla
de
Guara

Paloma
San
Salvador

Mata
Negra

Uracoa

San José

El Pelón

(Dyke)
El Cierre

Morichal

Paso Nuevo

Macareo

Pine   Plantations

Grande

Chaguaramas

Uverito

Barrancas

Isla Tórtola

Orinoco

*Orinoco
Heavy Oil Belt*

Piacoa

see page 231

Los Pozos

Los Castillos de
Guayana la Vieja

Los Barrancos

SAN FELIX
CIUDAD GUAYANA

BOLÍVAR

N

PTO ORDAZ

Bradt

Orinoco

AUTOPISTA

Ciudad Bolívar La Encrucijada

Caroní

Upata

0   25km

0   25 miles

Caruachi Dam

El Pao

MONAGAS & DELTA AMACURO

9

Monagas and the Orinoco Delta

Monagas is an oil state and Maturín, the capital, is the boomtown of Venezuela's great eastern oilfields where more than 10,000 reservoirs have already pumped four billion barrels of crude oil. The biggest attraction in Monagas is the Guácharo Cave, Venezuela's longest and largest, famed for its nocturnal oilbirds and the fresh climate of the forested hills around Caripe, many of which are planted with coffee. Monagas also has the only road to Tucupita, the capital of the Orinoco Delta, or Delta Amacuro, as the state is known. The delta is home to the Warao, an indigenous group who live in houses on stilts, like the ones that led the first Spanish navigators to dub the country 'Little Venice' or 'Venezuela'. Trips to jungle camps in the delta offer an unbeatable way to learn about the life of the Warao (called 'the boat people' for their skill on the water), and a chance to sleep in a hammock, fish for piranhas and maybe catch a glimpse of pink river dolphins or red howler monkeys.

CARIPE *Telephone code: 0292*

Located at an altitude of 900m, Caripe is a small mountain retreat with a cool climate perfect for coffee, citrus and vegetable production. For those coming from the coast, the fresh mountain breezes are a welcome relief. Caripe was founded in 1734 as a mission for Chaima Indians. The pace here is slow and the people are relaxed and friendly. Jeep roads climb through coffee plantations to woods filled with birdsong. Local flora includes giant tree ferns, festoons of orchids and philodendrons. Caripe is the main starting point for mountain hikes in the region and visits to the spectacular Guácharo Cave, located about 12km away, north of the village of El Guácharo. Trails criss-cross the area and local guides can lead you to the 80m waterfall of Salto Chorreron or to Cerro Negro, which at 2,400m is the highest peak around.

GETTING THERE
By bus Buses from Cumaná leave at 07.15 and 12.30 and pass in front of the Guácharo Cave (117km) on the way to Caripe (127km, 3 hours). They drop passengers at the bus depot behind the market. Buses leave for Cumaná at 06.00 and 12.00 (check times). Buses and *por puestos* leave throughout the day for Maturín (105km, 3 hours, US$5–8).

By car Caripe is just off the main road from Cumaná to Maturín and is clearly signposted on the left after passing the town of San Antonio.

WHERE TO STAY
In Caripe
Hotel Samán (24 rooms) 29 Av Enrique Chaumer; 0292 545 1183; e hotelsaman@ cantv.net; www.hotelsaman.com. One of the first hotels in Caripe & still one of the best, it provides clean, pleasant rooms with TV, fan, hot water, some with mountain views, around a central courtyard

The Cueva del Guácharo is named for, and is home to, approximately 18,000 guácharos or 'oilbirds' (*Steatornis caripensis*). The Spanish name refers to their cries or laments; the English name refers to the young birds' tremendous fat content for which they were once hunted. The adult bird weighs about one third that of the young, the difference being solid fat. The young fatten on the oil-rich nuts of seje palm, and at adulthood purge the oil by eating the fruit of the cobalonga tree.

This unique bird, which has a wingspan of a metre, has several features found in no other bird. It is the only bird known to fly in complete darkness, finding its way like a bat by the echo of sounds made by clacking its beak. You will hear this sound in the cave. It is the only nocturnal bird that is not carnivorous and it eats only on the fly, grabbing food in its beak. There has been much speculation, often conflicting, about the habits of the *guácharo*. The birds were once thought to fly as far as Brazil in their nightly search for the 32 kinds of fruit that make up their diet. It is now thought that they fly no more than 50km. *Guácharos* live in a number of other caves, 30 to 87 by various counts. They share their home with other cave-adapted creatures. There are fearless smooth-furred brown rats. Bats, unable to manage a peaceful coexistence, live in their own part of the cave. This is the Hall of Silence, so named for the abrupt absence of bird sounds. The entrance is a bottleneck through which the birds cannot pass.

The cave has been known to Europeans since 1660. In 1799 Alexander von Humboldt, the famous German explorer, visited the cave and described and named the oilbirds. His Indian guides would only permit him to go as far as the entrance to the Hall of Silence – to them the entrance to the world of the dead. In 1953 electric lights were installed. The birds abandoned the cave in great numbers and only returned when the lights were removed.

decorated with local handicrafts. Good information on local sights, hikes, can contact guides. $$
🏠 **Pueblo Pequeño Vacation Villas** (18 rooms, 23 cabins) Cocollar Amanita district; ☎ 0292 545 1887, 0292 545 1256. This is a large, attractive complex with pool, playgrounds & *tasca* restaurant. Rooms with TV & hot water. Dormitory used by kids for summer camps. Often booked up so reserve ahead. $–$$

🏠 **Posada Madre Emilia** (8 rooms) Av Libertador with Av Enrique Chaumer; ☎ 0292 545 4619. Located just behind the large monument of the guácharo bird at the entrance to town. Rooms with hot water, TV, bathroom & 2 cabins with kitchen, 3 bedrooms for 8 people. $

Around Caripe

🏠 **Cabañas Turisticas Luciernaga** (10 cabins) ☎ 0292 414 8970; m 0416 499 5824. Mariflor & Luis Leopardi run a fruit & coffee farm 3km beyond La Cuchilla, where they rent out rooms in pleasant cabins. The country restaurant is open to all at b/fast & the farm is open to visitors interested in coffee production during the Nov–Jan harvest period. Horseriding, hiking & birding trails. $$
🏠 **Finca La Coradeña** (10 rooms) ☎ 0292 414 9409; m 0416 299 0519. A 60ha working farm about 3km southwest of the town of El Guácharo, offers lodging, meals, horseriding & a chance to see how the farm works. Owners Lesbia & Corado Machuca make a popular liqueur from their roses,

oranges, passion fruit & coffee. Cabins with TV, hot water, bath, swimming pool. Meals on request in advance. Trips arranged to nearby waterfalls, forests. $$
🏠 **Hacienda Campo Claro** (12 rooms, 8 cabins) ☎ 0292 555 1013, 0292 414 6154; m 0414 770 8043; e campoclaro@cantv.net; www.haciendacampoclaro.com. This 70ha farm in the hills of Teresén–Santa Inés, has 12 rooms & 8 stone cabins for 5 guests. Owners Francisco & Nery Betancourt show guests how coffee is processed from picking beans to roasting & grinding during Nov–Jan harvesting period. There are horses for hire, birding & hiking trails to nearby *haciendas*. B/fast for guests &

non-guests: coffee, orange juice, bread & jam, butter, cheese, milk & eggs, all from the farm. They have built a chapel & cater for religious retreats. $$
🏠 **Cabañas Bellermann** (6 bungalows) east of San Agustín, 7km from the caves; 📞 0292 545 1326; 📱 0414 767 2968; 📧 bellerlicor@yahoo.com. Set among the shade trees of a working coffee

hacienda (altitude 1,200m). Bungalows for up to 6 people with hot water, dbl beds, TV. The Bellerman shop is famous for homemade cakes, jams, hot chocolate & liqueurs – especially coffee liqueur. They recommend a family restaurant, Las Delicias del Valle, further on. W/day prices nearly half w/end & holiday prices. $–$$

OTHER PRACTICALITIES There is a Bancesco bank on Avenida Guzmán Blanco and there's an internet place on Avenida Enrique Chaumer in the centre where you can make international calls.

WHAT TO SEE AND DO
Parque Nacional El Guácharo (⏱ *08.00–16.00; admission BsF15*) With its beautiful forest setting, large, gaping entrance, noisy colony of clacking and clicking oilbirds, shimmering stalagmite and stalactite formations and high-ceilinged galleries, the **Cueva del Guácharo** is the most spectacular and most easily visited cave in the country. Explored in 1799 by German scientist and naturalist Alexander von Humboldt, who first described the oilbird (*Steatornis caripensis*) to science, it was named Venezuela's first Natural Monument in 1949 and 627km² of the surrounding forest were declared a national park in 1975.

The entrance to the cave and car park are reached from the highway, and there is a small museum, a restaurant, a statue of Humboldt and the park office from where guided tours begin. All bags must be left here but take a jacket, because it gets cold, and wear shoes, because the first part of the tour passes through guano and soft mud. Cameras can be taken into the cave but no flash photography is permitted in the area where the birds roost. Tours of up to ten people take just over an hour to follow the stream in the cave to the Humboldt Pool, the furthest point allowed and some 1.5km from the entrance – a fraction of the 10.2km of tunnels that have been explored. The first chamber, named after Humboldt, is 40m tall and eyes adjust slowly to the darkness. The first thing you notice is the noise of the oilbirds roosting on high dim ledges. The constant clicking and squawking of the birds as they swoop

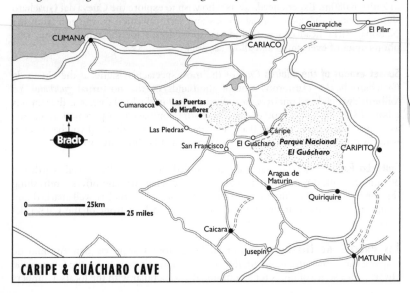

CARIPE & GUÁCHARO CAVE

overhead is a strange experience in the darkness, and it's easy to understand why the local Chaima Indians believed this place was charged with mythical significance. It seems incredible but there are generally some 10,000 oilbirds in the cave and the numbers increase in the nesting season from April to June. The birds are not the only inhabitants of the cave: stunted plants starved of light grow in the thick layer of guano and palm seeds on the cave floor. There are also tiny pink fish in the stream, an endemic spiny rat (*Proechimys guyanensis*), centipedes, spiders, beetles and bats, which live in the deeper recesses. The next chamber, called the Hall of Silence because there are no birds, is a tunnel of 759m where the guide will point out formations of stalactites (coming down from the ceiling) and stalagmites (coming up from the floor), such as the Tortuga (Turtle) and the Cabeza de Elefante (Elephant's Head). After this comes the Precious Hall, named for wonderful formations such as the oddly named 'Room of the Breasts' (Salon de Los Pechos). The Humboldt Pool marks the end of the tour. To penetrate further you have to pass a channel of water 2m deep, a semi-siphon and then use ropes up an 80m slope. But beyond lie the most magnificent galleries, reported to have breathtaking displays rarely seen elsewhere. The Guácharo Cave is considered to have a nearly complete range of geological formations, with an incredible variety of structures and crystals of all sizes. The spectacular Codazzi Hall was discovered as recently as 1967 by the Venezuelan Speleological Society. Cave guides are poorly paid, so if you get a good one, leave a tip. They can also arrange trips to nearby waterfalls such as Salto Chorreron or the Mata de Mango caves.

Speleological Museum This displays findings from over 40 years of exploration, including spectacular crystals, fossils, Indian bones and archaeological pieces from the Cueva del Guácharo, which was considered the entrance to the underworld by the Chaima Indians. The upper floor is dedicated to Alexander von Humboldt, his maps, drawings and works. There is also information about the Venezuelan Society of Natural Sciences, founded in 1952, and the Venezuelan Speleological Society, which continues field investigations today. The longest caves in Venezuela are: Cueva El Samán in Zulia, 18,000m (really the tunnel of an underground river); Cueva del Guácharo in Monagas, 10,200m; and the Cueva-Sumidero La Retirada in Zulia, 6,080m. Experienced cavers who wish to explore the Cueva del Guácharo should contact the speleological groups and secure written permission from the National Parks head office. Include passport details for the whole group, take photocopies of everything and allow six weeks.

Sunset exodus of the oilbirds One of the most spectacular sights at the Cueva de Guácharo is the clamorous exit of thousands of the nocturnal *guácharos*, or 'oilbirds', which head out *en masse* to feed on fruit in the local forests as the sun sets (about 18.30). If you decide to stay, make sure you have transport back to Caripe as public buses stop operating at about 16.00. Another possibility, if you have a tent, is to camp overnight for a small fee (US$5). Toilet facilities are available.

Salto La Paila This 30m waterfall surrounded by 70m walls is well worth the 30-minute walk through forest to get here. A pool at the base offers a refreshing dip for those brave enough to enter the icy water. The trail is well marked and signposted and starts at the entrance to the car park in front of the Cueva del Guácharo.

Las Puertas de Miraflores About an hour from Caripe via San Antonio de Capayacuar to the village of Miraflores is this dramatic canyon on the Guarapiche River, with a series of pools for swimming that is popular with the locals. Climbers

Alexander von Humboldt was not yet 30 in 1799 when he reached Cumaná in eastern Venezuela, almost by accident. His long-planned scientific journey to the Nile had been cancelled by Napoleon, as was an invitation to circumnavigate the world. But the baron from Berlin was unstoppable. With a young French botanist, Aime Bonpland, he hoped to catch a boat to Smyrna, and they set out for Spain on foot. Handsome and single, Humboldt charmed his way to King Carlos IV. More than his talents in Spanish, biology, astronomy and meteorology, it was Humboldt's knowledge of geology and mining that won passports from the Spanish king who envisioned lucrative findings. Humboldt was ecstatic. Until then, Spanish America had been off-bounds to foreigners, a scientific *terra incognita*.

They sailed on a ship bound for Cuba. When typhoid fever struck, the captain changed course for Venezuela. 'Had not the fever broken out on board the *Pizarro*, we should never have reached the Orinoco, the Cassiquiare,' he wrote. Before reaching the Orinoco Humboldt and Bonpland stopped in Caracas and Valencia, finally leaving for the Llanos in March 1800.

Humboldt's curiosity was insatiable. In the Llanos he was determined to measure the discharge of electric eels (*Electrophorus electricus* is not, in fact, an eel but is related to the carp). When he arrived at Calabozo in 1800 he had 30 horses and mules driven into a pool with electric eels; some horses drowned in the frenzy when they were 'electrocuted'. But when the *tembladores* exhausted their discharge, most animals recovered and Humboldt got his wish to make the first scientific examination.

'I do not remember ever having received from the discharge of a large Leyden jar a more dreadful shock than the one I experienced when I very stupidly placed both my feet on an electric eel that had just been taken out of the water. I was affected for the rest of the day with a violent pain in the knees and almost every joint.' However, the electricity remained a mystery: it didn't register on Humboldt's electrometer, it gave off no spark of light at night, nor was there a magnetic effect. And despite dissections, Humboldt could not answer the question: why don't electric fishes electrocute themselves?

Humboldt and Bonpland's Venezuelan route took them on the Orinoco to the great cataracts of the Atures and Maipures and against the current up to San Fernando de Atabapo. Ascending the Atabapo, they portaged to the Río Negro headwaters – finally reaching the Casiquiare Canal on 10 May. (For more, see *Chapter 12, Amazonas*, page 304.)

They later ascended Colombia's Magdalena River and Ecuador's volcanoes, then descended the deserts of Peru before heading to Mexico and the United States. When Humboldt returned to Europe in 1804 he had such a cargo of notes, dried plants, insects and minerals, that it took him decades and most of his family inheritance to classify 6,000 new species and write three volumes of *Travels to Equinoctial Regions of America*, and *Cosmos*, his 2,000-page masterpiece examining the physical world.

The German king made a medal in commemoration of *Cosmos* showing Humboldt, a sphinx and an electric eel.

come here to scale the canyon's near vertical walls, which offer climbing from beginner level to advanced. Iván Calderon (\ *0212 985 3132;* m *0414 254 6535*) takes climbers up the wall, as does Luis Roman Salaya (\ *0291 652 2955;* m *0416 498 7086*) of the Club de Escalada de Monagas. The **Posada Turistica Lago de Azul** (\ *0292 414 1948;* m *0416 488 0682*) has five simple rooms to rent.

Maturín, population 450,000, is an oil city, and just 25km from El Furrial, centre of the largest oil discovery in Venezuela in 30 years. As you drive west at night, you pass scores of drilling towers and wells, some 5,000ft to 6,000ft deep, brightly illuminated and topped by flares of burning gas.

The state capital, long the area's trading and oil centre, offers travellers broad, tree-lined streets and pleasant parks, but little reason to linger. The Guarapiche River, on which it was founded in the 18th century, was navigable to the Gulf of Paria and in 1797 a British force from Trinidad briefly occupied the city. For 200 years Maturín continued to trade with Trinidad, only 100km away by boat, until oil companies built the road to El Tigre. Now a large oil terminal is planned for the old river *pueblo* of Puerto Francés, named after French buccaneers.

The oil boom has brought drilling companies and service contractors and has transformed the city. Huge, shiny shopping malls have sprung up, including CC Petroriente and Monagas Plaza in the north, CC Bolívar in the centre, and La Cascada in the south. Inside you find multiplex cinemas, bowling lanes and restaurants.

GETTING THERE

By air The José Tadeo Monagas International Airport is 2km east of town, reached via Avenida Bolívar. There are a dozen weekday flights from Caracas and four on weekends by Conviasa (*www.conviasa.aero*), Aeropostal (*www.aeropostal.com*) and Avior (*www.avioairlines.com*); five from Margarita by Avior and Rutaca (*www.rutaca.com.ve*); and a service three times weekly from Barcelona and Puerto Ordaz. Rutaca flies to Trinidad on Monday, Wednesday and Friday (about US$115). Rutaca and Avior run charter flights, as does the local Yuri Air (✆ *0291 642 3387;* m *0416 792 5512*).

Car-hire agencies at the airport include Aco, Avis, Hertz and Quality Car Rental.

By bus The busy Terminal de Pasajeros serves as transport hub not only for Monagas but also the Delta Amacuro. It is located about 2km southwest of town where avenidas Orinoco and Libertador intersect. Caracas is served by *expreso* and *ejecutivo* coaches offering night departures. Buses and *por puestos* go to Tucupita (4 hours, US$10), Ciudad Guayana (3½ hours, US$8), Caripe (3 hours, US$7) and Carúpano (3½ hours US$8). The **Aeroexpresos Ejecutivos** (*www.aeroexpresos.com.ve*) has its own terminal on Avenida Libertador near Calle Principal Los Guaros; departures at 08.30, 22.30, 22.45, 23.00 for Caracas; 21.00 for Maracay and Valencia; and at 07.00 and 20.00 for Puerto La Cruz.

By car Maturín is reached by the main highway to Cumaná, where the coastal Route 9 continues to Puerto La Cruz and on to Caracas, and also on Route 10 from Ciudad Guayana.

TOURIST INFORMATION The main tourist office, **Corporacion Monaguense de Turismo (Cormotur)** (*Av Alirio Ugarte Pelayo;* ✆ *0291 643 0798, 0291 643 5949;* e *cormotur@cantv.net*), is located in Hacienda Sarrapial, a colonial house just outside town.

WHERE TO STAY Due to the area's economic boom, accommodation in this business city can be expensive during the week, but good rates are available at holidays and weekends. There are plenty of lodging options.

Best Western CCP (Casa Grande) (500 rooms) Av Ugarte Pelayo in the north; ✆ **0291 300 3350.**

Located in the Petroriente shopping mall, about 18mins' drive from the airport, this modern hotel has rooms with AC, hot water, cable, Wi-Fi, restaurant & gym. Safe option favoured by business travellers with sports bars & fast-food outlets close by. $$$$

⌂ **Morichal Largo** (210 rooms) Av Bella Vista; ℡ 0291 651 4222, 0291 651 4722, 0291 651 4322; www.venetur.gob.ve. A 5-star hotel about 3km out of Maturín now being run by the government, it has 2 magnificent pools & great views, restaurant, bar & sushi bar, fitness club, tennis courts, good discounts. $$$$

⌂ **Stauffer Hotel** (240 rooms) Av Alirio Ugarte Pelayo; ℡ 0291 643 1111, 0291 643 0622; e info@staufferhotel.com.ve; www.staufferhotel.com.ve. An attractive 5-star hotel popular with executives in the north of Maturín, it has pool with jacuzzi, restaurants & bar. $$$$

⌂ **La Trinidad** (10 rooms) 37 Carrera 8A; ℡ 0291 642 9356. A budget option half a block from Plaza Bolívar; the owners have another hotel close by. Dbl rooms with hot water & fan. Passable. $

OTHER PRACTICALITIES You can change money at any of the large hotels but if you need a bank there is a Banco Provincial on Calle Juncal with Carrera Monagas and a Banco Mercantil on Carrera Monagas near the Mercado Central.

You can surf the internet and make international calls at the CANTV call centre on Avenida Luis Del Valle Garcia, in the centre.

For everything under one roof, including banks, pharmacies, food court and internet access, head to Centro Comercial La Cascada. It's a few kilometres away from the centre, where Avenida Libertador meets Carretera Sur.

RÍO MORICHAL LAGO

Across the bridge over the Río Morichal Lago, 82km south of Maturín, there is a boat service and you can contract a boatman among the Warao people selling crafts on the east side. On the west, where cars park, tour operators moor their boats. The river flowing to the delta has an abundance of wildlife including troops of howler and capuchin monkeys, and the remarkable hoatzin. This bird, called *chenchena* or *guacharaca de agua*, is announced by its raucous call and musty odour. They are clumsy fliers and are easily heard as they flounder about in the trees. Several features single them out among birds: their diet (leaves), digestive process (two stomachs, like a cow) and the presence of a hook at the 'elbow' of the wings in fledglings which allows them to escape predators by dropping into the water then climbing back to their nests using these hooks and their strong feet. You may see caiman or *babas*, the maligned anaconda and piranhas, or *caribes rojos* as they are known locally. No swimming in the river!

On its way to join the Mánamo the river runs through gallery forests and *morichales*, stands of mauritia palms. This palm yields food and fibre for rope, baskets and hammocks for the Warao natives who live there. You will see the Warao in their stilt houses known as *palafitos* along the bank, and in their canoes. For those who do not have the time, endurance or money to go on a fully fledged river expedition, this is a good chance to see a bit of the delta.

Ideally, to take a day tour or longer, you should have a group of four minimum. However, you may be able to join a group so ask around.

WHERE TO STAY

⌂ **Campamento Rancho San Andrés** (26 rooms) 35mins by car from Maturín on the San José de Buja route; ℡ 0291 315 2523; m 0414 767 6114, 0414 394 2959; e ranch-san-andres@cantv.net; www.lodge-adventure.com. One of the most interesting options on the 200km road to Bolívar State & half an hour from the main delta port, this is more than a simple guesthouse. It is on a large dairy farm where owners Frédéric Janssen & Claude Baillie (who speak French & English) offer comfortable rooms with fans, private bath, hot water, plus less expensive rooms with shared bath (camping style) & hammock spaces, swimming pool & restaurant. Ranch activities include horse or bike riding on 12km of ranch roads. Delta trips may be organised to visit Warao villages, buy crafts, fish for piranhas. Transfers by arrangement; minimum party of 4. $$

THE ORINOCO DELTA

The Orinoco Delta is the newest of Venezuela's wilderness travel destinations, a vast maze of small channels and islands that branch out across an area larger than Belgium to form one of the largest deltas in the world. Previously, travellers would make their way to the capital of Tucupita and organise a boat trip to a Warao village on the Caño Mánamo, but increasingly tour operators in Mérida, Ciudad Bolívar and Santa Elena are offering all-inclusive trips to delta camps like Abujene, Mis Palafitos and Orinoco Delta Lodge in the north and Oridelta in the south (see *Delta camps*, page 235) for tourists who want to pack a lot into a short visit and prefer something organised. Organising a tour before you arrive makes good sense as many local operations won't take groups of less than four, or if they do will charge more.

Venezuela's 21st state (40,200km²) is called the Delta Amacuro after a river flowing from the eastern border near Guyana to the Boca Grande. Outside the capital of Tucupita (population 73,000), delta inhabitants (70,000) are widely scattered in over 280 settlements, most lacking basic services. This is the land of the Warao people, an indigenous group whose name means 'people of the canoe' for their skill in producing dugout canoes and their ability to travel large distances in them, even out at sea. Official figures put the Warao population at 36,000 but many have left their traditional stilt houses and dugout canoes to earn money in Ciudad Bolívar or Caracas by selling necklaces and handicrafts.

In the hot, humid estuary, 36 major rivers and some 300 lesser *caños*, most unnamed, fan over 25,000km². Of this area, 2,650km² of Delta Amacuro bordering the Atlantic were declared the Parque Nacional Mariusa in 1991. The park forms the core of a biosphere reserve. Thickly forested, the delta has a rich wildlife including some of Venezuela's largest mammals – tapir, jaguar, howler and capuchin monkeys, manatee, giant otter and river dolphin – as well as piranhas, anacondas and colourful birds led by the striking blue and yellow macaw. The world's largest concentration of scarlet ibis lives here, a truly amazing sight when they flock in to roost at sunset.

At the delta's apex near Barrancas, the Orinoco is 38km from shore to shore. From here the main channel and shipping route flows to the Atlantic through the southeastern river, the Río Grande. Incoming ships pick up a government river pilot at Punta Barima on the Atlantic who guides the ship to a port, which could be as far as Puerto Ordaz, 270km upriver. In the language of the Warao one name for this wide river is *wiri noko*, 'to row, place', perhaps the origin of the name Orinoco.

When Christopher Columbus arrived in the waters between the Orinoco Delta and Trinidad on his third voyage to the Americas in 1498, he was amazed by the 'mountain range' of freshwater waves flowing from the delta. This outpouring has been calculated at over 1,200,000 million cubic metres of fresh water a year, dumping as much as 50,000 million tons of sediments. Strong Atlantic currents prevent dispersal of these sediments, in effect adding new islands to the delta. Less than 15km beyond the Delta Amacuro lies the Caribbean island of Trinidad which Columbus named on his 1498 visit.

Temperatures here average a sticky 27°C, cooling a little at night. Average rainfall is a high 1,600mm, with the rainy season starting in April/May, pausing in July, then trailing into October and sometimes December.

☞ **WARNING:** This is malaria country; take anti-malaria pills before arriving if you are travelling in the wet season (see *Malaria* on page 36). You will also need a hat, long sleeves and long trousers for added mosquito protection and plenty of

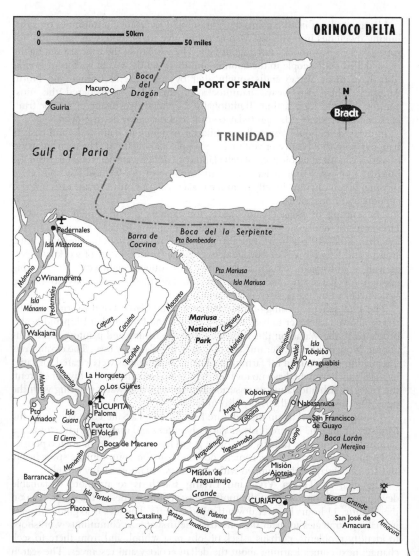

repellent, including a spray form for cuffs and collars. Surprisingly, there are few flying insects in the dry season.

THE WARAO The people who have lived in the Orinoco Delta for untold centuries are the Warao or 'Guaraúnos' in Spanish. Excellent fishermen, the Warao have kept intact their way of life as the 'canoe people', *wa arao* (outsiders are 'land people', *jota arao*), safe in the outer marshes. Using fire and axes, they make dugout canoes from logs, little ones for the kids, big ones for several families. Numbering about 36,000, the Warao are Venezuela's largest native group after the Wayúu (Guajiros) of Zulia State. Many do not speak Spanish. Neither Carib nor Arawak, the origin of their ancient language is still debated. Today under pressure from farmers moving in, many Warao families are moving out to Monagas and Bolívar states in search of a livelihood.

Using trunks of *manaca* palm, the Warao build riverside communities on stilts, linking dwellings into villages. *Moriche* palms give them food, wine and fibre for ropes, baskets, hammocks and dugout sails. The women of the tribe are among the most skilled craftspeople in the country and their tightly woven baskets of *moriche* fibre have made Warao crafts sought after by collectors in Europe and North America. They also weave hammocks of this fibre, considered the most comfortable and long lasting. Traditionally they used dyes made of *moriche* fruit, bark and other seeds although today commercial dyes may be employed.

In every delta house you will see children swinging in hammocks and baskets hanging from roof beams; or you may see people making them. The men are wood carvers, fashioning whole zoos of delta fauna out of light *sangrito* wood cut from the buttress roots of a large delta tree. Crafts are one of the Waraos' few sources of income. If you can buy directly from the maker, you not only provide cash but also support traditional skills.

The cutting of *manaca* palm hearts for canners provides men with work. However, the concession-holders not only exploit the Indians' situation, paying less than US$0.10 per heart, but also give them no instruction, allowing rotting stumps and felled leaves to damage new growths (future source of work and food as well as housing material). Each palm takes roughly eight years to grow big enough for harvesting and dies when cut. For these reasons, **avoid** buying Venezuelan palm hearts, tasty as they are.

The 1969 scheme closing off the Mánamo, second largest of the Orinoco Delta rivers, allowed saltwater to back up from the sea and brought hardship and health problems to the Warao on this river who find the fishing and planting conditions poorer. Now drinking water must be delivered to villages by boat. The closure was intended to reclaim land for farming and many delta islands were cleared for cattle by *criollo* ranchers, who have no love for the Warao. Lacking any freshwater current, the river, its fish and fauna were seriously affected by seawater entering with the tides. On the shores, soil fertility also suffered.

Among those working in the delta are Fe y Alegría, La Salle Foundation and the Ministry of Health. Tuberculosis, malaria, dysentery and undernourishment take a serious toll among the Indians who often get to hospital too late, or are too poor to make the long journey. Government doctors visit the communities sporadically and are not always well equipped with medicines. Infant mortality is high.

The goal of **Tierra Viva** and **Living Earth** is to promote sustainable development among some of the more remote communities in the outer delta on the Atlantic, 11 hours by river down the Río Grande. The idea is to guide villagers in making strategies to meet their needs. The first step is community workshops to identify problems, perhaps a lack of jobs or a school, and from there to seek change; next comes learning about the deltan ecology and resources. The search for solutions requires sharpening skills (dealing with bureaucracy, too) and working as a team for future results, not something that comes easily to fishermen. The Tierra Viva office (\ *0287 721 5669;* e *tierravivadel@cantv.net*) is in Tucupita on Calle La Paz between Mánamo and Petión.

MISSIONS AND DELTA TOWNS Capuchin missionary work among the Warao began in earnest when the Araguaimujo mission and boarding school were founded in 1925. The closest mission to Tucupita and Barrancas, Araguaimujo has a large craftwork centre. Other missions followed in Amacuro, Tucupita, Guayo, Nabasanuka and Ajotejana. You can ask the Capuchin priests in Tucupita for permission to visit these missions (go to the Casa Parroquial). Travellers are given shelter but are reminded that donations of school materials, clothing and medicines are welcome and food is scarce.

Southern towns on the Río Grande are the best supplied with services. Santa Catalina, on the right bank of a channel, is a *criollo* town on an open hill, boasting paved streets and a farm school. In the summer ranchers take their cattle across to graze on Isla Tortola. Guasina Island was where political prisoners were incarcerated by dictator Marcos Pérez Jiménez, and there is a monument in the village plaza honouring these prisoners. Curiapo, further down the Río Grande, is one of the most picturesque of delta towns; here the houses are all on stilts and the streets are bridges of planks. Curiapo has electricity, a school, library and even a jail (the town is more *criollo* than Indian).

On both banks of the Caño Asibujanoco, a town of some 2,000 people has grown up on stilts around the San Francisco de Guayo mission, not far from the Atlantic; it has a grade school and high school, doctor, police station and a museum of Warao crafts in the mission.

Caño Mánamo is the highway to the north, meeting the Gulf of Paria at Pedernales. This was the route taken in 1531 by Diego de Ordaz (the same conquistador who accompanied Hernán Cortez in Mexico) on the first exploration of the Orinoco River. Ordaz was followed in 1595 by Sir Walter Raleigh who went as far as the mouth of the Caroní (Ciudad Guayana).

Pedernales has the only airstrip in Delta Amacuro besides Tucupita, as well as a church, schools, hospital and a hotel. Pedernales is a major fishing centre, in particular shrimp fishing; at low tide you can see the boats resting on the mud bar. Why the *pueblo* is called the 'place of stones' is a mystery as in all the Orinoco Delta there are no rocks. The town is the communications centre for oil exploration by BP. Oil, in fact, has been exploited for over a century and the first wells in nearby Capure were drilled in 1901.

Tucupita (*Telephone code: 0287*) The capital of Delta Amacuro, with a population of 75,000, is the trading, supply and banking centre for the whole of the western delta, but in reality it's a rundown town with a sleepy air of abandonment. Public services are minimal and the power supply is intermittent. Oil exploration by foreign companies around Pedernales and Boca de Tigre is fairly quiet these days and tourism brings little benefit as most visitors are just passing through on tours to river camps in the delta. There is a shady Plaza Bolívar and an esplanade called the Paseo Mánamo where people watch the river go by. Businesses close from 12.00 to 15.00, while the town slips into a snoozy siesta. At night, it comes back to life for a short riverside stroll and a few beers down by the waterfront.

The river and the delta are the main focus here, especially the Caño Mánamo, which breaks away from the Tucupita River to head north to the Gulf of Paria and the Atlantic Ocean (110km). The only roads in the delta go from Tucupita to Los Güires and La Horqueta, 23km away.

Tucupita has been a strategic trading spot for centuries. Traditionally used by the Warao people, it was settled by Juan Millán and Regino Suira of Margarita in 1848 – when it was called simply '48'. Old ties between the people of Margarita and the Warao continue today. The settlement grew into a town with the arrival of Capuchin missionaries in 1919. The town's one-storey profile is broken by the securely locked and forbidding stone Cathedral of La Divina Pastora (finished in 1982) on Avenida Arismendi. Tucupita's oldest building is the attractive 1930s' church of San José de Tucupita on Paseo Mánamo.

Getting there and away
By air The Aeropuerto San Rafael is 3km north of Tucupita. Besides charter flights, mainly for tourism, there are currently no scheduled services. There is a *por puesto* service to town.

By bus Tucupita has a long-distance bus terminal about 1km from the centre. Many buses go to Maturín (212km, 4 hours), but you can save an hour by taking a *por puesto*. The same is true for Ciudad Guayana (189km), served by two departures only. Two bus lines, Los Llanos and Camargüí, drive overnight from Caracas via Maturín to Tucupita (730km, 11 hours). They return to Caracas around 19.00.

Local routes start from a terminus on Calle Tucupita, two blocks southeast of Plaza Bolívar.

By car Tucupita is best reached from Maturín, taking Route 10 to El Rosario and then Route 15 to Barrancas.

By boat A passenger service to Pedernales (110km, 5 hours) leaves daily from the Puerto Fluvial on Paseo Mánamo, five blocks north of San José Church. There is no regular service to the central delta by way of the Tucupita/Macareo rivers. (For the southern Delta Amacuro, see *River travel*, below.)

Tour operators

Fondo Mixto de Turismo Delta Amacuro Av Arismendi con Calle Petion; ☎ 0287 721 0326; e fondomixtodeltaamacuro@hotmail.com; ⏱ 08.00–15.00 Mon–Fri. Limited information on tours & operators is available.

Mánamo Tours East side of Plaza Bolívar; ☎ 0287 721 0179; e aciarcia@cantv.net. A travel agency with knowledgeable people who are problem solvers, & can help with getting air tickets, transfers, or river trips; travellers' cheques accepted. Italian & some English spoken.

🏠 **Where to stay** Accommodation choices are limited.

🏠 **Hotel La Rivera** (50 rooms) Av Rivera; ☎ 0287 721 0777, 0287 721 0578. 3 long blocks south of Plaza Bolívar, it has a restaurant. $$
🏠 **Hotel Saxxi** (95 rooms) ☎ 0287 721 2112, 0287 721 0175; e hotelsaxxi@cantv.net, mispalafitos@cantv.net; www.deltaorinocomispalafitos.com/hotelsaxxi/index.htm. On the main road 7km before Tucupita this large,

motel-style place has a swimming pool, *tasca* restaurant & disco. The hotel is on the Caño Mánamo & owner Alexis Marmanidis offers river excursions from here to Campamento Mis Palafitos (see *Delta camps*, page 236). $–$$
🏠 **Gran Hotel Amacuro** (25 rooms) Calle Bolívar; ☎ 0287 721 0404, 0287 721 0452. Near Plaza Bolívar, it has a restaurant. $

✗ **Where to eat** In town, restaurants north of Plaza Bolívar on the Dalla Costa include: the Laredo Grill and Marisquería Mi Tasca (seafood). The Capri Restaurant and the Bora Café on the Paseo Mánamo are reasonable alternatives.

Shopping The Warao Indians sell all sizes of baskets and hammocks at a row of shops on Calle Tucupita by the bus stop, three blocks from the river.

Other practicalities There's a Banco de Venezuela on Paseo Mánamo near Calle Delta with an ATM and there are several internet places in the Centro Comercial Delta Center on Plaza Bolívar. You can find a small supermarket, Automercado Unión, and a bakery on Calle Tucupita, where you can pick up last minute supplies.

RIVER TRAVEL Backpackers with a hammock and mosquito net should find it easy to spend the night in any remote deltan community. Ask the *comisario* or *prefecto* in each village for local orientation. These people have instructions to help visitors and tourists. Delta inhabitants are mostly simple, reserved people. Remember that they have only rudimentary shelter and the barest of supplies. Take bottled water, some coffee and sugar. You would do well to have a long shirt and trousers, hat, sunscreen, repellent, poncho or waterproof, and a plastic sheet (or bin liner) to protect your pack in the boat. A flashlight and head torch is essential as few places have electricity at night. Remember to carry all the money you will need.

As animals and birds disperse during annual floods, the best time for seeing life on the river is the dry season, usually November to April/May. There are beaches at this time of low water, and the trade winds, currents and waves are quite strong. By contrast, in rainy months when rivers are full and calm, travel is easier and faster.

Travel time also varies according to the motor used: with a 40hp, the run from El Volcán to Guayo takes seven to eight hours; with a 75hp, time is three to four hours. Most delta travel is by open boats with outboard motors: fishing craft called *peñeros*, dugout bongos (the larger ones are roofed) and the faster launches (less relaxed).

The port for travel to the southern delta is **Puerto El Volcán** on the Brazo Macareo, 22km south of Tucupita near the road over the Mánamo (there are local buses). Public launches leave for San Francisco de Guayo, and for Curiapo on the Río Grande, but this *transporte fluvial* is irregular. Large supply vessels to missions and towns of the eastern and southern delta leave from the Monagas port of **Barrancas**. Barrancas, although home to a hotel and an archaeological museum, has been rated as 'horrible'; travellers go to this *pueblo* to arrange a boat and return to Tucupita for the night.

Tours Trips of three days/two nights on the Caño Mánamo are standard and a minimum of four passengers is usually required. Prices start at about US$70–100 a day and comfort increases with price. As camps in the southern delta are more distant, the cost is higher from Tucupita. The camps are built on riverbanks with Warao-style stilt houses with palm-thatched roofs and boardwalks. You can choose beds with bath, or cheaper hammocks with mosquito net options. Even in camps with a generator, the electricity is normally shut off at night so bring a torch and plenty of repellent.

Delta camps Most camps are no longer primitive affairs but offer comfortable rooms or cabins with interior baths. Prices below are per person in a double room with bath and include all transfers, excursions, lodging and meals. Groups get booking preference.

Southern delta

⌂ **Campamento Maraisa** San Francisco de Guayo; ✆ 0287 721 0553. Abelardo Lara was one of the first people to organise delta tours & has guided lots of birdwatchers. His camp (hammocks or beds) has its own generator, some solar panels & water treatment plant; dbl/trpl rooms, plus a big room for hammocks, & 10 cabins with 2 beds plus hammock space, facing the river. The cost of 3 days/2 nights is US$250 pp. Passengers fish for piranhas & lunch at the Araguaimujo mission. Enquire at the Delta Surs office on Calle Pativilca at Mariño in Tucupita.

⌂ **Campamento Oridelta** ✆ 0287 400 2649; m 0414 868 2121; www.deltaorinoko.com.ve. Run by Roger & Ninoska Ruffenach, this nicely laid out camp is reached via Piacoa, 25km from the Castillos de Guayana & an hour's drive east of Ciudad Guayana where they have an office. The camp serves as a base for exploring the southern delta, missions & communities on the rivers Santa Catalina, Sacoroco & Caño Tulipane. 3-day/2-night packages, including transport to & from Ciudad Guayana, are about US$270.

⌂ **Oriwana Camp** San Francisco de Guayo; ✆ 0244 355 1683; e vivatrek@cantv.net; www.vivatrek.com. A co-operative run by native Warao is near San Francisco de Guayo. Arrangements can be made through Viva Trek Expeditions in Caracas.

⌂ **Tobé Lodge** ✆ 0286 961 7708; m 0414 864 8843, 0415 212 5087; e tobelodge@yahoo.com. Macaws squabble in trees every afternoon by this upmarket camp in the mission community of San Francisco de Guayo, less than an hour from the Atlantic Ocean. The area is known for its wildlife (*tobe* means jaguar in Warao) & guests can take a forest hike, observe crocodiles at night, go fishing for piranhas & visit Warao communities. The spacious palm-roofed compound has 24 dbl rooms with hot water, plus a room with hammocks & bath. Tobé's kitchen has an enviable reputation for French cooking, overseen by owners Arlette & Louis Carree.

Eastern/northern delta

🏠 **Aventura Turística Delta** Calle Centurión near Arismendi; ✆ 0287 721 4209; e a-t-d-1973@ hotmail.com; www.aventura-turistica-delta.com. Based in Tucupita, this agency offers economic river trips to the delta staying in hammocks at basic riverside camps for about US$100 a night.

🏠 **Campamento Abujene** m 0416 287 6964, 0416 102 3191, 0414 879 3947; e campamentoabujene@hotmail.com; www.campamentoabujene.com. The newest of the jungle camps, Abujene is the one used by most tour operators in Ciudad Bolívar. The style is typical of the local Warao houses on stilts, with a bridge & 26 cabins with beds & mosquito nets. Excursions include piranha fishing, Warao communities & jungle walk; boats use non-contaminating motors. Cheaper than other camps in the area, 2-day/1-night trips cost about US$110.

🏠 **Mis Palafitos** Local 16, CC Delta Center, Calle Petión, Tucupita; ✆ 0287 721 1733, 0287 721 5166; e mispalafitos@cantv.net; www.deltaorinocomispalafitos.com. Alexis Marmanidis of the Saxxi Hotel in Tucupita owns this camp, & the tours start at the hotel, Bica de Uracoa or in Tucupita. One of the closest camps, it has 30 nice new cabins raised on stilts above the water & a dry-season beach. Ask for an English-speaking guide. Excursions include jungle walks, piranha fishing, visits

Guests are transferred by launch from Piacoa near Los Castillos de Guayana, Bolívar State; or optionally by yacht from Puerto Ordaz. All-inclusive 3-day/2-night tours start at US$245 pp, & go up with fancier menus & more distant excursions.

to Warao communities & opportunities to buy handicrafts.

🏠 **Orinoco Delta Lodge** ✆ (Margarita) 0295 249 1823; m 0414 794 0172; e orinocodelta@ cantv.net, reservations@orinocodelta.cc; www.orinocodelta.com. Expect to be welcomed by a roaming ocelot or otters at this camp on the Mánamo 2hrs north of Tucupita & 1hr from Boca de Uracoa, which is home to various orphaned animals. This is one of the best-run camps, with gardens & an enormous palm-thatched dining area where the food is first class. Built by American Anthony Tahbou & his Venezuelan wife María Virginia, who run Tucupita Expeditions in Margarita, the camp has boardwalks linking the dock to 36 good cabins with twin beds. Staff speak English, German, Italian & Arabic. There is a small fleet of boats that are used for tourism & to take Warao children to a school that the lodge supports. Guests can explore camps that are more remote & more primitive for birdwatching & fishing *sábalo* (tarpon) & *morocoto* (damselfish). Rates from US$130 a day. They also offer tours from Margarita & have 2 other delta camps: the **Orinoco Atlantic Lodge** (*www.orinocodelta.net*), in the far delta, north of Pedernales & close to the Atlantic Ocean, which offers tarpon fishing; & **Jakara**, a more basic camp with hammocks & cheaper prices aimed at the backpacker market.

10

Los Llanos, Wildlife Paradise

Known as the Serengeti of South America for the incredible diversity of wildlife found here, the Llanos is a birdwatcher's paradise with some 360 species of birds. It is also home to giant anteaters, whooping howler monkeys, freshwater dolphins in various shades of pink, piranhas with a nasty nip, the magnificent but endangered jaguar, anacondas, the world's largest snake, and herds of capybara, the world's largest rodent. A vast area of seasonally flooded plains, the Llanos stretches north of the Orinoco to the Andean foothills, covering 300,000km² in Venezuela and another 220,000km² in Colombia. This is cattle-raising, cowboy country, lived from the saddle of a horse, and more cows than people live on the open plains. The Llaneros, as the inhabitants are called, grow up in a tough environment of extremes: drought and brush fires in the dry season are followed by heavy floods that create huge lakes in the rainy season. Ranches called *hatos* (the 'h' is silent) cover many thousands of hectares, populated by humped-back zebu cattle brought here from India by the British. The introduction of new forage crops, better breeds and artificial insemination have helped modernise the Llanos but Venezuelans still think of it as a place where brave, barefoot Llanero cowboys battle drought or

ALMA LLANERA (THE SOUL OF THE LLANOS)

The words of this very fast-paced *joropo*, perhaps the best-loved song in Venezuela, were written by Rafael Bolívar Coronado, to music by Pedro Elías Gutiérrez, as part of an operetta of the same name that opened at the Teatro Caracas in 1914.

I was born on this bank	*Yo nací en esta ribera*
of the rushing Arauca	*Del Arauca vibrador*
I'm brother to the foam,	*Soy hermano de la espuma,*
to the herons, to the roses	*De las garzas, de las rosas*
and to the sun, and to the sun.	*Y del sol y del sol*
I was roused by the lively call	*Me arrulló la viva diana*
of the breeze in the palms	*De la brisa en el palmar*
and that's why my soul	*Y por eso tengo el alma*
is like the fine soul	*Como el alma primorosa*
of crystal, of crystal.	*Del cristal, del cristal*
I love, cry, sing, dream,	*Amo, lloro, canto, sueño*
with carnations of passion	*Con claveles de pasión*
to adorn the golden mane	*Para ornar las rubias crines*
of my lover's steed.	*Al potro de mi amador*

Los Llanos map, showing locations including Guanare/Barinas, Arismendi/El Baúl/Hato Piñero/San Antonio, Calabozo/Hato La Fé/Caracas (400km), Guarico, Barinas, Pto de Nutrias, Campamento Turistico Rancho Grande, Bruzual, Caño Guaritico Wildlife Refuge, Hato El Frío, San Antonio, Apure, Camaguan, Uverito, El Samán de Apure, Apurito, San Fernando de Apure, Pto Miranda, Achaguas, Biruaca, (dykes), La Ye, Mantecal, Caño Coícara, Hato El Cedral (Matiyure), Lorenzo, La Trinidad de Arauca, Elorza, Arauca, Llanos Flood Plains, El Yagual, (Queseras del Medio), Aruacá, Cunaviche, Guachara, Payara, San Rafael de Atamaica, Cunaviche, Hato San Leonardo, Sta Rosa, El Lucero, Sta Ana, Los Tigres, Paso Capanaparo, Capanaparo, El Porvenir, Parque Nacional Cinaruco - Capanaparo, Cinaruco, Sta Rosa, Paso Cinaruco, Apure, Buena Vista, Orinoco, Puerto Páez, Meta, Puerto Carreño, Colombia, El Burro, Orinoco, Puerto Ayacucho (95km). Scale: 0-30km, 0-30 miles. Bradt.

LOS LLANOS

floods, jaguars or piranhas, to round up scattered herds. Perpetuating the romantic image of the Llanos is the music of the region, the sound of harp, *cuatro* (a small four-string guitar) and maracas, accompanied by a nasal, slightly off-key vocal. The galloping rhythm of *joropo* is only generally heard in the rest of Venezuela at folk events or in restaurants selling barbecued meat, but in the Llanos it is everywhere, blasting out from car stereos, shops, restaurants and every bar in every town and village. *Alma Llanera*, an early *joropo* is Venezuela's unofficial national anthem and a stirring hymn to the wild plains.

NATURAL HISTORY

FLORA Although the plains are flat, their topography is broken by communities of taller plants: evergreen gallery forests on the banks of *caños* or creeks, isolated copses called *matas*, and burned-over patches of hardy, twisted *chaparro* trees. In central Apure, floods leave a watery mosaic of *bajíos*, literally shallows. In water as deep as a frog's knees, a rapid cycle of plant and animal life thrives only as long as rain falls.

Grasslands are interrupted by dense stands of Mauritia palms called *moriches*. Among the Llanos's most distinctive features, these clumps or *morichales* form in boggy hollows. At first one or two palms grow, then more along a course of clear streams. Some old *morichales* extend 50km in length and are the source of clean water year-round for adjacent towns.

A whole ecosystem depends on the *esteros*, marshes whose clay bottoms retain floodwaters to form shallow lakes. Then the Llanero poles his boat along, with a harpoon at hand, seeking the shadow of a catfish moving under a floating carpet of water hyacinths. The seasonal cycle of the marsh and its animal life, water ferns and reeds, as it comes to an end with dry weather, nourishes thousands of birds and predators, until by January or February the clay bottom is exposed to the sun, picked clean.

FAUNA A census in the Llanos found 323 bird species, more than 50 mammals, 354 kinds of fish, 67 reptiles and 26 amphibians. Many animals and birds on the Llanos are adapted to water. You can spot river dolphins in muddy rivers when they surface to blow. The first reptile seen is usually the spectacled caiman or *baba*, 2.3m in length. The biggest, the Orinoco crocodile, which grows to over 6m, has been hunted almost to extinction and is now being reintroduced in one or two areas. Both males and females defend their young and will carry them to safety in their mouth. You won't see a crocodile in the wild, and the chances of seeing an anaconda are slim, except at *hatos* with hunting bans, such as Hato El Cedral. This is also the place to find piranhas, called *caribes* (which means 'flesh eater' and is the root of the words 'Caribbean' and 'cannibal'). Piranhas live in most of the plains' rivers and are the easiest fish to catch. In small concentrations they do not attack water fauna unless bleeding. Nevertheless, this is one reason not to swim in Llanos rivers, another being the presence in the muddy bottoms of stingrays and electric eels.

You will see family groups of what look like rotund, giant guinea pigs. These are *chigüires*, or capybaras, the world's biggest rodents weighing up to 60kg. Lifting comic snouts to sniff danger, they munch plants at the water's edge. The Llanos species is called *Hydrochoerus hydrochaeris* and a second species, *Hydrochoerus isthmius*, lives in Zulia State. *Chigüires* have slightly webbed feet, swim and dive like beavers and are a local source of meat – at one time declared to be suitable Lenten food by

---

ANTEATERS

Anteaters belong to an order of animals called Edentata, which they share with sloths and armadillos. The giant anteater (*Myrmecophaga tridactyla*) is the largest Edentate and among the largest of the rainforest animals, up to 2.8m long and weighing 39kg. Strictly terrestrial, it searches the forest floor where ants and termites are most plentiful. Insects are no match for the anteater whose claws rip open nests in seconds, while tough hairy skin protects it against stings and bites. With a long snout and sticky tongue it probes for its abundant food. If you walk off a forest track a short way you often see holes where an anteater has dug through an ants' nest. Its digging tools also come in handy to defend itself and it can easily kill a dog. Anteaters are easiest to see in grassland savanna habitats such as the Llanos.

Tamandua (*Tamandua tetradactyla*), sometimes misleadingly called the honeybear, is a small arboreal anteater, a specialist predator on ant and wasp nests. Related to the giant anteater, they share adaptations: powerful claws, long snouts and jawbones fused into a tube for the long, sticky tongue. Thick fur and small eyes and ears provide protection against aggressive stinging insects. Tamanduas are primarily arboreal and have a coiling, prehensile tail, adapted for grasping.

The smallest anteater is the silky or pygmy anteater (*Cyclopes didactylus*). No more than 20cm long and weighing 283g, it scores high on the cuteness quotient, with lustrous, silky, grey-gold fur. Pygmy anteaters are rarely seen; they live solitary, mainly nocturnal lives out of sight in the rainforest canopy.

the Catholic Church as 'amphibians'. Because they have been hunted for 300 years, *chigüires* are now seen in great numbers only on ranches where hunting is controlled or banned. According to studies by Viviana Salas, capybara groups of several families will defend a certain territory, including water. In this area only the dominant male has mating rights. Females, all subordinate, bear four young, which may be breastfed by more than one lactating mother.

On rivers in protected areas you may see families of giant otters (or hear their snorts); they are called *perros de agua*. A mature male measures 2m from head to tail. Shyer, more solitary and rarer are the land mammals – tapir, giant anteater, tamandua, armadillo, fox, tayra and spotted cats, big and small. Peccaries run in bands, and people climb trees to avoid their ire. You can hear howler monkeys from a great distance: the *araguatos*'s howl is more like a roar than the jaguar's call, or cough. Venezuelans call jaguars *tigres* and they have a wide distribution, although their numbers have been much reduced by hunting and habitat loss. The opossum is so ordinary as to be despised, while the porcupine with prehensile tail is charming though formidable; both are nocturnal.

Birds Water and wading birds gather by the thousand to feed at shrinking ponds. Herons, egrets, scarlet ibis, glossy ibis, roseate spoonbill, jabiru, wood storks, boatbilled herons, anhingas, cormorants, jacanas, gallinules, Orinoco Geese, whistling treeducks, as well as many birds of prey such as hawks, falcons, kestrel and osprey, may be viewed on a single ranch. The odd, prehistoric-looking hoatzin is a bird often seen in riverside bushes. The chicks can swim and are born with

THE HOATZIN

The unmistakeable hoatzin or *chenchena* (*Opisthocomus hoazin*) is a large, portly bird about the size of a turkey. Its head bears a prominent scruffy Mohican crest. Large blue eye-rings of bare skin add to its comic appearance.

They are poor flyers, as the pectoral muscles of the hoatzin are too small for sustained flight, limiting the seemingly clumsy bird to short, gliding flights. The reduced musculature makes room for the bird's oversized crop, which stores its diet of 60% leaves. Gut bacteria ferment the material for up to four times longer than most birds. Fermentation by-products are believed to be responsible for the hoatzin's unpleasant smell and its rather unkind nickname, the 'stinkbird'.

Raptors and arboreal predators can make an easy meal of the weakly flapping hoatzin, which therefore is quite wary, and often flies off as soon as it is disturbed. But when the prospect of mating comes along, hormones throw caution to the wind and shyness is reduced. Flocks of up to a dozen birds squawk clumsily among trees, especially along borders of permanent varzea swamp, co-operating in nesting with the mating pair assisted by a number of helpers.

The nest is built over water and, when threatened by a predator, the chick flings itself into the water below. It swims back to the nest tree where it uses its bill, feet and special wing-claws to climb back up. This latter unique and apparently primitive characteristic is believed to have evolved independently and is not evidence for the widespread belief that the hoatzin is related to the fossil bird archaeopteryx – one of the first birds that evolved 120 million years ago – or is itself a living fossil. Indeed egg protein analysis suggests it may be recently evolved from cuckoos. However, the bird is still weird enough to be classified in a family of its own, Opisthocomidae.

In some places where there's ideal habitat, hoatzin are very common. During non-breeding periods they form flocks of 25 or 30 at times, seeming to ignore benevolent human presence.

hooks on their wings so they can scramble back up to their nest if they fall in the river (see box opposite).

WILDLIFE CONSERVATION Among large animals that have been severely endangered by hunting are the Orinoco crocodile (*Crocodylus intermedius*), giant otter (*Pteroneura brasiliensis*), manatee (*Trichechus manatus*) – a 500kg relative of the seacow, giant anteater (*Myrmecophaga tridactyla*) and the nearly extinct giant armadillo or *cuspón* (*Priodontes giganteus*). The owners of Hato El Frío and El Cedral helped to set up the **Guaritico Wildlife Refuge** along a river between their lands to protect such species.

None of these animals has suffered such loss as the large *arrau* turtle which grows to 1m in length. In 1745 Jesuit priest José Gumilla wrote in his *Orinoco Ilustrado*, 'It would be as difficult to count the grains of sand on the Orinoco's shores, as to count the immense number of tortoises.' He believed that their great number would make the Orinoco unnavigable if eggs were not taken. Stopping at Pararuma in 1800, Alexander von Humboldt estimated that 33 million eggs were laid every dry season. Several hundred Indians of different tribes would assemble in late March for the egg harvest. Some tribes even came from the upper Orinoco. Turtle egg oil was sold for lamps in Ciudad Bolívar.

Today, at low water, some turtles still come to nest on the same sandy islands. The half-dozen park rangers have a next to impossible job stopping nest robbers as distances are great and the laying season covers three months.

There are also other, more serious threats to wildlife habitat: a government plan to dredge and channel rivers to make the Orinoco–Apure navigation route, and schemes to build dykes and drain land for farming, with all the dangers of impoverishing already acidic soils and encouraging land speculation.

PLANNING A VISIT

Despite being prized as a unique environment with an abundance of wildlife and amazing birding opportunities, visiting the Llanos is not easy. Visitors have two choices: to stay at an expensive cattle ranch and take a package including accommodation and safari-style trips by jeep and boat; or to take one of the cheap and cheerful adventure trips organised by tour operators in Mérida to a small *hato* close to Barinas with lodging in hammocks and basic facilities.

Frustratingly, there are now fewer options since the government decided in 2009 to take over the three main ranches offering safaris, Hato El Cedral, Hato El Frio and Hato Piñero. While Hato Cedral is still operating fully, it is not known yet if the government will maintain tourist services to Hato El Frio and Hato Piñero.

The best time to see wildlife is in the dry season, from December to April/May. This is called *verano*, 'the summer'. Grass withers, cracks open in the ground and cattle are moved to waterholes. It is the time when most visitors come for the drama unfolding in shrinking lagoons where too many fish succumb to too little oxygen, drawing thousands of wading birds to a feast. Spectacled caimans and fishermen also take advantage of the trapped fish.

Spring comes in May with the first rains. Frogs, turtles, and even fish emerge after months in a dormant state called aestivation under the baked mud. New grass sprouts; creeks turn into rivers and rivers into lakes; fish disperse over the Llanos to spawn; and egrets and ibises congregate to nest in huge rookeries. By July, the Orinoco is in flood. On Apure's floodplains, the Llaneros give up horses and jeeps in favour of boats and aircraft. Cattle that have not been rounded up to higher ground may drown. This season is called the *invierno*, or 'winter', well suited to water buffalo farms.

San Fernando, altitude 75m, is on the south shore of the Apure about 150km before it joins the Orinoco. The river port is the capital and only sizeable town in this state of some 400,000 people and 76,500km². As the traditional trading centre for ranchers of the lower Llanos, it is a thriving city of 175,000 inhabitants. Its main livelihood is beef, followed by some farming. There is a modern tannery, and caiman leather is also processed and exported. Good roads link the state's small towns of Achaguas, Elorza, Mantecal and Guasdualito, but all unsurfaced roads are virtually impassable during the rainy half of the year.

San Fernando was founded in 1788 as a little mission base for Franciscan monks. A century later it had grown into an important, even rich, river port with Italian, French and Corsican immigrants. In its heyday there were steamships and sailing boats going to Barinas and Ciudad Bolívar trading hides, dried meat and fish, tobacco, cotton and coffee. When a road was opened to Maracay and the north, San Fernando lost its trade to truckers and has not recovered its glory since World War II. Today the port has some fishing activity. San Fernando's main draw for travellers is as a base for seeing Llanos wildlife.

GETTING THERE

By air Las Flecheras Airport is 3km east of town; it's best to take a taxi. From Caracas, San Fernando is a 50-minute flight away. At present there are two daily flights by Avior (*www.aviorairlines.com*) from Caracas: at 08.00 except Sunday; and at 15.00 except Saturday. The same plane returns to Caracas.

By bus As you cross over the bridge into San Fernando, the Terminal de Pasajeros is on the west side of the road near the river and within walking distance of the famous crocodile/cornucopia fountain. There are both morning and evening buses to Caracas (400km, 8½ hours). Buses go throughout the day to Barinas (550km) and Maracay (315km, 7 hours). Expresos Los Llanos travels to San Cristóbal at night (950km, 13 hours). Buses to Puerto Ayacucho (303km, 8 hours) travel through the Cinaruco–Capanaparo park on an all-weather road along an embankment above the floodplain. New bridges are replacing the old flatbed ferries over the Capanaparo, Cinaruco and Orinoco rivers.

By 4x4 Adventurous cross-country drivers can go south of the Apure River, *llano adentro*, in the dry season of December–April. If using this option, take a 4x4 and make sure to pack six spare fuel cans and a compass (there are places named on maps that just don't exist). The sandy tracks or *trillas* that appear most worn often lead to ranches, visible miles away as clumps of mango trees. When getting directions don't ask how far you need to go, but how long it takes (remembering that Llaneros have no watches) to reach the next *hato*. (Don't ask locals the way to a distant goal such as Elorza.)

Take food supplies, as well as rope and hammocks; there are no hamlets or country stores anywhere. This is hot, flat savanna interrupted by beautiful dunes. As the drought advances the lagoons and creeks evaporate and animals and even birds become scarce. In the rivers, however, there are fat *pavón* (bass) and large *payara*, game fish with fangs. Here you sometimes meet Pumé Indians (Yaruro); they fish, and carve pieces of jet (*azabache*), which they find in the dunes.

North of the Apure lie the 'wet' Llanos. Even in the dry season they are greener with *morichales* or palm stands in swampy hollows, and lagoons where birds gather. However, the dust on roads is so terrible that drivers wear masks. Dust, combined with ruts and runnels, cuts progress to 15km/h.

TOURIST INFORMATION Tourist information can be found at the **Corporación Apureña de Turismo** (*Calle Rodriguez Rincones;* ☎ *0247 341 2362, 0247 342 1142*).

WHERE TO STAY

🏠 **Gran Hotel Plaza** (49 rooms) Plaza Bolívar; ☎ 0247 341 1245, 0247 341 1504; www.granhotelplaza.com. Rooms with TV, AC, hot water, bathroom. $$

🏠 **Nuevo Hotel Apure** (29 rooms) Av Maria Nieves; ☎ 0247 341 4483, 0247 341 4759. By the crocodile fountain opposite the petrol station, this motel-style place has a good restaurant & a range of rooms. $$

🏠 **Hotel Trinacria** (14 rooms) Av Miranda; ☎ 0247 342 3578, 0247 342 2566. A clean, economical, newer hotel 5–6 blocks west of the crocodile fountain. $

FESTIVALS Everyone gathers at San Fernando's week-long *feria* and agricultural exhibition in mid-April. There are bulldogging contests (*toros coleados*) without which no fair in the Llanos is complete. Cowhands from distant ranches compete in these rodeo skills, with four or five riders pursuing a bull down a long, narrow enclosure and trying to grab it by the tail (*cola*) and flip it onto its back. While young Llaneros show off their riding skills, *joropo* singers compete for the 'Florentino de Oro', a prestigious award given for the best composer of couplets in a battle between two singers called *contrapunteo*, in which they take it in turns to improvise verses and outdo each other in wit and lyrical skill, like a pair of rappers in a face off.

OTHER PRACTICALITIES There is a Banco Provincial on Plaza Páez and a Banco Mercantil on Paseo Libertador, on the corner with Carrera Colombia.

There is a Movistar call centre at the bus station with internet and international phone calls and a CANTV call centre on Avenida Paseo Libertador, between Calle Bolívar and Calle Comercio.

There are plenty of pharmacies in town with several on Avenida Carabobo and a Farmacentro on Calle Comercio. The main Pablo Acosta Ortiz hospital is on Avenida Caracas.

WHAT TO SEE AND DO For those passing through, there isn't much to see except for a couple of monuments to the bravery of the Llanero lancers who fought with distinction in the Independence wars under their leader José Antonio Páez, known as the Centaur of the Llanos. Páez played a key role in Bolívar's victory at the Battle of Carabobo in 1821 and went on to become Venezuela's first president. On the Paseo Libertador there is the **Monumento a los Llaneros** and eight blocks north, stands a statue of **Pedro Camejo**, known as 'Negro Primero', who died at General Páez's feet in the key battle of Carabobo. A fountain covered in coloured tiles and concrete crocodiles stands beside it.

The **Palacio Barbarito**, an ornate, two-storey house at the crocodile plaza, dates back to the late 1800s and early 1900s, when San Fernando flourished from the export of egret feathers. The house was built by the Barbarito brothers, Italian merchants who held a virtual monopoly on the feather trade. Back then, the best heron and egret rookeries were owned by dictator Juan Vicente Gómez, the Barbaritos and the Lancashire Trust, a British company. Exports, which were more valuable than gold, continued until the Audubon Society denounced the cruel trade.

The **Casa de Bolívar**, Carrera 3-Comercio at Independencia, a block north and west of Plaza Bolívar, is the restored house where Bolívar stayed in 1818 and is now the seat of the Centro Bolivariano.

Museo Rómulo Gallegos (*Calle Negro Primero;* ⊕ *08.00–12.00 & 14.00–18.00 weekdays; admission free*) A museum dedicated to the life of novelist Gallegos (1884–1969), one of the outstanding Latin American writers of his time and author of *Doña Bárbara*, a classic tale of love and passion in the Llanos (1929). The museum houses the Doña Bárbara public library and a few antiques. Gallegos was also a political leader who in 1947 won Venezuela's first universal, direct elections for president with 74% of the vote, only to be toppled by a military coup in 1948.

Cinaruco-Capanaparo Park Officially called the Parque Nacional Santos Luzardo, this 5,840km² tract is bounded on the east by the Orinoco, on the north by the Capanaparo and on the south by the Cinaruco. The nearby Orinoco islands of Pararuma, Ramonera, Loros and Isla del Medio have been declared a wildlife refuge. It is hoped that the endangered *arrau*, or Orinoco turtle, and rare Orinoco crocodile will nest there.

AN INQUISITIVE TRAVELLER'S GUIDE TO THE LLANOS
Edward Paine

I worked in Venezuela for four years, most of them spent between the Apure and Arauca rivers, in the heart of the Llanos, and my addiction for the area developed slowly as I worked first as a cowboy, progressing to manager of a 100,000-acre ranch. As with all the remote parts of the world, you have to work hard to get beyond initial impressions and begin to understand the local culture and traditions.

Firstly, as a transient visitor there is the problem of access: only one paved road loops its way through these immense plains and you won't see much from a vehicle. However, here are some of the ingredients that make up the Llanos.

THE CATTLE The large white ones with humps are probably brahman. Descended from the zebu cattle of India they have revolutionised the local cattle-breeding industry with their resistance to ticks and heat, and are replacing or being crossed with the *criollo* animals brought over from Europe by the early colonists.

THE COWBOYS Still fiercely independent, the Llaneros share with their Argentine cousin the *gaucho* a reluctance to go anywhere on foot when a horse or mule is available. Their main diet is, of course, meat, although as killing day is normally weekly the menu progresses through thinner and thinner *sopas* until there are a few bare bones and some spaghetti swimming around in hot water. As in all people who live by the hours of the sun and do not depend on watches, they are early risers. While you may find everyone asleep by 20.00, there will be activity in the bunkhouse several hours before dawn, soon after the cock crows. I soon learned not to place too much trust in this natural alarm clock: one morning, after a night at an outlying corral, we rose when the cock crowed, caught the horses, saddled up and set out on the eight-hour ride back to the farm centre, only to find that after five hours riding the sun still had not risen!

THE WILDLIFE By a happy chance the ranch economy has not conflicted with their habitat, so take a good guide and wonder at the bright colours and sheer numbers of birds as they fly from one lagoon to another.

THE MUSIC So often a short-cut to a good understanding of other cultures, you should plan to stop at any of the scruffy towns on the Llanos during the patron saints' fiestas, and listen to the same cowboy who that morning was up at dawn training his favourite fighting cock as he sings his heart out to his companions – companions whose agility on a horse has been converted to agile fingers moving over the strings of a harp, accompanied by the four-stringed *cuatro* and maracas.

Edward Paine runs the tour operator Last Frontiers – see page 30.

In practice, the Orinoco is out of the reach of visitors and there are no facilities of any sort, although the highway itself is an open invitation to campers. At the Capanaparo River, just beyond the old ferry crossing, a park visitors' centre is planned. Visitors will be requested to get a permit. In the meantime enquire about the fishing season and limits at Inparques (*Edificio Pasquali opposite the Palacio Barbarito, San Fernando;* ✆ *0247 341 3794*).

☞ **WARNING:** There are no mosquitoes in the dry season but chiggers await anyone on foot. By other names these microscopic ticks are called *chivacoa*, harvest mites or *bête rouge* because they are pink. Tuck your trouser legs into your socks or boots and spray repellent on the outside. If you already have chigger bites, to lessen their itch take a long bath and lather well (three minutes) with an antiseptic soap.

🏠 Where to stay

🏠 **Las Churuatas del Capanaparo** ✆ 0247 511 4315, 0212 235 1287; **m** 0414 327 4224. A rustic compound with restaurant, this is a good, inexpensive, stopover on the road from San Fernando through the national park. Set back 500m from the ferry access on the Capanaparo's south bank, near an inviting beach, the *churuatas* are 6 unscreened, palm-roofed structures with beds for 4 people, plus hammocks, private bath & electricity. You can take excursions by dugout canoe, or on horseback. Ask about the hammock-camp near Caño Pica. Go in the Dec–Apr dry season as there are many mosquitoes & midges once rains begin. ⑤

Wildlife lodges and camps

Several working cattle ranches have turned to ecotourism and photo safaris to support conservation (and bring in hard currency). Most lodges accommodate about 20 people in comfort, no more. As there is great interest among birdwatchers and nature lovers in general, it's best to book well in advance for the dry season, November–April. Tours with accommodation cost around US$100–150 a night per person based on double occupancy (always check if taxes are included before you reserve). Prices may be 30% lower in off-season, and Venezuelan residents sometimes get discounts. Included are excursions both morning and afternoon by safari truck and boats, usually with an English-speaking guide, but make sure before you book. Swimming in the rivers is discouraged because of piranhas, rays and electric eels, so a swimming pool, however small is a welcome treat after a hot, dusty day of wildlife watching. Transfers by car or plane from San Fernando or Barinas may be arranged at a separate cost. For a party of five or more, ask if there is a charter plane service from Caracas.

Of the *hatos* listed below, most are in Apure State. However, smaller ranches in the Llanos north of the Apure River, in Barinas State, offer more economical choices and easier access.

🏠 **Campamento Turistico Rancho Grande** ✆ 0240 808 7434; **m** 0416 873 1192. This modest option has been run for years by Ramon Guillermo Aveledo – known locally as 'Barriga' ('Big Belly') – who offers low-priced wildlife tours on the Río Guaritico from a camp with native-style thatched *churuatas*. Guides speak Spanish but have plenty of experience of foreign tourists, having taken many a backpacker horseriding or fishing for piranhas. Prices for 3-day/2-night tours staying in (hard) camp beds or (softer) hammocks are about US$100 pp with pickup from Mantecal. A great place to get that anaconda shot. Ring for reservation.

🏠 **Hato El Cedral** ✆ 0212 577 5174, 0212 893 6663, 0212 893 6659; **m** 0416 502 2757; **e** info@elcedral.com, reservacionescedral@hotmail.com; www.hatocedral.com. The top destination for bird & wildlife watching in Los Llanos, this immense *hato* was owned by the Rockefellers in the 1950s, when it was called the King Ranch. They invested in levées (*módulos*), which provide water in the dry season & high ground during the rains, making it the perfect place to see wildlife year round. Nesting time (May–Oct) is impressive as herons, egrets, spoonbills & ibises literally cover the trees in the *garceros* or rookeries. The ranch of 530km² has some 25,000 of the humped zebu cattle, 20,000 capybaras, 10,000 caimans, and over 300 species of birds have been observed here. (One section along the Matiyure River is advertised as a sanctuary but is really the same ranch.) 2 guided excursions are offered per day, including jeep safaris & boat excursions, with piranha fishing (make sure you ask). Night tours cost extra. Facilities are good: small pool, bar, 25 rooms with AC, some with hot water. Prices are high in the dry season, 15 Nov–30 Apr, but a 4-day/3-night stay offers better value. You pay extra for a sgl, and for transfer from San Fernando or Barinas. The camp is located 225km from San Fernando, west of the main road between Mantecal & Elorza & 10km south of a major junction called La Ye. To get there by bus from Caracas, take an express Los Llanos bus from La Bandera to Elorza & ask the bus driver to drop you on the road in front of the *hato*. Reservation only.

⌂ **Hato La Fé** Corozopando; ☏ 0247 514 6263; m 0414 468 8749, 0414 325 4418; e info@posadahatolafe.com; www.hatolafe.com. The closest place to Caracas for wildlife observation is a 1,000ha farm in Corozopando in Guarico State, on the road to San Fernando de Apure. A working farm with a rustic restaurant & guesthouse. Managed by the friendly Sorelia Franco, who shows guests how the milking & cheese making are done, among other

activities. Trips are offered to Hato Masaguaral, where biologists study fauna including foxes & howler monkeys, & over 230 bird species are listed for the areas visited by boat & on horseback from the farm. With a 2-day/1-night plan you get 3 Llanos forays, 3 meals & lodging in 1 of 8 rooms, some with private bath, for about US$100 pp.

⌂ **Hato Piñero** m 0426 358 0567, 0424 131 3694; e reserva@hatopinero.com, marketing@hatopinero.com, hatoecotours@gmail.com. This cattle ranch in the Llano Alto or central plains of Cojedes State enjoys a remarkable cornucopia of wildlife due to the hunting ban imposed here 50 years ago. As a result, you see many more animals & birds, including owls, macaws, hoatzin, iguanas, caiman, capuchin monkeys, agoutis, curassows, foxes, ocelots, giant anteater, fishing bats, herds of capybara & over 300 species of birds. However, the ranch was taken over by the government in 2009 & has been renamed the Centro Técnico Productivo Socialista Florentino, in line with the government's aim of ensuring the country's 'food sovereignty'. According to the people running the lodge, it is going to continue offering tours & accommodation for about US$100 a day, but no other information was available at the time of publication. Piñero is 370km (5–6hrs) from Caracas via Tinaco–El Baúl.

BARINAS STATE

The road from Apure to Barinas is perhaps the country's top wildlife route. Leaving San Fernando de Apure, the highway swings west through the heart of the Llanos. The best close-up views of thousands of birds and beasts, including howler monkeys, are along the roadside after El Samán de Apure (west of Achaguas), on the Mantecal–La Ye route, and up to Bruzual, where the road passes the Caño Guaritico Fauna Refuge. The other road at La Ye continues west to Guasdualito, an area best avoided due to the presence of Colombian rebels on the other side of the border.

A good road, well travelled by buses, continues north from the Apure River with many opportunities to see plentiful birdlife along the first part. The highway leads 133km to the upper plains and three agricultural states: Barinas, Portuguesa and Cojedes. Their large rivers flow from the Andes to the Apure: the Santo Domingo and Masparro in Barinas, and eastward the Guanare, Portuguesa and its tributary, the Cojedes. Barinas stretches from the Apure to the Andes. Its 600,000 inhabitants live mainly from raising cattle and water buffalo, and farming maize, cotton, tobacco and coffee.

Barinas State has a number of ranches with guest facilities offering wildlife observation at rates lower than those charged by the large Apure *hatos*. As a bonus, they are much closer to airports and bus routes and many tour operators, such as Guamanchi, Fanny Tours, and Arrasari bring travellers here from Mérida.

Across the Apure from Bruzual, Ciudad de Nutrias still shows traces of the era when the town, founded in 1774, boasted the region's principal river port. From the northern plains came not only cattle and hides, but also the tobacco so valued in Europe that the name of Barinas (or Varinas) was better known than that of Venezuela. As in San Fernando, the feather trade brought sudden growth in the early 1900s.

EN ROUTE TO BARINAS
Where to stay

🏠 **Finca Santa Maria** (11 rooms) ✆ 0273 415 6042, 0273 511 2994; m 0414 568 1980. A working farm on the Pagüey River, south of the farming town of San Silvestre & 53km from Barinas. Home to one of the biggest concentrations of capybaras in the Llanos, & an abundance of wetland birds, it is green year round thanks to a system of lagoons & irrigation canals. Within the ranch, day tours visit woods where you will see howler monkeys, anacondas & with luck a giant anteater. They have a swimming pool & guest rooms have AC, hot water. Good meals. Pricey in high season & off the beaten track, enquire about low-season & group discounts. $$$$

🏠 **Hato El Cristero** (12 rooms) Via Torunos, San Silvestre; ✆ 0273 223 5060; m 0414 454 4193; e hatocristero@yahoo.es; www.circuitodelaexcelencia.com. Just 20mins from Barinas this attractive working farm has nice rooms with hot water, bathrooms, AC, use of swimming pool. Horseriding, milking, piranha fishing & wildlife tours are offered, with a good chance of seeing anacondas, & there is an enclosure with rescued animals. Pickup from Barinas can be arranged. Run by the Concha family with a strong commitment to conservation. Check for low-season offers. Recommended. $$$

BARINAS (*Telephone code: 0273*) The biggest city of the three upper Llanos states, Barinas is a pleasant capital of over 276,000 inhabitants, and a transport hub for Caracas, the plains, Mérida and Táchira. The main draw for tourists is the nearby rafting and kayaking camps on the Acequias, Siniguis, Santo Domingo and Canagua rivers, offering white-water rapids at levels 2, 3, 4 and 5 from May to November, and the nearby petroglyphs in Bum Bum, mysterious symbols inscribed on large boulders in the distant past by long-lost Indian tribes.

History Barinas was originally founded in 1577 at Altamira de Cáceres, on the route to Mérida. Fifty years later a second site was chosen in Moromoy (near Barinitas), and finally in 1759 it moved to its present location on the banks of the Santo Domingo. At one time the country's second city, Barinas was devastated by revolutionary campaigns and a century of *caudillo* wars until the 20th century. In 1810, when Independence was declared from Spain, the population was 10,000; in 1900 there were fewer than 1,000 inhabitants living in 167 houses. Effective malaria controls and oil exploitation on the upper plains kick-started the growth of the city, which continues to expand and modernise.

Getting there

By *air* The airport on Avenida Adonay Parra is within walking distance of Plaza Bolívar (1.5km). If you have heavy bags catch a bus going down Avenida 6-Medina Jiménez/Avenida 23 de Enero. At the moment there are only a few flights to and from Caracas by Avior (*www.avioairlines.com*) between 07.00 and 19.00. Conviasa (*www.conviasa.aero*), the state-owned airline has five flights a day to Caracas during the week, with one flight on Saturday and two on Sunday. In 2008, President Chávez laid the foundation stone of Barinas International Airport, located 10km from the city in Barranca, Municipio Cruz Paredes. The airport is expected to be finished in 2013.

By *bus* The Terminal de Pasajeros is on Avenida Cuatricentenario, seven blocks north of Avenida 23 de Enero. Buses to Guanare run constantly throughout the day. There is also frequent service by various lines to San Fernando de Apure by normal or express coaches. Transporte Barinas goes to Mérida morning and afternoon (163km, 4 hours). Unión Táchira and other lines go to San Cristóbal (316km). Expresos Los Llanos has a *buscama* service to Caracas (525km, 8–9 hours). Don't forget to take a fleece, jacket or jumpers on board for the arctic air conditioning.

By car Barinas can be reached from San Fernando de Apure on Route 19. At the crossroads of La Ye you take the right fork via Ciudad de Nutrias to Libertad, where there is a turning to the city of Barinas. From Mérida the route follows some high passes to Barinitas before descending to the city. From Caracas you take the main highway to Valencia and then Route 5 all the way to Barinas.

Tourist information Visit **Corbatur** (*Calle Azobispo Mendez, Edif Vifran;* \ *0273 552 7091;* e *corbatur@gmail.com; www.descubrebarinas.com.ve*) for good maps of the city and information on tours, rafting and places to stay. They have kiosks at the airport and the bus terminal.

Where to stay

Hotel Mastranto Suite (56 rooms) Av Cuatricenteria; \ 0273 541 4126, 0273 532 1876; e mastrantosuite@yahoo.com, mastrantosuite@hotmail.com; www.hotelmastrantosuite.com. The swankiest option in town has all mod cons & tastefully decorated rooms have AC, cable TV, hot water, Wi-Fi. $$$

LLANOS FOLKLORE – JUST PLAIN FRIGHTENING

Some of Venezuela's scariest myths and legends come from the great plains of Los Llanos, where the dark nights and remote location of the cattle ranches create the perfect setting for ghost stories around the campfire. Many of these spine-chilling tales, such as the story of the spooky Silbón (the Whistler), or the seductive Sayona, date back to the 19th century and the Independence wars against Spain.

Even today these spectral figures strike fear into the hearts of the superstitious Llanero cowboys, who are quick to attribute the strange noises of the night to frightening mythical beasts that come out after dark to prey on the unwary. The most famous of these local characters have been immortalised in Llanero songs, making them known throughout the country.

EL SILBÓN Originally from Portuguesa State, El Silbón is a bad young man who killed his father with a machete, was damned for this vile act by his mother, and now roams the Llanos at night looking for new victims. Tall and lanky, his knees are said to reach above his head when he squats down and he carries a bag over his back with the bones of his father that clack together as he walks. Called the whistler, he announces his presence with a 'doh-reh-mi-fa-so' whistle that is heard close by when he is far away and gets more distant sounding as he approaches. Some say that the young man was a drunkard, a womaniser and wife beater who now seeks the company of others who do the same so he can 'correct' their actions with his razor sharp machete. Given the presence of so many birds in the Llanos, there are plenty of eerie whistles in the night to unsettle the superstitious. Every year, the Festival Internacional de Música Llanera 'El Silbón' is held in Guanare, Estado Portuguesa in October and brings together singers, musicians and dancers from the Venezuelan and Colombian Llanos to compete for prizes.

LA SAYONA La Sayona is a beautiful woman called Melissa who lived in the Llanos with her husband and child. Every day she would go to the river to bathe unaware that a neighbouring rancher who was smitten by her charms would secretly watch her. One

Hotel Bristol (69 rooms) Av 23 de Enero; ☎ 0273 532 1425, 0273 532 5213; e hotelbristol@cantv.net. The closest option to the centre, this 3-star hotel has a swimming pool, restaurant, *tasca* & convention hall. $$

Hotel Comercio (94 rooms) Av Marqués del Pumar at Calle 16; ☎ 0273 532 0782. Halfway between Plaza Bolívar & the airport. $$

Hotel Turístico Varyná (43 rooms) Av 23 de Enero; ☎ 0273 533 2477, 0273 533 5094. This motel-style complex has inexpensive rooms close to the airport. $$

Hotel Internacional (53 rooms) Calle 4-Arzobispo Méndez, Plaza Zamora; ☎ 0273 552 1749, 0273 552 2343. Built by dictator Marcos Pérez Jiménez over 50 years ago, this veteran hotel is located by the Santo Domingo River & is good for the price. $

Hotel Residencias El Marqués (50 rooms) Av 6-Méndez Jiménez at Calle Bolívar; ☎ 0273 552 6576. A good budget option close to Plaza Bolívar. $

See also *Rafting and adventure sports* on page 250 for lodges that offer accommodation as part of an activity package.

Shopping Barinas now has three new modern shopping malls on Avenida 23 de Enero, which have all the usual shops, fast-food outlets and internet and phone centres. When it comes to local culture, nothing beats the lively strains of *joropo* and music CDs and DVDs sold on the street for less than US$1 make great souvenirs. For those who fancy making their own sweet music, instruments are on sale at a number of stores and workshops around Calle 7 Cedeño.

day, desperate to get his hands on her, the neighbour convinced Melissa with lies and coincidences that her husband was having an affair with her own mother. Angry and vengeful she returned home, set fire to the house killing her husband and child and then dispatched her mother with a machete. On learning that the neighbour's words were false Melissa was overcome with grief and remorse but before dying her mother cursed her to forever wander the Llanos, entrancing unfaithful men with her beauty before turning into a ghoulish spectre and devouring them. Her name comes from the long tunic or *sayo* that she is said to wear. Over the years the legend has evolved and la Sayona is sometimes represented as a vampire-type figure.

EL CHIGÜIRE FANTASMAL This is a giant capybara that roams the dark Llanos nights emitting terrifying grunts and trampling underfoot unsuspecting cowboys who've drunk too much firewater at local fiestas. Told in a popular song from Cojedes, the story goes that a brave but seriously sozzled Llanero horseman was coming home from a dance when he heard the strange grunts of the giant rodent. Unfazed by the fearful racket he managed to lasso the dark shadow as it loomed towards him, spooking it to rush off and drag him and his horse behind it. Falling asleep in the saddle he awoke with the dawn to find himself hundreds of miles from home in Valencia and the giant rodent nowhere to be found. Well, that's what he told his wife.

FLORENTINO AND THE DEVIL This is a very popular Llanero legend about a cowboy known for his inventive and witty songs who meets El Diablo on a lonely stretch of road one night. The devil has heard of Florentino's ability to improvise *coplas*, or verses to *joropo* songs, and challenges him to a singing contest. Luckily, the hero wins the contest and the devil is vanquished. The story was immortalised in a poem by the Barinas poet Alberto Arvelo Torrealba and later made famous as a song recorded by Romero Bello, who sang the role of Florentino, and a Llanero legend in his own right El Carrao de Palmarito, who sung the devil's part.

Other practicalities There is a Banco de Venezuela on Avenida Marquéz del Pumar with Calle Plaza and other banks can be found in the shopping malls on Avenida 23 de Enero.

There is a Movistar call centre with internet and international calls on Avenida Márquez del Puma, between Avenida Cruz Paredes and Calle Camejo.

What to see and do In the historic centre you will find the imposing **Palacio del Marqués** on Plaza Bolívar, home to José Ignacio del Pumar, the grandson of a Spaniard who settled in Barinas in the late 1600s and was named Marquis of Boconó and Masparro by the Spanish king in 1787. A hugely wealthy planter and rancher, Pumar was variously mayor, judge and royal ensign in the colonial administration. However, he later gave his fortune to the patriot cause in which three of his sons fought with Bolívar. In 1814 royalist forces burned the house and took Pumar, aged 76, prisoner. He died in Guanare's prison the same year.

The **Casa de la Cultura**, also on Plaza Bolívar, was the town hall in the Marquis's day and had a jail from which patriot leader José Antonio Páez once escaped. The cultural centre presents exhibitions, recitals and concerts. The austere **cathedral**, built in 1760–80 is dedicated to Our Lady of Pilar, the patron saint of Barinas.

A spanking new **Palacio de Gobierno** abuts Plaza Bolívar on Avenida Marqués del Pumar at Calle 4. From this corner walk 1½ blocks north on Calle 4 to the **Museo San Francisco de Asis**; its collection of 30,000 eclectic pieces covers religious, historical and folk items from Barinas.

The **Jardín Botánico**'s (*Unellez, Av 23 de Enero;* \ *0273 546 4555;* e *jardinbotanico@unellez.edu.ve;* ☉ *08.00–15.00 weekdays*) collection of trees, landscaped grounds, plant nursery and small zoo of native animals is worth a visit and makes a pleasant outing. It's part of the spacious grounds of the Universidad Nacional Experimental de Los Llanos Ezequiel Zamora (Unellez).

Rafting and adventure sports Since the Mérida adventure companies started offering white-water rafting trips on the Acequias, Siniguis, Canagua and Santo Domingo rivers, a number of camps have sprung up offering level 2–5 rafting and kayaking during the May–November season, as well as canyoning, hiking, mountain biking and birding. Take a swimsuit, camera, flip-flops with straps or canvas shoes, hat, sunscreen, repellent, towel, change of clothes, top with long sleeves and long trousers for the evenings and a head torch or flashlight if you plan to stay overnight.

Campamento Aguas Bravas Río Acequias; m 0414 114 5818, 0416 726 0881; www.raftingbarinas.com. Run by Alejando Buzzo & his wife Fabiana in a fine camp by the Acequia River formerly owned by Guamanchi Tours. Alejandro is a champion rafter & kayaker whose father started the white-water craze in Venezuela in the 1980s when he operated rafting trips on the Atures rapids in Amazonas. Alejandro now operates May–Nov in Acequias & Dec–Apr on the Orinoco where he has another camp close to Puerto Ayacucho. 2-day packages for about US$150, include accommodation at the camp, meals, instruction, rafting or kayaking. Optional trips to petroglyphs in Bum Bum recommended.

Campamento Arrasari Trek La Acequia, Cano Grande; \ 0274 252 5879; m 0414 746 3569; e info@ arassari.com, arassari1@hotmail.com; www.arassari.com. Another Mérida-based adventure company & a pioneer of rafting on the Acequias runs this large camp with cabins, dorms, hammocks, restaurant & rafting, tubing, kayaking, mountain biking, hiking & birding. Their 3-day–3-river rafting package includes trips on the Acequias, Canagua & Siniguis rivers. They can also organise fishing for peacock bass (*pavon*) or piranhas in the Ticoporo forest reserve.

Campamento Grados Alta Aventura Altamira de Cáceres on the road from Barinas to Calderas; m 0416 877 4540, 0414 740 8512; e contacto@grados.com.ve; www.grados.com.ve. This very well-appointed river camp is run by Gregorio Montilla & Fabiola Berrio close to the picturesque mountain town of Altamira de Cáceres, where they have an office. Rafting trips to the Santo Domingo (level 3), Acequias (level 3) & Siniguis (levels 4 & 5) rivers are offered in 2-day/1-night packages for about US$130. They also offer kayaking, canyoning, mountain biking, hiking & fishing trips. A highlight of birding tours to the local forests is the brightly coloured Andean cock of the rock.

Campamento Guamanchi La Acequia, Via Cano Grande; \ 0274 252 2080; m 0426 673 6469; e info@ guamanchi.com; www.guamanchi.com. One of the biggest adventure sport operators in Mérida, Guamanchi don't disappoint at their large camp on the Siniguis, which has a climbing wall & offers level 3–5 rafting, kayaking, canyoning, canopy climbing, mountain biking, horseriding & birding.

GUANARE *Telephone code: 0257*

To visit the spiritual capital of Venezuela, travellers should to go Guanare, a quiet, provincial city of 235,000 souls and the capital of Portuguesa State. Founded in 1591 with the name 'City of the Holy Spirit of the Valley of St John of the Guanaguanare River', it would be unremarkable except for the miracle that is said to have taken place near here on 8 September 1652, when the Virgin Mary appeared to an Indian chief, Cacique Coromoto, causing him to convert to Christianity (see box below). Now, every September millions of Catholics come from all over the country to observe the day of the **Virgen de Coromoto**, who was canonised as the patron saint of Venezuela by Pope Pius XII in 1944.

DIVINE INTERVENTION BRINGS INDIAN CHIEF TO CATHOLIC FAITH

The story of the apparition of the Virgin Mary to an Indian chief in Guanare has been likened to the story of the Guadelupe Virgin in Mexico. It has also been interpreted as an allegory of the victory of Catholicism over the Cospes Indians, who resisted the Spanish conquest for more than 100 years. The legend says that in early 1652, the fiercely independent Cacique Coromoto of the Cospes Indians was crossing a stream with his wife Isabel when they saw a radiant lady with an infant in her arms walking over the stream towards them. She urged Coromoto in his own tongue to go to the white men and be baptised with water so he could go to heaven. The chief told his story to a settler named Juan Sánchez who gave his permission for the tribe to move to his plantation on the Guanaguanare River. All the tribe members were baptised except Coromoto, who refused.

After a few months of toiling away on Sánchez's plantation and receiving religious teaching, on 8 September 1652, Coromoto decided he had had enough of working for the Spanish. Angry, and yearning for his old life in the forest, where he answered to no-one, he went back to his village. That evening, his wife Isabel was making supper and Coromoto was resting in his hammock when the Virgin appeared to them again – as dazzling as the sun, reported Isabel. The chief picked up his bow and arrow and pointed them at the Virgin as a warning to come no further, but she entered the hut anyway. Dropping his bow he went to throw her out, when suddenly the light and the Virgin vanished. The chief's fist burned like fire and, as he opened his hand, rays of light shone from a small scrap of papyrus; on it was a painted image of the beautiful lady. Terrified, he threw it down and ran off into the night while his son went to fetch Sánchez.

The next day, while running through the forest, Coromoto was bitten by a snake. When by another miracle a Christian from Barinas happened upon him, the chief asked to be baptised. This done, he died with a final wish that all his people should be baptised, become Catholics and worship the Virgin Mary, who ever since, in this incarnation, has been called the Virgin of Coromoto.

10

GETTING THERE The Terminal de Pasajeros is about 2km out of town, following Calle 8/Avenida Unda via Guanarito. Buses go regularly to the Santuario Nacional de la Virgen de Coromoto (12km, 15 minutes) from Carrera 9, Calle 20 in Guanare.

If driving, you can reach Guanare by the Route 5 highway from Barinas.

TOURIST INFORMATION

Corporacion de Turismo de Portuguesa (Corpotur) Av Industrial, opposite Institute Nacional de

Deporte; 📞 0257 253 3194; 🕐 08.00–12.00 & 13.00–16.00 Mon–Fri

WHERE TO STAY

Reservations are needed during Carnival as Guanare celebrates this in a big way, and also during the first week of September at the time of the pilgrimages to the Virgen de Coromoto. Although most hotels only have cold water, it is so hot in Guanare that it is not a problem.

Hotel Italia (48 rooms) 19–20 Carrera 5; 📞 0257 253 1213, 0257 251 4277. Budget option with restaurant & bar, rooms with hot water. 💲

La Góndola (42 rooms) 2–80 Calle 3; 📞 0257 253 1480, 0257 251 2802, 0257 251 5445. A decent option with a good restaurant, this fills up quickly so reserve if possible. 💲

Posada del Cabrestero (15 rooms) Av Principal, Barrio San José; 📞 0257 253 0102; e posadadelcabrestero@hotmail.com. Located in the grounds of the Museo del Llano, west of town, this B&B *posada* is a typically Llanero house but the spacious rooms have individual patios with garden &

hammock, plus fridge, rather fierce AC, nice bathroom, cold water. 💲

Posada del Reo (30 rooms) Calle 16 at Carrera 3; 📞 0257 808 0373, 0257 808 9193. A restored 18th-century building that once housed the jail was transformed with labour, love & vision into a hotel with a small shopping centre in front. After closing for a while it has reopened with new management, who aren't as fussy on the details, but it is still the best option in town. The rooms – each with cell number – are arranged around a central patio; dbl rooms with AC, private bath, cold water, restaurant. 💲

FESTIVALS

Apart from the 8 September celebrations in honour of the Virgen de Coromoto, Guanare is also an important cultural centre, keeping alive the music, song and dance of the Llanos in its annual **Festival Internacional de Música Llanera El Silbón** held at the end of October. Over 350 artists from Venezuela and Colombia take part in the festival, which is named after the spooky whistler, 'El Silbón', who roams the Llanos at night (see box on page 248).

The popular Carnival celebrations here, known as **La Mascarada**, include street processions, fancy dress and even groups playing Brazilian samba.

OTHER PRACTICALITIES

There are several banks on Carrera 6, including a Banco de Venezuela on the corner of Calle 15 and a Banesco on the corner of Calle 16.

There is a CANTV call centre on Carrera 6, between Calle 16 and Calle 15 and a Movistar call centre on Carrera 5, between Calle 10 and Calle 11.

A health clinic, the Centro Medico Portuguesa, can be found on Carretera 4.

WHAT TO SEE AND DO

Most people come here to visit the basilica of the Virgin of Coromoto in Guanare and travel 12km out of town to the huge concrete sanctuary built on the site where the Virgin Mary appeared to the Indian chief Coromoto and where the miraculous image of her is kept.

Basilica de Nuestra Señora de Coromoto

Built in 1710–42, the basilica stands on Guanare's main Plaza Bolívar. Inside there is a gilt retable with the statue of the Virgin in the centre and the Christ Child on her lap. Scenes from Cacique Coromoto's conversion are painted under the dome. The famous painting of the

Virgen de Coromoto is in a massive gold and glass shrine on the right aisle. It contains a reliquary in the form of angels above a tree, the Arch of Carabobo and a hut, inside which the 350-year-old piece of bark was kept until it was moved to the sanctuary in 1999. You will also see thousands of gold and silver offerings given to the Virgin in return for favours granted.

The **Plaza Coromoto**, seven blocks east of Plaza Bolívar, has a monument to the Virgin and a group of marble statues of the Virgin appearing before Cacique Coromoto and Isabel.

Santuario Nacional de la Virgen de Coromoto (08.00–17.00; *masses held at 08.00, 11.00, 14.30 Sat–Sun*) This immense concrete structure is built on the exact spot that the Virgin Mary appeared to Cacique Coromoto, known as La Aparición, 12km from Guanare. Designed by Venezuelan architect Erasmo Calvani, and astonishingly out of place in this rural setting, it rises out of the ground like a nuclear bunker, with two tall towers of 68m and 76m reaching up into the sky, like two unfinished ladders to heaven. Like many modernistic churches designed in the 1970s, the severity of the concrete is softened by the brightly coloured stained-glass windows by local artist Guillermo Marquez, which reflect shimmering light into the vast interior, which has seating for 2,500. Building of the sanctuary, also known as El Templo Votivo, began in 1980 but it was officially opened in 1996, after being blessed by Pope John Paul II. On 8 September, thousands of pilgrims flock here to file past the reliquary and see the tiny image of the Virgin Mary.

Guanare's historic centre Some 18th-century buildings have been handsomely restored in Guanare's colonial district. On Plaza Bolívar the former Spanish jail now houses a little shopping centre and the Posada del Reo. The Ateneo, where music and folklore classes are held occupies an 18th-century house on Calle 14 between Carreras 3 and 4. The Museo de Guanare exhibits some pre-Columbian pottery, early photographs of Guanare and the safe of the Royal Tobacco monopoly. The Casacoima on Carrera 3 at Calle 16 also dates from the 1700s when it was headquarters of the Royal Tobacco monopoly.

Museo de Los Llanos (08.00–17.30 *Tue–Sun; admission free*) Located southwest of Guanare past the stadium, this fine new complex is part of the Parque Ferial José Antonio Páez. The idea of Edgar Cadet, restorer of the old Guanare jail, was to recreate a typical Llanos *pueblo* in order to display all its customs, from games, folklore and cooking through literary research. A big permanent exhibition is devoted to local archaeological finds. There is a ranch house with guest accommodations, **Posada del Cabrestero** (see *Where to stay*, opposite).

Bolívar State

THE GRAN SABANA, *TEPUIS* AND ANGEL FALLS

South of the Orinoco, extending east to the Republic of Guyana and all the way down to the border with Brazil is a vast area of forests, savannas, rivers and uplands known as La Guayana, or the 'Guiana Shield'. It covers nearly half of Venezuela and encompasses parts of the Delta Amacuro and Bolívar and Amazonas states. It does not appear on maps, except in the name of Ciudad Guayana, the largest city in Bolívar State, divided into two distinct parts, Puerto Ordaz and San Félix.

The cities of Ciudad Bolívar and Ciudad Guayana are the gateways to this fabulous region of piranha-filled jungle rivers in the Delta Amacuro, intriguing Indian villages on the Río Caura, and mysterious table-mountain *tepuis* of the Gran Sabana. It is from the vast, craggy plateau of Auyantepui, the largest of these sheer-walled mountains, that the highest waterfall in the world is born. Reached only by dugout canoes to remote jungle camps at its base, Angel Falls is 19 times higher than Niagara Falls, cascading 979m into the record books. The ancient rainswept uplands of the Guiana Shield contain some of the oldest rocks on earth and offer unique ecosystems to explore. The tallest of the *tepuis*, Mount Roraima, presents hikers with the unique experience of discovering the strange wonders that fired the imagination of the makers of the recent Pixar–Disney cartoon *Up*. A hundred years ago, these same giant mesas inspired the creator of Sherlock Holmes, Arthur Conan Doyle, to write his *Boy's Own* fantasy tale of derring-do and dinosaurs, *The Lost World*. Conan Doyle was fascinated by naturalists' reports of the walled mountains that defied ascent. When Roraima was finally climbed in 1884, he attended a packed meeting of the Royal Geographical Society in London to hear firsthand about this mountain plateau with its unique ecosystem. The *tepuis* are just as fascinating today, and regular tours from Santa Elena take hundreds of people to the top of Roraima every year.

Tales of fabulous golden cities first drew the Spanish conquistadors to Guayana, followed in 1595 by the English gentleman pirate Sir Walter Raleigh. They searched in vain for El Dorado and the lost city of Manoa. Then at last in the 19th century gold was struck in a big way in El Callao and in 1886 Venezuela became the world's largest producer. Today gold fever runs hot again as estimates put recoverable gold as high as 11,000 metric tons or 10% of known world reserves. Local and foreign companies explore concessions in a few places, but it is the thousands of small prospectors and illegal wildcat miners who scour and pit the forest, sluicing soil and mercury into rivers. Many are illegal Brazilian miners known as *garimpeiros*. Diamonds, too, are sought by miners who painstakingly wash sediments with sieves called *surrucas*, producing most of Venezuela's 300,000 carats a year.

CIUDAD BOLÍVAR *Telephone code: 0285*

Historically important as the Orinoco's major port and capital of Bolívar State, Ciudad Bolívar is a hot, colourful, and easy-going city, which is home to some

The river that rules Venezuela's vast interior breaks no records for length at 2,200km (number three in South America). It is, however, judged to be the world's third largest in volume of water – after the Amazon and Congo rivers – discharging an average of 36,000 cubic metres of water per second into the Atlantic through its huge delta.

Geologists date the early formation of the Amazon–Orinoco system to the first uprising of the Andes. This caused a long north–south trough to form between the Andes and two great stable slabs of continental crust, the Guiana and Brazilian shields, once part of the Gondwana supercontinent. In this trough the granddaddy of the Amazon–Orinoco rivers flowed north towards the Caribbean. By 15 million years ago, the fishes of this great river were similar to today, including the goliath catfish, electric eels, piranhas, arapaima and morocoto. Some ten million years ago the eastern Andes rose, creating (and separating) the Magdalena basin and later Lake Maracaibo. This uplift eventually blocked the river's outlet to the sea (near present-day Coro) and about eight million years ago the Orinoco and Amazon split into two rivers; each changed course from south–north to west–east towards the Atlantic. Perhaps as a souvenir of its geological past, the Orinoco sends a portion of its water to the Amazon via the Casiquiare, a unique river linking two great systems.

Today the Orinoco drains a basin of nearly a million square kilometres, a quarter of which is in Colombia. Into it flow over 30 large rivers and 2,000 lesser tributaries in Venezuela, making up 90% of the country's water resources. The Caroní alone provides two-thirds of the country's electricity. The Orinoco basin also contains vast mineral wealth: iron, bauxite, gold, and oil, as well as bitumen for Orimulsion.

While the Caroní's cataracts are deterrents, the 60km-long Atures and Maipures rapids on the Orinoco effectively block the passage south of all river craft. Spain's royal Expedición de Límites spent years in preparations before finally reaching the Río Negro (Brazil) by way of the Casiquiare in 1761. It was not until 1951 that a Franco–Venezuelan expedition pinpointed the Orinoco's source at 1,047m altitude in the Sierra de Parima near the Brazilian border.

400,000 people. It has a beautifully restored colonial centre on Plaza Bolívar and good *posadas* for overnight stays. In centuries past, it was a port-of-call for traders, gold seekers, missionaries and travellers to Indian domains. It's still like that, but now with tourists bound for Angel Falls, *Lost World* trekkers to Mount Roraima and those seeking cheap jungle trips to the Delta Orinoco and Río Caura. The airport has flights to Canaima, the starting point for all Angel Falls trips, and local tour operators and agencies can arrange good-value packages of three days/two nights in the rainy season from May to December – as well as circuits of the country taking in Mérida, Los Llanos and Los Roques.

The old town is on a hill overlooking the mighty Orinoco, and the massive boulders that squeeze the river into 'narrows' (*angosturas*). The river is only 1.6km (1 mile) wide at Ciudad Bolívar; downstream by Ciudad Guayana it spreads to 5km. During the August floods, the Orinoco rises as much as 15m to lap at the wall of the riverside promenade, known as El Paseo. But in April beaches appear and in midstream the Piedra del Medio is used to measure the water's descent. Diamond and gold buyers operate here and you can browse their wares at the jewellery shops in the passageways near the Hotel Colonial through to Calle Venezuela.

Ships used to sail up the Orinoco, 450km from the Atlantic, with oil, wheat and wine from Spain. Later came the wood-burning paddle steamers. Dealers once bought tonka beans, copaiba oil, rubber and chicle (gum) from southern

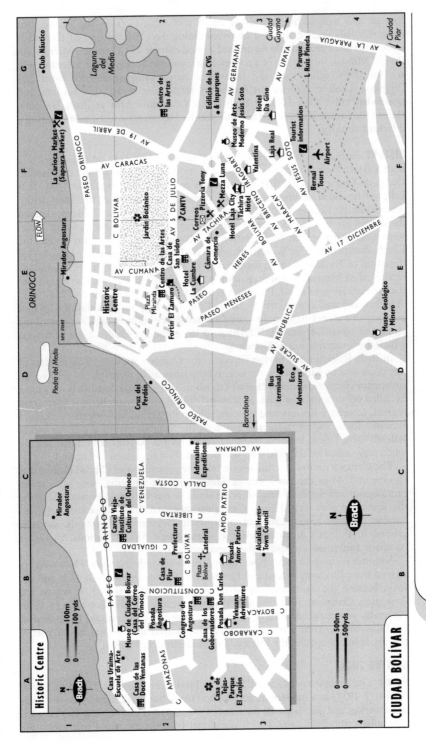

CIUDAD BOLÍVAR

Historic Centre

ORINOCO

- Mirador Angostura
- Casa Uraima-Escuela de Arte
- Casa de las Doce Ventanas
- Casa de Tejas-Parque El Zanjón
- Museo de Ciudad Bolívar (Casa del Correo del Orinoco)
- Posada Angostura
- Congreso de Angostura
- Casa de los Gobernadores
- Yekuana Adventures
- Cárcel Vieja-Instituto de Cultura del Orinoco
- Casa de Piar
- Prefectura
- Catedral
- Plaza Bolívar
- Posada Don Carlos
- Posada Amor Patrio
- Alcaldía Heres-Town Council
- Adrenaline Expeditions

C AMAZONAS
PASEO
C IGUALDAD
C BOLÍVAR
C CONSTITUCIÓN
C BOYACÁ
C CARABOBO
C VENEZUELA
C LIBERTAD
AMOR PATRIO
DALLA COSTA
AV CUMANÁ

0   100m
0   100 yds
0   500m
0   500 yds

N

Brdct

ORINOCO

FLOW

- Club Náutico
- Laguna del Medio
- Centro de las Artes
- La Carioca Market (Sapoara Market)
- Mirador Angostura
- Piedra del Medio
- Cruz del Perdón
- Historic Centre (see inset)
- Plaza Miranda
- Fortín El Zamuro
- Centro de las Artes
- Casa de San Isidro
- Hotel La Cumbre
- Jardín Botánico
- Edificio de la CVG & Inparques
- Museo de Arte Moderno Jesús Soto
- Hotel Da Gino
- Correos
- Pizzería Tony
- Mesza Luna
- CANTV
- Cámara de Comercio
- Hotel Laja City
- Valentina
- Laja Real
- Tourist information
- Airport
- Bernal Tours
- Parque L. Ruiz Pineda
- Bus terminal
- Eco Adventures
- Museo Geológico y Minero

PASEO ORINOCO
AV 19 DE ABRIL
AV CARACAS
C BOLÍVAR
AV CUMANÁ
AV 5 DE JULIO
PASEO
PASEO MENESES
AV TÁCHIRA
HERES
AV BARCENA
BOLÍVAR
TÁCHIRA
AV MARACAY
AV GERMANIA
AV UPATA
AV JESÚS SOTO
AV REPÚBLICA
AV SUCRE
AV 17 DICIEMBRE
AV LA PARAGUA

Barcelona
Ciudad Guyana
Ciudad Piar

N

Brdct

forests; and mules, hides, indigo, cacao and tobacco from the plains. But modern roads spelled the end of river-trading days. By the end of the 1950s trade with San Fernando de Apure had ceased completely. From the Mirador on Paseo Orinoco, former site of a colonial fort, you can look over the river but will see no ships, other than the occasional barge bringing bauxite from Los Pijiguaos. Look west to see the Angostura suspension bridge, 1,678m long and somewhat taller than Ciudad Bolívar itself (altitude 54m at Plaza Bolívar). Before the bridge was opened in 1967 you had to cross by ferry, as if entering a different country.

HISTORY Early Spanish explorers, lured by tales of El Dorado on the shores of a mythical lake Parima, used the Orinoco as a convenient 'highway' into the interior. Diego de Ordaz was the first conquistador to explore the region in 1531. It is believed he sailed against the flow of annual floods as far as the Meta River. Antonio de Berrío, on his third expedition from Bogotá to the Orinoco, claimed the Caroní for Spain in 1591, then made the region's first settlement, Santo Tomé, some leagues downriver. While Berrío was planning another Orinoco voyage, the Elizabethan privateer Sir Walter Raleigh arrived in 1595 and took him prisoner on the island of Trinidad. Raleigh was fired up by Berrío's reports of a city of fabulous wealth called Manoa, hidden deep in the jungle. Unable to pass the Caroní because the cataracts were in flood, Raleigh was forced to return to England without gold or riches and was imprisoned by James I for upsetting Spain. It didn't stop him penning an instant bestseller, his part-fact, part-fancy book on the discovery of the empire of Guiana, featuring: 'a relation of the great and Golden Citie of Manoa which the Spanyards call El Dorado'.

In 1618, Raleigh made his last voyage to the Orinoco, undaunted by 13 years of imprisonment by King James. As soon as he was released, although not absolved of conspiracy charges and under threat of death should he attack Spanish possessions, he sailed off to search for gold. Reaching Trinidad a sick man, he sent his trusted captain, Lawrence Keymis, and his own son up the Orinoco. They met resistance at Santo Tomé, and in taking the fort both the Spanish governor and the young Raleigh were killed. It was a tragic fiasco all round. Keymis committed suicide when reproached by Raleigh, who was beheaded on his return to England.

The Orinoco narrows are the reason why the present site of Ciudad Bolívar was chosen in 1764 as the last home of Santo Tomé de Guayana, built on a rocky prominence and renamed Angostura for short. It was known in Europe mainly as the source of a medicinal bark, *Cortex angosturae*, used by Capuchin monks to combat constant fevers. Later, an enterprising German serving as the surgeon general in Bolívar's army created the secret recipe for the famous Angostura Aromatic Bitters used to spice up gin and cocktails.

Angostura was a strategic base during the Independence wars. Here soldiers arrived from England, Ireland and Germany to fight with Simón Bolívar and the town became the alternative capital of Venezuela from 1817–21. It was at the Angostura Congress, held in 1819, that the creation of the Republic of Gran Colombia was declared, uniting Venezuela, Colombia and Ecuador. In honour of the Liberator, Angostura was renamed Ciudad Bolívar in 1846 and the old part of the city is still steeped in the history of the Independence period.

GETTING THERE

By air The Aeropuerto Nacional Tomas de Heres (*Av Jesus Soto;* \ *0285 632 4803, 0285 632 4978*) is a modern airport with a snack bar, travel agency booths, car-rental offices and gift shops. At the front of the airport is Jimmie Angel's Flamingo monoplane, the *Río Caroní*, which put Angel Falls on the world map when the

American bush pilot and prospector got his wheels stuck in a bog while landing on Auyantepui in 1937 (see box, page 269). The air force later lifted it off in parts and reassembled it in Maracay, before bringing it here.

The airport used to be buzzing with activity when the regular DC3 service from Caracas and regular flights from other Venezuelan cities brought tourists on their way to Canaima and Angel Falls. Incredibly, given the tourism potential of the falls, the only airline flying to Ciudad Bolívar from Caracas currently is Rutaca (\ 0285 632 4465; www.rutaca.com.ve), which has a daily flight, except Saturdays, arriving at 20.15. This means a night in Ciudad Bolívar for anybody wanting to fly on to Canaima.

There are currently no scheduled flights to Canaima but a couple of aerotaxi firms fly there in light aircraft (1 hour, US$160 return) every morning (06.00–09.00). The main company is Transmandu (\ 0285 632 1462; e info@ transmandu.com; www.transmandu.com), which flies five-seat Cessnas. If you want a flyover of the falls there is a surcharge of about US$35. The best option from Margarita is Aereotuy (www.tuy.com) who offer package tours including flights.

Travellers need to produce a passport or cédula for all flights and there is a strictly enforced 10kg weight allowance for luggage plus a small carry-on bag. If you book your flight or tour through Bernal Tours (www.bernaltours.com) at the airport they provide a safe deposit for luggage.

Airtaxis also offer flights to Puerto Ordaz, the mining centre of La Paragua, the Pemón villages Kamarata and Wonquén, and Santa Elena de Uairén (2½ hours, about US$150 one way) on the border with Brazil.

By bus The Terminal de Pasajeros [257 D3] is on Avenida República at Avenida Sucre, about 1.5km west of the airport and 2km from the Paseo Orinoco. There are frequent buses to Caracas (590km, 11 hours, US$15) and Santa Elena (760km, 12 hours, US$13). Long-distance express buses and *buscama* (literally 'bed bus', with reclining seats and more leg room) have the air conditioning set to Arctic and will be uncomfortably cold if you don't take a fleece, blanket or sleeping bag on board with you. You get the idea when you see Venezuelan families lining up in the blistering heat with woolly hats and duvets. There is a large internet centre in the bus station (1 hour, US$1).

By car Ciudad Bolívar is reached by the Route 16 highway from Puerto la Cruz via El Tigre and on Route 19 from Upata, where the road joins the Route 10 highway to the Gran Sabana.

TOURIST INFORMATION Information on local sights and maps of the historic centre can be found at **Corporacion de Turismo** [257 B2] (*Paseo Orinico, between Calle Constitucion, Calle Igualdad; www.turismoBolívar.gob.ve;* ⊕ *08.00–12.00 & 14.00–17.00*). There is also a booth at the airport.

Inparques [257 G3] (*7 Calle Vargas, Santisima Trinidad;* \0285 632 9908) provide camping permits for the Gran Sabana. No permits are needed for Canaima (BsF35 fee paid on arrival in Canaima airstrip) or Roraima.

☞ *WARNING:* While it is safe to explore the historic centre during the day, taking usual precautions against wearing watches, jewellery or flashing around expensive cameras, it is not advisable to walk around the old city or the Paseo Orinoco after dark. The *barrio* west of the Casa de Doce Ventanas on Paseo Orinoco should not be visited even in daytime and caution should be exercised on Avenida 5 de Mayo and the Jardin Botanico around the neighbourhood of Mango Asado.

TOUR OPERATORS Tours to Angel Falls, Río Caura and the Delta Amacuro are easy to arrange in Ciudad Bolívar and generally more reasonably priced than if arranged elsewhere. Ask around to get the best deal and try and get a group of four or more together. Roraima treks are best organised in Santa Elena.

Adrenaline Expeditions [257 C2] Bd Calle Igualdad, Calle Bolívar; \ 0285 632 4804; m 0414 886 7209; e adrenalinexptours@hotmail.com; www.adrenalinexpeditions.com. English-speaking Ricardo can arrange trips to Angel Falls, Delta Amacuro, Gran Sabana. Good maps, information, friendly.

Bernal Tours [257 F4] Aeropuerto Nacional Tomas de Heres; \ 0285 632 6890; m 0414 893 4905, 0414 854 8234; e bernaltours@terra.com.ve; www.bernaltours.com. Tomas Bernal was a Peruvian Indian who lived in Canaima camp, near Salto Sapo & pioneered the trail behind the falls before setting up his own camp on Isla Anatoly. His family now run the firm, formerly Sapito Tours, & offer some of the best-value deals to Angel Falls by boat on 3-day/2-night excursions (but always shop around for prices). If you arrive at the airport before 07.30 there's every chance they can get you on a flight to Canaima. They also sell plane tickets to other destinations & can help change cash.

Eco Adventures [257 D3] Office 33, bus terminal; \ 0285 651 9546; m 0414 851 3656, 0414 871 7188; e ecoadventuresbess@hotmail.com; www.adventurevenezuela.com. Leyland Bess runs this small outfit at the bus station, which offers cheaper Angel Falls trips via the airport of La Paragua, 30mins by road from Ciudad Bolívar. His groups stay at Churun Vena camp.

Gekko Tours Posada La Casita; \ 0285 617 0832; m 0414 854 5146, 0414 856 2925; www.gekkotours-venezuela.de. Run by Peter Rothfuss, who has his own light aircraft & can arrange flights to Canaima, Kavak & other destinations in the Gran

Sabana. Also organises circuits of the country to Mérida, Los Llanos, Los Roques, Roraima.

Jonas Tours Ciudad Bolívar; \ 0285 651 0918; m 0414 099 5904; e jonastours54@hotmail.com. The pioneer of Río Caura trips, Jonas Camejo is something of a legend in these parts. Guide 'Jungle' Junior speaks English & 5–6-day tours to Para Falls include visits to El Playon, & Sanema & Yekuana Indian villages. Good rates.

Turi Express Dorado Aeropuerto Nacional Tomas de Heres; \ 0285 632 7086, 0285 617 0166; www.turiexpressdorado.com.ve. Based at the airport, they do city tours, jeep tours of the Gran Sabana, Delta Orinoco & can book Canaima camps, arrange flights.

Vivatrek www.vivatrek.com. Run by British tour leader Doug Pridham, organise trips to the Río Paragua, a huge tributary of the Caroní River feeding Guri Lake, which has many small gold & diamond mines. A 4-day expedition, negotiating the rapids in a motorised *curiara*, takes you to the remote Ichún Falls, a dramatic cascade of white foam & deep black water. On the way you fish at Uraima rapids, visit diamond camps, & sling your hammock on sandy banks.

Yekuana Adventures [257 B3] Posada Don Carlos; m 0424 901 7710, 0412 184 6458; e miguelestaba@gmail.com. Miguel Estaba, whose Yekuana Indian name is Dichenedu, organises boat trips to the Río Caura & a circuit of the Nichare, Icutu & Tabaro rivers, staying in indigenous villages & sleeping in hammocks. Miguel is very passionate about the Yekuana culture & keeping the pristine forests of the Río Caura free from illegal mining.

WHERE TO STAY There are plenty of lodging options close to the airport, which is handy for eating out in restaurants on Avenida Tachira and catching morning flights to Canaima. Around Plaza Bolívar and the historic centre there are several good budget options but shops and restaurants shut after 18.00.

Hotel La Cumbre [257 E2] (24 rooms) Av 5 de Julio; \ 0285 632 7709; e lacumbre@cantv.net; www.hotellacumbre.com.ve. Panoramic views from this hotel between the airport & the old town on Cerro La Esperanza near the Casa San Isidro. Rooms with AC, hot water, views of Orinoco. Swimming pool, restaurant. $$$

Hotel Laja City [257 F3] (37 rooms) Av Bolívar near Av Táchira; \ 0285 632 9920. Owned by the Laja Real & only a couple of blocks away. Rooms with refrigerator & hot water. Restaurant, piano bar. Guests may use all services of the Laja Real including swimming pool. $$

Laja Real [257 F3] (73 rooms) Av Jesús Soto; \ 0285 632 7944, 0285 617 0100;

www.lajareal.com. Directly opposite the airport, modern motel-style lodging with swimming pool (open to non-guests for a fee), snack bar & decent restaurant, disco, shops, car rental, travel agency & money exchange. Close to restaurants on Av Táchira. Good value for great location. $$

🏠 **Posada Angostura** [257 B2] (7 rooms) 8 Calle Boyacá; m 0414 851 2295; e salesccs@cacaotravel.com; www.cacaotravel.com. A beautifully restored 2-storey colonial house around a patio in the old town run by Cacao Travel. An upper-level terrace looks over the Orinoco to the bridge. Rooms with AC, hot water, private bath. $$

🏠 **Valentina** [257 F3] (15 rooms) ☎ 0285 632 2145, 0285 632 7253. Another clean, modern option close to the airport with TV, AC, hot water. Il Vesubio restaurant next door serves good Italian fare. $$

🏠 **Hotel Da Gino** [257 G3] Av Jesús Soto; ☎ 0285 632 0313. Only a block from the airport. Rooms with hot water, AC, TV. Italian restaurant. $

🏠 **Hotel Táchira** [257 F3] (18 rooms) Av Táchira; ☎ 0285 632 7489. Spacious old house with tasca, restaurant, newer rooms in a rear wing with parking; refrigerator in room. $

🏠 **Posada Don Carlos** [257 B3] (10 rooms) Calle Boyaca; ☎ 0285 632 6017; e soanatravel@gmx.de; www.hosteltrail.com/posadadoncarlos. Martin Haars & wife Yourlenis run this friendly budget posada in a restored colonial house a block from Plaza Bolívar with large central patio, shared kitchen, laundry, TV, internet, secure parking & an antique bar brought over from Germany. Can arrange Angel Falls trips, Roraima, & Río Caura with local indigenous guide Dichenedu Yekuana. $

🏠 **Posada La Casita** (7 rooms, 3 cabins, 10 hammocks) Av Ligia Pulido, Urb 24 de Julio; ☎ 0285 617 0832; m 0414 854 5146, 0414 856 2925; e info@posada-la-casita.com; www.posada-la-casita.com. This attractive camp 11km from the airport is run by Peter & Maria Rothfuss, who offer transfer from the airport/bus terminal in their own vehicle. Lodging in cabins with AC, en-suite, rooms with fan, hammocks for budget groups, Wi-Fi, internet, churuata for meals, small zoo with monkeys, swimming pool. Peter has his own planes for trips to Angel Falls at reasonable rates including flyover (www.gekkotours-venezuela.de). Good option for a rest between adventure trips. $

✖ WHERE TO EAT AND DRINK

Sapoara, eaten baked, fried or stewed, is a local fish eaten in August. Beware, there's an old saying that any man who eats a sapoara head will marry a local girl. Other good river fish are bocachica, curbinata and morocoto. *Palo a pique* is a dish of beans, rice and salted meat. Traditional *carne mechada* or shredded beef is called *trapo viejo* ('old rags'). Sample local dishes at the informal restaurants in the **Sapoara Market** [257 F1] (also called La Carioca) at the east end of the Paseo Orinoco. The market bustles from 06.00 to about 13.00 but the restaurants and food stalls stay open for lunch until 16.00. Try the *lau-lau*, a type of catfish cooked in garlic on the griddle, which is a local speciality.

Bolívar State is also famous for its cashews, called *merey*: a nut praline is called *mazapán de merey* and the red fleshy cashew fruit is stewed with sugar to make a sweet, jammy dessert called *merey pasado* or *mermelada de merey*.

☞ *WARNING:* If you pick red fruit from a cashew tree, never put the protruding nut near your mouth as the shell contains cardol and it will burn your skin.

✖ **Hotel La Cumbre** [257 E2] (see *Where to stay*) ⏱ 07.30–24.00. You can have b/fast, lunch & dinner by the pool at this hilltop hotel, which has some Pemón Indian dishes on the menu. The **Bambu Sushi Bar** (⏱ 19.00–23.00) serves local fish Japanese-style washed down with tropical fruit & Angostura bitter cocktails. What else? At w/ends they have live music & dancing around the pool. $$

✖ **Mezza Luna** [257 F3] Av Táchira, Av Bolívar; ⏱ 12.00–22.00. An Italian eatery with rooms around a central patio, with reasonable prices & standard pizzas, pastas, juices & ice creams. $

✖ **Pizzeria Tony** [257 F2] Av Táchira; ⏱ 12.00–22.30. A decent range of pizzas, pastas & main courses at this shiny diner on the main road for restaurants in town. $

FESTIVALS

August is fiesta month on the Paseo, celebrating first the city's patron saint, **Nuestra Señora de las Nieves** whose day is 5 August, then in the third week the **Feria del Orinoco** when everyone feasts on sapoara (or zapoara) fish, caught in circular nets called *atarrayas* cast from dugouts. Besides an agricultural fair, there are song sessions, food booths, arts, crafts, cultural and sports events held all over town.

OTHER PRACTICALITIES There is a Banco de Venezuela on Paseo Orinoco on the corner with Calle Piar.

There are several internet places on Paseo Orinoco and a large call centre and internet place with fast access at the main bus terminal.

Clinica San Pedro (\ *0285 632 1951, 0285 632 5895*) is on Avenida Mario Briceño Iragorri near the junction with Paseo Heres.

WHAT TO SEE AND DO Walking around Ciudad Bolívar is like a history lesson on the Independence wars, and the buildings in the colonial centre have been beautifully restored with help from the government of Spain.

Paseo Orinoco Shoppers jostle through arcades under balconied old buildings where vendors sell pirate CDs and DVDs, batteries and knick-knacks. In the shops looking out over the river there are small passages leading to kiosks selling gold nuggets and diamonds. Unfortunately, the road separates the riverbank promenade from the buildings but you can sip a juice at the **Mirador**, a round building where the promenade juts out into the river. The river itself is the big star. In August, the river is high and the sapoara fish migrate *en masse* to spawn in the floodlands. From the Paseo you can see fishermen out casting their circular *atarraya* nets.

Carcel Vieja [257 C2] (⊕ *09.00–17.30 Tue–Sun; admission free*) The reconstructed colonial jail faces the Paseo Orinoco; its entrance is on Calle Igualdad. Its dungeons have been transformed by the Instituto de Cultura del Orinoco into an excellent **Ethnographic Museum** which displays photographs and crafts of the region's Indian cultures: the Yekuana (Makiritare), Pemón, Kariña and Warao. Ciudad Bolívar is the seat of active indigenous movements and the state government was the first to appoint an Indian to head the Indian Affairs Bureau.

Casa del Correo del Orinoco [257 B2] (⊕ *09.00–17.30 Tue–Sun; admission charge*) This stately 18th-century residence two blocks west on the Paseo is named after a newspaper, which Bolívar created to boost the revolutionary cause – the *Orinoco Mail*, or *Correo del Orinoco*, published in Spanish, French and English (1818–30). Now the **Museo de Ciudad Bolívar**, it displays the original press and artefacts, as well as a large art collection.

La Casa de las Doce Ventanas [257 A2] Boats once moored at the steps of this restored landmark two blocks west on the Paseo Orinoco. The elegant 'House of Twelve Windows', anchored atop a huge rock called the Laja de Sapoara, was the home of a patriot ship captain, José Tomás Machado. His son married Cecilia Siegert, daughter of Dr J T B Siegert, the German doctor to the Liberation army who marketed his Angostura Bitters formula for years in Ciudad Bolívar. The house now belongs to the Universidad Nacional Experimental de Guayana and is open as a gallery; entrance is on the street behind, Calle Venezuela.

Parque El Zanjón [257 A3] To discover this surprising hillside park with its piles of boulders, climb the steps up Calle Carabobo to Calle Amor Patrio (coming from Plaza Bolívar) and turn west. Here the city vanishes into a maze of hot granite boulders, desert flowers and trees. A small art school functions in La Casa de Tejas. Visitors are welcome.

Plaza Bolívar [257 B2] Five statues in the square personify the countries that Bolívar liberated: Venezuela, Nueva Granada (modern-day Colombia and Panama), Ecuador, Peru and Bolivia. To the west stands the imposing pink structure of the **Congreso de Angostura** where Bolívar was elected President of the Third Republic and proposed the creation of Gran Colombia. Guides show visitors around the well-kept building dating from 1766. Once a school, today it houses exhibitions as well as some 450,000 folios of the Guayana Historical Archives. Beside it, the Government Palace, seat of the state government, is a colonial building where the royal treasury or Real Hacienda collected taxes for Spain; a second storey was added to the building in 1869.

Casa de los Gobernadores [257 B2] Another handsomely redone 18th-century mansion, it was once occupied by Spanish governors. On Plaza Bolívar's upper side, it now houses state offices. Next to it is the Parish House, also colonial.

Cathedral [257 B2] Resplendent in pale yellow, the cathedral was begun in 1771 and took 70 years to build. It is still at the heart of city life, particularly on 8 August, the feast day of Our Lady of the Snows. The cathedral wall facing the plaza is pointed out as the place where Manuel Piar, a young and popular general, faced a firing squad in 1817. Piar, who had taken the city from the Spaniards after an eight-month siege, rejected Bolívar's authority and was tried and executed. **Casa Piar**, the house where he was imprisoned on the lower side of Plaza Bolívar, is kept as a museum. Many locals consider him a greater Independence hero than Simón Bolívar.

Alcaldía de Heres [257 B3] Just up from the cathedral you can't miss the aerial walkway spanning Calle Igualdad. It joins the two buildings of the mayor's office, once the city hospital. Continue south three blocks to the **Biblioteca Rómulo Gallegos**. The restored house with its stone walls and wooden floors was formerly a governor's residence.

Plaza Miranda [257 E2] Two blocks west between Calles Progreso and Lezama, the Plaza Miranda is at the edge of the historic district. The large **Centro de las Artes** (⊕ *09.00–17.00 Tue–Sun; admission free*) occupies a building which was variously a theatre, army barracks, and police headquarters before its restoration. Drop in for an art show or ask permission to take a rooftop photo of the city panorama.

Fortín El Zamuro [257 E2] (⊕ *09.00–17.00 Tue–Sun; admission free*) For a vulture's eye view of the old town, climb to a hilltop crowned by a tiny colonial battery. The little fort was pivotal during a 1903 battle, when the city was taken by the forces of Juan Vicente Gómez who was to become dictator of Venezuela (1908–35). Look for the entrance on **Paseo Heres**. Bronze busts of members of the Congreso de Angostura adorn the park, with Francisco Zea and Simón Bolívar at the top.

Casa de San Isidro [257 E2] (⊕ *09.00–17.00 Tue–Sun; admission free*) While writing his speech for the 1819 Congress of Angostura, Bolívar stayed with a friend in what was then a coffee *hacienda*. The lovely house built on a huge boulder, the Laja de San Isidro, is on Avenida Táchira at 5 de Julio. With its tall ceilings, simple elegance, period furnishings and ample gardens it makes a nice stop for a picnic. Check out the small turtles in the pool near the entrance.

Museo de Arte Moderno Jesús Soto [257 F3] (*Av Briceño Iragorry at Av Germania;* ⊕ *09.30–17.00 Tue–Sun; admission free*) One of the great abstract artists of the 20th

11

century, local boy Jesús Rafael Soto (5 June 1923–14 January 2005) was a founder member and leading light of the Kinetic art movement. The museum has a good collection of his large 'penetrables', sculptures made of coloured strings of plastic you can walk through, and smaller shimmering cubes and other pieces that trick the eye. There are also works by masters such as Mondrian, Kandinsky, Albers and others. Soto's work was collected all over the world and continues to sell at international auctions. In 1995, he was awarded France's highest sculpture prize, the *Grand Prix National de l'Esculture*.

CIUDAD GUAYANA Telephone code: 0286

Ciudad Guayana is actually two separate towns linked by three bridges at the confluence of the Caroní and Orinoco rivers and the main Avenida Guayana. On the Caroní's left bank is the new town of **Puerto Ordaz**, founded in 1952 as an iron ore port; on the right bank is old **San Félix**, founded in 1576, and a workers' town. When they were joined in 1961 the population was 40,000; today it is 940,000. Ciudad Guayana is Venezuela's heavy industry centre, powered by the turbines of the massive Guri Dam, which produces 73% of all Venezuela's electricity. Outside San Félix's small downtown area, low-cost housing, mechanics shops and businesses spread untidily along broad highways. Rural migrants have thrown up shacks of zinc, cardboard, wood and plastic in over 100 unplanned and under-serviced *barrios* spreading south of the old *pueblo*. More modern and home to most of the hotels, Puerto Ordaz is effectively run by the Corporación Venezolana de Guayana (CVG), which has interests in everything from gold and hydropower, to parks and pine plantations. In fact, Puerto Ordaz is a company town. It has one of the highest cost-of-living indices in the country. Large malls in the centre have boutiques, electronic and sporting goods outlets and restaurants that reflect the tastes of a mostly middle-class population of whitecollar workers. There are supermarkets, nightclubs, good roads and services. But the planned city lacks something that gives most towns a heart and soul, and has little to offer tourists except a visit to the Parque Cachamay, Llovizna waterfall park and the CVG museum. Most buses arrive in San Félix; most accommodation options are in Puerto Ordaz. Be aware that bus and plane schedules always refer to Puerto Ordaz and San Félix separately, never as Ciudad Guayana.

GETTING THERE

By air Aeropuerto Internacional del Orinoco Manuel Piar (*Av Guayana, Matanzas;* \ *0286 951 3697*). There are a dozen flights on weekdays to Caracas by Avior (*www.avioairlines.com*), Aserca (*www.asercaairlines.com*), Conviasa (*www.conviasa.aero*), Laser (*www.laser.com.ve*) and Rutaca (*www.rutaca.com.ve*) and fewer on weekends. Other inter-city flights link Puerto Ordaz to Porlamar Barcelona, Maturín and Valencia.

Aereotuy (*www.tuy.com*) flies from Margarita to Puerto Ordaz and Canaima and there are also daily charter planes to Canaima. Puerto Ordaz is a better option for a return flight from Canaima, given the amount of onward flights available (something to bear in mind when planning your trip). The airport is 5km west of the city centre. There are *por puestos* to the centre along Avenida Guayana or Avenida Las Américas. Buses to Castillito will take you to the hotel district.

By bus In Puerto Ordaz a modern bus station on Avenida Guayana at Avenida Norte-Sur, a 20-minute walk east of the airport, handles some through buses for the main terminal in San Félix, but not all lines stop here. Service to Ciudad Bolívar is frequent (120km, 1½ hours).

In San Félix the Terminal de Pasajeros is on Avenida Gumilla, 1.5km from the old centre, with buses to Caracas throughout the day and evening (730km, 10–11 hours) Santa Elena de Uairén, Tucupita (305km), Maturín (285km), Carúpano and Güiria. *Por puestos* and city buses link the terminal with downtown San Félix and Puerto Ordaz, but only until 20.30.

By car Ciudad Guyana is on the main Route 10 highway between Gran Sabana and the coast.

By ferry Car and passenger ferries cross the Orinoco from San Félix to Los Barrancos every half hour or so during the day. Passengers travel free. There can be long lines to board, especially in the early morning. The new terminal is at the end of Avenida Manuel Piar, east of downtown San Félix.

TOURIST INFORMATION There is a tourism kiosk at Puerto Ordaz Airport (\ *0286 974 2667*), and another in San Félix facing the Orinoco at the bottom of Carrera 1 (closed weekends and lunch hours).

WHERE TO STAY
Puerto Ordaz

Intercontinental Guayana (193 rooms) Av Guayana, Parque Punta Vista; \ 0286 713 1000; www.ichotelsgroup.com. A good 5-star hotel set in splendid isolation by the Caroní Bridge, with its own entrance to Cachamay Park for guests who want to jog. Refurbished in 2007 it offers executive services, Wi-Fi, internet, bar, restaurants, spa, pool, tennis; river excursions leave from the hotel jetty. Guests may use the Club Naútico's golf links. The hotel recently opened the Fiesta Casino (⊕ 17.00–01.00). $$$$

Hotel Dos Rios (82 rooms) Av México, near Av Ecuador; \ 0286 922 0679, 0286 922 9188. With 1 tower of refurbished rooms & a cheaper, older tower, this hotel near the Brazilian consulate is popular with businessmen & has a pool & restaurant. $$

Posada Turistica Kaori (23 rooms) Quinta Kaori, No 73-1, Calle Argentina, Campo 'B' Ferrominera Orinoco; \ 0286 923 4038, 0286 923 2269; e kaoriposada@cantv.net; www.posadakaori.com. A reliable, simple option, plain white rooms with AC,

hot water, TV, small fridge, internet in lobby. Like many *posada* options in Puerto Ordaz, this is like a small house in a residential area. $$

Residencias Tore (52 rooms) Calle San Cristobal at Carrera Los Andes; \ 0286 923 0679, 0286 923 1780; e tore@cantv.net, residenciastore@hotmail.com. 2 houses on both sides of a residential street meet travellers' needs for a good value B&B. Airport pickup is provided by arrangement. The original Tore is on the west side of the street behind a wall with big metal doors. There is no sign. Rooms with AC, hot water, cable TV, phone, pleasant, open bar/restaurant for guests. Owners Salvatore & Miriam Gravante are both knowledgeable & interested in regional tourism. $$

Embajador (60 rooms) Av Principal de Castillito at the corner of Calle Urbana; \ 0286 922 5511. An 8-storey block with good restaurant, conference room & tour services. $

San Félix Bus travellers may find central lodgings useful for an early start. There are several hotels that no taxi driver at Puerto Ordaz Airport would know about. Most do duty as *hoteles de cita* (Love Hotels) renting rooms by the hour, and are overpriced by comparison with hotels in Puerto Ordaz. Within four blocks of Plaza Bolívar are:

Hotel Aguila Calle 4 near Carrera 1. $
Hotel Orinoco Calle 2 near Carrera 3. $

Hotel Yoli Calle 1 near Carrera 5. $
The Excelsior Calle 3 near Carrera 6. $

WHERE TO EAT AND DRINK
Puerto Ordaz

If you need something more substantial than an *empanada* from the bus station, head over to the **Orinokia Mall**, which has everything from McDonald's to gourmet restaurants with prices to match.

✖ **La Casa Bote** Club Náutico Caroní; ✆ 0286 923 5289; www.puertorinoco.com; ☺ 09.00–06.00 Tue–Sun; music 20.00–03.00 Thu–Sat. A fish restaurant serving *lau-lau* & peacock bass by day, a bar in the evening & club on w/ends, this converted house boat is a good alternative for a night out. Open late Wed & Thu for international cuisine & dancing into the early hours at w/ends. Run by the owners of the Puerto Orinoco river boat. $$

✖ **Tasca Restaurant Jai Alai** Av Las Americas; ✆ 0286 717 3072; ☺ 12.00–15.00 & 18.00–23.00 Mon–Sat. An upmarket Spanish-style restaurant serving seafood & steaks. $$
✖ **Trattoria Da Giulio** Av Las Americas; ✆ 0286 923 5698; ☺ 12.00–15.00 & 19.00–21.00 Wed–Sat. A traditional Italian restaurant with good pastas & meat dishes. Pizzas served at night. $

SHOPPING
Puerto Ordaz One of the largest shopping malls in South America, **Orinokia Mall** (*Av Las Americas, Urb Villa America; www.orinokiamall.com*) has over 300 shops, a bowling alley, seven cinemas, fast-food outlets, restaurants and bars. It is a one-stop shop for pharmacy supplies, supermarket, banking and grabbing a fast bite. Over 55,000 people visit this mall every Saturday.

OTHER PRACTICALITIES There is a Banco de Venezuela on Avenida Las Americas and Avenida Monseñor Zabaleta. Other banks can be found in the massive Orinokia Mall (see above).

There is a CANTV call centre with internet and international phone calls at the airport and another at the Orinokia shopping mall.

Clinica Chilemex (✆ *0286 713 2201, 0286 923 8739*) is on Calle Chile in San Félix and offers 24-hour emergency services.

The **Brazilian consulate** (*Edf Eli-Alti, Ofic 4, Carrera Tocoma;* ✆ *0286 961 2995;* e *info@consbrasguayana.org.ve;* ☺ *09.00–12.00 & 14.00–18.00 Mon–Fri*) arranges visas.

WHAT TO SEE AND DO
Puerto Ordaz
Parque Cachamay (☺ *07.00–17.30 Tue–Sun; admission free*) A forested park leading to a view of the splendid Saltos Cachamay waterfalls, where the dark Caroní races down 200m of cataracts between islands. The spray from the falls and the shade under tropical trees offer cool relief from the sweltering midday heat. The lovely park lies between the highway and the river, ending at the Hotel Intercontinental.

Zoológico Loefling (☺ *07.00–17.30 Tue–Sun; admission free*) Adjacent to Parque Cachamay, it has a zoo of native fauna including anteaters, sloths and armadillos. Some of the larger animals such as tapirs and *chigüires* (capybara) wander free, and cheeky capuchin monkeys swing down from the trees to snatch food from unsuspecting visitors. The park is named after Pehr Loefling, a young Swede who came to Venezuela in 1754 as head botanist on a scientific expedition sponsored by the Spanish crown. He was collecting plants on the Caroní when he fell ill with fever and died in 1756 at the age of 27.

Parque La Llovizna (*Av Leopoldo Sucre Figarella;* ☺ *09:00–17.00 Tue–Sun; admission free*) The spectacular Salto La Llovizna is named for the spray (*llovizna*) created by the powerful waters of the Caroní thundering 20m down a gorge. The beautifully kept park has pathways over many little islands, and lookouts giving different views of the waterfalls. There is a soda fountain open from 05.30 for joggers. The entrance is over the Leopoldo Sucre Figarella causeway linking Macagua Dams I and II.

River trip on Puertorinoco catamaran to the falls (*Club Náutico Caroní;* ✆ *0286 923 5289;* e *info@puertorinoco.com; www.puertorinoco.com*) You can feel the spray in your face at the impressive La Llovizna falls as Jorge Yanez takes his catamaran up close on river trips that start from the Club Náutico Caroní pier near the Hotel Intercontinental Guayana. The two-hour trips leave at 10.30 and 14.30 Tuesday–Sunday and include the unusual meeting of the two main rivers, where you can see the dark Caroní merge with the milky coffee-coloured waters of the Orinoco, eat a snack lunch on a river beach and view the falls. The Friday sunset cruise lasts two hours, with dinner, and costs less.

Ecomuseo del Caroní (*Macagua II, between Av Pedro Palacios Herrera, Leopoldo Sucre Figarella;* \ *0286 964 7656; www.edelca.com.ve/ecomuseo;* ⏰ *09.00–21.00 Mon–Sun; admission free*) Across the road from Parque La Llovizna, and part of the Macagua Dam complex, there are art exhibits, pre-Colombian ceramics and exhibits on the history of hydro-electric power in the region. A round tunnel at the bottom of the four-storey building gives a peek at the massive turbines of the dam, which came on stream in 1995 and produce up to 2,540 megawatts. The Café del Ecomuseo serves good Venezuelan breakfasts, lunches and tea. A pedestrian path along the causeway links the parks of La Llovizna, Cachamay and Loefling.

Dam and factory visits (*Corporación Venezolana de Guayana, CVG, development agency; Edificio CVG, Calle Cuchivero, near the Plaza del Hierro, Alta Vista;* \ *0286 922 6155; www.cvg.com*) To visit the big steel and aluminium industrial plants around Ciudad Guayana and to enquire about trips to the Guri Dam (see *Around Cuidad Guayana*, below) contact the CVG. The big steel and aluminium plants in Matanzas district offer free guided tours, usually on weekdays; you'll be impressed by their huge scale. The Matanzas industrial zone is the size of a small city. The enormous steel mill, Sidor, occupies 87ha of construction, plus 27km^2 of grounds including docks on the Orinoco handling about 6,000,000 metric tons of steel a year. Some 150 buses are needed to transport its 19,000 workers. Sidor uses iron produced by Ferrominera Orinoco, whose ore trains run here from the mines of El Pao, San Isidro and Cerro Bolívar, the astonishing iron mountain that launched Guayana's industry when discovered in 1947. If you are travelling to La Paragua, you will pass this terraced mountain. Venalum and Alcasa together produce some 650,000 metric tons of aluminium a year. The metal is second to oil as a foreign exchange earner. Like steel, the industry is entirely integrated within the Guayana region. From Los Pijiguaos mine, 650km up the Orinoco, bauxite is barged down to Interalumina, which turns the raw material into alumina.

San Félix The old centre of San Félix faces the Orinoco and its Plaza Bolívar is just a block from the Mirador on the riverbank, where you can see the waters of the Caroní and Orinoco flowing side by side for kilometres before mingling. Or your visit may coincide with the annual Orinoco race in mid-April, when over 700 swimmers gather very early at the ferry terminal on the opposite shore to make the 3,100m crossing to San Félix in some 35 minutes. With its church, noisy market and small hotels, downtown San Felix is like a myriad other scruffy towns in Venezuela. There are no historic buildings and little to recommend.

AROUND CIUDAD GUAYANA

Castillos de Guayana (⏰ *09.00–12.00 & 13.00–17.00 Tue–Sun; admission free*) These imposing fortresses on the Orinoco are 38km (45 minutes) east of San Félix in Delta Amacuro State. The fort of San Francisco de Asis, or Villapol, was built from 1676–82 and San Diego de Alcalá, or Campo Elías, dates from 1734–47 and is on higher ground, up a steep incline. The forts were built to protect the city of Santo Tomás, which eventually moved upriver to become Ciudad Bolívar. There isn't much to see

11

inside the castles but the thick walls and panoramic views of the river from San Diego fort are impressive. *Por puestos* for the Castillos leave from El Mirador in east San Félix.

Caroní Mission Church (⊕ *09.00–17.00 Sat–Sun; admission free*) A testament to the power of the Catholic Church in the New World, the building, now in ruins, was once part of a chain of wealthy Guayana missions of the late 18th century. The roofless church reveals a prosperity that was the monks' undoing when patriot armies seized thousands of their horses, mules and cattle to support the 1817 Independence campaign. About 5km from La Llovizna, it can be reached by taxi or on a local tour.

Guri Dam (*Central Hidroeléctrica Simón Bolívar;* \ *0286 960 3521, 0286 960 8448;* ⊕ *Mon–Sun for guided tours*) The second largest hydro-electric dam in the world after the Itaipú Dam between Brazil and Paraguay, the Guri Dam is a manmade construction of epic proportions. Edelca, who run the dam, offer free guided tours of the installation at 09.00, 10.30, 14.00 and 15.30 – just show your passport at the gate. The tours last an hour, with videos explaining the whole operation. To create Guri Lake, an area of 4,250km² (roughly the size of Trinidad) was flooded about 100km before the Caroní River joins the Orinoco. Started in 1963, Guri Dam took 23 years to complete. Tours to Represa de Guri from Ciudad Bolívar or Ciudad Guayana cost about US$60. A full-day tour may include a visit to Cerro Bolívar.

The tour will take you below the concrete face of the dam (162m tall) and past large plazas with a huge aluminium 'Solar Tower' by sculptor Alejandro Otero and a great sundial by Esther Fontana and Lisette Delgado. You get a look into the powerhouse whose turbines supply over 70% of Venezuela's electricity. A serious drought in 2010 saw the lake shrink to a historic low, creating an electricity crisis that forced the government to make drastic cutbacks on consumption, introducing rolling blackouts across the country and forcing shopping malls and offices to shut early to conserve energy. Hydro-electric power was seen as a way of maximising the country's income from oil exports, but the crisis showed that relying almost exclusively on hydro-electric power leaves Venezuela vulnerable to the effects of freak weather conditions and climate change.

Fishing in Guri Dam The manmade lake, seventh largest in the world, is internationally known for peacock bass, or pavón, weighing up to 10kg; they feed in 'wolf packs' and readily strike top-water lures. Fanged payara, or 'vampire fish' also slash and leap. Other sport species are *caribe* (piranha), aymara, coporo, curbinata. Fishing boats on the lake can be arranged for US$100 a day. The long-time fishing specialist is Linda Sonderman of Alpitour in Caracas (*www.alpi-group.com*). A new group working with an air charter company, Chapi Sport Fishing operates the Pavon Lodge (*www.chapisportfishing.com*).

Cerro Bolívar In 1947 this landmark mountain of iron ore signalled the beginning of the region's industrial development when the compasses went haywire on a prospecting plane, so the story goes. It is no longer 590m high after continuous terracing, but its silhouette is still impressive on the palm-dotted savanna as you go south to La Paragua. The mountains of San Isidro and Los Barrancos in the east contain 600 million tons of high-grade ore, a third of Venezuela's iron deposits. Trains haul the ore to Puerto Ordaz.

ANGEL FALLS

If one place alone draws travellers to Venezuela it is Salto Angel, or 'Angel Falls', the highest waterfall in the world and Venezuela's greatest natural treasure. With a drop of 979m (3,212 ft), 19 times higher than Niagara Falls, it dramatically cascades from the sheer walls of a massive heart-shaped mesa mountain called Auyantepui in the Parque Nacional Canaima, a UNESCO World Heritage Site.

Part of the appeal of a visit to the base of Salto Angel is the boat trip in a dugout canoe from Canaima Camp through lush rainforest rivers, and a jungle trek to El Mirador de Laime, a vantage point below the falls in the Cañon del Diablo (Devil's Canyon). Here, in palm-thatched camps, tourists can spend a night or two in hammocks, swim in the soft tannin-rich waters, and appreciate the falls from a distance. Boat trips aren't always guaranteed. In the dry season from January to May the falls turn to mist before reaching the ground and dugouts can't make it past the rapids and up the rivers. In the rainy season, a short downpour can turn the single chute of Salto Angel into a thundering combination of three or four rivers rushing off the craggy ramparts of the *tepui*. After heavy rain, so many waterfalls pour off the cliffs that even experienced Indian guides can find it hard to identify Salto Angel from a distance.

In a nod to the local Pemón Indians and a dig at the 'Yankee Empire', President Hugo Chávez recently announced that the indigenous name for the waterfall, Kerepakupai Merú (waterfall of the deepest place), should be used. However, the

A MESSAGE LEFT BY JIMMIE ANGEL

When Jimmie Angel landed on top of Auyantepui, he made a mistake. Not only was there no gold, but also the surface was so boggy that the plane remained stuck. Gold-less (and largely food-less), Angel, his wife Marie, Gustavo Heny and his gardener Miguel, survived only because the route down had been scouted for them in advance by explorer Félix Cardona and Gustavo Heny himself. Is the fact that the escape route already existed evidence of thoroughness, or perhaps of Angel's willingness to abandon the Flamingo (which was not his)? Perhaps Angel was as much a publicity hound as fortune seeker. Before the little group started trekking down – it took them 11 days to get off the mountain – Angel left a piece of paper in the cockpit with a scrawled message. Who was the message for; an air rescue team? Years later it was found and kept by Aleksandrs Laime and is reproduced here.

11

269

president stopped short of issuing a formal decree, so it continues to carry the evocative name of American bush pilot and prospector Jimmie Angel (1 August 1899–8 December 1956). For many years Angel's abandoned monoplane glinted in a bog atop Auyantepui where he landed in 1937 looking for gold. But Angel's widely publicised exploits, which are the stuff of legend (he first saw the falls in 1933), have eclipsed their earlier discoverer, a prospector and rubber hunter named Ernesto Sánchez La Cruz. In 1910 Sánchez reported visiting the falls he called Churún Merú in the language of the Pemón Indians, who of course knew it was there all along. The name is now used to identify the Churún River headwaters, a set of falls at the very end of the canyon. Four years after Angel died in a plane accident in Panama, his son returned to Venezuela to scatter his ashes over the falls. Jimmie's plane, the *Río Caroní* (it was borrowed), was removed from the top of Auyantepui by the air force in 1970. Restored, it is now on display outside the Ciudad Bolívar Airport. The height of the falls was only established in 1949, when plucky US photographer Ruth Robertson led a *National Geographic* expedition to the base with the Latvian prospector and explorer Aleksandrs Laime. It was Laime who cut the trail to the Mirador used by tourists today.

Angel Falls still draws adventurers who scale the canyon's face, walk across it on tightropes and base jump off the top. The oldest person to base jump from the top is Welshman Eric Jones, who proved age is no obstacle to adventure when he parachuted down in 1998 aged 61. But, aside from a barricade of permits, the hazards are terrible. In 1990 French climber Jean Marc Boivin lost his life in a tragic paraglide jump from the falls.

Photographers should note that the falls face east, hidden deep in Devil's Canyon in the heart of Auyantepui. After midday they are in shade (and cloud, as often as not).

CANAIMA (*Telephone code: 0286*) The starting point for all trips to Angel Falls is Canaima, an isolated jungle camp reached only by plane that exists purely because of tourism. The setting on Canaima Lagoon couldn't be more spectacular, with the tea-coloured waters of the Carrao River thundering over the Hacha–El Sapo waterfalls in the distance and beautiful pink sandy beaches fringed by palms along the shore. Some 1,000 people, mostly Pemón Indians, live in the village behind the airstrip, and several hundred people work in the handful of tourist camps spread out around the lagoon. Sixty years ago there was nothing here, only river and savanna. There was no Indian village and the lagoon did not even have a name. Everything changed in 1947 when Charlie Baughan, a US pilot, fell in love with the place and christened it with an Indian name. Unfortunately, he chose the Pemón name for a vengeful spirit and died before he could realise his dream of opening a resort here. Baughan's Dutch partner, Rudy Truffino, went on to develop the resort and eventually opened his own camp above the Hacha Falls at Ucaima, creating a name for himself as 'Jungle Rudy' and playing host to Prince Charles and a host of Hollywood stars. Today, Canaima has mobile phone reception and (slow) internet service but its isolation has stopped it from growing too fast. The trips to Angel Falls are the same as they were 20 years ago. Although Canaima's main lodge, tour camps and souvenir shops are touristy, they are dwarfed by the magnificent panorama of waterfalls, savanna and jungle. With the *tepuis* in the distance and the lagoon in front, this is still an idyllic setting.

Visiting Angel Falls is a once in a lifetime experience but boat trips and overnight stays in Canaima can seem expensive for what you get, which in most cases is a hammock and a chicken dinner without alcoholic drinks. However, if you decide it's worth the price, there's not much point flying in to Canaima without having a tour or accommodation already organised. The best deals are to be had in Ciudad

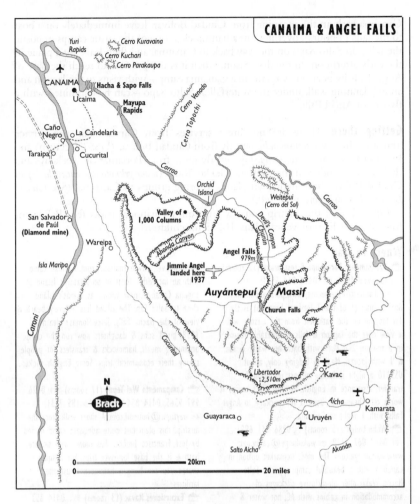

Yuri Rapids

Cerro Kuravaina
Cerro Kuchari
Cerro Parakaupa

CANAIMA

Hacha & Sapo Falls

Ucaima

Mayupa Rapids

Cerro Venado

Caño Negro

La Candelaria

Cerro Topochi

Taraipa

Cucurital

Carrao

San Salvador de Paúl (Diamond mine)

Orchid Island

Weitepuí (Cerro del Sol)

Carrao

Wareipa

Valley of 1,000 Columns

Ahonda

Devil's Canyon

Churún

Isla Maripa

Ahonda Canyon

Angel Falls 979m

Jimmie Angel landed here 1937

Auyántepuí   Massif

Churún Falls

Coroni

Cucurital

N

Bradt

Libertador 2,510m

Kavac

Aicha

Guayaraca

Uruyén

Kamarata

Salto Aicha

Akanán

0 ———————— 20km
0 ———————— 20 miles

Bolívar (see *Cuidad Bolívar, Tour operators*, page 260), where a group of five people in are in a perfect position to bargain, because they can fill a Cessna. The days of flying in and haggling for a bargain in Canaima as a solo traveller are long gone as visitor numbers are now so low that there are few other boat trips to put you on. It makes little financial sense for tour operators to take two or even three people in a large dugout canoe, unless they're paying full price. One-day excursions to the falls are not recommended unless you're really pressed for time, as so many hours sitting on the hard wooden seats can be torture, particularly if it is rainy and cold. The Angel Falls route is so beautiful it's a pity to take the fun away by rushing.

The cost of a three-day/two-night river trip varies from a low of US$180 per person to US$400, not including air fare. All the camps offer boat trips to Angel Falls but there is little to keep visitors in Canaima for longer than it takes to do a three-day/two-night trip to the falls. Given the fact that you spend most of the trip on a boat, there is little real difference between the tours on offer except the cost. Most of the Canaima camps can now be reached by email and will respond relatively rapidly, giving time to compare prices and last minute deals. The cheapest way to do Angel Falls in the rainy season is on a package where you fly in to

Canaima early in the morning from Ciudad Bolívar, leave immediately on a boat to the falls (4 hours), overnight in a hammock at one of the rustic camps opposite the falls, do Salto Sapo on the way back to Canaima, and then leave on a plane in the early afternoon. In the dry season, when it is not possible to reach the base of Angel Falls by boat, a few nights in a Canaima camp – with visits to the lagoon and an exhilarating walk under the waterfall at Salto Sapo – can be combined with a flyover of Angel Falls.

Getting there There are no direct services from Caracas. Air taxi service Transmandu (*www.transmandu.com*) fly from Ciudad Bolívar (US$250 return) and Puerto Ordaz. Aereotuy (*www.tuy.com*) fly tours from Porlamar on weekdays and flights are included in the package. Gekko Tours (*www.gekkotours-venezuela.de*) in Cuidad Bolívar have their own planes to bring groups to Canaima. (See *Ciudad Bolívar, Tour operators*, page 260.)

On arrival at the airstrip you pay Inparques a national parks fee (BsF35 for foreigners, BsF25 for Venezuelans, BsF15 for children).

⌂ Where to stay

⌂ **Campamento Parakaupa & restaurant** (12 rooms) \ 0286 961 4963; m 0414 864 5541; e parakaupa@etheron.net; www.parakaupa.com.ve. Run by Juan (1 of the 7 Jiménez brothers), is the 1st lodging on the path left from the airstrip with a view over the lagoon & falls. Comfortable rooms in a row on 2nd floor with bath, hot water & fan, & 1 with jacuzzi. Meals & lodging only, about US$110 a night including airport reception & transfer, assistance in English. As with most camps it works out cheaper to book a full package to Angel Falls, with 1 night in Canaima. $$$

⌂ **Waku Lodge** (15 rooms) \ 0286 961 6981; m 0414 867 6138; e wakulodge@cantv.net; www.wakulodge.com. The most upmarket option in Canaima with a beautiful camp opposite Salto Hacha, Waku offer all-inclusive packages of accommodation in cabins with AC, hot water & buffet-style dining in a central *churuata* & river trips to Angel Falls. Boat tours of the lagoon include visits to Salto Sapo & Salto Hacha. Wi-Fi & internet available for short periods at reception. $$$

⌂ **Campamento Canaima Venetur** (65 rooms) m 0416 685 0186, 0426 520 6912; e veneturecohotelcanaima@yahoo.com; www.venetur.com. The 1st hotel built on the lagoon still has the best location, with an elevated dining area with thatched roof overlooking the sandy beach facing Hacha Falls & 3 *tepuis* in the distance. Bungalow rooms face onto beach, with private bath & hot water. Recently taken over by government-run Venetur, which aims to benefit indigenous community. $$

⌂ **Campamento Tomás Bernal** (8 rooms, hammocks) m 0414 854 8234; e bernaltours@

terra.com.ve; www.bernaltours.com. A small camp with an incredible location on Anatoly's Island in Laguna Canaima, now known as Tomás's Island, close to Salto Sap. The island has a lovely beach & view of the Hacha Falls. Since Tomás's death in 1998, his 4 sons & daughters now run the camp, organising meals, hammocks & transfers for people taking their economical trips. Some English spoken. $$

⌂ **Campamento Wei-Tepuy** (17 rooms) m 0426 997 9565, 0414 854 6900, 0416 185 7231; e weytupu@hotmail.com. A short walk from the airstrip, this plain but quite adequate camp owned by José Francisco Jiménez has rooms with private bath & is the base for river trips. For a small charge you can hang a hammock & use the facilities. $$

⌂ **Excursiones Kavac** (13 rooms) m 0414 853 2338; e excursioneskavak@hotmail.com. A camp run by the Pemón in the heart of the indigenous community behind the lake. Rooms have fan, some AC, cold water. Economical boat trips to the falls include 1 night opposite Angel Falls, 1 night in Canaima. $$

⌂ **Ucaima** (16 rooms) \ 0289 808 9251, 0286 962 2359; www.junglerudy.com. On the banks of the Carrao above Hacha Falls, 1km south of Canaima, is the area's pioneer camp, built in 1958 by 'Jungle Rudy' Truffino, the expedition guide who died in 1994. The Dutchman's family still runs the camp, transferring guests from Canaima's airstrip. It has a bar, library with lots of information & videos about Angel Falls. Small, smart & attractive still, Prince Charles stayed here & a suite is named in his honour. $$

Camping There is no campsite in Canaima and camping is no longer allowed on the beach but if you ask at Wei-Tepuy, they will let you camp – a small fee is charged for using the facilities. Check with Inparques at the airport on arrival.

✗ Where to eat

✗ **Mentanai** In the Pemon village at the back of the Venetur camp (see above) is a bar with pool table where you can get reasonable (by Canaima standards) drinks & snacks. Expect to pay double what you would pay for a can of Polar in an expensive Caracas restaurant. $

Other practicalities

Money There are no banks in Canaima although some *posadas* will change dollars for you at a poor rate. *Posadas* will also charge you for the privilege of using your credit card so try and bring all the cash you need with you.

Internet In the Pemon village there is an internet place by the church with a slow connection that charges about US$2 an hour. You can also try the office of KavacExcursiones who may let you use the internet there. A government infocentre is planned that should provide free internet service to the Pemon village so stroll over and see if it's operating. If you don't fancy walking you can try the internet at Posada Morichal by the airstrip for US$5 an hour.

Shopping Everything is very expensive in Canaima. There are a couple of very pricey handicrafts stores selling indigenous beads and baskets, plastic rain ponchos and touristy T-shirts but if you want a bargain try the stalls at the airport shack where Eunice Jimenez is prepared to haggle over the price. She also offers international calls from the phone in her drawer.

What to do

Upriver to Angel Falls Large dugout canoes with bench seats leave from the port above Salto Hacha at Ucaima. There's no roof to protect you, rain or shine, so take a hat and waterproof in case of rain and a bag to keep your camera dry. Boats follow the Carrao River, with a short walk at Mayupa if the river is too low to negotiate the rapids. Marvel at the sheer *tepui* walls and craggy battlements at the top, like a giant abandoned castle as the boat gets closer to Auyantepui and joins the smaller Churún River flowing into the Devil's Canyon. Tying up at Ratoncito Camp facing Angel Falls, you walk the last hour or so over tangled tree roots, up muddy steps and through forest to a lookout point called Mirador de Laime, named after the Latvian explorer who first cut the trail. Coming out of the forest to this breathtaking view of the falls is a highlight of the trip and anybody who takes the trail up here slowly should be able to make it. If the falls are not too powerful there is a five-minute trail from the Mirador down to a pool fed directly by the freezing waters from the falls where you can bathe – a once-in-a-lifetime experience that shouldn't be missed. Once a canoe-load of Japanese tourists, who had not realised they would be able to swim and had not brought swimming costumes, put modesty aside and simply stripped down to bra and pants and dived in! Generally, Angel Falls receives most sun in the morning and can get cloudy by afternoon, so an overnight stay in hammocks is recommended as it gives you another chance to see the falls in the morning.

☞ **REMEMBER:** Be sure to take a hat and long-sleeved shirt for sun/insect protection, swimsuit and sun block, extra footwear such as old canvas shoes for river and camp use, plastic poncho and plastic bags for yourself and belongings as it often rains. For emergencies, a torch (*linterna*) and lighter, and snacks such as nuts, raisins and chocolate as a reward on the walk. Insect repellent is a must.

Angel Falls by air Light planes from Ciudad Bolívar or Canaima make breathtaking tours to the falls, flying past the sheer walls of the Devil's Canyon, which carves Auyantepui nearly in half. The 40-minute Cessna flights from Canaima cost about US$100 each for four passengers. However, there's no money-back guarantee if the falls are covered in cloud. Pilots will not take off if the ceiling is low, and even in sunny weather they cannot guarantee a good view of the falls as clouds form rapidly over the table mountain. You may have to be content with a close look at Auyantepui's fantastic walls and moonscape summit. If flying from Margarita on a tour organised by Aereotuy (*www.tuy.com*) a flight over Angel Falls is included, weather permitting.

Salto El Sapo This is a powerful waterfall on the eastern branch of the Carrao River, which is reached by boat from Canaima Lagoon and a short hike through forest. The name refers to the *sapito minero*, a tiny, yellow and black poison-arrow frog (*Dendrobates leucomelas*) found close to the falls. What makes the 20m falls extra special is a rocky passage that takes you behind the curtain of water, a truly exhilarating experience when the river is in full flow and the spray blows back into the tunnel. Wear a swimming costume and take a bag for your camera. Salto El Sapo is usually included at no extra cost in boat trips to Angel Falls, either at the start or when you return.

CLIMBING AUYANTEPUI   *With Peter Ireland*

Auyantepui is huge. The 700km² summit is as big as the island of St Lucia. The ancient tabletop mountain rises from 1,000m elevation at Guayaraca on the savanna, to over 2,500m on top. In shape Auyantepui resembles a heart about 40–50km long, with a deep central gorge called Devil's Canyon; this is where Angel Falls plunges over a cleft in the cliff. Rock climbers such as David Nott have scaled the face near Angel Falls. However, the only trail up Auyantepui for hikers is the southern route, which was opened by Félix Cardona and Gustavo Heny in 1937 in preparation for Jimmie Angel's attempt to land and explore.

Few people hike to Auyantepui because of the distances and time involved and the degree of difficulty, as it is more physically challenging than hiking up Roraima and involves climbing up knotted ropes. Mounting an expedition depends on hiring Indian guides in Kamarata, a day from the head of the trail, or closer in Kavac or Uruyén, which both have airstrips – another reason why most people prefer to go on an organised expedition. Kamarata is a large Indian settlement where people are still genuinely very friendly. Porters charge about US$30 a day and the main guide will require more. There is a well-stocked shop in Kamarata, a place to eat, even 'hotels'. You can also camp in front of the big stone Capuchin mission. There are several taps with drinking water, and you can swim or bathe in the river.

A typical hike can take eight–ten days so it's important to stock up on supplies before you come, unless you're in an organised expedition. It's a two-hour walk to Kavac (10km), easy but hot, and there's a river halfway.

On **Day 1** the hike starts on the savanna, which is hot walking in the dry season, and the path is hard. About four hours from Kavac you can bathe in the last river before the trail starts to climb; hard work in the sun. In about two to three hours from the river you reach the top of the first level and in another hour a river and campsite called **Guayaraca**. The river is beautifully refreshing (fine for drinking, as is all the water on the *tepui*). Some wooden frames have been constructed where you can use plastic sheeting for a roof, convenient because all other sites up the mountain are under huge rocks. Explore the forest here for huge purple orchids and timid hummingbirds.

Salto El Hacha This is the furthest set of falls from the beach at Canaima Lagoon, which can also be walked under when the river is not too full and is an alternative to Salto El Sapo in the dry season.

Yuri Falls Downriver on the Carrao, these falls are reached by a 20-minute jeep ride across savanna to Puerto Verde, a boat trip in a dugout, then a walk through gallery forest. The reddish waters of Yuri Falls descend in steps to a fine dry-season beach of squeaky pink sand.

Kamarata to Angel Falls An alternative way to visit Angel Falls is from the Pemón community of Kamarata, southeast of Auyantepui, on the Akanan River. The Capuchin mission is served by airtaxis from Ciudad Bolívar, but organising something yourself can be difficult as it requires finding a boatman in Kamarata and haggling over the price. The river trip down the Akanan to the falls takes longer than from Canaima, and skirts the eastern cliffs of Auyantepui, before joining the Carrao and the turn to the falls on the Churún. The return trip is via Canaima and a flight back to Ciudad Bolívar. Most tours include Kavac on this trip. Akanan Adventures (*www.akanan.com*) pioneered this trip many years ago and it is also offered by tour operators in Ciudad Bolívar.

On **Day 2** the hike climbs from forest through dense *tepui* vegetation on a shoulder called Danto, then up more steeply to **El Peñón** (1,700m). This is a huge rock with ten 'beds' cut in the sand underneath. A perfect shelter but chilly because wind funnels through it. There's a stream five minutes away. Below, you can see the plateau and the savanna path and other *tepuis* in the distance, while Kamarata and Kavac are already out of sight.

This is a good place to leave behind some food for the return. The path goes up steeply, then over a tangle of wet tree roots, emerging at the base of a huge vertical wall. There is a steep climb up ropes (already in place). Scaling the final rocks to the *tepui's* top is exhilarating. The huge columns of rock are incredibly shaped and pitted, mysterious in the clouds. On the rock to the right as you come up is a bronze bust of Bolívar, brought up by the Universidad Central de Venezuela in 1956; hence this point (about 2,400m) is known as **Libertador**. Breathtaking views are available here, both into and out of the *tepui*. There is a rock you can camp under, or you can continue on to **El Oso** (The Bear), another overhang. Each pool of water on the ancient black sandstone is full of mosses or plants. The water on top of the *tepui* is red like tea and is alright to drink (the colouring comes from tannin, especially from the Bonnetia trees).

Day 3 is a four-hour hike to **Borrachito** (meaning 'Little Drunkard', perhaps for the weird rock shapes). There is a fair amount of small forest, orchids and birds. Hummingbirds dart around. Borrachito is on the banks of a lovely, deep-red river, the Churún, which eventually passes over Angel Falls. There is a dark cave to pass the night. **Day 4** is spent scrambling through forests and around crevasses to **Boca de Dragón** where the river disappears under the rocks for a space. About an hour's walk downstream there is a lovely waterfall about 30m high. **Day 5** is for exploring. **Day 6** is for the return. To have enough time to get back to El Peñón in a day, you need to be at El Oso by noon and Libertador by 15.00. **Day 7** is an easy downhill to Guayaraca by noon, leaving a four-hour slog to Kavak to try and pick up a flight or spend the night. A pricey can of Polar never tasted so good. **Day 8** is the return flight back to Porlamar, Ciudad Bolívar or Canaima in an airtaxi. Akanan Adventures (*www.akanan.com*) organise seven-day trips following this route for groups of four or more.

Kavac Canyon Most flights and tours to Kavac originate in Ciudad Bolívar (US$200 return, 1 hour) or Canaima (US$50 return, 25 minutes) and include a fly over Angel Falls. Gekko Tours (*www.gekkotours-venezuela.de*) based at Posada La Casita do two-day tours to Kavak in their own planes (US$500). Kavac stands in open savanna with Auyantepui looming above it in the background. The dozen thatched Indian roundhouses were built exclusively for tourism by the Pemón Indians of Kamarata, a village 10km away. Pemón guides lead tours to the main attraction, Kavac Canyon and its waterfall. A trail towards Auyantepui follows the little Kavac River, where there is a passage of high, black rocks washed smooth by aeons of floodwaters and walls so narrow you can touch both sides. The idea is to swim or slide up the tunnel against the flow of the river to a dark pool where a waterfall plunges from a hole in rocks overhead. It's quite an adventure. The trip visits another waterfall and climbs to a lookout point on Auyantepui with views over the savanna. If you are not on a day trip, you can pay to join a group but it's easy enough to follow the trail up to the gorge. After the visitors are gone, it is very quiet. Most of the Pemón return to their homes in Kamarata (2 hours on foot) and there is very little in Kavac apart from the palm-roofed *churuatas* that provide shelter. If you have a hammock you can string it up for a small fee but you have to bring your own food. A small shop sells expensive beers and a few basics but generally there's no action unless a tour party is booked in.

Uruyén Another idyllic spot some 12km west of Kamarata, Uruyén has a little river that emerges from the flanks of Auyantepui in a very cool private waterfall, not as dark as Kavac. There is a landing strip where small planes bring tourists and trekkers heading for the summit of Auyantepui as Uruyén is the closest community to the trail up Auyantepui. On the banks of the river Valentino, Victorino Carballo (m *0415 212 0717*) has built one of the most beautiful lodges south of the Orinoco made from the baked yellow clay of the Gran Sabana. It has a dining area and five thatched houses, each with two double rooms with private baths. About US$80 a night including meals.

Bicycle trek Akanan Adventures (*www.akanan.com*) organise a splendid five-day mountain bike trek to Canaima starting from Ciudad Bolívar. On the first day bikers cross the Río Paragua by ferry and make camp. Then begins the adventure of crossing savannas and creeks on the earth road to the Chiguao ferry and entering the forested area called La Tigrera, for a second night in tents. The ride on day three begins with an ascent from the humid rainforest to open grassy lands characteristic of the Gran Sabana with views of *tepuis* including Auyantepui rising in the east. Camp is made near the Pemón village of **Las Bonitas**. At this point, the cyclists arrange with the Pemón Indians for dugout canoes to carry them and the bikes across the powerful **Caroní River** to camp on a beach on the opposite bank.

The last day is an easy ride over the savanna to Canaima where the beach and lagoon end the biking tour – although there's time enough to explore El Sapo Falls, or to take a light plane to see Angel Falls the following day.

GOLD COUNTRY AND GRAN SABANA

Beautifully graded and surfaced, the Gran Sabana highway is among the best in the country. Buses travel regularly from Caracas and Ciudad Bolívar to Santa Elena de Uairén, with some continuing to Boa Vista in Brazil. The road covers 331km from the fork at El Dorado to the border, passing through the Imataca Forest Reserve before entering Parque Nacional Canaima and the savannas and *tepui* mountains of the Gran Sabana. These giant table mountains are actually part of a giant plateau

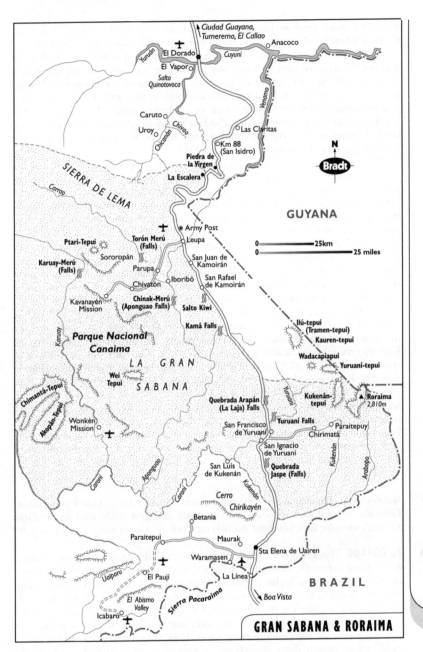

GRAN SABANA & RORAIMA

called the Guiana Shield, an igneous and metamorphic formation of some of the world's oldest rock, two to three billion years old. The *tepuis* themselves are made of sandstone sediments washed from the granddaddy of all continents, Gondwana (Pangaea). Layers of these sediments are over 2,700m thick in places such as Roraima, and on the mesa tops you can see the ripple marks of ancient lakes. Such isolated remnants, left standing after aeons of erosion by water and wind, are known as the Roraima Formation. Diamonds and gold may be one of Venezuela's links with the time when South America and Africa were part of the same supercontinent.

In 1991 25 *tepuis* were declared natural monuments, placing them under the wing of the national park system. Only a few have been scientifically studied, as most are remote and devoid of game or nourishment for sustaining human visitors. Soils are very poor in nutrients and high in iron and aluminium oxides, and remaining forests survive in a state of continual 'stress'. Their ecosystem is fragile, vulnerable to periodic drought and manmade disasters such as mining, roads, logging and fire. Burnt stumps can still be seen from great fires that swept through the Gran Sabana in 1927–28 and 1940.

The *tepui*-top habitats, collectively called Pantepui, support many endemic plants found nowhere else, especially epiphytes, which can survive on air, water and minimal nutrients. Plants common to the *tepuis* can be seen throughout the Gran Sabana. In boggy areas you can find carnivorous pitcher plants (*Heliamphora*) that trap insects in slippery, champagne-glass tubes and gradually digest them to obtain nitrogen, and tiny pink sundews (*Drosera*), with sticky beads to attract unlucky insects. A bromeliad, *Brocchinia reducta*, also traps insects to survive. The best-known member of the bromeliad family is the pineapple, native of the Guayana region, while the vertical cylinders of another bromeliad can store enough water to see it through dry periods, and rescue travellers from thirst. A great variety of orchids are found here too, enduring extremes of hot days and cold nights, as the temperature on *tepui* tops, which retain no heat, can go down to a chilly 0°C.

The Gran Sabana is the ancestral land of the Pemón, a Carib-speaking indigenous group divided between Arekuna in the centre (Kavanayén), Kamaracotos in the west and Taurepán in the south. The names of the mountains, rivers and towns are all Pemón in origin and are linked to a rich mythic tradition that has been passed down through shamans. Although many Pemón have converted to Catholicism and the region has been fought over by many Protestant sects from English-speaking Guyana and even from Brazil, the Pemón have maintained their language and are proud of their homeland. When the government began building electricity pylons across the Gran Sabana to supply Brazil, there were serious protests by the Pemón and they continue to defend their interests. The Pemón also lead tours to local waterfalls and the hike to Roraima would be a lot harder without the Pemón porters who carry all the gear.

☞ **WARNING:** Distances are far and facilities limited once you leave Ciudad Guayana. A local saying goes: 'about as much use as a credit card in the Gran Sabana', so make sure you have enough cash before you set out.

EL DORADO This town is a four-hour drive from Ciudad Guayana. The entrance to the town before the Cuyuní Bridge is counted as Km 0 for measuring distances on the Gran Sabana highway. Many buses continue over the Cuyuní Bridge without stopping here. At the confluence of the Cuyuní and Yuruari rivers, El Dorado does not face the river but is built around a large shady plaza. It has some food shops, restaurants, a petrol station and many gold buyers' booths, as the town is a major port for independent prospectors. El Dorado got its name during earlier gold strikes, which drew steamboats of fortune hunters and supplies up the Cuyuní from Georgetown in British Guiana. Its most famous visitor was Henri Charrière, better known as Papillon, a Frenchman who spent over ten years in the penal colonies of French Guiana before escaping to Venezuela in 1944. Papillon was imprisoned for a year here at the El Dorado penal colony on the east side of the river before settling in Caracas for many years. Plane-loads of criminals still arrive at El Dorado bound for Las Colonias.

EL CALLAO Northwest of El Dorado by 112km, El Callao was the site of a major gold rush in 1849 when gold was discovered on the Yuruari River. In 1855 alone the yield was eight tonnes. Today, the hot, scruffy town is famous for its cheap gold shops, its annual carnival and its calypso music – a legacy from the thousands of Caribbean workers who came here from Martinique and Trinidad to work the mines. The carnival starts a week before Ash Wednesday and is wild, wild, wild with calypso groups on floats, steel bands, carnival queens, and crazy characters dressed as white and red devils with whips and tridents. Women called *Madamas* dress in old Antillean-style with turbans and robes, and characters covered in black gloopy paint called *Mediopintos* demand cash or they splash you with gunge. The name comes from an old coin called a *medio* and the phrase '*o te pinto*' ('or I paint you'). An institution at Carnival is The Same People (*www.thesamepeople.com*), a calypso group who continue the tradition of singing in English. A sign at the entrance to the town says: '*Welcome to El Callao, land of gold, calypso and football*' as the country's first football and cricket teams once played in lively leagues here during the golden days of the boom.

There is a National Guard post as you leave El Callao where identity papers are checked whatever the hour.

Where to stay The only decent place in town is **Hotel El Arte Dorado** (*Calle El Rocio;* ☎ *0288 762 0535;* $$), but you can also try **Hotel Restaurant Italia** (*Calle Ricaurte;* ☎ *0288 762 0770;* $).

LAS CLARITAS This town is in the Imataca Forest Reserve. Another gold town, Las Claritas is full of '*Compro Oro*' signs on tinroofed shacks. Ciudad Bolívar buses stop here for refreshments at the rows of restaurants offering fried chicken, *arepas* and rice.

Where to stay

Barquilla de Fresa (6 rooms, cabin for 4) Km 84; ☎ 0212 256 4162; m 0416 709 7205; e barquilladefresa@cantv.net; www.strawberrybirds.com. A must-do birdwatching lodge for serious twitchers interested in Gran Sabana endemics & the Imataca Forest, this pleasant lodge is run by naturalist Henry Cleve. The birds on his 35ha property & lagoon include 8 different parrotlets & parrots, 3 kinds of cotingas, aracaris, jacamars & puffbirds. Cleve can advise on birding the Gran Sabana route, one of the best birdwatching roads in the whole country & can arrange birding tours. Rooms with bath & cold water. $$

PARQUE NACIONAL CANAIMA Shortly after San Isidro at Km 88 the road begins to wind up Cerro Venamo, leaving the hot country of the plains for cool hills. At 410m altitude, the granite bulk of the **Piedra de la Virgen** looms at the eastern boundary of the Parque Nacional Canaima. The park stretches 30,000km² west as far as the Caroní River, south to Roraima and the Kukenán River, and east to Guyana. UNESCO declared the park a world heritage site for its beauty and biodiversity.

From here **La Escalera** (literally 'The Stairway') rises sharply, gaining 1,000m elevation in 37km. Wet montane forest here is the home to fabled birds such as the cock of the rock, scarlet horned manakin, white bellbird and paradise tanager, among others; deer and jaguar are occasionally seen crossing the road.

At Km 122 there is a National Guard checkpoint, or *alcabala*, where all identity papers are checked and vehicles may be searched. The checkpoint is only a few kilometres from the Essequibo territory disputed with Guyana. The road continues up to the **Monumento al Soldado Pionero** (1,350m), the highest point, which honours the army engineers who built this road, opened in 1973 by President Rafael Caldera. The Brazilians built a road simultaneously from Boa

11

Vista to the border at Santa Elena, where the two presidents met. It is still the only road link between the two nations.

The first of the Gran Sabana's many campsites is by a bend in the dark **Aponguao River**, at Km 140, and is one of the few with toilet facilities. Across the road are offices of Inparques, followed by the army post of Fuerte Manikuyé or **La Ciudadela**. This is a frontier zone and vehicles are checked carefully, not only for firearms and drugs, but also illegal plants and rock samples. Petrol is available here, which is a necessity for people owning vehicles in Kavanayén as the mission is often without fuel.

Kavanayén Mission and waterfalls

A dirt road turns right by the military landing strip in Luepa at Km 147 and leads 70km west to a Pemón community and the Catholic mission of **Kavanayén**, which serves as a base for guided trips to spectacular waterfalls. Without a car the only way to continue from the turn-off is to hitch a ride or organise something with the Pemón in Kavanayén, which is hard because they lack their own transport. There is very little traffic, so be prepared for a night out in the cold.

If you want to camp along the road seek out a windy campsite as the drawback to this region is the legion of gnats or biting midges in the early morning and late afternoon known as *jejenes* or simply *plaga*, the plague. The worst are the night species, *puri-puri*, so small they can penetrate mosquito netting. Make sure you bring plenty of repellent, long trousers, a long-sleeved top and a hat.

On the way to Kavanayén With a 4x4 you can take the rough track for 17km to **Torón Falls**, by a right-hand fork at Km 23. At the first ford, explore the lovely rocky creek downstream; a few kilometres further are the 75m-high Torón Falls.

Salto Aponguao Falls or **Chinak-Merú**, is a spectacular waterfall of tea-coloured water that turns to white foam as it cascades 109m from a broad cliff about 100m wide. A popular destination with Venezuelan families, it is reached by dugout *curiara* from a stop on the Kavanayén road at Km 32. The *curiara* ferries tourists across to the trail for the falls for a small fee of US$3, which includes a guide for the savanna path (40 minutes) to the top of the falls. Another trail leads down to the lagoon at the base where it is safe to swim. Be sure to start early as the falls get sun in the morning only. The dirt road continues on to **Iboribó**, a remote Pemón community on the Aponguao River. Some of the Pemón here make baskets and calabash bowls and others prepare simple meals. The only accommodation is in hammocks, and there are bathrooms and camping spots. There is no phone to make bookings in advance but prices are reasonable.

🏠 Where to stay

🏠 **Campamento Mantopai** (12 stone cabins) ✆ 0286 963 4585; e turismoPemón@yahoo.com. Hidden at the foot of Sororopán-tepui, east of Kavanayén. The 12 fine Indian-style *churuatas* made of stone were built by the Calcaños, an enterprising Kamaracoto family. Each house has 2 comfortable beds, private bath, electricity, restaurant. This is now being run as part of the Pemón co-operative tourism project E'Masensen II run out of Kavanayén (see below). $

🏠 **Chivatón** (12 rooms) ✆ 0298 808 1002; e chivaton@cantv.net. On the Kavanayén road at Km 47, this offers accommodation but prior reservation is essential. Rooms have 2–4 beds each, bath, cold water; generator for light. There's a creek for swimming if you like very cold water. Windswept Chivatón has few gnats. $

Kavanayén The Franciscan Mission of Santa Teresita de Kavanayén (the Pemón name means 'Place of the Cock of the Rock') was founded in 1942 on this remote plateau (altitude 1,160m). The imposing mission and boarding school, as well as village houses, are made of stone. There is an infocentro with internet connection, a phone service, a rural clinic or *medicatura*, a mechanic, a petrol pump sometimes in service, an airfield and heliport. Holiday residences have been built near the heliport for the President of Venezuela, and presidents of Edelca and PDVSA, the state hydro-electricity and oil companies. From the airfield at the west end of Kavanayén, ringed by dramatic mesas and attendant storm clouds, you can see an amazing array of *tepuis*. In the northeast is Sororopán-tepui, north is Ptari-tepui, northwest is Aparamán, southwest are Chimantá and Akopán-tepui, and south is the cone-shaped Wei, the 'mountain of the sun'. These ancient weather makers account for Kavanayén having one of the highest rainfalls in the country, over 3,000mm a year.

Tour operators Recently, the local community created the **Pemón Tourism Cooperative E'Masensen II** (✆ *0286 963 4585, 0286 963 4584;* e *kusariwara@ gmail.com, ricardochani2@hotmail.com, turismoPemon@yahoo.com; www.andestropicales.org/ gransabana/Mantopai.html*). They have been working with Andes Tropicales (*www.andestropicales.com*), the same NGO that developed the Mucuposadas in Mérida, to put together a similar tourism project to benefit 14 Pemón villages in the surrounding region, consolidate their sense of identity and help preserve ancestral traditions. The programme was initially funded by the state-firm CVG Edelca, who helped Andes Tropicales prepare the Pemón, design and test the routes, train the guides and create publicity material. For travellers who want to make a difference and give something back, this is the ideal opportunity. They have two 4x4 vehicles for ten passengers each and *curiaras* for river trips. Excursions can be anything from day trips to seven-day circuits of the region combining jeep, hiking and river trips. Using expert local guides such as Ricardo Chaní and Eusebio the idea is for tourists to live a few days with the Pemón, learn about their customs and myths, their food and how they live off the land and, of course, travel with them to the magical *tepuis*, rivers, waterfalls and sacred petroglyphs that most people never get to see. The excursions are particularly suited to birdwatchers as the region is rich in *tepui* endemics.

Where to stay The Capuchin mission has spartan dormitory rooms with five beds and hot water (US$10). The mission does not provide meals. Two or three other houses in the village rent out inexpensive rooms and will cook for guests. The village football field can be used for camping. All accommodation and excursions are arranged through the E'Masensen II tourism co-operative.

Other practicalities Kavanayén is very basic. There are no banks, very limited shopping and while you can arrange to eat food cooked by local people you should bring some basic supplies, as well as all the cash you will need.

What to see and do The lovely **Karuay Falls** and pools, 23km west of Kavanayén, are reached by a track so rutted that it takes jeeps over an hour in dry weather (impassable in rain). As the Karuay descends over increasingly large shelves from the Gran Sabana, it forms higher and higher waterfalls. Indian guides with *curiaras* equipped with lifebelts and jackets offer to take you downstream to **Salto Hueso**. It is 2½ hours there and back plus half an hour for swimming. A trip to **Salto Techinén**, a lot higher, requires advance planning because of the distance and time involved.

From Kavanayén there is a six-day trek to **Kamarata**, southeast of Auyantepui. This kind of hike is only for the really fit as the trail winds up and down across the valleys between the Marík, Murauri and Yromún rivers. The terrain is virtually uninhabited and there are no emergency facilities. E'Masensen arrange meals, hammocks, porters, and a *curiara* for river crossings (about US$50 a day per person).

11

Gran Sabana highway waterfalls

San Rafael de Kamoirán At Km 171, this waterfall is located by a set of rapids on the river Kamoirán behind a basic accommodation option with a good restaurant and petrol station, called **Rápidos de Kamoirán** (*32 rooms;* \\0289 808 1505, 0286 951 8665). You can also ask to camp for a small fee. From here you can see the mountains Tramen, Ilú and Karauréntepui towards Guyana in the east. A community of Guyanese refugees live here so don't be surprised to hear English spoken.

Salto Kawi At Km 194–5, Salto Kawi is hidden off the east side of the road and is less visited. Here, the water from the falls spills onto a red jasper riverbed. A large sandy area is cleared for camping (US$2.50) and there is a shelter for slinging hammocks.

Salto Kamá Also known as **Kamá Meru**, on the west at Km 201, Salto Kamá slips over a rocky ledge to create a beautiful 55m curtain of white foaming water. By the river a Pemón family rents rooms in **Kama Wena**, a stone house with beds for six people, private bath and four thickly walled *churuatas* with shared baths (US$30). Nearer the river the **Karanao Restaurant** has a cluster of nicer *churuatas* (US$20) with beds, shared bath and a camping area (US$4).

Salto Arapán At Km 237, this waterfall is also known as **Quebrada Arapán (or Pacheco)**, or **La Laja**, for the river and its stony riverbed. There is an Inparques post where you can get local tourism information and a few Pemón houses, with a restaurant and souvenir shop. There are toilet facilities but washing is done in the river. Two *churuatas* have simple rooms to rent (US$20) or you can rent hammock space for a small fee.

Balneario Soruape 1.5km west of the highway at Km 243, there is a nearly perfect campsite in front of the rippling river, with smooth boulders and mauritia palms popular with weekend bathers from Santa Elena. There is a Parador Turístico with very basic bathrooms and an Inparques office. A number of sturdy native kiosks offer shelter for campers – if you can find the owner – or just come for the day.

Salto Yuruaní Upstream from the bridge at Km 247, this waterfall is wide rather than tall. When waters are low, pools invite swimming and you can duck behind the fall's curtain of water. But this spot, reached from the south end of the bridge, is marred by midge clouds all year. Mysteriously, there is no *plaga* if you take a trail on the north side of the bridge for maybe 700m to its end where the river has good swimming places and lovely views of Kukenán and Roraima.

San Francisco de Yuruaní At Km 250, San Francisco de Yuruaní is best known as the start of the trail to Roraima (see *Roraima* opposite). This fast-growing Pemón village has a police post on the highway, high school, Evangelical church, *medicatura*, football field, restaurants serving barbecued chicken and rice, and a few places offering basic lodging. A row of stalls bordering the road sells souvenirs. Ask for the spicy ant and termite sauce, a local speciality. To camp on the football field ask for 'El Capitan', the headman of the village, Hector Hernández.

⌂ Where to stay

⌂ **Arapena Guest House** (12 rooms) \\ 0241 866 4339; e arapenatours@hotmail.com. Basic rooms with beds, cold water, ask for Ovelio. Like everybody else in town can help arrange guides & porters for Roraima. $

⌂ **El Caney de Yuruaní** (12 rooms) m 0416 289 2413. Run by Hector Hernández, this simple *posada* has basic rooms with cold water, some with bunks. $

⌂ **Hospedaje Minina** (20 rooms) \\ 0289 808 2513; m 0414 886 6771. Another basic option with simple dorm-like rooms with cold water behind El Caney, restaurant serving fried chicken. Run by Dilia & her husband Eleuterio, who also organise Roraima treks. $

San Ignacio de Yuruaní At Km 259, San Ignacio de Yuruaní has a Guardia Nacional post that checks all travellers and vehicles.

Quebrada Jaspe At Km 273, this is the last set of waterfalls by the road. Small and intimate, it is much photographed for its red and yellow jasper bed. The creek hidden among trees is shallow, glowing as the sun strikes on wet jasper (go on a sunny day). There is good camping at Km 278, on the east side; walk about ten minutes to a smaller set of falls, the **Pozo de Agua Fría**.

The road leaves Canaima Park at the Kukenán Bridge, 15km before Santa Elena.

RORAIMA Roraima is the most mysterious, the most important and the best known of all the *tepuis*. At its top is a threeway boundary marker, the triple point, with Venezuela on the west, Guyana on the east and Brazil on the south, meaning you can visit three countries in under a minute. With a summit that reaches 2,810m, Roraima is also the tallest of the *tepuis*, giving hikers a climb of 1,700m from the savanna to the top. No special mountaineering skills or equipment are needed to climb Roraima, although a six-day hike to the summit and back is physically challenging. The local Pemón named the *tepui* Roraima, meaning 'Mother of All Waters', as the rivers that form on its ancient sandstone summit drain into three watersheds: the Orinoco, the Essequibo and the Amazon.

In 1912 geologist Leonard Dalton classified the sandstone that forms the plateau of the Guiana Shield and the *tepuis* as the Roraima Series. It was also the year that Arthur Conan Doyle, inspired by accounts of expeditions to the mountain, published his adventure classic of derring-do and dinosaurs, *The Lost World*. In

---

LA GUAYANA ESEQUIBA

Venezuela and Guyana must work to settle a century-old quarrel over La Guayana Esequiba, which appears to have no realistic solution. By an 1899 decision of an arbitration court in Paris, Venezuela lost claim to 150,000km² (61,500 square miles) west of the Essequibo River. It was one of the weightiest tribunals ever convened internationally: the American Chief Justice and a US Supreme Court judge represented Venezuela, and Lord Chief Justice Russell represented Britain. Both parties accepted the decision as final.

However, in 1982 a memorandum sealed more than 37 years earlier prompted Venezuela to reopen the case. In it, the ex-secretary to the original boundary commission, then an old man, stated that the British had unfairly influenced the court's decision by bribing its president.

The mediator in the boundary dispute – affecting two-thirds of the former British colony – is appointed by the United Nations Secretary-General under a 1996 agreement. Feelings escalated in the year 2000 when President Chávez threatened to grant oil concessions in La Guayana Esequiba in retaliation for Guyana signing a contract with a Texas aerospace company to build a commercial rocket launch site in the Essequibo. In the event, neither project materialised and the dispute was put on the back burner. However, Guyana has granted some 100 mining and lumbering concessions in the area to foreign enterprises.

The area, rich in forests and minerals, is sparsely populated. Many inhabitants are English-speaking Indians of the Arawak and Akawayo peoples. They are automatically dual nationals as citizens of land claimed by Venezuela.

reality, you're unlikely to find soaring pterodactyls or a giant T-Rex on the top of a *tepui* as the sparse vegetation and harsh conditions are unable to support anything larger than a rat. But, however tiny the inhabitants of the *tepui*, it doesn't stop the feeling of wonder you get from setting foot in this otherworldly place, which still feels like a real-life *Jurassic Park*. You trudge along white-sand trails through misty labyrinths of eroded black rock topped by weird silhouettes of fantastical creatures, passing sinkholes filled with tea-coloured waters and valleys strewn with quartz crystals. It's not surprising that the *tepui* summit is so unique, considering these huge outcrops are some of the oldest rock formations on the planet, formed over two billion years ago and exposed to sun, wind and rain for millennia.

Only hardy plants can eke out a living on the nutrient-deficient surface, including tiny orchids that stand out as intense spots of colour against the black rock. Wedged into cracks and crevices are mosses and lichens, while shallow pools host tough-leaved shrubs and twisted trees; even the black appearance of the rocks, which are naturally pink in unexposed areas, is caused by microscopic algae. But the true masters of survival are the carnivorous plants, the sticky sundews, pitcher plants and bladderworts that feed on the few insects to be found. Many of the tiny plants are exclusive to the *tepui* and have evolved for millions of years in isolation. The cutest creature has to be the tiny Roraima bush toad (*Oreophrynella quelchii*), a primitive black toad with a warty skin that can't hop or swim and appears to have adapted to *tepui* conditions by pretending to be a stone.

Dominating the landscape with its neighbour Kukenan, Roraima features in indigenous Pemón myth as the trunk of an ancient tree of plenty that was cut down by Ma'nápe, the brother of the hero Makunaima, unleashing a devastating flood and creating rivers and fish. Some anthropologists believe the mountain's reputation as the mother of all waters is linked to the myth.

Roraima came to international attention in the 19th century after reports were published by Robert Schomburgk of his adventures on a Royal Geographical Society expedition to map the boundaries of British Guiana, which were in dispute with Venezuela. A host of explorers and naturalists followed him to see this magical mountain for themselves and to try and ascend to its summit. Approaching from British Guiana, they all failed to scale the 600m cliffs and were driven back by storms, cold, fog and lack of food. Excitement ran high in Darwin's England, and the *Spectator* in 1874 challenged: 'Will no one explore Roraima and bring us back the tidings which it has waited these thousands of years to give us?' Finally, in 1884, Everard Im Thurn and Harry Perkins made it to the top after a two-month expedition. It was 18 December and very wet. Over a century later, hikers still follow the route taken by Perkins and Im Thurn. The only other route, pioneered in 1974 with great difficulty, involves climbing the north prow of the *tepui* on the Guyana side.

Today, any reasonably fit person can hike to Roraima's summit and back in four to six days from the base village of **Paraitepuy**. Although guides and porters can be hired in Paraitepuy and San Francisco de Yuruaní on the main Gran Sabana road, most tours began in Santa Elena de Uairén (see *Organising a trek* opposite).

Getting there Four- to six-day treks to Roraima start from the Pemón village of Paraitepuy, reached via a 27km dirt track from the roadside village of **San Francisco de Yuruaní**. About a dozen bus lines cross the Gran Sabana highway from Ciudad Guayana and Ciudad Bolívar to Santa Elena de Uairén on the border with Brazil and will drop hikers off at San Francisco, just south of the Yuruaní Bridge at Km 250. Jeeps can be arranged in San Francisco to take you to Paraitepuy (US$55 for a six-seater jeep), or you can walk there across shade-less savanna for seven hours. Many hikers on guided tours start from Santa Elena, which is about an hour south of San Francisco (66km) by bus and has an airport where charter planes from Canaima and Ciudad Bolívar land (US$100–120 one way). From Santa Elena it is also possible to contract a jeep and driver to take you straight to Paraitepuy (US$80 for a six-seater jeep), about 95km.

Organising a trek Hiking to the top of Roraima is not something you can do solo. Firstly, the Inparques post in Paraitepuy will not let you proceed unless you have a guide. Secondly, it is easy to get lost on the summit, which is covered in labyrinths of rock with deep ravines. It is also difficult to find the few sheltered overhangs that provide sandy camping spots – laughably referred to as 'hotels'. Fog can envelop you in an instant if cloud passes over the mountain, and hang there for hours, making progress dangerous. A slip while walking solo could result in a broken ankle or worse.

Hire your own guide You can hire guides and porters in San Francisco de Yuruaní at any of the *posadas* in town (see *Where to stay*, page 282) or Paraitepuy (ask at the Inparques post), who charge about US$30 and US$20 a day respectively. Porters will carry up to 20kg but you will have to provide your own food, which it is cheaper to buy before you arrive. Prices of all supplies are high in San Francisco and higher still in Paraitepuy, where options are limited to crackers, pasta and tinned sardines. You'll also need a cooker, waterproofs and warm clothes for the mountain-top. Anything you do not require for the hike you can leave in a locked hut in the village for a fee. Guides in San Francisco also rent out tents and sleeping mats but quality can be poor. Shop around, agree everything to be included before setting out and pay the bulk of the money when you get back. Typical complaints are that guides lag behind, especially if they're carrying significant weight, and hikers are left to follow the trail alone. One argument for hiring a local guide is that you are giving something back to the community.

Join a guided tour This is the easiest option and allows you to travel lighter as tents and sleeping bags are provided and carried by porters. The best place to join a tour is in Santa Elena, and the larger the group the more chance you have of getting a good deal on the price. Another important consideration, given that several thousand people climb Roraima every year, is that tour operators are obliged to provide chemical toilets, which significantly reduce contamination on the summit, while private guides do not.

All the tour operators offer the same six-day package, so price, quality of equipment and ability of guides make all the difference. Backpacker Tours, Mystic Tours and Kamadac are all recommended tour operators in Santa Elena (see *Santa Elena*, pages 289–90). Six-day/five-night tours range from about US$300 to US$500 per person depending on size of group. It definitely pays to shop around.

Permits and Inparques Officially, the summits of all *tepuis* are off limits in Venezuela but hikers who sign in at the Inparques office in Paraitepuy and are accompanied by a guide are allowed to make the trek. Arrive in Paraitepuy early, as nobody is allowed to start the trek after 14.00, to allow enough time to reach the first campsite at Río Tek, about four hours away. Inparques have the right to limit the number of hikers starting the walk and can close the trail at any time if they feel that too many people are on the mountain. At Christmas, Easter and Carnival, the summit can get overcrowded as campers cram into the available 'hotels'. Roraima is an environmentally sensitive area and the authorities are not keen to encourage people to climb it. And rightly so: too many unscrupulous guides and solo hikers have in the past shown little respect for this unique ecosystem and have dumped their garbage along the trail and on the summit. Annual clean-ups prove that some people continue to treat the mountain as a rubbish dump. Joining a guided tour

11

can be less environmentally damaging as the large tour operators use chemical toilets and dispose of all waste in Santa Elena.

What to take Pack as little as possible to keep weight down but plan for rain, hot days and cold nights. The most important things to bring are a light raincoat or poncho, plastic bags to keep clothes and camera dry, and a big plastic bin bag to line your rucksack. A flashlight is essential for moving about at night and a head torch makes life much easier. Bring enough batteries for your torch and digital camera as there is no electricity beyond Paraitepuy and it would be a shame to miss that final clear view of the mountain as the rain stops for the first time in six days! Boots should be thoroughly worn in before setting out, and a pair of flip-flops with straps make good camp wear and an alternative to the boots if blisters get too bad. Venezuelan *jabon azul*, available in supermarkets and small grocery stores, is eco-friendly for washing in pools on the summit. Repellent is a must on this trek, as are a hat, long-sleeved top and a pair of long trousers. A bottle of cheap rum purchased in Santa Elena (US$2.50) might sound like an extravagance on a mountain trek but you will appreciate the warming effects when poured into a hot drink before turning in to sleep.

UP AND AWAY TO RORAIMA

When director Pete Docter and the creative team at Pixar–Disney were looking for a location to set their cartoon adventure *Up* they initially considered a desert island. However, after seeing an old documentary about Angel Falls and the *Lost World tepuis* of the Gran Sabana they were inspired enough to fly down to Venezuela in 2004 and spend several weeks exploring the region. To make sure they got the feel of such an otherwordly place, the director Pete Docter and 11 Pixar artists climbed to the top of Roraima to see it for themselves.

'We hiked up to the top of the mountain and stayed there for three nights, painting and sketching,' Docter said in an interview, adding 'it was great' and 'everybody made it out alive'.

Up, a heartwarming tale of a grumpy old man who hitches thousands of balloons to his house and flies away to Venezuela with a young boy as his unintended companion, came out in 2010 to rave reviews and a slew of awards.

The story revolves around a curmudgeonly old balloon salesman called Carl Fredricksen (voiced by Ed Asner), a 78-year-old widower who had promised his late wife Ellie that he would take her away to 'Paradise Falls' (based on Angel Falls), the most beautiful and awe-inspiring waterfall in South America. Feeling he has nothing to lose after his house is targeted for demolition he finally plucks up the courage to set out on his adventure, unwittingly taking a an eight-year-old Wilderness Ranger called Russell with him. The two have lots of adventures on the *tepui*-top and although they don't find Conan Doyle's *Lost World* dinosaurs, they do meet a rare bird.

Not surprisingly, the film has sparked renewed interest in Angel Falls and Roraima and the strange landscape of the mountain top – with its carnivorous plants and spooky, prehistoric rock formations, which feature heavily in the movie.

Ronnie del Carmen, a story artist who worked on the film, writes on his blog that visiting Roraima was: 'the grand daddy of all research trips. Easily the most adventurous, rigorous trip I've ever been involved in (and I've been in a few. They are a walk in the park by comparison).'

According to del Carmen there was: 'danger at every turn: snakes, falling off cliffs, lethal bugs, spelunking under a crumbling cave ceiling... you know, fun.'

☞ **WARNING:** The rocks on Roraima may have been formed two billion years ago but the *tepui* summits are fragile ecosystems that should be respected. It is strictly forbidden to bring any stones, plants or crystals down from the mountain. The bags and pockets of all hikers returning to Paraitepuy are thoroughly searched by an Inparques ranger. If anything is found that belongs on the *tepui* the tour company is fined and the tour guide can be banned from working for up to two months.

The trail Most Roraima treks start in Paraitepuy early to mid morning and sign in at the Inparques post before setting off along a former jeep track down into the valley, up a ridge, across hills and through open savanna. As you walk east, the massifs of Kukenán on the left and Roraima on the right draw steadily closer. The footpath follows an old jeep trail and is impossible to lose, with occasional short cuts on the steep uphill and downhill bits. Have repellent handy for stops at the rivers as *puri-puri* bites can accumulate fast and slap on sunblock from the beginning as it's easy to burn.

After about three hours' trek, you come down to a generous stream with beautiful deep, blue swimming holes. You can usually cross this stream without removing your shoes. The Río Tek, about 30 minutes further on, is often used as the first night's camp and there are two shelters, with good views of Roraima and Kukenán beyond. The local Pemón sometimes carry crates of beer to this point, which they sell at exorbitant prices. Half an hour beyond this is the biggest river of all, the Río Kukenán. If it has rained within the last 24 hours this can be quite a difficult crossing, especially with a full pack on your back, as the rushing water can be thigh deep and the stones on the bottom are uneven and slippery. If you do need to cross in the water keep your socks on for grip and face upstream. Some treks are forced to stop if the water is too high, but experienced guides will use ropes if necessary to make crossings safe. If you set out from Paraitepuy at around midday, you should arrive at the Kukenán River in good time to have a swim and set up camp as the sun goes down. Most organised tours camp here for the first night or at Río Tek. If, however, you started early in the morning, you can have a snack and continue for another four hours or so up a steep final stretch to another campsite known as the **Campamento Abajo** or 'base camp', at 1,870m, where the Roraima foothills begin. After a fairly stiff climb you reach a flat meadow right under the shadow of Roraima's sheer cliffs. Below the campsite is a clear stream with freezing water from the mountain where you can bathe and freshen up. At night, there are fireflies. The view back over the route you have come is superb.

From the Campamento Abajo to the top of Roraima it is about four hours' gruelling climb, scrambling through dripping trees and over boulders, all the time going relentlessly upwards. For the first two hours you work your way up the cliff on a diagonal ledge covered in vegetation. Finally you descend to a cascading icy waterfall, which you pass under to reach a rocky gully. From here, the final two-hour ascent is up a series of steep steps leading to the top and your first glimpse of the fantastical rock formations on the summit.

It is not easy to move around on the summit, with its huge rock mushrooms, pillars and crevasses surrounded by boggy ponds, and camping is tricky. There are several sheltered areas known as 'hotels' but don't expect the Hilton: they are simply rock overhangs or caves carved into the sandstone with a sandy floor and enough space for two or three small tents at most. Other areas which look flat enough to camp on can quickly become water-logged if it rains, which is often, and the bare rock retains no heat when the sun sets making for very cold nights.

Once on top, the 9km walk to the **triple boundary** marker is not too tough, about eight hours there and back. But it is complicated and should not be attempted without a guide. Just before the marker, there is a large pool known as

El Foso (The Pit), where you can climb down into the sinkhole and bathe in the freezing waters and waterfall. Nearby is the famous **Valley of the Crystals**, a spectacular gully paved with white and pink quartz crystals. (Please do not pick the crystals – it is prohibited to take anything from the area and you may be fined.) Twenty minutes beyond the marker an idyllic cascade makes rainbows as it falls 10m into an amber pool.

Another place that can be visited from the hotels is La Ventana, a rock window that gives vertigo-inducing views of the sheer walls of the *tepui* and over the forested valley towards Kukenán, also known as Matawi Tepui, meaning 'the place of the dead' and considered sacred by the Pemón. The highest point on Roraima is marked by a small cairn and also has great views of Kukenán, especially in the afternoon when the valley between the mountains fills with cloud and you get the sensation of being in a plane.

On the way down, the descent from the *tepui* can be hard on the knees and slippery when wet. Most treks head straight for Río Tek on day five, arriving in the late afternoon. The last day is a short two- to three-hour walk to Paraitepuy, where bags are searched at the Inparques post for crystals and plants.

Roraima the quick, easy and exciting way If you are short of time, and funds are not too tight, then you can follow Hollywood stars like Harrison Ford and fly to the summit of Roraima in a helicopter. Instead of a six-day trek, the flight to the Triple Point boundary marker takes less than an hour and you can visit more distant points on top of the *tepui*, which would take too long to reach on foot. Being flown in by helicopter may not seem like the proper way to trek to Roraima, but it's a valid option for those who can't physically make the trek, have little time to spare, or just want to see the *tepui* from the air and get a different perspective on the *Lost World* plateau and a panoramic view of the other tabletop mountains. Return flights cost over US$1,300 for four people and you can arrange drop off and pickup (see *Helicopter and plane charters*, page 291).

SANTA ELENA DE UAIRÉN (*Telephone code: 0289*) Just 15km from the border with Brazil, you're as likely to hear Portuguese as Spanish in the small frontier town of Santa Elena, which feels safe and secure compared with many Venezuelan cities. Surrounded on all sides by spectacular savanna, with tabletop mountains and towering waterfalls within easy reach, it is also an important base for tourists planning to climb Roraima, explore the Gran Sabana or visit the remote artistic community of El Paují. For Brazilian tourists from Manaus and Boa Vista it's the gateway to the central coast and Margarita Island, the closest beaches they can drive to from their home in the heart of the Brazilian jungle, even though the distances might seem incredible. Santa Elena is a good place to change money and stock up on supplies. Besides well-stocked supermarkets, there is a hospital, two banks, a disco with a karaoke machine, three pool halls, and countless liquor stores and gold brokers. Good restaurants and bakeries are reasonably priced and there is a definite Brazilian flavour to the town, with some restaurants selling buffet-style food by the kilo. Crossborder trade thrives, especially when it comes to Venezuelan petrol, which is so cheap in relation to Brazilian petrol it has to be rationed. The town is also an important trading point for miners, who come in from Icabarú looking to sell gold and get some weekend action. If you buy any diamonds or gold be sure to get a receipt to avoid any problems with the Guardia Nacional. Santa Elena also attracts Venezuelan and foreign settlers seeking a healthier life and a new start. Many have opened guesthouses, tour companies and restaurants, and there is a volunteer programme working with indigenous groups and disabled children run by a German expatriate. In this far-out place of 30,000 inhabitants you can meet sociologists, anthropologists, practitioners of acupuncture and hatha yoga, Evangelist missionaries and even followers of the Indian guru Sai Baba, whose followers have two temples.

The town is fairly recent, founded in 1924 by a settler called Lucas Fernández Peña, and his family. He named the place after the little Uairén River and his daughter Elena (and went on to have 27 more children). A Capuchin mission at the Pemón (Taurepán) community of Manakruk (1km west of Plaza Bolívar) dates from 1931.

Getting there and away
By air The airfield is on the road to El Paují some 7km southwest of Santa Elena. The terminal consists of one waiting/control room. Across the street are a small restaurant catering for would-be passengers, and a Guardia Nacional desk where you register. The only regular service is an Aereotuy (*www.tuy.com*) flight every Monday, Friday and Saturday leaving Santa Elena at 12.30, which stops in Canaima and continues to Porlamar in Margarita (US$500 return). There are no *por puestos* serving the airport; taxis from the centre cost about US$5. Chartered flights to Canaima or Ciudad Bolívar cost about US$120 per person for a group of four.

By bus The terminal is on the highway about 2km north of town. Buses of Expresos Guayana, Línea Orinoco, and others leave daily for Ciudad Bolívar (11 hours, US$20), the cheapest being Transbolivar (US$10), the government-run service to Ciudad Bolívar Airport. A direct service to Caracas by Expresos Los Llanos leaves at 11.30, arriving in La Bandera at 08.00 (US$35). Tickets must be purchased on day of travel. There is a small terminal tax and you must present your luggage to the Guardia Nacional desk at the entrance so it can be checked before you leave. Buses to Boa Vista (230km) and Manaus (760km) in Brazil must be taken on the other side of the border in the Pacaraima bus terminal.

Jeeps for El Paují leave at 07.00 from Plaza Bolívar and take less than two hours (US$25).

By car Santa Elena is the last town on the Gran Sabana highway, also known as Route 10. If driving down from Ciudad Guayana make sure that you fill up with fuel before you start your journey and have all the paperwork in order for the car as there are three or four National Guard checkpoints along the way.

To/from Brazil Travellers entering or leaving Venezuela have to go through immigration at the border called La Linea on the Venezuelan side and Pacaraima on the Brazilian side. Be sure to have your passport stamped by ONI (Oficina Nacional de Inmigación) officials as you enter or leave and all travellers entering Brazil must have a yellow-fever vaccination certificate or they will vaccinate you free of charge at the border. Travellers in Brazil heading for Venezuela should try to get their Venezuelan visa in Manaus or Boa Vista. Don't get a 72-hour transit visa, which cannot be extended once you get to Venezuela. Travellers from Venezuela visiting the border town of Pacaraima only need their passport and yellow-fever certificate. The Brazilian consulate (*Edifício Galeno, Calle Los Castanos;* \ *0289 995 1256;* ⊕ *08.00–12.00 weekdays*) should issue visas the same day, but don't count on it.

Tour operators
Backpacker Tours Calle Urdaneta; \ 0289 995 1415, 0289 995 1430; m 0414 886 7227; e info@ backpacker-tours.com; www.backpacker-tours.com. Run

by a German called Eric Buschbell & his Venezuelan wife, this tour company offers some of the best Roraima excursions in town, with good prices &

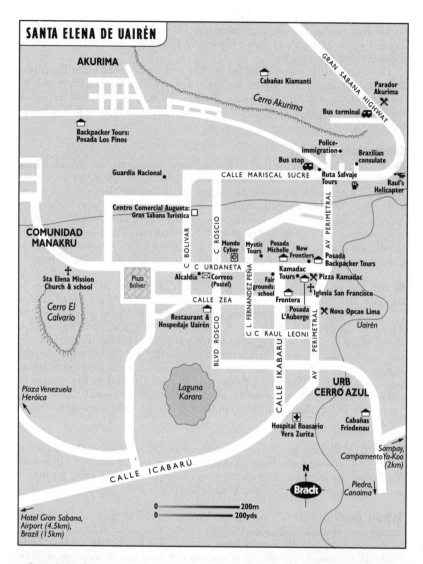

SANTA ELENA DE UAIRÉN

AKURIMA

Cerro Akurima

Cabañas Kiamanti

GRAN SABANA HIGHWAY

Parador Akurima

Bus terminal

Backpacker Tours: Posada Los Pinos

Police-immigration

Brazilian consulate

Bus stop

Guardia Nacional

CALLE MARISCAL SUCRE

Ruta Salvaje Tours

Raul's Helicopter

COMUNIDAD MANAKRU

Centro Comercial Augusta: Gran Sabana Turística

C BOLIVAR

C ROSCIO

AV PERIMETRAL

Mundo Cyber

Mystic Tours

Posada Michelle

New Frontiers

Posada Backpacker Tours

C C URDANETA

Sta Elena Mission Church & school

Plaza Bolívar

Alcaldía

Correos (Postel)

C L FERNANDEZ PEÑA

Kamadac Tours

Pizza Kamadac

Cerro El Calvario

Fair grounds: school

Frontera

Iglesia San Francisco

CALLE ZEA

Restaurant & Hospedaje Uairén

BLVD ROSCIO

C C RAUL LEONI

Posada L'Auberge

Nova Opcao Lima

Uairén

AV PERIMETRAL

Plaza Venezuela Heróica

Laguna Karara

CALLE IKABARU

URB CERRO AZUL

Hospital Roasario Vera Zurita

Cabañas Friedenau

AV PERIMETRAL

CALLE ICABARÚ

Sampay, Campamento Ya-Koo (2km)

N

Bradt

Piedra, Canaima

0 ————— 200m
0 ————— 200yds

Hotel Gran Sabana, Airport (4.5km), Brazil (15km)

quality equipment. Can also arrange accommodation, charter flights & trips to Angel Falls, Gran Sabana, circuits of Venezuela. Eric speaks English.

Kamadac Tours & Expeditions Calle Urdaneta; 0289 995 1408, 0289 888 994; m 0416 187 7216, 0424 963 7832; e tour@kamadac.de; www.kamadac.de. A German–Venezuelan operation with bilingual English-speaking guides, Kamadac is located opposite Backpacker Tours on Calle Urdaneta & has a popular pizza restaurant. Roraima treks are the bread & butter of this outfit but they also offer Angel Falls & trekking to remote *tepuis*, such as Akopan.

Mystic Tours Calle Urdaneta, casa No 6; 0289 416 0558, 0289 416 0686; e robertomarrero52@gmail.com; www.mystictours.com.ve. Roberto Marrero has been running tours in the Gran Sabana for years & has an efficient & friendly team of Pemón guides & porters. He has also published several books & maps documenting the history of the Gran Sabana & the Pemón Indians & has a wealth of knowledge about the region, which he is happy to share. Those who are attuned to extra-dimensional vibrations, may fancy taking one of his mystic tours spotting UFOs in the Gran Sabana. Good Roraima tours at cheap prices.

New Frontiers Adventure Hotel Michelle at the east end of Av Urdaneta; \ 0289 995 1443, 0289 995 1583; e info@newfrontiersadventures.com. Has an excellent mountain team headed by guides Mario Rojas & Kendall Donald Mitchell, an English-speaking Pemón (he owns the Arapán restaurant & shop in Quebrada de Pacheco).

Helicopter and plane charters Raúl Arias has a heliport and hangar on Avenida Mariscal Sucre by the new bus terminal, and an office in the Hotel Gran Sabana (\ 0289 995 1912, 0289 995 1711; e raularias@cantv.net; www.raulhelicopteros.com). For travellers with over US$1,000 to spare, this is a fantastic way to get around. Raúl can put his Bell five-seater helicopters on top of Roraima. He even visits Angel Falls. There's little Raúl doesn't know about what to see or do. He has organised three parachuting events 12,500ft over the Gran Sabana and can arrange charter flights.

Where to stay

At an elevation of 900m, the area is cool at night and hotels need no air conditioning; those listed below have rooms with fan and private bath. The more expensive places are likely to have higher prices at holiday times, particularly during the dry season and the town's *fiestas patronales* in August.

Cabañas Friedenau (8 cabins, 8 trpls) Av Principal, Cielo Azul; \ 0289 995 1295; m 0414 894 7171; e friedenau@cantv.net. Just out of town in the Cielo Azul sector, the walled grounds have cabins for up to 6 guests with hot water, TV, kitchen (bring your own pots) & restaurant serving vegetarian food. Ask in advance if there is food service. Good for large groups. $$

Campamento Ya-Koo (17 rooms) Lomas de Piedra, via Sampai; \ 0289 995 1742; e yakoo@cantv.net; www.ya-koo.com. This by-reservation guesthouse built by Manfred & Xiomara Frischeisen has a wonderful savanna view. Set on the hill above an opensided restaurant are pretty oval cottages for 5–9 guests with hot water, an open-sided dining area, oxy swimming pool & a natural pool formed by damming the river. Offer special low-season rates in a dbl, with b/fast & dinner. Pickup from bus station, Santa Elena. Can arrange tours & treks in Gran Sabana. Very friendly. $$

Posada L'Auberge (8 rooms) Calle Urdaneta; \ 0289 995 1567; m 0416 628 0836; e l.auberge@hotmail.com; www.l-auberge.net. This new, French-run place in the main tourist street in town has clean, simple rooms with hot water, AC, fridge, TV, internet in lobby & parking. Owners can give advice on organising Roraima treks & visits to Gran Sabana waterfalls. $$

Posada Backpacker Tours (10 rooms) Calle Urdaneta; \ 0289 995 1415; m 0414 886 7227; www.backpacker-tours.com. Basic but nice rooms with hot water upstairs & internet, bar & restaurant downstairs, make this one of the main meeting places for backpackers looking for others to make up numbers on Roraima trips. Eric, who runs Backpacker Tours, has another house called Posada los Pinos, with a small swimming pool, bar & restaurant for guests only. $–$$

Posada Michelle (25 rooms) Calle Urdaneta, a few doors down from Backpacker Tours; \ 0289 416 1257. A good budget option with kitchen privileges, cheaper rooms have shared bathroom. A place to meet other travellers. $

Where to eat

Nova Opcao Lima Av Perimetral, opposite Iglesia San Francisco; \ 0289 995 1013; ⏰ 11.30–21.00. A very popular Brazilian restaurant, where you pay for your plate by the kilo from a buffet of meat & vegetable dishes. Cheap & filling. $

Pizza Kamadac Calle Urdaneta, next to Kamadac tour agency; \ 0289 995 1408; m 0414 889 1196; ⏰ 12.00–22.00. A cosy corner to meet for a beer or a Cuba Libre & a pizza. $

Restaurant Michelle At Posada Michelle — see above; \ 0289 995 1628; ⏰ 12.00–22.00. A Chinese restaurant serving heaped portions with a menu list the length of your arm. Good value. $

Other practicalities

Money You should have little trouble changing dollars in shops or hotels, but travellers' cheques will be harder, except perhaps American Express. Small exchange houses and street dealers on Calle Urdaneta and Calle Bolívar (known as Cuatro Esquinas) change US dollars and Brazilian reales. There is a Banco Guayana on Plaza Bolívar and a Banco Industrial on Calle Urdaneta.

Internet There are several connection centres offering internet for US$1 an hour. Mundo Cyber on Calle Urdaneta stays open late and there is a CANTV Communications Centre in Calle Zea.

Medical The Rosario Vera Zurita hospital (📞 *171*) is on Calle Icabarú.

Shopping There isn't much to buy in Santa Elena but if you fancy owning a fancy Brazilian hammock the stores around Plaza Bolívar have a good selection of Brazilian goods.

AROUND SANTA ELENA
La Línea There's a statue of Emperor Dom Pedro at La Línea, as the border is called, and some roadside restaurants and shops. **Pacaraima**, the Brazilian community some distance down the road, is small and colourless, depending on Santa Elena for petrol and many other necessities. In return, Venezuelans go there to buy medicines and mining gear, and to eat at small restaurants. There are undistinguished hotels; Hotel Palace Pacaraima lacks paint and patrons. The asphalted highway goes 220km to Boa Vista.

El Pauji At Km 75 from Santa Elena, El Paují is a Bohemian Shangri-La of artists, dancers, painters, and other New Age types who have abandoned the rat race of the big city to live among native Pemón and local miners, and devote themselves to an alternative lifestyle more in tune with the rhythms of nature. The village is at the edge of a savanna, enjoying hot days and cool nights at an altitude of 860m. It is named after a turkey-sized forest bird, the guan. Here, far from modern comforts (there is radio communication but no phones), settlers have built quirky homes, a thatched chapel, a village school, clinic, water system, and now a theatre and very active cultural centre. The football field also sees plenty of action. People make a living as small-scale farmers, miners or bee-keepers – El Paují's 'wild' honey is famous. Others have set up *posadas* and are promoting tourism to the village and the surrounding countryside, including the spectacular views from a small *tepui* called El Abismo that looks over a huge swathe of Brazilian rainforest.

On the way from Santa Elena to El Paují, the jeeps pass two Pemón communities, Maurak and Betania, and the mixed mining community of Peraitepuy near the Surucún River reached by a track at Km 55. The Surucún has been known for its diamonds since 1931 and in 1942, back in the days when the journey from El Dorado took six weeks, a miner there named Jaime 'Barrabás' Hudson found a huge 154-carat diamond which had been passed over as a rock. The diamond was bought by the famous New York-based diamond dealer and jeweller Harry Winston, who cut it into three stones. The largest, the 40-carat 'Libertador', is part of the Winston collection. Hudson, who was driving a taxi in Tumeremo when interviewed in 1989, said he quickly spent his US$10,000 fortune and went back to work in the mines.

Getting there The road from Santa Elena to El Paují (75km) is now paved and jeeps take only two hours (US$25) to make the journey, continuing on to Icabarú (121km). There is an airstrip with regular airtaxi service to Santa Elena.

🏠 **Where to stay and eat** Most lodging takes the form of rustic cabins and rooms with bath, imaginatively built and run by the owners who often cook meals, too.

🛏 **Hospedaje Chimantá** (7 rooms) ✆ 0289 995 1431; m 0416 926 9091; e chimanta@cantv.net. Owned by bee-keeper Luis Scott, who speaks English & German. Luis serves guests who stay on packages 2 or 3 meals a day with whole-wheat loaves that he makes himself at his nearby bar/restaurant **La Comarca**. Rooms for 2–5 guests, with solar hot water & lighting, private bath. Luis & his wife will also take reservations for other *posadas* & organise local excursions. When he's not collecting honey, he milks venom from snakes for serum makers. $$

🛏 **Posada Maripak Tepuy** (3 cabins) ✆ 0289 808 1033, 0212 234 3661; m 0414 886 7144; e maripaktepuy@hotmail.com. Located near the airfield, has a well-patronised restaurant/bar where Marielly Gil presides. The cosy cabins have hot water, use of kitchen & there are places to camp for a small fee, & somewhere to cook. $$

🛏 **Campamento Manoa** (8 cabins) 1km east, makes the international marketplace with expeditions, local tours, transfers & 8 very nice cabins with solar lighting, trpls & dbls; cabin only, or package deal for US$70 a head. (Reservations, contact Luis.) $

Other practicalities This is a very rustic place with no banks or big supermarkets, so take the cash and supplies you need with you. A head torch is always useful in case of power outages and for trips to an outdoor restroom. A spare battery for the digital camera always comes in handy out in the wilds.

What to see and do

Visit the Casa de Cultura A respected theatre and dance centre directed by Marlene Morillo and Ali Rangel where international festivals are held, entitled *Nature, Art & Frontier*. Marlene also runs a guesthouse with ten rooms in cabins to accommodate visitors ($$).

Trek to El Abismo An hour's walk uphill takes you to the Mirador, at 930m elevation on an eroded massif, which marks the edge of the Gran Sabana Plateau. Looking south, the abyss falls away 400m down forested slopes to Brazil. The valley, some 30km wide, forms the upper Icabarú basin. Other less demanding attractions near El Paují are waterfalls and natural swimming pools hidden in the forest, such as the beautiful Pozo Esmeralda, an easy walk from El Paují, and La Catedral, a waterfall with a 15m drop some 12km east of El Paují.

Icabarú Icabarú is 121km southwest of Santa Elena by this road through forested hills. It has an airfield and you can fly in by airtaxi. The *pueblo*, which began life as a 1947 diamond strike or *bulla*, is again the centre of mining activities today (both legal and illegal), mostly gold. It is a rough place, without adequate accommodation, basic stores and the bars sell over-priced beer. As many as 20,000 miners work this region in the headwaters of the Caroní. A place to get a taste of the mining life on a day trip visit from El Paují.

CAURA RIVER AND PARA FALLS
The Caura is a mighty Guayana river, third in volume after the Orinoco (of which it is a tributary) and the Río Caroní. It is doubly valued as one of the last great 'wild' rivers, its pristine waters untainted by mining or farming run-off. Racing darkly over boulders and rapids, the Caura descends 500km through virgin forests from mountains bordering Brazil to a spectacular chain of falls 50m high, the Saltos Para, seldom visited and all the more special as a result.

The Caura basin catches some of the country's heaviest rains, over 3,000mm a year, emerging as a black-water river – stained a tea-red by the tannins from a zillion fallen leaves. Black Guayana rivers run swiftly over bedrock, bearing little sediment, and as a result support fewer insects and wildlife (meaning fewer nasty mosquitoes) than white-water Orinoco tributaries, which are slow and muddy.

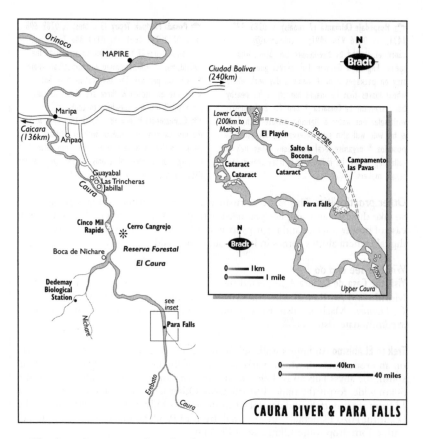

CAURA RIVER & PARA FALLS

The best time to travel is the dry season, December to April, when rock formations, superb beaches and the absence of mosquitoes contribute to idyllic camping. This is truly the best off-the-beaten-track river.

The Caura is also an important river for the Yekuana, a proud Carib-speaking group formerly known as Makiritares. The Yekuana are stocky and strong. Many Yekuana trace their origins to the upper reaches of the Caura and consider it their cultural heartland. Yekuana means 'Men of the River' and these Indians are indeed master makers and handlers of dugout canoes – durable, slim craft hollowed to a 3cm shell from a solid trunk. Such *curiaras* may measure over 14m. Because of the Caura's many intricate rapids, the Yekuana are the only real navigators of its changing currents. The Yekuana are also famed for their wood-carvings of shaman's benches in the forms of jaguar and armadillo, and intricate basketwork designs. The Sanema, an ethnic group related to the Yanomami, also live along the Caura, traditionally in a subservient role to the Yekuana. Few outsiders penetrate above Para Falls.

Maripa The only town of any size along the Caura, Maripa makes a good travel base as it is on the Caicara highway 234km west of Ciudad Bolívar. The *pueblo* is famous for making and selling *curiaras* and men can often be seen hollowing out camphorwood and sassafras trunks with axes and fire. For a riverman, however, the big investment today is his outboard motor as many of Maripa's 9,000 inhabitants depend on fishing or farm plots upriver.

In 1773 the Franciscans founded a settlement to the north called San Pedro de Alcántara. In the 19th century rice was widely grown and there was a rice mill nearby. At the turn of the 20th century Maripa was an export centre for rubber and tonka beans – the seed of the *sarrapia* tree, which was used in perfume and cigarette manufacture (Lucky Strike), as it contains a fragrant substance called coumarin. Today the mango-like fruit is mostly left to the pigs but can be found all along the river.

Maripa's wide streets are lined with government-built houses shaded by large mango trees. Some shops sell basics such as corn flour for *arepas*, oil, tinned sardines, soft drinks, beer, hats and rope. The town's airstrip is on the northern outskirts. Phones have barely reached Maripa, but the Yekuana community maintains radio contact with Ciudad Bolívar, Para Falls and settlements on the upper Caura.

Because malaria is a problem in the rainy season, visitors should take preventive medicine before arriving. The village has no permanent doctor although there is a medical dispensary with a nurse.

Getting there Maripa is easy to reach by bus or by car from Ciudad Bolívar (240km, 4 hours) over the good highway to Caicara (126km) and Puerto Ayacucho. The road is hot and dusty in the dry season but passes through miles and miles of picturesque savannas dotted with palms.

✗ Where to eat There are two restaurants, one at the east end of town and one at the west, serving reliable chicken (*pollo a la parrilla*) where beer flows freely, as well as newer establishments towards the river.

Caura tours Most river boat tours leave from Las Trincheras to Para Falls, saving about three hours' river travel compared with departures from Maripa. Trincheras is 74km from Maripa and 52km from the highway and takes four hours from Ciudad Bolívar. A 4x4 is needed in the rainy season when the final section of dirt road can become impassable. Tours can take five, four or three days but having come so far it's a shame to rush when there are so many indigenous villages to visit, jungle walks to make and rivers to swim in. Tours cost US$300–500 per person and the more people in your group the cheaper it gets.

Tour operators

Akanan Travel www.akanan.com. This Caracas-based adventure tour operator can arrange 6-day tours starting in Ciudad Bolívar with a minimum of 2 passengers, making a leisurely exploration of the Caura with nights at Para Falls & the beach at El Playón, sleeping in hammocks with mosquito nets.

Cacao Travel www.cacaotravel.com. This operator has the best Caura base in Las Trincheras, overlooking the river, with good swimming. The lodge has 4 cabins for guests & a large thatched building equipped with hammocks, shower, cold water. Their trips to Para Falls leave from Ciudad Bolívar, with a minimum of 2 passengers. Sleeping in hammocks with mosquito nets, they spend 2 nights in Las Trincheras & 2 at El Playón.

Jonas Tours Ciudad Bolívar; \ 0285 651 0918; m 0414 099 5904; e jonastours54@hotmail.com. The pioneer of Río Caura Trips, Jonas Camejo is something of a legend in these parts. Guide 'Jungle'

Junior speaks English & 5–6-day tours to Para Falls include visits to El Playon, & Sanema & Yekuana Indian villages. Good rates.

Terekay Adventure Av Perimetral, Puerto Ayacucho; \ 0248 809 6581; m 0414 487 2123, 0416 543 7556, 0416 838 5637; e Terekayadventure@hotmail.com; www.Terekay.com.ve. From his base in Puerto Ayacucho, jungle-guide Vicente Barletta now offers Caura trips that start in Amazonas, travelling in speedboats (*voladoras*) to the Río Caura & Para Falls.

Yekwana Adventures Posada Don Carlos; m 0424 901 7710, 0412 184 6458; e miguelestaba@gmail.com. Miguel Estaba, whose Yekuana Indian name is Dichenedu, organises boat trips to the Río Caura & a circuit of the Nichare, Icutu & Tabaro rivers, staying in indigenous villages & sleeping in hammocks. Miguel is very passionate about the Yekuana culture & keeping the pristine forests of the Río Caura free from illegal mining.

Up the Caura to Para Falls Most trips begin at the *criollo* community of **Las Trincheras**, a sleepy town dotted with mango trees where people take life easy. From here, on **Day 1**, dugout canoes take three hours to the mouth of the Nichare, passing islands, jagged rocks and rapids, such as the **Mura Rapids** and **Raudal Cinco Mil**, where a man's *curiara* sank along with his fortune over a century ago. A stop for a picnic lunch allows time to cool off with a swim in the brandy-coloured waters. The first advice you get is that the Caura is relatively free of mosquitoes, a good thing, but the river is home to rays, which can sting if disturbed, and electric eels (which are really fish), so as you enter the shallows you have to shuffle your feet.

As the boat travels upriver keep an eye out for kingfishers darting across the water close to shore, or macaws, which squawk overhead in pairs. The cormorant-like birds sunning themselves on rocks in the river are anhingas, you see toucans flapping hard to keep their beaks up, fishing eagles, black hawks, white egrets, and grey skimmers dipping into the black waters.

The first night is normally spent in hammocks at one of the islands along the river like Doufrumi, which has a thatched shelter, Yokore, which has a menagerie of tame birds, or the Yekuana village of Nichare, at the mouth of the Nichare River. Now a village of nearly a hundred people, Boca de Nichare has many thatched huts, a large central roundhouse, and a medical dispensary. The Yekuana cultivate yuca for making cassava bread, and maize, yams, sugarcane, pineapple, pawpaw, coffee and cacao. A small research station, supported by the Amigos del Nichare and the New York Zoological Society, studies the area's birds, animals and fish. Wildlife is greatly depleted on the river, and fish are under pressure too. Fishermen from Ciudad Bolívar use 100m-long nets called *trenes*, taking tonnes of peacock bass, morocoto (*pacú*) and cachama.

Howler monkeys, turtles, giant otters, freshwater dolphins and spectacled caiman, once seen everywhere up the Caura, are now very shy; crocodiles have been all but eliminated.

On **Day 2** you pass more Yekuana and Sanema communities, such as Soapire, before reaching the end of the navigable section of the lower Caura: **El Playón**, a shining expanse of white beach. Here, there is a 5km series of cataracts and waterfalls rising to Para Falls. At the top of the beach stands a large wooden sculpture of the Yekuana creator Wanadi dreaming the world into being, taken from the small carvings on the handles of shaman's maracas. The beach now has five huts for visitors to hang hammocks, a shack selling beer and a shop selling artworks inspired by traditional Yekuana wood-carvings and baskets by Daniel Torres. The beach is good for swimming, free of mosquitoes and you can watch as the Yekuana fish from the rocks at the far end towards the falls.

On **Day 3** it's an early start to climb from El Playón to the Para Falls along a 6.5km portage trail, used by Yekuana and Sanema to transport goods up and down. Even loaded with 70kg tanks of fuel and barefoot, they can climb the trail in less than two hours. However, the uninitiated should plan for closer to three hours as the steep forest path, which is slippery in places, rises 210m. Take your swimsuit, water and a picnic and follow the well-beaten trail. Halfway, a boat portage bisects the path; you follow straight on for **Campamento Las Pavas** (3km). This camp at the top of the trail is a pretty surprise: prefabricated cabins set in a neat park. Engineers making a dam feasibility study built the 'temporary' camp and helipad in 1975.

From here you get a panoramic view over the seven sets of 50m falls and smaller cataracts. Follow a trail to the bottom and you can swim in the river below the falls and in the rainy season the Yekuana will rent out a boat to take you into the spray of the falls. The return journey to El Playón is easier than the ascent and allows time to look out for the feared 24-hour ant, or *veintecuatro*, in the leaf litter or on the trunks of trees. These large ants give a bite that is so painful locals say it will induce a fever that lasts a full day, hence its name.

Day 4 sees a return down the Caura, travelling direct for five or six hours to Trincheras, or spending another night on the Caura and visiting **Cerro Cangrejo**, a lookout point on a high ridge that gives a spectacular view of the Caura River and the expanse of green forest canopy that stretches out as far as the eye can see.

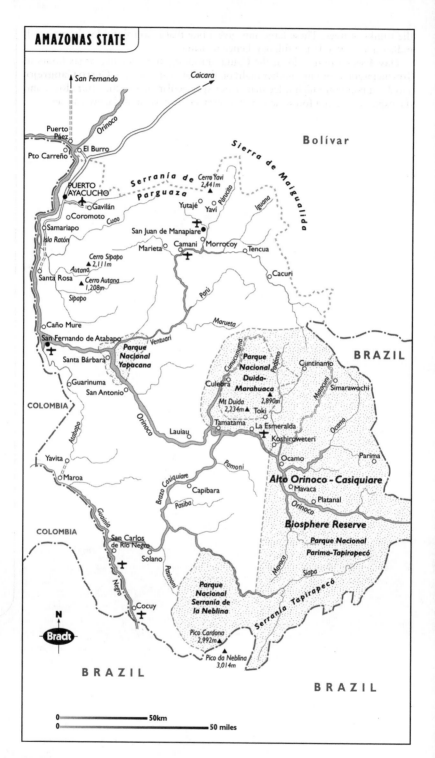

AMAZONAS STATE

San Fernando

Caicara

Orinoco

Puerto Páez

Pto Carreño

El Burro

Bolívar

Sierra de Maigualida

Serranía de parguaza

Cerro Yavi 2,441m

PUERTO AYACUCHO

Gavilán

Yutajé

Yavi

Panacito

Iguana

Coromoto

Cuao

Samariapo

San Juan de Manapiare

Isla Ratón

Marieta

Camani

Morrocoy

Tencua

Cerro Sipapo ▲ 2,111m

Autana

Parú

Cacuri

Santa Rosa

Cerro Autana 1,208m

Sipapo

Marueta

Caño Mure

San Fernando de Atabapo

Ventuari

Parque Nacional Yapacana

BRAZIL

Santa Bárbara

Cunacunuma

Parque Nacional Duida-Marahuaca

Cuntinamo

Padamo

Guarinuma

San Antonio

Culebra

2,890m ▲

Simarawochi

Matacuni

COLOMBIA

Mt Duida 2,234m ▲

Toki

Orinoco

Lauiau

Tamatama

La Esmeralda

Koshiroweteri

Ocamo

Ocamo

Parima

Atabapo

Pamoni

Yavita

Alto Orinoco - Casiquiare

Maroa

Brazo Casiquiare

Capibara

Mavaca

Platanal

Guainía

Pasiba

Orinoco

Biosphere Reserve

COLOMBIA

San Carlos de Río Negro

Parque Nacional Parima-Tapirapecó

Mavaca

Solano

Negro

Pasimoni

Siapa

Parque Nacional Serranía de la Neblina

Serranía Tapirapecó

Cocuy

N

Pico Cardona 2,992m ▲

Bradt

Pico da Neblina 3,014m

BRAZIL

BRAZIL

0 ————— 50km

0 ————— 50 miles

Amazonas

A wild, untamed and still unexplored region with a total population of just 150,000, Amazonas is Venezuela's 22nd state, covering a territory of 180,000km² and extending south to 0°40', just short of the Equator. From here, rainforests stretch south towards Brazil in a green carpet unbroken by roads but criss-crossed by the tributaries of the mighty Orinoco River that take the place of highways for travellers.

Home to remote rainforest tribes, national parks and a protected biosphere reserve, Amazonas offers travellers the opportunity to raft the famous Atures rapids at Puerto Ayacucho, follow the pioneering river routes of explorers like Alexander von Humboldt, visit mystical *tepui* mountains, fish for sabre-toothed payara and pretty peacock bass or go birdwatching at upmarket camps in the remote jungle of San Juan de Manapiare.

Puerto Ayacucho, the state capital and gateway to the region, is relatively developed and provides all mod cons, with several well-organised tour operators running road and river trips to ancient petroglyphs, Indian villages and rainforest camps, as well as air links in small planes to the more remote communities in the state. Travellers who want to explore the region can use Puerto Ayacucho as a base to learn more about the many indigenous tribes who live in the area and plan trips further afield to the mission station of La Esmeralda on the Orinoco, or the Casiquiare Canal, made famous by von Humboldt, and the distant San Carlos de Río Negro, set on a river of the same name which flows into the mighty Amazon.

NATURAL HISTORY

Four national parks in Amazonas cover a total of 53,000km², protecting (mostly on paper) the tablelands and mountains of the Yapacana, Duida–Marahuaca, Serranía La Neblina and the Parima–Tapirapeco, which at 34,200km² is the largest park in Venezuela. All but the Yapacana fall within the **Upper Orinoco Casiquiare Biosphere Reserve** (83,000km²), created in 1991 to restrict illegal mining and logging in the area and protect over 8,000 plant species.

Geologically, the area forms the western part of the Guiana Shield, whose pre-Cambrian sediments are over 1,000 years old. What you see today are the eroded remains of striking *tepui* tablelands, such as the isolated and majestic **Autana**, sacred to the Piaroa Indians, which rises vertically 1,220m out of green forest only 100km southeast of Puerto Ayacucho. **Cerro Marahuaca** (2,890m) and **Pico Cardona** (2,992m) in the Serranía La Neblina on the border with Brazil, are the tallest points of the Guiana Shield.

HISTORY

LAND OF EXPLORERS In 1761 the first and very large official Spanish expedition to the upper Orinoco, the Expedición de Límites, reached the Río Negro via the

Casiquiare Canal to settle the border with Brazil. Voyages by travellers and naturalists followed, including the German scientist Alexander von Humboldt and the French botanist Aime Bonpland in 1800, who explored the Casiquiare Canal. Jean Chaffanjon and Auguste Morisot followed in 1886 and Theodor Koch-Grünberg in 1912.

The source of the Orinoco was only officially discovered in 1951 in the Sierra de Parima and it was not until 1954 that a botanical expedition led by Bassett Maguire of the New York Botanical Garden reached and named **Cerro Neblina**. The Neblina range has two adjacent peaks, Pico Cardona in Venezuela and Pico de Neblina in Brazil. When measured at 3,014m, Neblina proved to be Brazil's highest mountain. Together the peaks are South America's tallest mountains east of the Andes.

Other than explorers, the forested interior remained largely unknown except to collectors of quinine, cacao, tonka beans (*sarrapia*) and later rubber (*balatá*). The forest workers who received a pittance for this labour were by and large the original Indian inhabitants.

MISSIONARY POSITION Given the history of the region, many of the communities along the rivers are run by missionaries. The Salesians, a Catholic order, have missions in Colonia Coromoto, Isla Ratón, San Fernando de Atabapo, San Juan de Manapiare and Ocamo. Evangelist missions set up shop in Tama Tama, Padamo and Mavaca in the 1950s but the Venezuelan government ordered all members of the US-based New Tribes Mission to leave the country in 2006 and only a few Venezuelan-born missionaries remain. Many such mission centres, old and new, have led to permanent communities. The mission in La Esmeralda has a long history, starting with Franciscans in the 18th century and, much later, the Salesians. This order has run a large school and mission in La Esmeralda since the 1940s. La Esmeralda has an environmental research station, the Centro Amazónico Alejandro de Humboldt, on the savanna behind the airstrip.

PEOPLE

The major ethnic groups in Amazonas are the Guahibo (Hiwi), Piaroa, Yekuana (Makiritare), Panare, Yanomami (Waika) and related Sanema, perhaps 40,000 people in all. The history of white men's contact with the Yanomami, beginning in the 1960s, is one of good intentions with doubtful benefits and at times disastrous consequences for the forest people's health and independent survival.

Today many ethnic communities living on the Ventuari, Manapiare, Paru, Orinoco and Atabapo rivers work with the forest, planting cacao (Yekuana and Piaroa), bee-keeping (Sanema, Piaroa, Guahibo), collecting *chiquichiqui* broom fibre, or processing *seje* palm nut oil. The Yekuana also herd water buffalo on grasslands.

The Yekuana are admired for their elegant dugout canoes, bigger types of *bongos* and beautifully designed communal houses. These huge conical structures accommodate several families. Like the Yekuana, the Piaroa, too, build a central roundhouse. Their traditional *churuata* is spectacular: it is like a 100-person seamless hat, 12m tall and thatched from ground to tip. Baskets, stools, carved jaguars and anteaters made by various ethnic groups are sent downriver for sale at Puerto Ayacucho's lively craft market. One of the lasting impressions most visitors to Amazonas take with them is a visit to the market and the different indigenous tribes encountered there.

However, although many visitors want to visit indigenous communities, Venezuelan law requires special permits to visit Indian territory and contact is limited to a few road and river routes; tour operators in Puerto Ayacucho (see page 302) can advise on permits.

Remember that this is a malaria region so begin taking anti-malaria medication before arriving if you intend to take a trip into the jungle, although for a short stay in Puerto Ayacucho you should have no problems. Bring insect repellent in spray and cream forms, and pack a long-sleeved shirt and long trousers or tracksuit to cover up with in the evenings. Electricity is variable so always have a flashlight; a head torch is worth its weight in gold in jungle camps. If you're travelling by boat to the Autana, or further afield, bring a swimming costume and canvas shoes or flip-flops with straps as the rivers, Orinoco included, are fast and clean and good for swimming. The sun is fierce and downpours unpredictable so bring a sun hat, rain poncho or cagoule and line your pack with a large plastic bag to keep kit dry on river boat trips.

GETTING THERE AND AWAY

By air The airline **Conviasa** (*www.conviasa.aero*) flies from Caracas to Puerto Ayacucho at 13.55 (1 hour 40 minutes, US$60–80) and from Puerto Ayacucho to Caracas at 16.05, daily except for Saturday. Taxis from the airport, 7km south of town, cost about US$3.

Airtaxis Based on Calle Evelio Roa, **Wayumi** (*\ 0248 521 0635*) is a co-operative of pilots running an airtaxi service. They make regular early morning flights, except on Sundays, to small towns in Amazonas State, including daily flights to **San Fernando de Atabapo** and **San Juan de Manapiare**, twice weekly to **La Esmeralda** and **Maroa** and once a week to **San Carlos de Río Negro**. They also make trips to smaller places such as the Yutajé jungle camp (45 minutes away; see page 303). Charter costs are calculated at about US$240 an hour for a five-seater Cessna. When estimating costs for flights to jungle camps, add 25% of an hour's flying cost for every hour the plane waits for you. Weight allowance is 10kg. A copy of your passport is needed in advance for the permit issued by the state government, which is arranged by Wayumi.

By bus The Terminal de Pasajeros is on the highway 6km from downtown, via Avenida 23 de Enero where there are local buses into town. Coaches leave in the evening for Ciudad Bolívar, 709km away (10–11 hours). Direct Caracas service is provided using the Orinoco ferry at Caicara (355km); this route takes at least 11 hours. The Llanos route to San Fernando de Apure, with connections to Maracay and points west, is a journey of 297km (8 hours) by way of the Orinoco ferry at El Burro and two more ferry crossings. This will be significantly reduced when planned bridges replace the picturesque river ferries or *chalanas*. There are *por puestos* from Puerto Ayacucho to El Burro.

By car The Route 19 highway from Ciudad Bolívar joins Route 12 at Caicara del Orinoco, where it follows the Río Orinoco south to Puerto Ayacucho.

To/from Brazil From the village of **San Carlos de Río Negro**, served by light planes from Puerto Ayacucho, you may find river transport to Brazil. The Venezuelan border post, San Simón de Cocuy, is about 100km south on the Río Negro and is linked to its Brazilian counterpart Sao Gabriel da Cachoeira by road. Brazilian three-decker river boats travel from Sao Gabriel to Manaus. However, it is exorbitantly expensive and time consuming to follow this route to Manaus. Better instead to travel from Puerto Ayacucho to Santa Elena in Bolívar State and cross into Brazil there. Travellers aiming to return to Venezuela will find a consulate in Manaus that issues visas, or can get a tourist card from their airline.

To/from Colombia Travellers entering or leaving Venezuela should have their passports stamped by Immigration. If you have not done this, go to the SAIME office on Avenida Aguerrevere, three blocks west of Avenida Orinoco (🕐 *08.00–12.00 & 14.00–17.00 w/days*).

By river, you can take the passenger launches from the dock in Puerto Ayacucho to **Casuarito** on the opposite bank. There you can catch a Colombian speedboat, or *voladora*, that goes every afternoon to Puerto Carreño (1 hour), at the confluence of the Meta and Orinoco rivers.

Alternatively, by road, head north of Puerto Ayacucho to El Burro and cross the Orinoco on a ferry-barge to **Puerto Páez**. This small Venezuelan port lies at the junction of the Orinoco with the Meta. It has an army post and SAIME office; make sure you get your passport stamped out of Venezuela. From the port, frequent passenger launches cross the Meta to Colombia. **Puerto Carreño**, a little town, has the necessary DAS office to stamp you into the country. Puerto Carreño is connected to Bogotá by a dry-weather road. There is an air service (Satena) three times a week. Among various hotels is the Samanare with a genial owner, Jairo Zorro, and a restaurant and disco.

TOUR OPERATORS Sightseeing tours to nearby indigenous communities, petroglyph sites and popular three–five-day boat trips to Autana, Cuao and San Fernando de Atabapo can easily be arranged in Puerto Ayacucho. Costs are usually quoted in dollars at US$30–35 for half a day, and US$50–60 for a full day. Longer trips where you sleep over in hammocks with mosquito nets will be more expensive, but the more people in your group the cheaper the price. Most agencies will be able to tailor an itinerary to your interests, be they birds, fishing or Indian villages, but if you want to do sport fishing you should bring your own equipment. While a two-day/one-night excursion – for instance to the Piaroa villages on the Río Parguaza – may cost roughly US$120, a four-day/three-night trip at US$220 works out relatively cheaper. Costs go up if there are fewer than four people in a group. Always shop around and bargain for a discount.

Axel Tours Valle Verde Triangulo; \ 0248 414 5036; m 0416 785 5033; e cruisingtours@hotmail.com; www.axeltours.info/index.php. German adventurer & tour leader Axel Keleman is a larger-than-life character who has spent some 25 years in the jungle leading both lengthy expeditions for prestigious scientists searching for new species and short individual tours with amateur Anthropology buffs who just want to visit the Yanomami for a few days after watching a *National Geographic* special on the rainforest tribe. Keleman can arrange most things, at a cost, & is enthusiastic, engaging & informative.

Coyote Expediciones Av Aguerrevere west of Av Orinoco; \ 0248 521 4583; e coyotexpediciones@cantv.net. A small company offering adventure tours for 1 or more people at very competitive prices. They organise travel (& permits) to rivers near & far: the Atabapo, Sipapo, Autana, Casiquiare, Río Negro. The *bongo* is your home by day, hammocks in a riverside camp by night. With a local guide you can trek through the forest, sleeping in hammocks, fishing & hunting.

Expediciones Selvadentro Via Alto Carinagua, Puerto Ayacucho; \ 0248 414 7458; m 0414 487 3810; e info@selvadentro.com; www.selvadentro.com. Friendly husband & wife team Luis 'Lucho' Navarro & Natalia Bird are the only tour company in Amazonas with a Brazilian houseboat, the *Iguana*, which once belonged to Jacques Cousteau. On it, they take travellers to the Casiquiare Canal on the so-called Ruta Humboldt from San Carlos de Río Negro to Samariapo, passing through the Casiquiare Canal, in 8–10 days. They also do trips to the Autana, the Cunucunuma River & offer tailor-made trips in the region to visit Yanomami villages. Tours cost about US$120–150 pp per day. Lucho & Natalia took authors Richard Starks & Miriam Murcutt on their recent adventure to the Casiquiare described in their book *Along the River that Flows Uphill: From the Orinoco to the Amazon*. (See *Appendix 2, Further information*, page 435).

TADAE Av Orinoco, C C Maniglia, Loc 13; \ 0248 521 4882; m 0414 486 5923; e tadaevenezuela@hotmail.com. Ruth & Javier Vielma take travellers to all the usual riverboat destinations from their small store on the Plaza de Los Indios, & Ruth goes the extra mile to make the meals interesting. A real bonus when you're out in the jungle.

Terekay Adventure Av Perimetral, Puerto Ayacucho; ✆ 0248 809 6581; m 0414 487 2123, 0416 543 7556, 0416 838 5637; e Terekayadventure@ hotmail.com; www.Terekay.com.ve. Vicente Barletta grew up visiting indigenous communities with his father, an Italian doctor. Now he takes tourists on very professional river trips to Autana, Cuao, Lago de Leopoldo, the Parguaza & Pijigua, & to visit the Yutaje waterfall & Hoti Indian villages in the Sierra de Maigualida from San Juan de Manapiare. Vicente is also pioneering speedboat (*voladora*) trips from Puerto Ayacucho to the Río Caura & Para Falls in Bolívar State, & has an incredible collection of indigenous art & artefacts.

Adventure camps Distant camps are reached by light planes working as airtaxis from Puerto Ayacucho Airport. The camps give a real opportunity to explore rainforests, rivers, and sometimes Indian cultures, or to go birding and fishing. The fees of such camps cover all activities and food, but not usually the transfer flight (on which you can carry 10kg only). Several camps have closed down since the last edition but check with tour operators in Puerto Ayacucho for updates.

Yutajé In the San Juan de Manapiare region; ✆ 0212 472 0502, 0248 521 5002, 0248 521 2550. Pioneered 40 years ago by an Italian, José Raggi; today the camp is run by his son. It lies some 45mins by plane northeast of Puerto Ayacucho in the Manapiare headwaters. Yutajé means 'Water which comes down from high' referring to the 700m falls not seen from the camp. The Raggis' wilderness base now offers satellite TV & telephone, 6 simple thatched *churuatas* & cabins with dbl & trpl rooms, cold water shower, ceiling fan. You can explore the clear, dark Corocoro River where curious giant otters poke heads out of water, & river dolphins surface to blow. Good bass fishing in dry season. Current price of US$80 per night includes taxes, excursions & meals (extra for bottled drinks & ice flown in by air). To reserve from Caracas contact Alpitour (see *Tour operators*, page 31).

Fishing tours Alpitour (*www.alpi-group.com*) can organise fishing tours in the Pasiba and Pasimoni rivers, famous among sport fishermen for producing world-record-breaking peacock bass. This is a lowland of virgin rainforest, lagoons and dry season beaches. Alpitour have an experienced crew that pick up visitors in San Carlos de Río Negro or Tama Tama, depending on river conditions, and use 16ft aluminium boats equipped with swivel seats and electric motor for catch-and-release fishing, with two anglers per boat. A five-day plan, sleeping in tents with cots in a moveable camp with generator and propane refrigerator, includes the two-hour charter flight from Puerto Ayacucho (see *Tour operators*, opposite).

River tours Permits are needed for any river trips to the Orinoco headwaters, the Alto Orinoco Biosphere Reserve, or beyond La Esmeralda, and these can be applied for by local tour companies who will need the names and ID or passport details of all the members of a group in advance. The Inparques office is in Edificio Funeraria Amazonas (*Calle La Guardia & Av Unión;* ✆ 0248 521 4771). As all river trips leave from Samariapo or Venedo ask local operators to include visits to Cerro Pintado and Tobogan de la Selva in any package you buy to the Autana or Cuao (see *Around Puerto Ayacucho*, page 308).

PUERTO AYACUCHO *Telephone code: 0248*

Full of street vendors and Indians selling trinkets, there is a border-town feel to Puerto Ayacucho, with a large boost in recent years to its small population of 40,000 from immigrants from the Colombian town of Casuarito on the other side of the Orinoco. The town follows a conventional plan: the church, Salesian mission school, town council and government offices surround Plaza Bolívar.

Amazonas State is not only linked to Brazil by its name. A unique river, the Casiquiare Canal, in fact joins the Orinoco and Amazon basins. The 320km-long river meets the upper Orinoco near the Catholic mission of La Esmeralda and, depending on the season, carries roughly one fifth of the Orinoco's waters to the Río Negro, a tributary of the Amazon. The two rivers join near the village of San Carlos de Río Negro, a day's journey from the frontier post of San Simón de Cocuy.

In 1800 German explorer and scientist Alexander von Humboldt and the French botanist Aimé Bonpland set out on a historic jungle adventure to discover more about this strange river. With porters toting trunks of instruments and boxes for plant and animal collections, they went by mule over the Llanos, and by boat to the Orinoco where their dugout had to be hauled through the Atures and Maipures rapids. They then travelled up the Atabapo to its headwaters, where 23 indians from the mission of Yavita dragged their large canoe 11km over to the Guainía's headwaters. After reaching the Río Negro, they followed the length of the Casiquiare to the Orinoco. It was a groundbreaking journey by Humboldt, who became the first person to prove that the Casiquiare Canal linked the Amazon and Orinoco basins. Tour operators in Puerto Ayacucho still organise similar trips for adventurous traveller's who want to follow 'Humboldt's Route', as it is known (see *Tour operators*, page 302).

Be warned. The Casiquiare has an evil reputation for clouds of biting midges and mosquitoes that have made life miserable for travellers for centuries. Humboldt and his party were distracted from the insect torture only by their floating menagerie of toucans, parrots and monkeys. Luckily, times have changed and travellers using outboard motors can now move faster than the mosquitoes. Modern-day explorers who have followed Humboldt along the Casiquiare Canal include Redmond O'Hanlon, who penned a hilarious and very informative account of his travels in the book *In Trouble Again*, and the writers Richard Starks and Miriam Murcutt who recently published *Along the River that Flows Uphill: From the Orinoco to the Amazon* (see *Appendix 2, Further information*, page 435).

Most tourism activity takes place in and around Plaza de Los Indios, where the ethnological museum is located, a few tour companies have their offices, and the Indian market bursts into life at weekends.

The first thing most visitors notice is the heat. The town is hot and humid most of the year and not surprisingly, given its location north of the biggest rainforest in the world, receives very heavy rains, more than 2,300mm a year, falling mostly during May–June and October.

Puerto Ayacucho is an important regional administrative centre and there is a strong National Guard and army presence to control river and air traffic to all points south, with an emphasis on intercepting cocaine shipments from Colombia and monitoring illegal mining.

HISTORY For all its sleepy indolence and creeper-covered walls, Puerto Ayacucho is a relatively modern town, founded in 1924, by the dictator Juan Vicente Gómez to mark the hundredth anniversary of the Battle of Ayacucho. By moving the capital to this site at the lower side of the Atures rapids where all travellers on the Orinoco are obliged to halt, the dictator could control the whole of the Amazonas territory. Here the great Atures and Maipures rapids, with their giant black boulders, are a natural obstacle to river navigation from the lower Orinoco, 900km or so from the Atlantic coast, and the headwaters of the upper Orinoco, with its source in the Sierra Parima Mountains over 1,100km away. Today cargo bound for the upper Orinoco must still be trucked 63km south of the rapids on a road built in the times of Gómez. Orinoco barges once brought all the town's fuel, vehicles, beer and cement, while planes supplied perishables, but the opening of the Caicara road has helped to bring down prices.

TOURIST INFORMATION The main office of the **Tourism Secretariat** (\ *0248 521 0033;* e *turismo@gob.ve; www.amazonas.gob.ve*) is opposite the airport and has information on the main sights, accommodation options and maps of the area.

WHERE TO STAY Given the importance of Puerto Ayacucho as a gateway to the region, there is a surprising lack of decent accommodation options. The best places in town are:

Hotel Gran Amazonas (25 rooms) Calle Amazonas, con Calle Evelio Roa; \ 0248 521 5633. Rescued & revamped, this iconic hotel is now run by the government & rates as one of the best in town. It has a large swimming pool with poolside bar, *tasca* restaurant serving food all day & pleasant entrance hall decorated with indigenous crafts. Rooms have AC, en-suite bathrooms & TV. $$

Posada Turistica Manapiare (15 rooms) Calle Principal de Alto Parima, 2 entrada, Casa Numero 1, Puerto Ayacucho; \ 0248 686 0062, 0248 521 3954; e posadamanapiare@hotmail.com; www.posadamanapiare.com.ve. This is the best place in town, with AC & TV in rooms, laundry service, a small restaurant serving b/fasts, lunch & dinner & a small pool for cooling off after a hot day of adventuring. Yesenia & José who run the place put

the competition to shame with attention to every detail. Very busy, ring well in advance to reserve. $$

Residencias Miramar (18 rooms) opposite Cadafe, Av Orinoco; \ 0248 521 4521. New & attractive, motel-style option with large rooms with AC, TV, bath. $$

Hotel Mawari (10 rooms) Calle Evelio Roa, near Plaza Bolívar & Hotel Gran Amazonas; \ 0248 521 3189. Another very basic option, with AC & fans in some rooms. $

Residencias Internacional (30 rooms) 18 Av Aguerrevere; \ 0248 521 0241. A haunt for backpackers seeking a cheap & cheerful base, who aren't too fussy about the amenities. Rooms around a central patio have AC, or fan; friendly owners offer meals, laundry service. $

Other mid-range options with air conditioning if you're stuck are:

Hotel Apure (17 rooms) \ 0248 521 0516. About 1km south of Plaza Bolívar on Av Orinoco. *Tasca* restaurant. $$

Hotel City Center (20 dbls & 2 trpls) Av 23 de Enero opposite the Marina; \ 0248 521 0639. $$

Hotel Mi Jardin (66 rooms) \ 0248 521 4647. Further south than Hotel Apure, one of the few hotels with suites & a restaurant. $$

Hotel Tonino (5 rooms) Av 23 de Enero, 100m from Av Orinoco; \ 0248 521 1464. A small hotel with plain rooms, bath & AC. Less expensive than the 3 hotels above. $

Camps

Campamento Orinoquia (10 *churuata*-style huts) 23km south of Puerto Ayacucho on the Samariapo road; \ 0212 977 1234; e ventas@ casatropical.com.ve; www.casatropical.com.ve. These indigenous-style cabins on the banks of the Orinoco at Garcitas rapids are perhaps the best of the lodges run by Caracas-based Casa Tropical. The thatched cabins have twin beds, cold water & bath & overlook the river (bring repellent). A larger *churuata* has a dining area & office. At low water there are good pools for swimming. Boat excursion

to Garcitas Island, ancient Indian cemetery, photo & bird safaris; also expeditions to the upper Orinoco & Ventuari rivers. Room prices pp in a dbl; also offer packages with tours & transfers. $$

Camturama \ 0248 521 0266, 0212 943 5160; m 0414 937 2531, 0416 269 9265. This jungle camp, also near Garcitas rapids, is 20km south of Ayacucho. It has ample grounds, ponds, a huge social centre with restaurant, disco, bar & games room, & comfortable lodging in 46 dbls in bungalows with hot water. Good low-season rates. Package deals

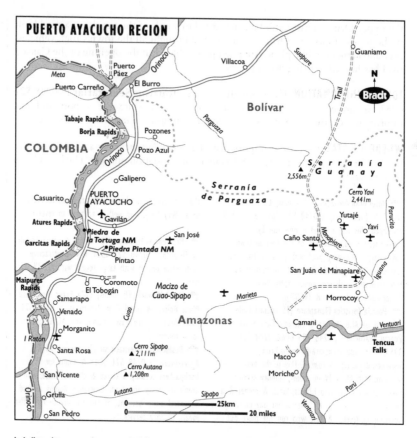

including airport transfers, taxes & daily tour about US$100 a day. $$

⌂ **Nacamtur** South of Puerto Ayacucho, located at Km 1.5 on the road to Gavilán, 5km from the airport; ☎ 0251 263 1739; m 0414 521 5117, 0414 521 6472. A large camp within walking distance of petroglyphs. There is a sizeable *criollo* restaurant, a separate disco that gets busy at w/ends, & a house providing 8 large suites with private bath, AC, for 2–6 guests; dbl bed. The late owner's son Yonny has taken over the camp; ask about local tours & river fishing. $$

✗ **WHERE TO EAT** There are no standout food places in Puerto Ayacucho and many people eat at the restaurants in their hotel, such as the *tasca* in the Hotel Gran Amazonas, which has slow service, or the better offering in Posada Manapiare. Keep in mind that Sundays are dead in Puerto Ayacucho so eat early.

On Saturday mornings it's worth trying the Indian market on Avenida Perimetral near the bus station, where river fish and *plátanos* or cooking bananas are fried on the spot. Look for seasonal palm fruits such as the *pijiguao* or peach palm boiled with salt like a potato and the *moriche* palm nuts used in fresh drinks.

✗ **Cherazad** 3rd flr, Av Aguerrevere con Río Negro; ☎ 0248 521 5679. Beside the museum on the corner, it has generous, tasty meals with Arab touches, pizzas & chicken. Very economical. $

✗ **Karam El Amir** Av Orinoco; ☎ 0248 521 1610; ☉ noon–midnight Mon–Sat, 05.30–11.00 Sun. A block from Plaza Bolívar this is a reasonable Arabic food place run by Syrians, always good for *tabaquitos* or stuffed cabbage rolls, hummus & falafel. $

La Pusana Av Orinoco, Via Aeropuerto; ☏ 0248 521 6534; m 0416 747 8842. The name comes from the magical mixtures of herbs used by local Indian ladies to bring them love. What better name for a restaurant housed in an Indian *churuata* dedicated to making its clients fall in love with the indigenous food of the region? This is the place to try spicy *katara* sauce, made from ants, exotic palm fruits & all manner of local fish served with rice & plantains. Run by an Indian co-operative. Thoroughly recommended. Take a taxi from Puerto Ayacucho. $

SHOPPING The main market in the Plaza del Indio has plenty of indigenous crafts and in the streets branching off the plaza you can find small stores selling fruit and vegetables. For specialist purchases of indigenous crafts from specific tribal groups, such as a Yekuana shaman's halluginogenic snuff-grinding set or 6ft-long Yanomami bow and arrows, contact Vicente Barletta of Terekay Adventures (see *Tour operators* above) who specialises in hard to get handicrafts.

OTHER PRACTICALITIES Access to the **internet** is very slow in Amazonas and answering emails can be frustrating. There are a number of cyber cafés in town, which are open all day, except Sundays when the town is dead. Try Cibercafé on Calle Evelio Roa by Hotel Maguari, and El Navegante in the Centro Comercial Maniglia on Avenida Orinoco. The central office of CANTV on Avenida Orinoco at Avenida Aguerrevere has the usual **phone service** for local and international phone calls and there are a number of stalls in the street around Plaza de Los Indios and at the bus terminal offering mobile phone calls at reasonable prices.

There is a Banco de Venezuela on Avenida Orinoco opposite the corner with Calle Union and a Banco Provincial on Avenida Aguerrevere near the corner with Avenida la Guardia.

The main Hospital José Gregorio Hernández on Avenida 23 de Enero offers basic public hospital facilities.

WHAT TO SEE AND DO
Museo Etnológico del Amazonas (*Ethnographic Museum; Plaza de los Indios, Av Río Negro;* ☏ *0248 521 2842;* e *musetamaz@cantv.net;* ⊕ *08.30–11.30 & 14.30–18.00 Tue–Fri, 09.00–12.00 & 15.30–19.00 Sat, 09.00–13.00 Sun; admission US$0.50*) In need of some TLC, this interesting museum is still the best place to learn about the 40,000 indigenous inhabitants of Amazonas, including the Hiwi (Guajibo), Yekuana, Yanomami, Sanema and Piaroa Indians. Even if you can't understand Spanish you can enjoy the exhibits of blowpipes and baskets, ceramics and traditional dress. Models of Indian villages and old photographs give a sense of the vanished world of many of these tribes.

Indian Market The market in Plaza de Los Indios, outside the museum, is a fantastic mixed bag of local talents, mostly Piaroa and Hiwi, with a few true gems among the many kitschy items made to sell to tourists. The best days to visit are Thursday through to Saturday, although the market is open every morning, even on Sunday when everything else is shut. Early birds will find the best-made model animals, pottery and baskets. Look out for juices made from local *seje* palm fruit and bottles of *catara* (or *katara*), a spicy Indian sauce made from leafcutter ants and chilli that is reputed to have strong aphrodisiac qualities. Other shops selling crafts nearby are Artesanías Topocho on Avenida Río Negro just across Avenida Aguerrevere, and Artesanía Amazonas on Calle Evelio Ríos, a block from the Gran Hotel Amazonas.

Boat trip to Colombia From the port in Puerto Ayacucho, *bongos* and launches take day shoppers across the Orinoco for about US$1 to Casuarito on the

12

Colombian side, where jewellery and fine leather goods are plentiful. The *pueblo* has a reputation for bars and brothels, but there are nice places to sit and have coffee and snacks. Casuarito appears to be built on a single huge slab of rock or *laja*. Formalities are limited to showing your passport.

Walk up to El Mirador Cerro Perico has a broad overview of the Atures rapids and is a good place to enjoy a great sunset panorama overlooking Puerto Ayacucho and the Orinoco. It's a 500m walk from the Museo Etnológico by way of Avenida Aguerrevere. Ask for directions.

White-water rafting on the Atures

Aguas Bravas m 0414 114 5818, 0416 726 08 81; e info@raftingbarinas.com; www.raftingorinoco.com. Venezuelan kayak champion Alejandro Buzzo has resurrected his father's white-water rafting tours of the Atures & Maipures rapids in the river in front of Puerto Ayacucho under the name Aguas Bravas. This is in addition to the rafting tours he offers in Barinas State on the Acequias River. These highly recommended trips are run from an island camp on the Orinoco where guests stay in hammocks & visit ancient petroglyphs & spectacular sandy river beaches as they negotiate these very powerful rapids. Aguas Bravas operates Dec–Apr in Puerto Ayacucho & May–Nov in Barinas.

AROUND PUERTO AYACUCHO

Piedra de la Tortuga Seen from the road to Samariapo, 8km south of Puerto Ayacucho, this gigantic granite boulder with its smaller 'head' looks like a tortoise. It has been declared a Natural Monument. Nearby there is an Indian cemetery, reached by river when waters are low.

Piedro Pintado This immense boulder, about 17km south of town on the road to Samariapo, is carved with prehistoric petroglyphs of a giant, 50m-long serpent and other figures. Like Humboldt, you can wonder how they were carved so high up. The petroglyphs can be hard to make out without a guide, so consider visiting on a tour (see *Tour operators*, page 302).

Parque Tobogán de la Selva This is a giant natural water slide down a smooth, slippery rock about 25 minutes' drive from Puerto Ayacucho to the south. Picnic tables and shelter are provided and snacks sold at weekends when it is busy with locals. It becomes crowded and noisy during holidays. It is possible to camp during the week; ask for the caretakers at the food kiosks. It is also possible to visit the nearby **Coromoto** community of Guahibo Indians.

Autana Also known as Autana Tepui or Cerro Autana, Autana is a magnificent tabletop mountain that rises 1,220m out of the jungle like the stump of some enormous petrified tree. More spectacular, perhaps, is that below Autana's truncated top (1,300m), a cave runs right through the middle that is big enough to enable a helicopter to fly through the mountain. The Piaroa Indians who still inhabit the forests of the region revere it as sacred and it was declared a Natural Monument in 1978. Boat trips from the port of Samariapo take travellers on a three- or four-day trip up the Sipapo River to the Piaroa village of Raudal de la Ceguera, from where a two-hour hike through jungle leads to the top of the adjacent Uripica Tepui, for breathtaking views of Autana.

Lago Leopoldo A five-day adventure trip to this isolated lake in the middle of a low-lying *tepui* named after Belgian King Leopold III, includes navigating a small tributary of the Orinoco, sleeping in hammocks and tents and trekking in rainforest. The mysterious lake is 240m in diameter and some 35m deep. It is not fed by any rivers and has no discernible outlet and geologists now believe it is actually a *sima* or *tepui* sinkhole. It gets its name from the ELATA expedition organised in 1952 by Leopold, who one year earlier had abdicated the throne in favour of his son. An amateur anthropologist and explorer, Leopold was so enamoured of the rainforest and Venezuela's Amazonas region that he called his daughter Esmeralda, after the Orinoco mission post. The name Lago Leopoldo first appears on the maps published in 1956 by Venezuelan archaeologist and explorer José M Cruxent after the lake showed up on aerial photographs. The first expedition to actually reach the lake was in 1973, although the indigenous Piaroa guides, who call the lake Paraka Wachoi refused to go all the way as they feared a Loch Ness-style water serpent lives in its depths. This is a fairly new offering from Puerto Ayacucho tour operators and can be combined with a trip to Cerro Autana.

San Fernando de Atabapo The old capital of Amazonas, founded in 1758, is today a sizeable town of 15,000 people. You can either come here with a tour operator, arrange a *por puesto* ride from Samariapo with the locals (US$20 for a 3-hour journey in a *voladora*), or fly in a Wayumi airtaxi (US$80 one way in a six-seater plane). San Fernando came to fame in the *balata* rubber boom when Tomás Funes, the 'Terror of Río Negro', took over in 1913, killing the governor, his family and hundreds more in an eight-year reign of terror. Funes's house and the place where he was executed in Plaza Bolívar are still pointed out by locals and even now indigenous people scare their children into obedience by threatening them that 'Funes is coming'. In the dry season, the riverbanks are lined by beautiful white beaches and it is here that you can see the black waters of the Río Atabapo mingling with the brown waters of Colombia's Río Guaviare as they merge with the Orinoco. A sleepy town that's home to gold miners, you can stay at the Posada Atabapo ($) on Calle Piar or the more expensive Posada Turistica Pendare on the Plaza Bolívar ($). Take a hammock in case they are full.

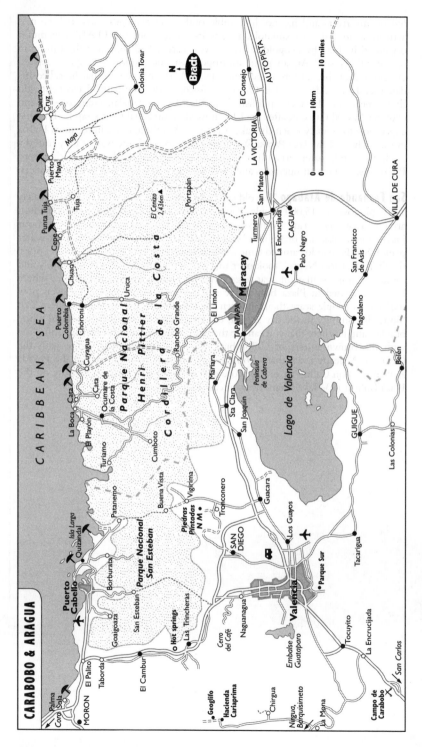

CARABOBO & ARAGUA

CARIBBEAN SEA

Bradt

N

0   10km
0   10 miles

Palma Sola
Coro
MORON
El Palito
Taborda
Puerto Cabello
Goaigoaza
Borburata
Isla Larga
Quizandal
San Esteban
El Cambur
Parque Nacional San Esteban
Las Trincheras
Hot springs
Geoglifo
Hacienda Cariaprima
Chirgua
Niagua, Barquisimeto
La Mona
Campo de Carabobo
Cerro del Café
Naguanagua
Embalse Guataparo
Valencia
Parque Sur
Tocuyito
La Encrucijada
San Carlos
Tacarigua
Las Colonias
GUIGUE
Belén
Magdaleno
San Francisco de Asís
VILLA DE CURA
Palma Sola
Puerto Cruz
Colonia Tovar
El Consejo
LA VICTORIA
San Mateo
Turmero
La Encrucijada
CAGUA
Palo Negro
Maracay
TAPATAPA
El Limón
Lago de Valencia
Península de Cabrera
Sta Clara
San Joaquín
Guacara
Los Guayos
SAN DIEGO
Troncronero
Vigirima
Piedras Pintadas N.M.
Buena Vista
Cumboto
Rancho Grande
Maracay
Mañara
Portapán
El Cenizo 2,436m
Parque Nacional Henri Pittier
Cordillera de la Costa
Uruca
Choroní
Puerto Colombia
Cuyagua
Cata
Ocumare de la Costa
La Boca
El Playón
Turiamo
Patanemo
Panenemo
Chuao
Cepe
Punta Tuja
Tuja
Puerto Maya
Maya

310

13

Aragua and Carabobo

Traffic from Caracas courses through Aragua's low valleys on broad highways built alongside sugarcane fields and rum distilleries to **Maracay**, the capital of Aragua State (110km), and **Valencia**, the capital of Carabobo State (159km). There is little to detain tourists in either city but they serve as important hubs for trips to popular beaches, historic cocoa plantations, excellent birding in cool cloudforest, and steaming hot springs.

Separating the hot valley of Maracay from the Caribbean is a thickly forested mountain range, protected in 1937 by the country's first national park, the Parque Nacional Rancho Grande. In 1974 it was enlarged to 1,078km^2 and renamed **Parque Nacional Henri Pittier** after a Swiss naturalist who worked to preserve it from deforestation. Still threatened by bush fires every dry season, the park is Venezuela's top birdwatching spot in terms of the numbers of endemics and migratory birds recorded here and an irreplaceable refuge for the mammals, trees, ferns and orchids of the Cordillera de la Costa. Down on the Caribbean side, beautiful crescent bays and Afro-Venezuelan drums lure hordes of weekend sun-seekers to brave the hair-raising roads over the mountain to the beaches of Choroní, Ocumare, Cata and the surfers' favourite Cuyagua. Other more isolated bays, such as Chuao and Cepe, are reached only by fishing boat from towns on the coast or on long treks following ancient mule trails still used to transport cocoa beans to market.

ARAGUA STATE *Telephone code: 0243*

MARACAY The fourth largest city in Venezuela, Maracay has a population of more than 1.3 million Maracayeros and once you get through the rings of factories is a pleasant city with broad, tree-lined avenues. Founded in 1701, it prospered for many years as a centre for cacao, tobacco and indigo, produced on surrounding plantations. Under the 1908–35 dictatorship of Juan Vicente Gómez it became the country's unofficial capital. Many of the city's main monuments are linked to Gómez, as is the heavy presence of the military, with Venezuela's two largest air force bases, army and tank units and National Guard barracks. There are a few museums and some nice restaurants, but for most visitors it is merely a jumping-off point for the popular beach towns of Choroní (northeast) and Rancho Grande-Cuyagua (northwest) or other destinations.

Getting there and away
By air Maracay's airport, the Aeropuerto Nacional de Aragua Florencio Gómez, fell into disuse in the early noughties and stopped operating. There are now projects underway to reopen the airport and an international airport at the Libertador Air base.

By bus Maracay is a convenient hub for many long-distance lines. The main bus terminal is south of Avenida Constitución at Avenida Fuerzas Aéreas [312 B5],

Aragua and Carabobo ARAGUA STATE

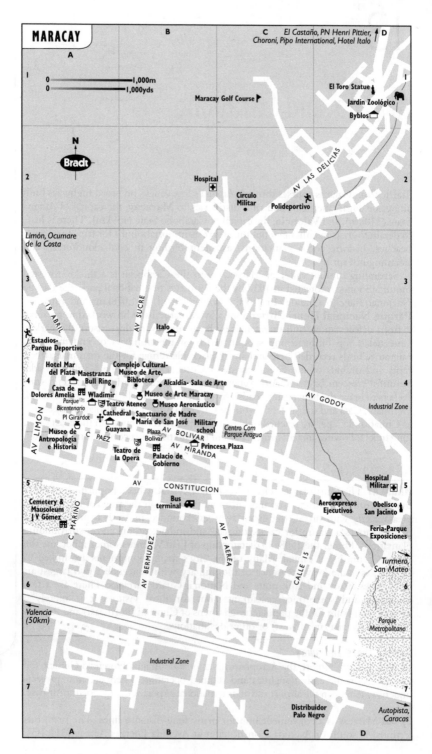

MARACAY

A
B
C   El Castaño, PN Henri Pittier,
D
     Choroní, Pipo International, Hotel Italo

0 ——————— 1,000m
0 ——————— 1,000yds

Maracay Golf Course

El Toro Statue
Jardín Zoológico
Byblos

N
Bradt

Hospital
Círculo
Militar
Polideportivo
AV LAS DELICIAS

Limón, Ocumare
de la Costa

AV SUCRE

19 ABRIL

Italo

Estadios-
Parque Deportivo

AV GODOY
Industrial Zone

Hotel Mar
del Plata   Maestranza
             Bull Ring   Complejo Cultural-
                          Museo de Arte,
Casa de   Bibloteca   Alcaldía- Sala de Arte
Dolores Amelia   Wladimir   Museo de Arte Maracay
             Parque   Teatro Ateneo   Museo Aeronáutico
             Bicentenario
             Pl Girardot   Cathedral   Sanctuario de Madre
                                         María de San José   Military
Museo de   Guayana   school
Antropología   Plaza   AV   Centro Com
e Historia   C PAEZ   Bolívar BOLIVAR   Parque Aragua
                          Teatro de   AV   Princesa Plaza
AV LIMON   la Opera   MIRANDA
                          Palacio de
                          Gobierno

Hospital
Militar

AV
         CONSTITUCION
Cemetery &
Mausoleum   Bus
J V Gómez   terminal   Aeroexpresos   Obelisco
                                     Ejecutivos   San Jacinto
C MARINO
                                                     Feria-Parque
                                                     Exposiciones

AV BERMUDEZ
AV F AEREA
CALLE 15

Turmero,
San Mateo

Valencia
(50km)
                                                     Parque
                                                     Metropolitana

Industrial Zone

Distribuidor   Autopista,
Palo Negro   Caracas

A
B
C
D

with frequent *por puesto* buses to the centre and Plaza Bolívar. Buses go frequently to Caracas (1½ hours, US$4), Valencia (1 hour, US$3), Barquisimeto (4 hours, US$4); less often to Coro (6½ hours, US$7), San Fernando de Apure (6 hours, US$10), Mérida (11 hours, US$15) and San Antonio del Táchira (12 hours, US$20–25). Longer journeys usually depart at night to arrive in the morning.

Local buses take the winding route along tight switchbacks over the mountains of the Parque Nacional Henri Pittier to the beach towns of the coast, leaving every hour to Ocumare (US$3), where you can continue by *por puesto* to Cata and Cuyagua. Service to Choroní–Puerto Colombia is every two hours but buses leave when full during peak holidays. The last bus is about 17.00 (2 hours, US$3).

The fast buses of **Aeroexpresos Ejecutivos** [312 D5] (*www.aeroexpresos.com.ve*) leave from a private terminal on Avenida Bolívar Este, opposite Ingeniería Militar. Service are to: Caracas at 06.30, 10.45, 12.45 15.00, 16.00 and 18.30; Valencia at 06.30 and 21.30; Maracaibo at 21.30; Maturín 21.00; Puerto La Cruz 22.00.

By car Maracay is on the main highway between Caracas and Valencia.

Where to stay Many of the seedy-looking hotels by the bus station are Love Hotels, rented by the hour and it is not recommended to walk about at night in this area looking for a room.

Byblos [312 D1] (232 rooms) Av Las Delicias; \ 0243 242 3454; e contacto@hotelbyblos.com.ve; www.hotelbyblos.com.ve. A 12-storey tower with restaurant, nightclub, comfortable rooms. $$$

Hotel Italo [312 B4] (98 rooms) Av Las Delicias; \ 0243 242 8664; e info@hotelitalo.com.ve; www.hotelitalo.com.ve. Large hotel close to restaurants in Las Delicias with pool, sauna, restaurant. $$$

Pipo Internacional [312 D1] (119 rooms) Av Las Delicias; \ 0243 241 3111; e hpipoint@telcel.net.ve; www.hotelpipo.com. The furthest hotel north on the road to Choroní–Puerto Colombia. Rooms with AC, cable TV, swimming pools, bar, restaurant. $$$

Princesa Plaza [312 B5] (100 rooms) Av Miranda by the Torre Sindoni; \ 0243 232 0177, 0243 233 2571; e hotelprincesaplaza@cantv.net; www.hotelprincesaplaza.com.ve. A mid-range option 2 blocks east of Plaza Bolívar. All rooms have AC, cable TV, some better than others, ask to see room before checking in. $$

Mar del Plata [312 A4] (28 rooms) Av Santos Michelena; \ 0243 245 4313, 0243 247 2001. Simple, central, dbls with AC. $

Wladimir [312 A4] (36 rooms) 27 Av Bolívar, just east of the cathedral; \ 0243 246 2566; e hwladimir@cantv.net. Rooms with AC, TV, good Italian restaurant. $

Where to eat If you just want a snack while waiting for the bus to Choroní, there are plenty of places in the main bus terminal [312 B5] selling fruit juices, toasted sandwiches of ham and cheese, and empanadas.

Other practicalities There is a 24-hour Farmatodo pharmacy on Avenida Las Delicias on the road to Choroní.

What to see and do Maracay bears the stamp of dictator **Juan Vicente Gómez** who turned the bucolic town into his private capital from 1910 until he died in 1935. An illiterate, Gómez was so tyrannical that his motto of '*Paz y Trabajo*' ('Peace and Work') was experienced by many as 'Peace in the Cemetery and Work on the Roads'. Eldest of 13 children of an Andean farmer, he had a Bolívar fixation. He was born on Bolívar's birthday (he said) and died on the day of Bolívar's death, having already prepared his family **mausoleum** [312 A5], a florid affair in the cemetery, eight blocks south of the cathedral. He was the one who raised the triumphal arch at the Campo de Carabobo honouring Bolívar's victory there in 1821.

Plaza Bolívar [312 B5] is one of the biggest in Venezuela and another Gómez project, as are the big barracks on its north side. The dictator's pride, the once-elegant Hotel Jardín with its Alhambra-like tiles, is today the **Palacio de Gobierno** on the south side of Plaza Bolívar. On the plaza's southwest corner stands the building he lavished a fortune on, the grand **Teatro de la Opera** designed by Luis Malaussena. But Gómez died before it was ready and for 38 years it stood shuttered until in 1973 the city finally found the resolve to finish and open it. Today it functions as one of the country's best theatres.

Plaza de Toros La Maestranza [312 A4] is a handsome bullfighting ring built by the great dictator, three blocks northeast of the cathedral. It was designed in 1933 by Carlos Raúl Villanueva and is based on one in Seville, Spain. Outside there is a statue of renowned matador César Girón.

Sanctuario de Madre María de San José [312 B4] (*Calle López Aveledo, up from Av Bolívar;* ⊕ *09.30–12.00 & 14.00–17.00 Tue–Sun*)
One of the most visited sites in Maracay is the sanctuary of Venezuela's first (and only) saint, beatified by Pope John Paul II in 1995. Laura Evangelista Alvarado Cardozo was born in Choroní in 1875 and died here in 1967 at the age of 92. An Augustinian nun, she devoted her life to the poor and sick and founded Maracay's first hospital. The building holds the sarcophagus with the saint's surprisingly intact remains.

Iglesia de San José [312 A4]
Maracay's cathedral is a well-restored colonial structure bearing the date 1743. It stands on **Plaza Girardot**, the historic town centre. On and around 19 March every year, Maracay honours its patron saint in the **Feria de San José** with parades, bullfights and an agricultural fair. Plaza Girardot's obelisk and bronze eagle were raised in 1897 to the American volunteers who joined Francisco Miranda's ill-fated expedition in 1806. The patriots landed in Ocumare, but Spaniards captured one ship, and hanged the ten American officers. The statue to Atanasio Girardot who died in the Battle of Bárbula, in 1813, stands on the pedestrian boulevard.

Museo de Antropología e Historia [312 A4] (*Plaza Girardot; www.museodemaracay.com.ve;* ⊕ *08.00–15.30 Mon–Fri, 09.00–12.30 w/ends; admission free*)
A well-arranged museum with displays of pre-Columbian pots and finds from local archaeological digs, including the intriguing 'Venus of Valencia' figurines with wide heads and coffee-bean eyes. The history section has oil paintings of Independence heroes, Bolivariana and some of the dictator Gómez's riding gear. A basement salon houses a collection of craft by ethnic groups including the Yanomami, Sanema, Yekuana, Panare, Guajiro and Warao.

Casa de Dolores Amelia [312 A4]
North of the adjacent **Parque Bicentenario** (with underground parking) is this restored Andalusian mansion built by Gómez on Avenida Santos Michelena for a favoured mistress (one of many). Although he never married, Gómez fathered many children and considered himself a family man. You can ask permission to see the tiled patio.

'Culture row'
Walk along the 'culture row' from Parque Bicentenario east on Avenida 19 de Abril, ending at the aeronautic museum. In a block you'll find the post office and the **Ateneo** in a Gómez-era theatre [312 A4]. The **Complejo Cultural** occupies the block between Avenida Sucre and the foot of Avenida Las Delicias. Gathered here are the public library, Casa de Cultura, school of visual arts, youth orchestra and, on the east end, the **Museo de Arte Maracay** [312 B4], with rotating exhibitions.

Museo Aeronáutico [312 B4] (*Av 19 de Abril;* ⊕ *10.00–18.00 Sat–Sun; admission free*) The air force school opened by Gómez in 1920 now operates as a museum with some three dozen aircraft including antique craft from 1910–20 and a replica of Jimmie Angel's Flamingo monoplane *Río Caroní* (the original stands outside the airport in Ciudad Bolívar). It's the only place you'll find a statue of Gómez (raised in 1995). The dictator was a passionate fan of aviation and the founder of Venezuela's air force. The US aviation pioneer Charles Lindbergh was invited to land here in the *Spirit of St Louis* in 1928.

Jardín Zoológico [312 D1] (*Av Las Delicias;* ⊕ *09.00–16.30 Tue–Sun; admission free*) This small zoo on the road out of town on the way to Choroní started as a repository for exotic animals given to General Gómez and was later opened as a formal zoo under the dictator Marcos Pérez Jiménez in 1952. Its enclosures are being revamped to make it more eco-friendly. Animals include a variety of native species such as the spectacled bear, capuchin monkey and capybara, plus a hippo, elephants, tigers and llamas. A large central lagoon has an island of nesting herons and egrets, and many iguanas, turtles, ducks and pelicans. Close to the zoo is a bronze statue of a bull, known as **El Toro de Las Delicias**, a reference to Gómez who treated Venezuela as his personal ranch.

CHORONÍ AND PUERTO COLOMBIA (Telephone code: 0243)

From the national park post at Parque Nacional Henri Pittier directly north of town, a narrow mountain road spirals up along tight switchbacks to cool heights before dropping through lush cloudforest to the Caribbean, some 56km in all. It is not for the faint-hearted. It was built by convicts in the Gómez era as an escape route from Maracay to the little fishing port of Puerto Colombia. Today it is an escape from urban chaos into enchanting forests where mists veil the ridge at 1,830m and fords cross crystal streams splashing down lush green slopes. At the bottom in the hot Choroní Valley you can see red-fruiting cacao trees under the shade of giant plantation trees, a key to the wealth that was generated here from the early 17th century, when the local cacao was exported to Europe to make the finest chocolate. The large cocoa *haciendas* are all but gone although a few still produce quality cocoa beans, highly prized by top-end chocolatiers in Italy, Belgium and the UK. Some visitors are confused when they ask for Puerto Colombia and get directed to a bus saying Choroní. That is because for Venezuelans, the colonial village, fishing port and beach are all known as Choroní.

On the way down, the road passes **Uraca** at Km 48 where an old hydro-electric plant dating to 1922 once supplied Maracay with electricity. The old **Cadafe** electricity plant is still there, its turbines now part of a Museum of Electricity and cultural centre, which has erratic opening hours. This is a good place to explore the river, which has a number of small falls and pools for bathing amid large round boulders. Uraca is also the setting of a six-day annual guitar meeting, the **Encuentro Guitarrístico**, held in April or early May. Guitarists travel here to attend workshops by master players and international guest artists.

Just 2km from the sea and the little port of Puerto Colombia, is the colonial village of **Choroní**. Founded as a parish in 1622, it is so well preserved that historical dramas and soap operas are filmed here. On the shady Plaza Bolívar is the 300-year-old church of Santa Clara, Choroní's patron saint whose fiesta is in August. Trimly painted cottages line two quiet streets around the plaza. There are a couple of *abastos* (food shops) selling supplies but most of the hotels and restaurants are to be found in Puerto Colombia. Venezuela's first saint, Madre María de San José, is honoured by a statue at the entrance to the village. She was born here in 1875 and there is a plaque on her family house, which is a site of pilgrimage for devotees. As a girl she started a school for poor children here, and went on to work with the poor in Maracay until she died in 1967. She is famous for having founded Maracay's first hospital.

Puerto Colombia is an attractive fishing village with a *malecón*, or 'sea wall', with rusting cannon, and a sandy beach by the river where the fishing boats are harboured. The village is small and laid back during the week but at weekends and during Christmas, Easter and Carnival, it can get raucous, throbbing into the early hours to the sounds of salsa, reggaeton and *tambores*, the local Afro-Venezuelan drums. The narrow colonial streets contain one of the highest concentrations of accommodation options in Venezuela, a clear mark of the village's tourism appeal. But the isolation of being reached by one road over a mountain and restrictions on building in the four blocks leading to the Malecón, have somehow preserved the village's charm. Fishermen hang out drinking beer in the mornings after selling their catch and most people walk about barefoot. There is a strong Afro-Venezuelan identity here and black pride expresses itself in the annual festivities dedicated to San Juan Bautista, known as '*el santo negro*' ('the black saint'), and the drum dancing every weekend under the statue of the saint on the *malecón*. Local fiestas are fuelled by a homemade concoction called *guarapita*, a highly effective yet innocuous-tasting mix of passion-fruit juice and raw cane alcohol, or *aguardiente* (literally, 'fire water'). Best to go easy on the *guarapita*.

In the mornings, fishermen ferry visitors to solitary beaches along the coast. You can travel *por puesto* like the locals and wait for a boat to fill up, or hire a whole boat and set the time you're picked up. A return trip to the beach and historic cocoa plantation of Chuao is about US$10, or US$110 for the boat. The further beach of Cepe is about US$12.

About ten minutes' walk from Puerto Colombia, across a bridge over the river, is the beach of **Playa Grande**, a lovely crescent bay backed by tall palms with high bluffs at each end. There are snack bars selling *empanadas*, fried fish and soups, and changing rooms with showers open Friday–Sunday. The first part of the beach has sunshades and beach chairs for hire and there are plenty of shady coconut palms to hang hammocks from in the middle of the beach. Be careful in the sea and heed the warnings of local lifeguards, who patrol the sand at weekends. Bodysurfing is easier than swimming in the waves, which can be rough, especially in the centre of the beach where there is a dangerous undertow or *resaca*. It is unwise to go out beyond waist-high waves and the best area for bathing is at the start of the beach.

Getting there

By bus Buses to Choroní–Puerto Colombia leave the terminal in Maracay every two hours, or when full during peak holidays from 07.00 until about 17.00 (2 hours, US$3). If you miss the last bus it is better to hook up with other stranded passengers and haggle for a good price in a taxi (about US$35 for the car) than stay a night in Maracay. Some *posadas* arrange transfers from Maiquetía Airport (see below).

By car If driving your own car, follow the signs in Maracay to the Las Delicias sector of town. Once past the zoo and the Pipo Internacional hotel the road starts to ascend the Parque Nacional Henri Pittier along switchback curves that barely leave room for one car in places. First timers should drive during the day as it is more dangerous at night, and be alert for buses as they drive the road at speed.

Tour operators Tours to Henri Pittier National Park for birdwatching or a night in the cloud forest are organized by English-speaking guide Virgilio Espinal (m *0416 747 3833; www.cocuy.org.ve*) who has a rustic camp on the mountain called El Cocuy and takes tourists from Puerto Colombia to different areas of the park in a Toyota Land Cruiser.

Where to stay Travellers will find an astonishing four-dozen *posadas* and converted *hacienda* houses, ranging from basic options with a bed and a fan to boutique-style places with small pools and prices to match. Prices rise steeply during holidays and long weekends. Be sure to check for weekday bargains, especially when staying a few days. A website with a useful map of *posadas* is www.choroni.info.

Choroní

Hacienda Monterosa (4 rooms) Sector La Planta; m 0412 732 7032; www.cacao.travel. Before the entrance to Choroní, in La Planta, is this colonial house on an 18th-century cocoa plantation shaded by giant trees. A great opportunity to experience the life of the 'Gran Cacaos', as the cocoa-exporting elite were once known, & understand the workings of a cocoa plantation using traditional techniques to harvest internationally coveted local beans. Birders will also find plenty to do in the shady forest of the plantation. The rooms are rented for 2 nights' minimum & parties of up to 9 can be accommodated, reservations in advance. $$$$

La Casa de Las García (15 rooms) Calle El Cementerio; ✆ 0243 991 1056; m 0412 235 6894; www.posadalasgarciachoroni.com. This wonderfully restored *hacienda* house has been in the family since the late 1800s: it has tall ceilings, walls 2ft thick, verandas, red-tiled roof, gardens, swimming pool & restaurant for guests or by reservation. B&B rooms have comfortable beds, en-suite bath, hot water, AC, hammock. $$$

Hacienda El Portete (24 rooms) Calle El Cementerio; ✆ 0243 991 1255; m 0414 345 7768; e portete@telcel.net.ve; www.elportetechoroni.com.

A less traditional update of a colonial house on a road that passes the cemetery & leads off to an isolated beach at Playa El Diario. B&B rooms have bath, hot water, AC, corridor with hammocks, restaurant for guests & adult & kids' swimming pools. $$

Hostería Río Mar (9 rooms) ✆ 0243 991 1038; m 0416 639 9280; e riomar@cantv.net. Rooms with bath, cold water, AC, some with TV. $$

Mijao Suites (14 rooms, suite) Calle El Cementerio; ✆ 0243 991 1114; m 0414 329 2518; e shutneyvill@hotmail.com; www.mijaosuites.com. B&B rooms with hot water, AC, TV, porch, swimming pool, outdoor jacuzzi. The 1st place on the road to El Cementerio, close to Puerto Colombia, good midweek deals. $$

Hospedaje del Pueblo (6 rooms) Calle Miranda, 1 block north of Plaza Bolívar; ✆ 0243 991 1008. Spartan rooms with fan, bath, cold water. $

Posada Colonial Choroní (4 rooms) ✆ 0243 991 1296; m 0416 743 1454; e posadacolonial@cantv.net. Near Plaza Bolívar, rooms have fan, cold water. There's an internal patio & another behind giving on to a brook forming a natural bathing pool & a restaurant (⊕ 08.00–21.00). $

Puerto Colombia

Hostal Casa Grande (17 rooms) 33 Av Morillo; ✆ 0243 991 1251; m 0416 845 5534; e hostalcasagrandechoroni@hotmail.com; www.hostalcasagrande.net. A very upmarket option in a red-roofed colonial-style house with columned verandas, furnished with mahogany antiques & pieces made by owner Julian Bulfón. Large rooms with AC, good bathroom, hot water, around a central patio with a shallow pool. Includes b/fast. Italian, French, English & German spoken. $$$

Posada Mesón Xuchytlán (14 rooms) 22 Av Morillo; ✆ 0243 991 1234; e xbteado@hotmail.com. Done out in Mexican colonial-style, with dark terracotta walls & cane ceilings, this elegant *posada* has a an open kitchen-diner where b/fast is served, some suites with private garden & jacuzzi, others with showers opening on to mini-garden. Lovingly decorated with paintings & antiques to

delight the eye, this is very swanky & priced accordingly. $$$

Club Cotoperix (18 rooms) ✆ 0212 977 2703; m 0416 815 0627; e cotoperixchoroni@hotmail.com. This colonial *posada* on the main street towards the bay, did much to launch Choroní's fame in the late 1980s when owner Polo Casanova restored a historic 6-room house & stocked the kitchen with Choroní's excellent fish, fruit, coffee & chocolate, offering a package with meals, beach picnic & barbecue, boat to remote bays, mountain excursions & often local music at night. This formula was so successful that the Cotoperix grew to 4 locales. Today the hotel operates the original house & another with a 2-floor addition. Packages include excursions by boat. $$

Hostal Piapoco (12 rooms) Walled garden just along from the Pittier; ✆ 0243 991 1108;

e info@hostalpiapoco.com. Large, modern *posada* on 2 storeys with small swimming pool, bar, restaurant. Rooms with bath, hot water, AC. Some English & French spoken. $$

🏠 **Posada Del Sol** (10 rooms) ✆ 0243 219 2263; 📱 0414 455 8434. Reached by an unpaved road leading west past the Posada Pittier. Rooms with AC, hot water, TV, nice swimming pool, bar serves b/fast for w/end guests only; some English spoken. $$

🏠 **Posada Pittier** (9 rooms) ✆ 0243 991 1028; 📱 0414 462 4643; e posadapittier@gmail.com; www.posadapittier.com. A colonial-style house with B&B rooms around central patio with AC, TV, hot water, Wi-Fi, swimming pool. Lower w/day rates. $$

🏠 **Posada Tom-Carel** (11 rooms) 11 Calle Trino Rangel; ✆ 0243 991 1220; 📱 0414 321 3022; e tomcarel@cantv.net, tomcarel@hotmail.com; www.posadatomcarel.com. A comfortable base for beach or mountain excursions. Rooms with private bath, hot water, 2 upstairs with balcony, b/fast optional, internet, Wi-Fi. Owners Tom & Carmen Elena can arrange tours & airport transfers. $$

🏠 **Casa Luna** (5 rooms) 35 Calle Morillo; ✆ 0243 951 5318; e jungletrip@choroni.net; www.jungletrip.de/en. Another backpacker option by the bus stop run by German woman Claudia & her Venezuelan husband Emilio. Simple rooms with fan, shared bathroom & kitchen, cold water. Organise tours & trips to Henri Pittier forest, cocoa plantation. Can arrange taxi transfer from Maiquetía Airport. $

🏠 **Hostal Colonial** (20 rooms) On the main street opposite Calle Trino Rangel; ✆ 0243 218 5012; e colonialchoroni@gmail.com; www.choroni.net. Good value rooms around patio with fan, cheaper ones with shared bathroom, some with equipped kitchen, Wi-Fi area. Popular with backpackers. German & English spoken. $

🏠 **Posada Don Miguel** (15 rooms) Near the police checkpoint or *alcabala*; ✆ 0243 991 1081; 📱 0414 446 1665. Rooms with bath, cold water, some with AC, & midweek discounts. A budget option if nothing better available. $

🏠 **Posada La Montañita** (20 rooms) 2 doors from the waterfront *malecón* at 6 Calle Morillo; ✆ 0243 991 1132; 📱 0416 231 3801; e malecon@telcel.net.ve. A 2nd floor plus a rooftop terrace have been added to the pleasant old part. Rooms with fan, cold shower, some with AC, TV, b/fast. Taxi transfers, excursions can be arranged by the friendly Rodríguez family. $

🏠 **Posada La Parchita** (4 rooms) Calle Trino Rangel; ✆ 0243 991 1259; 📱 0414 225 5705. Dbl rooms (plus bunks) with bath, hot water, around a central courtyard. Backs on to river, so bring repellent. W/day discounts, reservations required at w/ends. $

🏠 **Posada Los Guanches** (9 rooms) Side street off Calle Trino Rangel; ✆ 0243 991 1209. Simple, plain dbls with fan, anti-mosquito device, en suite in a 2-floor house that has the name painted in large letters seen from afar. Friendly owner Aridani lives in front & keeps it very clean. Good value, long-stay discounts. $

✗ **Where to eat** Waiters from the kiosk restaurants by the beach will try and entice you to sit at their tables and eat an *empanada* and drink a coffee to start the day, or a full meal of fried fish such as red snapper, grouper or a swordfish steak served with *tostones*, rice and a chopped side salad. Ask to see the fish first. Cheaper options are seafood soups. Homemade hot sauces on the tables pack a mean punch so take it easy. If you just want to chill out and watch the crowds, order a cold beer. In the evening there are several restaurants worth seeking out.

✗ **Boku Tapas & Grill** Downstairs in Posada La Montañita; ⏰ 08.30–22.00 Fri–Sun. Lighter b/fasts, such as muesli & yoghurt, whole-wheat bread, sandwiches during the day & fusion food in the evenings, such as *ceviche* served in pitta bread & tempura, supplemented with pastas, fried fish & surf & turf. $$

✗ **Willy's Place** ⏰ 17.00–22.00 Fri–Sun. On the other side of the river by the bridge is this bamboo-sided terrace where German chef Willy & his wife Evelyn serve up seafood such as squid & shrimps in garlic, fried fish & a European range of potato side orders for those sick of plantains. Only open at w/ends & high season. $$

Other practicalities There is a **Banco Nacional de Credito** near the bus terminal but the ATM does not always work so bring all the money you need with you. Several of the *posadas* will change dollars so ask around for the best rate.

There are two cyber cafés in town (about US$2 an hour) but the connection can be slow.

A small *medicatura* can deal with minor injuries and there is a pharmacy down near the malecón, but the nearest hospital is in Maracay over the mountain.

There are a couple of stores selling beach gear and street vendors selling pirate CDs but check out the small store by the bridge to the beach that sells locally made bars of chocolate.

For drivers, there is a petrol station just before Choroní.

CHUAO A remote cocoa plantation reached only by sea or after a two-day walk following a mule trail over the mountains, Chuao is like an El Dorado for chocolate lovers, a place steeped in myth and trapped in a time warp. Even today European chocolate makers fight over Chuao's precious cocoa beans, the main ingredient in chocolate, which are still produced using traditional harvesting, drying and fermenting techniques that hark back to the 17th century. The village started life in 1568 as a Spanish *encomienda*, when local Indians were forced to work for the Spanish conquistadors. A century later African slaves were put to work on the plantation and it became an important exporter of cocoa beans. In 1826 it was expropriated from the Catholic Church by Independence hero Simón Bolívar and slavery was abolished. Today, the plantation is run by a co-operative and the Afro-Venezuelan heritage of the 2,300 inhabitants is expressed in the *tambores* drum dancing, which takes place at weekends and the important festivals in June in honour of Saint John the Baptist. Just like Choroní, Chuao is set back some 5km up a valley from the beach, a protective measure employed by the Spanish when cocoa beans were worth more than gold pound for pound and these coasts were plagued by pirates in search of plunder.

The first view most people get is of Chuao's wide, curving beach, empty except in peak holidays with just a few shacks at the back offering cold drinks and hot *empanadas*. There is little shade as the palm trees are not at the water's edge and the sea can be unpredictable and rough. When swimming, stick to the area near the river where the fishing boats moor as there are dangerous undertows. After a splash in the sea, head towards the cocoa plantation and the village, a 40-minute walk through the giant shade trees of the plantation along a dirt road. If you're lucky, the one *por puesto* bus in the village will be passing and give you a lift; if not, it's a pleasant walk and you can observe the cocoa pods growing straight out of the trunks of the trees. As you enter the sleepy village and approach the squat, whitewashed 17th-century church with its patio used for drying cocoa beans, you can smell the unmistakeable aroma of fermenting cocoa. There is a museum on the plaza with a few historic pieces relating to slave days and devil dancing masks, but you need to ask around to get the key. A refreshing cold beer is a nice reward after a hot walk and at the end of the village you find women washing clothes in the river, naked kids splashing about and a pool for swimming. Have some repellent to hand, as biting flies come out in the late afternoon.

Getting there Fishing boats, or *peñeros*, work as taxis from Choroní. You can hire the whole boat for a return trip, but it is cheaper to do what the locals do and pay by the seat (*por puesto*, US$10), leaving when the boat is full and hoping to get a return seat on another boat.

It is still possible to trek down to Chuao following the colonial mule trail from Turmero, near Maracay, but it takes two days with a night camping in the Parque Nacional Henri Pittier, and the trail is not clear in places. A few hours before Chuao, the trail passes the spectacular 70m waterfall of Chorreron, which is seldom visited. Akanan Tours (*www.akanan.com*) in Caracas lead Turmero–Chuao treks and local kids will show you the way to Chorreron.

⌂ Where to stay

⌂ **Hosteleria Playa Chuao** (3 rooms) ☎ 0243 872 5039, 0243 218 2063; m 0412 893 6736. Overlooking the beach, with a good fried fish restaurant below. Rooms with fan, bathroom, cold water. $$

⌂ **Posada del Morocho** (3 rooms) ☎ 0243 246 6127; m 0414 450 3341. House behind the church with roof terrace for hanging hammocks, cable TV, rooms with AC, use of kitchen by arrangement. $$

⌂ **Posada La Luzonera** (6 rooms) ☎ 0243 242 1284; m 0412 723 1987; e posadalaluzonera@ yahoo.com. On the main street in front of the plaza, run by Morella Luzon, B&B rooms with AC, cold water, restaurant in front. Reserve in advance. Can arrange trips to Chorreron. $$

⌂ **Posada Doña Mirian** previously **La Casona del Río** (16 rooms) m 0412 669 9465. At the entrance to the upper village, by the Chuao River. An old 2-storey house, rooms with fan & shared bathrooms, restaurant. Can arrange excursions to Chorreron. $

Festivals Chuao's big festival is **Corpus Christi**, which is the ninth Thursday after Holy Thursday, and often falls in early June. On Wednesday morning, announced by drums and church bells, the 'devil dancers' gather. Many village men belong to a religious society of '*diablos danzantes*', some of whom have danced since boyhood. Greatest prestige goes to La Sayona, the devils' mother figure (a man). In brightly patterned costumes and masks with staring eyes and grinning mouth, the dancers form a cross, offering themselves to God as humble servants. They advance on the church, but entry is repeatedly denied; the culmination comes with a mass in which their sins are forgiven. Celebrations end on Friday with a huge pot of fish *sancocho* over a wood fire, a stew to restore life after days fuelled mainly by *aguardiente*. The fiesta of the big drums celebrating **St John the Baptist** follows on 23–24 June; then everyone in the village takes to the streets, dancing lasts all night and fishermen take the statue of San Juan out to sea to meet other statues of San Juan from Cepe, Puerto Maya and Choroní.

CEPE From Choroní, the next bay after Chuao is Cepe, with a smaller beach backed by palms and enclosed by rocky bluffs, inhabited by a few fishermen. There are shacks selling food that open at weekends. Snorkelling off the rocks is good. The village is set back from the sea on a path through forest and there are petroglyphs on a trail up the valley following the river. A trail from the back of Posada Puerto Escondido leads to Playa Escondida, a small secluded bay with a sandy beach.

⌂ Where to stay

⌂ **Posada Puerto Escondido** (8 rooms) ☎ 0243 241 3614, 0243 241 4645; m 0414 123 5225; e info@puertoescondido.com.ve; www.puertoescondido.com.ve. Just behind the beach is this surprisingly elegant *posada*, the base of scuba divers César & Freddy Fischer, both experienced dive instructors. Scuba equipment is available for hire & they run PADI courses with initial immersion in the swimming pool & diving off Chuao & Tuja. The colonial-style house has a thatched dining shelter for guests and B&B rooms have private bath, hot water. The Fischers also lead hikes into the national park. $$$

PARQUE NACIONAL HENRI PITTIER The park stretches from Pico El Cenizo (2,436m) and Punta Tuja in the east to Pico Jengibre (1,500m) and the Bahía de Turiamo in the west. There are two roads through the park from Maracay to the coast. The one to Choroní–Puerto Colombia starts in Las Delicias. A lower and wider road starts in **El Limón** and passes the **Rancho Grande Biological Station** before descending to the beach town of **Ocumare**. Both roads give the traveller a close-up view of changing flora. A birdwatcher's paradise, Henri Pittier is home to an astonishing 550 bird species and birders from all over the world flock here to see violet-chested hummingbirds, white-tipped quetzals, rufous-cheeked tanagers, helmeted curassow, groove-billed toucanets, black-throated spinetails and handsome fruiteaters, among many others, from the tiniest of hummingbirds to the largest of raptors such as solitary eagles and the mighty harpy eagle. The forests are also home to howler monkeys, sloths, ocelots, tapirs, deer, peccary and the rarely seen jaguars, which are the largest denizen of the park. Over half the 136 mammal species are bats, which do valuable work fertilising forest flowers and spreading seeds. There are 74 kinds of reptiles and 38 amphibians.

The park covers a wide variety of ecosystems, which change with altitude. Mangroves grow in sea-level swamps, cactus scrub clings to the dry foothills of the coast, while inland, huge trees shade cacao plantations along the river valleys. At about 500m, deciduous forests grow where the soil and increased humidity permit. Above 900m or 1,000m, the evergreen begins, with hundreds of different tree ferns, philodendrons and orchids feeding off the dripping moisture as the average humidity hits 92% in misty cloudforest.

Rancho Grande Biological Station The road to Ocumare passes the gates of Rancho Grande Biological Station (⊕ *07.00–18.00; admission on small fee to gatekeeper*) 28km from Maracay at 1,100m in the cloudforest. The biological station operates from a derelict hotel, built in the 1930s by the dictator Gómez. Workers apparently downed tools when they got news of the dictator's death and the project was abandoned. The forest has reclaimed much of the structure and it's an extraordinary, unforgettable, spooky place inhabited mainly by bats. Some people say that executions took place here and others have seen ghosts. Most people come, however, to see some of the 550 bird species recorded here, 38% of Venezuela's total of 1,417. The biological station was created in 1966 by the Universidad Central de Venezuela's School of Agronomy to study the dynamics and evolution of tropical mountain ecosystems. It offers researchers basic kitchen facilities and four dormitories with bunk beds, shared bathrooms and cold showers. Campers will need a good rainproof tent, sleeping bag (it gets cold at night), warm clothes, candles and food. For more details on the possibilities of staying at Rancho Grande contact the Venezuelan Audubon Society (*www.audubonvenezuela.org*) or Posada El Limón (see *Where to stay and eat*, page 322).

Veteran birder and a founding member of the Venezuelan Audubon Society, Mary Lou Goodwin, wrote this about Rancho Grande in her book *Birding in Venezuela*:

> Rancho Grande at dawn is, without doubt, one of the rarest, most exquisite experiences a birder can have anywhere in the world. Veiled in mist, the rainforest emerges from the darkness and the silence at night's end into joyful bird songs and crystal clear light… You may expect to see some of the endemics, such as the handsome fruiteater; it is also possible to see harpy eagle (check the sky, especially around 10.00 to noon). Around the main grounds you should see blood-eared parakeets as well as white-tipped swift, which nest under the balconies… In the mating season, February/April, it is easier to see the white-tipped quetzal from the terrace of the station.

Trails Behind Rancho Grande there is an iron staircase leading to the forest, the start of the Andrew Field Interpretation Trail named for an English botany student who died from a fall while studying the huge Niño trees of Rancho Grande. There is a brass plaque dedicated to Field (1954–84) 'whose imagination, love and perseverance resulted in the creation of this trail'. Some 150m past this plaque a trail leads left. This is the **Guacamaya Trail** going up to Pico Guacamaya, 1,828m. Since you start walking at an elevation of 1,100m, the hike up is not so hard. The

Henri François Pittier (1857–1950) was a Swiss civil engineer and botanist who grew up among the mountains of Bex, in the east of Switzerland. After teaching in France, he went to Costa Rica in 1887 as director of the Physio-Geographic Institute, overseeing road and railway mapping and studying flora and fauna. He came to Venezuela aged 62 in 1919 and before he died 30 years later, he had compiled a manual (still in use) of 30,000 common plants, established a national botanical service and herbarium, co-founded the Venezuelan Society of Natural Sciences, and successfully urged the creation of Venezuela's first national park in 1937, now named in his honour.

path, at times faint, continues down a ridge north to the coast, and eventually comes out at the village of Cuyagua. For twitchers seeking endemics, it's an easy trail to bird for an hour or so.

Up the road from the station you will see a wire mesh fence and gate (sometimes locked) on the left. This is the trail for **Portachuelo Pass**. At some 700m below Guacamaya Peak, it is a main flyway for insects and birds, including migrants from North America, which begin to arrive in October, and leave again in April. At these times ornithologists from the Audubon Society band as many as 100 birds a day.

Where to stay and eat

Posada El Limón (19 rooms) 64 Calle El Pinal; \ 0243 283 4925; e caribean@telcel.net.ve; www.posadaellimon.com. One of the best ways to explore the Parque Nacional Henri Pittier, especially for birdwatchers, is from the back garden of the house in a quiet residential zone near the mountains, which has a path leading into the park. Owner Bernardus van den Hurk, who runs Caribean Eco Tours, & his wife between them speak 6 languages, including Arabic, & offer custom tours for birdwatchers & insect collectors, as well as more distant tours, & transfers from Caracas. The *posada* has a small pleasant pool, comfortable rooms with good beds, private bath & hot water, some with AC. Other services include laundry, internet, fax, cell-phone rental, & meals by arrangement with the chef. $$

OCUMARE DE LA COSTA AND EL PLAYÓN (*Telephone code: 0243*) From the Rancho Grande Pass, the road descends through forest and for a good way runs parallel to the Ocumare River; there is a recreation area at La Trilla with picnic shelters and changing rooms for bathers, and further on, roadside places to stop by the river. Shortly below, the road forks: the left-hand turning leads to **Cumboto** and **Turiamo** by another Gómez-era road. Cacao plantations along the Cumboto River are shaded by huge rubber trees; you can see incisions in the bark for collecting sap. The cacao-producing communities here are Las Palmitas and Cumboto. Traffic to Turiamo is restricted as it is a naval base.

Go right for **Ocumare de la Costa**. This little town was a well-established settlement of the Parica Indians when the Spaniards arrived in 1595 to cultivate cacao, and as such it is one of the few towns where credit is given to an Indian, Chief Martín, as founder. Ocumare has two plazas, Miranda and Bolívar. Another 3.5km further on is the beach of **El Playón**. Its official name is Independencia in memory of Francisco Miranda's attempted landing in 1806, a disaster ending in the capture of two ships. El Playón, with its popularity pegged to weekend sun-seekers, has guesthouses, rooms to let, restaurants, bakeries and various food stores. It is the centre for local park excursions on foot or bicycle. Scuba divers and snorkellers go west by boat to the reefs of a bottle-shaped bay called **La Ciénaga** with beautiful, clear waters and a shimmering coral lagoon.

Where to stay

🏠 **De La Costa Eco-Lodge** (24 rooms) Calle California/La Playa, El Playón; ☎ 0243 993 1986; m 0414 460 0655; e dlcecolodge@hotmail.com; www.ecovenezuela.com. Popular with foreign travellers, the Eco-Lodge has a pool, jacuzzi & restaurant, rooms with AC, cable TV, offered independently or in a package with excursions. A 3-day/2-night package includes all meals, transfers & excursions to Cata, La Ciénaga & Rancho Grande. Owner can organise scuba diving, birdwatching, kayaking, & fishing trips. English, German & Italian spoken. $$

🏠 **Hotel Costa de Oro** (4 suites) On the beach, Calle California/Calle La Playa, El Playón; ☎ 0243 993 1957; m 0414 463 0004; www.hotelcostadeoro.com. New rooms & apts with kitchen, AC, TV, hot water, sea views. Italian & a little English spoken. $$

🏠 **Posada Bocono** (8 rooms) 44 Calle Fuerzas Armadas, El Playón; ☎ 0243 993 1434; m 0414 463 5652; e info@posadabocono.com; www.posadabocono.com.ve. Located on the beach, this is one of the 1st posadas in El Playón, now run by a Dutch owner. Rooms with bath, AC, cable TV, beach chairs, umbrellas included, restaurant for guests serves b/fasts, meals in peak season only. $$

🏠 **Posada Los Helechos** (7 rooms) Calle Santander, El Playón; ☎ 0243 993 1385; m 0414 477 5777; e phelechos@gmail.com;

www.posadaloshelechos.blogspot.com. Good value in a white house with green ferns (helechos). Rooms with bath, cold water, AC, cable TV. Small pool. Restaurant open to public (🕐 08.00–21.00). $$

🏠 **Posada Villa de Loly** (8 rooms) Calle Fuerzas Armadas at Urdaneta, El Playón; ☎ 0243 993 1252; m 0414 457 4040; e loley-enlacosta@hotmail.com. A block from the beach, it has basic rooms with bath, cold water, AC, cable TV for up to 4 guests. There's a barbecue grill outside, a pool & restaurant-dining area for guests. Excursions by arrangement, transfers from Caracas. Some English & German spoken. $$

🏠 **Residencia Doña Elisa** (9 rooms) 32 Calle Aragua, El Playón; ☎ 0243 993 1305. Another option for 3–6 people in apts with AC, kitchen, dbl bed & bunk beds, ask for a sheet or bring your own. Min 2 days' stay during long w/end holidays. $$

🏠 **Restaurant & Posada María Luisa** (20 rooms) Near the plaza in Ocumare; ☎ 0243 993 1073; e posadamarialuisa@cantv.net; www.posadamarialuisa.com. An 1884 house furnished with antiques & a restaurant serving typical Venezuelan dishes. Rooms with en-suite bath, hot water, AC & a new section with suites around swimming pool. B/fast & dinner included as package in high season. Birding tours offered to Henri Pittier, boat trips to beaches. $$

CATA Cata's almost perfect crescent bay fringed by coconut palms is 5.6km east of El Playón. It is only 'almost' perfect because two apartment towers loom on the beach. It has changing rooms, open-air restaurants, parasols, lifeguards and a parking lot. Campers pay a small fee to set up tents, but it's free to hang a hammock. Most people just come for the day. Fishing boats ferry bathers to the smaller beach of Catita at the end of the same bay, where there is a beautiful coral reef and good snorkelling, or you can walk there in an hour; take a hat, water and sunscreen.

The village of Cata is 4.7km inland. This is a very quiet place until the drums sound on fiestas such as **San Juan** (24 June) and **Corpus Christi** (ninth Thursday after Holy Thursday) when the devil dancers perform in front of the old Iglesia de San Francisco. Then people come from the hills around and cities far away to join in street processions.

CUYAGUA The broad bay of Cuyagua, 13km beyond Cata, is popular with surfers who drive their 4x4s onto the sand, crank up the reggae music and set up camp for the weekend. The beach is backed by a coconut plantation and there are food stalls serving hot arepas on weekends, but few other services. The waves are big enough for surfing, and at times are too rough for swimming. Fewer people go as far as Cuyagua and the beach is wonderfully empty on weekdays. That the beach is clean is a tribute to conservation-minded villagers who have a community action group. The village itself is a short distance south, up the valley, and has just two streets: one for entering, one for leaving. Cuyagua's river is called simply Río Grande.

People go to picnic and take a dip at a little *balneario* in the national park called Pozo de Arena (ask in the village for directions).

Getting there Travelling by *por puesto* from Ocumare de la Costa takes 40 minutes (US$2.50).

Where to stay

Posada Cuyagua Mar (26 rooms) Calle La Cruz, on the street past the plaza in the village; \ 0243 217 7896; m 0416 802 6070, 0414 944 3182; e cuyaguamar@posadacuyaguamar.com. Rooms with bath, fan, some with AC, off a leafy courtyard. $$

La Posada de Doña Meche (10 rooms) Calle La Cruz, near the plaza; \ 0243 219 5991, 0243 951 5400. Simple rooms with fan, shared baths (2) upstairs, use of kitchen downstairs where the family live. Can organise boat trips, excursions. $

Posada Cuyagua Beach (12 rooms) Near the entrance to the beach; \ 0243 236 2853; m 0414 343 6466, 0412 890 4220; e posadacu@hotmail.com. Basic rooms with AC, cold water, cable

TV & small fridge in this 3-storey *posada* with top-floor terrace & minibar. $

Posada Fernoys (16 rooms) Between the beach & village by the basketball courts; m 0412 963 8855, 0412 639 2563. Simple dbls with AC, cold water, use of kitchen. $

Posada La Casa Grande (8 rooms) Calle La Cruz; m 0414 317 0868. A very large house at the end of the road to the Pozo de Arena picnic area on the river, which the Quijano family helped to design & make as it is on their land. The 3-storey house has basic rooms with bath & fan for 3–6 guests & use of kitchen in low season. In a stone house on the wooded property with its own little pools, there are also 2 good apts with kitchen. $

CARABOBO STATE

The central state of Carabobo offers travellers a modern and lively capital city with good restaurants and nightlife, an excellent mountain park, ancient petroglyphs, the seaport of Puerto Cabello and good beaches nearby. The area around Lake Valencia was once the site of an important pre-Colombian civilisation and archaeological excavations over many years have revealed that the lake's shore was thickly settled by Indian tribes. Many fine ceramic artefacts have been dug up here, including examples of the enigmatic female figures with coffee-bean eyes and large heads, known as Venus de Tacarigua figurines. The 34km-wide lake has also yielded important fossils of animals such as the giant sloth, mastodon, primitive horse and the giant crocodile, megasaurus. Now nearly halved in volume, the lake has no natural outlet and is seriously contaminated by water piped in from industries in Cojedes.

The name Carabobo comes from an Indian word for a palm-like plant (*Carludovica palmata*) that grows on the shores of the lake, according to local historian Torcuato Manzo Núñez. When Simón Bolívar's army of Venezuelan patriots and British, Irish and Scottish volunteers ended Spain's military control at the Battle of Carabobo, 24 June 1821, effectively securing Venezuela's independence, that name was extended to the whole area and the State of Carabobo was born.

VALENCIA (*Telephone code: 0241*) Valencia is the country's third largest city, with some 1.5 million inhabitants, and the biggest centre of light industry, where hundreds of companies make everything from animal feed to automobiles. In 2006 it opened its own subway system, with seven stations in operation and more planned. The valley, 479m above sea level, has a hot climate (average 26°C) pleasantly cooled by evening breezes from the surrounding hills. There's little to hold the visitor on a tight schedule rushing through to somewhere more exciting, such as the Parque Nacional Morrocoy.

Valencia is important historically and was on three occasions Venezuela's capital. As all records were burned during a 1667 attack by French pirates, it is hard to pin down the date of the town's founding to 1553 or 1555. By then Captain Alonso Díaz Moreno had chosen the valley as a good place to live as well as a staging point for further conquest. A successful rancher, he was able to provision Diego de Losada on his expedition to found Caracas 11 years later. His family portrait (see *Casa de los Celis*, page 329) shows seven daughters and one son. The fifth daughter married a Spaniard called Simón de Bolívar and became one of the Liberator's early Venezuelan-born ancestors. Valencia hung on through assaults by the tyrant Lope de Aguirre, by Carib Indians, earthquakes and, most terrible of all, the wars of Independence. There were not many of Valencia's 'finest' left after 35 battles fought in the area. The year after Venezuela's Declaration of Independence on 5 July 1811, Valencia served as the seat of government for the short-lived First Republic. In 1830 Valencia became the capital a second time when a congress met in the Casa de la Estrella to dissolve the Gran Colombian union so cherished by Bolívar (who died a few months later). Then in 1858–59 the city again became capital after the fall of President José Tadeo Monagas.

Getting there and away

By air The international airport, Aeropuerto Internacional Arturo Michelena, is 7km southeast of Valencia. Aserca (*www.asercaairlines.com*) has a daily flight to Caracas (30 minutes, US$50). There are daily flights by Aeropostal (*www.aeropostal.com*) to Porlamar. Aserca links Barquisimeto, Barcelona, Puerto Ordaz and Maracaibo. The Dutch Antilles Express (*www.flydae.com*) flies between Curaçao and Valencia. Aserca flies three times weekly to Aruba and Curaçao.

By bus Valencia is 2½ hours from Caracas by the *autopista*, making it a good springboard for western and central states. The large and very busy bus terminal lies 4km east of downtown Valencia in the Centro Big Low. This development of phoney turrets and towers has an amusement park and a shopping centre. Behind the shops is the Terminal de Pasajeros. Buses leave throughout the day for Maracay (1 hour, US$3), Caracas (2½ hours, US$5) and more distant points south and west: Barquisimeto, 193km (3 hours, US$6), Coro, 288km (5–6 hours, US$10), and San Fernando de Apure, 368km (7–8 hours, US$15). There is frequent service to Puerto Cabello (50 minutes, US$2), Tucacas (2 hours, US$4) and Chichiriviche (2½ hours, US$3). Express coaches to Mérida, 525km (9–10 hours, US$22), San Antonio del Táchira, 700km (11½ hours, US$18) and Maracaibo, 549km (8 hours, US$15), usually travel at night.

The executive bus service to Caracas is gaining popularity. You pay more but get there faster. The air-conditioned coaches have curtains sewn shut for screening videos that usually take a little longer than the ride so you don't get to see the end. You can't see the countryside or open a window, but then many *expresos* travel at night. **Aeroexpresos Ejecutivos** (*www.aeroexpresos.com.ve*) will reserve you a seat on one of ten daily departures to Caracas (2½ hours, US$6). There are seven departures to Barquisimeto, four to Maracay, two to Maracaibo and Puerto La Cruz and one to Maturín.

By car Valencia is on the main highway, about 2½ hours from Caracas and about an hour from Maracay.

Getting around The **Metro de Valencia** (*www.metrovalencia.gob.ve*; ⊕ *06.00–20.30 Mon–Fri, 06.00–19.30 Sat–Sun & public hols; ticket US$0.23*) is a spanking new subway system that started operating in 2006 as a trial and opened fully in 2007. The seven stations on Line 1 linking the south of the city to the centre are:

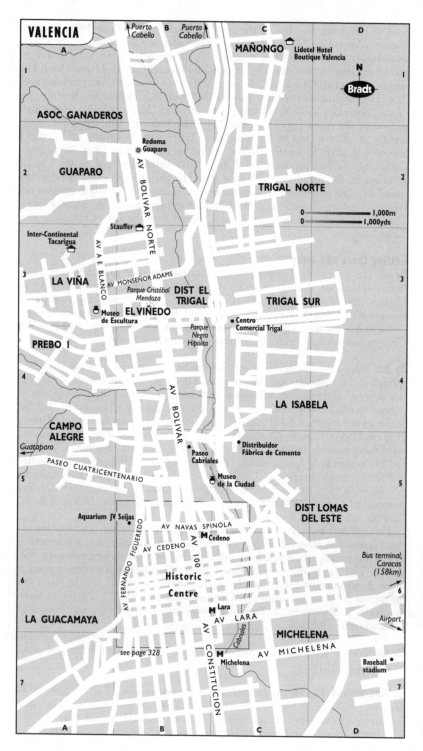

VALENCIA

A   Puerto   B   Puerto   C   D
     Cabello   Cabello

MAÑONGO   Lidotel Hotel
           Boutique Valencia

N

Bradt

ASOC GANADEROS

TRIGAL NORTE

1,000m
1,000yds

Redoma
Guaparo

GUAPARO

AV BOLIVAR NORTE

Stauffer

AV A E BLANCO

Inter-Continental
Tacarigua

LA VIÑA   AV MONSEÑOR ADAMS

Parque Cristóbal   DIST EL   TRIGAL SUR
Mendoza   TRIGAL

EL VIÑEDO
Museo
de Escultura   Centro
                Comercial Trigal

Parque
Negra
PREBO I   Hipólita

LA ISABELA

AV BOLIVAR

CAMPO
ALEGRE

Guataparo   Distribuidor
             Fábrica de Cemento

Paseo
Cabriales

PASEO CUATRICENTENARIO   Museo
                          de la Ciudad

DIST LOMAS
DEL ESTE

Aquarium JV Seijas

AV NAVAS SPINOLA
M Cedeno

AV FERNANDO FIGUEREDO   AV CEDENO

AV 100

Historic

Bus terminal,
Caracas
(158km)

Centre

Airport

M Lara

AV LARA

Cabriales

MICHELENA

LA GUACAMAYA

AV MICHELENA

AV CONSTITUCION

see page 328   M
               Michelena

Baseball
stadium

A   B   C   D

Monumental, Las Ferias, Palotal, Santa Rosa, Michelena, Lara and Cedeño. Two more lines are currently being built. The final plan envisages four subway lines linked to the projected Ezequial Zamora railway line, which is being built between Puerto Cabello and Maracay.

Where to stay Hotels in this commercial city, whether expensive or modest, are less busy on weekends. All are air conditioned and have private bath unless noted. Around Plaza Bolívar there are some budget options and a few Love Hotels that charge by the hour, but it's not recommended to walk around this zone at night.

Inter-Continental Tacarigua [326 A3] (162 rooms) La Viña district; ☎ 0241 824 2476, 0241 824 4435; www.venetur.gob.ve. Run by the state tourism agency Venetur & about 4km from the city centre, this 70s' style hotel is on 6 floors, overlooking a large pool, gym, buffet restaurant, & sushi bar. Ask about w/end rates with b/fast. Look out for the large green iguanas that inhabit the gardens. $$$$

Lidotel Hotel Boutique Valencia [326 C1] (133 rooms) Av Numero 4, Ciudad Jardin Mañongo; ☎ 0241 841 1999; e reservasval@lidotel.com.ve. New hotel annexed to the Sambil shopping centre, with all amenities, business centre, Wi-Fi, restaurants, bar, swimming pool, gym. $$$$

Stauffer [326 B3] (188 rooms) Av Bolívar Norte; ☎ 0241 823 4022; e vtasval@staufferhotel.com.ve; www.staufferhotel.com.ve. Huge 18-storey tower is fairly charmless inside, top rooms with good views, swimming pool on 4th floor, restaurant. About 4km from city centre. $$$

Don Pelayo [328 B2] (144 suites & rooms) Av 101 near Calle 103; ☎ 0241 857 9222; e hoteldp@cantv.net; www.hoteldonpelayo.com. Good mid-range option 4 blocks from Plaza Bolívar with gym, internet centre, café, *tasca* bar & restaurant. $$

Hotel Carabobo [328 C3] (52 rooms) Calle Libertador, Plaza Bolívar; ☎ 0241 858 8860, 0241 858 4467. A basic option in the centre. $

Where to eat and drink Valencia is a large city spread out from north to south along Avenida Bolívar. In the centre things close down early and so you should plan to eat early or head out to Avenida Monseñor Adams in the area of El Viñedo where many of the city's trendiest bars and restaurants can be found. If you are staying in the north of the city you need go no further than the Sambil shopping mall in Mañongo, which houses everything from fast food joints in the food hall to fine dining establishments and popular sports bars.

Bambu Lounge Av Monseñor Adams, in front of the Plaza de Las Esculturas; ☎ 0241 825 5180; ⊕ 19.00–24.00 Mon–Wed, 18.00–03.00 Thu–Sat. A young crowd frequent this lounge bar & restaurant with open-air patio in the trendy area of El Viñedo. Informal atmosphere extends to bean bags & laid-back tunes played by house DJ. A safe, friendly place to start the evening, preferably with a cocktail.

Meals include pizzas & seafood dishes. From Thu to Sat the tempo picks up after 22.00 when the lounge tunes are replaced by reggaeton. $$

Guarda Tinajas Av 91, Urb La Trigaleña; ☎ 0241 842 5413; www.guardatinajas.com. A bastion of hearty old-school Venezuelan fare such as *pabellón criollo*, & chicken & beef *sancocho* soups. $

Other practicalities In the centre there is a Banco de Venezuela on Calle Libertad, on the corner with Avenida Díaz Moreno, and a Banesco opposite. The Sambil shopping centre has several banks, such as Banesco and Banco Mercantil.

There are many CANTV and Movistar call centres offering internet and international calls, including in the main bus terminal, in the Big Low centre and in the Sambil shopping mall.

There are several 24-hour pharmacies in the old centre and the main shopping centres, and a public hospital in Naguanagua.

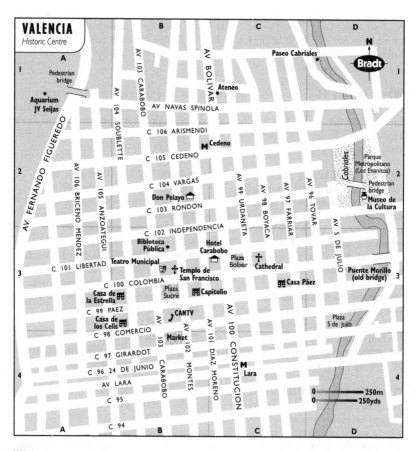

What to see and do
Historic Valencia

Plaza Bolívar [328 C3] The unusual bronze statue of Simón Bolívar in the plaza stands on top of a 15m marble monolith, similar to Nelson's Column in London's Trafalgar Square. The Liberator is not brandishing a sword but points towards Carabobo, where the decisive battle against the Spanish was fought in 1821.

Cathedral The cathedral [328 C3] on Avenida 99 Urdaneta is a mixture of styles, with a large dome, added in 1955, and some original colonial features that are 420 years old. Two large oil paintings by Antonio Herrera Toro, a renowned Valencia painter, and the 16th-century carving of the Virgen del Socorro are worth seeing. The sad-looking Socorro, her head draped in a black shawl, is the patron saint of Valencia. She was the first statue crowned by the Church in Venezuela and her jewel-encrusted crown is only taken out of the safe for the celebrations of her feast day on 13 November.

Capitolio [328 B3] (*Calle 99 Páez;* ⊕ *09.00–16.00 Mon–Fri*; *admission free*) The seat of government was originally a Catholic hospital and operated as a convent before it was destroyed by fire in 1795 and rebuilt as a girls' school run by Carmelite nuns. In 1874 all religious orders in Venezuela were expelled by President Guzmán Blanco and their properties confiscated. The front pillars were added in 1877 when the state moved in. Ask to see the famous painting by Arturo Michelena of Bolívar on his white horse, Paloma, in the assembly hall.

Casa Páez [328 C3] (*Av Boyacá, Calle 99 Páez;* ☏ *0241 857 0685;* ☉ *09.00–14.00 Tue–Sun; admission free*) A well-restored colonial mansion built by General José Antonio Páez, who became Venezuela's first president in 1831 after the dissolution of Gran Colombia. On the patio walls are murals of the battles in which his army of fierce Llanero horsemen helped to defeat the Spanish. His favourite maxims (such as 'Without virtue, there is no country') are painted on the outside walls. You can infer his rough Llanos background from a rustic leather chair. He was elected again in 1839 and later refused a third term. Admired wherever he went for his zest, sense and self-taught culture, Páez spent 20 years in exile in Argentina, France, Germany and the United States. He died in 1873 in New York where his funeral cortege was accompanied to the docks by Generals Sherman and Sheridan before his remains were borne to Venezuela by a US warship.

Teatro Municipal [328 B3] (*Calle 100 Colombia*) Opened in 1894, it was designed as a smaller version of the Paris Opera House by French architect Antonio Malaussena, whose son made the theatres in Maracay and Puerto Cabello. The splendid ceiling murals in the large dome were painted by Antonio Herrera Toro, who included his self-portrait among the European heroes of music and drama.

Casa de la Estrella [328 B3] (*Calle Colombia at Av 104;* ☉ *10.00–17.00 Tue–Sun; admission free*) A national monument for its importance in the Independence Wars, this historic house is where the Congress of 1812 drew up the constitution of the First Republic, naming Valencia its capital. In 1830 another congress here decreed Venezuela's sovereignty, withdrawing from Gran Colombia, which then included Ecuador, Colombia and Panama. The oldest surviving building in Valencia (1710) and one of the oldest in the country, it was originally a hospital and later housed the Colegio Nacional de Carabobo, precursor of the Universidad de Valencia. There are a few exhibits on Valencia's history but the building itself is the real attraction.

Casa de los Celis [328 B3] (*Calle Soublette, Calle Comercio;* ☉ *09.00–14.00 Tue–Sun; admission free*) One of the most beautiful colonial mansions in Venezuela, the large house and central patio with its big shade trees was built in 1765 by a Spanish mayor who abandoned it 40 years later to the Independence forces. Colonel Pedro Celis bought it in 1837 and sold half, it was so big. The **Museo de Arte e Historia** and the extensive archaeological collection of the Fundación Lisandro Alvarado are all housed here in spacious rooms displaying pre-Columbian ceramics from the Valencia basin, colonial furniture and artworks by three fine painters of the late 19th century: Arturo Michelena, Antonio Herrera Toro and Andrés Mujica. A nice place to escape the city streets for an hour.

Palacio de los Iturriza (also known as **Quinta La Isabela**) (*Calle Rojas Queipo at Av Paseo Cabriales;* ☉ *09.00–17.00 Tue–Fri, 10.00–17.00 Sat–Sun; admission free*) Another colonial mansion, about 1.5km north of the centre. Built in 1867 for Juan Miguel Izturriza, in a mishmash of styles inspired by Spanish colonial and French Baroque, it fell into disrepair when sold in 1976 to a bank that failed, but has been restored and reopened as the Museo de la Ciudad.

Other attractions
Aquarium J V Seijas [328 A1] (*Av Fernando Figueredo;* ☏ *0241 857 4739; www.aquariumdevalencia.com;* ☉ *09.30–16.30 Tue–Fri, 10.00–17.30 Sat–Sun;*

admission US$1.25) A popular aquarium and zoo housed in a converted waterworks in the west of the city. There's plenty to occupy several hours, and you can eat at the soda fountain or restaurant. The main attraction is the family of pink dolphins (*toninas*) from the Orinoco River. During feeding times in the large central tank (10.00, 13.30 and 17.00) the dolphins jump, dive and play ball. Among displays of 300 native species of fish, are piranhas and electric eels (*tembladores*). A terrarium has poisonous snakes and the aquarium sells antivenom serum for snake and scorpion bites. A **zoo** is built around a ravine behind the aquarium. In semi-natural settings live a large manatee (only seen at feeding times), tapirs, peccaries, jaguar, puma and crocodiles. From the bus terminal in Centro Big Low, city buses and *por puestos* take you west across Avenida Cedeño (Calle 105); ask to be let off at the pedestrian bridge (*pasarela*) leading to the aquarium.

Museo de Beisbol and Hall of Fame (*Centro Comercial Sambil, Mañongo district;* \0241 841 1313; *www.museodebeisbol.org;* ⊕ *12.00–20.00; admission US$3*) Opened in 2002, this innovative museum offers a chance to explore Venezuela's fanatical love for baseball, the national sport, which has been played since the 1930s, and the careers of home-grown players in the American big leagues. There are five salons on two floors covering the origins of the game, the big stars past and present, and the eight national teams, as well as an auditorium for screening videos, a library, sports shop and art gallery, topped with a pitching-machine practice area. It's easy to find, under a half-round dome like a giant baseball at the **Sambil** shopping mall in the Mañongo district, north of El Trigal.

Plaza de Toros Monumental About 3km directly south of Plaza Bolívar, the bullring is indeed monumental. Opened in 1968, it is classed as one of the world's top three, along with arenas in Spain and Mexico. Peter Albers who designed the bullring was in charge 30 years later of remodelling it for sports exhibitions and public spectacles such as ice-skating, with eight floodlight towers, new access ramps, 4,000 seats in boxes and barriers, 38 bathrooms, and fire-fighting hoses and tanks. From the original capacity of 27,000, seating was reduced to 25,000. Carlos Cruz Diez painted the circular *Physichromie* artwork of aluminium, and Vladimir Zabaleta created the 27m bull of concrete for the re-inauguration in 1998 when nine matadors fought on three afternoons of bulls.

Around Valencia

Guacara and the Vigirima petroglyphs The **Cerro de Piedras Pintadas** (*park centre;* ⊕ *09.00–16.00 Mon–Sun*) is a collection of prehistoric engraved stones in the Parque Nacional San Esteban on two hills close together in the sunny countryside near Tronconero, north of Guacara. Covering dozens of weathered rocks are shallow engravings of anthropomorphic figures, animals, hands, lines, dots and swirls, some of them very elaborate, including a woman giving birth. Who made them, and when, are matters of conjecture as such exposed glyphs cannot be dated. On the slope behind the main hill a low wall of upright megaliths leads up the ridge. Centuries roll back as you climb the grassy foothills and wonder at the prehistoric people who, from here, may have looked over a fuller Lake Tacarigua (now Lake Valencia). There is a visitor's centre with information on the petroglyphs but there have been robberies by local delinquents, so for reasons of security visitors are advised to view the more isolated megaliths in groups. Obvious damage to some of the petroglyphs and graffiti carved into the rocks is a sad sign of the neglect they've suffered, despite being a unique link to the indigenous people who carved them hundreds, maybe thousands, of years before Columbus arrived.

Getting there To drive, head for Guacara, near the *autopista*, some 13km east of Valencia. From the Plaza Bolívar of Guacara, follow signs north for Vigirima. In 6.3km you will see Bodega La Esmeralda on the left; 500m beyond, turn left at Los Tres Samanes, another *bodega* or country store. A broad road leads west about 2km to the shady Tronconero River. After crossing the bridge, take a right fork after 500m at the Escuela Rural No 49. You are now facing north on a rough jeep track running through maize fields for 1.5km towards the hills. There it veers right, past the visitor's centre to the two low hills covered in petroglyphs and the megalith hill up on the right. The other option is to take a Valencia bus from Maracay, ask the driver to let you down in Guacara on the highway bridge, go down to the road below and wait for a *por puesto* to Tronconero. Walk the last ten minutes.

Campo de Carabobo The nation's most famous battlefield is located 32km southwest of Valencia, on the road to Tinaco. Here Venezuela, the first colony to revolt against Spain, won the battle for Independence on 24 June 1821. There is a great **Triumphal Arch** guarding the Tomb of the Unknown Soldier with its eternal flame. The imposing allegorical monument called the **Altar de la Patria** has seven steps for the seven original provinces, bearing likenesses of Independence heroes with the Liberator's equestrian statue crowning the top. The monument, commissioned by dictator Juan Vicente Gómez, was unveiled in 1930.

At the **Mirador** overlooking the battlefield, there's a model of battle forces: the Spanish troops under General de la Torre commanding the plain, versus Bolívar's forces, superior in number but in a weaker attack position until Bolívar sent Páez's Bravos de Apure and the British Legion to surprise the Spaniards from the rear. There is a **diorama** of the events. The guards of honour wear period uniforms and bearskin hats, a reminder that the battle was considered so crucial by all the forces that they fought in ceremonial dress. Support given by British legionnaires on that

---

CARABOBO BATTLE BROKE ROYAL POWER

After a decade of wars for Independence, the battle that put Venezuela's reins firmly in patriot hands began on the morning of 24 June 1821 on the plains of Carabobo. The adversaries were led by wealthy Caracas aristocrat, Simón Bolívar (aged 36), and a Spanish nobleman, Miguel de la Torre. The two knew each other and had married Spanish girls who were cousins (Bolívar's wife died eight months after their marriage).

Holding the plains were 4,279 royalists, half of them Venezuelans. Bolívar summoned his forces: Urdaneta from Coro, Páez (who then was about 25) from the Llanos, Cruz Carrillo from the Andes; in all 6,400 men. Fighting under Páez was the British Legion composed of veterans of the Napoleonic Wars. The Rifles Battalion, led by Arthur Sandes, was in the third division.

When Colonel Ferrier and his second, James Scott, were felled, Captain Charles Minchin took command; he, too, was killed. The legion's resistance is credited with giving Páez's lancers the opening needed to attack the enemy's rear. At the battle's end 100 legionnaires were dead. More than half of the royalist troops had been killed or captured and Spanish power was broken. Triumph was not complete, however, until the Battle of Lake Maracaibo on 24 July 1823, and the Battle of Puerto Cabello on 10 November 1823.

Bolívar went on to the distant Andes with Sucre, another young (29-year-old) Venezuelan, routing the Spaniards at the battles of Junín and Ayacucho in Peru, 1824. Upper Peru formed its own state, naming it Bolivia in honour of the Liberator, and voted Sucre its president.

day earned the British armed forces the honour of being the only foreigners permitted to bear arms (ceremonially) in Venezuela.

There are places to snack, several *parrilla* restaurants and crafts shops on the road approaching Campo Carabobo.

Getting there Buses from Valencia marked Campo Carabobo leave from Avenida Lara and drop you at the entrance to the park, from where it's a long walk to the monuments.

Chirgua geoglyph Unique in Venezuela, a reclining figure with two legs, no arms and a large head bearing antennae is dug into the side of a ridge up the Chirgua Valley, 52km from Valencia. The mysterious 35m-long geoglyph can be seen from the road. Its outlines, formed by trenches today 40cm deep, were dug in prehistoric days and the figure's significance is a matter of conjecture. Unfortunately, a clay idol and potsherds excavated from the figure's body area vanished soon after their discovery in 1946 by owners of the site on Hacienda Cariaprima, leaving archaeologists without the possibility of doing carbon-dating tests. The Chirgua River has various boulders carved with petroglyphs of figures and faces.

Getting there In a car, from Valencia follow the highway southwest 15km to the main Tinaco/Barquisimeto junction and take the right fork towards Nirgua–Barquisimeto. In about 18km, opposite the petrol station of La Mona, a small road goes north 11km to the village of Chirgua. The geoglyph is located on Hacienda Cariaprima, 4km north of Chirgua.

Las Trincheras Centro Termal y Spa (✆ 0241 808 1502; e trincheras@ trincheras.com; www.trincheras.com.ve; ◷ 07.00–21.00 Tue–Sun, 07.00–16.00 Mon; day pass US$3) Just 15 minutes' drive from Valencia on the Puerto Cabello road, the modest installations at Las Trincheras boast the second hottest thermal waters in the world after Japan, and attract devotees of sulphur waters and mud baths from all over the world. The mineral waters are *hot*. In 1800, it took the German naturalist and explorer Alexander von Humboldt less than four minutes to boil an egg in water over 90°C. The reputed curative powers of the waters led to the opening of a spa hotel in 1889. Today, the hot springs are diverted into three swimming pools graded from warm to hot. The day pass includes the use of the pools, mud bath, natural sauna and vapour inhalators. A new spa provides some 30 professional services including anti-stress massages, facials, physiotherapy, aquatherapy and reflexology.

⌂ **Where to stay**

⌂ **Hotel Spa Las Trincheras** (120 rooms) ✆ 0241 808 1502; e trincheras@trincheras.com. Surrounded by gardens with macaws & animals, the hotel is divided into the original Gómez-era building & new rooms overlooking the pools. Rooms are basic with AC, some suites with TV, kitchenette, fridge & balcony. Room price includes use of thermal pools, sauna, mud baths but not individual spa treatments or meals. There is an annex with snack bar. $$

PUERTO CABELLO (*Telephone code: 0242*) Most visitors come here for the colonial charm of the historic centre, access to beaches and diving off the coast, but Puerto Cabello makes a living from the sea, with the country's largest commercial port and most important naval base. As the best harbour in the country and principal port for the industries of Valencia, Maracay and Barquisimeto, Puerto Cabello handles twice as much tonnage as the rest of the nation's ports combined, and is ranked the seventh most active port in Latin America. The town's satellite districts now extend as far west as the airport and the population is estimated at 200,000 inhabitants.

The port began life in the 16th century as a smuggler's anchorage, was attacked by pirates, became a hub for illegal trade with Curaçao and boomed in the 18th century with exports of Venezuela's famous cocoa beans, or *cacao*, grown on the lush plantations bordering mountain rivers such as Río Aguas Calientes, San Esteban and Borburata. In 1800 Alexander von Humboldt described Puerto Cabello as 'quite modern, and the port is one of the finest in the world'. He described the town of 9,000 as having a cheerful and agreeable aspect, despite the scourge of yellow fever. He visited the costly new aqueduct that conveyed the Río Esteban's waters to every street. At the time it was disputed whether the port's name derived from the harbour's tranquillity, 'which would not move a hair (*cabello*)', or from Andrés Cabello, a fisherman who traded with Curaçao smugglers when the port was no more than a hamlet.

Now restored and brightly painted after long neglect, the colonial centre has become a beacon for travellers. A seaside walk, the **Malecón**, has broad open spaces for strolling from the Concejo Municipal on Plaza Bolívar to the Monumento del Aguila. Cherubs and fountains grace the plazas where pink poui trees (*apamates*) bloom in April. Stop for an ice cream at an 18th-century house, or have juice and pizza under multi-coloured awnings.

Getting there and away
By air Puerto Cabello's airport is on the main road, 8km west of town. There are no scheduled flights but the airport handles a lot of cargo.

By bus The main Terminal de Pasajeros is on Avenida La Paz where it turns into Calle Urdaneta at Avenida 10/11. Take care in the area outside the bus station after dark, especially the area north towards Playa Blanca where there have been armed hold-ups. Take a *por puesto* or taxi to your destination. Bus service is frequent to Valencia, 64km (50 minutes), less so to San Felipe, 184km (2 hours), and Barquisimeto, 257km (3 hours). There are several buses a day to Tucacas, 60km (1¼ hours), but service to Chichiriviche is not frequent.

Local buses to San Esteban, Patanemo, El Palito and Morón leave from a central street corner called La Alcantarilla, about 300m east of the bus station. You can't miss it, as there is a large mural of a priest holding a casualty during 'El Porteñazo' (the 1962 insurrection at the naval base). Passengers for Tucacas, Chichiriviche in the Parque Nacional Morrocoy and Coro may take one of the frequent buses to Morón (30 minutes) and pick up a bus coming from Valencia.

By car From Valencia it's 58km on Route 1 towards Morón, then follow the signs back along the coast on Route 11.

By train The Ferrocar station is on Avenida La Paz west of the bus terminal. This line, built by dictator Marcos Pérez Jiménez in the 1950s, covers the 173km (3 hours) to Barquisimeto. The train stops at El Palito, Morón, San Felipe, Boraure, Chivacoa and Yaritagua. Only freight trains currently run but construction is underway on the government's ambitious plan to build a passenger railway service to Maracay and the Tuy Valley that will link to Valencia's subway system.

Tourist information The **tourist bureau** (*Calle Puerto Cabello;* \ *0242 361 3921;* ⏰ *08.00–17.00 Mon–Fri*) at the end of the Malecón has some useful local information.

13

Where to stay

🏠 **Hotel & Restaurant Isla Larga** (55 rooms) Near the bus terminal on Calle Miranda; ☎ 0242 361 3290. One of the most modern accommodation options in the centre, this 4-storey hotel has a pool, rooms with AC, TV, fridge. $$

🏠 **Hotel Cumboto** (44 rooms) Av La Playa, Cumboto; ☎ 0242 364 0672; e hotelcumboto@ yahoo.com. A new option by the beach. Rooms with sea view & AC, swimming pool, restaurant, Wi-Fi. $$

🏠 **Hotel Suite Caribe** (139 rooms) 21 Av Salóm, on the highway; ☎ 0242 364 2286; www.hotelsuitecaribe.com. Located in La Sorpresa district towards the airport, this 3-star hotel is in a safe area but could do with refurbishment. Rooms

have AC, TV, hot water, there's a restaurant, bar & pool. $$

🏠 **Posada Santa Margarita** (7 rooms) 4-36 Av Bolívar; ☎ 0242 361 7113; m 0412 597 4829; www.ptocabello.com. Near the beach & the historic centre, the owners have joined 2 250-year-old colonial houses, meticulously restored them & fitted them out with modern comforts, such as a lap pool, an internet point, Wi-Fi. From the rooftop terrace there are good views over the bay, mountains & forts. B&B rooms with private bath & fan, some with AC. Can arrange boat trips to nearby beaches & islands. $$

Where to eat

✗ **Lunchería La Fuente** ⏰ 08.00–20.00. In a fine 18th-century house with tall ceilings near the Templo de Rosario, facing Parque Flores. The grilled red snapper is excellent, fresh fruit juices. $$

✗ **Briceño Ven** ⏰ 11.00–15.00 & 17.00–22.00 w/days. Next to the Prefectura on the Malecón, has a 40-year reputation for excellent *criollo* dishes, pork, goat, cheese from Falcón State, *pabellón criollo*. $

✗ **Restaurant Los Lanceros** ⏰ 12.00–22.00. A popular *tasca* bar on the Malecón around the corner from Calle Lanceros serves good seafood every day in a lovely 2-storey building. Get a sea view upstairs & enjoy fried fish with rice & plantains or a paella for 2. $

Festivals Puerto Cabello celebrates **Carnival** riotously, with street dances on the Malecón, water balloons (paint is outlawed) and carousing. An old custom, '**La Hamaca**', closes festivities on Carnival Tuesday when a group proceeds through town to the Malecón bearing a hammock with a 'dead' dummy. They chant a toneless dirge to the lamenting of horns, literally cow and deer horns, and the beating of drums by the **Tambores de San Millán** group. Street dances, particularly mock battles with long poles, follow.

The **Blessing of the Sea** on Easter Sunday fills the entire Malecón with the faithful from many parts of the coast. Some arrive at dawn for a front-row view of the fleet of fishing vessels escorting the image of the Virgin of the Valley. At 07.30 the diocesan archbishop leads the religious ceremony from a barge in the bay. Some of the faithful, not content with a distant sprinkling, dive into the bay to receive the blessing.

Other practicalities There's a Banco de Venezuela on Calle Colón down by the malecón. A CANTV call centre offering internet and international calls is located on Avenida Bolívar between Calle Sucre and Calle Miranda.

What to see and do

Calle Lanceros Behind the Malecón, this was the first street restored by the city and is famous for its much-photographed and very colourful house fronts. On this street in 1823 General Páez and his brave Llanero lancers routed Spain's last troops in Venezuela and the besieged San Felipe Fort surrendered.

Museo de Historia (⏰ *08.00–18.00; admission free*) Built in 1790, this costly mansion is supposed to have collections of antique maps, weapons and photographs, but these rooms are closed. There are rooms devoted to Bartolomé Salóm, a native of

San Esteban who fought the entire 15 years of Independence wars until the liberation of Peru, and to a Puerto Cabello-born general, Juan José Flores, who was President of Ecuador three times. A second-storey walkway bridges the street; the museum goes all the way through to Calle Bolívar and is actually the centre for a very active group of local painters.

Templo de El Rosario This is a small yellow church with a copper dome and a unique wooden bell tower, on Calle Bolívar and the end of Los Lanceros. It dates from 1780 but incorporates walls of an earlier salt storehouse.

Monumento del Aguila On Plaza del Aguila, this is a monument honouring the American volunteers who were captured in Francisco Miranda's failed attempt to land in Ocumare in 1806. Ten of the officers were hanged, 53 others imprisoned. The 'eagle' is actually a condor.

Casa Guipuzcoana Built around 1730 on Plaza del Aguila, the Casa Guipuzcoana was the headquarters of the Basque company that exercised the royal trading monopoly in Puerto Cabello. Today it is a library.

Teatro Municipal The former elegance of this theatre as a stage setting for Anna Pavlova has also been restored. This grand edifice by the Malecón, a block south of Plaza Bolívar, was designed by Antonio Malaussena and built in the 1880s.

Castillo del Libertador or Fuerte San Felipe (⊕ 08.00–16.00; admission free) Built by the Guipuzcoana company to protect its interests, this fort was the last Spanish stronghold in the Independence wars until it was taken in 1823 and renamed in honour of Bolívar. One patriot executed here was Vicente Salías (1776–1814), a doctor and revolutionary writer born in Puerto Cabello who wrote the words to *Gloria al Bravo Pueblo*, declared Venezuela's national anthem in 1881. In the 27 years of Juan Vicente Gómez's dictatorship the fort was an infamous prison. When closed on Gómez's death in 1935, 14 tons of chains and leg irons were pitched into the bay. Today it is part of the naval base and you have to ask at the gate for a guided tour after taking a free navy shuttle boat at the end of the Malecón near Paseo Flores.

Mirador Fortín Solano (⊕ 09.00–17.00) For the best view of the whole port, go to the reconstructed Fortín Solano. Take a taxi or a San Esteban *por puesto* to the entrance to the fort, reached up a steep ramp. One of the last colonial forts built in the country, it is named after the governor who ordered its construction (1763–71) at great expense to the Guipuzcoana company.

Scuba diving

La Tienda de Buceo Centro Comercial HS, Av Bolívar Norte, Valencia; \ 0241 825 5624; m 0414 941 5801; e latiendadebuceo@ hotmail.com; www.venezueladiving.com. Operates 3 boats going to reefs around islands of the Parque Nacional San Esteban from the Marina of Puerto Cabello opposite the Malecón. 20mins away off Isla Larga there are 2 World War II sunken ships at 60ft depth, & a 3rd at 70ft depth that harbours an aquarium of different fishes. There is another ship sunk at 100ft, the *Mejillón*, by Isla Alcatraz (20mins). This coastguard boat was dynamited, leaving a perfect entrance for groupers. An excellent coral reef by Guayacán (25mins) has visibility of 50ft. The *King Fish*, *Tiempo* & *Paraiso II* are 30–38ft craft with twin outboards, captained by PADI & SSI instructors. Dive packages include 2 immersions, tanks, weights & a snack. Dive trips to Guabinas (40mins–1hr) off Parque Nacional Henri Pittier enjoy 60ft visibility, exploring a wall or the *Carmen Fabiana* sunk at 140ft in 2000.

San Esteban Shaded by splendid trees the old village retains a frayed elegance from the 19th century when Puerto Cabello's high society, including German merchants, built fine estates by its cool river. One of the first walled properties on the left belongs to the family of Henrique Salas Romer. A bit further, near the village school, stairs lead to the birthplace of **Bartolomé Salom**, a house opened to visitors but only partially restored. Here the patriot, who fought in almost every major campaign and was in charge of logistics for the march over the Andes to Peru, retired to live in peace – if not prosperity. Today, peace and nostalgia are banished by weekend motorcyclists and parties of bathers who arrive with canned salsa music and beer. Indian tribes once lived by the river and made many petroglyphs on a house-sized boulder, the **Piedra del Indio**. Look for the figure of a man in a boat; it's on your left, following a path above the east bank ten minutes beyond the village.

Parque Nacional San Esteban In colonial times goods were transported from Puerto Cabello by way of the cobbled Camino Real to Valencia. Today most of this forested area forms the Parque Nacional San Esteban. The San Esteban River basin has long been protected as the watershed supplying Puerto Cabello with drinking water.

The ascent of two to three hours from the Caja de Agua or waterworks to the arched **Puente de Paso Hondo**, built in 1808, is a beautiful hike by the rushing river. There are fine campsites. In the late dry season, April/May, the loud 'kong, kong' of the bearded bellbird reverberates at elevations between 300m and 800m. The bellbird, whose clang sounds more like an anvil stroke, is the forest ventriloquist. You have to be very sharp to spot these birds in the high canopy.

Beaches City beaches such as Playa Blanca and others to the west should be avoided, as they are not only contaminated but also unsafe (there have been hold-ups). By contrast, the coast and islands east of Puerto Cabello have excellent beaches. Most facilities are in **Quizandal**: go about 5km on the road towards the naval base, then follow signs 1.5km east through thorn scrub to the parking lot, restaurants and changing rooms of this *balneario*. From Quizandal, many bathers head for the white sands and clear protected waters of **Isla Larga**, the largest offshore island, 15 minutes away by *peñero* (US$4 round trip, leaving between 08.00 and 13.00 and returning at 16.30). An Italian and a German freighter, scuttled here in World War II, are now encrusted with coral, inviting snorkellers. Some *kioscos* sell food at weekends. It is possible to camp, except in windless periods when *plaga*, biting midges, make life impossible from dusk to dawn. During the week fewer boats operate, according to demand, and you may have to contract the whole boat.

El Huequito is the next beach, 1km south of Quizandal. It is less developed and the entrance road of rutted earth (no shade) starts from the Borburata crossroads. You can also reach this beach by walking along the Quizandal shore.

Borburata is the name of the next bay, valley, its river and village. The *pueblo*, about 3km south of the coast road, is said to be the fourth oldest in Venezuela, dating to 1549. Most of the cacao plantations that made it famous have fallen into ruin and the farmlands have now become middle-class suburbs of Puerto Cabello. Every year on the **Fiesta de San Juan**, 23–24 June, villagers rejoice in their African roots with big drums and street dances. A statue of St John the Baptist heads a procession from the church (1751), first to the river to be 'baptised', then to each village as far as Patanemo. Borburata Bay is largely occupied by army/navy housing; to use the well-kept beach and restaurant show your passport.

Rincón del Pirata, the next seaside community, has little appeal but has some restaurants. It is on the way to Patanemo, a beautiful curving bay backed by lush green hills 13km from Puerto Cabello. **Patanemo beach** is part of Parque Nacional San Esteban; you cross salty marshes for 1.2km to ample coconut-shaded sands. The beach has informal fried-fish stands and is popular at weekends when campers set up tents.

The coastal road ends in another 2km at the *pueblo* of Patanemo, a long street of small simple houses. On the plaza stands an unassuming little blue church with two old bronze bells. This is the scenario for masked devil dancers on the Thursday of Corpus Christi, nine weeks after Easter. The rites of submission to the church are rooted in medieval Europe.

Where to stay

▲ **Eden Casa de Playa** (14 rooms) On the road to Patanemo past La Fortaleza; ✆ 0242 808 4565; m 0416 442 4955. Nicolas Cipriani & his son Arturo (who is also chef) run a complex including a swimming pool by a pizza restaurant, *bolas criollas* court, camping area, & comfortable B&B rooms with bath, hot water, AC for 2–10 guests in colourful cottages. Italian spoken. $$

▲ **La Fortaleza** (3 cabins, 5 rooms) Av Principal Los Caneyes on the road to Patanemo; ✆ 0242 421 7145; m 0412 538 3685; e lafortaleza@ guiapuertocabello.com. On the main street, Rodolfo Martínez (he speaks English) has 2 cottages set in tropical gardens with equipped kitchen, the larger for 8 guests, the smaller for 4 min, & rooms with bath, cold water, AC, TV. $$

14

Yaracuy and Lara

The states of Yaracuy and Lara are the agricultural and spiritual heartlands of western Venezuela and an important crossroads between Caracas, Maracay, Valencia in the east and Coro, Mérida and Maracaibo in the west. Steeped in history and a fertile breeding ground for myths and mysteries, the green valleys of Yaracuy between the Sierra de Aroa and Nirgua mountains are home to the Cult of María Lionza, a uniquely Venezuelan cocktail of spiritual expressions that has been compared to Haitian Voodoo and Cuban Santeria. The area is also known for its dairy farms, sugarcane and tropical fruits, particularly mangoes, papayas and bananas. Lara borders the vast cattle plains of the Llanos to the south and the deserts of Falcón to the north. The southern hills, at the tail end of the Andes, produce coffee and potatoes, while the central valleys produce sugarcane, maize and black beans – the staples of the nation. Barquisimeto, the rapidly modernising capital of Lara with its shiny malls and ambitious transport plans, is the fourth largest city in Venezuela and host to one of the country's most important religious festivals. The week-long celebrations centre around the 14 January procession in honour of the Divina Pastora (the Divine Shepherdess). On that day, over two million of the faithful accompany a venerated statue of the Virgin Mary holding the infant Christ and a sheep, as it is carried from the village of Santa Rosa to the cathedral in Barquisimeto. Tradition is also the keyword in the town of Quíbor, which preserves a flourishing ceramic and handicraft tradition that dates back to pre-Columbian times, and the surrounding villages where there is a thriving trade in locally produced hammocks, wood carvings and musical instruments.

The musical and gastronomic influence of the Llanos is strong in Yaracuy and Lara. Both states swing to the *joropo* sound of harp, maracas and *cuatro* (a small four-string guitar) and beef and chicken are prepared on the *parilla* (barbecue). For a complete blowout try the *parilla especial* served with beef, chicken, spicy chorizo, French fries, slices of *cachapa* (thick savoury maize pancake), avocado and fried cheese.

YARACUY STATE

Named after the Yaracuy River, which flows from southwest to northeast and into the sea close to Tucacas, this small state is home to Venezuela's most enigmatic and interesting spiritual phenomenon. The **Cult of María Lionza** is centred on the sacred cult sites of Sorte, Quibayo and El Oro on a forest-draped mountain near the town of Chivacoa, known as the **Cerro de Sorte**. Every year on 12 October, the Day of Indigenous Resistance in Venezuela, believers from all over the country make a pilgrimage to Yaracuy to pay their respects to María Lionza and the other figures worshipped by the cult, including Indian chiefs from the time of the Spanish conquest and even Simón Bolívar, the Independence hero. The Cult of María Lionza is a fascinating Venezuelan cultural expression that is gradually gaining wider exposure outside the country, attracting more and more curious outsiders seeking to find out what this strange cult is all about.

The jump-off point for Chivacoa is Barquisimeto in Lara State or San Felipe, a quiet city with a historical past and a world famous flora park.

SAN FELIPE (*Telephone code: 0254*) The origin of San Felipe, today's capital, was a farming community called El Cerrito that already had a church in the year 1693. By the early 1700s these pioneers had thriving cacao groves and tobacco plantations. In those days boats plied the Yaracuy River and harvests were shipped to Dutch traders established in Tucacas, earning the enmity of the authorities in Barquisimeto who repeatedly burnt down the settlement. The village was rebuilt a league away and in 1725 at last received permission to found a town. In 1729 Philip V granted it the status of city and in honour of the Spanish king and the saint's day, on 1 May 1735 it was renamed San Felipe El Fuerte.

The town grew rapidly as the regional headquarters of the Guipuzcoana Company, a Spanish monopoly holding exclusive rights to trade between Venezuela and Spain. Spain's main concern was cocoa beans as Venezuelan beans, the world's most sought after, were a valuable commodity, outranked only by gold and silver. Venezuelan shippers preferred to trade with Mexico, which bought large quantities and paid in silver and gold coins, and the closer Dutch-controlled Antilles, with the result that Spain was forced to buy high-priced chocolate from Holland. However, the Guipuzcoana ships, armed with cannons to control smuggling, doubled cacao exports to Spain and held the monopoly for 50 years, despite revolts by cacao growers and exporters forced to accept low prices.

When the worst earthquake in Venezuela's recorded history struck on 26 March 1812, half of San Felipe's 7,500 inhabitants died and the town was destroyed (in Caracas and La Guaira deaths reached 10,000). This time the ruins were left untouched and a new town was built, called simply San Felipe.

Today the pleasant city of 220,000 inhabitants, the largest in the state, enjoys broad, tree-lined avenues and an unhurried pace. The ruins of San Felipe El Fuerte are now a tourist attraction. There are various good guesthouses around San Felipe and in the mountains, serving a growing tourism interest in the city and the nearby Cult of María Lionza.

Getting there
By bus The Terminal Nuevo at the end of Avenida Libertador, serves long-distance routes, with regular buses throughout the day to Morón on the coast, where buses can be taken to Coro and Tucacas, and less often to Puerto Cabello. Buses to Barquisimeto and Valencia leave hourly. Express coaches also go to Caracas, 277km (4 hours). The old downtown bus station, Terminal Viejo, Avenida La Patria at 2nd Avenida, is the terminus for urban routes.

By car The main Route 1 highway between Morón and Barquisimento passes through San Felipe.

By train There is a railway line linking Barquisimeto with the coast but it no longer takes passengers.

🏠 **Where to stay**

🏠 **Posada Turistica Granja Momentos** (2 rooms, 4 suites & 2 cabins) ☏ 0254 231 0153, 0254 231 4729; ☎ 0414 547 0414; e posada@ momentos.com.ve; www.momentos.com.ve,

www.circuitodelaexcelencia.com. Friendly hosts Aura & Efraín Pérez run this highly recommended *posada* on Av Alberto Ravell, in La Montaña at the foot of the mountain. Rooms are immaculate with bathroom,

AC, fan, & there is a small swimming pool, large thatched *caney* restaurant, a spring bringing fresh mountain water & landscaped gardens with tropical birds. Horseriding can be arranged as well as guides to the Cerro María Lionza. $$$

⌂ **Gran Hotel El Fuerte** (33 rooms) Av La Patria between Av 2 & the Panamericana; ✎ 0254 234 5473. There is a restaurant. $$

⌂ **Hostería Colonial** (60 rooms) Av La Paz; ✎ 0254 231 2626, 0254 231 5650. Rooms are around the swimming pool, popular restaurant. $$

⌂ **Hotel Marimon** (42 rooms) Calle Cascabel with Av Cedeno: ✎ 0254 231 6655, 0254 232 5356; e hotel_marimon@yahoo.es. Clean, functional motel

rooms with bathroom, TV, Wi-Fi, snack bar & secure parking. $$

⌂ **Hotel Yaracuy** (44 rooms) Av Yaracuy at Cedeño; ✎ 0254 234 3784, 0254 231 0102. This is a motel-style place with decent rooms. $$

⌂ **Río Yurubí** (49 rooms) End of Av La Fuente; ✎ 0254 231 0802, 0254 231 0798. Large hotel at the entrance to Parque Leonor Bernabó, has a swimming pool, restaurant, bowling alley. There is a funky bar/restaurant next door with a terrace overlooking the river. $$

⌂ **El Virrey** (16 rooms) Calle 13 at 12-12 Av Veroes; ✎ 0254 231 4621. Budget option, dbls with fan, some with private bath. $

Other practicalities A Banco de Venezuela with ATM is on Avenida Libertador (Avenida 5) on the corner with Calle 15.

There is a call centre providing internet and international calls in the main bus terminal on Avenida La Patria.

What to see and do

Catedral de San Felipe On the large paved Plaza Bolívar, opposite the neoclassical government house is this modern angular, asymmetrical structure of bare concrete lit up inside by fine stained-glass windows.

San Felipe El Fuerte (⊕ 08.30–17.30 Tue–Sun) The ruins of the colonial town of San Felipe El Fuerte, which was completely destroyed in the 1812 earthquake are preserved in a pleasant archaeological, historical park four blocks from Plaza Bolívar. You can see the former cobbled streets running off the central Plaza de las Aguillas and the pillars, altar and baptismal font of the 1748 cathedral, which were uncovered in archaeological excavations that began in 1971. A big tree in the centre of the nave has been left to grow, providing welcome shade. An attractive, colonial-style whitewashed house with a columned veranda displays pieces excavated from the ruins. Take repellent if you plan to wander around the ruins.

Monument to Yaracuy This dramatic statue at the head of Avenida Yaracuy, 2.2km north of the centre, shows the Indian leader Yaracuy, a leaping jaguar at his side, about to smite his enemies. A great chief of the Jirajara or Yara people, Yaracuy successfully defended these lands against Spanish conquistadors in the 1560s until he was eventually defeated by Diego de Losada (the founder of Caracas). The sculpture is by Alejandro Colina who also made the famous statue of María Lionza riding a tapir, seen on the Francisco Fajardo freeway in Caracas.

Parque Leonor Bernabó (*Av La Fuente;* ⊕ *08.00–16.30 Tue–Sun; admission free*) Named after a 19th-century poetess, this 7ha park gives easy entry to the larger **Parque Nacional Yurubí**, which became a protected area in 1960. The recreational area has swimming pools, playgrounds, shelters and barbecue grills. Filled with joggers in the early morning and families at weekends, there are many pleasant forest walks up the hill following the Yurubí River, the city's main source of fresh water.

Parque de la Exótica Flora Tropical (✎ *0254 600 0000, 0254 614 5124, 0254 614 5123;* e *comercializacion.parque@hotelantiguamision.com: www.tropicalpark.com.ve;* ⊕ *08.00–17.00 Mon–Fri, 08.00–18.00 Sat–Sun; admission US$15 per adult including* *golf-cart tour of gardens, child & family discounts available*) This popular, privately owned park located a few kilometres east of San Felipe has been hailed as one of the biggest and finest botanical gardens in Latin America. Spread over 10.5ha, it specialises in flowering plants from tropical regions around the world, including water lilies, ferns, flowering vines, heliconias, orchids, bromeliads and a good selection of Venezuelan plants. Designed by French landscape architect and botanist Jean Philipe Thoze, it is fast gaining an international reputation since opening in 1996.

The central whitewashed building is the **Misión Nuestra Señora del Carmen**, a faithful re-creation of the Capuchin mission that was founded here in 1720. The modern owners accidentally uncovered the chapel floor of the mission while carrying out building work and decided to reconstruct the whole building using traditionally produced adobe bricks, red clay roof tiles and wild cane for the ceilings. In the mission are an impressive chapel, two restaurants, a craft shop, small museum, and meeting and baby-sitting facilities. Tours of the sprawling gardens, which are laid out artistically to take advantage of the colours and textures of the plants, can be done on foot, in electric golf carts or by horse-drawn carriage.

The five-star **Hotel Antigua Mision** (81 rooms), built around a central patio in ochre tones to complement the colonial architecture of the mission, opened in 2009. The two-storey structure has a swimming pool, conference rooms, snack bars and Wi-Fi.

Around San Felipe
The mountain of María Lionza To visit the Cerro de Sorte, where devotees of the Cult of María Lionza practise their colourful rituals, take a bus to Chivacoa, about 40 minutes from San Felipe. From there a regular jeep service runs to Quibayo, the largest of the cult sites, which has an Inparques post and stalls selling hot food. (See *Chivacoa*, page 344.)

Parque Las Minas de Aroa This park is 77km from San Felipe, via Marín and Yumare in the Aroa Valley. It includes the remains of the mining camp, copper smelter, railroad, the English cemetery and, 3km further up the gorge, the crushers and mine itself. Known of since 1605, the copper mine was owned by Simón Bolívar's family. Bolívar leased it to a British mining company to finance the Independence struggle. After his death the mine was sold to the Bolívar Mining Association, another English company that barged the ore down the Aroa to the coast for shipping. Finally, a third company took over, installed smelters and in 1877 built Venezuela's first railway, the Ferrocarril Bolívar, to Tucacas. Aroa later became the first town in Venezuela to have electricity and telephones, as well as a cableway between the mine and the camp. The English company operated the mine until 1936. There is a small, rundown museum with photos and information about the mine, and the English cemetery can still be visited. Locals, some of whom preserve the surnames Prince and Bowen, are happy to point out the site.

Where to stay
Campamento El Jaguar (6 rooms & cabin) \ 0251 254 0449; m 0414 529 2658, 0416 123 5455; e ecoaveneljaguar@cantv.net. Well off the beaten track, the camp is near Aroa but isolated by virgin forest at the end of a 10km penetration road in the mountains to the east. Topping a ridge at 900m the camp is the home of Maurice Daludier, a French ex-oilman delighted to have nothing in view but trees & the distant Caribbean, & no sounds other than birdsong – 350 species live in these mountains. Monkeys, tapirs, coatis & climbing porcupines live here, & the jaguar, too, is seen by his tracks. On the 15,000ha of Daludier's private reserve there are 10 different trails, cascading rivers, pools for cooling off & hammock shelters for serious hikers who like a night in the

forest. Guides are Maurice, his son Morgan & local experts. Non-walkers have the choice of a pool for swimming or horse for riding. The guesthouse has 6 rooms with twin beds & thick blankets & a cabin for 8 with bunk beds; toilets are separate & showers are in a different building. Call & ask for a map to guide drivers via the coast & Morón, or Barquisimeto–Duaca to the meeting point of El Hacha. Daludier provides a locked shed & watchman for your car & transfer by 4x4 to the camp. $$

CHIVACOA (*Telephone code: 0251*) This town of 59,000 inhabitants surrounded by sugarcane fields, is 37km from San Felipe, 133km from Valencia and 60km from Barquisimeto. Its main claim to fame is as the entry point for visitors to the Cerro de Sorte, home to the Cult of María Lionza, a unique Venezuelan combination of Indian, African and Catholic beliefs that combines devotion to historical and mythical figures with spirit mediums and cleansing rituals. Plaster images of cult figures crowd the windows of dozens of 'perfume' shops. Las Tres Potencias (The Three Powers) are the holy trinity of the cult: María Lionza is in the middle, flanked by a 16th-century Indian chief called Guaicaipuro, and El Negro Felipe, a black slave who led a 1552 revolt at a gold mine in Nirgua. A figure resembling Charlie Chaplin with a black hat and moustache is José Gregorio Hernández, a doctor devoted to the poor who died in Caracas in 1919. Other figures include Venezuela's patron saint the Virgen de Coromoto, a group of blonde-haired Vikings, a gang of criminal kids known as La Corte de Los Malandros, and the Independence hero Simón Bolívar. The perfume shops offer a complete introduction to the cult and make for an interesting hour of browsing.

THE MYTH OF MARÍA LIONZA

According to believers, María Lionza is a beautiful Indian princess with green eyes who was converted into a spirit of the forest, the protector of nature and animals. A famous statue in Caracas from the 1950s shows a naked María Lionza sitting astride a tapir, holding aloft a human pelvis, and this is the image that is often reproduced in paintings. Many statues of her in the shrines at Sorte, however, show her as a European-looking princess with a golden crown. For some, she was the daughter of an Indian princess and a Spanish conquistador. For others, she was the daughter of an Indian chief who had her guarded in a locked house when a shaman foretold disaster if she were not put to death. One day, when the guards slept the girl escaped. Coming to a lake, she gazed for the first time at her reflection in the water but an evil spirit, a giant anaconda who lived in the lake, desired her and dragged her underwater in its coils. The girl's body swelled and grew so large that the anaconda was killed but the water flooded from the lake drowning her people and bringing to pass the tragedy prophesied by the shaman. María Lionza lived on as a spirit.

The three main cult figures are María Lionza – known as La Reina (the queen) or La Madre (the mother) in a clear link to the Virgin Mary – the Indian chief Guaicaipuro and El Negro Felipe (also referred to as El Negro Primero, an Independence war hero). They are accompanied by a bewildering pantheon of spirits, whose number and power grow with inspiration from African, Indian, Christian and now Oriental sources. The cult has no higher authority, no taboos except against taking what belongs to María Lionza or killing animals without reason. From Christianity the cult takes incense, candles, religious images and songs (most adepts consider themselves to be Catholics). From Africa come the drums, trances and possession by spirits. Indian sources provide shamanism, the belief in nature spirits and the use of tobacco for healing and divining. More recently, Cuban *santería* practices have influenced the cult with rites involving animal sacrifices and invocation of Yoruba divinities. Popular herb medicine also plays a part.

Getting there

By bus There are direct buses and *por puestos* to Chivacoa from Barquisimeto (1 hour) and San Felipe (40 minutes). Toyota jeeps costing less than US$1 leave regularly from the Plaza Bolívar in Chivacoa (07.00–20.00) for the 25-minute journey to Quibayo.

By car Chivacoa is just off the main Route 1 highway between San Felipe and Barquisimeto, and can also be reached on Route 11 from Valencia.

Where to stay
A few simple hotels in the centre provide restaurant, bed, bath and air conditioning at reasonable prices.

El Lusitano (22 rooms) Calle 10 between Av 12–13; \ 0251 883 0366. $

Hotel Abruzzese (21 rooms) Av 9 between Calles 10 & 11; \ 0251 883 0419, 0251 883 1563. $

Hotel Restaurant Venecia (45 rooms) Av 9 between Calles 11 & 12; \ 0251 883 0544, 0251

883 0810. Rooms for 2–6 people with AC, TV, hot water. Restaurant serves good pizzas. $

Posada Maguaife (20 rooms) La Bartola, via San Pablo; \ 0254 614 5808. Rooms in this *posada* dedicated to María Lionza have AC, TV & bathroom. Swimming pool, restaurant, children's play area. $

Other practicalities There is a Banco de Venezuela on Avenioda 9 between Calle 12 and Calle 13, and there are a couple of internet places off the main plaza.

What to see and do
Visit the Cult of María Lionza in Cerro de Sorte The best way to visit Sorte is on a day trip, starting early from San Felipe or Chivacoa to the main cult site at Quibayo (or Quiballo) and returning by jeep before nightfall. It is best to visit at weekends when there are more people and to travel in a group. During the run-up to the Indigenous Resistance Day celebrations on 12 October, the Cerro de Sorte is packed solid with 20,000 worshippers. While it can be harder to get transport or accommodation, there is no better time to experience the incredible devotion of the cult's followers, as whole families descend on Quibayo for a week of rituals. The events culminate on 12 October with a night of fire dancing, involving all the major figures in the hierarchy of the cult.

☞ *WARNING:* There have been robberies here, but if you stick to the area near the Inparques post, don't stray too far from the main shrines on the other side of the bridge, and show respect for the beliefs of the practitioners of the cult, you will come away with a very rewarding experience. Although the rituals look bizarre and can sometimes be bloody, and the loud noise of drums and shouts and speaking in tongues can be unnerving, Marialionceros welcome curious visitors to Quibayo. Remember to take bottled water, suncream, repellent and an open mind. Leave behind any valuables or jewellery that might attract attention and avoid dark or black clothes, which are not welcome on the mountain.

LARA STATE

Two and a half times larger than Yaracuy, Lara has a prospering economy driven by farming, agro-industry, wholesaling and distribution. Although lacking a major river and access to the sea, Lara has the advantage of good roads to the east, west and south. And although much of central Lara is so arid it is almost a desert, valleys south and west of Barquisimeto flourish under irrigation, producing melons, onions and tomatoes. Coffee, potatoes, avocados, papayas, pineapples, guavas, flowers and ornamental plants are grown on cooler pre-montane slopes formed by

Believers, from the humblest street vendor to high government officials, go to the Cerro de María Lionza, also known as Cerro de Sorte, in search of healing or help with practical problems, personal and work relationships – needs that in times of crisis are hard to fill elsewhere.

At weekends and on important dates, people arrive at Quibayo around the clock, often in groups or 'brotherhoods', young and old, carrying statues, fruit, flowers, candles, perfume, cigars and alcohol, all essential for communicating with the spirits. Tobacco is said to be holy because it has the four elements of life: carbon, oxygen, nitrogen and (very little) hydrogen; believers smoke cigars outside the altars as a form of meditation and as an offering. Perfume helps to attract the right deities, while rum is used as an aid during trances and is used for anointing the mediums before ceremonies or is spat over them in a spray as they work. Worshippers stop first at the Altar Major to make an offering and to ask for permission to cross the river, where there are more shrines and altars. Following the path uphill, the Marialionceros mark out spaces in clearings in the woods or overlooking the stream, where they make camp and build shrines. At the top are Las Tres Casitas, shrines to María Lionza, Guaicaipuro and Negro Felipe, known as Las Tres Potencias (The Three Powers).

In the makeshift camps of tents and hammocks, where areas are roped off to allow rituals to take place, the *bancos* or 'guides' serve as intermediaries between those who come with problems or questions and the mediums who channel the spirits. Many of these mediums are said to have visionary or healing powers but their main purpose is to allow María Lionza, Guaicaipuro, or one of the Viking spirits to enter them. Once the medium is possessed, the *banco* identifies the spirit and asks for help or advice for the gathered devotees. Some spirits are more aggressive than others and the Viking spirits are known for inducing mediums to cut and pierce their cheeks and tongues, creating bloody spectacles. As they work, the *bancos* chant spells and the rituals are accompanied by large groups of young men singing, clapping and playing African drums, which makes for a cacophony of noise as hundreds of groups – thousands on important days like 12 October – carry out their rituals side by side. Other ceremonies involve cleansing rituals in which strange symbols are drawn around devotees who lie prostrate on the ground surrounded by candles while a banco and medium purify them with tobacco smoke and rum. To show respect and avoid confrontation in the highly-charged atmosphere of these rituals, turn off the flash when taking photos. Some bancos say camera flashes cause pain to the spirits and physical danger to the medium in a trance. Tourists are also advised to avoid dark clothes, especially black. It is best to visit in a group, and to stick to the area near the Inparques post and Altar Major. You can cross the bridge but don't venture too far. Ask at the Inparques post if you want to find someone who knows the zone and the customs to lead you further up the mountain. The way to the top of the Cerro de Sorte mountain is not clear; there are many portals (shrines) and at each one permission to pass must be sought by lighting candles and smoking cigars.

the eastern end of the Andes. There are three mountain parks: **Terepaima**, **Yacambú–El Guache** and **Dinira**, which is shared with Trujillo State. The people of Lara are practical, lively and open. They love making music and dancing the local dance, the Tamunangue. They weave excellent blankets and hammocks, make interesting clay pots, exquisite wooden furniture and tasty cheese, and are the country's only serious wine producers.

BARQUISIMETO *(Telephone code: 0251)* Barquisimeto is the capital of Lara State and the country's fourth largest city. A busy trading and agricultural centre, the city is home to more than a million people, roughly 60% of the state's population. It is centrally situated on main routes to Maracaibo, the Andes and Colombia via the Panamericana; to Acarigua and the western plains; to Coro in the north; and to Valencia and points east.

Dotted with shady parks, the centre of Barquisimeto is clean and well kept. Streets are user-friendly, laid out on a Spanish pattern of *calles* running north–south, and *carreras* going east–west. First settled in 1552, the infant town went through three moves before arriving at its present site by the Turbio River (altitude 566m). Variquecemeto (Barquisimeto), an old Indian word, means 'river of ash-coloured water'. Because the city was shaken to its foundations by the 1812 earthquake, few Spanish structures remain.

Today's Barquisimetanos prefer to go modern; the cathedral is the most surprising example of this. The city's trademark is the **Obelisco** at the west entrance, a 70m tower raised for Barquisimeto's 400th anniversary. In the east the many new shopping malls are led by the giant Ciudad Las Trinitarias, a shiny temple to consumerism with shops, cinemas, pharmacies and fast-food outlets.

What history that remains is to be found in the city's excellent museums and its musical traditions, which keep local culture alive. So many people, young and old, make instruments, play them or sing in choirs that Barquisimeto is known as the 'music capital of Venezuela'.

Half of the country's pineapples, onions, tomatoes, potatoes and a third of its sugar are produced here, much of it sold through a giant wholesale centre in Barquisimeto called Mercabar which covers ten acres and moves 700,000 tonnes of food yearly, fresh and processed.

Getting there

By air The Aeropuerto Internacional Jacinto Lara is about 4.5km southwest of the bus depot, or 3.2km south of the Obelisco via Avenida Rotaria. Aeropostal (*www.aeropostal.com*) has morning and evening flights to Caracas, except Sundays, Avior (*www.aviorairlines.com*) also flies to Caracas and Aserca (*www.asceraairlines.com*) has daily flights to Barcelona, Caracas, Maturín and Puerto Ordaz.

By bus The Terminal de Pasajeros is on Carrera 24 at Calle 43 in western Barquisimeto, between Avenida 20 Pedro León Torres and Avenida Venezuela. Local buses to Quíbor, Sanare, Chivacoa and San Felipe leave regularly through the day. Long-distance express services generally travel at night to the main destinations of Valera (4 hours, 234km), Caracas (5 hours, 351km), Barinas (5 hours, 258km), Maracaibo (5 hours, 322km), Coro (7 hours, 279km), Mérida (8 hours, 410km), and San Cristóbal (9 hours, 574km).

Aeroexpresos Ejecutivos (*www.aeroexpresos.com.ve*) runs buses that are faster, more expensive and in better condition but the air conditioning is set to arctic. Express departures for Caracas (US$15) leave at 07.30, 09.15, 11.00, 13.30, 15.15, 00.30, and 00.45. Other routes cover Maracaibo, Valencia, Maracay and Puerto La Cruz. The terminal is located by the huge Las Trinitarias shopping mall on Avenida Herman Garmendia, via El Ujano (\ *0251 254 6809, 0252 254 7907*).

By car The highway from Morón passes through Barquisimeto *en route* to Carora, and Route 7 joins Barquisimeto with Mérida.

By train The Terminal de Ferrocarril is 1km north of the Obelisco traffic circle, hub of western Barquisimeto. You will see several old engines and carriages on the grounds. Ferrocar's passenger service to Puerto Cabello by way of Yaracuy and Carabobo states has been suspended for overhaul. There's a pleasant restaurant in front of the station.

Getting around
By trolleybus An ambitious new trolleybus system being created by the firm Transbarca aims to ease the gridlock on Barquisimeto's main streets and link all parts of the city.

Tourist information This is available from **Direccion de Turismo del Estado Lara** (*Av Libertador, Edif Funda Lara, piso 2;* ☎ *0251 255 7544;* e *cortulara@cantv.net; www.cortulara.gob.ve*).

🏠 Where to stay

🏠 **Hotel Jirahara** (136 rooms) Carrera 5 between Calles 5 & 6, in the eastern district of Nueva Segovia; ☎ 0251 710 6111, 0251 710 6103; www.jiraharahotel.com.ve. This well-situated hotel, formerly the Barquisimeto Hilton, is still popular for its landscaped grounds, restaurant, swimming pool, tennis courts & access to golf club. $$$$

🏠 **Hotel Trinitarias Suites** (144 rooms) Av Los Leones, Centro Comercial Las Trinitarias; ☎ 0251 230 4000, 0251 267 6747; www.hoteltrinitarias.com. This is the most expensive option in town but offers the comfort & safety of being located in the shopping centre & having all facilities to hand & a taxi rank for airport transfers. Rooms smaller than the name might suggest but clean & modern, lobby bar, swimming pool. $$$$

🏠 **Lidotel** (164 rooms) Av Venezuela with Av Argimiro Bracamonte; ☎ 0251 713 8333; e reservasbar@lidotel.com.ve; www.lidotel.com.ve. Sparkling new hotel at the Sambil shopping mall, the Lidotel has Wi-Fi, business centre with internet, restaurant, bar & swimming pool. $$$$

🏠 **Lancelot Hotel Suite & Bar** (36 rooms) Av 20 between Calles 11 & 12; ☎ 0251 252 2021, 0251 252 2510; e administracion@lancelotsuites.com. Don't be put off by the fake castle walls outside or the Arthurian theme-park feel inside; this is a comfortable if pricey option. Rooms with AC, TV, minibar, Wi-Fi. $$–$$$

🏠 **Hotel Ibiza** (14 rooms) Calle 3 between Carreras 1 & 2, Urb Nueva Segovia; ☎ 0251 252 6407, 0251

267 9221; e posadaibiza@cantv.net; www.posadaibiza.com.ve. A small, modern, reasonable option in Nueva Segovia with Wi-Fi in lobby, & restaurant: La Perla Negra. $$

🏠 **Hotel Principe** (150 rooms) Calle 23 between Carreras 18 & 19; ☎ 0251 231 2111, 0251 231 1131; e reservacion01@cantv.net. An old stalwart with a good Italian restaurant, convention & business facilities, swimming pool. $$

🏠 **Posada La Segoviana** (29 rooms) Calle 7 between Carreras 2 & 3, Urb Nueva Segovia; ☎ 0251 252 8669, 0251 252 4841; e posadalasegoviana@hotmail.com; www.posadalasegoviana.com.ve. A safe, comfortable option close to the Jirahara. Offers internet service & laundry, has a conference room & restaurant & is recommended. $$

🏠 **Yacambú** (48 rooms) Av Vargas with Calle 18 at Carrera 19; ☎ 0251 252 6746, 0251 252 1077; e hotelyacambu@gmail.com. For over 40 years the Yacambú has been offering lodging in the central business area. Rooms with TV, AC & bathroom are reasonably priced & *tasca* restaurant offers good meal option. $$

🏠 **Hotel Evelyn** (70 rooms) Av Vargas with Calle 18 at Carrera 21; ☎ 0251 251 3529, 0251 251 3986. A basic option close to a trolleybus station a few blocks from the centre. Rooms with AC, hot water, TV. $

🏠 **Hotel Florida** (18 rooms) Carrera 19 between Calles 31 & 32; ☎ 0251 232 9804. Has a good Italian restaurant. $

✕ **Where to eat** Barquisimetanos eat well and at reasonable prices. For those just passing through all the fast-food options are available at the Las Trinitarias and Sambil shopping malls. Larger hotels have their own restaurants. In the busy centre around Avenida Vargas (Calle 18), there are many small restaurants but they are closed on Sundays.

Local Lara specialities include roast goat (*chivo*) and goat cheese (*queso de cabra*); try these at:

✕ **El Portal del Chivo** Calle 50 at Carrera 13A–13. $$
✕ **La Mansión del Chivo** Carrera 21 at Calle 17. $$

✕ **Suelo Larense** Calle 6 at Carrera 11–12. Further east than the above options. $$

Venezuelan staples are also found at:

✕ **La Perla Negra** In Hotel Ibiza (see above). Has a good menu. $$
✕ **Caney de Amelia** Carrera 17 between Calles 20 & 21. $

✕ **D'Isabel** Carrera 19 between Calles 31 & 32. $
✕ **Restaurant Carlos** On the corner of Carrera 19 & Calle 29. A good *arepera*, with an outdoor café & more tables inside. $

Tasty Middle Eastern food at reasonable prices is served by:

✕ **Restaurant Basil** Calle 19 at Carreras 22–23. $$

✕ **El Aladino** Carrera 23 at Calle 19. $

Seafood houses in the centre include:

✕ **La Vieja Taberna** Av Vargas at Carreras 17–18. $$
✕ **Los Faroles** Carrera 22 at Calle 14. $$

✕ **Rio Mar** Calle 17 between Carreras 17 & 18. Slightly more expensive than others & does big business on Sun. $$

For vegetarian fare, try:

✕ **La Berenjena** Carrera 21 at Calles 9–10. $

✕ **La Mesa Vegetariana** Carrera 24 at Calles 13–14. $

The best ice cream is found at **Delight Cream**, Carrera 19 at Calles 10–11: blackberry, peach yoghurt, macadamia and other flavours are made by a family who began with a pushcart.

Shopping Several villages and small towns southwest of Barquisimeto are known for their excellent handicrafts, such as the woven hammocks and rugs from Tintorero; pots, bowls and pre-Columbian reproductions from Quíbor and Cubiro; hardwood furniture and carved fruits and animals from Guadalupe, Quíbor and Sanare. (See *Crafts – the Quíbor route*, pages 351–5.) You will find a good selection of these crafts in Barquisimeto shops:

Artesanía Sanjón Carrera 17 between Calles 24 & 25
Ciudadela Artesanal In the Complejo Ferial on eastern Av Libertador

Mercado Terepaima Av Venezuela
Variedades Nacionales Artesanía Calle 23 between Carreras 18 & 19

Festivals Barquisimeto celebrates its annual festival in honour of the **Divina Pastora** (Divine Shepherdess), an image of the Virgin Mary, every January with a week-long series of events that brings some two million visitors. In the main procession on 14 January, the statue of the Divine Shepherdess leaves her 18th-century church in the village of Santa Rosa (at the eastern outskirts of Barquisimeto) and is taken to the cathedral and then paraded around all the city's churches in a religious festival considered to be one of the most important in Latin America.

In the lead up to the procession a musical festival, sports events and an agricultural show are held at the **Complejo Ferial**, or fair complex, on Avenida Libertador by the circular **Monumento al Sol Naciente**, a massive structure in colours by Carlos Cruz Diez. Just to the east is the long *manga de coleo* where traditional bull-dogging events are held, with mounted cowboys competing to throw bulls to the ground after catching their tails.

Other practicalities Banks and internet services can be found in the main shopping centres: the massive Las Trinitarias, on Avenida Los Leones, and the Sambil on Avenida Venezuela. There is also an internet place in the main bus terminal that stays open to 22.00.

What to see and do

Museo de Barquisimeto (*Carrera 15, Calles 25 & 26;* ☉ *09.00–12.00 & 15.00–18.00 Tue–Fri, 10.00–17.00 w/ends; admission free*) A restored convent and hospital with a colonnaded central courtyard from 1918 houses the La Salle collection of pre-Columbian pottery, one of the best archaeological collections in Venezuela. Regular exhibitions of local artists, plus a good bookshop. Well worth a visit.

Mercado Terepaima West of the cathedral on Calle 36, the busiest day for the market is Saturday. You will not only get the full flavour of Lara's cornucopia of fruit and vegetables, meat, cheese and beans sold at a hundred booths, but you can also buy crafts, cotton work-clothes and dresses. Sometimes, too, you'll see alms collectors carrying an image of their namesake, San Benito. Beating drums, the San Beniteros work their way around the market; donations go to charities.

Cathedral On Avenida Venezuela (Carrera 26) at Calle 29 is this modernistic concrete mushroom built in the 1960s by John Bergkamp, a Dutch–Venezuelan architect. To see its blue stained-glass, central stone altars and a Christ suspended from the ceiling, pass by on Sunday, or at 18.00 on weekdays.

Biblioteca Pío Tamayo The Biblioteca Pío Tamayo on Avenida Vargas (Calle 20), three blocks north of Avenida Venezuela, is a large library that holds free concerts on Sunday.

Parque Bararida Zoo (*Carrera 29 at Calle 19;* ☉ *08.00–18.00 Tue–Sun; admission US$1*) A spacious park with cactus garden, playgrounds, artificial lake with rowboats, amphitheatre and zoo housing tapir, jaguar, capybara, spectacled bear and anaconda from Venezuela, alongside rhinos, tigers and kangaroos.

Historic centre Founded in 1552, after two false starts the settlement put down roots above the Río Turbio near what is now **Plaza Bolívar**. On the plaza's north side is the contemporary Alcaldía or town hall, on the east more public offices in the Edificio Nacional, and on the south the **Iglesia de La Concepción**, formerly the cathedral. Dating from 1605, it was largely destroyed by an earthquake in 1812 and slowly rebuilt, opening in 1853. The cathedral, however, was moved to **Iglesia de San Francisco**, three blocks east on **Plaza Lara**; it was completed in 1865 after five decades of construction, only to be damaged by an earthquake in 1950 (prompting the building of today's cathedral).

On Plaza Lara you will find a statue of Jacinto Lara, the Independence hero for whom the state is named, and the city's remaining colonial buildings. The handsomely restored two-floor **Centro Histórico Larense** is on the west side. Here you can browse among historical remnants, weapons, colonial furniture, art and coins, all displayed in rooms around two paved patios (☉ *08.00–12.00 & 14.00–17.00 w/days, 08.00–11.00 Sat*).

Lastly, there's a historic and really splendid old forest of native royal palms called **Bosque Macuto**, a 30-minute walk south down Avenida Vargas (Calle 18); turn right at the bottom of the hill, and cross the Río Turbio Bridge (this road leads to the town of Río Claro).

CARORA (*Telephone code: 0252*) Founded in 1569, Lara's second city is famous for its music, crafts and food and has one of the best-preserved colonial centres in Venezuela, giving it an antique charm. Set in the dry central part of Lara, 102km west of Barquisimeto, it has a population of 105,000. The land is parched and many hills are fiercely eroded. Goats scramble up gullies by the road. A small national park east of Carora, **Cerro Saroche**, conserves a desert-like ecosystem in among the hills where the little rain evaporates before it can touch the ground; seven of its plants are said to be endemic species. There are other surprises. Dairymen here have bred a strain of Carora cows tough enough to thrive among the thorns (ask to try the Carora *fuerte* cheese).

A recent source of pride is **wine** produced since 1990 by Bodegas Pomar (a joint venture by beer makers Polar and French company Martell) from grapes grown on irrigated slopes near the old village of Altagracia (see *Wine tasting*, opposite).

Getting there

By bus Most through buses bypass Carora. There is a Terminal de Pasajeros on the southeast side of town served principally by buses to Caracas (453km, 7½ hours), Maracaibo (220km, 3½ hours) and Barquisimeto (103km, 1½ hours).

By car Carora is reached by following the main Route 1 from Barquisimeto, then turning onto Route 17 at San Pablo for the final leg of the journey. It can also be reached from Cabimas and Maracaibo on Route 17.

Where to stay and eat

Posada El Cuji (3 rooms) Calle 2, between Carabobo & Contreras; ⧵ 0252 421 2910; m 0414 360 6705; e posadaelcuji@hotmail.com. This colonial-style house has been completely restored since the devastating flood of 1973 & has a small pool for guests to use in the attractive patio. Rooms with AC, TV & internet available. This is a very smart option. $$

Hotel Irpinia (36 rooms) Carrera Lara; ⧵ 0252 421 6362. Large rooms with AC, bath. $

Posada El Amparo (18 rooms) Vía Lara–Zulia, near the Indio Mara; m 0416 421 0111. Modern place with motel-style rooms with TV, AC, telephones. *Tasca* restaurant open to the public. $

Posada Madrevieja (16 rooms) Av Francisco de Miranda; ⧵ 0252 421 2590. A central option opposite Banco Central, the *posada* has had a well-needed spruce up. Rooms have AC, TV, hot water & there is a large terrace with a good restaurant. $

Other practicalities There is a Banco de Venezuela with an ATM on Avenida Francisco de Miranda, on the the corner with Calle Coromoto, and a Banesco on Calle Lara and Calle Rivas.

The main bus terminal on Avenida Francisco de Miranda has a call centre that provides internet and international calls.

What to see and do

Historic centre Photographers are spoilt for choice in the historic town centre, or *casco historic*, considered to be one of the oldest and best restored in Venezuela, where several blocks of restored churches and houses on neat streets with patterned tiles offer a host of great shots.

With church records going back to 1587, the handsome, domed **Catedral de San Juan Bautista** is a real colonial treasure; there is a retablo behind the altar glowing with gold. The top storeys of the bell tower were added in 1883. Carora's *fiestas patronales* are celebrated here on St John's Day, 24 June.

Balcón de los Alvarez, a house next to the church, dates to 1741. Simón Bolívar stayed at this colonial residence in 1821, two months after the Battle of Carabobo on his way to Bogotá.

Casa Amarilla, on the south side of the plaza, is Carora's oldest house, noted for its iron balconies. Its first owner sold it in 1650 to the town council. Until recently it was still used as the police headquarters; now it's a public library.

Casa de la Cultura or Carora Museum, on Calle 2, exhibits pre-Columbian pottery and idols from cultures that once flourished in Lara State. The colonial building was used as a jail until its restoration. **Capilla del Calvario**, a chapel standing with its little side bell tower in the centre of an empty square, was built in 1787 by a townsman enamoured of the Baroque 'horned' façade. Damaged by flood in 1973, it was restored by architect Graziano Gasparini, who earlier restored the San Juan Bautista church and has the credit for preserving many colonial structures around Venezuela.

The latest restoration job is the ornate **Capilla de San Dionisio**, Carrera 11 between Calles 2 and 3, two blocks north of the cathedral, dating from 1743. Opposite it is the **Casa de Jacinto Lara**, birthplace of the patriot and later general who served in almost every Independence campaign through to the Liberation of Peru.

Crafts Carora is the birthplace of a number of famous musicians, including classical guitarist Alirio Diaz. There are many workshops, or *talleres*, making stringed instruments, specifically the four-stringed guitar or *cuatro*, such as Cuatros Navarro in Barrio Las Mercedes, and the Fábrica de Cuatros in Palo de Olor on the Barquisimeto highway. You can also find a leather and harness workshop, Taller El Establo, Calle Lara opposite the Club Italo.

Wine tasting Group visits to the winery of **Bodegas Pomar** (\ *0252 421 2191, 0252 421 2225 in Carora, 0212 202 8907, 0212 202 8908 in Caracas;* e *clubpomar@empresas-polar.com; www.bodegaspomar.com.ve*), some 3km south of Carora, can be arranged through the Caracas office. Day trips (US$120) include transport and lunch. The most expensive visits are during the harvest period (*la feria de la vendimia*), when they also have ballooning over the vineyards.

CRAFTS – THE QUÍBOR ROUTE *Telephone code: 0253*
Tintorero Colourful hammocks and rugs hanging outside houses and workshops announce this humble village on the western highway at Km 25, just after El Rodeo, the junction for Quíbor. Craft shops around El Rodeo sell rustic furniture, hammocks, *cuatros* and other stringed instruments.

Tintorero is the closest craft centre to Barquisimeto and can be easily reached by taxi or bus in an hour and a half. By buying directly from the weavers, you not only get first choice but also contribute to their art and survival. Here the art of weaving blankets (formerly of local wool) has been handed down from generation to generation, starting with spinning and dyeing (a *tintorero* is a dyer). Today most weaving is done with cotton. By working as a team, the men weaving and the women assembling, production is faster. Look for the hammock 'chairs'.

Each family has its own style and favourite colours. Some of these are displayed at the **Casa de la Cultura Sixto Sarmiento**, named after a master weaver who lived and worked here into his nineties. The cultural centre is a display case for potters, too. Since Sixto died, the Sarmiento family across the street began making miniature earthenware houses and model churches, today much in demand. Tintorero is the site of a **Feria Artesanal** in August that draws craft workers from around Venezuela as well as international participants.

Quíbor Quíbor lies 34km southwest of Barquisimeto in the hot, arid Tocuyo Valley where melons, onions and tomatoes grow to perfection. The town is home to about 55,000 people. It was founded in 1620 on the site of an Indian settlement recorded as early as 1535, whose name means planting/harvesting. An Indian burial ground under Plaza Bolívar was accidentally uncovered during excavation for a sewer in 1965. Containing the remains of more than 100 tombs, the archaeological site has produced a large quantity of pre-Columbian pottery dating to AD200. Plans exist for a museum on site at the **Cementerio Indígena** where visitors will use an aerial walkway while archaeologists work at the dig, still in progress.

The **Museo Arqueológico** (*Calle 12 at Av 10; ⌚ 09.00–12.00 Tue–Fri, 10.00–17.00 Sat–Sun*) has a good display of pottery pieces, funerary urns and mortuary offerings from local excavations, considered the most important in the country. There is also a reference library and research centre.

Huge copies of the prehistoric artefacts from the museum line a walkway located in front of the church between Plaza Bolívar and Plaza Florencio Jiménez. The **Iglesia de Nuestra Señora de Altagracia** was built in 1808 and had to be reconstructed after an earthquake in 1881. Much older is **La Ermita de Nuestra Señora de Altagracia**, originally a shrine, which attracts many pilgrims to its venerated painting of the Infant Jesus, Mary and Joseph (dated 1606). The singular church with massive walls and a round tower with arrow-slits, stands on Calle 13 at Avenida 19/20. It dates to Quíbor's founding in the early 1600s and was reconstructed in 1799–1810.

Where to stay

Hostería Valle de Quíbor (73 rooms) Av 5 de Julio at Calle 7; 0253 491 0601, 0253 491 0602; m 0414 054 9437; e hosteriavalledequibor@hotmail.com; www.hosteriavalledequibor.com. The most popular lodging in town, this busy, motel-style option has cabins & rooms with TV, AC, hot water, swimming pool, parking, restaurant & disco. $$

Hotel Gran Duque (27 rooms) Av Florencio Jiménez by La Ceiba service station; 0253 491 0149. Rooms with fan or AC, restaurant, pizzeria. $

Crafts The **Centro de Acopio Artesanal** (⌚ *09.00–17.00*) craft centre contains the largest collection of handicrafts in Lara. The entrance is marked by a gigantic clay tripod pot at the Redoma Rotaria traffic circle as you enter Quíbor, the junction for roads to Cubiro and El Tocuyo. They sell rugs, tapestries, fine woodwork, boxes, furniture and miniature houses, as well as pottery figures, churches and painted saints, bowls and jugs from Tintorero, Guadalupe, Cubiro, Sanare, Quíbor and other centres.

The kilns of Quíbor work overtime in a dozen **ceramic workshops** (*talleres*) to fire the clay bowls and reproductions of archaeological pots for which the craftsmen and women are renowned here. You are welcome to visit these workshops; all double as shops. Some of those around Calles 11, 12 and 13 are: Taller El Indio (*Av 18 at Calle 13*); Taller Tierra Indígena (*Av 18 at Calle 12*); Taller Eladio Morales (*Av Pedro León Torres (Calle 11) between Avs 18 & 19*); and Taller El Trípode (*Av 16 between Calles 11 & 12*).

Guadalupe, a village 12km north of Quíbor, is famous for its wood carvers. The land is arid and the trees, which used to provide semi-precious hardwoods such as *vera*, *roble*, *puy* (Araguaney or yellow poui), are no longer here. Yet the craftsmen keep going, travelling further to find hardwoods in different colours suited to animals, snakes, flowers, or polished fruit such as pineapple, cacao pods and grapes. Pottery, too, is made in Guadalupe.

Cubiro With great views over Barquisimeto and Quíbor, and fresh mountain air at an altitude of 1,600m, the farming village of Cubiro (population 7,000) is a popular escape for city dwellers, many of whom take a picnic up to the open, grassy **Parque**

Las Lomas, 2km above Cubiro. The narrow 20km road to Cubiro leaves the highway just east of the turn for Quíbor.

Like Quíbor and Sanare, Cubiro began life as an Indian settlement and was formally founded in 1620 as a *pueblo de doctrina* or 'Indian town' ordered by the Spanish king to replace the *encomienda* system under which pacified Indians laboured for their Spanish protectors. The first *encomendero* to hold lands in Cubiro was Diego de Losada, a conquistador who not only founded Caracas in 1567 but was also earlier the Mayor of Carora where his descendants still live. After his exploits conquering Indian lands for the Spanish crown, he returned to live in Cubiro and was buried in full armour in the church.

Where to stay Cubiro has more *posadas* and cabins than any town in Lara; many have spectacular views. More than a dozen comfortable options offer economical lodgings, many with restaurants.

Hotel Diego de Losada (10 rooms, 8 suites) Calle Sucre; 0253 444 8142, 0212 781 4241 in Caracas; e fleitz@etheron.net. The restored colonial house has a restaurant, while a new colonial-style building has a terrific balcony & views as far as the Catatumbo lightning in Zulia State. $$

La Flor Serrana (20 rooms) Calle Consuelo; 0253 444 8194. This is a popular inn with a restaurant downstairs, best avoided on noisy w/ends. $$

Posada Nuestra Fumarola (7 rooms) Calle Comercio by the police station near Plaza Bolívar; 0253 444 8131; m 0416 351 7031, 0416 353 3084; e frank_koban@hotmail.com. In front there is a restaurant, Mi Terrón, & behind it owner Frank Koban has built a traditional house with good views of rolling hills. Rooms have hot water, satellite TV. $

Residencias El Milagro (19 rooms) Calle Independencia, east of Plaza Bolívar; 0253 444 8123. Good, simple option with large, clean rooms & restaurant, 3 simple apts with kitchen. $

Residencias Paramito (14 rooms) 13-422 Calle Comercio, opposite La Montaña restaurant; 0253 444 8085. Rooms with bath, hot water; dbl with TV. $

Crafts Cubiro's Feria Agro-Artesanal y Turística is held in the last week of August. Although this is a good time to see local crafts, production is year-round, boosted by the influx of weekend visitors from Barquisimeto. Pottery in all its forms: dishes, mugs, hanging mobiles and decorations, are found in shops all along the main street.

Sanare A growing farming centre, Sanare is 22km south of Quíbor by a road climbing from near-desert into the mountains. It is the closest town to the Parque Nacional Yacambú and to the fumarole, a kind of volcanic gas vent found nowhere else in Venezuela. At an altitude of 1,358m, this temperate region is well suited to growing coffee, potatoes, green vegetables and flowers. Sunday is the day when farmers come down to trade from the surrounding hills – where they still plough with oxen in some parts.

Where to stay

Hotel La Fumarola (5 rooms, 2 suites, cabins) in Palo Verde at the entrance to Sanare; 0253 449 0754; m 0414 352 2199. Has a swimming pool, games room, & cabins for 3–6 people. Restaurant open w/ends. Nice views. $

Hotel Taburiente (26 rooms) Av Miranda between Calle La Fe & José Silva; 0253 449 0148. Has a restaurant, bar & economical rooms with bath & hot water. $

Posada El Cerrito (15 rooms) Calle Providencia, Urb El Cerrito near Plaza Bolívar; 0253 449 0016; m 0414 550 4077. Old colonial-style house, simple rooms with hot water, TV, around a central courtyard. Large restaurant serves snacks & lunch, including local goat dishes, open ⊕ until 19.00 w/ends. Good option. Book well in advance for holidays & folk festival w/ends. $

Posada Los Sauces (16 rooms) South through town on the Yacambú route; 0253 449 0653. Rooms with bath & hot water, restaurant, kids' park. $

Festivals Crowds of costumed people gather on 28 December, *Día de los Inocentes* (the Venezuelan equivalent of April Fool's Day), for mass at the church of Santa Ana, followed by the big **Fiesta de la Zaragoza**. With songs and street dances, they proceed through the village. Other important festivities celebrated here include San Isidro Labrador on 15 May when farmers bring their garlanded oxen to the plaza, San Pascual Bailón in early May and there is a Passion play during Easter week. The colourful Tamunangue music and dancing on 12–13 June in honour of San Antonio de Padua is really worth seeing, especially the mock stick fighting as the men dance. The *Fiestas Patronales* in July honouring Santa Ana also bring the town to life.

Crafts Sanare's artisans are known particularly for saints and Nativity scenes in pottery and wood. At the northern end of this long, narrow town is a craft shop known for miniature Nativities, churches and houses, the Artesanía Uniminarro on Avenida Lara, La Loma. Other workshops include: Artesanía Accarraza (*Av Lara at Calle Sucre*); Artesanía Ideal (*Calle La Fe between Av Lara & Av Bolívar*); and El Rincón de los Muñecos (*Calle José Silva between Av Miranda & Comercio*).

El Volcán de Sanare The *fumarola*, also locally called Sanare's volcano, is located in Parque Nacional Yacambú but is rarely visited. Emitting volcanic gases and mud, this is the only fumarole in Venezuela. The two-hour trek through forest starts from a hamlet on Bojó Peak reached by a jeep track, to the east of Sanare. You will need to contract a local guide, or *baqueano*, in Bojó and take along a rope for the final descent.

El Tocuyo One of the oldest towns on the continent (1545), El Tocuyo is 30km southwest of Quíbor. Long ago the town was reached by boat up the Tocuyo River all the way from the coast near Chichiriviche and was a natural launching point for Spanish colonisers who set out for Barquisimeto and Caracas. It became known as the 'Mother City of Venezuela'. One of the most important towns of the colony, El Tocuyo was the capital of the province from 1547–77, when it was moved to Caracas. The first sugarcane in Venezuela was planted in El Tocuyo, and it is still the major agricultural crop.

Sadly, only a few examples remain of El Tocuyo's historic churches and spacious colonial buildings after an earthquake in 1950 destroyed nearly the whole town. Instead of restoring these colonial gems the dictator Marcos Pérez Jiménez ordered the majority of them bulldozed.

Where to stay

Posada Colonial (24 rooms) Av Fraternidad behind the Casa de la Cultura; ℡ 0253 663 0025. Rooms with hot water, AC. $

Festivals Announced by chiming bells and popping rockets, **the Tamunangue fiesta** – the year's biggest folklore event in El Tocuyo – takes place on 13 June in Plaza Bolívar when the Tamunangue dancers celebrate the day of **San Antonio de Padua**. This is preceded by prayers on 13 consecutive Tuesdays, attended by members of the San Antonio Brotherhood who meet in the Convent of San Francisco. Their promise to the saint is to dance in his honour, in return for a cure, lost things found, couples united, rain received…

Barquisimeto, Quíbor, Sanare and other towns in Lara and Portuguesa where there are brotherhoods also dance the Tamunangue.

The Tamunangue has the most complex musical and dance figures in Venezuelan folklore linked, according to some, with the summer solstice, and according to others with centuries-old African rituals and Spanish dances. To the underlying beat of the biggest drum, the *tamunango*, calling up the maracas, *cuatro* and other stringed instruments, the seven different rhythms, their songs and dances, begin with *El yiyivamos*, a courting dance in 6/8 tempo; followed by *La bella*, a light-hearted flirting sequence; *La perrendenga* when both men and women engage in mock battle using staves; and *El galerón*, a festive dance with four dozen combined steps, passes, waltzes, stomps and clapping. In the difficult *Seis corrido* three couples execute a weaving dance said to have 36 different steps; next, the steps of *La juruminga* are called out by a soloist, preceding the last dance: *Poco a poco*, a humorous struggle between the partners in which the man prancing like a horse is finally tamed by the woman.

The **Fiesta del Garrote Tocuyano**, a mock battle and dance, marks Tocuyo's Founding Day on 7 December.

What to see and do The beautiful **Iglesia de La Inmaculada Concepción**, noted for its unique exterior bell tower with three tiers (square, columned and round), stands alone on a plaza between Calles 17 and 18. It is the last survivor of the 17th- and 18th-century churches. Although severely damaged by the 1950 quake, it was reconstructed under the direction of master restorer Graziano Gasparini. Unscathed are the original wonderfully carved altar screen and the statue of the Virgin which was sent to El Tocuyo as a gift by Philip II in 1547 and has been there ever since.

The **Convento de San Francisco**, today the only old building left on Plaza Bolívar, withstood the quake, although the church next to it fell. Some parts of its unusual two-floor colonnade around a courtyard are original, some reconstructed. Today it houses the **Casa de la Cultura**. You can look around its salons where there are before-and-after photos of the earthquake.

Well disguised among government offices on the north side of Plaza Bolívar, the **Museo Arqueológico J M Cruxent** (⊕ *09.00–16.00 Tue–Fri, 09.00–11.00 w/ends*) has changing exhibits on ancient Indian cultures and archaeology. There is also the **Museo Histórico Lisandro Alvarado** on Calle 17 by Carrera 11, dealing with local literary and historical events.

TEREPAIMA AND YACAMBÚ NATIONAL PARKS In striking contrast to the state's arid regions, primary forest survives in southern Lara where two national parks have been formed in an attempt to halt destruction and protect watersheds: Terepaima, 169km^2, and Yacambú, 145km^2. Terepaima is the lower and hotter, dropping from 1,175m to some 300m at the Sarare River. The forest here covers a third of the park only, the rest being savanna and old fields. Although animal life is severely depleted, this area is home to the ocelot and puma, deer, armadillo, agouti, opossum, monkey, kinkajou, tamandua and climbing porcupine – most of which were hunted and eaten. Turning the tables, snakes such as rattlers and corals, and ants including the infamous army ants, are feared.

The tip of **Terepaima Park** is half an hour from Barquisimeto by road. Old earth roads climb up from Cabudare to Terepaima village providing splendid views; the Camino Real to Río Guache Seco and Caserío Los Aposentos crosses an area of pre-Columbian burial sites. Cartography map No 6245 covers the park. For more information, check with the Inparques officer in Barquisimeto (*Instituto Nacional de Parques, Av Los Leones facing CC Las Trinitarias;* \ *0254 254 3577*).

In **Yacambú**, mountains rise to 2,200m along an Andean spur called the Sierra de Portuguesa. Flora typical of the Andes mix with plants from the coastal cordillera and rare palms, tree ferns and local cloudforest species. Some plants grow nowhere else (like the lovely *Fuchsia tillettii*). Rains from April to November feed rivers such as the Yacambú. The Yacambú Reservoir provides irrigation for the Quíbor Valley and water for Barquisimeto.

Getting there A jeep service provides public transportation from Sanare. The paved road runs to Yacambú, continuing through the park to a mirador or lookout above the reservoir, 30km in total from Sanare. The entrance to El Blanquito administrative centre and campsite is well before this; stop at Km 21 and walk half a kilometre from the main road.

What to do

Birding Tracking the birds of Venezuela, Mary Lou Goodwin reports that Yacambú Park has: 'what I consider to be one of the best birding roads north of the Orinoco River... wherever you stop on this road you will find birds, but my favourite spot is the lagoon. In one short day I sighted 68 species.' Her list includes oropendula, oriole, warbler, four wrens, 11 tanagers, antpitta, redstart, parakeet, hummingbird and toucanet.

Hiking to Río Negro Canyon in Yacambú The Parque Nacional Yacambú is little known to walkers although it has a pleasant climate, beautiful cloudforest down to about 850m, and a relatively easy trail to the Río Negro Canyon. This route descending by way of Quebrada El Chorro takes six hours' walking time there and back (not counting a splash at the bottom). There is an excellent campsite with flowers and grass at **Laguna El Blanquito** at the start: picnic shelters, panorama, gardens, elegant willows and eucalyptus trees.

The Andes

PÁRAMOS AND PEAKS

The Venezuelan section of the Andes, with its charming mountain villages, friendly *campesinos* and striking natural beauty, offers visitors well-maintained hiking trails to high meadows, lakes and valleys, a host of adventure sports for adrenaline junkies, and a safe base from which to explore the rest of Venezuela. Highlights include the world's highest and longest cable car (*teleférico*), which runs from the city of Mérida to Pico Espejo, just 242m below Venezuela's highest mountain, Pico Bolívar (5,007m). The *teleférico* offers quick access to the picturesque but isolated village of Los Nevados and cuts days of trekking time to the glaciers of Pico Humboldt and Pico Bolívar. The highest peaks of the Sierra are often covered in snow, leading the ancient Timote-Cuica Indians to dub them the Five White Eagles. Glaciers at one time covered the entire Mérida Valley, with tongues of ice reaching Timotes and Santo Domingo. Leftovers from this last ice age are V-shaped valleys, dark lakes and glacier remnants called *timoncitos* (now shrinking dramatically due to climate change). Maize dominates the diet in the mountains and many high-country streams are stocked with trout, making a tasty change from red snapper and swordfish. Travellers will need one or more layers of warm clothing as temperatures can change quickly from tropical lowlands to high valleys above 3,000m, where it can fall below freezing at night. These high Andean valleys between 3,000m and 5,000m represent a unique ecological zone, known as *páramo*, with plants adapted to living in the seasonally frozen peat soils by developing deep roots and waxy leaves covered in downy fluff to withstand harsh sunlight in the mornings, as well as cold winds, fog and occasional night frosts.

MÉRIDA STATE

MÉRIDA (*Telephone code: 0274*) The state capital of Mérida is a city of 350,000 people where one in every six inhabitants is a student. Although traditional in their customs, courtesy and strong work ethic, Merideños are upbeat and open-minded. Travellers will find themselves at home in the lively university atmosphere of a town where the cost of living is low, food and lodging can be had at reasonable prices, internet access is cheap and plentiful, buses go everywhere, nightlife throbs to a salsa beat and beer is sold at supermarket prices in student bars.

Long a popular mountain destination famous for its beautiful setting at the foot of the Sierra Nevada and its cable car or *teleférico*, the state capital Mérida is Venezuela's best-developed tourist spot after Isla Margarita, with a good selection of hotels and *posadas*, a helpful state tourism office, and a smile for travellers, especially *mochileros* or 'backpackers'.

Visitors from Europe and the Americas, drawn first by the Sierra Nevada's peaks, can now enjoy the white-knuckle thrills of paragliding, white-water rafting, bridge jumping and canyoning (see *Chapter 3*). Local tour operators have expanded their itineraries to include a much wider array of excursions, from wildlife refuges in Los Llanos to boat trips to Lake Maracaibo to watch the amazing lightning show known as El Relámpago del Catatumbo. By taking advantage of Mérida's reputation as a safe place to stay in Venezuela, and keeping profit-margins low, local tour firms now offer budget circuits of the country, including Angel Falls, the Orinoco Delta, Río Caura and Roraima.

Although Mérida is the highest city in the country (1,650m) it's in the tropics, and far from being chilly has an average temperature of 19°C with hot sunny days and brisk nights.

Raised up on a plateau above the Río Chama, the city stretches from the historic city centre in the northeast to the airport and Jardín Acuario in the southwest. New districts occupy former coffee and sugarcane plantations to the north, separated by the little Albarenga River from the old town.

Mérida is the seat of the **Universidad de Los Andes**, second oldest in the country, which has some 60,000 students and branches in Trujillo and San Cristóbal. With some 250,000 tourists a month during the peak season (July–September), you get an idea of Mérida's growing importance as a cultural and travel centre.

History Although few historic buildings remain, the city is proud of its Spanish roots dating to 1558. Captain Juan Rodríguez Suárez, sent from Pamplona in search of gold mines, ran up against opposition in the Valley of the Mocotíes from Indians whose style of attack earned them their nickname of dancers or *bailadores*. He founded the first settlement near Lagunillas, called it Mérida after his birthplace in Spain and, harried by insects and heat, in a few days moved it to La Punta. Accused of mistreating Indians and exceeding orders by founding a settlement, he was pursued and arrested by Captain Juan Maldonado on orders from Bogotá. It was Maldonado who, in 1559, decided Mérida's final location facing the Sierra Nevada where it was named Santiago de los Caballeros (Saint James of the Knights).

The Spaniards, clinging to a narrow foothold along the Chama River, quickly saw the advantages of co-existence with peaceful groups such as the Mucuchíes, Jajíes, and Timote-Cuicas who planted 'roots and maize for sustenance because the multitude of people did not allow a patch of land to lie idle, even in the cold *páramos'*. A site with 63 pre-Columbian terraces used for cultivation has been identified near Escagüey along the Estití stream. According to one early reference such terraces were called *andenes*, suggesting the name Andes. Even now, Andeans are the hardest working people in the country. They are aware that their customs are different (and their Spanish clearer), and they like it that way. Andeans pride themselves on being *gente correcta* (proper).

For over two centuries Mérida was under the colonial jurisdiction of Nueva Granada (Colombia) rather than the Captaincy General of Venezuela. The Jesuits, arriving in 1628, founded a school, then the Seminary of San Buenaventura in 1788, which was made into the university as one of the first measures of the revolutionary patriots after proclaiming Independence. This occurred in 1810, scarcely five months after the proclamation in Caracas.

The province of Mérida was connected to Caracas and the rest of Venezuela by way of Lake Maracaibo and its ports of Bobures and La Ceiba. Early exports to Colombia included wheat flour, cheese, ham, beef, honey and sugar. A road for mule and horse carts was opened from Mucuchíes across the *páramo* and down to Torondoy south of the lake. Another road went from Tovar via El Vigía to the Sur del Lago ports. In the coffee boom of the 1890s, the French invested in construction of a 63km railway from El Vigía to Santa Bárbara, a river port. Mérida had both electricity and telephone lines by the end of the century. Finally, the Trans-Andean route was completed in 1925 (although not paved until the 1960s).

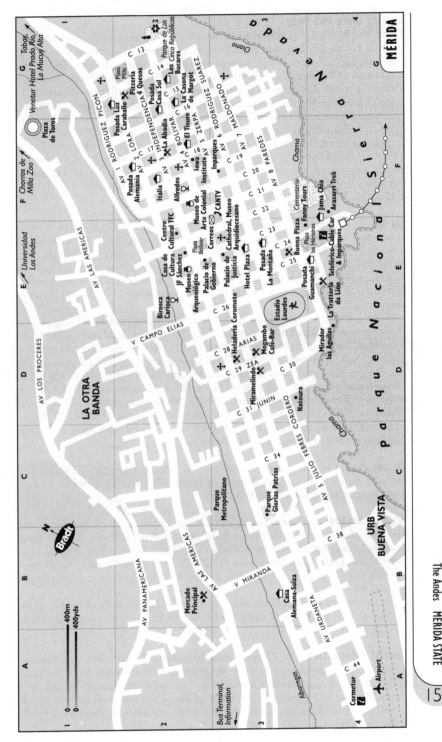

MÉRIDA

Taboy,
Veneluri Hotel Prado Río,
La Mucuy Alta

Chorros de
Milla Zoo

Universidad
Los Andes

Parque de Los
Cinco Repúblicos

G Chama

N e v a d a

Plaza
Milla

C 13

Plaza
de Toros

F

RODRIGUEZ PICON

Posada Luz
Caraballo
Pizzeria
4 Quesos
C 14
Posada
Casa Sol
La Casona
de Margot

AV 1
AV 2
C

Posada
Alemania
LORA

INDEPENDENCIA
17
C 15
La Abadia
El Tisure

Bucarres

AV 3
AV 4
Italia
Alfredos
Iowa
Institute

BOLIVAR
ZERPA
AV 5
AV 18
6

RODRIGUEZ SUAREZ

Inparques
AV 6

MALDONADO
C 19
AV 7
C 20

PAREDES
C 21
AV 8
C 22

LA OTRA
BANDA

AV LOS PROCERES

AV LAS AMERICAS

Centro
Cultural TFC

Museo de
Arte Colonial
Museo
Arqueológico

Casa de
Cultura
JF Sánchez

Birosca
Carioca

Plaza
Bolívar

Palacio de
Gobierno

Museo
Arqueológico

V CAMPO ELIAS

C 26

Heladeria
Coromoto

C 28

C 29
ZEA

Miramelindo
C 31

JUNIN

Mogambo
Café-Bar
C 30

ARIAS

AV LAS AMERICAS

AV PANAMERICANA

Mercado
Principal

Parque
Metropolitano

Parque
Glorias Patrias

C 34

AV JULIO FEBRES CORDERO

AV 5

C 38

V MIRANDA

Casa
Alemana-Suiza

URB
BUENA VISTA

AV URDANETA

Corretur

Airport

Bus Terminal,
Information

Albarregas

CANTV

Correos

Cathedral,
Palacio de
Justicia
Arquidiocesano

Hotel Plaza

Posada
La Montaña
C 25

C 23
C 24

Estadio
Lourdes

Mirador
las Aguilas

La Trattoría
da Lino

Posada
Guamanchi

Buona Pizza
Plaza
las Heroínas

Teleférico-Cable Car
& Inparques

Jama Chía

Fanny Tours

Cementerio

Arasarri Trek

Chama

P a r q u e   N a c i o n a l   S i e r r a

N e v a d a

Chama

Bradt

N

400m
400yds

0

0

The Andes MÉRIDA STATE

15

359

Getting there and away

By air The **Aeropuerto Alberto Carnevalli** [359 A4] is in southwest Mérida on Avenida Urdaneta, 3km from Plaza Bolívar. At the time of writing it was still not receiving flights from the major airlines since a Santa Barbara Airlines (SBA) flight crashed on 21 February 2007 shortly after taking off. Flights to Mérida have been redirected to the **Aeropuerto Internacional Juan Pablo Pérez Alfonso** in El Vigía (70km from Mérida, 30 minutes by bus), where SBA (*www.sbairlines.com*) and state airline Conviasa (*www.conviasa.aero*) have morning and afternoon flights from Monday to Saturday to Maiquetía Airport in Caracas (1 hour, US$90 one way).

Another alternative is to fly to the airport in Barinas, which has flights to Caracas (1 hour, US$70 one way). *Por puestos* to Mérida (3½ hours) and buses (5 hours) depart throughout the day, swinging around hairpin bends up to Laguna de Mucubají and Apartaderos and then down to the main terminal in the city. (See *Chapter 10, Barinas*, page 247.)

By bus The Terminal de Pasajeros is on Avenida Las Américas, 3km west of downtown Mérida. To get there and back take a bus or *por puesto* from Avenida 2 Lora and Calle 25 or a taxi (US$5). Minibuses to many *pueblos* in Mérida State such as Santa Cruz de Mora park in the loading bays; they leave when full and you pay on arrival. Although you need no ticket, you must have a tax receipt: before boarding, all passengers pay a small tax or *tasa de salida* of US$0.50 at a booth in the terminal.

For the scenic but slow Trans-Andean route to Mucuchíes, Pico El Aguila and Timotes, take a Valera bus (5 hours, US$9). For Laguna de Mucubají and Santo Domingo, take a bus to Barinas (4 hours, US$7), which depart every 90 minutes. Buses to **San Cristóbal** (5 hours, US$10) leave every three hours during the day via El Vigía and the lowland highway; for the mountain route, take a local bus to Tovar-Bailadores. There is an evening bus to **Coro** (12 hours, US$20) and express services to **Barquisimeto** (6 hours, US$13), **Maracaibo** (8 hours, US$15) and **Valencia** (10 hours, US$19). Direct buses to **Caracas** (770km, 12 hours, US$15–19) are all air conditioned (wrap up warm). The Llanos route to Caracas (690km) requires a change of bus in **Barinas**.

By car From Caracas, the two routes are: via Valencia (see page 325), and then Route 5 through Guanare to Barinas; or on the Carretera Transandina Route 7 from Barquisimeto, via Trujillo and Valera.

Getting around Taxis are reasonably priced and hiring one for a day trip to visit the Trans-Andean *pueblos* may prove to be cheaper than car rental. Reliable firms include **Líneas Unificadas de Mérida** (☎ 0274 263 5335), which has a 24-hour service and **Taxi Tours Teleférico** (☎ 0274 252 1524), by the cable car. A short trip across town is about US$2, a full day about US$60. Higher rates are charged after 21.00.

At the airport, **Budget** (*www.budget.com.ve*) offer car rental. Read the fine print, and carefully read the list of equipment ticked by the agency, as you will have to pay for any missing pieces.

Tourist information The **Corporación Mérideña de Turismo**, or Cormetur [359 A4] (*Av Urdaneta at Calle 45 by the airport;* ☎ *0800 637 4300, 0274 262 1603, 0274 263 5918;* e *ggcormetur@hotmail.com*), has seven information booths open from Monday to Saturday. Well-stocked kiosks at the bus terminal and airport (⊕ 07.00–19.00) have maps and information about local sites. Another is by the cable car station (⊕ 08.00–15.00).

Tour operators Mérida's tour operators now offer much more than hiking trips to the main peaks and *páramos* of the surrounding Sierra Nevada mountain range. World-class paragliding is offered at a short distance from the city in Tierra Negra near Las Gonzales and horseriding and mountain bike trails to remote villages are available for all levels of skill. Tours to the nearby rivers of Barinas provide white-water rafting, as well as tubing, canyoning and kayaking. Mérida is also a good starting point for cheap wildlife tours to Los Llanos and boat trips to Lake Maracaibo to see the amazing wildlife and thunder-less lightning of the **Ciénagas del Catatumbo**. Increasingly, operators are linking up with *posadas* and jungle camps in Canaima, the Río Caura and Orinoco Delta to offer reasonably priced circuits of Venezuela that offer travellers the security of having someone to pick them up on arrival at airports and bus terminals as they travel around the country. (See box on page 363 for more details of some of the activities on offer in Mérida.)

The top operators are found on Calle 24 near the cable car station and most have English- or German-speaking staff, qualified guides, and equipment for mountaineering and other sports. Clearly, there is a risk attached to paragliding tandem for 45 minutes over rocky terrain and rushing rivers so make sure your insurance covers you for extreme sports and stick to the main agencies. Guides should be registered not only with Inparques but also Cormetur for mountaineering (*montañismo*) and rock and ice climbing (*escalada*). Ask to see the equipment used. Is it professional? Is there a back-up in case of failure or adverse weather? Always check and compare a few agencies before signing up for anything.

Arasarri Trek [359 F4] At the bottom of Calle 24 alongside the Teleférico; ☎ 0274 252 5879; e info@arasarri.com; www.arasarri.com. A pioneering tour operator offering white-water rafting on the Canaguá, with a class 5–3 rating from 700m elevation down to 200m, & canyoning from their camp on the Acequia River in Barinas during the Jun–Nov rafting season. Paragliding or *parapente* is arranged on fine mornings or late afternoons for US$60 pp. Wildlife trips to Los Llanos, including horseriding & night time observation of caiman alligators. Guides are very knowledgeable on natural history & great cooks as well.

Cocolight m 0414 756 2575; e alanconda@gmail.com; www.cocolight.com. Mérida-based tour guide Alan Highton has been leading groups to Los Llanos & the Catatumbo for over 20 years & is an expert on local wildlife. His 2-day Catatumbo tours spend the night at a house on stilts in the lake village of Ologa in Sur del Lago in the Parque Nacional Ciénagas del Catatumbo, from where the lightning is spectacular. This natural phenomenon is best seen Jun–Dec, during the rainy season, when electrical storms of up to 280 flashes an hour can light up the sky with bright streaks of electricity that last until dawn.

Colibri Expediciones Av 2 at Calles 17–18; ☎ 0274 252 4067; www.posadaalemania.com. Run by Ricardo Torres through the Posada Alemania, a friendly & helpful guide who prepares suggestions, with bus routes for DIY *páramo* walks to hot springs & also arranges tours to Los Nevados, the Catatumbo & Los Llanos.

Fanny Tours [359 E3] Calle 24, No 8–30; ☎ 0274 252 2952; e info@fanny-tours.com; www.fannytours.com. Mountaineer & mountain biker José Albarran is better known to his friends as 'Piojo' ('Flea'), because of his ability to cling to sheer rock walls. A pioneer of paragliding in Venezuela he now runs this tour agency with his Swiss wife Patrizia, offering tandem flights in Tierra Negra, mountain trekking, mountain biking, Catatumbo tours & circuits of Venezuela. He says the rather unusual name of his tour agency comes from the lady he bought it from, Señora Fanny.

Guamanchi Expeditions No 8–39 Calle 24, near Plaza Las Heroínas; ☎ 0274 252 2080; e info@guamanchi.com; www.guamanchi.com. Another pioneer of adventure tourism run by mountaineer John Peña & his Swiss wife Joelle. Their qualified climbers will guide you (alone or in a group) to Pico Humboldt, Pico Bolívar or Los Nevados. Guamanchi has its own *posada* in Los Nevados & a white-water rafting camp on the Acequia, which is also good for birding or biking. Suggested biking itineraries (tours or bikes for hire) depend on the biker's experience, with a lift by vehicle to starting points such as Pico El Aguila, cycling down to Timotes, Piñango or Torondoy south of Lake Maracaibo.

15

Natoura [359 D3] Calle 31, between Av Don Tulio & Av 6, No 5–27; ☎ 0274 252 4216; e info@ natoura.com; www.natoura.com. Run by Renate Reiners & José Luís Troconis this is the leading tour operator in Mérida. They can arrange international & national flights, transfers & accommodation from outside Venezuela, tailoring trips for small groups to Los Llanos, Los Roques, Roraima, Angel Falls & Amazonas as well as biking, birdwatching & trekking throughout Venezuela. They use good quality sleeping bags, helmets, boots, crampons, ice axes & harnesses for their Sierra Nevada tours & rent out equipment. Natoura also offers tandem paragliding at Tierra Negra above Las Gonzáles (US$60), & from the cable car station at Loma Redonda. Visa & MasterCard accepted & can help change money.

Montaña Adventure Local I, Residencias Las Américas, Av Las Américas; ☎ 0274 266 2867; e info@ venadventure.com; www.venadventure.com. One of the senior tour agencies. Run by Jerry Keeton, an American who organises tours to Venezuela's top destinations such as Angel Falls & Los Roques for US, English & Japanese travel companies. Among the tailored tours offered in Mérida are *pueblo-to-pueblo* trekking, overnight trips to Los Nevados, mountain biking circuits with support jeeps to carry gear up the 'awesome Andes' to Pico El Aguila, El Morro & Jají, tandem paragliding flights, trout fishing & birding in both the Andes & the Llanos.

Where to stay
Mérida has plenty of good hotels and *posadas* to choose from with several backpacker places clustered around the area near the cable car and in the old part of town and more spacious, more expensive options north of Plaza Bolívar and along Avenida Urdaneta towards the airport. Travellers do not usually need to book in advance except during Easter, Carnival and the Feria del Sol (see box, *Fairs and fiestas in Mérida*, page 366) when it is almost impossible to find a room. At other times be sure to ask for off-season rates, *la tarifa de época baja*, and always verify whether rates cover all taxes (*impuestos*).

Hotel Tibisay (81 rooms, presidential suite) Av Universidad; ☎ 0274 244 4455; e reservas@hoteltibisay.com; www.hoteltibisay.com. 6-storeys of shiny glass mark the difference at this ultra-modern hotel, which opened in 2008. Rooms have nice touches such as hairdryer, minibar & cable TV & the presidential suite has a jacuzzi. A small heated pool is a nice treat & there is a bar & restaurant, Wi-Fi & internet access. $$$

La Pedregosa (104 rooms, 24 cabins) Pedregosa Norte district; ☎ 0274 266 6749, 0274 266 4295; e pedregosa@telcel.net.ve. A large place with sauna & spacious grounds with artificial lake. $$$

Venetur Hotel Prado Río [359 G1] (13 rooms, 80 cabin rooms) Av 1, Hoyada de Milla; ☎ 0274 252 0633, 0274 252 0775; e informacion@ hotelpradorio.com.ve; www.hotelpradorio.com.ve. At the northeast end of Av 1 where the Trans-Andean route enters Mérida, this government-built hotel from 1958 was Mérida's 1st luxury hotel. Today it is run as a hotel school, with grill restaurant, snack bar, games room, Wi-Fi area & internet. Rooms with AC, hot water, cable TV, 25m swimming pool with view of the Sierra Nevada. $$$

Belensate (25 rooms) Av Las Americas, La Hacienda; ☎ 0274 266 3722; e reservaciones@ hotelbelensate.com; www.hotelbelensate.com. Near the west end of Av Las Américas in a green residential district that was once a sugarcane plantation, it has an art centre, playground, swimming pool & Italian restaurant. $$

Casa Alemana–Suiza [359 B3] (10 rooms) Av 2 between Calles 38 & 39 (across from Hotel Caribay); ☎ 0274 263 6502, 0274 263 9629; e info@casa-alemana.com; www.casa-alemana.com. A big house reconditioned by Swiss owner Markus Twerenbold. Comfortable rooms with bath, hot water, cable TV. Communal area with pool table, honour bar, internet access, Wi-Fi. Airport, bus transfers. Good value. $$

El Tisure [359 F2] (34 rooms) Av 4 Bolívar at Calles 17–18; ☎ 0274 252 6072. Another good choice, run by a French woman. *Tasca* bar/restaurant downstairs, parking, security. $$

Hotel Plaza [359 E3] (46 rooms) Av 5 at Calle 23; ☎ 0274 252 1315; e reservaciones@ hotelplazamerida.com; www.hotelplazamerida.com. A block from Plaza Bolívar, this reasonable option has internet, Wi-Fi in lobby & parking. Rooms are variable, ask to see a few before deciding. $$

Posada Alemania [359 F2] (14 rooms) Av 2 between Calles 17 & 18; ☎ 0274 252 4067; info@ posadaalemania.com; www.posadaalemania.com. A magnet for international backpackers, this friendly *posada* in a colonial house offers kitchen & laundry privileges, buffet b/fast, small garden, internet. Low-

PARAGLIDING Excellent gliding conditions have brought international competitions to Mérida. Starting with the *teleférico*'s Loma Redonda and La Aguada stations, take-off points include Loma de Los Angeles on the way to Jají and the best, Tierra Negra above Las Gonzáles southwest of the city about 20km. Tandem flights as long as 30km and lasting 1½ hours are not uncommon; they cost about US$50–60 per person with transport to launch site. Wear long trousers, solid trainers and a fleece to keep warm while soaring. 'Piojo' of Fanny Tours is a recommended pilot.

BIRDWATCHING For birdwatching try **Gravity Tours** (*Calle 24 between Avs 7 & 8;* \0274 251 1279; m 0424 760 8327; e *gravityxtreme@hotmail.com; www.gravity-tours.com.ve*), a small outfit headed by Gustavo Viloria, a biologist, birder and Audubon member, who knows the birds of various ecosystems and can organise three-day trips to primary forest around La Azulita and south of Lake Maracaibo. Using playback sound equipment, he has listed 250 species. Birding tours in the Llanos are by 4x4 and riverboat in the ranches of Apure.

Joe Klaiber who runs the **Posada Casa Vieja** (*www.casa-vieja-merida.com*) in Tabay is also a recommended expert who can arrange tours to the top birding spots.

HORSE TREKKING Stables and pastures at a mountain farm called Finca La Yegua Blanca (\ 0274 657 4018; m 0416 874 5607; e *yeguablanca@yahoo.com; www.fincayeguablanca.com*) are run by a wiry Swiss horse-lover and mountaineer named Jackie. He arranges to bring the horses to a meeting place for day treks to Páramo La Culata; US$60 per person, lower rate for groups. Treks of three to five days in the Sierra Nevada or La Culata cost about US$80 per day, sleeping in caves, deserted houses or tents on the *páramo*, or overnighting in *posadas* for an extra US$10. The cook-out menu is often trout fresh from mountain creeks. These longer treks require a fortnight's advance notice, and a minimum of four people. Arassari (*www.arassari.com*) can also arrange horseriding with Yegua Blanca.

TROUT FISHING The fishing season runs 15 March–30 September. Rushing mountain streams, white with oxygen, are perfect for rainbow and brook trout, which were first introduced in the 1930s. Andeans fish many streams such as those tumbling over the *páramo* to the Santo Domingo highway, from Mucubají down to Hotel Los Frailes. The state of Mérida has at least 150 high lakes (3,000–4,000m), periodically restocked. In the Sierra Nevada across from Mucuchíes there are well over a dozen lakes. Some of the *lagunas* are Los Patos, Saisay, Montón, the three lakes of Rollal, Santo Cristo, Verde. Experts advise that the best fishing time is early in the morning or on overcast afternoons, so be prepared for biting cold. The government bureau in charge is Inapesca (El Instituto Nacional de Pesca y Aquicultura) on Avenida Urdaneta in Mérida.

---

price dorm & rooms with bathroom, hot water. Manager Ricardo Torres runs Colibrí Expediciones, speaks English & German & can give pointers on what to do, where to go. $$
⌂ **Posada Casa Sol** [359 G2] (19 rooms) Av 4, Calle 15–16; \ 0274 252 4164; e info@ posadacasasol.com; www.posadacasasol.com. Stylish, charming & stuffed with quirky artworks & features,

this old colonial house has been thoroughly remodelled into a boutique-style hotel offering great rooms at a good price in the old part of town. Rooms & suites with AC, hot water, Wi-Fi. B/fasts available on demand, internet near reception. $$
⌂ **Posada Luz Caraballo** [359 G2] (36 rooms) Av 2 on Plaza Sucre (Milla); \ 0274 252 5411. Known for its popular restaurant serving tasty snacks, this

3-storey *posada* is at the top of town near the cheap & cheerful **Pizzeria El Sabor de Los 4 Quesos**. Rooms with bath, hot water, cable TV. $$

🏠 **Jama Chía** [359 F4] (10 rooms) Calle 24 near the cable car station; ✆ 0274 252 5676. Living area with kitchen privileges downstairs, terrace & hammocks upstairs & nice but spartan rooms, including dorm rooms with shared bathrooms. Señora Benedicta, the owner is used to backpackers on a tight budget. $

🏠 **La Casona de Margot** [359 G2] (11 rooms) Av 4, between Calles 15 & 16; ✆ 0274 252 3312; www.lacasonademargot.com. Comfy rooms with bath, hot water, cable TV, in colonial house with central patio. Free coffee for guests, Wi-Fi. $

🏠 **Posada Guamanchi** [359 E4] (18 rooms) Calle 24 No 8–86, near cable car; ✆ 0274 252 2080; e info@guamanchi.com; www.guamanchi.com. Good value rooms with bath, hot water, use of kitchen,

mainly used by foreign backpackers on their tours. New rooms at back have view of mountains, hammock area on upper terrace for hanging out. Friendly owners. $

🏠 **Posada La Montaña** [359 E3] (19 rooms) Calle 24 between Avs 6 & 7; ✆ 0274 252 5977; e posadalamontana@hotmail.com; www.posadalamontana.com. A traditional 2-storey house near the cable car station offering simple rooms with fan, hot water, cable TV. Good restaurant (🕐 07.30–22.30) with inventive menu, sun terrace, laundry service, Wi-Fi. $

🏠 **Posada Los Bucares** [359 G2] (16 rooms) Av 4 at Calle 15; ✆ 0274 252 2841; e info@losbucares.com. Simple rooms with bath, hot water, cable TV in an old colonial house set around a central patio. Friendly, helpful staff, some English spoken. $

Spa

🏠 **Hosteria & Spa La Sevillana** (12 rooms) 5km north of La Pedregosa Alta where the road meets the mountain; ✆ 0274 266 3227, 0274 266 2810; e sevillana@telcel.net.ve; www.andes.net/lasevillana. This is a very special 12-room *posada* with gardens, pond, an old *trapiche* or sugar mill, tree ferns & the source of a spring, all sitting at the edge of a forest rising another 1,000m in altitude. The owner Ilse Gasser, a retired tour operator from

Germany, has built a mountain refuge with wide verandas, patios, fireplace & open kitchen, run by excellent cook Erika. The revitalisation centre, or 'vitalispa', gives anti-stress treatments from hydrotherapy, oxygen therapy & steam baths to cosmetology, reflexology & exfoliation. Basic spa plan includes massage, medicinal mud, aroma/music therapy. 7 languages spoken. $$

Campgrounds

Prepared campgrounds with bathrooms are a rarity. **La Mucuy Alta** is an Inparques recreational area at the entrance to the Parque Nacional Sierra Nevada; trails to Laguna Coromoto and Humboldt Peak start here. A line of *por puesto* Toyotas parks on the Plaza Bolívar of Tabay and covers the 6km route to the park. There are well-kept grounds, pools for bathing in the pretty Quebrada del Oro, picnic shelters, bathrooms and a dormitory-style cabin that can be reserved for groups through Inparques. Above the ranger station there is a trout farm, which raises sprats for seeding the Sierra lakes.

✖ **Where to eat** Restaurants are plentiful, practical and reasonable. If you're on a budget, do as the locals do and go for the *menú popular*, a low-priced set lunch of soup, main course and juice or coffee offered at many no-frills restaurants such as the **Margarita** which serves three meals every day at Calle 19 between Avenidas 5 and 6. Look out for trout, which is inexpensive as it's raised on fish farms and available virtually everywhere.

Some restaurants are closed on Mondays during low season. The four-storey **Mercado Principal** [359 B2] (*Av Las Américas*) at Viaducto Miranda has a large, inexpensive dining room (breakfast, lunch) on the top floor. Tables are served by various kitchens with different menus, mostly *criollo*, plus standard pork chops, chicken and trout. Try a glass of local blackberry (*mora*) wine or, if you're feeling really brave – or hungover – find the juice stall downstairs that sells *Levantón*

Andino, a fearsome concoction of mixed fruit, powdered milk, quails eggs, rum, beer, brandy and a couple of bulls eyes. Local people swear that there is no better hangover cure and insist it has aphrodisiac qualities to rival Viagra (if you can stomach it).

✗ **La Abadia Cyber Café** [359 F2] Av 3 between Calles 17 & 18; ⊕ 12.00–23.30. Attracts internet surfers as well as diners with a restaurant in the mysterious old monastery building serving hearty chicken, beef & fish dishes at 5 tables on an upstairs terrace with a pretty view of angels trumpeting on a church roof, & 5 more tables by a garden patio. $$

✗ **La Trattoria da Lino** [359 E4] Pasaje Ayacucho; ⊕ 12.00–22.00. Lino makes excellent *carpaccio*, pasta & profiteroles at this romantic Italian restaurant. $$

✗ **Miramelindo** [359 D3] Av 4 at Calle 29; ☎ 0274 252 9437; ⊕ 12.00–15.00 & 19.00–23.00 Mon–Sat. A Basque restaurant under the Chama Hotel run by chefs Miren & Jordi serves good seafood & has a sushi bar that opens in the evenings. $$

✗ **Mogambo Café-Bar** [359 D3] Av 4 at Calle 29; ☎ 0274 252 5643; ⊕ 08.00–11.00 & 17.00–23.00. A good option for a light lunch, they serve *panini* sandwiches, salads, desserts & coffee. Live groups sometimes perform in the evenings. $$

✗ **Buona Pizza** [359 E3] Av 7 at Calles 24–25; ⊕ 12.00–24.00. As the name suggests, good pizzas

at reasonable prices in a small place 2 blocks from the cable car station. $

✗ **Heladería Coromoto** [359 D3] Av 3 at Calle 28; ⊕ 14.00–21.45 Tue–Sun. Fancy a trout-flavoured ice cream? A neon sign outside announces this place is in the *Guinness Book of Records* for its world-beating 860 flavours of ice cream, although only a selection are available each day. Alongside vanilla, chocolate & fruit flavours are weird combos of meat & vegetables dreamed up by owner Manuel da Silva Oliveira. Try an ice cream version of Venezuela's national dish, *pabellón criollo* (shredded beef, rice, black beans & plantains) & finish off with a fruity *mora* (blackberry). $

✗ **Pizzeria El Sabor de Los 4 Quesos** [359 G2] Av 2 at Plaza Milla; ⊕ 17.30–20.30 Mon–Thu, 11.30–20.00 Fri–Sun. A cheap & cheerful pizzeria in an old house on the plaza popular with students. Order a couple of beers at a time as service can be slow. $

✗ **T'Café** Av 3 at Calle 29; ⊕ 08.00–24.00. An open-air restaurant with Wi-Fi opposite Heladería Coromoto [359 D3] serving typical b/fasts, pizzas, speciality coffee. Run by a hang-glider and popular with a young crowd. $

Nightlife

♀ **Alfredo's** [359 F2] Av 4 & Calle 19. A noisy, popular beer hall & meeting place with a travellers' bulletin board & internet service.

☆ **Gradas** Av 4 & Calle 19; ⊕ 12.00–02.00. On the '*esquina caliente*' or 'hot corner' of town, next to Alfredo's & the Hoyo del Queque, this is the starting point for a night out in the old part of town. A self-styled sports bar, cyber café & grill, on Mon & Tue it sells beer at supermarket prices, & is packed with local students & foreign tourists.

☆ **Hoyo del Queque** Av 4 & Calle 19. A small hangout run by a French tour operator & paraglider, where 90% of travellers pop in for

conversation, a cheap beer, internet & overseas telephone calls.

♀ **La Birosca Carioca** [359 E2] Av 2 at Calle 24, CC Las Tapias. Tremendously popular, informal, European-style bar-disco with a stand-up bar, reasonable drinks & music for all tastes, drawing a Bohemian crowd. Local bands & DJs at w/ends.

☆ **La Cucaracha** Centro Comercial Las Tapias; www.lacucaracha.com.ve; ⊕ 14.00–06.00. Salsa, vallenato, rock & thumping techno are all on offer at this massive club with bars & dance areas near the centre. A young crowd fill the place to bursting at w/ends. 2 related clubs **Cucaracha Café** & **Cucaracha Racing** are in the CC Alto Prado shopping mall.

☞ *WARNING:* The presence of so many young people provides a market for drugs. Penalties for drug possession in Venezuela are heavy, with prison sentences of eight to ten years.

Shopping Head to the **Mercado Principal** [359 B2] on Avenida Las Américas (⊕ 07.00–17.00) which has a wealth of local handicrafts to browse through on four

The **Feria del Sol** is the biggest festival in Mérida State, an annual week-long bash that takes place in the run-up to Ash Wednesday. Originally focussed around the bullfights in the Plaza de Toros, it now includes concerts by the top rock and pop bands, as well as folk groups from all over the country, many performing free in the city's many squares. There are also a host of beauty pageants to elect the Reina del Sol, Miss Tourism, even a Miss Internet. During the *feria* pubs and clubs put on special events and the whole city has a party atmosphere.

At other times you may see costumed villagers celebrating traditional festivals and saints' days with street processions and ritual dances. In the capital, Christmas is preceded by a fortnight of celebrations with impromptu street gatherings and evening song contests around Plaza Bolívar. Mérida also puts on a very popular International Jazz Festival in June, and a large, successful book fair or Feria Nacional del Libro.

January (all month)	Paradura del Niño, a widely celebrated search for the lost Infant Jesus, with costumed Indians, angels, shepherds and dancers.
1 January	Baile de Las Locaínas in Pueblo Llano.
6 January	Day of the Kings in Santo Domingo, Tabay.
12 January	Los Giros de San Benito in San Rafael de Mucuchíes. Festividad del Santo Niño de Cacute, Cacute.
January (last Sunday)	San Benito closing fiesta in San Isidro, Mucutujote near La Venta-Chachopo.

floors, from the cute little ceramic houses that Venezuelans like to hang on the wall, to carved saints, indigenous baskets and local produce such as jams and spicy sauces. You can also eat at the market at one of the cheap and cheerful food stalls – see opposite.

Other practicalities

Money Italcambio at the airport (⊕ *08.00–18.00 Mon–Fri, 08.00–13.00 Sat*) is the only money exchange house but most hotels and *posadas* can help with changing dollars. Banks will change dollars, but expect long queues and take your passport. To change travellers' cheques, you may be requested to show the original purchase slip. CorpBanca on Avenida Las Américas, a block east of the Mercado, will change Amex. Banco Mercantil, Avenida 5 at Calle 15, handles Thomas Cook. There is a Banco de Venezuela with ATM a block south of Plaza Bolívar on Avenida 4 between Calle 23 andCalle 24. Most ATMs in town accept Visa and MasterCard.

Inparques [359 E4] (*Calle 2;* ℡ *0274 262 1356; www.inparques.gob.ve;* ⊕ *08.30–12.00 & 13.30–17.00*) Tucked away in a street one block south and running parallel to Avenida Las Américas, midway between the main Mercado and the bus terminal. It's easier to get camping permits from the Inparques office at the cable car station (⊕ *07.30–14.00 Mon–Fri*). You need a passport, and a small sum per night's stay in the park. Permits must be handed back on return as a control on lost hikers.

Internet Internet access is available all over town for as low as US$0.70 an hour. A good place to get a bite to eat while surfing is **La Abadía Cyber Café** [359 F2] (*Av 3 between Calles 17 & 18;* ⊕ *10.00–23.30 Mon–Sun*), which has 27 terminals and restaurant service (see *Where to eat*, page 365).

2 February	Los Vasallos de La Candelaria in La Punta, Bailadores. In La Parroquia at the western edge of Mérida seven dances, chants, celebrate the patron saint's day.
Easter (Holy Thursday– Good Friday)	Passion Play in La Parroquia, Lagunillas.
15 May	San Isidro Labrador in Apartaderos, Mucurubá, Cacute, Bailadores, Jají, Lagunillas. San Antonio de Padua in Chiguará.
22 May	Los Locos de Santa Rita in Pueblo Nuevo.
14–17 June	San Buenaventura in Ejido.
25 July	Santo Apostol (St James) in Lagunillas, Ejido, Jají.
11 September	La Virgen de Coromoto in Chachopo.
24 September	Archangel Michael's Day in Jají and Mérida.
30 September	Los Negros de San Jerónimo in Santo Domingo.
12 October	La Virgen de Coromoto in the capital of Mérida.
24 October	Fiesta de San Rafael in San Rafael de Mucuchíes.
8 December	Fiesta de las 19,000 Velas honouring the Virgin of Immaculate Conception in Mucurubá.
28 December	Los Chimbángueles in Palmarito. Los Giros de San Benito in Mucuchíes (also 29 Dec).
29 December	Los Giros de San Benito (the black saint) in Chachopo, Timotes.

Post office The main post office is **Ipostel** [359 E3] (*Calle 21, between Avs 4 & 5*).

Bilingual doctor Aldo Olivieri (↘ *0274 244 3834;* m *0414 374 0356*) is an Italian doctor who speaks English and works from the Centro Profesional El Buho (*Edificio Centro Profesional, Av Principal El Llanito, Sector la Otra Banda*).

Language centres Mérida is probably the best and cheapest place to learn Spanish in Venezuela, with year-round courses and homestay lodging options with local families.

Iowa Institute [359 F2] Av 4 at Calle 18; ↘ 0274 252 6404; e www.iowainstitute.com. Organises group classes, one-to-one instruction & homestays with local families from their base in a colonial house in the old part of town.
Jakera Calle 24, Casa No 8–205, Plaza Las Heroinas; ↘ 0274 252 4732; e jakera@jakera.com;

www.jakera.com. Spanish classes are given in a *posada* with dbl rooms, dorm beds & kitchen facilities aimed at gap-year kids & young adults. They run another *posada*–school in Playa Colorada in Parque Nacional Mochima & offer adventure travel & language learning while travelling between the two.

Climbing equipment
5007 Escalada Libre Av 5, betweens Calles 19 & 20; Planta Baja, Centro Comercial Mediterráneo; ↘ 0274 252 6806. A small shop with good mountain gear, boots, backpacks, tents, torches, sleeping bags & ice picks. Note however that all the

top adventure tour operators provide equipment for their trekkers, agencies like Natoura can hire out equipment if needed & most things will be cheaper in your home country.

What to see and do
Plaza Bolívar [359 E2] Dominating the square is the large **cathedral**. Begun in 1800, it was modelled on the cathedral of Toledo. Destroyed by earthquake and

finally finished in 1958 it is a hotchpotch of styles but retains some nice touches, including the bronzes of the sacred heart on the massive doors and the crypt holding the remains of a Roman soldier, St Clement, who was beheaded as a Christian.

Museo Arquidiocesano [359 E3] (*Av 4, Plaza Bolívar;* ⊕ *15.00–18.00 Tue–Fri, 09.00–16.00 Sat–Sun; admission US$0.30 adults*) Displays religious art and treasures, including a bell dated AD909, one of the world's oldest.

Museo Arqueológico [359 E2] (*Corner of Av 3 at Calle 23; www.vereda.saber.ula.ve/museo_arqueologico;* ⊕ *10.00–18.00 daily; admission US$1*) A small but interesting exhibition of stone and ceramic figurines with coffee-bean eyes from Mérida's pre-Columbian past, examples of burial techniques and ethnographic displays. Although all the information is in Spanish, it is still worth visiting. Housed in the rector's office of the Universidad de Los Andes (ULA), founded in 1785 by Jesuits and raised to university level in 1810.

Casa de Cultura Juan Félix Sánchez [359 E2] (*North side of Plaza Bolívar;* ⊕ *09.00–21.00 Mon–Fri*) Housed in the north side of what was once an elegant mansion, this provides a showcase for works by Mérida's artists and craftsmen; home to several music and dance schools.

Centro Cultural Tulio Febres Cordero [359 E2] (*Av 2 between Calles 21 & 22;* ⊕ *09.00–17.00 Tue–Sun*) A modern performing arts complex occupies the block northeast of Plaza Bolívar. This is where the old Mercado stood until destroyed by fire. In size alone the complex is one of the city's most important buildings after the cathedral. There is a concert and lecture hall with 1,500 seats, art gallery, craft area, and café.

Museo de Arte Colonial [359 F2] (*Av 4 at Calle 20;* ⊕ *08.00–12.00 & 14.00–18.00 Mon–Fri; 08.00–16.00 Sat–Sun; admission US$0.50*) A colonial house built between 1689 and 1710 where Juan Antonio Paredes, a patriot general, was born. The museum has a small collection of period pieces up to 1811 (Independence), including furniture, art works and 17th-century bas-reliefs.

Biblioteca Bolivariana (*Av 4, Calle 20*) Independence documents, some of Bolívar's medals, a jewel-encrusted sword and gold sheath presented by a grateful Peru can be seen here.

Parque de las Cinco Repúblicas [359 G2] (*Upper end of Av 4*) The park has the world's first monument to Bolívar, erected in 1842, although it is no longer the original one.

Plaza Las Heroínas [359 E4] A block west of Plaza Bolívar and six blocks south, the Plaza Las Heroínas is surrounded by hotels, restaurants, a craft market and a climbing wall. After Plaza Bolívar, it is the city's most important square because the *teleférico* terminal and small Inparques office are here, also the major adventure tourism operators.

Mercado Principal [359 B2] (*Av Las Américas;* ⊕ *07.30–18.00 Mon–Sun*) One of Mérida's most popular attractions where you can easily spend a morning if crafts, souvenirs, sweaters and even silk scarves interest you, and then have lunch at the top floor restaurant. On the ground floor there are vegetables, meat and fish stalls, and crafts including pottery and many kinds of baskets. On the second floor, more crafts, furniture, trinkets, toys and textiles, including cotton, wool and fine silk. Mérida has a home-grown silk industry, from growing silkworms to dyeing and weaving. On the third floor there are sweaters, ponchos, T-shirts, blankets and woven bags made in Mérida, Colombia and Ecuador. There is a tourism module here. Buses for the Mercado leave from Calle 26 near Avenida 1 in the centre.

Parque Jardín Acuario (*Av Andres Bello, near Centro Comercial Las Tapias;* ⊕ *08.00–17.00 Tue–Sun; admission BsF1*) Just 2.2km past the airport this aquarium displays 300 species of fish, including those native to the Andes and the Llanos. There are two modules showing the state's cultural, folk and tourism attractions.

Taller Morera (*Av Principal de La Pedregosa;* ✆ *0274 266 1545;* ⊕ *08.00–12.00 & 14.00–17.00 daily, w/days only in low season*) The silk-weavers' workshop is a fascinating place where María Eugenia and Eduardo Dávila raise the silk worms in greenhouses, grow mulberry trees to feed the larvae bales of leaves, collect thousands of cocoons, and wash these to obtain and spin the silk. It's definitely a labour of love as the silk thread, once dyed, yields a limited quantity of cloth – albeit prize-winning – through the skills of the Dávilas and three other weavers of their company.

Museo de Ciencia y Tecnología (*Av Andrés Bello, Bd Cinco Águilas Blancas;* ⊕ *10.00–18.00 Mon–Sun; admission US$2 adults*) Exhibits on earthquakes, mechanised dinosaurs, planetarium, climbing wall and cafeteria. An artificial lake with digitally controlled 'legosaur' and 'elasmosaur' adds a bit of fun. One for the kids.

Parque Zoologico Chorros de Milla [359 F1] (*Av Principal de los Chorros de Milla, La Hechicera district;* ⊕ *08.00–18.00, in low season closed Mon; admission US$1.50*) In the far north of the city, this small, pleasant zoo with shady walks to natural falls is the most popular attraction in town. The zoo has around 150 animals, including most of Venezuela's mammals, from small agoutis to the endangered spectacled bear and jaguars. Some of the cages could definitely be bigger but the animals generally look well cared for. A captive breeding programme for the condor begun in 2000 with the co-operation of Cleveland Zoo has already produced a chick, the first condor born in Venezuela for 40 years.

The teleférico [359 E4] Reaching 4,765m altitude at Pico Espejo, this four-stage cable car is the world's highest and longest and is a central focus of tourism activity in Mérida. However, after a series of technical issues affecting service, the government decided in 2009 to completely overhaul the system, replacing the cables, cars and motors. The new system is not expected to be operational before 2012.

The cable cars cover 12.5km in an hour-long ride starting from **Barinitas** station at the bottom of Calle 25, 1,638m elevation. Swinging over the Chama Gorge, the *teleférico* begins a dramatic ascent over banana, sugarcane, then coffee plants up to dense forest at **La Montaña** station, 2,442m. There is a cafeteria here. As the next stage rises steeply, more than 1,000m in 3km, the landscape changes from forest to *páramo* and *frailejón* flowers and the temperature drops correspondingly at **La Aguada** station, 3,452m, where you can just see Pico Bolívar. At **Loma Redonda** station, 4,045m, hikers bound for Los Nevados get off, awaited by guides with mules. Guides can also take you for a ride to Laguna del Espejo. The last stage ascends 725m over stark ridges without any midway towers, while below gleam lakes – a pair of round ones called Anteojos (eyeglasses), Laguna Negra and Laguna Colorada. Weather permitting, the **Pico Espejo** station has spectacular views: north to La Culata range, east to the double peak of Humboldt

15

and Bonpland, south to the plains, and west as far as the Sierra de Cocuy in Colombia. There is a bronze bust of Simón Bolívar atop Bolívar Peak and, close to the station, a marble statue of the Virgin of the Snows, patroness of climbers. The *teleférico* system was engineered by the French and built under dictator Marcos Pérez Jiménez in 1958.

Because clouds often close in after midday, try to be early so as not to miss the stunning views. Make sure you have warm clothes and heavy socks as it is very cold up there; jackets and gloves may be rented at the *teleférico* shop. If you are asthmatic or suffer other breathing problems, take extra care. There is a doctor and mountain rescue team at Pico Espejo.

Around Mérida

Andean theme parks An enterprising *Andino* named Romer Alexis Montilla has turned his nostalgic dreams of a high mountain childhood into a string of ambitious theme parks and a movie about his own life. Very popular with Venezuelan tourists who pack out the places during peak holidays, there is plenty to see and learn on a half-day trip.

Los Aleros (*www.losaleros.net;* ☉ *09.00–18.00; admission US$30 adults, US$20 children 4–12*) A traditional village of adobe houses set out to recreate the Andes of the 1930s, complete with working radio station, cinema with silent films, newspaper office, bakery, restaurant and post office. The itinerant photographer is at work, as are wool spinners, school pupils and village barber. The setting is a wooded hillside at 2,150m. *Por puestos* take 30 minutes from Calle 26 in Mérida.

Venezuela de Antier (*www.lavenezueladeantier.net;* ☉ *09.00–19.00; admission US$30 adults, US$20 children 4–12*) 5km up the Mérida–Jají road, the same man who made Los Aleros created an equally successful park re-creating scenarios from all over Venezuela, this time in the 1920s' era when Juan Vicente Gómez was dictator. Visitors can sample regional dishes from around the country, listen to local bands playing harp music from the Llanos or drums in Barlovento, take part in a mock bullfight, see the devil dancing of Yare and dress up as the general for a period photo. Colourful sights include Indian dwellings from Amazonas, Guajira ladies dressed in long *mantas*, old Plaza Bolívar in Caracas, cockfights, even the Lake Maracaibo Bridge.

Montaña de Los Sueños (*www.montanadelossuenos.com;* ☉ *16.00–22.30; admission US$30 adults, US$20 children 4–12*) Near **Chiguará**, a charming little town 45km southwest of Mérida, is the third theme village dreamed up by Alexis Montilla, revolving around movie-making and taking advantage of several 1950s' buildings, including a cinema dating to the construction of Mérida's cable system under dictator Pérez Jiménez. A bus to **Chiguará** leaves from the main terminal in Mérida.

THE SIERRA NATIONAL PARKS

Sierra Nevada de Mérida The highest peaks in Venezuela rise south of Mérida's state capital. The chain culminates in **Pico Bolívar**, 5,007m (a bronze bust of the Liberator was placed up there in 1951). In a cluster to the east are **La Concha** (the Shell), also known as **La Garza** (the Heron), 4,922m; and **La Corona** (the Crown) whose two peaks, 4,942m and 4,883m, honour a pair of 19th-century naturalists, **Humboldt** and **Bonpland**, who never saw the Sierra Nevada. Continuing east is the Sierra de Santo Domingo where the massif of **Mucuñuque** reaches 4,672m. Directly west of Pico Bolívar is **Pico Espejo** (Mirror), 4,765m, served by the cable car system. Also to the west are **El Toro** (the Bull), 4,755m, and **El León** (the Lion), 4,740m.

These peaks form the spine of the Parque Nacional Sierra Nevada. The park covers 2,760km² stretching just east of Santo Domingo to El Morro in the west, and from close to the Chama River over the peaks to Barinas State at around 600m. The less-freqented Barinas slopes still have undisturbed cloudforest with deer, coatis, agoutis, porcupines, pumas and monkeys. Ornithologists have spotted the rare Andean cock-of-the-rock near cascading brooks, as well as crested quetzals, nightjars, cotingas and collared jays.

The moor-like *páramos* range from about 3,000m up to 4,300m; above this, the barren scree is called desert *páramo*. Perfect for hiking in fine weather, the *páramos* are open, windswept and largely treeless. But in hollows or by lakes such as the Laguna Negra grow thickets of short, red-trunked *coloradito* trees (*Polylepis sericea*). Their twisted branches shade lichens, ferns and dark green mosses shining with dew. Evergreen *coloradito* forests are not hangers-on from warmer times: they like the climate and are said to be among the highest-altitude trees in the world, up to 4,500m. However, their ecosystem, once axed, never regenerates. This is quoted as one reason why pine trees are used for reforestation despite being quite out of place.

Sierra del Norte or La Culata North of Mérida a mountain chain runs parallel to, and slightly lower than, the Sierra Nevada. It is called the Sierra del Norte or La Culata (the 'butt' or 'rear' because from Lake Maracaibo it is seen as the Andes' back). Its highest points are Piedras Blancas, 4,762m; Pan de Azúcar, 4,660m; Tucaní, 4,400m; and La Culata, 4,290m. In 1989 over 2,000km² of this northern range was declared a national park in an effort to halt degradation of habitat. The park stretches from near Timotes in the east to La Azulita in the west.

Ecosystems in the Parque Nacional Sierra de La Culata vary with altitude and climate, from rainforest at 400m to *páramos* so high and dry they are called desert *páramo*. Endangered species include the largest bird, the vanished condor now being reintroduced (see *Mifafí Condor Centre*, page 373), and the spectacled bear (*Tremarctos ornatus*), severely threatened by local hunters. A park study lists 59 mammal species and 61 reptiles and amphibians, including nine endemic frogs and toads. The park is also known for its endemic flora, particularly several *frailejón* species (see *The páramo, an Andean garden*, page 372).

These plants range from ground-hugging velvety rosettes to centuries-old trunks with tufted tops whose silhouettes reminded Spaniards of a procession of friars or *frailes*.

To reach the principal trailhead you can take one of the El Valle–La Culata buses whose Mérida terminal is on Calle 19 between Avenidas 1 and 2. **El Valle**, northeast of Mérida, is the name given to the Mucujún Valley. The road ends at the park in 25km. Along the way there are inns, small restaurants and a trout hatchery.

The hike into the park follows northeast to the top of the Mucujún River up a long stony path. Rain and fog are frequent here and the vegetation is dark and lush for the first hour's walking. The goal in another three hours is El Refugio, a bare-bones shelter at 3,700m altitude. The trail continues over stark *páramos* to Pan de Azúcar. Consult the trekking companies for this three-day trek, returning via Mucurubá or Mucuchíes.

Hiking the Sierras The two national parks, La Culata and Sierra Nevada, provide infinite opportunities for hiking. Ascents of Pico Bolívar or Pico Humboldt should not be attempted in wet months except by experts. According to interests (and weather), you can spend a week on the trails without retracing your route; you can cross the Sierra Nevada to Barinas and the plains, or cross Sierra de La Culata to the basin of Lake Maracaibo. Mérida has many expert mountain guides (who must be registered with both Inparques and Corpoturismo, and you can ask to see their

The Andes **MÉRIDA STATE**

15

carnet to prove this) for rock, ice or mountain climbing. In the event of an emergency, these are the people who know what to do. The two best known climbing associations are the **Grupo de Rescate** or GAR (✆ *0274 416 7811*) and the **Asociación Merideña de Andinismo** or AMA (✆ *0274 252 1666*). Trek operators are numerous and highly competitive (see *Tour operators*, page 361). Don't hesitate to ask them for advice; they give it freely. Better still, join one of the treks and get the advantage of their equipment and food.

Climbers and hikers are required to have at least one partner and to obtain a permit (US$1) from Inparques in Mérida by the cable car station or from the Inparques ranger stations at La Mucuy and Laguna de Mucubají, which also issue camping permits (US$1 per tent). Hikers heading out to high peaks should sign in before setting out and sign back out when returning as hikers have been lost in fog in the past, sparking search and rescue missions.

Weather The seasons – wet, called *invierno* (winter), and dry, called *verano* (summer) – are no longer predictable with some years having constant rain and others drought. It used to be accepted that light rains began in May and June, then trailed off, with the proper wet season lasting from August to November or December when storms buffet the *páramos* with snow, often melting on a sunny

THE *PÁRAMO*, AN ANDEAN GARDEN

To many plant-lovers the best time to see the Andes is October to December when the *páramos* are in bloom. Bees, butterflies and birds, even hummingbirds, revel in the bright floral tapestry. Insect pollination might seem a bit chancy at 3,000–4,000m, but the spectacular profusion of colours is a kind of over-compensation. One botanist compares the Andean *páramos* to the rhododendron belt of the Himalayas.

Some of the Andean flowers prized in Europe are the calceolaria with its yellow-pouched blooms, nasturtiums, quilted-leaved gesnerias, asters, clematis, saxifrage, gentian, salvia and befaria. Dotting the *páramos* are violet or yellow tabacotes (*Senecio sp.*), blue lupins (*Lupinus meridanus*) or chochos, white *páramo* chicory (*Hypochoeris*), yellow huesito shrubs (*Hypericum laricifolium*), red 'Spanish flag' (*Castilleja fissifolia*) related to the Indian paintbrush, and pale blue lobelias called avenita.

The contrasts of summer-by-day and winter-by-night require special adaptation. Some plants must resist not only sub-zero temperatures and wind but also radiation so intense that moisture is sucked into the atmosphere, stunting growth. Many species grow in a tight rosette or cushion form as protection against the elements. Others have specially adapted leaves – thick, hard-skinned, waxy or furry.

The best example is the *frailejón* (*Espeletia sp.*) found everywhere on the *páramos*. A velvety fluff covers the leaves, apparently giving the plant protection against sun, ice and evaporation, and leading local children to call the plants 'rabbit ears'. Most species of *frailejón* have rosettes of soft, silvery leaves and heads of yellow flowers that stick up out of the plant like the antennae of a triffid. One kind of *frailejón* lives at great elevations (4,500m) and takes the place of trees. It reaches 3m in height, growing at a rate of a few millimetres a year, and there is evidence that it lives for over 100 years. There are 65 endemic species of this daisy relative in Venezuela and some botanists believe that the genus originated in the Andean valleys surrounding Mérida and dispersed out from here.

From afar the tall, slightly bent stacks resemble chubby men dressed in brown, hence the name '*frailejón*' (big friar).

Reintroducing the condor to Mérida's skies is an old dream of María Rosa Cuesta who founded this breeding station in Mifafí at 3,550m with backing from the Banco Andino. The centre is off the Trans-Andean highway, 7km from the Pico El Aguila Monument and some 65km from Mérida. The entrance is less than a kilometre up the mountain by a rough track. The biggest structure is an enclosure for condors born in captivity and raised for release in the wild. After ten condors were released in 1996, donated by the San Diego zoo for this programme, they were surprisingly joined by two wild birds. This good news was later offset by the shooting of some released birds; a great setback. However, young condors hatched here are being successfully raised.

day. Campers may find the *invierno* to be wet and miserable or snowy and miserable. The dry season is traditionally from about December to April (sunny spells again in June and July). Then the Andes are at their most inviting, sunny and bright. December to February are the coldest months.

WARNING: Because of afternoon fog, it is best to start treks in the mornings. Night temperatures may plunge to freezing above 3,500m (for every 100m rise in altitude, the mercury drops about 0.6°C). By contrast, the midday temperatures may soar to over 30°C. You'll see that Andinos, even small children, have leathery faces burnt by sun and wind. Sunburn occurs at high altitudes because thin oxygen permits more radiation, so trekkers should use sunblock. Lack of oxygen may also cause mountain sickness, known as the *soroche* or *mal de páramo*. In the Andes, to feel depressed is to be *emparamado*. And 'to pass over the *páramo*', or '*pasar el páramo*', means to die. So go slowly, rest often and always take a light waterproof, warm fleece, head torch, some water, high energy snacks and extra food in case of accident or emergency.

Hiking trails

Los Nevados One of the most popular trails from the city of Mérida is to the mountain village of Los Nevados at 2,750m, a collection of old adobe houses along a steep central street clustered around a tiny church with excellent views over the valleys below. In this isolated village the only sounds are birdsong and the chatter of gossip in the tiny Plaza Bolívar in front of the picturesque church, with its tall bell tower dating to 1916. Founded in 1591 by the Spanish, the village makes a living from farming and tourism nowadays and a number of houses have been converted into *posadas* that serve meals. The only bar is in the Posada Bella Vista where you can enjoy the view and the fresh evening breeze with a few beers. Don't expect a big night out – most places are shut by 21.30 except on the feast day of San Isidro, when the village parties all night. There are two ways to reach Los Nevados. The easiest is to walk downhill from the *teleférico* station of **Loma Redonda** at 4,065m (when the cable car is in service) on a five-hour hike through the *páramo* past fresh mountain streams and *frailejónes*. There are also mules for hire at the start of the trail in Loma Redonda, if you don't fancy the walk. The trail itself is not difficult with an initial climb to the pass at 4,200m and then a descent all the way to Los Nevados. The trail can be tackled by any fit person with a little backpacking experience and the common sense to go slowly at high altitude. Take water, food, sunscreen, repellent, hat, waterproof and a fleece or something warm for the cold nights.

You get your first bird's-eye view of this enchanting little village about three hours from the pass. Once you've spotted the village the easiest route down is by way of the white cross to your right. You can buy a few basic necessities in the village's two shops, including beer and soft drinks.

The second way to reach the village is by jeep with **Línea Mérida–Los Nevados** (*Calle 24, Plaza Las Heroinas*), which costs about US$10 per seat for the four-hour journey on a steep dirt road that skirts the edge of the valley with some scary sheer drops in places. Jeeps leave Los Nevados very early in the morning and after lunch and depart from Mérida at 07.00 or when full.

Where to stay Things have changed a lot from the early days of tourism when the locals would pull out a cowhide and let hikers sleep on the floor. You can now get hot water, there's electricity and *posadas* provide evening meal and breakfast for US$15–30. The **Posada Bella Vista** (℡ *0274 416 9823;* m *0416 657 4909*) by the church has 12 rooms and the best views in town. **Guamanchi Expeditions** (*www.guamanchi.com*) also has a nice *posada* with 19 rooms and hammocks on a roofed terrace, where Zoraida and Jorge attend to guests. If you want a sense of what daily life is like you can also stay in more simple accommodation at the **Posada Buen Jesus** (℡ *0274 252 5696*), which has five rooms around a courtyard or the very rustic **Posada Florencia**, the very first house in town to offer lodging, run by Omar and Rosa, who still have no phone. Their kitchen with its wood stove is like stepping back in time.

Laguna Mucubají to Laguna Negra The one-hour walk from Laguna Mucubají, at 3,540m, to the beautiful Laguna Negra (Black Lagoon) is the easiest way to experience the Parque Nacional Sierra Nevada. The trail starts at the Inparques ranger station at the foot of Pico Mucunuque (4,672m), which dominates the skyline and the picture perfect Laguna Mucubají, where there is a camping site (US$1 per tent). From here well-marked paths lead to Laguna Negra, Laguna de los Patos, Laguna Victoria and the waterfalls and peak of Mucunuque.

You can walk to the Laguna Negra or go by mule or horse (US$7). The trail is easy enough to walk and it can easily be done in T-shirt and shorts on a sunny day, although afternoons can be less predictable in the coldest months of October–December when fog and freezing mist can drop quickly, so bring a waterproof, warm hat and fleece. The rainy season is also the blossom period for the *frailejónes*, when the drab highland tundra comes alive and is carpeted in the colours of these hardy flowers and shrubs that eke out a living here. From the visitor centre – the last place to enjoy a warming cup of hot chocolate – the trail takes you up through rolling fields of *frailejónes* into dense pine forest. These Canadian pines, an ongoing experiment by the Universidad de los Andes, were first planted in 1942 and have taken well to local conditions, although critics say they have edged out *páramo* plants. The pines end just before the last ascent, giving great views of the Barinas road and Pico Aguila. Laguna Negra is reached through an ancient stone gate, evidence of the importance of the mountain lakes to the pre-Columbian tribes who built it. Mountains, lakes and large stones had an important place in the mythology and beliefs of pre-Columbian people and there is archaeological evidence of offerings and sacrifices at the region's glacial lagoons. Looking down into the glassy, black waters of the lake it's easy to understand why local people still believe in the existence of spirits or *duendes* that live here and that they can cause sudden downpours if rudely disturbed. Think about that before you skim stones off the water… From the Laguna Negra it is an hour's walk up to the higher Laguna Los Patos.

To get to the park take a Barinas bus or *por puesto* from the main terminal in Mérida and ask to be set down on the main road by the park entrance. Start early, as *por puestos* back to Mérida from the junction at Apartaderos dry up after 16.00.

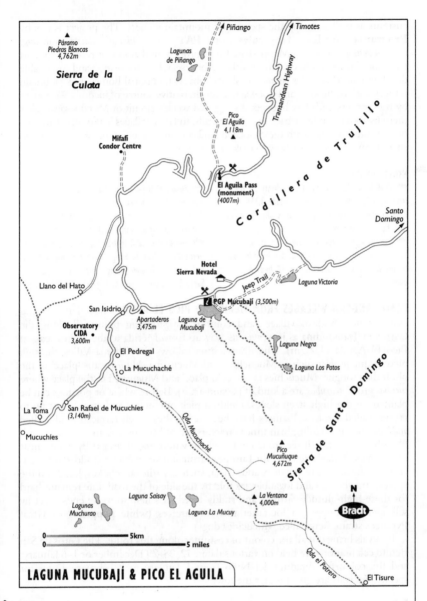

Piñango

Timotes

Páramo
Piedras Blancas
4,762m

Lagunas
de Piñango

**Sierra de la
Culata**

Pico
El Aguila
4,118m

Transandean Highway

Mifafí
Condor Centre

C o r d i l l e r a   d e   T r u j i l l o

El Aguila Pass
(monument)
(4007m)

Santo
Domingo

Hotel
Sierra Nevada

Jeep Trail

Laguna Victoria

Llano del Hato

PGP Mucubají (3,500m)

San Isidrio

Apartaderos
3,475m

Laguna de
Mucubají

Laguna Negra

Observatory
CIDA
3,600m

El Pedregal

Laguna Los Patos

La Mucuchaché

S i e r r a   d e   S a n t o   D o m i n g o

La Toma

San Rafael de Mucuchíes
(3,140m)

Qda Mucuchaché

Mucuchíes

Pico
Mucuñuque
4,672m

N

La Ventana
4,000m

Lagunas
Muchurao

Laguna Saisay

Laguna La Mucuy

Bradt

0 ———————— 5km
0 ———————— 5 miles

Qda el Potrero

El Tisure

LAGUNA MUCUBAJÍ & PICO EL AGUILA

Where to stay

Hotel Sierra Nevada (10 rooms) ☎ 0274 888 0075. An old standby since the 1970s, about 800m from the entrance to Lake Mucubají. Rooms with private bathroom, hot shower & some heating. The attached Restaurante Mucubají is often closed in low season (late Sep–Nov). Ⓢ

High valley trails to Mucuposadas Designed as a way to promote regional tourism and pump tourist dollars into the most remote farming communities in the high valleys, the Mucuposadas are traditional Andean farmhouses refurbished with beds and other facilities to accommodate overnight stays. Trails between the Mucuposadas allow hikers to spend several days up in the *páramo* getting to know local people and customs as well as seeing the spectacular mountain scenery. The project is run by **Programa Andes Tropicales** or **PAT** (e *ekkaia@andestropicales.org; www.andestropicales.org*), a Mérida-based non-profit foundation that receives support from the European Union, among others, for research, conservation and sustainable development. PAT helps *páramo* residents convert traditional homes into mountain refuges with bathrooms and hot water as an alternative source of income. Welcomed by backpackers with low budgets, a suggested week's circuit of Mucuposadas takes them by foot or on horseback over mule trails, to lakes, villages and peaks. A unique opportunity to lodge with these isolated Andean families, enjoying opportunities to share home life, learning how to make *arepas* or milk the cow.

⌂ Where to stay

⌂ **El Nidal del Gavilán** (the Hawk's Nest) On the road from Mucuchíes to Misintá, altitude 3,358m, Rosa de Balza & her son Juan Carlos offer 2 rooms with bunks, 1 with dbl bed. $

⌂ **Posada Agüita Azul** High above La Toma in Sector El Banco, altitude 3,400m, this *posada* run by Iris & José Eliseo Sánchez has 10 beds & bunks. $

⌂ **Posada El Trigal** In the hamlet of Mitibibó, altitude 3,400m, below the observatory of Llano del Hato, Irene & Venancio Sánchez pioneered the Mucuposada circuit with this 4-room *posada*. $

⌂ **Posada Michicabá** In Gavidia, at 3,350m, Rosalía Hernández & Rómulo Rangel have 2 rooms with dbl bed & bunks, & offer hiking to the high Laguna Santo Cristo, the largest of Mérida's glacial lakes. $

TRANS-ANDEAN VILLAGES FROM MÉRIDA TO PICO EL AGUILA

Travellers will find easily visited Andean villages and comfortable stopping points all along the Carretera Transandina as it weaves its way up from Mérida to the highest pass at Pico El Aguila (4,007m). The Transandina follows the Chama Valley through picturesque *pueblos* such as Mucuchíes and Mucurubá. *Mucu* means 'place' in the old Indian tongue: Mucuchíes is 'the cold place' and Mucurubá is 'the place where *curubas* grow' (*curubas* are a kind of passion-fruit). Before wheat or potatoes can be planted on the high steep slopes, children pick out stones and stack them up to create walled terraces. Farmers have been using these high terraced fields called *andenes* since pre-Columbian times. Tractors are of little use, so men or oxen pull ploughs. You can still see stone circles where wheat was threshed by horses near Mucuchíes. Today's demand for European fruit and vegetables has added different crops to the staples of potatoes and wheat, such as garlic, artichokes, leeks and the apples, strawberries and loganberries sold by the side of the road. Life remains hard for these high-altitude farmers and ruddy-faced kids help to make ends meet by selling fluffy puppies a lot fatter than themselves (white puppies of a Great Pyrenees strain, here called Mucuchíes dogs).

Festivals bring out all the colour of costumes along this route. The Giros de San Benito celebrations are held on various dates: 12, 28–29 December or 1–6 January; and the colourful Paradura del Niño from 1 January to 2 February. Dates for specific festivals are given under the towns.

Tabay Only 12km from Mérida, Tabay was founded in 1689 on lands of the Tabay Indians and maintains vestiges of its colonial character. A large twin-towered church (whose chimes are digital recordings) dominates the plaza shaded by Australian casuarina pines. From Plaza Bolívar *por puestos* go to the entrance to the national park (and campground) at **La Mucuy** (2,130m). Here there is an Inparques office and trails to the highest peaks begin, via the mountain lakes of Laguna Coromoto (3,200m), Laguna Verde (4,000m), Laguna el Suero (4,200m) and then on to the glacier and the ascent to Pico Bolívar (5,007m). The hike from La Mucuy ranger station to Laguna Coromoto can be done in a morning if you start early and takes you through thick rainforest with excellent birding.

For a swim and sauna visit the **hot springs** or *aguas termales* above Tabay. You can hike 40 minutes up by way of a track to the left of the cemetery; ask in town, it's a popular spot with locals at weekends.

Both Tabay and **La Mucuy Baja** across the Chama River are famous for wood craftsmen and naïve sculptors, some of whose work has been exhibited internationally. Look out for the carvings of virgins, saints and Venezuelan generals favoured by the local *artesanos santeros* and blocks of wood whittled into bottle-shaped triptychs of saints.

Where to stay

Cabañas Xinia & Peter (16 rooms, 6 cabins) La Mucuy Baja; \ 0274 283 0214; m 0416 874 7698, 0414 975 7319; e xiniaypeter@hotmail.com; www.xiniaypeter.com. A touch of luxury in the mountains. Peter Lauterbach who is something of a gourmet & his wife Xinia, an artist, have created this complex of beautiful cottages filled with fine details, from paintings gracing the walls to comfortable sofas & landscaped gardens. Cabins have kitchen diners & guests who want meals can eat b/fast & dinner at their Gazebo restaurant. A programme of day tours covers Mérida State from the condor centre & astrophysical observatory, a hike or horse ride to Laguna Negra, to La Victoria coffee *hacienda*, Jají & the Pueblos del Sur. These form the base of a vacation package with all meals. Xinia & Peter speak English & German. $$

Posada Doña Rosa (10 rooms) La Joya-El Arenal, 5km west of Tabay; \ 0274 252 8355; e posadadonarosa@hotmail.com; www.andes.net/ donarosa. This delightful guesthouse occupies the 140-year-old *hacienda* house called La Mesa that served as the cable car offices during the building of the *teleférico*. The big quadrangle has been reconditioned with rooms around the central patio, all with hot water bathrooms. Price includes b/fast & supper. There are stables, a swimming pool & hiking trails up to the first station of the *teleférico*. For the more energetic, paragliding & bungee jumping can be arranged. One of the owners, María Rosa Cuesta, who speaks English, is an ornithologist involved in reintroducing the condor to the Venezuelan Andes. $$

Posada Casa Vieja (7 rooms) El Paramito, 1km from Tabay on the Transandina; \ 0274 417 1489; m 0414 179 8541; e info@casa-vieja-merida.com; www.casa-vieja-merida.com. Close to the hot springs & the entrance to the Parque Nacional Sierra Nevada, this beautiful 18th-century house is run by German birdwatching enthusiast Joe Klaiber & his Peruvian wife Alejandra. A favourite with twitchers because of the gardens, which attract hummingbirds, & access to nearby birding trails, it offers comfortable B&B rooms with bath, hot water, cable TV. Joe has recorded the songs of 100 local birds & organises trips to see endemics, such as the Andean cock-of-the-rock, & quetzals, trogons & antpittas. Highly recommended as a base for hikes to nearby colonial towns & lakes. Transfers, plane tickets & circuits of Venezuela arranged through Joe's travel agency Caiman Tours. Buses to Los Aleros from Mérida bus terminal pass by the door. $

Posada La Casa de La Mano Poderosa (4 rooms, hammocks) San Rafael de Tabay, la Plazuela; m 0416 576 5636; e lamanopoderosa@gmail.com; www.lamanopoderosa.com. An old, tile-roofed *posada* aimed at European trekkers about 1.5km from the bus stop at la Plazuela near San Rafael de Tabay, reached on foot down a 300m jeep-only path. There's a laid-back hippy vibe on the open verandas with hammocks all around to take in the view. The rooms for 2–6 people have dbl beds, bunks, & shared bathrooms. The *posada* is run by Venezuelan & French trekking operators passionate about paragliding, rafting, climbing & horse trekking. Ask about excursions. $

Cacute Take a look around this old riverside village on a left fork towards the Chama River, where villagers are proud of their restored colonial centre. Their big popular events are a religious celebration of the Christ Child, the *Festividad del Santo Niño de Cacute* on 12 January, and week-long fiestas around San Isidro's day, 15 May, involving processions with horses and oxen.

Where to stay

Posada Tasca La Casa Grande (8 rooms) In the village centre; \ 0274 511 4202; m 0416 874 9813. The rooms occupy 3 sides of a quadrangle, with cane ceilings, tree-trunk bedsteads, hot showers, dbl & bunk beds for 2–6 people. On the 4th side is the restaurant, open in peak season only, & a *tasca*. $

Mucurubá This is the next village on the Trans-Andean highway with its Plaza Bolívar and square-towered blue and white church facing the road. The Fiesta de las 19,000 Velas (it began with *mil* (a thousand) candles) draws more and more people every year bearing candles on the feast day of La Virgen de la Inmaculada Concepción. Watch out on 8 December when the fiesta chaotically blocks all car (and people) traffic.

Where to stay

Aposentos del Baquiano (17 rooms) 4km south of Mucurubá; m 0416 674 9329; e posada_elbaquiano@hotmail.com; www.alexismontilla.com. The creator of the Los Aleros theme park, Alexis Montilla, has now moved into *posadas* with this old Andean-style tile-roofed house. Rooms have 4-poster beds, hot water, bathtub & traditional Andean dishes are served at tables around a courtyard. $$

Monocoque This hamlet has one of the oldest trout farms in Mérida **Truchicultura Moconoque** (open to visitors) and a centuries-old house where, on his 1813 march, Simón Bolívar is said to have been given Nevado, a Mucuchíes dog bred here, which was his faithful canine companion, staying by his side until it was killed by a lance on the battlefield in 1821. These dogs, descended from Pyrenean mastiffs brought to Venezuela over 400 years ago by Augustinian friars, are sold by the side of the road here and in Mucuchíes by children who hold them up as you drive past.

Mucuchíes This village (altitude 2,980m), 7km from San Rafael, was founded in 1596 around a large Indian community. In its streets around the church on Plaza Bolívar popular and religious rites take place, such as the blessing of oxen on the morning of 24 November, the many Christmas observances, and on 28–29 December the whirling Giros de San Benito. Honouring the black saint, men in white wearing black face paint and streams of coloured ribbons dance in intricate patterns, revolving around a pole.

Where to stay

Castillo San Ignacio (30 rooms) At the town's entrance; 0274 872 0021; www.hotelcastillosanignazio.com. You can't miss the turreted stone battlements of this *Shrek*-style fantasy castle. True, it is an eyesore, but it is also royally decorated inside with antiques, carvings & timbered dining hall. The suites, all different, are sold in B&B packages. $$$

Hotel Restaurant Carillón (20 rooms) Av Carabobo; 0274 872 0160. Next to a stone-clad restaurant of some renown, this small hotel is decked out with elegant furnishings & vast bedrooms with high ceilings, antique touches & suites with jacuzzi. $$

San Rafael de Mucuchíes The village (altitude 3,140m) is famous for the rough stone chapel that local artist Juan Félix Sánchez (1900–97) built at the entrance in honour of La Virgen de Coromoto. This devout self-taught man made the chapel stone by stone with his bare hands when he was in his eighties, earning him the National Prize for Art (1989). The house he shared with his wife Epifania is now a little museum where you can see the blankets he wove. Sánchez's first chapel in El Tisure, 12 km away, is even more astonishing but can only be visited by hiking up the Mucuchache Valley, and you need a tent to camp out the night. Ask in the local shops about renting mules to El Tisure or for directions to the start of the trail.

Where to stay

Posada Llano de Trigo (10 rooms) Micarache; 0274 262 2992; m 0414 745 8613; e llanodetrigo@hotmail.com. Up past the Páramo de Gavidia at 3,200m this attractive & remote *posada* with its stone walls, cane ceilings & indoor heating, combines valley views with comfort &

simplicity. Rooms with hot water & all meals sold in a package. The road to this *posada* leaves the Trans-Andean highway at the last curve before Mucuchíes, descending to the bridge across the Chama & rising to the village of Gavidia, 30mins by jeep. Then it is another 5mins east to Micarache, a tiny village complete with church, plaza, school & medical dispensary. The owners offer transportation from Mérida. $$

🏠 **Posada San Rafael del Paramo** (14 rooms) ☎ 0274 872 0938; e posadasanrafaeldelparamo@ hotmail.com. As you leave the *pueblo* at the northern end, this reconstructed old Andean house dating to 1868 once belonged to Juan Félix Sánchez's father & is full of rustic details & traditional local artworks & carvings. Rooms with hot water, heaters & balconies that overlook the valley. Restaurant serves b/fast in high season. Owners Mary & Omar Monsalve can arrange horseriding excursions. $

The **Mesa Redonda Ecological Refuge** (*adjacent to the Páramo Piedras Blancas Biological Reserve with access by a narrow road up the mountain above La Toma at the last curve & little bridge before Mucuchíes;* $) can be booked through Andes Tropicales in Mérida (*www.andestropicales.org*). Usually, a minimum of six people per group is required. The refuge makes a great base for *páramo* hikers who enjoy spectacular views of the Sierra Nevada. At 3,750m, the house was built simply of dry stone by experts in the old Andean ways. It has solar power, modern kitchen and hot water, private baths. There are two comfortable, heated double rooms and one with seven two-tier bunks. Campers are also welcome.

Apartaderos Literally a crossroads, Apartaderos is just below the fork in the road, with one branch heading on to Timotes and Valera in Trujillo over the pass at Pico el Aguila and the other to Santo Domingo and Barinas. There are several hotels and souvenir shops here. At the lower end is the town of **San Isidro** (altitude 3,342m, average temperature 6°C). The village church draws throngs on 29 January as farmers bring their oxen, horses and dogs to the plaza to be blessed on the *Fiesta de San Benito*. Horse races are the high point of the festivities.

Where to stay

🏠 **Residencias Parque San Isidro** (4 cabins) ☎ 0274 888 0012. Down a short driveway, the splendid cottages accommodate 3–5 people, with fireplace, nicely equipped kitchen, hot water. Call in advance. $$

🏠 **Refugio Turístico Mifafi** (20 rooms, 9 cabins) ☎ 0274 888 0131; e refugioturisticomifafi@ hotmail.com. Simple rooms with hot showers adjacent to a large restaurant serving Andean dishes. $

Observatory In the Sierra del Norte, at 3,600m, is the three-domed observatory run by the **Centro de Investigaciones de Astronomía**, or **CIDA** (☎ 0274 245 0106; *www.cida.ve*). The observatory is open to the public on some weekends in holiday periods but there is no public transport and you should call in advance if planning a trip to avoid disappointment. It has four optical telescopes, a Schmidt camera with 1m-diameter lens, and a library open for consultation. Through a computer-aided search of images recorded on the night of 15 March 2000, a team of astronomers from Yale and Indiana universities and the Universidad de Los Andes spotted a new minor planet, or planetoid, in the outer fringes of the solar system between Neptune and Pluto. They dubbed it Plutino, as it measures 650km in diameter, a quarter of Pluto's size. It will take Plutino some 243 years to complete its orbit of the sun.

CIDA is reached by an entrance road west of the Trans-Andean highway, 3km from the Apartaderos junction towards Pico El Aguila.

From the observatory it is 2km down to **Llano del Hato**, the highest town in Venezuela at 3,510m. By way of a fair, although narrow, road you can continue

15

southwest from Llano del Hato to rejoin the Carretera Transandina at La Toma just east of Mucuchíes.

Pico El Aguila Standing at 4,007m, Pico El Aguila is often blanketed in snow and has an average temperature of 6°C. It's all the more impressive when you discover that the monument (whose bronze bird is not an eagle but a condor) marks the passage in 1813 of Bolívar's poorly equipped, half-frozen army on its way from taking Mérida to liberate Caracas. The tourist *parador* or stopping place, Páramo Aguila, is a good place to catch your breath and warm up with a hot chocolate. If you lack time or the right transportation, try in any case to hike as far as the CANTV antennas on Pico El Aguila, 2km, to see the remarkable stands of tall, ancient *frailejónes* growing well above tree level.

Jají A whitewashed colonial village with a pleasant climate at 1,780m, Jají was founded in 1610 by Bartolomé Gil Naranjo and completely reconstructed in the 1960s.

There are inns, restaurants, craft and souvenir shops. Although quiet in the low season, traffic builds up during holidays and fiestas. There are three important feast days with processions: 15 May, San Isidro Labrador; 25 July, St James's Day – Santiago Apostol; and 24 September, the feast day of Jají's patron saint San Miguel Arcángel.

Regular buses leave from the main terminal in Mérida to cover the 43km (US$1).

🏠 Where to stay

🏠 **Posada Aldea Vieja** (7 rooms, 5 cabins) ✆ 0274 266 0072; m 0414 717 3137; e reservaciones@ aldeavieja.com; www.aldeavieja.com. Half a block south of Plaza Bolívar, this 2-storey whitewashed *posada* with wooden balconies has a good restaurant on an outer terrace. Large rooms on 2nd floor have en-suite hot showers, cable TV. $$

🏠 **Posada Araguaney** (5 rooms) Plaza Bolívar; ✆ 0274 417 4028. Rooms with hot shower at the rear of a craft shop. $

🏠 **Posada de Jají** (6 rooms) Opposite the church; ✆ 0274 416 6333. A typical 2-storey Andean house, with a bar & restaurant (⏰ 09.00–21.00). Upstairs rooms with hot showers, TV, fan. $

🏠 **Posada Papá Miguel** (10 rooms) ✆ 0274 417 4315; m 0414 654 2438; e posadapapamiguel@ hotmail.com. Owned & attended by the genial Señora Arminda, whose grandfather was Papá Miguel, this lovely old complex of buildings is in La Mesa de Los Indios, about 8.5km from Jají, an area of coffee hills known for its excellent hot springs. A dining room, café & *tasca* are set around the courtyard & a new 2-storey structure in the same Andean style with balcony has rooms with bath & hot water. A 3-night plan includes outings to hot springs & the Pueblos del Sur, & evening sessions by local storytellers & musicians. $

Lagunillas Just north of the Trans-Andean highway, southwest of Mérida, is Lagunillas, the first village founded in the Andes in 1558. Visit the **Laguna de Urao**, a shallow lake fed by subterranean waters. It was declared a Natural Monument for its local importance as a source of soda crystals (*urao*), a key ingredient of *chimó*, a kind of spicy chewing tobacco used since prehistoric times. The viscous black tobacco paste is still used by old-timers, who put it between the lip and gum as a nicotine stimulant and to stave off cold and hunger.

Buses from Mérida take about 30 minutes (US$1) from the terminal.

TRUJILLO STATE

The great Andean chain descends from its peaks in Mérida State to the mountains of Trujillo, a state that offers a northeasterly approach to the Andes within easy distance of Barquisimeto. Foreign travellers rarely visit this part of the country, which is popular with Venezuelan pilgrims visiting the birthplace of famous doctor and folk saint José Gregorio Hernández in Isnotú and the giant concrete statue of the Virgin Mary towering over Trujillo. Those who do come will find Andean villages stuck in a time warp such as Burbusay, Niquitao, Santa Ana and San Miguel reached by country roads winding over hills cultivated with coffee and pineapple. They are worth seeing by bus, car or bike. Called the 'garden of Venezuela' Boconó has pleasant rural hotels. Flowers and vegetables grow well as farmers rely on two rainy periods: April–June and August––November. Trujillo is bordered by Lara, Zulia, Mérida and the Llanos states of Barinas and Portuguesa. The capital is Trujillo, a small city surrounded by mountains, but the largest city is Valera.

VALERA (*Telephone code: 0271*) A hot, bustling commercial centre, Valera is the biggest city in Trujillo State (population 240,000). It was founded on an alluvial terrace in the broad Motatán Valley (altitude 540m), first as a parish in 1819 and then as a town in 1860. There's not much to see or do in this modern city but some travellers may want to lodge in Valera as it is convenient for the state's only airport, and for destinations along the Pan American and Trans-Andean highways. The smaller, cooler and more colonial state capital of Trujillo (36km) makes a better base for exploring. Valera has several decent hotels, pleasant plazas and shopping malls. **Plaza Bolívar** is between Calles 7 and 8, three blocks west of Avenida Bolívar. The **Iglesia de San Juan Bautista** is on the plaza's south side. Walk south on Avenida Bolívar to the **Plaza de Los Estados** shopping mall flying the banners of Pan American nations. In the shopping centre are craft booths, an outdoor café and a tourist information stand on the first floor. However, this and other tourism modules in the airport (7km north) and bus terminal only operate at holiday times.

Getting there

By air Aeropuerto Nacional Antonio Nicolás Briceño on Avenida Principal la Hoyada is 4km northeast of the centre of Valera. Currently, there is only one scheduled daily midday flight to Caracas (1 hour 10 minutes, US$70) with the state airline Conviasa (*www.conviasa.aero*).

By bus The interstate bus terminal is about 1km southeast of downtown 7. There are regular buses to Caracas (9 hours, US$19), mainly leaving at night, stopping at Barquisimeto or Maracay for early morning arrival in La Bandera. Buses to Barquisimeto (US$8), Maracaibo (US$8) and Mérida (US$9) via the Carretera Transandina, leave throughout the day.

Buses for the Carretera Transandina route and Jajó leave from Avenida 4 at Calle 7, known as the 'Punto de Mérida'. *Por puestos* service the routes to Trujillo (35 minutes, US$1) and Boconó (2 hours, US$3.50).

By car Valera is reached from Mérida on the Route 7 highway, along the Carretera Transandina, in about four to five hours. From there the road continues on to Barquisimeto.

Tourist information The office for **Fondo Turismo de Trujillo** (*www.fondoturismotrujillo.com.ve*) is in Avenida Bolívar between Calles 10 and 11.

⌂ **Where to stay** Hotel space, inclined to be tight on weekdays, is at a premium during the last half of August when Valera hosts the state-wide Feria Agrícola.

Flamingo Palace (30 rooms) ☎ 0271 225 2815; e hotelflamingopalace@hotmail.com. Restaurant, bar, motel-style rooms. $$

Hotel Camino Real (60 rooms) Av 5 Independencia; ☎ 0271 225 2815; e hcr@hotelcaminoreal.com.ve; www.hotelcaminoreal.com.ve. A tall, brightly painted 10-storey tower with rooftop restaurant & *tasca* with good views. Rooms with AC, hot water, cable TV, parking. $$

Hotel Hidrotermal San Rafael Hot springs (13 rooms) ☎ 0271 249 2934. Contact the Camino Real (above) as it has the same owners. The hot spring waters of the Aguas Termales Motatán were discovered by accident in 1945 by an oil firm drilling exploratory wells. The waters are piped directly into the swimming pool of the hotel & the rooms, which have AC, some with showers & others with tubs for soaking. Also cabins for 2–6 people. Professional massages & spa services are provided by the Heisi Institute. Non-guests may use the pool for a small daily fee, making a pleasant outing from Valera. An informal restaurant serves food at w/ends. About 12km northwest of Valera via Motatán, follow the signs for 'El Baño'. $$

Hotel Valera (140 rooms) Calle 6 with Av Bolívar; ☎ 0271 225 7511. 5 blocks west of the bus terminal, rooms have AC, hot water, cable TV, restaurant. $$

Aurora (40 rooms) Av Bolívar at Calles 10–11; ☎ 0271 231 5675. The best of the budget hotels in the centre. Rooms with AC, decent restaurant. $

Other practicalities There is a Banco de Venezuela with an ATM on Avenida 10 where it intersects with Calle 8 in front of Plaza Bolívar, and another in the CC Pineda shopping mall on Avenida México, on the corner with Calle Americo Briceño.

There is a CANTV call centre with internet and international calls in the CC Jabreco shopping mall on Avenida 9, between Calle 8 and Calle 9.

Several pharmacies in the centre stay open late and the Hospital Central de Valera is on Calle 6.

ISNOTÚ – BIRTHPLACE OF JOSÉ GREGORIO HERNÁNDEZ A little town 15km northwest of Valera, Isnotú owes its fame to Doctor José Gregorio Hernández who was born here on 26 October 1864. Pilgrims come to Isnotú by the hundreds on weekends and by the thousands on the anniversary of the good doctor's birth, as well as on the feast day of Santa Rosalía on 7 October. José Gregorio grew up in Isnotú where he helped his father raise six younger children upon his mother's death when he was nine. A humble, devout doctor, he is one of Venezuela's best-loved figures for his work among the poor in Caracas, whom he treated for free, often buying the medicines himself. A small, neat man with a moustache, he cuts a Charlie Chaplinesque figure with his black suit and trilby hat, his arms behind his back or carrying an umbrella as he hurries on his rounds to patients and hospitals. Tragically killed in a car accident in 1919 by one of the first cars in Caracas, his fame grew as a worker of miracles, and he is widely regarded as a saint by Catholics and followers of the Cult of María Lionza (see *Chapter 14, Yaracuy and Lara*, page 344). In 1985 the Catholic Church elevated him to the status of Venerable.

His statue in front of the memorial chapel in Isnotú is heaped with flowers and surrounded by candles and testimonials to cures. A small museum by the church displays his bed and personal belongings. Paintings portray his life: as a medical student at the Central University of Venezuela, as a brilliant researcher in Paris where he studied under leading specialists and as a doctor in Caracas. A pioneer of modern medicine in Venezuela, the young doctor taught experimental physiology and bacteriology on his return to Caracas in 1891. A fervent Catholic, he twice attempted to enter the Church, once in a monastery in Italy in 1908 and again in 1913 when he entered a seminary in Rome to become a priest; both attempts were ended by poor health. He continued to receive mass daily and was known to have offered his life to God in exchange for an end to the Great War in Europe. In fact, the day he was killed by a car, 29 June 1919, was the day after the signing of the Versailles peace treaty.

Where to stay

🏠 **Hospedaje Popular** (3 rooms) Calle La Paz; ☎ 0271 663 2446. A dorm-style place that charges for the bed. Rooms with bath & cold water. $

🏠 **Posada Turistica El Parque** (4 rooms) Av 3 with Calle 1; ☎ 0271 663 2408; 📱 0416 403 2921. Dbl rooms in a pleasant family-run *posada* with AC,

bath, hot water & cable TV. $

🏠 **Posada Turistica Isnotú** (12 rooms) On the plaza; ☎ 0271 554 6934. Forms a complex with restaurant, shops & a post office. Large, no-nonsense rooms with hot water, fan, TV, are aimed at pilgrims & sleep up to 6, extra beds can be added. $

TRUJILLO (*Telephone code: 0272*) The state capital was one of Venezuela's first settlements, founded in 1558 and moved seven times before arriving at its final site in 1570 in the Valley of the Mucas, sandwiched between steep green hills. Its official name is Nuestra Señora de La Paz de Trujillo – named after Trujillo in Spain, birthplace of the conquistador Diego García de Paredes who came to Venezuela after taking part in the conquest of Mexico with Hernán Cortés and Peru with Francisco Pizarro. The town's early importance arose from the wheat and hides produced here and shipped to Curaçao, and from its strategic position on the trade route between the Llanos and the ports of Lake Maracaibo which exported cacao and Varinas tobacco sought after by Dutch, English, French and German consumers. At 958m, Trujillo is warm, unhurried and provincial. Unlike its bigger rival Valera, it has little in the way of commerce and only 50,000 residents. The old town has only two long streets, Avenida Independencia leading up the narrow valley and Avenida Bolívar leading down, with Plaza Bolívar and Plaza Sucre in between.

Getting there

By bus Intercity buses and *por puestos* stop at Plaza Bolívar on their way to the bus terminal, 2.5km north of the historic centre. There are regular buses to Valera (US$1.30, 40 minutes) and a few night buses to Caracas (US$15, 10 hours), although it's quicker to travel to Valera and on to Caracas from there.

By car Trujillo is reached via the main Route 7 highway between Valera and Barquisimeto.

Tourist information The **Corporacion Trujillana de Turismo** (☎ *0272 236 6151*; ⊕ *08.00–17.00 Mon–Fri*) is in La Plazuela, 3km from Trujillo on the Valera road.

Where to stay

🏠 **Hotel Country Trujillo** (52 rooms) Av Carmona; ☎ 0271 236 3576; e trujillo@hotelcountry.com.ve; www.hotelcountry.com.ve. Pleasant & well-maintained old house on 2 floors with a restaurant, disco, swimming pool with slide, poolside restaurant. Rooms with hot water, AC, fridge. There is a park along the river in front. The best place in town, so call ahead to book. $$

🏠 **Hotel La Paz** (26 apts) Av Carmona, Calle 15; ☎ 0271 236 4864. Roomy economical apts with bath, hot water, refrigerator (no kitchen) in a 7-storey block. $

🏠 **Hotel Los Gallegos** (32 rooms) 65 Av Independencia; ☎ 0272 233 3193; 📱 0416 979 5338; e hotellosgallegos@hotmail.com. A block from the Centro de Historia, this the best value for clean rooms with bath, hot water, cable TV. $.

🏠 **Posada La Troja-El Portal del Encanto** (9 rooms) 1.3km from Trujillo towards La Virgen de la Paz; ☎ 0272 236 0292; 📱 0414 971 2990, 0414 723 1959. An attractive rustic inn & restaurant (⊕ *09.00–21.00 Wed–Sun*), built & attended by the friendly owners. Rooms have dbl beds, bath, hot water, TV, some with bunk beds & upper sleeping lofts. $

✘ **Where to eat** Try **Valle Los Mukas**, an attractive patio restaurant in a colonial house on Calle 11 near Avenida Bolívar; or **El Damasquino** and **Pastas Mama Mía** on Avenida 19 de Abril. There are two vegetarian restaurants on Avenida Colón: the **Alcachofa** and the **Girasol**.

Other practicalities There is a Banco de Venezuela with an ATM at Calle Independencia, on the corner with Calle Colón.

A CANTV call centre with internet and international phone calls is located at the intersection of Avenida Bolívar and Calle Comercio on Plaza Bolívar.

What to see and do You can see Trujillo's colonial past in the low houses with tiled roofs around the tree-lined Plaza Bolívar.

Cathedral The cathedral was built in 1662 and is a traditional squat, whitewashed colonial edifice with a bell tower on one side and a very simple interior that sets off the Baroque gilt altarpiece perfectly.

Convento Regina Angelorum On the northeast corner of Plaza Bolívar and Miranda, this is a former convent converted into a public library. The building dates from the early 1600s and has an impressive central courtyard.

Casa del Decreto de Guerra, or Centro de Historia (*Av Independencia, 1½ blocks up from Plaza Bolívar;* ⊕ *09.00–12.00 & 14.00–17.00 Mon–Sun; admission free*) A restored colonial house with traditional kitchen housing weapons, antiques, maps and mementos of the Independence wars. It was in this house in 1813 that Simón Bolívar decreed a 'War to the Death' to all enemies of the revolution including prisoners. You can see the table he used for signing the decree, and his bed.

Museo Salvador Valero (*Av Carmona, university campus;* \ *0271 236 4870; admission free*) Famous for hosting a big biennial show, on even years, of naïve art and crafts called Arte Popular. The state is home to many self-taught potters, weavers and carvers and the show is open also to artists from abroad.

Virgen de La Paz (⊕ *09.00–17.00; admission US$1.50*) The colossal concrete statue of the Virgin Mary, known as La Virgen de La Paz because of the dove of peace she holds in her hand, is Trujillo's most famous landmark and stands atop a hill at 1,700m overlooking the city. Designed by Manuel de la Fuente and erected in 1983, the concrete monument has internal stairs with 226 steps for those who want a bird's-eye view from the dove or the Virgin's hand, waist or eye. At 46.7m, this is the tallest statue of the Virgin Mary in the world, standing as tall as the Statue of Liberty. On the right day there are incredible views as far as Lake Maracaibo and the Sierra Nevada. *Por puestos* from a stop opposite Hotel Trujillo at the top end of town take 20 minutes to cover the 11km to the base of the statue.

JAJÓ Less than 10km from the highway is a lovely village safely tucked a million miles away from modern Venezuela. Founded in 1611, Jajó is set at 1,796m among terraced farms, flowers and eucalyptus trees. It is still delightfully off the beaten track. Simple white houses with red roofs line cobbled streets curving down to the plaza and church built in 1990. Buses from Valera take an hour and a half to cover the 48km (US$1) to Jajó through mountain valleys.

🏠 **Where to stay**

🏠 **Posada de Jajó** (6 rooms) Plaza de Jajó; \ 0271 414 4143, 0271 225 2977. A balconied old house on the south side of the plaza, also known as the Posada de Amparo for the Señora Amparo Carrillo who runs it. Basic rooms with hot water. Meals cooked by arrangement. $

🏠 **Posada Marysabel** (8 rooms) Calle Páez (Real); \ 0271 511 7947; m 0416 171 9687;

www.posadamarysabel.com.ve. Simple rooms for up to 5 people, with hot shower, TV. Marysabel & her husband Jesús also run the restaurant downstairs & a *tasca* in the cellar; ask for a *calentaito*, a local drink prepared with spices & alcohol fit to warm your heart. Enquire here about renting a 4-bedroom colonial house on the plaza. $

What to see Local lore and antiques are gathered by Pedro Sánchez in his **Museo Casa Colonial** on Calle Real. Peace and quiet are interrupted during the annual fiesta on **San Pedro's Day**, 29 June, and the nearest weekend, when locals join processions and the San Beniteros perform traditional dances such as the Sebucán.

NIQUITAO Nestling in a high valley at 1,917m, Niquitao is a mountain village with cobbled streets founded in 1625 by two Spanish brothers who daringly brought their wives with them to the New World.

Niquitao is some 62km from Jajó. There are frequent jeeps to **Boconó** (25km, US$1.50) a 'garden town' on the main route from Guanare in the Llanos to the city of Trujillo, passing centuries-old mountain towns such as **San Miguel**, **Santa Ana** and **Burbusay**.

Where to stay

Posada Turística Niquitao (16 rooms) Plaza Bolívar; \ 0271 885 2042; m 0416 771 7860; e posadaniquitao@yahoo.com. Besides a popular restaurant known for Andean specialities, Sr Enriques & his wife maintain a family museum with archaeological & historical relics. Rooms with private bath, hot water, cable TV. They organise excursions to the Teta de Niquitao & Pico Güiriguay. Food for guests by arrangement only, so call ahead if you want an evening meal on day of arrival. $$

What to see and do The church on Plaza Bolívar is called San Rafael de La Piedrita after a small stone that was found in the hills bearing a painted likeness of the saint. At Easter, villagers dress up and act out a live Passion play, with scenes of Christ's Passion, the Last Supper and the Stations of the Cross.

A local speciality is the *vino de mora* (blackberry wine) sold in dry, medium and sweet varieties from a family business in Avenida Bolívar.

TÁCHIRA STATE

Táchira, the country's leading coffee producer, has one of the country's highest ratios of people living in rural areas, with small villages widely scattered among the hills and valleys. The state produces much of its own food starting with potatoes and dairy products in the mountains, rice and sugar cultivated around Ureña and bananas, papaya and other fruit near Lake Maracaibo. Farmers are self-reliant, tough and resistant to change – one of the reasons why so many local traditions survive.

LA GRITA A prosperous farming centre of some 25,000 inhabitants, La Grita was founded in 1578 on a narrow plateau at 1,457m above fertile alluvial terraces. A pair of one-way streets runs the length of the narrow town past the three plazas, and Avenida Cáceres, a broad, parallel road outside the centre. The top of La Grita's three squares is Plaza Sucre.

Getting there The Carretera Transandina highway between Bailadores (altitude 1,750m) in Mérida State and La Grita passes over the beautiful **Páramo La Negra** and is an entertainment in itself as it loops up to 2,800m. At the crest, the road splits into two routes, both going to La Grita: the left, lower and faster, and the right (the Carretera Transandina) across the 3,000m-high *páramo* in an exhilarating series of zigzags with spectacular views and little villages where farmers still plough with a yoke of oxen. It is worth starting out early to beat the fog. La Grita is 83km from San Cristóbal, 37km from Aeropuerto Internacional Francisco García de Hevia in La Fría, where Conviasa flies from Caracas (US$70).

🏠 Where to stay

🏠 **Hotel La Montaña** (25 rooms & cabins) Las Porqueras; ✎ 0277 881 2938. Pleasant lodging next to a popular travellers' restaurant called Campo Alegre, high on a mountain 6km out of town towards the Páramo del Batallón Park, off the road to Bailadores. The hotel was designed by Venezuelan architect Fruto Vivas, rooms have hot water, TV. $$
🏠 **Hotel Los Naranjos** (36 rooms) Calle 2; ✎ 0277 881 2678; e hotellosnaranjos@cantv.net. This 3-

storey motel-style place close to Plaza Bolívar is an architectural sore thumb among the colonial houses of the centre but has good, clean rooms with hot water, TV, bar & restaurant. $$
🏠 **Posada Calle Real** (9 rooms) Calle 2; ✎ 0277 881 1023. Next to Los Naranjos, this more modest guesthouse has rooms with bath, hot water, cable TV & a family-style restaurant (🕐 07.30–21.00). $

Other practicalities There is a Banco de Venezuela with an ATM on Calle 2 in the centre and a CANTV call centre on Carrera 6, between Calle 2 and Calle 3. Several pharmacies stay open late in the centre of town.

What to see Here a two-floor colonial house, the **Balcón de La Grita**, is noted as the place where Bolívar began his Admirable Campaign in 1813. Next is Plaza Jáuregui surrounded by a convent school and the twin-spired **Iglesia de Los Angeles**, built on the earthquake ruins of an earlier monastery. The **Iglesia del Espíritu Santo** on Plaza Bolívar, dating from 1836, has been remodelled after various earthquakes.

The 17th-century image of **Santo Cristo de La Grita** is venerated as miraculous, specifically during the 6–10 August festivities. These are combined with a big regional fair starting in mid-July, opening with a rally and gymkhana, and including cycling races, afternoon bullfights, evening dances and popular music concerts.

Stop at the **Mercado** near Plaza Jáuregui to see wood crafts and pottery as well as farmers' produce; open morning and afternoon but the earlier you go the better, especially on Saturdays.

Around La Grita

Birdwatching on the Páramo Zumbador At a windy mountain pass 2.5km south is the Zumbador *alcabala* or National Guard checkpoint, marking the crossroads for Michelena, 37km to the west and the serpentine road to **Páramo Zumbador** and **Queniquea**, 33km to the east. This forested stretch of road is popular with birdwatchers and Venezuelan Audubon founder Mary Lou Goodwin described the scenery and birdlife here as 'spectacular, mind-boggling' in her book *Birding Venezuela*. Over 60 species have been recorded here, including flower-piercers, tanagers, tyrannulets, woodpeckers, parakeets, wrens and warblers. Streams from Zumbador form the Torbes River headwaters, flowing eventually to the Orinoco. The views southward are magnificent and it is even possible to see San Cristóbal on a clear day.

SAN CRISTÓBAL (*Telephone code: 0276*) Many roads lead to San Cristóbal, a thriving city of 315,000 people with a pleasant climate (average 22°C). For foreign travellers the main reason for stopping here is when travelling to or from Cúcuta in Colombia at the nearby border town of San Antonio. The capital of Táchira State sits on a mesa at 825m on the western slopes of Venezuela's Andes. Its river, the Torbes, flows south. The city owes its importance as a centre of commerce to roads from the southern plains, the Andes, central Venezuela, Zulia and Colombia, only 50km away. Its proximity to one of the most active border areas in South

America, Cúcuta–San Antonio, is a major impulse of industrial growth. Indeed, San Cristóbal's flavour is reminiscent of Colombia: industrious, orderly, clean and quiet in comparison with most Venezuelan cities.

The annual **Feria de San Sebastián** changes all this. For two weeks around 20 January, the city's saint's day, there are street processions and dances, big-time bullfights, cattle and industrial fairs, international bicycle races and folk and cultural events. If you plan to be around at this time, be sure to be in place well ahead. August is the month for festivities in the nearby towns of **Táriba**, **Lobatera** and **Peribeca**.

History San Cristóbal is different in many ways. It was never sacked by pirates or racked by Independence wars. There are few colonial structures: the Iglesia San Sebastián and other old buildings fell victim to earthquakes. Historically, it had few powerful citizens, no *latifundistas* or holders of huge estates. For 200 years after it was founded in 1561 as a station between Pamplona and the Sierra Nevada, little happened: the poor agricultural village remained subject politically to Nueva Granada, today's Colombia. The introduction of coffee in the late 18th century was Táchira's biggest pre-Independence event. Táchira remains the country's leading coffee producer and the biggest employer of Colombian migrants for coffee-picking.

The early Spanish settlement on Indian lands was closer to Bogotá and had no road communication with Caracas. The journey to Caracas took two weeks by way of the Táchira, Zulia and Catatumbo rivers to Lake Maracaibo, then by sea. This was the route for coffee exports (from Colombia, too). Help came briefly from a small railway built from La Fría to Encontrados in 1894. In 1925 the first road linking Caracas with Táchira, the Trans-Andean route, was opened, although paving was still incomplete by 1960. In 1955 the lowland Pan American highway was built south of Lake Maracaibo, and the Llanos highway came soon after, making San Cristóbal one of the cities best connected by road today.

Two presidents of Venezuela and two dictators came from Táchira: dictator Cipriano Castro (1899–1908), born in Capacho; dictator Juan Vicente Gómez (1908–35), born in La Mulera; President Eleazar López Contreras (1935–41), born in Queniquea; and Carlos Andrés Pérez, born in Rubio, president in 1974–79 and 1989–93.

Getting there and away

By *air* There is no airport in San Cristóbal. The **Aeropuerto Internacional de Santo Domingo**, about 40km from the centre has daily flights to Caracas on Conviasa (*www.conviasa.aero*), Aserca (*www.asercaairlines.com*) and Rutaca (*www.rutaca.com.ve*) (US$60–70). The **Aeropuerto Internacional Francisco García de Hevia** is in La Fría about 37km north (35 minutes away) where Conviasa flies to/from Caracas (US$70).

Another airport is in **San Antonio**, the **Aeropuerto Internacional Juan Vicente Gómez** near the Colombian border, also 40km distant. Rutaca has two flights a day (US$65) between Caracas and San Antonio daily except Saturday.

By *bus* The big concrete and brick Terminal de Pasajeros is at the south end of Avenida 5 where it becomes Avenida La Concordia, towards the Barinas exit from town. Buses to Mérida (US$9) via the Panamericana leave throughout the day, 05.30–19.00, and there are also *por puestos* (US$10). The Llanos route is preferred by express coaches to Caracas, 825km (13 hours, US$20) with about ten departures a day. The fast air-conditioned coaches can get really cold on long journeys so take a heavy sweater or blanket.

The Andes TÁCHIRA STATE

15

Travellers to Colombia can take a minibus or taxi *por puesto* to San Antonio on the border throughout the day (1 hour, US$3). Expresos Bolivarianos leave every half hour for San Antonio and Cúcuta in Colombia.

By car San Cristóbal is on the main Route 7 highway, which passes through La Grita, and Route 5 from Barinas, which skirts the Andes.

By taxi Taxis are not expensive and you can contract them by the day. Three reliable lines are: Servitaxi (\ *0276 344 9416*); Serviturismo (\ *0276 341 1033*); Taxi Visión (\ *0276 344 2011*). Taxis have a standard fare to Cúcuta in Colombia (about US$10–15) and will wait while you cross the border and continue to Cúcuta.

Tourist information The **Corporacion Tachirense de Turismo**, Cotatur (*Av España, Av Carabobo, Edificio Cotatur;* \ *0276 357 9655; www.cotatur.gob.ve; www.traveltachira.com*), has good maps of the city and information on local sights.

The **Inparques** office is on Avenida 19 de Abril (*Parque Metropolitano;* \ *0276 346 6544;* ⊕ *08.00–12.30 & 14.00–18.00*).

🏠 Where to stay

🏠 **Hotel Lidotel** (121 rooms) Sambil shopping mall, Av Antonio José de Sucre, Sector Las Lomas; \ 0276 510 3333; e reservasc@lidotel.com.ve; www.lidotel.com.ve. A bit out of town in the massive Sambil shopping mall, but with banks, pharmacies, restaurants, bars & fast-food outlets within easy reach, this is the most modern & best-appointed hotel in the city. Rooms with Wi-Fi, all mod cons, swimming pool, gym, business centre. $$$

🏠 **Hotel Parador del Hidalgo** (23 rooms) Calle 7 at Carreras 9–10; \ 0276 343 2839. An economic

central hotel with restaurant & simple, clean rooms with fan, hot water, cable TV. $$

🏠 **Posada La Araguena** (9 rooms) Av España, Campo Alegre; \ 0276 356 4786; m 0414 704 6721; www.laaraguena.com. Just 300m from the Feria complex in an area with banks, pharmacies. $$

🏠 **Posada Los Pirineos Doña Josefina** (15 rooms) Av Francisco Cárdenas, Pirineos; \ 0276 355 6528. One of the few *posadas* in town, it has rooms with hot water, TV, in odd colours & is quite pricey. $$

✗ Where to eat

The main concentration of restaurants, cafés and bars is in Barrio Obrero.

✗ **Restaurant La Vaquera** Av Libertador; ⊕ 12.00–15.00 & 19.00–22.00. One of the best steak restaurants in San Cristóbal & perhaps the country; follow Av Libertador north, it's just past Motel Las Lomas. $$

✗ **La Píccola Távola** Barrio Obrero, Pasaje Acueducto, Carrera 24; ⊕ 18.00–01.00. A popular nightspot with live w/end music on the street going up beside the church. $

✗ **Restaurant Brócoli** Barrio Obrero, Pasaje Acueducto, Carretera 23; ⊕ 12.00–19.00. Great for eggplant & mushroom dishes. $

Other practicalities The best place to make overseas calls and check emails is at the **CANTV** telecommunications centre on Calle 11, a block down from Plaza Libertad.

The **Sambil shopping mall** (*Av Antonio José de Sucre, Sector Las Lomas; www.tusambil.com;* ⊕ *11.00–21.00 Mon–Sat, 12.00–20.00 Sun*) has a wide range of shops, pharmacies, banks, communication centres, restaurants and bars.

Ipostel is on Calle 5, between Carreteras 2 and 3.

What to see and do The imposing twin-spired **cathedral** is at the heart of historic San Cristóbal on Plaza Maldonado, Carrera 3 at Calle 4. Built of brick in 1688, the church was destroyed by an earthquake and rebuilt c1908; look inside for the statue of San Sebastián, martyred by arrows. The plaza is dedicated to city founder Juan de

Maldonado. On its north side the ageing Edificio Nacional shelters courts of law, public offices and the post office, Ipostel. It takes up a whole block, also giving on to Plaza Urdaneta. Lawyers occupy many fine old houses nearby.

If you walk up from the cathedral seven blocks (east) you come to Plaza Sucre and the block-long **Palacio de Los Leones** named for its rooftop lions, favourite icon of Eustoquio Gómez who finished this government palace around 1920. He was appointed President of Táchira by his cousin, the dictator Juan Vicente Gómez, and was, if possible, even more tyrannical.

The city's newest plaza is really a double square, **Plaza Libertad**. It has an amphitheatre and a pantheon designed by Fruto Vivas, containing the remains of citizens who fought for freedom.

The **Complejo Ferial** encompassing spacious fairgrounds, sports and exhibition complex, is situated near the foot of the mountains, reached by way of Avenida España and Avenida Universidad. It is worth a trip to the tourist bureau, Cotatur, to ask for the latest pamphlets, maps or information on *posadas*. The large **bullring** is here, also the stadium and velodrome for cyclists.

The **Museo Antropológico del Táchira** (*Av Universidad;* ⊕ *09.00–17.30 Tue–Fri, 10.00–18.00 Sat–Sun*), a kilometre north of the fairgrounds, is housed in the restored Hacienda de Paramillo. The one-floor colonial building, formerly a convent school has exhibitions of Andean archaeology, folklore, history and art.

FURTHER AFIELD

San Pedro del Río The popularity of this tidy village in its beautiful valley has soared since the opening of the new freeway north of the capital, putting it at 45 minutes from San Cristóbal. San Pedro, between San Juan de Colón and Michelena, lies at the start of the road west to Ureña. The rivers of its name are the Quebrada Chirirí and Río Lobaterita. At weekends San Pedro is invaded by people from the capital who come to eat or dance at two capacious *criollo* restaurants, but during the week peace and quiet return.

What makes San Pedro unique is not its restoration but the dedication of a local doctor, Pedro Granados, who saw his village declining from a once-prosperous coffee centre founded in 1840 to a petroleum-age derelict. He called in the colonial-era expert, Graziano Gasparini, to plan its rebirth. The whole village pitched in, and today San Pedro is an example that all Tachirenses take pride in.

Two cobblestone streets run up and down; the plaza and church are tranquil oases. There is a small museum, library and a music school (consequently there's a children's band and a student band). Kids also have a basketball court, football field, and even a stadium.

Easter is an especially solemn event. Nightly processions begin a week before Holy Thursday, culminating with an all-night vigil; on Good Friday the Stages of the Cross are re-enacted. A procession and mass mark the annual *fiestas patronales* of **San Pedro** and **San Pablo** on 29 June, followed by competitions such as the *palo encebado* or 'greased pole', sack races and *novilladas* in which youths tackle young bulls or cows. **Christmas** is observed with carols, hot spicy *calentado* (punch) and *candela*, literally 'fire': a football of kerosene-soaked rags, or a bull-mask lit in the same manner are borne by a runner in a hurry. On 30 December there is a big fireworks display.

Where to stay

Posada Mi Vieja Escuela (8 rooms) 3–61 Calle Real; \ 0277 291 3720; e miviejaescuela@ hotmail.com. The village schoolhouse converted into a 2-storey *posada* with simple rooms around a central patio, with hot water, AC. A restaurant provides b/fast & traditional sweets are sold in front. $

Posada Paseo La Chiriri (4 rooms) Calle Los Morales; \ 0277 291 0157. Above a craft shop, rooms with hot showers. $

TRAVEL TO/FROM COLOMBIA

San Antonio del Táchira San Antonio is 42km from San Cristóbal via Rubio, and 36km via Capacho and the Pan American highway which bears heavy traffic. On the east bank of the Táchira River, San Antonio is hot and low (438m). Although founded as early as 1730, there is little to see here. Most people come to shop, in particular Colombians who get bargains such as subsidised corn flour, petrol, cement and some appliances. Buses from both countries go as far as the Simón Bolívar International Bridge and you can just walk across. However, if you are carrying a backpack be advised that you are a mark for thieves working in teams; avoid trouble by taking the buses from Carrera 4 at Calle 6. San Antonio is not the only place to cross the frontier but has the best communications, being only 15km from Cúcuta, which has a busy airport.

Venezuelans may go as far as Cúcuta and, like Colombian shoppers, need only to present identification. Drivers of Venezuelan cars must have vehicle ownership papers.

Getting there and away

By air The Aeropuerto Internacional Juan Vicente Gómez, San Antonio's busy airport is just northeast of town on the road to Ureña. There is a regular bus service to the airport from Calle 6 at Avenida Venezuela in the centre. Rutaca (*www.rutaca.com.ve*) has two flights a day (US$65) to and from Caracas daily except Saturday.

By bus The new Terminal de Pasajeros is located between the centre and the airport on the same road. City buses to the terminal leave from Calle 6 at Avenida Venezuela. Four lines go to Caracas, (825km, US$25, 14 hours) via the Llanos route, leaving in the afternoon. For travel to Mérida, Maracaibo and Barquisimeto, take a bus to the Terminal de Pasajeros in San Cristóbal; *por puestos* go there from Avenida Venezuela at Carrera 10.

By car There is a good paved highway between San Cristóbal and San Antonio.

Where to stay San Antonio is just a transit point between Venezuela and Colombia, which is reflected in the poor quality of most of the accommodation on offer. Luckily most travellers will just be breezing through.

Hotel Adriático (43 rooms) Calle 6 & Carrera 6; \ 0276 771 5757; e hoteladriatico@hotmail.com. Rooms with hot water, AC, cable TV, restaurant, conference rooms. $$
Hotel Don Jorge (27 rooms) Calle 5 a block east of Plaza Bolívar; \ 0276 771 4089. Smaller than

the Adriático with clean, simple rooms with hot water, AC & cable TV. $$
Terepaima (10 rooms) Carrera 8 at Calle 2; \ 0276 771 1763. This is a very basic budget option, some rooms with AC & an inexpensive restaurant downstairs. $

Crossing the border into Colombia Leaving or entering Venezuela, travellers need to get passports stamped by ONI, the immigration office, at the DEX office (*Carrera 9 at Calles 6–7;* ⊕ *06.00–20.00*). Foreign nationals must pay an exit tax of US$16. To enter Colombia, nationals of most European countries, the USA and Canada do not need visas, just a valid passport. On crossing the bridge go to the Colombian immigration office DAS (⊕ 07.00–19.00) to get stamped in. Remember that there is a time difference of half an hour, so if it's noon in Venezuela it's 11.30 in Colombia. DAS also has an office in Cúcuta and at Cúcuta Airport for air passengers only.

Frequent buses to Cúcuta and *por puesto* taxis, called *colectivos*, leave from the centre of San Antonio, Calle 6 at Carrera 9, and Avenida Venezuela.

16

Falcón and Zulia

Falcón State has much to recommend it to travellers. The state capital of Coro, at the foot of the long isthmus and peninsula of Paraguaná, is the most important and best conserved colonial city in Venezuela and a UNESCO World Heritage Site. The island beaches of Parque Nacional Morrocoy attract Venezuelans and foreigners alike with their palm trees, white sand and calm, translucent waters (see *Chapter 6, Los Roques, Morrocoy and Mochima*). The arid coast, dotted with dusty villages with more goats than people, continues west to Zulia State and the oil-rich capital of Maracaibo, the second largest city in the country. Maracaibo is reached by a bridge across Lake Maracaibo, the largest lake in South America. Zulia also shares a border with Colombia in the sparsely populated desert region of La Guajira, homeland of the Wayúu or Guajiros, the nation's largest and best organised ethnic group.

FALCÓN STATE

CORO (*Telephone code: 0268*) Santa Ana de Coro, to give it its full name, is a hot, drowsy town, with an excessive number of shoe shops and hairdressers and a population of some 235,000. The main draw for visitors is the immaculately preserved historic centre of Santa Ana de Coro, between Plaza Bolívar and Plaza Falcón, which was declared a World Heritage Site by UNESCO in 1993 for its well-conserved colonial buildings. About 60 or 70 of the top Coro families built their *bahareque* (wattle and daub houses) here on the Spanish grid-pattern of streets, around squat churches with thick walls to protect against Indian and pirate attacks. In 2005, following two years of heavy rains that caused damage to buildings in the historic centre, UNESCO placed Coro on its list of World Heritage Sites in Danger. The name Coro is believed to come from the Caquetío word '*curiana*', meaning 'place of winds', for the strong trade winds that constantly blow in from the sea. In the evening, those winds bring a welcome respite from the dry heat of the day. The average temperature is 28°C, with highs over 40°C and lows of 14°C.

History Founded in 1527, Coro is the oldest continuous Spanish settlement on the continent. When King Carlos I of Spain signed a decree creating the Province of Venezuela in 1528, Coro became its capital. Unlike the founders of Cumaná – who were forced out three times by Indians outraged by slavers seeking pearl divers – Coro's founder Juan de Ampíes got along well with the local Caquetíos. The land, though arid, was healthy, and refreshed by pleasant breezes. The Pope made Coro South America's first bishopric in 1531 and its church became the first cathedral. The only missing ingredient was the riches that *conquistadores* had found in Mexico and Peru, and so the search for El Dorado began and the first overland expeditions set out from Coro in search of cities of gold. Extraordinary in scope, hardship, as well as barbarity, most of these follies ended in death. The gold-seekers were not

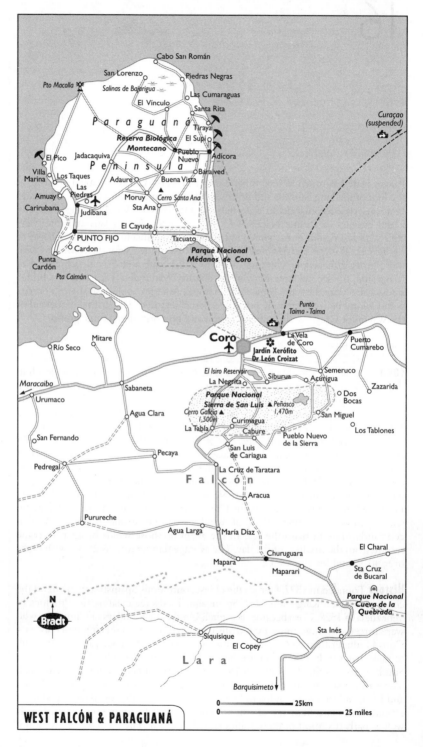

Cabo San Román
San Lorenzo
Piedras Negras
Pto Macolla
Salinas de Bajarigua
Las Cumaraguas
El Vinculo
Santa Rita
P a r a g u a n á
Tiraya
Reserva Biológica
El Supí
Montecano
Pueblo
Adícora
El Pico
Jadacaquiva
Nuevo
Villa
Los Taques
P e n i n s u l a
Bararved
Marina
Adaure
Buena Vista
Amuay
Las
Piedras
Moruy
Cerro Santa Ana
Carirubana
Judibana
Sta Ana
El Cayude
PUNTO FIJO
Tacuato
Cardon
Parque Nacional
Punta
Médanos de Coro
Cardón
Pta Caimán

Curaçao
(suspended)

Punta
Taima - Taima
Coro
La Vela
de Coro
Mitare
Puerto
Río Seco
Jardín Xerófito
Cumarebo
Dr León Croizat
Semeruco
Maracaibo
Sabaneta
El Isiro Reservoir
Siburua
Acurigua
Zazarida
Urumaco
La Negrita
Dos
Parque Nacional
Peñasco
Bocas
Sierra de San Luis
1,470m
Agua Clara
Cerro Galicia
1,500m
San Miguel
San Fernando
La Tabla
Curimagua
Los Tablones
Cabure
Pecaya
Pueblo Nuevo
San Luis
de la Sierra
Pedregal
de Cariagua
La Cruz de Taratara
F a l c ó n
Aracua
Pururéche
Agua Larga
María Díaz
El Charal
Churuguara
Sta Cruz
Mapara
de Bucaral
Maparari
Parque Nacional
Cueva de la
Quebrada

N
Bradt
Síquisique
Sta Inés
El Copey
L a r a
Barquisimeto

0 ————————— 25km
0 ————————— 25 miles

WEST FALCÓN & PARAGUANÁ

Spanish, however, but German: by the time Ampíes founded Coro, Carlos I (who was also Charles V of the Habsburgs and the Holy Roman Emperor) had made a deal with the banking house of Welser, leasing them the Province of Venezuela to cover his war debts.

Upon arrival in Coro Welser's agent, Ambrosius Ehinger (called Alfinger in Venezuela), arrested Ampíes and deported him to Curaçao. He then explored Lake Maracaibo and founded the settlement of Maracaibo. A ruthless killer, Alfinger pursued his golden idol as far as the Magdalena in Colombia where he was killed by a poisoned arrow. The next German governor, Georg Hohemuth of Speier (called Jorge Spira in Venezuela), set out with 361 men and got as far as the Río Meta in the Llanos but missed the kingdom of El Dorado and, starving, returned with a few survivors. Nikolaus Federmann got all the way to Bogotá, only to find Jiménez de Quesada had arrived before him. German efforts ended in 1545 when Bartholomew Welser and Phillip von Hutten were assassinated by Juan de Carvajal, who had forged the governor's credentials.

With no golden cities or mines to be found, Coro struggled to survive. Some inhabitants, coerced by Carvajal, left Coro with him to found El Tocuyo (where justice caught up with him and he was hanged). In 1578 the governor moved to Caracas, in effect taking the capital with him. The bishop did the same in 1637. An English privateer, Christopher Mings, looted and burned Coro as late as 1659, leaving it in smoking ruins. Small wonder it appeared on some maps as 'destroyed'.

Gradually Coro took hold as a supply centre for Curaçao and Aruba through its port, La Vela. Exports were mainly cacao, tobacco, horses and mules. Such trade thrived despite being illegal, and the town prospered. Most of its important buildings and houses date from the 18th century.

Falcón State is named after **Juan Crisóstomo Falcón** who was President of Venezuela in 1863–68. General Falcón and his brother-in-law, Ezequiel Zamora, led the federalist cause against the centralist party. Accompanied by Antonio Guzmán Blanco, they fought in Barquisimeto, Barinas and San Carlos where Zamora was shot. Falcón never liked Caracas, although he created the Federal District. He appointed various interim presidents, including Guzmán Blanco, so he could spend time in Coro and Paraguaná. Falcón renounced the presidency in 1868 only to die two years later in his native state.

Getting there and away

By air The **Aeropuerto José Leonardo Chirino** is so close to the centre of Coro you can walk to the colonial district. State-run airline Conviasa (*www.conviasa.aero*) has one flight a day to Caracas at 08.45 (50 minutes, US$65). Another airport, the **Aeropuerto Internacional Josefa Camejo**, in Las Piedras on the Paraguaná Peninsula, about 90km away, has flights on national airlines to Caracas and Maracaibo and international flights to Aruba and Curaçao.

By bus The Terminal de Pasajeros is on Avenida Los Médanos, six blocks south of Calle Falcón. There is frequent service to Valencia via Morón, 290km (5 hours, US$10); Caracas, 450km (7 hours, US$15); and Maracaibo, 255km (4 hours, US$10). Fewer buses go to Mérida and San Cristóbal (12–13 hours, US$20–25). For the Paraguaná Peninsula, there's a choice of buses to Adícora on the east coast (50km, US$2); or Punto Fijo on the west, services all day (1 hour, US$3). For the mountains of the Sierra de San Luis, ask for buses or *por puesto* jeeps to Curimagua, Pueblo Nuevo or Churuguara.

By car Coro is reached on the main Route 4 highway from Barquisimeto or by the Route 3 highway that links Maracaibo to Morón.

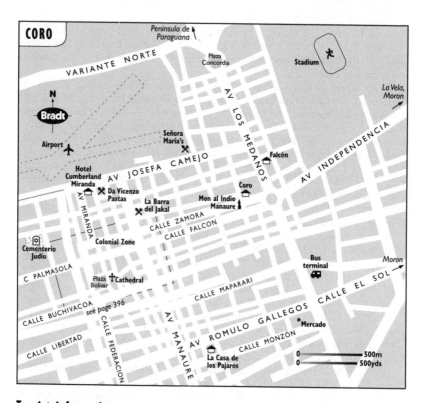

Tourist information CorFalTur, or the **Corporación Falconiana de Turismo**
(\ *0268 253 0262, 0268 252 4198;* e *corfaltur@gmail.com; www.visitfalcon.com;*
⊕ *weekdays*) is on Paseo La Alameda, near Plaza Bolívar and has state tourism maps
and pamphlets on sites of interest. A tourism booth is open ⊕ from 08.30 to 17.00
in the main airport and another in Las Piedras Airport in Punto Fijo.

Inparques (\ *0268 277 8582*) has an office at the Jardín Botánico Xerófito,
Avenida Intercomunal, halfway to La Vela de Coro.

Where to stay

Hotel Cumberland Miranda (91 rooms) Opposite
the airport; \ 0268 252 2111; e reservas@
hotelescumberland.com; www.hotelescumberland.com. A
3-star hotel with restaurant, pool, gardens, travel
agency, gym, sauna & free Wi-Fi. Clean comfortable
rooms & suites with AC, cable TV, b/fast included. $$
La Casa de los Pájaros (7 rooms) Calle Monzón, in
front of Plaza Monzón; \ 0268 252 8215; m 0416
668 1566; e rstiuv@hotmail.com;
www.casadelospajaros.com.ve. A labour of love on the
part of Roberto Stiuv & Marnie, his wife, who have
decorated their colonial house in warm tropical
colours to appeal to foreign visitors. Rooms with AC,
bathroom, TV, dorm with fan, hammocks in the large
patio. B/fast is included & there is a small charge to
use the kitchen to prepare meals. Can arrange trips

to Paraguaná, San Luis & Tama Tama, sandboards for
guests to use on the dunes of Los Médanos. $$
Casa Tun Tun (7 rooms) Calle Zamora, in historic
centre; \ 0268 404 4260; e casatuntun@
hotmail.com. Pretty colonial house & a good
backpacker option with dorm rooms, rooms with
shared bath & dbls with en suite, all with cold water,
fan, some with AC, hammocks in patio area, central
courtyard. Free use of kitchen, honour bar & washing
machine charged by the load. French spoken. $
Posada El Gallo (7 rooms) 26 Calle Federación, a
block north of Calle Zamora; \ 0268 252 9481;
e posadaelgallo@hotmail.com. Entirely rebuilt from
floor to ceiling by French artist Erick Migliore, the
colonial house gives the feel of what a secluded
Coro home was like before AC – tall ceilings &

rooms giving on to an open corridor around a planted patio where you can hang out in hammocks. Rooms with shared bath, fan, kitchen privileges, Wi-Fi & internet. Owner can arrange trips to the Sierra de San Luis & Paraguaná. French & English spoken. $

✗ Where to eat Visitors should not leave Coro without trying the local dishes such as roast kid (*asado de chivo*), kid cooked in coconut (*chivo en coco*) and goat's milk cheese (*queso de cabra*). *Queso coriano* is a fresh local cheese made with milk, *nata*, a delicious cross between butter and salty cream, and *dulce de leche* is a soft fudge made of condensed milk and sugar.

✗ Da Vicenzo Pastas Av Josefa Camejo; ⊕ 12.00–22.00. Pastas & pizzas at this popular Italian restaurant with a coffee bar near the Cumberland Hotel. $$

✗ La Barra del Jakal Calle Union, near Av Manaure; ⊕ 12.00–23.00. A local hangout in the evenings with tables on a terrace, serving pizzas, cold beers, *tasca* bar inside, seafood specials. $$

✗ Dulcería Katy 10 Calle Colón, between Urdaneta & Miranda; ⊕ 08.00–19.00. A little upstairs shop about a block & a half from Urdaneta, that sells every kind of *dulce de leche*, made with guava, pineapple & chocolate. $

✗ Fonda Tuística Sabor Latino Paseo Alameda; ⊕ 08.00–20.00. Good b/fasts, eggs with toast or *arepas*, juices, tables outside for watching the world go by. Light lunches, snacks. $

✗ Rincón de Cabure Av Prolongación Los Médanos with Calle Ramón Antonio Medina; ⊕ 08.00–15.00. A small place selling local dishes & one of the best places to try kid (*chivo*) & goat (*cabrito*). $

✗ Señora María's Av Aeropuerto; ⊕ 06.30–13.00 & 17.00–21.00. On the road to the airport, sells traditional *arepas de maíz* made from maize ground in a *pilon* with a variety of fillings from grated cheese to shredded chicken. $

Festivals Shops shut on 2 January, as well as New Year's Day in Coro, for the **Día del Comerciante**, when shopkeepers and merchants organise music, parties and contests on the streets. Federation Day is 2 February; most state offices are closed. The last week in July is filled by Coro's *fiestas patronales*. November is the month of the annual Falcón Exhibition and Fair at the Feria Industrial grounds east of town. In early December the **Feria del Pesebre** is a competition for the best Christmas Nativity scene and includes a live re-creation of the Bethlehem stable with Mary, Joseph and the wise men, complete with choirs, carol singers and musical groups. Food, arts and crafts are sold.

Other practicalities There is a Banco de Venezuela with an ATM on Paseo Talavera, behind the cathedral. There is a pharmacy on Calle 13 Urdaneta on the intersection with Avenida Manaure. The main hospital is the Hospital Universitario Dr Alfredo van Grieken (\ *0268 252 5700*) just off Avenida José Leonardo Chirino.

What to see and do
Cathedral The cathedral or **Templo de Santa Ana**, on the main plaza, is Venezuela's first church. Originally built in adobe in 1583, it was being rebuilt in masonry in 1595 when it was burnt to the ground by English privateer Amyas Preston. Finally completed in 1632, the imposing white structure has massive walls, gun slits like a fortress and an impressive gilded altar. It is the oldest building in Coro and the oldest church in Venezuela.

Iglesia de San Francisco On Calle Zamora, with its 50m tower that can be seen from all over town, this church sits on the foundations of a 1620 building burnt down by pirates and rebuilt a century later. The neo-Gothic façade was added in the 1900s, belying its antiquity. The adjacent **Museo Diocesano de Coro Lucas Guillermo Castillo** (⊕ *09.00–12.00 & 15.00–18.00 Tue–Sat, 09.00–14.00 Sun; admission free*) is a large museum housed in a former Franciscan monastery with an

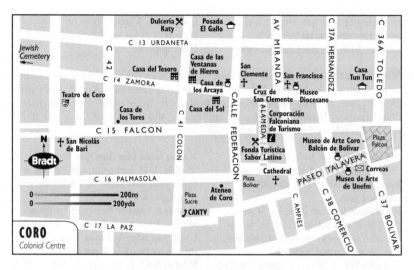

CORO
Colonial Centre

important collection of religious art in gold, silver, glass, tapestry, as well as colonial bells, furniture, sculpture and paintings by important Venezuelan religious artists such as Juan Pedro López. There are guided tours in Spanish.

Iglesia de San Clemente On Calle Zamora, with its yellow walls, is another church that was destroyed by pirates in the 16th century and rebuilt around 1750 and is one of the few churches in Venezuela laid out in the form of a cross. Go inside to see the richly painted blue, red and gold altar screen, and the ceiling anchor of Saint Clement, an early Bishop of Rome who was martyred in the Crimea by being tied to an anchor and drowned. The **Cross of San Clemente**, as old as the city itself, is across from the Alameda in a shelter. According to tradition, the cross is made from hard *cují* wood from the mesquite tree under which the first mass in the new Province of Venezuela was held.

Museo de Cerámica Histórica y Loza Popular (*Calle Zamora & Calle Federación;* ⊕ *09.00–12.00 & 15.00–18.00 Tue–Sat, 09.00–13.00 Sun; admission free*) Housed in the **Casa de Los Arcaya**, a fine two-storey mansion with a wooden balcony built in the 1740s. The museum contains fine china, local pottery and pre-Columbian ceramics as well as fossils and other archaeological finds.

Casa del Sol On the south side of Zamora is a single-storey house from the early 18th century, and one of the oldest in Coro. The name comes from a plaster sun above the door, a symbol of God. The fine residence belonged at one time to José Garcés, who built the Casa de las Ventanas de Hierro. It later served as a school and today is a courthouse.

Casa de las Ventanas de Hierro This house has a plaster doorway considered the finest of its kind in the Caribbean, nearly 8m tall. It was built in 1764–65 by the Mayor of Coro, Don José Garcés, and has never been sold – a rarity among colonial structures. The heirs, the Tellería and Zárraga families, have restored the bedrooms, library, chapel, coach yard, kitchen and slave quarters as the **Museo de Tradición Familiar** (⊕ *09.00–17.00 Mon–Sat*). Don't miss the old family photos, swinging cradle, four-poster bed, toilet chair and polychrome ceilings. Fat-bellied columns known as *panzudas* surround a breezy patio where mockingbirds sing.

Casa del Tesoro (*Calle Zamora & Calle Colón*) Casa del Tesoro was built in the 1770s for Andrés de Talavera, a *Coriano* whose wealth disappeared when he died, giving rise to tales of buried treasure (hence the name 'House of Treasure'). Many generations have dug for, and even found, tunnels, but no gold has surfaced. Mariano de Talavera y Garcés, orator, intellectual and Bishop of Guayana, was born here so the house is also known as the Casa del Obispo.

Cementerio Judío (*Calle Zamora & 23 Enero*) Dating to 1830, this is the oldest Jewish cemetery still functioning in South America. It is usually locked, so ask for Pedro Roberto García who lives opposite (after 17.00 or at weekends). When the Sephardic Jews were banished from Spain many found a safe haven in Dutch Curaçao. During the Independence wars Joseph Curiel left Curaçao and travelled to Ciudad Bolívar to offer Jewish support to Simón Bolívar. After Independence, those who came to live in Coro, however, had to overcome discrimination serious enough for Holland to demand reparations for damages. Curiel built the cemetery and the oldest grave, dated 1832, is that of his young daughter who died aged ten.

San Nicolás de Bari A block south of Zamora on Calle Falcón at Calle Ayacucho, there's an unadorned colonial church, with a door into the old Catholic cemetery. The façade shows what San Clemente and other churches looked like before they were remodelled. Below the roof is the date 1741.

Museo de Arte de Coro (*Paseo Talavera;* ⊕ *09.00–12.30 & 15.00–19.30 Tue–Sat, 09.00–16.00 Sun; admission free*) This museum is housed in the **Balcón de Bolívar** (Bolívar's Balcony), or Casa de Los Senior after the Curaçao merchants who bought it in 1896 to use as a warehouse. The name refers to Simón Bolívar's only visit to Coro, on 23 December 1826, when he greeted his cheering supporters from the wooden balcony. Now completely restored, it doubles as the Coro branch of the Caracas Museum of Contemporary Art, holding top-notch exhibitions. There is a fine craft shop.

Museo de Arte de Unefm (*Paseo Talavera;* ⊕ *09.00–12.30 & 15.00–19.30 Tue–Sat, 09.00–16.00 Sun; admission free*) An art museum housing the **Alberto Henríquez** collection of modern art and religious and indigenous artefacts. Behind the 19th-century mansion is a little **synagogue**, the oldest in Venezuela.

Around Coro

Los Médanos de Coro For a Lawrence of Arabia experience head for Los Médanos de Coro, an extensive area of shifting sands and 35m dunes whipped by constant trade winds that cover the road at the northern edge of Coro and the entry to the Paraguaná Peninsula. To get to the dunes take a bus from Calle Falcón to Avenida Los Médanos and ask to be dropped at the Monumento al Madre. From there it's a ten-minute walk. The highway to Paraguaná runs right through the Parque Nacional Los Médanos, the largest of Falcón State's four national parks, covering 912km² on the isthmus of Paraguaná with the sea on either side. Salt flats stretch along the west border and on the windward side the sea is rough and not good for swimming.

☞ *WARNING:* Be aware that tourists of any nationality stick out like a penguin on a sand dune. Groups of kids have mugged tourists at knifepoint so travel in a group and don't stray too far from the road.

Jardín Xerófito León Croizat (⊕ *08.00–12.00 & 13.00–16.00 Tue–Sun*) On the road halfway from Coro to La Vela, this fine botanical garden of desert plants has a fascinating array of cacti, palms, shrubs and flowers on its 32ha, as well as laboratories and salons for study and teaching and visitor installations. **Inparques**, the National Parks Institute, has its regional headquarters here (see *Tourist information*, page 394).

La Vela de Coro A little seaport, 12km northeast of the city, La Vela de Coro was used in the past to transport goods to the Paraguaná Peninsula as well as for all trade, particularly with Curaçao. Naviarca (*www.grancacique.com.ve*) used to run a popular ferry service from La Vela to Aruba/Curaçao from the pier at Muelle de Muaco, which may be reopened in the future. A sandy bay some 2km long provides Coro's nearest beach. Although the waves are often rough and the water turbid, the beach is crowded at weekends.

La Vela, founded in 1528, was declared a World Heritage Site in 1993 along with Coro. The town continues a programme to restore its old houses and beautify the historic centre with trees, benches and statues. The biggest structure is the 17th-century **Aduana** or customs house, now home to a **Museo Marítimo**. There is a monument to **Francisco Miranda** atop the ruins of an early fort, commemorating the landing he made in 1806 when the red, blue and yellow flag he designed was unfurled for the first time on Venezuelan soil. The statue of a Dutch woman on **Plaza Antillana** by the pier honours Venezuela's good relations with the neighbouring islands of Curaçao, Aruba and Bonaire.

Once a year the town gives an all-out bash aided by any outsider who can get there on 28 December: the **Fiesta de los Locos de La Vela**. Historically, the date marks the slaughter of the innocents by Herod, but today in Venezuela it is the

FOSSILS FROM AN ANCIENT DELTA

Eons before the eastern Andes were uplifted some eight million years ago, a great river poured into the Caribbean, some 100km west of Coro. Evidence of its huge delta comes to light in major fossil finds from the Urumaco area: huge turtles, crocodiles and monster fish. In 2000 an almost complete skeleton of an ancient ancestor of the water-loving capybara was found. Called *Phoberomys pattersoni* after palaeontologist Brian Patterson, this giant measured some 3m long from nose to tail, making it one of the biggest rodents ever to roam the earth.

The ancient river that flowed to the sea here in the Miocene era was the ancestor not only of the Orinoco but also the Amazon. The great system flowed north in a trough at the foot of the first Andean chain. When continued uplift formed the Venezuelan Andes and the Sierra de San Luis, the river was cut off from the Caribbean. Forced eastward, the waters divided into the Orinoco and the Amazon, each turning 90° to the Atlantic.

A simple house in the roadside village of Urumaco, 72km west of Coro on the highway to Maracaibo, serves as Falcón's fossil museum, **El Museo Paleontológico de Urumaco** (*www.paleobio.labb.usb.ve*), until a better one is built. It is currently home to a 3m fossil carapace found north of the highway. This once belonged to the giant turtle, called uruma, now returned from its years under study at Harvard's Museum of Comparative Zoology where it was qualified as the world's oldest and largest turtle fossil. Sadly, the almost-complete skeleton of *P. pattersoni* found in 2000 by a team from Coro's Universidad Experimental Francisco de Miranda in conjunction with archaeologists from the USA and Germany, is not on display in Urumaco. The so-called 'Guinea-zilla', a distant relative of capybaras and guinea pigs, lived when Paraguaná was an island and this area was a delta. To give an idea of its size, a modern-day capybara weighs 50kg, while *P. pattersoni* would have weighed 700kg and stood 1m tall.

equivalent of April Fool's Day. The people of La Vela prepare bizarre costumes, food and lots of drink. Parades and street dances are led by 'Cucurucho', a figure clad in a cone hat, mask and suit of bells.

Where to stay

Posada Granja El Ojito (10 rooms) On the Coro to Cumarebo highway; \ 0268 774 1050; e granjaelojito@cantv.net; www.granjaelojito.com. Agronomist Dierk Demant chose this well-watered spot for his farm & guesthouse because of its natural springs (ojos de agua) & coconut palms, as well as the beach. He put in a swimming pool with dressing rooms, jacuzzi & clay tennis court, conference room with audiovisual aids. The restaurant with changing daily menu of Falcón specialities is a top attraction. 10 rooms have bath, AC, satellite TV, phone, veranda & hammock. Tours to Coro, Paraguaná, Sierra de San Luís & Morrocoy are offered, as well as airport transfers from Coro & Punto Fijo. German, English & French spoken. $$

THE PARAGUANÁ PENINSULA (*Telephone code: 0269*) Famed for its windsurfing and colonial villages, the dry and windswept Paraguaná Peninsula was once an island and has much in common with the nearby Dutch Antilles. It is separated from the mainland by a narrow isthmus of sand and the large dunes, or *médanos*, that blocked entry until the modern highway was built. An aqueduct bringing water from the Sierra de San Luis has transformed the semi-arid land, where rainfall averages 500mm, the lowest in the country. Where before only cactus grew, farms now produce melons, tomatoes, onions and aloe vera (*sabila*). An oil pipeline paralleling the aqueduct is a clue to the peninsula's importance as the site of the world's largest oil refinery, a massive complex at Amuay and Cardon.

At the tip of Paraguaná is **Cabo San Román**, the most northerly point in Venezuela, named in 1499 by Spanish navigator Alonso de Ojeda on his way to discover Lake Maracaibo. For the next 450 years the few hardy Spaniards who settled here eked out a living like the native Caquetío Indians, fishing, hunting rabbits and deer, and abandoning the peninsula during periods of prolonged drought. The biggest change (good and bad) was the introduction of goats, which eat the cactus and can in turn be eaten. There was also a flourishing smuggling trade with Curaçao. Then in 1949 the first oil refineries came to the west coast, bringing electricity, roads and the built-up suburbs of **Punto Fijo**, where the oil workers live.

The main attractions of the peninsula are the charming colonial churches of **Moruy**, **Jadacaquiva** and **Santa Ana**, at the foot of the only mountain. These towns and Pueblo Nuevo, Miraca and Baraived, were all originally pre-Spanish Indian communities. The beach town of **Adícora** has excellent windsurfing and kitesurfing and good accommodation options.

Getting there All the towns and villages on the Paraguaná Peninsula are easily accessible by local buses from Coro. Unless you can get a 4x4 vehicle or have a lot of time on your hands, forget about exploring the wilder north where roads are not signposted and tracks disappear altogether among scrub, thorns and rock. There are plans to make a road around the northern coast, but this may take years.

Santa Ana Some 35km from the isthmus at the foot of the cone-shaped mountain of Cerro Santa Ana lies the small village of Santa Ana. Watered by a mountain stream, it was inhabited long before the arrival of the Spaniards. The squat 17th-century **Iglesia de Santa Ana** was built to impress indigenous converts and resist pirates. It's a dazzling white church with a unique bell tower added in the 1750s. If it's a Sunday, you may be one of the lucky few to see the gilt altar piece with its naïve carvings, complete with saints, angels, St George and the dragon, and at the

Seen from afar, Santa Ana Mountain rises like a cone in the middle of the peninsula. Surrounded by dry scrub, it is an island of cloudforest topped at 830m by low windswept shrubs. Declared a Natural Monument in 1972, Santa Ana is a refuge of plants, birds and animals including rabbits, foxes and ocelots. It has three peaks: Moruy, in the north, is the highest point; Santa Ana, or *picacho en medio*, is in the middle; and Buena Vista is in the east. The main trail is from the Moruy side, but there is another trail from Santa Ana, longer and less frequented. In either case, be prepared for rain from September to January, and for possible cold wind and fog at the top.

TRAIL FROM SANTA ANA The Inparques office is on the street leading from Plaza Bolívar and the church towards the mountain. All hikers must sign in before 09.00 as the ascent takes three to four hours depending on the route. There is no telephone in the office but you can take down the mobile number of the park guard in case of emergency.

No other permission is needed and you can start walking right away. The asphalt road ends at a triangular plaza; follow the main jeep road past smallholdings and thorn bushes and keep left at all crossroads. You will arrive at a campsite and parking area in 2km. There is a 'Monumento Natural' sign where the trail starts to the left.

The first stage (25 minutes) is to the Caja de Agua (water tank), which for centuries supplied the village with its all its water. It begins hot and rocky, leading straight towards the mountain. After reaching some shady deciduous trees, the trail begins to climb and bears left (west), passing spiky sword-leaved bromeliads called *caracuey* – relatives of the pineapple that turn scarlet in the dry season – and trees covered with Spanish moss. The concrete water tank is fed by the pure waters of the Santa Ana River.

The second stage follows the Santa Ana River through deciduous forest alive with birdsong, so look out for troupials, red siskins and parakeets. The trail parallels the ravine, climbing first on its right, then crossing left to pass between two large boulders before you arrive at a clearing ideal for camping near a rivulet (20 minutes' walking).

top a charming oil painting of Santa Ana herself, reading the good book to the young Virgin. The church is usually locked.

There are several '*ambiente familiar*' restaurants in town serving good, inexpensive chicken, yuca and beer, but there are no hotels.

Moruy Seven kilometres northwest of Santa Ana, Moruy is just as old. Humble houses are dwarfed by the domed church tower of the Iglesia de San Nicolás. Colonists from Spain brought with them the image of San Nicolás de Bari, whose feast day is 24 December. The original church, dating from the 1760s, was enlarged by two 19th-century naves and the whole sparkles with fresh paint. Everywhere that the mainland aqueduct reaches (it hasn't failed in 35 years), new houses are going up and farmers are clearing plots to plant tomatoes, onions and aloe vera. Cactus is stacked to make thorny fences and local crafts, although the wood, *cardón*, grows quite slowly and is officially protected.

Jadacaquiva The Dutch influence on the peninsula can be seen in the stark white church, which is 250 years old and has an old painting on the altar showing a Venezuelan sailboat entering Willemstad harbour in Curaçao. The church has no tower; the bells hang in a frame outside.

Pueblo Nuevo From Jadacaquiva it is 24km east via a circle road to Pueblo Nuevo (not actually new – it was formally founded in 1734), the biggest peninsular focus

The vegetation becomes greener as the trail rises (the creek is on the right) and leads through lianas like a hanging door to the next, more humid vegetation zone. Here the trail is not very clear as there appear to be two watercourses; the remains of the old concrete aqueduct on the left lead to another clearing and possible campsite. Shaded by huge trees, the trail skirts muddy spots by the aqueduct, more runnels of water and goes to the right of a big boulder, then left, seeking the **Piedra de Agua**, source of the Santa Ana River (20 minutes).

Bearing east the trail continues up and passes a big rock (*peñón*). In the dry season the cliff is visible ahead, the route passes below through lianas, ferns, mosses and bromeliads. Someone once lived at a flat spot, Los Naranjos, where an orange tree is now shaded by second-growth forest with red-flowering bromeliads. Soon the upward trail opens into a circular clearing, another camping spot. From here a path to the right leads down to Misaray, while the trail to the peak goes upward, at last emerging from the forest with a magnificent view stretching eastward. In a few minutes more, the peak looms above a grassy shoulder. Dwarf palms (*Geonoma paraguanensis*) grow at the top among ferns, orchids and shrubs recalling *páramo* flora.

TRAIL FROM MORUY The well-trodden trail on the west side of Cerro Santa Ana takes you to the top in something over two hours. To get to the trail, follow the road from the little town and church of Moruy to the main north–south highway and cross to the opposite side towards the mountain (2km), passing many houses, until you reach the Inparques campsite (sign in on the way up, and on returning); you should start by 09.00 according to regulations.

The trail starts out rocky and with little shade for the best part of an hour. However, once above 500m, the forest makes hiking cooler and views open southward. The final ascent to 830m is a scramble over roots and up rocks; a rope and chain have been left by other hikers. Clouds and fog add drama to the ascent, particularly in the afternoon. On a clear day you can see as far as the Sierra de San Luis and Curaçao.

of farm development. The church, although genuinely colonial, has been remodelled more than once. Houses near the plaza have been restored and there's a new bus terminal. Cottage industries include soaps, creams and shampoo made of *sábila* (aloe vera), *dulce de leche* made of goat's milk, and *cardón* chairs. Restaurants and pensions are beginning to appear. A good economical lunch place is the Restaurant del Pueblo on Plaza Bolívar: plain but satisfying *criollo* dishes such as stew, fried fish and pork chops. A splendid new Josefa Camejo Cultural Complex with a library, auditorium and rehearsal rooms is named for the Independence heroine of Paraguaná who was born in 1781 in the village of Aguaque, 7km north of Pueblo Nuevo.

Where to stay

Posada & Resturant de Luis (11 rooms) West of Plaza Bolívar, 23 Calle Falcón, Pueblo Nuevo; 0269 988 1072; e polloreyes@cantv.net. A pleasant old house with patio restaurant (& ice cream parlour next door) provides simple rooms for 2–4 guests, with private bath, AC. Dbls in price in high season, when b/fast & dinner are included. $

Posada Hidalgo (9 rooms) Av Bolívar, Pueblo Nuevo; 0269 988 1123; m 0416 767 8604. Fairly new *posada* with AV, TV, hot water. 5mins from Adícora. $

What to see and do

Reserva Biológica Montecano (*Pueblo Nuevo office at Av Arévalo González near Calle Páez;* 0269 988 1048; m 0416 668 0464; ⏲ 09.00–17.00; admission free) The reserve is

7km from Pueblo Nuevo via San José de Cocodite, west of the Pueblo Nuevo–Buena Vista highway. There's a cabin at the entrance with information and you can hike the trails, or go birding. Among the cactus you can find orioles, red siskin, spinetail, antwren, partridge, parakeets and hawks. Monte Cano protects some of the peninsula's last deciduous forest, home to threatened flora and fauna, including species found nowhere else but Cerro Santa Ana. Scientists are drawn here by the greenbottle blue tarantula (*Chromatopelma cyaneopubescens*), a strikingly colourful spider with blue legs, green carapace and orange abdomen that makes web-filled burrows near tree roots. The ridge takes its name from *cana*, meaning 'grey hair', referring to the abundant Spanish moss hanging from the trees. In Agua Sabrida, yet another biological reserve south of Miraca, investigators have found the world's smallest lizard, the Paraguanan ground gecko (*Lepidoblepharis montecanoensis*), measuring no more than 30mm, half the size of its name. Biologists also study a rare bat, the Paraguaná moustached bat (*Pteronotus paraguanensis*) known locally as *bigotudo*, found in the Cueva del Guano in the vicinity of Moruy. Bats have lived in the 118m cave for so long that the bat dung was exploited and sold to Aruba and Curaçao in the early 1900s. Bats are important pollinating agents on the peninsula.

Adícora With two beaches, strong trade winds and a growing number of *posadas* and restaurants, Adícora is becoming a popular destination for windsurfers and kitesurfers looking for a budget alternative to El Yaque in Margarita. The old fishing village was for centuries Paraguaná's principal port of trade with Curaçao. Salt was its big export, as well as guayacan (*Lignum vitae*), a wood so hard that the Dutch sent it home for windmill gears. Some of the original coral stone structures have been restored, and little houses with Caribbean Dutch influence are painted in bright pinks, blues and yellows. The old *faro*, lighthouse, stands by a tiny plaza. Stroll down the pretty waterfront boulevard to the small, rocky beach of Playa Norte with flat sea protected by a breakwater. The better sandy beach of Playa Sur, with strong winds and choppy waves, is through the town to the south and has plenty of informal restaurants serving fried fish. Another beach north of Adícora is popular with city people who have built summer homes. There are nearby coral reefs for scuba diving and the wrecks of two French galleons from the time when pirates and smugglers used Paraguaná as a refuge.

Where to stay Apart from the three windsurf *posadas* (see *Windsurfing and kitesurfing* opposite) there are few other choices:

La Troja (15 cabins) 72 Calle Santa Ana, paralleling the Pueblo Nuevo road (south of Montecano); ☎ 0269 849 1362; m 0416 621 5766, 0414 248 9368; e latroja@cantv.net; www.latroja.com.ve. Behind a stone wall, this massive complex around a 100-year-old stone house has a tree-filled garden, a big swimming pool, mini-zoo with birds & monkeys, sports fields & barbecue area, plus 4 large dorms for a children's summer camp. Cabins have bathroom, AC, cable TV, mini-fridge & hammocks outside. A good option in low season. Lodging includes 2 buffet-style meals. $$

Posada Montecano (7 rooms) On the Pueblo Nuevo road near the bus stop in Adícora; ☎ 0269

998 8174; m 0416 756 2425. A short hike from the Playa Norte beach is this *posada* & restaurant run by friendly owner, Francisco Palmese. Simple rooms have beds for 3–5 with AC, bath, cold water, TV. Good value meals available from the restaurant, which serves pastas & local seafood. Italian & a bit of English spoken. $$

Posada de la Familia Kitzberger or **Posada la Casa Rosada** (5 rooms) Boulevard, Playa Norte; ☎ 0269 988 8004; e andepaula@hotmail.com. Run by Franz & Alba Kitzberger who rent out rooms with AC, TV, bath, cold water & an apt for 6, set around a green patio with hammocks. A small restaurant open to the public serves good pizzas. $

Other practicalities There are no banks or *casas de cambio* in Adícora so bring all the money you need with you. In case of emergency there is a bank in the nearby town of Pueblo Nuevo.

Most *posadas* offer internet or Wi-Fi and can help you get connected.

The nearest hospital and private clinics are in Punto Fijo or Coro.

What to do

Windsurfing and kitesurfing Paraguaná is famous for its winds and enjoys a good reputation among European windsurfers. At Adícora the same trade winds that keep temperatures at a pleasant 28°C provide a dependable breeze for surfing. Winds are strongest between January and May; on most afternoons velocity reaches 4–7 on the Beaufort scale. Waves, too, are big, with 23m waves for training and 35m waves for crack surfers seeking jumps and bumps. There's also calm water for speed. The slack period, when winds are calmest, is July to October. The two main schools providing windsurfing and kitesurfing instruction, equipment rental and lodging are:

Adícora Kite – Adícora Wind Paradise Playa Sur; m 0414 501 3170, 0414 634 1039; e adicorakite@hotmail.com; www.adicorakite.com. Roberto Sierra runs this beachfront kitesurfing school, offering courses, equipment hire, storage & accommodation in the on-site *posada*. Lodging is in rooms & apts with Wi-Fi & meals are available at w/ends ($).
Archie's Windsurf Playa Sur; \ 0269 988 8285; m 0414 694 8175; e archies@ archies-surf-posada.com; www.kitesurfing-venezuela.com. German windsurfer & instructor Archie Wicher, offers courses Nov–May, when he enjoys 'winter' in Adícora. The school rents kites & boards, has a deposit for equipment & Archie runs a *posada* ($) from the same spot.
Windsurf Adícora Playa Sur; \ 0269 988 8224; m 0416 769 6196, 0414 684 3734; e pachi@ windsurfadicora.com, pachiadicora@yahoo.com; www.kitesurfingadicora.com. Instructor Pachi, a pioneer of kitesurfing in Paraguaná, offers courses, rent of sails, boards, diving gear & bikes & lodging in rooms or apts ($).

Further afield

Buchuaco, El Supí Although only 3km from Adícora by the sea, the beach of Buchuaco is reached by the road from El Supí, 6.7km. Both are largely summer home developments. The beaches are protected by coral reefs that act as natural breakwaters. There are often houses for rent, but without security; it's better to stay in a guesthouse in Adícora.

Boca de Caño Wildlife Refuge Also known as Laguna Tiraya, this wildlife refuge is 10km north of Adícora. Flamingos gather here to feed on shrimp in the shallow waters separated from the sea by reefs. The sun is merciless, however, and the birds are often distant; the best time to see them is November to January. (Another larger lagoon attracting very big flocks of flamingos is the **Salina de Bajarigua**, inland from Las Cumaraguas. But you may have to get a guide to find the way.) The *posadas* in Adícora can arrange trips to the refuge.

Tiraya This bare-bones beach community is reached by a paved causeway over the lagoon's north end. It's a popular swimming place at weekends but shuttered and without shade or facilities on weekdays.

A road parallels the coast northward past the **Salinas de Cumaraguas**, a series of lagoons exploited for salt. Their evaporating waters shimmer in lavender-rose hues, edged by brilliant salt crystals; it's an amazing sight. On the sea side, reached by a dyke over the lagoon, a large resort was built on Bahía Mata Gorda, with many signs announcing the Médano Caribe. However, as the hotel went bankrupt and

Falcón and Zulia FALCÓN STATE

16

the place has been closed for years, all you see are the three-storey skeletons of buildings deserted among the sands.

Another road continues further north via **Pueblo Nuevo–El Vínculo**, joins the coast road and continues further north where you pass another abandoned project for the shortwave radio station of La Voz de Venezuela. The coast just south is called **Piedras Negras** for its bluffs of jagged black rocks. There are dunes and some bungalows.

To reach **Cabo San Román**, another 8km or so, you will need an expert guide and jeep driver to negotiate the track through cactus and boulders. The northernmost point of Venezuela, the cape is named for the saint's day when Alonso de Ojeda touched here on 9 August 1499. The seas of the upper peninsula are calmer than the east coast and despite sharp black rocks you can find quiet beaches, even trees, and lots of washed up shells. Aruba is on the northern horizon.

WEST COAST (Telephone code: 0269)

Judibana, Punto Fijo and Cardón After travelling through the peninsula's interior of goats, cactus and centuries-old *pueblos*, the speedways and urban sprawl on the west coast come as a shock. The integration of Amuay and Cardón refineries into the **Paraguaná Refining Centre** makes this the world's largest refining complex, with a processing capacity of 940,000 barrels a day. Amuay, started by Standard Oil in 1947, is a skyscraper maze of pipelines, furnaces and cracking plants. Giant tankers berth at its port on Amuay Bay. Cardón, about 20km south, was built by Shell Oil. In fact, refineries are Falcón State's main engines of development and Punto Fijo–Judibana its biggest city. Secondary industries have grown such as a shipyard making and repairing steel boats, and a shrimp processing plant. A fishing fleet operates out of **Carirubana**, going after shrimp in the deep Gulf of Venezuela.

Judibana, a suburban centre near the airport of **Las Piedras**, has banks, restaurants, hotels, trees and parks. Pleasant enough, it is easy to drive around but there is little to do. The town was planned as part of Amuay refinery to house oil workers.

Punto Fijo, the old urban centre, has a population of 11,500 but the total population including Judibana is some 255,000 people. Horns blare and cars and people choke its main streets, Avenida Bolívar and Avenida Colombia. The only reason to come here for most people is for the shopping. Paraguaná is now a tax-free zone, with no import taxes on alcoholic beverages or electronic goods. This boost to the local economy has brought shiny new shopping malls, such as the massive Sambil Mall Paraguaná, which opened in 2009 and is built in the shape of a child's pinwheel. Just as in Margarita, visitors from outside Venezuela will not find many bargains among the imported goods on sale.

Cardón, immediately south, merges with Punto Fijo (the refinery itself is some 4km further down the coast). The ex-oil camp is an open, agreeable district of homes near a golf club, park, hospital, schools, and cultural and social centres. There's a good marina and sailing club.

Opposite the new Paraguaná Natural Science Museum is the **Zoológico de Paraguaná**. A private, non-profit foundation, it is one of the best zoos in the country, dedicated to conservation. Here, a pair of Andean spectacled bears, the endangered *oso frontino*, have reared three cubs.

Getting there

By air The Aeropuerto Internacional Josefa Camejo is referred to on airline schedules as Aeropuerto Las Piedras. It is 12km northeast of Punto Fijo. There are flights to Caracas, Maracaibo and Coro by state-run airline Conviasa (*www.conviasa.aero*), Santa Bárbara (*www.sbairlines.com*) flies to Caracas, Tiara Air (*www.tiara-air.com*) flies to Aruba and Insel Air (*www.fly-inselair.com*) flies to Curaçao.

By bus Peninsular buses stop at Calle 89 Perimetral, north of the **Mercado** in downtown Punto Fijo. They go to Pueblo Nuevo, to Santa Ana and other towns. Buses go to Coro (83km,1 hour, US$3), throughout the day. Airport buses leave from Avenida Bolívar and Calle 82. A service to Barquisimeto is provided by Transporte Federación, to Maracaibo by Transporte Bucaral and Expresos Guasa.

There is no central bus terminal in Punto Fijo, so long-distance coaches depart from individual bus offices. Expresos Alianza is located at Calle 85 and Avenida 18 Colombia; Expresos Occidente, Calle 78 Comercio at Avenida 21; Expresos San Cristóbal is on Avenida Colombia at Calle 90. There are various night departures to Maracaibo (337km, 5½ hours, US$15); Valencia (378km, 6 hours, US$17); and Caracas (552km, 8–9 hours, US$20).

By car From Coro follow the signs to Los Médanos and the highway that crosses the isthmus to Paraguaná. At the crossroads, turn left for Punto Fijo and all destinations west, with a turn-off at El Cayude to Santa Ana. Alternatively, carry on straight ahead to Adícora and Cabo San Román at the tip of the peninsula. Signposting is good.

Where to stay
Punto Fijo

Lidotel Hotel Boutique Paraguaná (66 rooms) Av Intercomunal Alí Primera, Sambil Paraguaná Ciudad Turística shopping mall; www.lidotel.com.ve. The latest in the Lidotel chain of Sambil hotels offers the same comfort & modern touches, including, internet, Wi-Fi, restaurant, bar. Part of the shopping mall, it is in easy reach of shops, fast-food outlets, restaurants, bars & nightclubs. $$$

Hotel Villa Mar Suites (110 rooms) Av Coro, Santa Irene; \ 0269 247 0211; e ventas@ hotel-villamarsuites.com, villamarsuites@gmail.com; www.hotelvillamarsuites.com. Modern rooms & apts, with restaurant, bar, swimming pool, laundry service, internet. Popular with Venezuelans making the most of the tax-free shopping in local stores, this is a good option if you need to stay in Punto Fijo. $$

THE SIERRA DE SAN LUIS Less than half an hour's drive from the baking streets of Coro, in the Sierra de San Luis the temperature is an astonishing 10°C cooler. Providing superb views, old villages, quaint *posadas*, caves, hikes and excellent birding, it's no wonder that these mountains attract a steady stream of travellers looking for a refreshing respite from hot beaches and desert dunes. From many points you can see far below the **Embalse de El Isiro** near the start of the road. This dam supplies not only Coro but also the Paraguaná Peninsula with mountain water. El Isiro is fed by the Siburúa, one of many mountain rivers. The Sierra de San Luis, formed of porous limestone, is tunnelled by as many as **1,000 caves**, some having underground lakes and rivers draining to these north slopes. Sugarcane is planted in the valleys and, higher up, coffee grows under the shade of *bucares*, the immortelle trees that burst into fiery orange blooms in the dry season. Cloudforest and mist clothe the top of the range.

Another hour takes you to the three main Sierra *pueblos*: the former sugarcane *haciendas* of **Curimagua**, dating to 1768, **Cabure**, 1773, and **San Luis de Cariagua**, founded in 1590 and the district capital. Curimagua is the starting point for a 7km hike to the highest point of the range at Cerro Galicia (1,500m) in the western part of the **Parque Nacional Sierra de San Luis**, officially known as the **Parque Nacional Juan Crisóstomo Falcón**. From Cabure there is a three-hour hike through countryside along an old Spanish road or **Camino de los Españoles**, to **La Negrita**. In San Luis there is an important religious festival on

11 October, honouring **Nuestra Señora del Pilar**, when the villagers take the statue of the Virgin in procession from neighbouring Zaragoza, and the next day take her back.

Getting there The main *por puesto* route from Coro bus station goes to Cabure and San Luis before joining the old highway south to Churuguara and Barquisimeto. From any village on this route it is easy to return to Coro. There are also jeeps to Curimagua from Coro (50 minutes, US$2.50).

If driving, you will find well-signposted roads from Punto Fijo to Judibana and the airport, continuing along the coast to Villa Marina and then on to La Macolla in the far north of the peninsula.

Posadas in Coro (see *Where to stay*, page 394) also organise day tours and longer trips to the Sierra de San Luis.

Where to stay

Curimagua

Casa de Campo (24 rooms, 4 cabins) 30km from Coro on La Chapa–Soledad road; \ 0268 416 0719; m 0414 685 4037; e casadecampo@casadecampo.com.ve; www.casadecampo.com.ve. Behind a Disney-style castle gate, this large complex with swimming pool, gardens & restaurant offers great views of coast & peninsula. Rooms with hot water, TV. $$

Finca El Monte (3 rooms) On the Curimagua–Soledad road; \ 0268 404 0564; e fincaelmonte@yahoo.com. A coffee plantation popular with twitchers run by friendly Swiss owners, Ursula & Ernst Iseli. Guest rooms have hot water, good blankets, hearty, economical meals, vegetarian dishes to order. Good views. Can organise hikes to nearby caves & waterfalls with map or guide, day tours by 4x4 vehicle, birdwatching. German, Swiss & English spoken. $

Posada Bosquetito (2 rooms, 5 cabins) Caserío El Carmen, off the Curimagua–Soledad road; \ 0268 252 3602, 0268 808 4906; m 0414 682 0656; www.posadabosquetito.com. Set among lawns & trees, rooms have bath, hot water, TV, cabins with fridge, *tasca* restaurant. Horseriding, hiking to nearby Ulua Caves (10mins). Owner Josefa de Chirinos can organise package with meals, advise on local attractions, transport from Coro. $

Posada El Conuquero (6 rooms) Santa María de la Chapa, between La Negrita & La Chapa; m 0414 256 7692; e valleros@cantv.net. A 6-room guesthouse in a village said to be the oldest of the Sierra; private bath, hot water, fan, TV & restaurant. Tours offered to the Sierra, Coro, Paraguaná. $

Cabure and San Luis

Posada Turística Don Aguedo (10 rooms) Calle Principal San Luis; m 0416 263 5949, 0416 966 189; e donaguedo@hotmail.com; www.posadadonaguedo.com. Rooms with bath, TV, AC, hot water, dorm room with shared bath. Small restaurant serving hearty fare at good prices. Can arrange excursions to local attractions. $$

Club Turístico Campestre Camino Viejo (12 rooms, cabins) Cabure; \ 0269 248 2418; m 0416 669 0816. A popular w/end place for its pool, restaurant, evening *tasca*, satellite TV, close to the *camino real*, the old Spanish road to La Negrita. Economical rooms with dbl bed, bath, cold water, AC, TV, as well as units with kitchen for 8 guests. Closed Mon. $

Posada La Cabureña (6 rooms) Calle Bolívar, near church, Cabure; \ 0268 661 1093; m 0414 696 2571. Place in centre of Cabure. Rooms with bath, hot water, AC, TV, fridge. $

Posada Turística El Duende (5 rooms) Cabure; \ 0268 404 9298, 0268 661 1079; m 0416 225 6491. A charming *posada* at the start of the centuries-old *camino real*, 1km north of the village. The rustic, tile-roofed restaurant & *posada* are built of adobe. Rooms for 2–6 guests, with bath, cold water. The venerable owner, Señor 'Muma' Coronado, can organise horseriding trips & advise on hikes to the Acurite Caves, the large sinkhole of Sima de Guarataro & the petroglyphs of Ramonal. $

Other practicalities The Sierra de San Luis is a rural area of small towns where access to banks and internet services is limited so plan accordingly and bring the cash you need. Informal internet places can be found in the bigger towns, such as Curimagua, San Luis and Cabure.

San Pedro de Maparari and Las Turas folk dancing

Celebrated every year on 23–24 September and harking back to ancient indigenous harvest traditions in honour of Mother Earth, the night-long **Baile de las Turas** is held in a large private courtyard. The celebrations begin in the afternoon when a queen is chosen, usually an important senior matriarch. Wearing a crown decked with maize and other grains, she leads the dancing around an altar topped with a cross, surrounded by maize and fruit. In a circle, the dancers link hands behind their backs, all moving forwards, then backwards. Men and boys play the traditional *turas* or cane flutes and maracas, while others blow on deer skull trumpets. The next day, all go to church and the procession starts again, led by the statue of the Virgin Mary. This is still a very local event, celebrated by rural families who trace their ancestors back to the Ayamanes and Jirajara Indians who fled to the mountains to escape the conquistadors in the times of Nikolaus Federmann and the search for El Dorado.

Where to stay

Posada El Pájaro Azul (5 rooms) 100 Calle Comercio, Maparari; 0268 993 1017. Another good option, also inexpensive. Behind a café & shop are spacious, attractive rooms for 2–5 guests, with bath, hot water & fan, facing a patio fountain. The *posada* fills up on 23–24 September when Maparari celebrates a harvest ritual that has changed little over time. $

Cueva de la Quebrada El Toro

A national park famous for its large **underground river**, cave and many *guácharos* (oilbirds), the Cueva de la Quebrada El Toro is reached by a road through cattle country, going east at a fork 10km south of Maparari, via Santa Cruz de Bucaral (this continues as a jeep road down to the Morón–Coro highway). Close to the Lara State border, the 85km² park encloses a beautiful limestone canyon with vertical walls and wonderful trees, immensely tall royal palms, the Toro River and the cave. Varied fauna in the canyon include deer, ocelots, puma, peccary and howler monkeys.

Access is by way of La Taza (1,000m) where there is an Inparques guard post (PGP); a 9km earth road descends to a second post in the canyon (300m). Campers here will need a permit from Inparques (*Santa Cruz de Bucaral;* 0268 277 8582), who can also recommend local guides; the maximum size of group allowed in the cave is five people. This fascinating park is well guarded because the river issuing from the cave is the only water source for La Taza and Santa Cruz. In the rainy season the swollen river stops all visits.

The Toro River flows out of the big cave entrance where *guácharo* birds nest. The river is navigable for some 200m by inflatable boat or inner tube. Swimmers should have neoprene suits and flippers, and boat passengers should wear a T-shirt or tracksuit and rubber shoes because of the cold. More oilbirds inhabit a hall 150m from the cave entrance where torchlight also reveals spiders, beetles and blind fish. The Sociedad Venezolana de Espeleología has mapped 1,602m of horizontal galleries.

ZULIA STATE

LAKE MARACAIBO First known by its Indian name of Coquivacoa, Lake Maracaibo is the largest lake in South America (13,000km²), and is unique in having a direct outlet to the sea. Alonso de Ojeda, leading four Spanish ships in 1499, spent nine days on the lake and found the Indians, who gave him a beautiful and very amicable girl. Isabel, as she became, went back with him to the royal court and

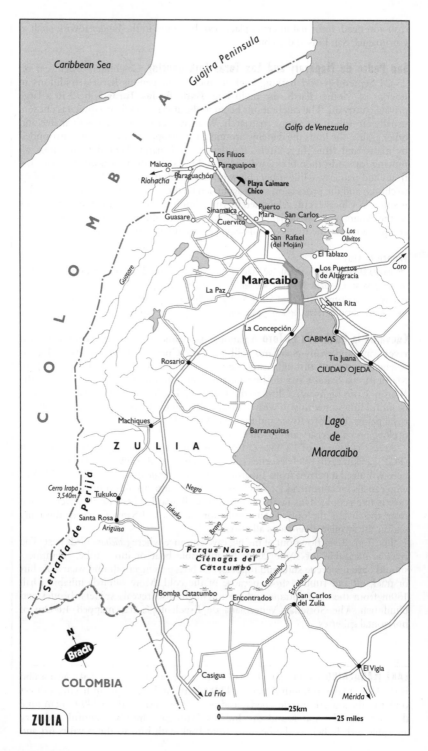

ZULIA

spent the rest of her life at his side. With their three children they lived in Santo Domingo where Ojeda died and was buried in 1516.

Historically, the lake served Spaniards as the most direct route inland to the Andes. They went south up rivers entering the lake: the Motatán to Trujillo, the Chama to Mérida and the Escalante to Táchira. All Andean exports and imports to Spain also travelled via Lake Maracaibo. **Zulia State** takes its name from an important southwest trade route from Colombia via the Zulia–Catatumbo rivers. In the days of steamboats (*estimbotes*) people and produce travelled on a small railway from Táchira to Encontrados, went down the Catatumbo and transferred onto paddle steamers for the trip to Maracaibo. Steamboats faded when the Pan American highway opened in the 1950s. Little lake ports linger on: La Ceiba (Trujillo State), Boscán, Gibraltar, Bobures, San Antonio and Palmarito (Mérida), Puerto Chama.

Fed by more than 135 rivers, the lake once had such a low salt content that the water served for drinking and irrigation. All that changed with the coming of oil, however. A channel dredged in 1954 to allow the passage of bigger ships into the lake more than tripled the amount of seawater coming in. Oil also makes the lake the richest in the world, with more than 10,000 wells producing over 700,000 barrels a day. Over 400 major deposits have been found in and around the lake. Some wooden derricks from the old days still stand. At night huge gas compression plants, pumping stations and gas flares light up the southeast. Underwater there lies a maze of 24,000km of pipelines, half carrying oil, half gas and oil-well water which today is re-injected into wells. A pipe transports oil 235km to the Paraguaná Peninsula, to feed the large refineries of Amuay and Cardón.

Fertile lands south of the lake have been cleared and drained by farmers and ranchers. The **Sur del Lago** is one of the country's main fruit, vegetable, milk and beef producing areas but deforestation has dried up watercourses and affected swamps that produce El Relámpago de Catatumbo (see *Catatumbo lightning*, page 421), a natural phenomenon of thunder-less lightning that lights up the sky for 140–160 nights of the year. The lake has also been affected by duckweed, with at least 12% of the surface covered by the aggressive aquatic plant at one point, and the only solution is to dredge it up and remove it more quickly than it can grow back. A long-term solution is definitely needed and the Environment Ministry, universities and oil industry are all working together on lake conservation (paid for by the state oil company PDVSA). Saline waters increase corrosion so the risk of oil spills is ever-present. Computer technology and sophisticated detection methods have been developed including the use of satellite images. However, the worst contamination comes from agricultural run-off, industrial and human waste. Since 2000 Maracaibo and other towns have started up sewage treatment plants, but there are still no safe swimming areas in the lake.

MARACAIBO (*Telephone code: 0261*) There is little in Maracaibo to attract most travellers, who generally pass through only when going on to Colombia via the border at Maicao–Paraguachón. The second biggest city in Venezuela, Maracaibo has a population of over 1.5 million, nearly half the total for Zulia State. A colourful city spreading northwest of the lake, it is famously hot (average 30°C/85°F) and known for serving the coldest beer in the country. On the bustling streets of the city you see oil executives in smart suits rubbing shoulders with colourfully clad Wayúu (Guajira) women in traditional flowing *mantas*. The people here are known for their good humour, quick wit and knack for giving everything a nickname. They call themselves Maracaiberos, although outsiders call them Maracuchos. Their city is fascinating to visit for its lake, bridge, oil fields, *gaita* music, markets, historic buildings and cultural centres. A new **metro system**

started limited operations in 2006 and opened fully in 2009. Line 1 has six stations linking Altos de la Vanega, in the southeast of the city, with Avenida Libertador in the centre of town. Maracaibo has only been linked by road to the rest of Venezuela since 1962–63 when the bridge was built, at that time the longest pre-stressed concrete bridge in the world. The **General Rafael Urdaneta Bridge**, one of the local sights, stretches 8.6km over the neck of Lake Maracaibo. Before the bridge, you had to take a plane, boat or ferry to reach Maracaibo. The road circling west via Machiques–La Fría was built ten years later.

Long isolation did not bother the ebullient Maracaiberos, many of whom would like their city to be capital of 'La República del Zulia'. After all, Zulia produces much of Venezuela's dried milk, *plátanos*, top grade beef, as well as sugar, tons of fish, excellent beer and half of the nation's oil. Maracaibo's port ranks third in the nation.

History The first settlement on the shores of the lake was founded in 1529 by the German conquistador Ambrosius Alfinger as a staging post for expeditions seeking El Dorado and Indian gold. Founded again by Pedro Maldonado in 1574, Maracaibo became the trading centre for the entire Andean region, including the eastern part of what is now Colombia. Until San Carlos Fort was built in 1683,

OIL, THE 'BLACK GOLD'

For over 70 years Venezuela has been among the world's biggest oil exporters. The state company Petróleos de Venezuela (PDVSA) is listed among the world's largest oil corporations, behind Saudi Arabia's Aramco. World attention was riveted in 1922 by the blowout on Lake Maracaibo's east coast of a well called Barrosos Number 2. For nine days the well spewed out a million barrels of oil before it was brought under control. Four years later oil took over as the country's leading export.

Even before the Conquest, Indians around Lake Maracaibo caulked their canoes with oil and used it as a curative. They called the oil seeps *menes*. Spaniards used oil for lamps as well as boat repair. As early as 1539 a barrel of oil was exported to Spain 'to alleviate the gout of Emperor Charles V'. It was shipped from Cubagua, which at that time had a seep. Then in 1878 a local Táchira company, La Alquitrana (*alquitrán* means 'tar'), first exploited oil near Rubio (operations finally closed in 1934). It was not until 1914, however, that Venezuela entered the oil age with the first big commercial well, Zumaque Number I in the Mene Grande field. Shell subsidiaries brought in this well and Los Barrosos.

From a primitive agricultural country, Venezuela rocketed into an oil economy. For the people used to *haciendas* bossed by a *patrón*, the new system was just bigger and easier. Some wealth filtered down from the top, and a centralised government controlled all power. For a long time there was a great deal of money and work. Three quarters of the population moved to cities. But oil dependency was too great; when prices fell in the 1980s the economy crumbled. By this time corruption had riddled the administration and public services were bankrupt. Despite democracy mayors and state governors were appointed, not elected, until 1989.

Oil fields extend north of the Orinoco from the Maracaibo and Apure basins in the west, to the Orinoco Delta in the east. In Monagas State a big discovery was made in 1986 in El Furrial. Such new finds bring proven reserves up to 99.5 billion barrels, placing Venezuela fourth in global terms. And these figures do not include the oil or tar sands of the Orinoco Oil Belt, the world's largest reserve of heavy crudes or naphthenes, with estimated reserves of 513 billion barrels.

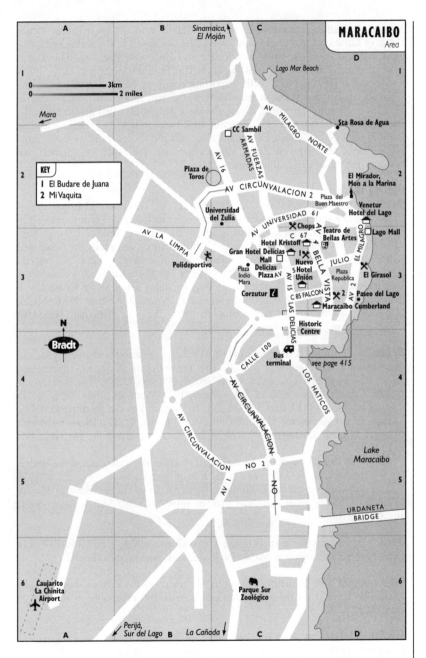

MARACAIBO
Area

Sinamaica,
El Moján

Lago Mar Beach

AV MILAGRO NORTE

Mara

Sta Rosa de Agua

0 ———— 3km
0 ———— 2 miles

CC Sambil

AV FUERZAS ARMADAS

AV 16

Plaza de
Toros

El Mirador,
Mon a la Marina

KEY

1 El Budare de Juana
2 Mi Vaquita

AV CIRCUNVALACION 2

Plaza del
Buen Maestro

Venetur
Hotel del Lago

Universidad
del Zulia

AV UNIVERSIDAD 61

Chops

Lago Mall

AV LA LIMPIA

C 67

Teatro de
Bellas Artes

EL MILAGRO

Hotel Kristoff

BELLA VISTA

Gran Hotel Delicias

Mall

JULIO

Polideportivo

Plaza
Indio
Mara

Delicias
Plaza AV

Nuevo
Hotel
Unión

AV 15

Plaza
Republica

El Girasol

Corzutur

C 85 FALCON

2

AV 2

Paseo del Lago

Maracaibo Cumberland

N

LAS DELICIAS

Historic
Centre

Bradt

CALLE 100

Bus
terminal

see page 415

LOS HATICOS

AV CIRCUNVALACION

Lake
Maracaibo

AV CIRCUNVALACION NO 2

AV 1

NO

URDANETA
BRIDGE

Caujarito
La Chinita
Airport

Parque Sur
Zoológico

Perijá,
Sur del Sur del Lago

La Cañada

however, the little port was a magnet for pirates of the Spanish Main and was repeatedly attacked. Gibraltar, the southern lake port for cacao and sugar growers was burnt and sacked three times by pirates: in 1665 by Jean Nim, a French pirate; in 1669 by Henry Morgan and in 1678 by another Frenchman, d'Estees.

Later, during the Independence wars, the **Battle of Lake Maracaibo** on 24 July 1823 ended Spain's hold over the Province of Venezuela. Spanish General Pablo

16

Morales had taken Maracaibo a year after Bolívar won the great Independence Battle of Carabobo, and it was only after a fleet was raised in Colombia and a ten-week blockade that the battle was fought and Zulia was liberated. The date is celebrated today as Armed Forces Day (as well as Bolívar's birthday).

Maracaibo flowered as a coffee exporting centre in the mid 1800s, attracting German, Italian and Curaçao merchants whose names are still active today in Venezuela: Blohm, Steinvorth, Zingg, De Lima. Venezuela's first private bank, the Banco de Maracaibo, was established in 1882 by shareholders including leading families such as the Belloso, D'Empaire, Troconis and Urdaneta. After coffee came oil and now, in northwest Zulia, mixed enterprises are exploiting gigantic coal reserves, proven at 938 million tons.

Getting there

By air Aeropuerto Internacional La Chinita [411 A6] is the second largest airport in the country and is also known as Caujarito for its location, 12km southwest of central Maracaibo (about US$8 in a taxi from the centre). Airlines making a total of 18 flights to Caracas on weekdays, and half as many on weekends, are Aeropostal (*www.aeropostal.com*), Aserca (*www.asercaairlines.com*) and Conviasa (*www.conviasa.aero*), which also has flights to Porlamar and Punto Fijo. International service to Barranquilla, Bogotá and Cartagena in Colombia is provided by Aires (*US$130–200; www.aires.aero*). American Airlines flies to Miami (*US$600; www.aa.com*) and Copa Airlines flies to Panama (*US$600; www.copaair.com*).

By bus The Terminal de Pasajeros [411 C4] is large, busy and conveniently located downtown, 1.5km southwest of Calle 100. Buses depart all day to Cabimas and eastern towns, to El Moján and to Coro, 260km (4 hours, US$8). The fastest route to San Cristóbal goes west of Lake Maracaibo, 445km (8 hours, US$15). To Caracas it's 745km (11 hours, US$20–24). To Valencia you can go either via Coro, 533km, or Barquisimeto, 511km (both about 6 hours, US$9). Buses to Mérida (9 hours, US$16), leaving mostly at night, take the route west of the lake via La Fría to El Vigía.

Por puestos to Altagracia, on the east coast of Lake Maracaibo across the bridge, leave from Avenida 100 Libertador at the foot of Avenida 10.

The quickest way to the Colombian border is to take a *por puesto* to Maicao (3 hours, US$10), where you can pick up buses to Santa Marta, Barranquilla and Cartagena.

By car Maracaibo is on the main Route 3 from Coro and Valera, and Route 17 from Barquisimeto, joining up at Maracaibo bridge and crossing into the city.

Lake launches The launches crossing to Altagracia on the eastern shore of Lake Maracaibo leave from the *embarcadero* on Avenida 100 Libertador at the foot of Avenida 10 [315 C4].

Tourist information The tourism office of the state development agency is **Corzutur** [411 C3] (*Edificio Lieja, Av 18 between Av 5 de Julio & Calle 78;* \ *0261 792 1411, 0261 783 4982;* ⊕ *08.00–12.00 & 14.00–16.00 Mon–Fri*). They will tell you what's new and provide city maps, folders and a schedule of local events.

🏠 **Where to stay** Hotels in Maracaibo run the gamut from dosshouse to luxury but for security reasons and for ease of eating out it's better to stick to the new centre and visit the historic downtown area during the day.

⌂ **Venetur Hotel Del Lago** [411 D2] (360 rooms) Av 2 El Milagro; ☎ 0261 794 4222; www.venetur.gob.ve. Nice gardens, poolside barbecue, 3 restaurants, bars, shops, gym, sauna & a beach on the lake at this 5-star hotel now run by the state. Rooms with minibars, internet. $$$$

⌂ **Hotel Kristoff** [411 C3] (300 rooms) Av No 8, Calle 68, Sector Santa Rita; ☎ 0261 796 1000; e info@hotelkristoff.com; www.hotelkristoff.com. A modern 4-star hotel on 6 floors with a beautiful pool, restaurants, bar & gym. $$$

⌂ **Gran Hotel Delicias** [411 C3] (188 rooms) Av 15-Las Delicias at Calle 70; ☎ 0261 797 6111; e hoteldelicias@telcel.net.ve; www.hoteldelicias.com. Located near Av 5 de Julio in the new centre with

small swimming pool, Italian restaurant, bar-disco, laundry, Wi-Fi. $$

⌂ **Maracaibo Cumberland** [411 D3] (87 rooms) Calle 86A; ☎ 0261 722 2244; e reservas@ hotelescumberland.com; www.hotelescumberland.com. A more reasonably priced midtown option with restaurant, laundry & internet. $$

⌂ **Hotel Caribe** [415 D2] (60 rooms) Av 7 near Calle 93; ☎ 0261 722 5986. A downtown budget option a few blocks from Plaza Bolívar, has rooms with fan & AC. Try & get one of the newer rooms. $

⌂ **Nuevo Hotel Unión** [411 C3] (14 rooms) 4–60 Calle 84; ☎ 0261 793 3278. A pleasant old-style house a block east of Bella Vista. Rooms with AC, tall ceilings & tiled floors, usually full so call to book. $

✘ **Where to eat** Maracuchos like deep-fried *arepas*, grilled meats, premium whiskys, ice-cold beers and restaurants with arctic air conditioning, which can be a shock when coming in from the heat of the street. Also be aware that many restaurants are closed on Sunday. The midtown area between Calle 67 and Cecilio Acosta in the north and Calle 77 and 5 de Julio in the south has a great variety of restaurants to choose from. Fast-food junkies will find all the burgers and chicken wings they crave in the city's many large shopping malls, including the Lago Mall [411 D3] on Avenida Milagro, next to the Hotel del Lago, Mall Delicias Plaza [411 C3] in Avenida Las Delicias Norte and the brand new Sambil mega-mall [411 C2], north of the city in Avenida Goajira.

✘ **El Girasol** [411 D3] Av 1B at Calle 74, top floor of Hotel El Paseo; www.hotelelpaseo.com.ve; ⌚ 12.00–15.00 & 19.00–24.00. The only revolving restaurant in Maracaibo, with excellent views over the city & the lake, there's a real novelty factor to the Girasol, which is popular with couples & heavy on the romantic mood music. The food is more pedestrian, with a pricey menu of international cuisine featuring few nods to local dishes. $$$

✘ **El Zaguán** [415 D2] Calle Carabobo 94 at Av 6; www.restaurantelzaguan.com; ⌚ 12.00–19.00 Mon–Sat. A good downtown option decorated like an old Maracaibo house (*zaguán* is the entry of a colonial house). A nice place for a coffee & snack under great bombax trees or for an early dinner in the inner sanctum with AC, where traditional Zulian dishes are served. Try the *carnero en coco* (ram cooked in coconut) or the *torta de plátano* (plantain cake). $$

✘ **Mi Vaquita** [411 D2] Calle 76 at Av 3H, near Plaza La República; www.mivaquita.com; ⌚ 12.00–23.00. For serious carnivores, this Texan-style steak house is something of an institution with caesar salads & a list of grilled meats as long as your arm. The bar turns into a disco after 11.00. $$

✘ **Chops** [411 C2] Av 10 & Calle 65; ⌚ 11.00–23.00. A local fast-food chain that pops

up all over the city, try this one or the one on Calle 72. They sell hamburgers but the highlights are the large portions of *tequeños* (deep-fried cheese & pastry twists) eaten with ketchup & the *patacones* (green plantains flattened & fried) served with pork & avocado. They even have a *platiburger*, a hamburger served between 2 fried plantains. $

✘ **El Budare de Juana** [411 C3] Av 8, Calle 70; ⌚ all hours. Hearty soups & *arepas* stuffed with a host of fillings in any combination you want at this small locale in Santa Rita. A popular place to head off a hangover after a night on the town. The nearby **San Benito** sells the less than appealing sounding *aguita e sapo* (toad water), a mouth-watering combo of fried cheese & cooked ham dripping with juice served in a deep-fried *arepa*. $

✘ **La Matera** 14 Calle 71, Las Delicias; ⌚ 11.30–22.00 Mon–Sat, 11.30–18.00 Sun. You only have to see the many workers, oilmen & executives eating side by side to be aware of its 30-year position as a leading *criollo* restaurant; rustic, tree-shaded & reasonable, serving specialities such as coconut-bean soup, *mojito* of coconut & shredded fish, curried goat, crab with fish sauce, *huevos chimbos* — not eggs but a rum-pumpkin dessert. $

Festivals Zulia's patron saint is La Virgen de Chiquinquirá and the whole state turns out for the big **Feria de La Chinita** leading up to religious observances on 18 November. The fair starts out with a parade of floats on Avenida 5 de Julio headed by the Fair's Queen. She also presides at the opening of a bike race and a bullfight. Concerts and exhibitions are staged at the Centro de Bellas Artes. There's an art and craft fair, and even a night-time lake cruise, the 'Feria del Ferry' – all to the rhythm of *gaita* bands resounding night and day.

Another Maracaibo tradition comes in the run-up to Christmas with the arrival of *gaitas*, an infectious local music style that has spread from Zulia throughout the country. In every district, almost every street, *gaitero* groups compose and rehearse songs for Christmas and the competition to have the most popular *gaita* of the year. Downtown, Maracaibo's streets become a big bazaar as stalls go up along the Paseo de Las Ciencias, Plaza Baralt, Avenida Padilla and Calle 100. The **Festival de San Benito** over 27–31 December is observed by the people of El Mojan, Altagracia, Cabimas, Lagunillas, Gibraltar, Bobures and San Antonio with processions and costumed dances honouring the black saint. In Sinamaica, the native Paraujanos proceed in launches around 17.00 on 27 December to the opening ritual; each group is led by an image of San Benito held high. Around an altar, under a palm thatch, drummers lay down a solemn beat as the men dance still carrying their own San Benito.

South of the lake, the fiestas in Bobures and Gibraltar are famous for their conical African drums, costumed *vasallos* and *esclavos* (vassals and slaves), and all-night vigils to fulfil promises made to the saint who is given shots of rum and is believed to enjoy a good party.

Other practicalities There is no problem finding a bank with an ATM in Maracaibo, both in the shiny new shopping malls and in the historic centre.

There is a Movistar call center with internet and international calls at the main bus terminal [411 C4]. A CANTV call centre is in the CC Plaza Lago shopping mall on Avenida Libertador.

The Hospital Central is on Avenida El Milagro between Calle 94 and calle 95.

What to see and do Within a small downtown area near the docks you can catch the city's lively spirit. *Avenidas* go north–south, *calles* east–west. The lakeside drive, Avenida 2 El Milagro, starts at the **Malecón** or south waterfront boulevard. The main shopping district is around Avenida 4 Bella Vista and Avenida 5 de Julio (Calle 77). Bella Vista is the city's modern centre with large shops and restaurants.

Plaza Baralt [415 D3] Before the oil boom this plaza was the classy business and shopping centre, presided over by the statue of Rafael María Baralt, 19th-century writer and historian who wrote a Castillian dictionary. At the north end is the restored **Templo de San Francisco**, an 18th-century church declared a National Historic Monument.

Centro de Arte de Maracaibo Lia Bermúdez [415 D3] (*Plaza Baralt;* ✆ 0261 723 1286; *www.camlb.com*) This is housed in the old public market, a wrought iron structure dating from 1928 that was imported piecemeal from England. Elegantly restored, the centre has a museum, drama, dance and concert hall, information centre, craft shop and cafeteria.

Mercado de Las Pulgas [415 C3] (*On Calle 100, by the lake*) Everything under the sun is sold at this open-air marketplace, literally a 'flea market'. Look out for the Guajira women who come at dawn by bus, do their shopping and selling, then

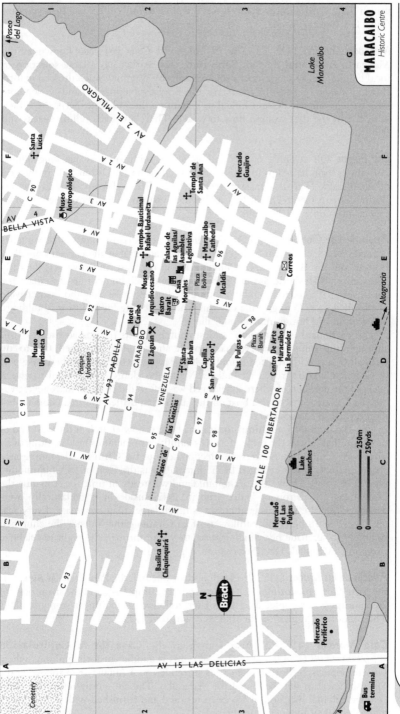

Cemetery

AV 15 LAS DELICIAS

Basílica de
Chiquinquirá

C 93

Parque
Urdaneta

Museo
Urdaneta

C 91

C 90

Santa
Lucía

Museo
Antropológico

AV
BELLA VISTA

AV 2 EL MILAGRO

Poseo
del Lago

Templo Bautismal
Rafael Urdaneta

Museo
Arquidiocesano

Hotel
Caribe

El Zaguán

CARABOBO

Palacio de
las Aguilas/
Asamblea
Legislativa

Casa
Morales

Teatro
Baralt

Templo de
Santa Ana

Mercado
Guajiro

Maracaibo
Cathedral

Plaza
Bolívar

Alcaldía

Correos

AV-93-PADILLA

VENEZUELA

Santa
Bárbara

Capilla
San Francisco

Paseo de
las Ciencias

Las Pulgas

Plaza
Baralt

Centro De Arte
Maracaibo
Lia Bermúdez

Altagracia

CALLE 100 LIBERTADOR

Lake
launches

Mercado
de Las Pulgas

Mercado
Periférico

Bus
terminal

Lake
Maracaibo

N
Bradt

0   250m
0   250yds

vanish homeward. However, this is not the place to buy crafts; with luck you may find a few baskets outside.

Mercado Guajiro [415 F3] (*Av El Milagro at Calle 96*) Also known as the **Mercado Artesanal de San Sebastián**, this market has a large selection of local handicrafts and hammocks sold on stalls by Wayúu women dressed in long flowing *mantas*. Stand-out items are the brightly coloured, hand-woven tote bags with geometric designs linked to Wayúu myths and Wale´kerü, the spider, who taught the first women how to weave. There are stalls selling snacks and fruit juices.

Las Pulgas On Avenida 6, Las Pulgas teems with vendors hawking almost everything from hair clips to books, clothes, CDs and DVDs but little in the way of handicrafts. The flea market extends from **Plaza Baralt**, behind the Lia Bermúdez Arts Centre, to the blue and white **Templo de San Francisco**, built by Franciscan monks (1699-1730).

Paseo de Las Ciencias [415 C2–D2] This is a pedestrian walkway that stretches between Maracaibo's two main churches: the cathedral at the east end on Plaza Bolívar, and the Basílica de La Chiquinquirá in the west. In between is the early 19th-century **Iglesia de Santa Bárbara**, the only building not razed to make the controversial Paseo. Many picturesque little houses of El Saladillo district were demolished in 1973 to give the city this spacious setting for its historic buildings. Some of the old houses remain on Calle 96.

The **cathedral** is Maracaibo's oldest church and its records go back to 1610 although the building is 19th century. It shelters the venerated **Cristo de Gibraltar**, a crucifix rescued from fire 400 years ago when the southern lake port of Gibraltar was destroyed by Indians. Maracaibo clergy later refused to give it back, so the decision of where it belonged was left to the charred image revered as the Black Christ. Placed in a boat on the lake it first drifted towards Gibraltar but then turned to Maracaibo.

The **Basílica de La Chiquinquirá** is a large yellow church at the west end of the Paseo that houses the pride of Zulia's faithful, a miraculous little painting of La Virgen de Chiquinquirá, known affectionately as **La Chinita**. Beginning as a chapel in 1686, it was enlarged in the mid 1700s as the Cult of La Chiquinquirá grew. The basilica took 20 years to build and was ready in time for crowning the Holy Image as patron of Zulia State in 1942. Inside, it is fantastically over-decorated and the Virgin's gold crown is much larger than her image. Every year on the eve of 18 November followers of La Chinita gather outside the church at midnight to serenade her. Singing *gaitas*, they wait through the night to celebrate mass on La Chinita's Day. (See *Festivals*, page 414.)

Palacio de las Aguilas [415 E2] North of the cathedral, the Palacio de las Aguilas is the State Government House. Construction began in 1841 and the main floor of 24 columns was completed 25 years later, followed by the upper storey in 1890. The condors or 'eagles' on the roof were added in 1929.

Casa Morales [415 E2] Also known as the **Casa de la Capitulación** (⊕ *09.00–13.00 & 14.00–18.00 Tue–Sat*), this is another historic building, where General Francisco Morales signed his surrender on 3 August 1823 following the Spanish defeat in the Battle of Lake Maracaibo. The city's only remaining 18th-century colonial mansion, it has been restored and furnished with period pieces and paintings of Independence heroes.

Teatro Baralt [415 E2] A handsome building dating to 1932, the Teatro Baralt has only recently been restored, uncovering remains of the previous theatre built in 1883.

Temple de Santa Ana [415 F2] This chapel was built in 1602 at the east end of Calle 94 by a devout couple, Doña Inés del Basto and Francisco Ortiz, who then built an adjacent hospital, Venezuela's first. The chapel is one of Maracaibo's few colonial structures, enlarged in 1774 with a wonderfully Baroque altar screen and pulpit. There is still a city hospital next door although not attached and not beautified.

Templo Bautismal Rafael Urdaneta [415 E2] (*Av 4*) This tiny chapel was where Maracaibo's Independence hero was baptised. His sad last words, engraved in the corner of Plaza de la Herencia were: 'I leave only a widow and 11 children in the greatest poverty.'

Museo Urdaneta [415 D1] (*Av 7A, near Parque Urdaneta; ⊕ 09.00–12.00 & 14.00–17.00 Tue–Fri, 10.00–13.00 Sat–Sun; admission free*) The house where the Independence hero Rafael Urdaneta was born (1788) no longer exists. In its place is a 1936 building containing many of Urdaneta's belongings, period weapons and paintings. There is a good historical library.

Santa Lucía [415 F1] The district of Santa Lucía, also known as **El Empedrado**, overlooks the lake to the east of Avenida 3 at Calle 90. Topped by a church on a hill, Santa Lucía is worth exploring as one of Maracaibo's last neighbourhoods of brightly painted typical houses. Steps lead down from the plaza to lower streets. *Gaita* music, trademark of Zulia, apparently originated here with bands playing on St Lucia's day, 13 December. The beat is insistent, pervasive; words are irreverent, satirical or devout but rarely romantic. The instruments traditionally used in *gaita* are the *cuatro*, or four-stringed guitar, maracas, *charrasca* (a scraped instrument), and the *furruco* whose deep insistent throb comes from rubbing an upright pole attached to a drumhead. Modern *gaitas*, played by groups like Maracaibo 15 and

Guaco, have taken elements of salsa and merengue and added electric bass and keyboards to create a dance form popular all over Venezuela at Christmas.

Santa Rosa de Agua [411 D2] Today part of Maracaibo, this lakeside village is on stilts. It is located about 2km north of Parque La Marina and lies some distance from Avenida Milagro Norte so that you do not see it from the road. People, imagining that perhaps this was the village that inspired Amerigo Vespucci to name the area Little Venice, have placed his bust in the plaza. Certainly Vespucci saw similar villages, although Santa Rosa is a *criollo* fishing village, not an Indian community. Here the houses or *palafitos* are built of planks with boardwalks linking one to another. This construction over the water makes houses cooler, but the lake is contaminated and drinking water must be supplied from land. For true Indian *palafitos*, take a trip to Sinamaica (see below).

Around Maracaibo

Los Puertos de Altagracia One of the easiest and best outings while visiting Maracaibo is to take a fast ferry (for less than US$1) across the neck of the lake to Los Puertos de Altagracia. Before the bridge was built people travelling from Coro to Maracaibo took a boat from one of several old ports around Altagracia. As the distance is a fifth of that by road, launches continue to ferry workers to jobs on either shore. The *flechas* (arrows) leave from the old pier at Calle 100–Libertador from dawn to dusk on the half-hour, returning on the hour.

Altagracia is an old town with brightly painted houses dating back some 200 years. In Plaza Miranda is the Museum of History, in one of the finest houses of its era. The Battle of Lake Maracaibo was planned here in 1823 and in 1826 Bolívar stayed on his fruitless journey to save the union of Gran Colombia.

Altagracia's beach, El Vigía, is considered to be one of the best on the lake but you can't swim here as it's too close to the huge oil terminal of Puerto Miranda, a few kilometres north, and the giant El Tablazo petrochemical complex.

San Carlos Island San Carlos, a headland rather than a true island, is being groomed for tourism for its fine beaches and restored fort. The star-shaped **Castillo de San Carlos** guarding the entrance to Lake Maracaibo was built in 1680–88. The fort last saw action in 1903 when its guns repelled warships sent by European powers to blockade Venezuelan ports for non-payment of foreign debts. Although the watchtower has disappeared, the fort's massive walls have withstood sun, wind and surf. The fortress was put to use by dictator Juan Vicente Gómez as a political prison and some cells still bear the scratched names of occupants. After Gómez's death in 1935 hundreds of unfortunates being held here were freed.

The dazzling beach facing the Gulf of Venezuela is broad, sandy, mostly deserted and worth the short trek for bathers. However, it is shade-less and as the sun is white hot you will be well roasted in half a day. The more popular beach is on the south side where food stalls serve snacks. This beach is near the pier.

Some people in San Carlos village are beginning to offer rooms for rent but there's little to keep visitors overnight.

Getting there Launch ferries run frequently from **El Moján** to Toas Island and San Carlos. El Moján is a growing town at the mouth of the Limón River. It is not very pretty, but has a new bus terminal with fast service to Maracaibo, 40km.

Sinamaica Lagoon A network of marshes and lagoons including Sinamaica drains into the Limón River. This is the territory of some 1,800 Paraujanos, fishermen and their families of mixed *criollo*-Indian culture. Their villages on stilts form one of the biggest tourist attractions near Maracaibo. The main embarkation point for tourist launches (six passengers, US$25–30) is called **Puerto Mara**, just down to the right before the Río Limón Bridge, 5km from El Moján. The busy time is weekends; if you go on a weekday (barring holidays) there will be little activity and you may have to hire the whole *lancha*, for an hour's outing. You can eat well at one of the two large open-sided restaurants and the alcohol list is almost longer than the menu.

The second port, **Cuervito**, is on the lagoon 5km from the village of Sinamaica (60km from Maracaibo, US$3 in a *por puesto*, US$10 in a taxi). If you arrive early on Wednesday you will see the boats of people coming to market. There are usually

AMERICA, OR WHAT'S IN A NAME?

If honours for discovering the New World go to Christopher Columbus, then how did the continents get labelled America?

In 1499, before Columbus returned from his third voyage, an expedition set sail from Spain under Alonso de Ojeda. Map maker Juan de la Cosa, who had twice accompanied Columbus, was official cartographer. Also along was Amerigo Vespucci, a Florentine merchant in the service of the Medicis and a friend of Columbus who had helped him with supplies. He had the Medicis' backing and commanded two of the four ships. The fleet was sent by King Ferdinand and Queen Isabella for the specific purpose of checking up on Columbus and finding new lands in Terra Firma (as Venezuela was called) as Columbus had rights to a tenth of royal income from his discoveries and their royal highnesses were unhappy.

When the ships sighted land (near the Guianas) Vespucci explored southeast along the coast as far south as about latitude 6° before turning back. They then passed the mouths of the Essequibo and Orinoco rivers, and next followed the coast west the entire length of Venezuela, discovering the Paraguaná Peninsula, Curaçao, Lake Coquivacoa (Maracaibo) and a large gulf which they named Gulf of Venezuela, or 'Little Venice' after native villages built on stilts over the water. In 1500 Juan de la Cosa made his celebrated *Mappa Mundi* on which the New World appeared with the name Venezuela, for the first time.

Vespucci's letter to Lorenzo di Medici describing new lands, translated and published as *Mundus Novus* in Augsburg, 1504, made him famous throughout Europe and went into 50 editions. Vespucci was the first to announce that the lands were not Asia but a new world and did not call its inhabitants Indians. He even proposed a trade route to the East Indies, going south and west around the continent (anticipating Magellan).

In 1507 a German professor, Martin Waldseemüller, at the Saint Dié University in Lorraine, was about to publish a new cosmography. He first put forward the name of America for the New World and added Vespucci's letters relating four voyages as an appendix. Although historians have found proof of only two of these reputed voyages, they admit Vespucci sailed the breadth of Venezuela in 1499 and sailed to Brazil for the Portuguese king in 1501. He went up the Amazon four days, continued south to Guanabara Bay, and was the first to go as far as Río de la Plata and beyond (latitude 50°) reaching a cold land, possibly Patagonia, which would make him the discoverer of Argentina. It was Vespucci who described the Southern Cross as a navigational guide. Pedro Alvares Cabral had already landed on 23 April 1500, on the coast of Bahía State and has the credit for discovering Brazil.

Ironically, it is Columbus who is most honoured in Venezuela although Ojeda and Vespucci discovered the entire coast from Margarita, west to Lake Maracaibo, and even named the country and the continent.

16

plenty of launches here all day to take you to lake communities such as Pueblo Barro, about 15 minutes away, or Caño Morita, La Boquita and Boca del Caño. Most visitors stop for refreshments at the Parador Turístico built for the purpose in the lake.

Shops, schools, even a church and police station, are all built over the water *palafito*-style, some linked by boardwalks. Dwellings have walls made of *esteras* or reed matting, and roof of reeds or palm-thatch. The traditional one-room house has hammocks for sleeping but few chairs and no door; ceiling beams provide storage and hanging space. Apart from their canoe, a Paraujano family's most prized possession is the TV set. Onshore, houses are often built with planks, tin roofs and room dividers. These may be the homes of Paraujanos who earn wages in oil and coal, coconut plantations or shrimp farms. Apart from being outside the money economy, the lagoon has other drawbacks for those living there: poor sanitation, lack of fresh water in the dry season when the lagoon becomes salty and mosquitoes in the rainy season.

Some 12km beyond Sinamaica is a side road to the old **Caimare Chico** development and a beach on the Gulf of Venezuela. It is popular at weekends with Maracaibo sun-seekers, with restaurants, two pools, bungalows and lively Saturday nights.

The Guajira Peninsula The road north enters arid lands where Wayúu women dress in billowing *mantas* and the men are clad in shirts, sash and loincloths as they tend their cattle. There are about 295,000 Wayúu in Venezuela, making them the largest indigenous group in the country, and another 200,000 live in Colombia. Traditionally nomadic herders, they roam freely through the Guajira Peninsula and have a reputation for smuggling, as they don't recognise the Colombian–Venezuelan border.

Belonging to the Arawak linguistic family, they were for many years known as Guajiros, but prefer the name Wayúu, which means 'people'. The language is thriving and many Wayúu grow up learning Spanish as a second language at school. The Wayúu are perhaps the New World natives who most successfully took advantage of the Europeans' arrival with cattle and horses, and soon developed a cattle-centred economy unique in the Americas. As early as 1550 they already had herds and were replacing hunting and gathering with cattle raising as a way of life. Formerly semi-nomadic, moving with cattle from well to watering hole, today the Wayúu live in scattered communities.

Families are tightly organised in *castas* or clans where authority rests with the matriarch's brother. Clan lines, including chieftains, descend through women. A bride's worth is calculated by the number of cattle the groom pays, and negotiations are long. Also, if blood is spilled, even in a work accident, then recompense must be paid in cattle or cash, and long and bloody feuds can ensue if accounts are not settled amicably.

Paraguaipoa, 95km from Maracaibo on the main road to the Colombian border, is the area's only sizeable town. It has grown, first as a business and barter centre for people as far away as Maicao and Ríohacha in Colombia, then as a funnel for contraband goods arriving by sea on the long coast. However, travellers rarely visit as electricity, health services and personal security are all precarious. The army has a post and car checks are frequent. **Los Filuos market** draws lines of *plátano*-laden trucks, herdsmen with goats and sheep, and hundreds of Guajiros coming by jeep and truck from the dusty Alta Guajira or 'upper peninsula' (mainly Colombia) to do their bartering. Held very early on Mondays, the market is located at the north outskirts of Paraguaipoa. Although this is not a tourist market, you may find for sale some Guajira sandals with soles made of tyre rubber, hats, bags crocheted in many colours and sizes, sashes and *mantas* of cotton, nylon and dacron.

Travel to the Colombian border and Maicao The best and fastest way to reach Colombia is by *por puesto* from Maracaibo (3 hours, US$10). Along the road to the border are some nine police and National Guard checkpoints where you may be asked for ID papers and your baggage could be searched. The Venezuelan border point is at **Paraguachón** where you go through passport control and must pay an exit tax of BsF65 (US$15). It is then a short distance to **Maicao** in Colombia where there are onward buses to Barranquilla, Santa Marta and Cartagena. Although the area is reputed to be a hotbed of drug runners, or *narco traficantes*, and there is a heavy police and military presence, this is a well-travelled border crossing into Colombia.

Catatumbo lightning A striking natural phenomenon known as **El Relámpago del Catatumbo** (Catatumbo lightning), or the **Faro del Catatumbo** (Catatumbo lighthouse), illuminates the sky above Lake Maracaibo and the Catatumbo Basin with flashes of thunder-less lightning that can last the whole night. This silent, intermittent light show has occurred for centuries and can be seen from as far away as the Andes with lightning activity for 140–160 nights a year, lasting up to ten hours a night and with up to 280 lightning flashes an hour.

This sustained electrical activity makes Catatumbo lightning a significant element in the regeneration of the ozone layer. The recent drought of 2010 saw a significant drop of dry-season activity and scientists believe the phenomenon is diminishing as a result of climate change and deforestation around the Catatumbo marshes.

To help protect the fragile environment of the Catatumbo River basin, in 1991 a large wilderness area was declared **Parque Nacional Ciénagas del Catatumbo**. The main generator of methane responsible for the phenomenon comes from the *ciénagas* (marshes) that border the south of Lake Maracaibo (Sur del Lago) and extend to the Catatumbo River.

One of the first to write an account of the phenomenon, and bring it to the attention of the wider world, was the German scientist and explorer Alexander von Humboldt, who visited in 1800 and described the powerful and sustained lightning flashes as 'electrical explosions that are like a phosphorescent gleam'.

Humboldt referred to the phenomenon as 'El Farol de Maracaybo', or 'The Lighthouse of Maracaibo', because navigators on the lake are 'guided by it as by a lighthouse'.

For centuries goods and travellers from the Andes (Colombian and Venezuelan) reached Maracaibo by riverboat via the Catatumbo and the lake but now that the Perijá highway runs west of the lake, there is little river traffic. There are no visitor facilities but one or two Mérida tour companies organise overnight trips by minibus and boat to the Sur del Lago area where visitors stay in houses on stilts to see this amazing natural light show. (See *Tour operators*, page 361.)

Appendix I

LANGUAGE

Spanish (or Castilian) is a fairly straightforward language, particularly in Venezuela where there is no lisping of the soft 'c' and 'z', as in *cerveza* (beer), that you find in most of mainland Spain. Venezuelans are quite informal as a rule and the second person pronoun *tu* is more commonly heard than *usted*, which is reserved for officials, elders and betters. There are many regional variations in speech and Caraqueños, as the inhabitants of the capital are called, speak fast and often leave the 's' off the end of words. Andeans, meanwhile, speak clearly and slowly. If you can manage only a little Spanish, start with '*Hablo poco español*'. Remember that 'h' is *always* silent, and you won't go wrong with '*Hace calor*', 'It's hot' (literally, 'it makes heat'), and '*¿Qué hora es?*', 'What time is it?' The letter 'j' *always* sounds like 'h' in English: '*Viajamos juntos*', 'We travel together'. And 'll' sounds like an English 'y' in '*calle*', meaning street. 'V' and 'b' sound so similar, like the English 'b' in 'boy' that you'll hear people differentiate them as '*v corta*' and '*b larga*' when spelling something out, or '*v de vaca*' and '*b de burro*', using the words for cow and donkey.

SIGN LANGUAGE Sign language is an important part of Venezuelan communication. Puckering up the lips as if readying for a kiss and pointing with them is an acceptable way of indicating where something is in a shop, for example, although it takes some getting used to. Venezuelans will also show that they don't understand something by crinkling up the nose and brow, in a rabbit-style twitch, which can also mean 'What's up?' or 'What's going on?'. Rude gestures include making an 'o' with the thumb and forefinger, as if to form an English OK but with the 'o' fingers facing forward, which is equivalent to calling somebody gay. Tapping the elbow indicates somebody is mean with money. Pulling down the lower eyelid with the forefinger, sometimes done surreptitiously as a warning so that others don't see, means 'be careful'. It is usually accompanied by the words '*ojo*' ('watch out'), or '*mosca*', (literally 'fly' but in Venezuela indicating danger). In restaurants you can avoid a whole host of words by catching the waiter's eye and writing an imaginary cheque on your hand, which means 'Could you bring the bill, please?'. You'll also hear Venezuelans making a hissing noise by blowing air through the teeth to catch the waiter's attention. However, take care with this one. Seedy men often try to get women's attention in the street by doing the same, usually throwing in a romantic line about angels falling from heaven. These '*piropos*', as chat up lines are called, typically come with a cheery wink or an expression of pained and besotted admiration. They are best ignored.

PRONUNCIATION
Consonants

c	as 'c' in cat before 'a', 'o' or 'u'; like 's' before 'e' or 'i'
d	as 'd' in 'dog'
g	like a strong English 'h' before 'e' or 'i'; like 'g' elsewhere
h	always silent
j	always like a strong English 'h'

ll	like the 'y' in 'yellow'
ñ	like the 'ni' in 'onion'
r	always pronounced as a strong English 'r' as in 'racket'
rr	a trilled 'r'
v	similar to 'b' in 'boy'
y	similar to English but with a stronger 'dj' sound
z	like an English 's'
b, f, k, l, m, n, p, q, s, t, w, x	as in English

Vowels

a	as 'a' in 'rat'
e	as 'e' in 'hen'
i	as 'i' in 'machine'
o	as 'o' in 'hot'
u	like the 'u' sound in 'rule'; when it follows a 'q' it is silent; after an 'h' or 'g' it's pronounced as 'w', except when it comes between 'g' and 'e' or 'i', when it is also silent

USEFUL WORDS AND PHRASES The list below gives a visitor with no knowledge of Spanish enough words to get around, find luggage, ask the time, look for food and communicate other basic needs.

Essentials

Yes	Sí
No	No
Hello	Hola
Goodbye	Adios/chao
Good day/morning	Buenos días
Good afternoon	Buenas tardes
Good night	Buenas noches
See you later	Hasta luego
Do you speak…?	¿Habla…?
…English?	¿Ingles?
Please	Por favor
Thanks	Gracias
How are you?	¿Cómo está? (Usted)
Very good	Muy bien
And you?	¿Y Usted? (formal)/¿Y tu? (informal)
You are welcome	De nada
Excuse me	Perdón
What is your name?	¿Cómo se llama?
My name is…	Mi nombre es…
What is your…?	¿Qué es su…?
Telephone number	Número de teléfono
I want/need	Quiero/necesito
Help	Ayuda

Directions

Where is…?	¿Dónde está…?	house, building	casa, edificio
address	dirección	to the right/left	a la derecha/izquierda
street	calle, avenida	straight ahead	derecho

At the hotel – *En el hotel*

bedroom	*la habitación*	telephone	*el teléfono*
bathroom	*el baño*	room service	*servicio de piso*
towel	*toalla*	the manager	*el gerente*
soap	*jabón*		

Days of the week – *Días de la semana*

Monday	*lunes*	Friday	*viernes*
Tuesday	*martes*	Saturday	*sábado*
Wednesday	*miércoles*	Sunday	*domingo*
Thursday	*jueves*		

Months – *Meses*

January	*enero*	July	*julio*
February	*febrero*	August	*agosto*
March	*marzo*	September	*septiembre*
April	*abril*	October	*octubre*
May	*mayo*	November	*noviembre*
June	*junio*	December	*diciembre*

Numbers – *Números*

0	*cero*	16	*dieciseis*
1	*uno*	17	*diecisiete*
2	*dos*	18	*dieciocho*
3	*tres*	19	*diecenueve*
4	*cuatro*	20	*veinte*
5	*cinco*	21	*veinte uno*
6	*seis*	30	*treinta*
7	*siete*	40	*quarenta*
8	*ocho*	50	*cinquenta*
9	*nueve*	60	*sesenta*
10	*diez*	70	*setenta*
11	*once*	80	*ochenta*
12	*doce*	90	*noventa*
13	*trece*	100	*cien*
14	*catorce*	500	*quinientos*
15	quince	1,000	*un mil*
		1,000,000	*un millón*

Public transport – *Transporte publico*

bus station	*terminal de pasajeros*
bus stop	*la parada*
Where is this bus going?	*¿Donde va este autobus?*
my luggage	*mi equipaje*
airport	*aeropuerto*
plane	*avión*
a flight today	*un vuelo hoy*
I want a ticket to...	*Quiero un boleto a...*
At what time is...?	*¿a qué hora es...?*
the flight/departure	*el vuelo/la salida*
boat	*barco*
ferry	*el ferry*

Health – *Salud*

ache	*dolor*	heatstroke	*insolación*
toothache	*dolor de muela*	insect sting	*picada*
altitude sickness	*mal de páramo, soroche*	pain	*dolor*
bite	*mordedura*	poisonous	*venenoso*
blood	*sangre*	poisonous snake	*ponzoñoso*
blood test	*examen de sangre*	prescription	*receta*
broken bone	*fractura de hueso*	rape	*violación*
constipation	*estreñimiento*	sea/airsickness	*mareo*
dehydration	*deshidratación*	unconscious	*sin sentido, desmayado,*
dizzy spell	*mareo*		*inconsciente*
I feel dizzy	*estoy mareado/a*	vaccination	*vacuna*
doctor	*médico, doctor*	wound	*herida*
earache	*dolor de oido*	I am hurt	*estoy herido/a*
fever	*fiebre*	yellow fever	*fiebre amarilla*

Making purchases – *Haciendo compras*

I need...	*Necesito...*	that's expensive	*es caro*
I want...	*Quiero...*	that's too much	*es demasiado*
I would like...	*Quisiera...*	What is the	*Cual es el tipo*
Can I see...?	*¿Puedo ver...?*	exchange rate?	*de cambio?*
Do you have ... ?	*¿Hay...?*	bigger	*mas grande*
this one	*ésto/ésta*	smaller	*mas pequeno/a*
How much?	*¿Cuánto es?*	a discount for cash	*un descuento por efectivo*
cheaper	*mas barato*		

Food and drink – *Comida y bebida*
Café *and restaurant*

breakfast	*desayuno*	bill	*la cuenta*
lunch	*almuerzo*	tip	*propina*
dinner	*cena*	tax, VAT	*impuesto, IVA*
dining room	*comedor*	take-away service	*servicio a domicilio*
menu	*menu/la carta*	fast food	*comida rapida*
knife	*cuchillo*	set lunch	*sopa y seco/*
fork	*tenedor*		*menu ejecutivo*
spoon	*cuchara*	glass	*vaso*
waiter	*mesonero/a*	cup	*tasa*

EMERGENCY – *UNA EMERGENCIA*

Help!	*Socorro!*
Help me please	*Ayudame por favor*
I am lost	*Estoy perdido(a)*
I have been robbed	*Me robaron*
Call...	*Llama...*
...the police	*...la policia*
...an ambulance	*...una ambulancia*
...a doctor	*...un medico*
...the embassy	*...la embajada*
Fire!	*Fuego!*
It's an emergency	*Es una emergencia*

Menu items – En la carta

avocado	*aguacate*
banana	*cambur*; tasty varieties are the small, plump *cambur manzano*, finger bananas *titiaros*, cooking bananas *plátanos*
beans	*caraotas*; black beans, *caraotas negras*, are a national staple. Larger red, brown varieties are called *frijoles*
beef	*res*; roast beef, *rosbif*; steak, *biftek* (often tough). Better cuts are rump *punta trasera*, sirloin *churrasco* or *solomo de cuerito*, tenderloin *lomito*. Ask for your beef rare *medio crudo*, *poco cocido*; medium *término medio*; well done *bien cocido*.
bread	*pan*; toast *pan tosdado*; whole wheat bread *pan integral*
butter	*mantequilla*; margarine *margarina* is widely used as a replacement
cheese	*queso*; especially good is a type of local fresh cheese, the creamy *queso guayanés* or *queso de mano*
chicken	*pollo*; roast *al horno*, fried *frito*, grilled *a la parrilla*
drink	*bebida*; non-alcoholic *bebida natural*, *refresco*; alcoholic *trago*
egg	*huevo*; fried *frito*, boiled *pasado por agua*, scrambled *perico* or *revuelto*
fish	*pescado*; mullet *lebranche*, hake *merluza*, mackerel or kingfish *carite*, red snapper *pargo*, shark *cazón*, sea bass or grouper *mero*
garlic	*ajo*
grapefruit	*toronja*
grill	*parrilla*; mixed grill *parrilla mixta*; grilled *a la plancha*
ham	*jamón*
juice	*jugo*; freshly made *jugo natural*, or a *batido* made of blended fresh fruit
lettuce	*lechuga*
lobster	*langosta*
maize	*maíz*; on the cob *jojoto*
milk	*leche*; sour milk *leche ágria* or *pasada* (off)
omelette	*tortilla*
orange	*naranja*
pancake	*panqueca*, also *crepe*
pineapple	*piña*
pork	*cochino*; chops *chuletas*, roast pork leg *pernil*
potatoes	*papas*; French fries *papas fritas*, mashed *puré*, baked *al horno*
prawn	*langostino*
salad	*ensalada*; fruit salad *ensalada de fruta*
salt	*sal*; without salt *sin sal*; over-salted *exceso de sal*
sandwich	*sandwiche*, *emparedado*
shellfish	*mariscos*
shrimp	*camarones*
snack	*merienda*
soft drink	*refresco*
squid	*calamares*
stew	*guisado*, *hervido*
sugar	*azúcar*; brown sugar *azúcar morena*, sugar loaf *papelón* or *panela*
sweet potato	*batata*
take-out	*comida para llevar*
tasty	*sabroso*; tasteless *desabrido*
tea	*té negro*; when ordering a cup, specify *leche aparte*, milk on the side, or you may get a cup of hot milk with a teabag. Iced tea *té frío* also *Nestea*. Herb tea *té de hierbas*.
tunafish	*atún*
turkey	*pavo*

vegetables	*vegetales, legumbres.* The word *verduras* covers roots, not greens.
vegetarian	*vegetariano*
water	*agua*; drinking *agua potable* or *pura*; boiled *hervida*; filtered *filtrada*; tap water *agua del chorro*. Bottled water is sold as *agua mineral*, either carbonated (*con gas*), or plain (*normal*).
wine	*vino*

SPEAK LIKE A VENEZUELAN

Venezuelans like a laugh and their colourful speech gets straight to the point. People are happy to call you by a nickname like '*flaco*' ('slim') or '*gordo*' ('tubby') as soon as you walk into their store or restaurant, although they might make it more endearing by adding a diminutive '*ito*' on the end, so '*mi amor*' becomes '*mi amorcito*' ('my little darling'). No matter how old you are you're likely to be addressed at some point as '*chamo*' ('boy') or '*chama*' ('girl'). Familiarity is the order of the day and it helps to understand a few words in the local lingo or '*venezolanismos*'. If you want to join in the fun throw in a few local phrases and you'll soon have your new friends rolling about. If you learn only one word it should be the catch-all term '*chévere*', meaning 'great', 'fantastic', or 'cool' and you can't escape the ubiquitous '*pana*' or 'mate', which is believed to come from the early oil days when the US contractors from Texas would refer to everybody as 'partner'. Whatever their own misgivings about the state of the country the one thing the locals want to hear when they ask visitors what they think of Venezuela is '*todo chévere! Todo fino pana!*'

Here are a few words with a local twist to help you on your travels:

abono	down payment, deposit
alcabala	police or army road checkpoint. It is an offence to be found without identification, passport.
arrecho	very difficult, tough, angry; or fantastic, terribly good
avisparse	to keep a sharp eye out, as in *Avíspate!* (Look lively!) (From *avispa*, wasp)
balneario	beach or bathing spot with parking, food, not always changing room
barrio	a district of poor shanty homes (*ranchos*) often built on invaded land lacking basic services
bicho	insect, general word for thing or being, especially crawlies. *Bicho!* (Wow!).
bochinche	uproar, commotion, disorder
bomba	petrol station, water pump, bomb
bonche	a party with alcohol (from 'punch')
bongo	large river craft hewn from single trunk, with raised sides, outboard motor
bulla	racket, confusion, row; a diamond or gold rush
caney	open-sided shelter with thatched roof
caño	small tributary or creek, at times drying up; a delta channel
caribe	piranha. The original Carib word meant 'meat-eater', whence 'cannibal'.
catire	blond or fair-skinned
chalana	flatbed river ferry carrying vehicles, passengers
chamo/a	boy/girl, kid (informal)
chévere	great, fine
chimbo	bad, of poor quality
chinchorro	hammock made with an open-net weave; fishnet
chivacoa	microscopic red ticks, the harvest mite; also called *bête rouge*, chiggers in the West Indies, USA
churuata	thatched Indian round house, sometimes open sided; loosely, any house with thatched roof
cola	tail; queue, as at the bank or in traffic. To hitchhike is to *pedir cola*.

colgadero	rope for slinging hammock
conuco	Indian farming plot, usually cleared by slash-and-burn
criollo	creole, native-born, but not indigenous
curiara	dugout canoe hollowed from a single trunk, now powered by outboard motor
excursionista	hiker, trekker. *Estoy de excursión*, 'I'm on an outing'.
falca	capacious dugout for carrying cargo, 13–15m long, with roof and outboard motor
fila	mountain ridge; *filo*, sharp edge of knife
Fino!	Excellent! Used to describe how you feel, a night out, a spectacular view, a great meal.
frailejón	furry-leafed plants (*Espeletia sp.*) of the *páramo*
franela	T-shirt, from the English 'flannel'
guachimán	watchman or gatekeeper (an example of Spanglish)
hato	large cattle ranch; *hatillo*, little ranch
invierno	winter: the rainy season, May to October
jefatura	police headquarters
jején	gnat with a very irritating bite, infesting savannas, riverbanks at certain times of year
ladilla	tiresome, boring person, literally louse. *Que ladilla!* What a drag!
limpio	clean; without money, as in *Estoy limpio*, I'm broke
liquiliqui	man's cotton suit with button-up neck, worn without shirt; traditional in the Llanos
Llanos	the great plains of the Orinoco; Llanero, cowboy
malandro/a	rogue, scoundrel, bad lot, wrong-doer, lawbreaker
marico/a	homosexual
mecate	rope for hauling, or for hanging hammock etc
mochilero	backpacker. A *mochila* is a backpack, also *morral*.
molestia	trouble, inconvenience. *No es molestia*, It's no trouble. But take care, officials get angry when you say *Estoy molesto*, I am upset, annoyed.
moreno/a	person of brown skin. It is not disparaging, and is used affectionately.
morro	a rounded peak, promontory
mosca	literally, a fly; beware, as in *Mosca con los malandros!* Watch out for the bad guys!
mosquitero	mosquito net
motorista	operator of a boat, engine driver
nailon	fishing line, monofilament (sounds like 'nylon')
nigua	sandflea, jigger (US), chigoe (West Indies)
palafito	stilt house like Lake Maracaibo houses that inspired the name 'Little Venice' or Venezuela
palanca	lever; by extension influence, strings. *Tiene palanca*, he's got influence
palo	a stick, tree; a drink or shot of alcohol (from the era when plantations gave workers wooden chits instead of money, so they bought a '*palo de ron*').
pana	friend, mate (from 'partner')
páramo	high moor-like Andean terrain with low vegetation, from about 3,000m to the snow line
peñero	wooden or fibreglass fishing boat with outboard engine
pica	trail cut by machete. *Picar*, to cut, slice; to sting (insects).
pirata	a car operating illegally as a taxi or *por puesto*
plaga	general word for biting insect, pests
por puesto	pay-by-the-seat cars (*carritos*, *colectivos*) or small buses (*busetas*) run privately

prepotente	overbearing, bossy, macho attitude
puri-puri	nocturnal biting gnats so small they pass through the finest netting
ranchos	shacks. Ranchos, often erected by urban migrants, may evolve into multi-storey houses. *Ranchería*, a group of shelters used by fishermen, Indians.
ratón	a mouse. Also, a hangover; *tengo un raton*, I'm hung over.
raya	sting ray. The spotted marine ray is called *chucho*.
real	money, formerly a 50 cent piece. *Cuesta mucho real*, 'It costs a great deal'.
rumba	swinging party. *Vamos a rumbear*, 'Let's go partying'.
rústico	any 4x4 vehicle
sifrino/a	a plastic person or snob, someone with superficial values
tepui	table mountain of the Guiana Shield (from the Pemón), also *tepuy*
tigre	jaguar. A *tigra* is a poisonous snake of the Bothrops family, *mapanare*.
toros coleados	bull-dogging, throwing a bull by its tail, practised in a *manga de coleo*
verano	summer: in Venezuela the dry season, December to April/May
zamuro	vulture. *En pico de zamuro*, in the vulture's beak – to be in mortal danger.
zancudo	mosquito
zaperoco	uproar, disorder

Appendix 2

FURTHER INFORMATION

BOOKS

Art

Lucie-Smith, Edward *Latin American Art of the 20th Century* Thames and Hudson, 2005. Soto and Cruz-Diez feature alongside more contemporary conceptual artists.

Sullivan, Edward *Latin American Art in the Twentieth Century* Phaidon Press, 1996. Chapter on Venezuela with colour illustrations gives overview of important movements and artists such as Armando Reveron, Jesus Soto and Carlos Cruz-Diez.

Birds and wildlife

Emmons, Louise *Neotropical Rainforest Mammals* University of Chicago Press, Chicago & London, 1990. Handy, compact, illustrated field guide with illustrations, descriptions and local names of 500 species of mammals, the majority found in Venezuela.

Goodwin, Mary Lou *Birding in Venezuela* Sociedad Conservacionista Audubon de Venezuela, Caracas, 2003. The fifth edition covers the haunts of more species than most twitchers could hope to see and is an excellent guide for wilderness travel from a real character who still goes birding in her seventies.

Hilty, Steven *Guide to the Birds of Venezuela* Helm Field Guides, New Jersey, 2002. The most complete up-to-date, illustrated field guide of Venezuelan birds with distribution maps, nomenclature of species and habits and habitats for 1,381 species.

Meyer de Schauensee, Rodolphe and Phelps Jr, William H *Birds of Venezuela* Princeton University Press, New Jersey, 1978. The forerunner to Hilty's book, this classic field guide has 52 colour plates.

Fiction

Conan Doyle, Sir Arthur *The Lost World* Oxford Paperbacks, 2008. This classic adventure yarn of intrepid explorers climbing to the top of a South American mountain plateau and encountering savage ape-like beasts and dinosaurs is based on accounts of the first ascent of Mount Roraima. The otherworldly nature of Roraima and its unique ecosystem only adds to the book's enduring appeal.

Garcia Marquez, Gabriel *The General in his Labyrinth* Penguin, 2008. The Colombian master of magical realism brings real tragedy and pathos to the last days of Independence hero Simón Bolívar as he makes his last journey, a broken man dying from TB, his dreams of a united South America in tatters.

Hudson, W H *Green Mansions: A Romance of the Tropical Forest* Gerald Duckworth and Co Ltd, 2008. Written in 1904 by the founder of the RSPB in Britain, this romantic tale of love and loss in the Venezuelan rainforest still evokes the mystery and magic of the tropical jungle and its peoples.

Kehlman, Daniel *Measuring the World* Quercus, 2005. German scientist and explorer Baron Alexander von Humboldt and his Venezuelan travels are fictionalised in this ambitious novel, which also tells the tale of stay-at-home mathematician Carl Friedrick Gauss.

Krol, Torsten *The Dolphin People* Atlantic Books, 2006. Nazis lost in the rainforest? Enigmatic novelist Krol pits a German family fleeing the aftermath of World War Two against a jungle tribe, piranha-infested rivers and the deadly 'willy fish' in a black comedy disguised as a *Boy's Own* book.

Food

Harcourt-Cooze, William *Willie's Chocolate Factory Cookbook* Hodder & Stoughton, 2010. Based on the Channel 4 TV series of the same name, this easy to use cookbook features sweet and savoury recipes using Venezuelan cocoa. The first half also tells the story of how Willie and his wife bought an old *hacienda* close to Choroní and the Parque Nacional Henri Pittier and turned it into a working cacao plantation.

Popic, Miro *Guía Gastronómica Caracas/Caracas Restaurant Guide* Miro Popic Editores, 2010. An invaluable bilingual guide to hundreds of restaurants, coffee shops, bars and discotheques in Caracas.

Health

Werner, David *Where There is No Doctor* Macmillan Education, 1993

Wilson-Howarth, Dr Jane *Bugs, Bites & Bowels* Cadogan, 2006

Wilson-Howarth, Dr Jane, and Ellis, Dr Matthew *Your Child Abroad: A Travel Health Guide*, Bradt Travel Guides, 2005

History

Chasteen, John Charles *Americanos: Latin America's Struggle for Independence* Oxford University Press, 2008. An easy introduction to the Latin American wars of Independence from Spain and the major players, including the Venezuelans Francisco de Miranda and Simón Bolívar.

Chasteen, John Charles *Born in Blood and Fire; A Concise History of Latin America* W H Norton and Co, 2006. A much wider overview of the history of Latin America and the major historical events that have shaped the region.

Ewell, Judith *The Indictment of a Dictator: The Extradition and Trial of Marcos Pérez Jiménez* Texas A&M University Press, 1981. Tells the story of Venezuela's last dictator, who ruled the country for ten years in the 1950s.

Harvey, Robert *Liberators: Latin America's Struggle for Independence* Robinson, 2002. An impressive attempt to bring the Independence wars in Latin America to life that makes for an enjoyable read.

Lynch, John *Simón Bolívar: A Life* Yale University Press, 2007. An authoritative biography of the great Venezuelan hero that can be enjoyed by scholars and non-academics alike.

Morison, Samuel Eliot *Christopher Columbus, Mariner* Meridian, 1983. A sailing man, Morison follows the voyages of Columbus by sea, especially the third voyage when he 'discovered' Venezuela's Paria Peninsula and Margarita Island.

Racine, Karen *Francisco de Miranda: A Transatlantic Life in the Age of Revolution* Scholarly Resources, 2002. Venezuelan Independence hero Miranda, who fought in the French Revolution and became the lover of Catherine the Great of Russia, is a fascinating character who had enough experiences to fill five lives.

Indigenous peoples

Allen, Benedict *Mad White Giant* Flamingo, 1992. Before he presented TV programmes about exploring the wilder regions of the world, Benedict went out into the wilds on his own. This is one of his first adventures, a walk into the Venezuelan jungle that he nearly doesn't survive.

Biocca, Ettore *Yanoama: The Story of Helena Valero, a Girl Kidnapped by Amazonian Indians* Kodansha, 1997. One of the best accounts ever of Yanomami life as told to an Italian journalist by a woman who was captured by a Yanomami raiding party and spent years in the jungle with them.

Chagnon, Napoleon *Yanomamo: The Fierce people* Thomson Learning, 1983. Now controversial for its emphasis on the warlike nature of the Yanomami, this was once the best-selling anthropology book of all time.

Civrieux, Marc de *Watunna: An Orinoco Creation Cycle* University of Texas Press, 1997. Translated by David M Guss, this book of Yekuana (Makiritare) creation stories is the most comprehensive cycle of indigenous South American myths yet compiled.

Dawson, Michael *Growing Up Yanomamo: Missionary Adventures in the Amazon Rainforest* Grace Acres Press, 2009. A well-written insight into what it's like to work as a US missionary with an isolated rainforest tribe.

Good, Kenneth *Into the Heart: An Amazonian Love Story* Penguin, 1992. Whatever the rights or wrongs, this anthropologist decided to forego detached observation and get romantically involved with a Yanomami girl. The relationship didn't last but the book is still worth reading.

Lin Yu, Pei *Hungry Lightning: Notes of a Woman Anthropologist in Venezuela* University of New Mexico Press, 1997. Little has been published about the Pume Indians of the lower Llanos but this anthropologist gives a lively account of her fieldwork among a people suffering on the margins of Venezuelan society.

Lizot, Jacques *Tales of the Yanomami: Daily Life in the Venezuelan Jungle* Canto, 1991. Daily life told from the Yanomami viewpoint by this French anthropologist is infused with magic and myth.

Parry, Bruce *Tribe: Adventures in a Changing World* Penguin, 2007. Enthusiastic TV adventurer Parry devotes a chapter from the book to his time among the Sanema of the Caura River, complete with hallucinogenic snuff-taking, which he describes in detail.

Tierney, Patrick *Darkness in El Dorado, How Scientists & Journalists Devastated the Amazon* Norton & Co, 2000. The negative impacts on indigenous rainforest people by missionaries and anthropologists is laid bare in this book, which has had doubts raised about its findings but still deserves to be read.

Maps

Venezuela map ITMB Publishing, 2001 0921463596. Still the best map available for planning trips in Venezuela it has a street plan of Caracas and inset maps of Margarita Island, and Auyantepui and Roraima in the Gran Sabana.

Guía Vial de Venezuela Miro Popic Editores CA, Caracas, 2001. This excellent spiral-bound road atlas includes not only maps of states and their capitals, but also lists (in Spanish) major attractions, historic sites, hotels, restaurants, garages and emergency numbers for all towns and some villages, too. A new edition is planned.

Music

Calvo Ospina, Hernando *Salsa: Havana Heat, Bronx Beat* Latin American Bureau, 1995. Venezuela is a salsa-obsessed country that can lay claim to coming up with this saucy umbrella term to describe Afro–Cuban rhythms. Good basic guide to the origins of the music.

Lindop, Grevel *Travels on the Dance Floor: One Man's Journey to the Heart of Salsa* Andre Deutsch Ltd, 2010. Not content with dance classes in rainy Manchester, this British writer went in search of the real thing, passing through Caracas on the way.

Politics

Ferguson, James *Venezuela in Focus* Latin American Bureau, 1995. This small booklet on culture, politics and economics is desperately in need of an update but has interesting sections on the social ills that led to Hugo Chávez becoming president.

Gott, Richard *Hugo Chávez and the Bolivarian Revolution in Venezuela* Verso, 2005. One of the best-written introductions to President Chávez's very personal political project for Venezuela.

Jones, Bart *Hugo! The Hugo Chávez Story: From Mud Hut to Perpetual Revolution* The Bodley Head, 2008. A biography that starts back in Sabaneta where the future president learnt important life lessons from his grandmother, through the army years, the failed coup attempt, jail and finally the presidency.

McCaughan, Michael *The Battle of Venezuela* Latin American Bureau, 2004. Focusing mainly on the attempts to oust President Chávez and his Bolivarian Revolution, this book also looks at the grass roots groups supporting Chávez.

Reid, Michael *Forgotten Continent: The Battle for Latin America's Soul* Yale University Press, 2007. Written by a leading editor at *The Economist*, this takes a less rosy look at Venezuela under President Chávez.

Tarver, Michael H and Frederick, Julia C *The History of Venezuela* Greenwood Press, 2005. Although dry in style this short trawl through Venezuela's history covers all the major events.

Prison stories

MacNeil, Donald *Journey to Hell: Inside the World's Most Violent Prison System* Milo Books, 2006. The message is simple: don't smuggle drugs because Venezuelan prisons are not nice.

Welsh, Natalie *Sentenced to Hell: The Incredible True Story of a Young Mother's Miraculous Escape from Venezuela's Notorious Prison System* Sphere Books, 2009. More horror stories of life behind bars.

Travel guides

Baguley, Kitt *Culture Shock: A Survival Guide to Customs and Etiquette* Marshall Cavendish, 2008. A dos and don'ts guide to Venezuelan society with some useful tips.

Kline, Elizabeth *Guide to Camps, Posadas and Cabins* Self-published, 2009. A guide to out of the way *posadas* and camps that expatriates would probably find handy for organising road trips.

Quintero, Valentina *Venezuela La Guia* Editorial Arte/Transhumante, 2009. Very good guide for Spanish-speakers seeking up-to-date travel information from a travel writer who spends her life criss-crossing the country.

Travelogues

Blessed, Brian *Quest for the Lost World* Boxtree, 2000. The big actor with the booming voice does his best Professor Challenger impersonation as he climbs Roraima. Good background information on the *tepui* mountains and Conan Doyle's inspiration for *The Lost World*.

Brokken, Jan *Jungle Rudy* Marion Boyars, 2004. A fascinating biography of the man who set up the first tourist operation in Canaima and pioneered the trips to Angel Falls before opening his own camp at Ucaima and playing host to international celebrities, including Prince Charles.

Charriere, Henri *Banco* Panther, 1975. This is the second volume of reminiscences by the famous French prisoner, better known as Papillon, following his release from El Dorado prison, a stint as a cook on oil exploration trips in Zulia and his exploits running bars and clubs in Caracas until the 1967 earthquake brings his life crashing down around him.

Goodman, Edward J *The Explorers of South America* Collier-Macmillan Ltd, London, 1972. A rundown of often incredible feats by Andean and Amazonian explorers, and the journeys of Columbus, Vespucci, Ordaz, Raleigh in Venezuela, plus later naturalists Humboldt, Bates and Spruce.

Gordon, Nick *Tarantulas and marmosets: An Amazon Diary* Metro, 1998. Sadly, wildlife filmmaker Nick Gordon had a heart attack in Venezuela while making a documentary. This book tells of his adventures in Venezuela and Brazil and the critters he went to such incredible lengths to film.

Helferich, Gerard *Humboldt's Cosmos* Gotham, 2005. A biography of the great German scientist and traveller.

Humboldt, Alexander von *Personal Narrative of Travels to the Equinoctial Regions of America* Penguin, 1995. German scientist Humboldt studied everything he could see, smell or touch in Venezuela during his 1799–1800 travels: Indian missions, adventurous escapades, electric eels, curare, the mysteries of Catatumbo lightning and the Casiquiare Canal. It's all here, and still valid today.

Jacobs, Michael *Andes* Granta, 2010. Landing in Caracas at the start of a mammoth journey following the mighty Andes all the way to the tip of South America, Jacobs sees little of Caracas but provides some insights into life under President Chávez. Travelling to Mérida, on his way to Colombia, the author tells the story of Simón Bolívar's epic march over the Andes. Well written and exhaustively researched, this is a good book for anyone with an interest in South American history, geography and politics.

Jordan, Tanis and Martin *Out of Chingford: Round the North Circular and up the Orinoco* Coronet, 1989. An entertaining account of the Jordans' adventures and misadventures in an inflatable boat. Angel Falls was a major expedition.

MacInnes, Hamish *Climb to the Lost World* Hodder & Stoughton, London, 1974. Lively account of the expedition to Roraima's north prow from Guyana, with notes on Everard Im Thurn's 1884 ascent, climbing techniques.

Nicholl, Charles *The Creature in the Map: Sir Walter Raleigh and the Quest for El Dorado* Virago, 1995. Taking Raleigh's ill-fated expeditions to Venezuela as a starting point, the author then goes on his own voyage of discovery through the Orinoco Delta to the Gran Sabana and Angel Falls.

O'Hanlon, Redmond *In Trouble Again: A Journey Between the Orinoco and the Amazon* Penguin, 1989. This is the best and certainly the funniest jungle adventure book on Venezuela.

Robertson, Ruth *Churun-Meru, the Tallest Angel* Whitmore Publishing, Pennsylvania, 1975. The plucky US photographer describes her 1948 *National Geographic* expedition, the first to measure Angel Falls and put it in the record books. Good details on Jimmie Angel and other old-timers.

St Aubin de Teran, Lisa *The Hacienda: My Venezuelan Years* Virago, 1998. Only 17 and recently married, the writer travelled to Venezuela to live in her increasingly mad husband's ramshackle *hacienda* in the Andes. Quirky and frustratingly wrong on some of the Venezuela background, it reads more like a magical realist novel than autobiography.

Starks, Richard and Murcutt, Miriam *Along the River that Flows Uphill: From the Orinoco to the Amazon* Haus Publishing, 2009. A contemporary expedition to the Casiquiare Canal follows the Humboldt route in reverse with some scares along the way.

WEBSITES
General
www.heedarmy.co.uk/1347/bogie-interested-in-venezuelan-keeper-mikhael-jaimez-ruiz

Politics
www.venezuelanalysis.com
www.zcommunications.org/znet/places/venezuela
www.lab.org.uk

Tourism
www.venezuelatuya.com/indexeng.htm
www.think-venezuela.net
www.margaritaonline.com

Travel warnings
www.travel.state.gov/travel/cis_pa_tw/cis/cis_1059.html (US Department of State)
www.fco.gov.uk/en/travel-and-living-abroad/travel-advice-by-country/south-america/venezuela (UK Foreign and Commonwealth Office)

Index

Page references in **bold** indicate main entries; those in *italics* indicate maps.
Abbreviations: NP for National Park, NM for Natural Monument